PATHWAYS TO PERSONAL GROWTH
ADJUSTMENT IN TODAY'S WORLD

GEORGE R. GOETHALS

Williams College

STEPHEN WORCHEL

University of Southern Maine

LAURIE HEATHERINGTON

Williams College

ALLYN AND BACON

Boston • London • Toronto • Sydney • Tokyo • Singapore

Vice President and Editor in Chief, Social Sciences and Education: Sean Wakely
Series Editor: Carolyn Merrill
Editorial Assistant: Amy Goldmacher
Senior Marketing Manager: Joyce Nilsen
Editorial–Production Administrator: Donna Simons
Editorial–Production Service: Matrix Productions Inc.
Composition and Prepress Buyer: Linda Cox
Manufacturing Buyer: Megan Cochran
Cover Administrator: Brian Gogolin
Electronic Composition: Omegatype Typography, Inc.

Copyright © 1999 by Allyn & Bacon
A Viacom Company
160 Gould Street
Needham Heights, MA 02194

Internet: www.abacon.com
America Online: keyword: College Online

Credits appear on p. 494, which constitutes a continuation of the copyright page.

Library of Congress Cataloging-in-Publication Data

Goethals, George R.
    Pathways to personal growth : adjustment in today's world / George
Goethals, Stephen Worchel, Laurie Heatherington.
      p.   cm.
    Includes bibliographical references and index.
    ISBN 0-205-13955-8
    1. Adjustment (Psychology) 2. Adaptability (Psychology)
I. Worchel, Stephen. II. Heatherington, Laurie. III. Title.
BF335.G595 1998
155.2'4—dc21   98-5941
                                        CIP

Printed in the United States of America

10 9 8 7 6 5 4 3   03 02 01 00

To Barbara and Natalie, and the memories of George and Doc,
To Dawna, Leah, Jessica, Hannah, and Elise,
To Keith, Rachel and Nathaniel, and Dan and Dorothy,
For all that you have contributed to our personal growth.

Contents

Writing a textbook on the psychology of adjustment leads to certain inevitable questions. "Adjustment to what?" for example. In its broadest sense, this is a book about adjustment to modern life. The search for happiness, security, and a healthy, meaningful life is something that concerns all of us. The area of adjustment is devoted to this search. More specifically, this area of psychology concerns adjustment to the natural changes and tasks that accompany growth and development, such as adjustment to adolescence, intimate relationships, work, parenthood, stress, and old age. People throughout history have faced these adjustments. But possibly no period in history other than the present has made adjustment so complex and challenging. We live in exciting yet frightening times. Modern life is fast-paced and offers more freedoms and choices than were previously available. Technology allows us to prolong our lives and create new life as never before. Computers allow us to shop, travel, make new friends, join groups, get advice, and find entertainment without leaving home. The media bring the global village, with all its problems and hopes, to our doorsteps. Changing roles and social mores present more choices than ever before about relationships, sex, marriage, divorce, jobs, and the shape of family life. The wider society and our communities not only provide tremendous support, but they can also be sources of stress. For example, unemployment and neighborhood violence, which some shoulder more than others, are societal factors that affect the well-being of individuals and families.

Overall, it is clear that we live in a period that poses great challenge to the ability of people to adjust and cope. We firmly believe that knowledge from the vast literature of psychology can be useful in helping people adjust. In writing this book, we asked ourselves, "What is it that we know as psychologists that might actually be helpful to people in understanding themselves and others?" On the pathway to personal growth, what information might help you chart your course? This book is not a "how to" guide for life. No one can provide that, as life involves unpredictability and requires that we adjust to ever-changing conditions. Rather, our aim is to bring psychological research and theory to a concrete and useful level, allowing readers to use it as a tool in charting their own courses. We begin each chapter with a case study to illustrate how the topic of the chapter relates to a real person's life and then weave that person's story into the chapter itself. We present opportunities for self-assessment (Self-Assessment Exercises), anecdotes from our personal and professional experience (Lessons from Life), and Questions for Critical Thinking to get the reader personally involved in the text. We show how psychological knowledge is generated, by providing an inside look at a specific study, and how it was done, rather than just what the findings were (Lessons from the Lab).

The initial chapters focus on the individual, first describing how people develop from infancy through old age. We discuss the contribution of inherited temperaments and other tendencies, which provide a set of possibilities, and the contribution of the environment, which interacts with those possibilities to determine their outcomes. We then examine the influence of gender on personality and behavior, looking carefully at common assumptions about what it means to be male or female in our society and analyzing those assumptions in comparison to psychological knowledge. As everyone knows from personal experience, the pathway to personal growth and happiness is sometimes rocky. Thus, we next examine stress and related topics. What is stress, what are its effects on our physical and psychological well-being, and how can we cope with it? How do we lose and regain control of everyday activities, such as eating and drinking? The group of chapters focusing on the individual includes chapters on psychological disorders and therapy. From disorders that are rare but fascinating to those that are very common but nonetheless distressing, we discuss symptoms, causes, and treatments. In every chapter of the book, we emphasize and illustrate the importance of culture on human behavior.

We live in a social world and are greatly affected by people around us. Thus, a later set of chapters focuses more directly on social influences by addressing the challenge of dealing with other people and developing friendships and intimate relationships. Why are we attracted to some people and not others? Why do some people fall in love and why do some stay in love? How does sexual intimacy figure into relationships? These topics, which focus on one-to-one relationships, are followed by chapters that examine the behavior of people in larger social contexts. The two most important of these contexts in modern adult life are the family and work. We discuss both of these settings in separate chapters. The question of how we can become accepted and useful members of groups, balancing independence and autonomy with interdependence and connectedness, reverberates throughout these later chapters. Finally, we focus on the physical environment. Humans both shape and are shaped by the environment that surrounds them. The challenge, especially for the 21st century, is to appreciate this relationship and make it a positive and sustainable one.

The authors of this text are diverse, but we share a common interest in adjustment of the individual in the context of social groups. We average more than 20 years each of teaching social, clinical, and personality psychology courses, from introductory courses to advanced seminars. Our research interests include social relationships, social influence, and social cognition, cross-cultural psychology, family therapy, gender and social behavior, leadership, violence and aggression, intergroup relations, and environmental psychology. Our work has also taken us outside the academic environment, to doing psychotherapy and consulting with schools, businesses, and community groups.

There are three of us who wrote the book. However, there are several other individuals whose work helped bring this book to press. We would like to thank Carolyn Merrill and her staff at Allyn and Bacon for creating a book out of the hundreds of manuscript pages we sent them. We would also like to thank Merrill Peterson for all of his help in the production phase. Jennifer Ford, Kim Cozzi, and Val Thurman helped type parts of the manuscript and kept us from butchering the English language. We are indebted to Denise Jordan for her timely and cheerful secretarial assistance. John Iuzzini, Hank Rothberger, Paul Boxer, Heather Weston, and Sheri McKay, and librarians Helena Warburg, Peter Giordanao, and Becky Smith were sleuths who tracked down important information or helped us organize it. We also want to thank the reviewers who gave us valuable suggestions and guided us throughout the work. They included Pearlene Breshears, Southwest Baptist University; Stephen Coccia, Orange County Community College; Richard Hardy, Central Michigan University; Sidney Hochman, Nassau Community College; Malia Huchendorf, Normandale Community College; Felicia Moore-Davis, Houston Community College; Connie Schick, Bloomsburg University; Velma Walker, Tarrant County Junior College; and Lois Willoughby, Miami–Dade Community College. We also appreciate the help of dozens of students who read the manuscript, served as sounding boards for ideas, and forced us to remain user-friendly.

Last, but certainly not least, we express deepest gratitude to our immediate and extended family members. They gave us time to write, encouragement, and inspiration throughout this project.

George R. Goethals
Stephen Worchel
Laurie Heatherington

ADJUSTING TO OUR WORLD

Leo Beuerman

Leo Beuerman

Each morning, Leo Beuerman wakes up, dresses, eats a quick breakfast, and heads off to work in the community near his home. These activities seem routine and hardly worth mentioning since millions of other Americans go through the same procedure. But Leo's actions assume a new significance when we learn more about him.

Leo Beuerman was born shortly after the turn of the century. His birth was not a happy occasion, however, because Leo was born deformed. His limbs were mere stubs that barely supported his tiny feet and hands. Later it was learned that Leo was also deaf. While other children were growing tall and straight, Leo's body remained twisted and small; he would never be taller than an average 3-year-old child.

In time, Leo became a captive of other people's fears. His mother, afraid some accident might befall her helpless son, always kept Leo at home. She tended to his every need: cooking his food, washing and mending his clothes, and even moving him around the house.

All this aid, though given with the greatest love and good intentions, could have further crippled Leo by adding to his dependency and helplessness. However, Leo was determined that this wouldn't happen; he wanted to be useful and to control his own life. He couldn't hear, but he could see. His arms were not long, but he could control his hands and fingers. His body was small, but his determination was great.

Leo learned to read and spent endless hours studying. He felt not only that it was important to learn, but also that communicating thoughts and feelings was crucial to a fulfilling life. Few people visited Leo, but he taught himself to use a typewriter and laboriously tapped out his thoughts. He learned to repair clocks and watches and supplemented the meager family income through this activity. His clock repair business gave him a sense of purpose and a feeling that he was making a contribution to his family and society.

The death of Leo's mother had an important effect on his life. He was now alone. There was no one to ensure that he was clothed and fed or that he could move from place to place. He could enter an institution where others would take care of his daily needs. Certainly no one would blame him for this decision; nature had treated Leo cruelly, and he had a right to request help.

Leo thought otherwise, however. Instead of dwelling on his misfortune, he chose to look at his fortune. He would use his talents and compensate for his limitation. He was determined to be useful and happy.

He built a small cart to serve as his legs and give him mobility. By turning the wheels of the cart with his hands, he could scoot from place to place. He designed a series of pulleys and chains that, when hooked to his ancient tractor, could hoist his cart and himself onto the tractor seat. This contraption freed him from the confines of home and allowed him to go into the neighboring community.

Leo was determined not to remain isolated. He felt that an individual can live a fulfilling life only if he or she learns to interact with and adjust to other people. So Leo decided to become a merchant; through this activity he could support himself and remain a free and independent individual among others. His size, deafness, and lack of capital prevented his owning a large store with a varied inventory. Leo reacted to these limitations by building a business that was suited to his situation; he sold pencils, pens, and other writing material from his little cart.

A common sight in the community near Leo's home is an ancient tractor slowly making its way down Main Street with a shriveled little man perched high on the seat. The tractor pulls into a parking space that, by custom, has become reserved for Leo Beuerman. Leo then goes through the long and tedious process of lowering himself and his cart onto the sidewalk. After securing his display case on the cart, Leo navigates to a shady spot on the sidewalk and opens for business. Proudly written in bold letters across the front of the display case is Leo's business code: "I guarantee it."

Leo Beuerman leads a useful, productive, and happy life. He is quick to supply the credo that has guided his own life: "I never did believe in being a quitter. Let nothing stop you until you get what you set out for or see your own mistakes." Leo also advises people to recognize the futility of self-pity and focus instead on the abundance of opportunities and abilities that they do have. Above all, he expresses the philosophy that people should concentrate on understanding themselves and mobilizing their forces for the supremely important endeavor of enjoying life. To accentuate this point, Leo proudly reports that he "is enjoying life very well."

WHAT IS ADJUSTMENT?

Leo Beuerman is different from most of us in many ways. Most of us are not forced to live in silence with a misshapen body. Most of us did not spend childhood totally confined inside our homes. Most of us have had far more formal education than Leo did. Yet despite all these differences, we all share something important with Leo Beuerman: We all face daily the task of **adjustment.**

The concept of personal adjustment has many definitions. In general, personal adjustment is the everyday task of coping with ourselves, our environment, and the people we encounter. Adjustment is a complex process. It involves (1) learning about and understanding ourselves and our social and physical environment, (2) using our understanding to set realistic goals for ourselves, (3) using our abilities to control our environment and destiny so that we can attain our goals, and (4) being sensitive to the needs and concerns of others so that we can also make positive contributions to the lives of others. In defining adjustment, we may well want to remember Leo Beuerman's life philosophy. In Leo's terms, personal adjustment involves the striving to enjoy life and to help others enjoy their lives. The specific demands faced by each individual differ, but we all must adjust to the world.

While our tasks are similar, it is clear that some of us do a better job of adjusting than others do. The well-adjusted individual is one who copes successfully and effectively with personal and situational demands. Achieving positive personal adjustment doesn't mean that we'll no longer experience problems, obstacles, or depression. Everyone experiences these conditions; they are a normal part of everyday living. In fact, we measure adjustment by the way we handle such experiences. We can't determine the degree of our adjustment by our status in the social world or the size of our bank accounts. Rather, the test of adjustment is how we'll cope with the conditions of our lives.

Leo Beuerman will never be a success story in terms of the amount of money he makes or the type of occupation he holds. His daily income is barely sufficient to meet his most basic needs, and he will never enter a profession such as medicine, law, engineering, or teaching. His twisted body excludes him from many social events; in fact, some people turn away or even cross the street to avoid having to stare at the little man. Thus, by many standards Leo's existence is not enviable. On another scale, however, Leo is a success. He has coped with his situation. He has learned to compensate for his physical deformities. He has developed friendships with people, many of them children, who are willing to stop and talk to him. Leo leads an independent and free life. He has developed a sense of purpose and self-esteem. Above all, in spite of feeling lonely and depressed at times, Leo enjoys life and strives to live it to the fullest extent allowed by his capabilities.

THE CHANGING LANDSCAPE: A CHALLENGE TO ADJUSTMENT

In many respects the challenges we face in adjusting to our world are similar to those Leo faces. We face decisions about school, social relationships, personal goals, career, and family. Although these domains are similar to those confronted by Leo in the early 1900s, the challenge of adjustment is becoming increasingly complex. At no time in history have people faced so much and so rapid change (Zastrow, 1992). In fact, if we had to choose one word to describe our world, the best candidate would be *change*. No matter where we turn, we face dramatic change, and each change presents a new challenge.

Changes in technology can be found in nearly every area of our lives. Computers change the way we work, play, and communicate. We must learn not only to talk to other people, but we must also "communicate" with machines. Our food is likely to be cooked in a few minutes by microwaves. Instead of telephoning each other from the confines of our home, we can call each other from our mobile phones while walking on the street or driving in our automobiles. We can fax documents rather than waiting days for them to be sent by mail.

Technology provides us with several challenges. One goal is simply learning how to use the new devices. Just when we get comfortable with one device, we find that it is obsolete and we must learn how to operate the new one. Technology also influences our day-to-day lives and our social interactions. Without care and consideration, we can fall into a lonely trap of isolation, carrying out daily activities from our homes. Our entertainment can be confined to in-home video tapes and computer games. We can have our meals delivered to our doorstep, and we can shop over the Internet. As we will see in Chapter 14, many of us will work at home, rarely going to a central office. Also, more of us will face the possibility of being replaced by machines in our workplaces.

Rapid change is equally evident in the health area. New drugs have prolonged our lives. As a result, we must learn how to make our additional years happy and fulfilling. It would be a hollow victory to find that our added years are characterized by loneliness and poverty. The increasing number of elderly people requires society to develop new opportunities for work, recreation, and living that are adapted to the abilities of the elderly. New technology in medicine allows us to create new life outside the natural route of reproduction (for example, test-tube babies) and to influence the sex and other characteristic of babies. These advances raise ethical questions about the degree to which we are comfortable with such interventions into our private lives. In addition, we can speculate about the possible effects on family structure of techniques for producing offspring that do not require the intimate union between a man and a woman. On the disease side, acquired immune deficiency syndrome (AIDS) is a deadly killer. As it becomes increasingly widespread, tens of thousands of people are directly affected by the disease, either because they have it or because a loved one is infected. And because AIDS can be sexually transmitted, its threat affects the sexual behavior of many people.

We have in our time witnessed a dramatic change in the structure of the family (see Chapter 12). Divorce is increasingly common, as is the incidence of single-parent families. Both adults and children must cope with different social relationships. French sociologist Emile Durkheim (1951) argued that mass confusion and depression result when a society is confronted with a lack of clarity about accepted rules of behavior (norms) or when masses of people are no longer interested in being guided by existing norms. He referred to this condition as *anomie*. Zastrow (1992) has suggested that the 1990s is a period of social anomie in which many people are unsure of the rules that govern social behavior or are unwilling to follow these rules. He suggests that there is confusion about "right" and "wrong" behaviors governing family and other social relationships. This confusion creates a tremendous challenge to personal adjustment.

As we will see in Chapter 5, any change (even positive change) is experienced as stressful. Each change requires that we adapt and cope. As a result, the decade of the 1990s presents greater challenges to our ability to adjust than any other decade in history. Although this message may seem foreboding, there is a comforting side. The rapid change we all face presents each of us with increasing opportunities and personal freedom to chart our own life course and the tools and skills to accomplish this. The real challenge of this decade of adjustment is to identify and use these opportunities to enhance our development without becoming overwhelmed by the changing physical and social landscape.

The Process of Adjustment

The beauty of human life is its diversity. Each of us is unique. Our experiences are different from other people's; the situations we face each day are unique to us; our attitudes, abilities, and values—however similar to those of others—are expressed in ways that are ours alone. So the requirements for, and the process of, adjustment are slightly different for each of us. This difference makes life exciting and challenging—and also makes it impossible for any book to lay out a plan of personal adjustment for everyone. No book or expert can tell you exactly what you should do to adjust to your world.

Despite our wonderful differences, however, we all have experiences and life requirements in common. We all belong to groups; we all love and are loved; we all face situations that lead to conflict and anger; we all achieve successes and experience failures. Thus, while we can't describe a sure formula for every person's success and happiness, we can examine some of the basic questions and processes involved in our adjustment to our special worlds.

What Is Human Nature?

One of the most basic questions that begins the process of adjustment is: What are people really like? Almost from the beginning of recorded history, people h.. pondered this issue. Poets, philosophers religious teachers, social scientists, political leaders, and even chemists have asked: What is human nature? The answer has remained elusive, and debate still rages. In our efforts to study personal adjustment, it is of interest to look briefly at the positions that have been advanced.

There are, in fact, two somewhat different questions to examine. One concerns whether we are by nature good or bad, self-centered or socially conscious. Put another way, if there were no laws or restraints on human behavior, would people act to help others and make positive contributions to society, or would people be evil and destructive and act only to further their own ends?

The view that people are basically good is best represented by **humanists** such as Abraham Maslow and Carl Rogers. They argue that we are naturally driven to make a positive impact and strive to be the best that we can be. People become depressed and do bad things because the rules of society thwart their natural development. The rules force people to live up to the expectations of others, and consequently they lose sight of their own goals.

Conversely, Sigmund Freud argued that we have a basic tendency for self-gratification, to do only what feels good for us, even if we have to destroy or hurt others. This tendency is represented in Freud's concept of the id that encourages us to eat, drink, be merry, and seek self-pleasure.

Note, however, that these positions argue that society and its rules play very different roles in our adjustment. One school holds that society should provide us a free and open environment to explore and develop ourselves. We should be encouraged to find ourselves, and in this way we will make important contributions to our society. In the other view, human nature is selfish, and society must serve as the police to make us more socially responsible. Its rules should limit and guide our actions and tell us how we should act. We must be controlled and forced to act for the good of the group.

There are actually a number of questions involved in the issue of choice. One is the age-old debate about nature versus nurture. To illustrate this issue, we invite you to look into a behavioral mirror that reflects your actions, thoughts, and feelings. Are the characteristics you observe in our magical mirror the result of inheritance or of the environment in which you grew up? In other words, did you enter this world with a preprogrammed road map that you are destined to follow, or did the particular situations you have encountered mold you like potter's clay? This is a fundamental question because it has wide-ranging implications. For example, if we find that biology determines our level of aggression, we should focus our efforts toward determining who will be aggressive and isolating them rather than developing programs to teach nonviolent solutions to conflict.

The methods employed to answer this question are almost as interesting as the nature/nurture debate itself. One approach has been to study identical twins, who have the same biological basis. These studies indicate that identical twins often have similar personalities and intelligence (Bouchard & McGue, 1990). However, there is a problem with this method: Identical twins are often raised in similar environments. Is it the biological basis or the environment that creates the observed similarity? To deal with this problem, studies have compared identical twins who were separated at birth and adopted by different families. Now we have individuals who have the same genetic make-up but are raised in different environments.

Studies along these lines suggest that genetics plays a role in determining a wide range of characteristics, such as intelligence, personality, and the likelihood of physical and mental illness (Bouchard et al., 1990; Plomin, 1989; Weinberg et al., 1992). Going a step farther, evolutionary psychologists have argued that being human and sharing a history of adaption creates a certain kinship among us that predisposes us to think and behave in prescribed ways. For example, David Buss (1989) argues that the natural desire to maintain our species by producing offspring leads males to be attracted to women with a certain body shape, one that typically signals an ability to conceive and bear children. At the same time, women have a tendency (natural, according to evolutionary psychologists) to be attracted to men who have the resources to protect them and their offspring (see Chapter 4).

These positions are subject to considerable debate and controversy, but they illustrate the extent of the importance accorded biology in influencing human behavior. Biology is not the only factor that plays a hand, however. Our physical and social environments as well as the decisions we make about our own behaviors also play a role in creating who we are. In a sense, our biological hard wiring may create predispositions or tendencies to behave, feel, or act in certain ways, and heredity may set limits for us. On the other hand, our situations play an equally important role in influencing how our lives develop.

A second issue related to human choice deals more directly with the role of environment. On one hand, **behaviorists** such as B. F. Skinner argue that humans have little choice in their behavior. Rather to the extent that environment influences behavior, they contend, we are controlled by the reward/punishment contingencies that are present. We learn which acts will be rewarded and which will be punished and behave to increase the chances of receiving rewards.

Humanists, on the other hand, recoil at this picture of the human as a puppet of the environment. Carl Rogers argues that humans have the freedom to decide how they will behave. They can think about the impact they wish to have; they can set their goals, develop their aspirations, and exercise freedom of choice in trying to attain these ideals.

Complicating this debate is the issue of permanence and change. Healtherton and Weinberger (1994) open the preface of their book on personality change with the Jesuit maxim, "Give me a child until he is seven, and I will show you the man." This phrase suggests that whether the determining factor is biology, environment, or choice, personality is established during early childhood, and little change takes place after that. On the other hand, many personality theorists, such as Carl Jung and Erik Erickson, argue that change can and does take place throughout life (see Chapter 2).

The point of all of this is not to identify the "right" position; there is probably some truth to all the positions. Rather, our aim is to demonstrate the range of thinking about the causes of human behavior. Each position has implications for the way societies should be structured, the role that learning will play, the course that efforts to adjust will follow, and the processes that will be useful in learning about ourselves.

Knowing and Accepting Ourselves

A recent newspaper story told of an elderly woman who, dying of cancer, lamented, "I have spent so much of my life worrying about other people and other things that I have never taken the time to know myself." This statement probably applies to many of us. Our world is changing at a very rapid pace, and we are constantly bombarded with new objects to possess, new places to go, and new ways to get there. Our increased mobility has brought us into contact with increasing numbers of people, and we spend a great deal of our time working to be accepted and liked by

them. With all these environmental and social demands, we spend very little time learning to know ourselves.

It is also a curious fact of life that our eyes are directed outward: We can easily observe others, but unless we stand in front of a mirror, we do not see ourselves. This is the point made by the Scottish poet Robert Burns as he observed a rude woman in church:

> *Would some power the gift to give us,*
> *To see ourselves as others see us,*
> *It would from many a blunder free us.*

Thus, we often know others better than we know ourselves. Who are we? Why do we think, feel, and behave as we do? Knowing who we are involves developing a **self-identity**—a definition or interpretation of the self (Osborne, 1996)—that is continuous in the sense that it is rather stable. Our self-identity differentiates us from others and makes us unique.

Our self-identity has three important parts (see Table 1.1). First, it contains our values and priorities: what we believe, what is important to us, and what goals we pursue. Second, it has an interpersonal aspect. It includes our relationships with other people, our position in groups (see Chapter 13), and our jobs or occupations (see Chapter 14). Third, it includes an estimation of our personalities and individual potentials: Are we friendly, outgoing, energetic, lazy? We also include information about our abilities that help determine how likely we are to reach our goals.

This picture may be viewed as your *actual self*. You may see yourself as being friendly, shy, lazy, and intelligent. Then there is the *ideal self*, the way in which you would ideally like to be (Higgins, 1990). In addition to these two selves, we often have views of our *ought* self, our *can* self, and our *future* self. It is important to distinguish between these selves when we ask who we are. When we find discrepancies, such as between our actual and ideal self, we

TABLE 1.1   Self-Identity

I. Components
   A. Values and priorities
   B. Interpersonal relations
   C. Personality, ability, and potential

II. Functions
   A. Helping us make choices
   B. Allowing us to form satisfying interpersonal relationships
   C. Furnishing us with a sense of strength and resilience

often become motivated to change or seek greater self-knowledge.

Knowing ourselves and defining our self-identity is important for a number of reasons. Our identity helps us make choices. When we know who we are and what we like, we can more easily decide what type of vacation we will take this year, where we will go to school, and what our major will be. We must know ourselves before we can form close relationships with other people. Then we can become intimate with others without losing our independence. Not knowing who we are makes it difficult to feel comfortable with and contribute to relationships. Finally, having a clear self-identity gives us strength and resilience. We can bounce back from misfortune and set new goals. We can incorporate our experiences into our identity rather than having our identity determined by temporary setbacks. Thus, knowing who we are plays a major role in adjusting and adapting to our world and our relationships.

While learning about ourselves may open new avenues for personal adjustment, it may also reveal some characteristics or limitations that don't please us. We may be able to change some aspects of ourselves, but there may be others we can't change. It's important to be realistic in making this distinction. Hav-

ing done so, we can mobilize our efforts to alter the changeable characteristics and avoid wasting energy struggling with insurmountable obstacles. Instead, we can focus on compensating for those unyielding aspects of ourselves.

There are two important points to remember as we attempt to answer the question: Who am I? The first is that our **self-appraisals** must be realistic. We must be able to distinguish the differences between the different selves (actual, ideal, ought, etc.). While we must be willing to accept that certain characteristics will be a part of us forever, we must avoid classifying a characteristic as unchangeable simply because it might take a great deal of effort to change. The second important point is that once we have made a realistic self-appraisal, we must accept ourselves. To succumb to self-pity or despair because we aren't who we would like to be will destroy our ability to adjust and lead happy and fulfilling lives.

Leo Beuerman clearly illustrates these points. When Leo's mother died, he had to decide whether to enter an institution where others would take care of him or to live as an independent person who would take care of himself. To make this decision, he had to make a realistic appraisal of himself and his capabilities. If he indeed lacked the capabilities for self-sufficiency, a decision to remain on his own would be sheer folly and would have serious negative consequences. On the other hand, if he did have the capacity to care for himself, he would waste his life by deciding to become institutionalized simply because it would have required too much work to compensate for his limitations.

Leo learned about himself and made his self-appraisal. He acknowledged his physical deformities and his lack of education. There was nothing he could do to change his stubby limbs or his deafness. Rather than dwelling on what he couldn't have, however, he focused on the opportunities that were available despite his impairments. His lack of education was a different story. He could overcome this deficiency. He could learn from books, and he could communicate his thoughts by typing them out on his small typewriter.

One of the aims of this book is to present information that will aid you in your search for self-understanding and self-acceptance. We will examine how environmental conditions and social relationships during infancy and childhood play a major role in determining the personality of the adult. We will dis-

cuss the way in which individuals experience emotions and why the same condition may lead different individuals to experience different emotions. We will also focus on the factors that influence the development and change of attitudes and values. These discussions should provide further insights into why human beings think, feel, and behave as they do. Addressing these questions will help you to know and accept yourself, and in doing this you will be taking an important step toward positive personal adjustment.

REVIEW QUESTIONS

1. T or F: Only negative change creates stress and challenge for adjustment.

2. _____ is a condition in which society is faced with a lack of clarity about rules and norms or in which people are no longer interested in being guided by existing norms.

3. _____ believe that humans can exercise considerable choice and free will regarding their behavior.

4. T or F: Concerning human nature, the evidence suggests that biology controls and dictates behavior and human potential.

5. Which self-image represents how you would like to be, given freedom of choice?
   a. actual self
   b. ideal self
   c. ought self
   d. future self

UNDERSTANDING OUR PHYSICAL AND CULTURAL ENVIRONMENTS

When we consider the objects and events that affect our behavior, some distinctions readily spring to mind. There are the people with whom we interact each day. There are our jobs, our schools, and our groups. In a sense, we can view each of these factors as props on the stage of our lives. However, in addition to these props, our lives and behaviors are also influenced by the stage itself. The stage is composed of our physical and cultural environment, which we often take for granted and rarely consider.

Looking first at physical environment (discussed in Chapter 15), think for a moment

how your life is affected by the size of town in which you live, the typical weather in your area, and how close people live to each other. The size of town affects how much time you spend going from place to place, the places you go, and the things you can do. If you live in a small rural town, for example, you probably do not go often to see plays, and you may order many of your clothes through catalogues. At the same time, you may spend much of your time outdoors, quite possibly with pets or farm animals. You take the trees and open space for granted. In contrast, if you live in a large city, your life probably revolves around theaters, malls, museums, and public transportation. Trees, horses, and cows are objects you most likely encounter on vacation.

Adjusting to different physical environments requires different skills.

Likewise, our culture has a strong influence on us. Most of us grow up in a Western culture that stresses independence, self-reliance, and personal privacy. Our families are small, consisting of one or two parents and siblings. This type of culture is considered *individualistic* (Hofstede, 1980; Matsumoto, 1996). However, if you grow up in China, Japan, or Latin America, you encounter a *collective* culture, one that stresses the group over the individual (Triandis, 1994). In these cultures, you most likely live with your family, which includes parents, grandparents, siblings, uncles, aunts, cousins, and other more distant relatives. You probably do not move away from home when you get married. Your privacy and your personal desires are secondary to the needs of your group and family. Interdependence, rather than independence, is stressed.

In addition to the collectivism–individualism dimension, cultures vary along many other dimensions, such as how strongly they stress traditional and separate roles for men and women. Within any single country many different cultures with competing or different viewpoints may coexist. For example, the predominant position in the United States is highly individualistic. However, the Hispanic and African-American cultures are strongly collective in their orientation. Therefore, African Americans may find themselves attempting to adjust to both collective and individualistic demands. Just as with adjusting to different physical environments, adjusting to different cultures requires separate skills and considerations.

Therefore, when we consider the process of adjusting and coping with our world, it is important to understand the impact of the physical and cultural environments. In addition, given the expanded opportunities we enjoy to travel and meet a wide variety of people, we will encounter people from many cultures and environments. Developing the most satisfying interpersonal relationships with these people requires that we understand their points of view and how their cultures and previous experiences have shaped their lives and beliefs. Without this understanding and appreciation, diversity can be frightening and threatening.

Taking Control of Our Lives

Some cultures have a strong belief that what happens to people is the result of fate. Individuals are born into a class or situation, and their challenge is to learn to accept their position or situation. In the United States and other Western cultures, however, many people believe that their destiny is in their hands. Such a culture stresses the need to take control and strive to reach our goals.

One of the most depressing and frightening things we can experience is the feeling that we don't have any control over our lives. Unfortunately, many people believe that they are the pawns of their physical and social environment. They fail to perceive the choices open to them and, instead of acting to control their situations, simply react as external conditions dictate. Such people never experience the joys of positive personal adjustment.

To be well adjusted in our society, we must make decisions about our behavior. Healthy personal adjustment is an active process that requires decisions and independent actions. Even in social relationships such as marriage, the more control people have, the happier they are with the relationship (Madden, 1987). A state of positive adjustment isn't something that happens to us; it's something we make happen.

Fortunately, human life is filled with both the freedom and the opportunity to make choices. Unlike many animals who possess instincts that program them to act in a predetermined manner, humans have few, if any, instincts. As we will see later in this book, hu-

Culture's Influence on Self Identity

One of the major distinctions that has been drawn between cultures is along the *individualism–collectivism* dimension (Hofstede, 1980). More individualistic cultures tend to place greater emphasis on the individual, valuing independence, personal rights, personal responsibility, and privacy. More collective cultures value the group and the individual's relationship to the group. The needs of the group are valued above individual rights or needs. Individuals gain satisfaction to the degree that they help their group. Bochner (1994) argued that these differences in culture should be reflected in the self-image of individuals in the different cultures. Specifically, he argued that the self-image of people from collective cultures should focus on their relationships to groups. On the other hand, the self-image of people from more individualistic cultures should consist predominantly of references to personal characteristics.

To examine this hypothesis, Bochner asked 78 subjects (Malaysia, 26 people; Australia, 32 people; and Great Britain, 20 people) to describe themselves by responding to 10 statements beginning with "I am...." A previous investigation (Hofstede, 1980) had identified the cultures of Australia and Great Britain as being individualistic and Malaysian culture as being collective.

Raters who were unaware of the subject's culture were asked to code the responses. The two categories of interest to our present discussion were idiocentric (personal) and group statements. Idiocentric statements were described as "statements about personal qualities, attitudes, beliefs, behaviors, states, and traits that *do not* relate to other people. Examples: 'I am honest'; 'I am intel-

ligent'; 'I am happy.'" Group statements involved responses "about group membership, demographic characteristics, and groups with which people experience a common fate. Examples: 'I am Roman Catholic'; 'I am a daughter'; 'I am a plumber'" (p. 279).

As can be seen in Table 1.2, culture did affect responses in line with Bochner's predictions. Although subjects from Australia and Great Britain gave more idiocentric descriptions of themselves than subjects from the collective culture of Malaysia, the Malaysian subjects used more group terms than subjects from the other two cultures. The results suggest that culture does influence the self-image we develop, and that people from different cultures emphasize different points in their self-descriptions.

TABLE 1.2 Self-References in Three Cultures

SELF-REFERENCES	NATIONALITY OF SUBJECTS		
	Malaysian	*Australian*	*British*
Group	11.38	5.53	5.10
Idiocentric	13.42	18.97	17.10
Collective	3.15	3.56	5.80

NOTE: The higher the score, the greater the salience.
Source: Adapted from S. Bochner *Journal of Cross Cultural Psychology, 25,* p. 281, copyright © 1994 by Sage Publications, Inc. Reprinted by permission of Sage Publications, Inc.

mans are influenced by various social and environmental situations. In spite of these influences, however, human beings have great potential to determine their own behaviors and attitudes toward life.

One of the best ways to identify and preserve our choices is to understand how and why specific experiences and situations in-

fluence us. Nowhere is the saying "knowledge is freedom" more applicable than in the area of personal adjustment. For example, we can know ourselves better by understanding the factors that have shaped our attitudes and values. This understanding will help us see why we choose to pursue certain occupations or why we feel guilty when performing certain actions. This understanding of our attitudes and values also helps us change or reshape those values with which we're uncomfortable. A case in point is Leo's childhood fear of leaving the house, which kept him confined indoors much of the time. Then Leo realized how he had developed his fear: It was based on his mother's overprotective concern about his getting hurt, not on the fact of real dangers lurking outside the house. Understanding the basis for his fear allowed Leo to change his attitude and venture outside with self-confidence.

Control is one of the major themes of this book. We will examine how we can control our **social interactions** and actively seek out friends. We will discuss the pitfalls of giving up our control and relying on crutches such as alcohol and drugs to mask problems and conflicts. We will examine positive ways of dealing with our life situations rather than hiding from our problems. By properly understanding the options we all have to control our own destiny, we can make great strides in personal growth and adjustment. In a real sense, control is one of the keys to making our lives live up to their potential.

Setting Personal Goals

Leo Beuerman had a purpose in life: to own his own business and live a life free of dependency on others. This goal not only guided him in his day-to-day activities, it also gave him the strength to carry on when his life became particularly trying.

Positive personal adjustment is aided when we have life **goals.** These goals give a sense of purpose to living and a direction toward which we can focus our energies. For example, the decision to become a nurse not only gives a person a future goal but also dictates present action. A person who has made such a decision will focus his or her school curriculum on science courses, may wish to choose medically related summer jobs, and

may choose friends who have the same goal or who already practice the profession. Goals should be set in many areas. We can have professional goals, social goals, and spiritual goals. By setting many types of goals, we can avoid becoming too preoccupied with any one aspect of our lives. Setting goals is a first step for reducing the stress of everyday life (Taylor, 1986).

While setting personal goals is important for forming a healthy personality, several points should be remembered in choosing these goals.

First, goals must be realistic. We must carefully evaluate our capabilities and potentials and set goals that, though challenging, are within our abilities. If we set unrealistically high goals, we will encounter frustration and disillusionment. If our goals are too low, we will suffer boredom. Thus, we must choose our goals carefully. To set realistic goals, we must first learn about ourselves and establish our self-identity. We must also remember that the goal-setting process is an ongoing one; we will be setting goals for ourselves throughout our lives. The attainment of one goal fosters the setting of a new one.

The second point to remember about goal setting is that even though goals give a direction to our behavior, we shouldn't become so obsessed with them that we fail to enjoy the present. Some people become so concerned with their future they fail to adjust to the present. College students who feel they can't spend time participating in sports or social activities because they must constantly prepare for a profession are not showing positive adjustment. In such cases, the obsession with the future goal may be the result of a lack of self-confidence. Either these people have failed to assess their abilities accurately, or their goals are unrealistically high. Another trap that some people fall into is the use of a future goal to excuse present behavior. People may hide behind a goal because they have no confidence in their ability to handle present situations.

LESSONS FROM LIFE

Freedom of Choice: Blessing or Curse

Several years ago a student and his father came to my office to discuss the student's difficulties in adjusting to the university. The father rattled out a long list of problems his son was having. His grades were not good; he had changed majors several times; he seemed to have no real direction; the student had been experimenting with drugs and alcohol; and he seemed to have no appreciation for all the things (automobile, stereo, clothes, computer) his father had given him. The father threw up his hands and exclaimed, "I just don't understand him. When I was a student, I never had the things he has. I went to college to be an engineer, and I couldn't have changed majors even if I wanted to. He just doesn't know how lucky he is, and, even though he has everything, he is floundering." The discussion went on like this for a period of time, the father pointing out his son's problem behaviors and the son attempting to explain and defend himself (and I sitting back like a voyeur peering into the soul of this family).

Just when I thought I was going to have to break in to keep these two from wrestling on the floor, the student stopped in midsentence as if dumbstruck by an idea. "You know," he said, "I think much of my trouble centers around the issue of choice. I do have a lot material things, options, and opportunities, many more than you ever had. You think this makes my life easier, but I think it makes it more difficult. I don't have a curfew in my dorm, like you did in college. So I have to decide when to come home. I often feel embarrassed telling my friends I want to leave a party just because I'm tired or think I *should* go home. In my dorm, it is easy to get alcohol or any other drugs. I have to make the decision about whether or not to use drugs. Unlike you, I've got a car and spending money. This allows me to go almost anywhere, but I have to make the choice." He continued listing the wide variety of choices he had, ones that were not open to his father in college. The student concluded, "Having all these choices and opportunities is great and I wouldn't want to give them up. But sometimes I'm so tired at the end of the day from having to make choices that I just wish someone would tell me what to do when."

The student's statement struck home with both his father and me. Like the father, I had viewed students of today as fortunate because they had so many more opportunities and so much more freedom that I had as a student. Yet it dawned on me, listening to my distressed student, that the additional freedom carries a price, sometimes a large price. Making decisions involves work—learning about the alternative and understanding the consequences of the various options. Making choices implies responsibility for the outcomes. Indeed, it is important to realize that the landscape of adjustment involves making choices, and as opportunities and options increase, so does the pressure associated with decision making.

Finally, some attention should be given to choosing goals whose attainment will result in personal satisfaction. Goals should represent a challenge, but achieving them should also be a source of pleasure. If your goal is to learn to play tennis, you should enjoy not only the learning process, but also the game itself once you've become a good tennis player. Unfortunately, some people are unable to experience satisfaction from their goals; their lives revolve around challenge only, and they fail to experience the joy of their past achievements. This problem often results when we allow others to set our goals rather than carefully choosing them ourselves on the basis of our own desires and abilities. A person is unlikely to enjoy being a lawyer if she or he chose that profession simply because of pressure from parents or friends.

Many of the topics discussed in this book will help you in setting realistic personal goals. We will examine human motives and how they guide and focus the individuals attention. We will also examine how people make decisions and what effects these decisions have on thoughts and behavior. In addition, we will examine some of the factors that prevent us from making decisions and setting goals. By understanding these topics, we should be better able to avoid the paralysis that some people experience when trying to set goals. Finally, much of the information covered in this text is aimed at helping you learn about yourself. The better you know yourself, the more you will be able to set personal goals that are within reach.

Interacting with Others

The human is a social animal. We are born into a social group (the family) and spend our lives interacting with others. As illustrated by John Donne's meditation, written in the seventeenth century, individuals live in a social network and are interdependent:

> No man is an island, entire of itself; every man is a piece of the Continent, a part of the main. If a clod be washed away by the sea, Europe is the less, as well as if a promontory were, as well as if a manor of thy friend's or of thine own were. Any man's death diminishes me, because I am involved in mankind, and therefore never send to know for whom the bell tolls; it tolls for thee.

Leo Beuerman clearly realized that the individual can't survive alone. One of his strongest impulses was to avoid a life of isolation. He longed for social interaction, and this longing motivated him to increase his mobility and venture into the world. Although it is clear that Leo wanted to be part of society, it is also clear that he realized that social interaction didn't mean social dependency. Leo felt that a satisfying social relationship must be based on give and take. Each individual must be able to participate in social relationships without becoming totally dependent on those

relationships and without giving up his or her identity and personal freedom.

An important part of personal development involves adjusting to the social world. We interact with a large number of people every day. In fact, it may be eye opening to count the number of people with whom you interact in a single day. All these people affect you to a greater or lesser degree, and in turn you have some influence on them.

In this book we will examine how others influence our attitudes and behaviors. We will discover some of the factors that motivate us to choose certain people as friends and to reject others. We will see how people influence the type of clothes we wear, the decisions we make, and the lifestyles we choose. We will also examine how our physical environment guides many of our social interactions.

An understanding of social influences is important for a number of reasons. First, we are often unaware of numerous factors that affect our behavior. We react unwittingly to social and situational influences. A greater awareness of the existence and effects of these factors will not only allow us to understand our behavior better but also give us greater ability to control our own actions. For example, a knowledge of how groups produce pressures for conformity will enable us to prepare better for group membership and to resist those pressures when necessary. To be forewarned is to be prepared.

A second reason to study the process of social interaction is that it will allow us to be better able to relate to others. We can become more aware of how our behavior affects others and more sensitive to the feelings of others.

Satisfying social relationships involve not only getting something for ourselves out of relationships but also meeting the needs of others. Thus we must be able to identify the needs of others. We must not only communicate our desires but also understand what others are communicating to us—that is, be a good receiver and sender of information (Fulmer, 1977). Social relationships, then, make us walk a tightrope between paying attention to and understanding ourselves and the people with whom we are interacting. This may, indeed, be one of the reasons that it is so difficult to build good interpersonal relationships.

A third reason for understanding our social world centers on a dilemma that most of us face every day of our lives. On one hand, we want to be liked and accepted by other people and to help make their lives happier. On the other hand, we want freedom to explore our world and learn about ourselves, free from social pressures and concerns about what others will think of us. In a sense, personal adjustment involves finding the right balance that will allow us both to have satisfying social interactions without becoming consumed by them and to act independently without becoming socially isolated.

On Becoming a Healthy and Happy Person

We have examined the process of adjustment. As we pointed out, one important step in this process is to set goals. One goal that most of us would set is being healthy and happy. Leo Beuerman, in fact, stated very clearly that his daily goal was to live his life so that he felt better about himself and his relationships with others than he had the day before.

Many writers and social scientists have tried to identify those characteristics that are common to happy and healthy people. Abraham Maslow, a humanistic psychologist, captures the essence of the well-adjusted person better than most who have tackled this task. Maslow studied the lives of famous people such as Eleanor Roosevelt and Albert Einstein, who were considered well adjusted and who made important contributions to society. We will discuss Maslow's work further in Chapter 2, but we can examine here the features that characterize these people.

1. They form close, caring interpersonal relationships. They are not afraid to be open and let others see how they feel. Interestingly, these well-adjusted people limited their close relationships to a few other people.

2. They perceive reality accurately and fully. They are good judges of people and can detect dishonesty and deceit. They have a similar ability to judge situations and can quickly determine both problems and solutions.

3. They accept themselves, others, and nature in general. They can accept situations that cannot be changed. They do not waste time worrying about what ought to be. Instead they make the best out of bad situations and personal imperfections.

4. They are creative and show a continued fresh appreciation of life and daily activities. They manage to find joy and excitement in even the most routine and casual activities. They allow themselves to feel, express, and experience.

5. They are willing to learn from anyone. They do not prejudge others or feel that only certain people have anything to offer them.

6. They are confident in their abilities and independent in thought and action. They have strong personal values and a sense of ethics. They do not strive to be what others think they should be. Rather, they strive to reach their own goals and live by their own code of ethics and morals.

7. They have a well-developed and nonhostile sense of humor.

The characteristics featured in this list may be difficult to emulate, but they can give us some direction in our own search for happiness and fulfillment. One important point to remember is that adjustment is a continuous process. We don't suddenly reach the point of adjustment. Rather it is a never-ending trip, with each day offering new experiences and new opportunities for personal development. We must take time to stop and smell the roses.

LEARNING ABOUT ADJUSTMENT

As we pointed out earlier, the path to adjustment is different for each of us. No two people have the same personal histories, nor do they face the same obstacles. The demands you face are different from those faced by the student seated next to you, and the demands on each of you will certainly be different from those faced by Leo Beuerman. No book can supply a program of adjustment to be followed by everyone; neither life nor adjustment is that simple.

However, you can facilitate your adjustment by understanding the factors that influence both your feelings and behavior and the feelings and behavior of others. One way of achieving this understanding is through careful reflection on the past and accurate observation of events and people in the present. These activities provide invaluable knowledge with which to guide personal adjustment.

Another important source of knowledge is the research and theory developed by social scientists. Their work aims to discover the factors that influence human behavior and emotion and to explain the process through which these factors work. A **theory** is a systematic statement that explains why events occur. Much of the research in psychology and other social sciences is directed at developing theories of human behavior and testing the validity of these theories.

The work of the psychologist is to understand why people act, feel, think, and react as they do. Psychologists attempt to discover and explain how and why certain factors affect most of the people most of the time. To accomplish this task, psychologists perform experiments, many of them in the laboratory, designed to test their explanations and rule out alternative explanations. This knowledge is invaluable from the standpoint of personal adjustment because it suggests why you become a particular type of person and why others behave as they do. Psychological theory

and research point out the important events and factors on which we should focus when trying to understand ourselves and others.

Moving toward Adjustment

The achievement of positive personal adjustment is a two-part process. The first part involves developing a clear and accurate understanding of yourself and others and of the physical and social factors that influence human behavior. This understanding can be achieved by examining the psychological literature presented in this book and supplementing it with observations of your own behavior and surroundings. The psychological literature should serve as a guide to basic processes and help you identify those factors in your personal life that deserve special attention. Your own observations can supplement the literature by pinpointing specific cases in which these psychological principles are relevant.

Once you have developed a more complete understanding of yourself and others, it is important to take the second step—applying your knowledge. The road to healthy personal adjustment is paved with trials and errors. You must experiment with new behaviors and new ways of handling problems. The specific nature of these behaviors should be guided by your understanding of social and psychological processes. Even with this guide, however, some of your new attempts at adjustment will not be satisfactory, whereas others will prove very satisfying. It's important not to be discouraged by your mistakes; add the lessons learned from the mistakes to your store of knowledge. The more you understand yourself and others, the more capable you will be of making wise choices. The adjustment process is a lifelong activity; and it is important to have the courage to attempt new behaviors, to have the wisdom to accept and learn from successes and failures, and to have the flexibility to meet the demands of changing personal, social, and physical environments.

ORGANIZATION OF THIS BOOK

The process of adjustment involves knowing yourself, coping with the stress of everyday life, understanding others, and being aware of the influence of the environment on social behavior. While these endeavors are interrelated, we have attempted to examine each of them in order.

Chapters 1 to 4 are organized around the theme of knowing the self. In these chapters we look at how the personality develops from birth to adulthood and what factors influence this development. We also discuss how we can learn about ourselves and form self-concepts. In addition, we examine the similar and different challenges faced by men and women as they adjust to their world. In a sense these chapters discuss the basic tools each person has for meeting the challenges of everyday life. These tools include personality, self-concept, attitudes, and beliefs.

Having the tools is still a long way from getting the house built. As we discussed, our world is filled with daily choices and challenges. The pathway to adjustment is paved with difficult decisions and stress. Understanding the types of stresses that we face and learning how to control our lives to deal effectively with these stresses is the topic of Chapters 5 to 8. These chapters examine how stress arises. You may be surprised to learn that some of the joys of life, such as getting a promotion or taking a vacation, create stress. We will find that stress affects both our mental and physical health. These chapters will also examine a wide variety of responses to stress. Some of these responses are maladaptive, such as alcohol or drug addiction and emotional disorders. Other responses that involve taking control of the situation and meeting the problem head on are adaptive and can lead to positive personal growth. In some cases, the stress may require us to seek the help of others to cope; knowing when and how to seek help increases our options in adjusting to our

world. Chapter 8 examines the wide range of opportunities we have in seeking the help of others in our quest for adjustment.

Chapters 9 to 12 focus on interpersonal relationships. As we have pointed out, a major portion of the adjustment process involves interacting with and relating to others. The chapters in this part deal with the factors that influence the relationship between two people. Chapters 9 to 11 focus on developing interpersonal relationships. These chapters examine how individuals get to know each other, how norms and unwritten rules guide the acquaintance process, and how certain factors determine with whom an individual will fall in love. We also discuss intimate relationships, sexual behavior, and marriage in these chapters. The final chapter in this group, Chapter 12, examines the changing face of the family and both healthy and unhealthy dynamics that occur in families.

Chapters 13 to 15 conclude the text with an exploration of ways our social and physical environments affect our behavior. Chapter 13 examines how belonging to a group can affect behavior. Issues such as conformity, dehumanization, and decision making in groups are addressed. Chapter 14 looks at factors that affect us in the work setting. Chapter 15 focuses on the physical environment. The effects of too few people and too many people are covered. We also look at how physical features such as temperature, noise, and building design influence behavior. The chapter concludes with a discussion of how living in a large city can influence our feelings for and responses to other people.

We believe that learning about others will also allow you to understand yourself better. Because of this belief, we open each chapter with a brief account of events in the life of some person or persons. Throughout the chapter we illustrate how a particular theory or research finding can lead to a greater understanding of this person or event. In this way we hope to broaden the perspective of human adjustment to include an understanding of both the self and other people.

A final note involves the philosophy of this book. As you can surmise from our earlier remarks, we don't believe that anyone or any book can tell you how to adjust. We feel that the purpose of a book such as this should be to supply the basic knowledge with which you can choose your own pattern of adjustment, so we refrain from saying: You must do this or that to adjust. Rather, we have tried to draw on the principles of psychology that should give you the greatest insight into human behavior. These principles are not just educated guesses; they have in most cases been tested through careful observation and experimentation. We have tried not only to present theories of human behavior but also to discuss the major findings that support them. The cited research should provide an understanding of how we learn about human behavior; it may also serve as a guide for your own experiments and observations.

LEARNING TO LEARN

Before we move on to the other chapters, there is one issue that we should briefly discuss. Although all of us know how to read, many of us don't develop effective ways to learn what we read. Nothing is more frustrating than spending hours reading only to draw a blank when we are tested on what we have read. There is no sure-fire formula that will ensure that you score an *A* on every test, but some pointers can help you better understand and retain what you have read.

First, remember that a book is a form of communication between the authors and the reader (Worchel & Shebilske, 1996). Authors develop an outline and fill in this outline as they write the book. Readers construct an internal representation of the material that they have read. This representation is also an outline. Effective communication results when the author and reader have the same outline.

Therefore, it is important that the two outlines be similar. Students who learn well from texts quickly develop internal representations that match the text structure.

A second goal in learning from texts is to get the material from short-term memory into long-term memory. *Short-term memory* contains information that we retain for only a short period of time. For example, when you make a call to inquire about a newspaper ad, you read the telephone number, dial that number, and quickly forget it. The telephone number was entered only into your short-term memory. However, the number of your best friend is committed into your *long-term memory*. You know this number and do not need to look it up in the telephone book, each time you want to call your friend. In a similar fashion, we want to get the important material in this text into your long-term memory.

Many procedures have been developed to achieve these desired goals. One of the better known is called the *SQ3R:* survey, question, read, recite, and review (Robinson, 1970). This learning technique begins with a *survey* of the material. You begin by surveying the outline at the beginning of the chapter to note generally what it covers. Next, skim the section titles in the chapter to get a more complete picture of the topics covered and the order of coverage. Finally, read the chapter summary provided at the end of the chapter.

The second step in SQ3R is to *question*. Ask yourself what you want to learn in each section. In addition, examine the questions that are provided in the boxes throughout each chapter. These questions will help you to focus your attention and anticipate what we will present in each section.

The third step is to *read* the material. For most people, the best reading procedure is to read in chunks. The size of the chunk will vary for different readers; for some it will be a section, whereas for others it may be a number of sections. Don't stop reading within the chunk; take your breaks after you have completed a chunk. After each chunk, ask your-self whether you understand the material you have read.

The fourth step is to *recite.* You don't have to walk across campus reciting out loud passages from your adjustment text. Rather, after each section, close the book and go over in your mind the material you have read. You can also use the questions within each chapter to guide you in this activity.

Finally, *review* the material after you have completed the chapter. Read the summary and review the key terms provided at the end of the chapter. Flip through the chapter again to review the basic points raised in each section. You may also find it helpful to review the material with a classmate.

We can add one further step to the SQ3R method; a step called *apply.* We have found that it is easier (and more fun) to read material that applies to our own lives. We pay more attention to this kind of material and can remember it better. Therefore, as you read, try seeing how the material helps you better understand the incident presented at the beginning of the chapter and how the material fits your own experiences. We aid these activities by referring back to the opening incident throughout the chapter and asking questions about your own life.

Our intent in providing this guide is to enable you not only to enjoy reading this text but also to retain and use its information.

REVIEW QUESTIONS

6. Individuals from _____ cultures tend to be more concerned with their groups and their role in the groups than with their own independence.

7. _____ are an important aspect of adjustment because they guide our actions and give us a sense of purpose.

8. T or F: Well-adjusted people are careful to learn only from those whom they admire and look up to.

9. Well-adjusted people have a _____ and _____ sense of humor.

10. SQ3R involves _____, _____, _____, _____, and _____.

SUMMARY

1. Adjustment is a complex process that involves (a) learning about and understanding ourselves, (b) using our understanding to set realistic goals, (c) using our abilities to control our environment, and (d) being sensitive to the needs and concerns of others. Each change in our world, whether positive or negative, creates new challenges for adjustment.

2. Several questions have been raised about human nature. One concerns whether people are inherently selfish or socially conscious. Another concerns the degree to which human characteristics, behavior, and potential are determined by biology (inherited) or by the so-

cial and physical environment (learned). A third deals with the degree to which they are controlled by environmental reward–punishment contingencies. Still another question concerns the degree to which personality can be changed after childhood. Each of these issues has important implications for how society should be structured to aid personal adjustment.

3. Self-identity includes our values and priorities, our relationships and position in groups, and our personalities and individual potentials. We have many views of ourselves. Investigators have identified many of these self-images, including the actual self, the ideal self, the ought self, the can self, and the future self. Adjustment is less often determined by the content of any of these self-images than by the relationship among them. It is important to undertake periodic self-appraisals to determine how you see yourself, how you would like to be, and how you possibly could be. In undertaking this appraisal, it is also important to separate images driven by your own desires and perceptions from images based on how others want you to be.

4. Our physical and cultural environment influence our adjustment process. For example, some cultures are more individualistic, emphasizing the independence and responsibility of the individual. Others are more collective, emphasizing the importance of the group (family, work, country) and the role of the individual in the group.

5. Adjustment often involves recognizing our choices and taking control over our lives. Setting realistic goals is an important function of adjustment because it gives us a sense of purpose, guides our actions, and helps determine our progress. Adjustment involves developing successful relationships, but we must ensure that we do not let others set our goals and determine what we should be.

6. One list of the characteristics of well-adjusted people includes (a) forming close and meaningful personal relationships, (b) perceiving reality accurately and fully, (c) accepting themselves, others, and nature, (d) being creative and holding a fresh appreciation of life, (e) being willing to learn from anyone, (f) being confident in their abilities and being independent in thought and action, and (g) having a well-developed, nonhostile sense of humor.

7. Adjustment is a two-part process. The first part involves developing a clear and accurate understanding of yourself and others. The second involves applying your knowledge to guide your actions and thinking.

CRITICAL THINKING QUESTIONS

1. Change poses new challenges for adjustment. We all like to look back at the "good old days" and remember how things were. Take a moment to compare the world you face today with that you faced ten years ago. What changes have there been in technology, in health issues, and in the work and social environment? What new challenges (good and bad) have these changes posed for adjustment?

2. There are various theories regarding human nature. Each of these has implications for how society should be structured to enhance adjustment. Assume that you accept the position that human behavior is totally controlled by inherited biological characteristics and that, once established, personality and behavior patterns cannot be changed. Given this position, how would you structure a society (education, social relationships, work settings, health care) to allow people to fit in and society to prosper?

3. Consider the various images you have of yourself. For the actual self, complete the sentence, "I am a person who...." For the ideal self, complete the sentence, "Given the opportunity, I would like to be a person who...." Compare your responses to the two sentences to determine the discrepancy between the two self-concepts. Next, determine how many of the characteristics you listed involve you as an individual (traits such as intelligent, beautiful, rich), and how many concern social relationships (a member of a group, a position in a group). This comparison will reveal another interesting aspect of the self-identity; some part of our identity is focused on personal characteristics and some on social relationships.

MATCHING EXERCISE_____

Match each term with its definition.

a. adjustment   **d.** humanists   **g.** self-identity
b. behaviorists   **e.** instinct   **h.** social interaction
c. goal   **f.** self-appraisal   **i.** theory

1. Innate program that determines an organism's behavior in a given situation
2. Relating or interacting with other people
3. Object or condition that a person desires to obtain
4. Complex personal process that involves learning about oneself, setting goals, and coping with social and situational demands
5. Systematic statement that explains why events occur

6. Self-examination aimed at identifying one's abilities, values, and goals
7. Psychologists who hold the position that people are basically good and society should give them freedom to choose their behavior and react their potential
8. Psychologists who believe that behavior is determined by rewards and punishments in the external environment
9. A definition or interpretation of the self

Answers to Matching Exercise

a. 4   b. 8   c. 3   d. 7   e. 1   f. 6   g. 9   h. 2   i. 5

ANSWERS TO REVIEW QUESTIONS_____

1. false
2. anomie
3. humanists
4. false
5. b

6. collective
7. goals
8. false
9. well-developed, nonhostile
10. survey, question, read, recite, review

THE DEVELOPING PERSONALITY

Dr. Martin Luther King, Jr.

Martin Luther King, Jr.

"That night will never leave my mind," Martin Luther King, Jr. recalled. "It was the angriest I have ever been in my life" (Oates, 1982, p. 16). The incident occurred in the early teenage years of the man who would become the greatest civil rights leader in American history. Young Martin had just won a prize in an oratorical contest in Valdosta, Georgia. Accompanied by a high school teacher, he was riding home on a bus. When the bus stopped and let on several white riders, the driver ordered King and the teacher, a woman, to stand so that the whites could sit. King at first refused. The driver flew into a rage and called Martin a "black son-of-a-bitch." The crisis passed when Martin's teacher signaled that he should move. It was one of the young King's most dramatic early brushes with out-and-out racism, and it left a lasting impression.

Compared with the experience of other African Americans, Martin Luther King's childhood in Atlanta, Georgia, was comfortable and secure. Born in 1929, he lived in a large house with his parents, his brother and sister, and his grandmother. As a child Martin showed great promise. He was healthy, popular, and fun loving; though small, he dominated his peers athletically and intellectually. His friends commented that there was a good chance of getting hurt playing basketball or football with Martin, but it was his ability to dominate with words that set Martin apart. Even as a young child he was fascinated with speaking. His mother recalled Martin saying at age 6, "You just wait and see, I'm going to get me some *big* words" (Bennett, 1968, p. 17). He quickly developed a strong, clear voice and the capacity to speak fluently and eloquently. These qualities made him a leader among his male friends and very attractive in his teenage years to a number of young women.

Martin's mother and father were both key figures in his early years. His mother had to explain the realities of race relations in the South after the parents of his white friends would no longer let Martin play with their sons when they reached school age. However, she always made him remember that he was somebody, that he was as good as anyone else, white or black. His father, the pastor of a Baptist church, was a stern disciplinarian who commanded great respect. Nonetheless, Martin always maintained a degree of independence, even defiance. His father recalled that "he was the most peculiar child whenever you whipped him. He'd stand there, and the tears would run down and he'd never cry. His grandmother couldn't stand to see it" (Oates, 1982, p. 14).

His grandmother, known in the household as Mama, was an extremely important presence in Martin's early life. She was a constant source of emotional support and would go off to her own room to sob at the sight of Martin's distress and determination when he needed to be whipped. Martin's attachment to Mama led him twice to jump out the second floor window of his house in apparent attempts to commit suicide. Once Martin jumped when his younger brother slid down the bannister and accidentally knocked his grandmother unconscious. Martin thought she was dead. The second time occurred when Martin was 12, and Mama did actually die of a sudden heart attack. Martin's emotions were strong, and his attachments were deep.

The young man who emerged from this close-knit, secure family had many talents. Martin was a precocious student who skipped the ninth and twelfth grades and entered Morehouse College at the age of 15. After finishing at Morehouse, he also graduated at the top of his class from Crozer Seminary near Philadelphia and then earned his Ph.D. from Boston University. After his graduate studies, Dr. King returned to the ministry, becoming pastor of the Dexter Avenue Baptist Church in Montgomery, Alabama. He was determined to use his many talents to make a difference. He always remembered the idea expressed by Henry David Thoreau in "Civil Disobedience" that one honest man, sticking by his beliefs, can have an enormous impact on his society and the world. King wanted to have that impact, and it was in Montgomery that he did.

The event that led to King's rise to leadership in the civil rights movement occurred on December 1, 1955. Rosa Parks, a black seamstress, boarded a crowded bus. She paid her fare and took a seat in the "Negro section" at the back. Six whites boarded the bus at the next stop, and the bus driver then went to the back and ordered the blacks to give up their places so that the whites could be seated. Three blacks yielded to this established custom and immediately rose, but Rosa Parks remained seated. The bus driver repeated his demand, and again she refused. For this act of insubordination, she was arrested. Her arrest provided the catalyst for the unification of the black freedom movement under King's leadership.

The African-American leaders of Montgomery felt that it was time to protest the treatment of Rosa Parks and of all African Americans in the South. A one-day, nonviolent boycott of the bus line by African Americans was planned by King. Encouraged by its success, the black leaders elected King to head the Montgomery freedom movement, and they decided to continue the boycott until the city's buses were desegregated. King's following grew, and the one-day boycott evolved into a 382-day struggle that finally ended on November 14, 1956, when the Supreme Court declared illegal the Alabama law requiring segregation on buses. It was a victory for the black freedom movement; for its new leader, Martin Luther King, Jr.; and for King's doctrine of nonviolent protest.

In the years after the Montgomery boycott, King led drives for African-American freedom and equality throughout the South, always with the goal of achieving his ends through civil disobedience and nonviolence. Despite great danger and loud protests from those who disagreed with his tactics, King persisted with his advocacy of nonviolence. He earned the respect of thousands, black and white alike, and won the right to create the defining moment in the civil rights movement of the 1960s. On August 23, 1963, he spoke to a crowd of 250,000 at the Lincoln Memorial. His speech in this culminating event of the march on Washington will never be forgotten. King said he dreamed of the day when all people would be able to sing together the words of the African-American spiritual, "Free at last! Free at last! Thank God Almighty, we are free at last!"

Within a year of the march on Washington, thanks in great part to King's tireless efforts, the Civil Rights Act of 1964 was signed into law. In the following years King became active in opposing the American war in Vietnam and in mobilizing protests against poverty in the United States. He was in Memphis, Tennessee, on April 4, 1968, organizing a march of sanitation workers demanding better working conditions, when he was shot down by an assassin's bullet. He was only 39 years old.

UNDERSTANDING PERSONALITY

How can we understand Martin Luther King? What forces contributed to his development from a young child to a grown man? How can we account for his capacity to move people and to help move the nation? In this chapter we will consider the nature of personality and the way it develops in the early years.

A personality is a complex construction. Many forces shape it, from before birth to the present. These forces include people's biological inheritance and their environment and culture at home, in their community, and in their society. They also include the consequences of a person's own behavior and initiatives. The theories and research that help us understand personality development are also complex and varied. We think that each of the approaches to personality that has emerged in psychology can help us understand individuals like Martin Luther King and the rest of us as well.

We will consider the four major approaches to personality in this chapter and what each contributes to our understanding of Dr. King. These four approaches are the *psychodynamic approach,* which emphasizes the internal and unconscious psychological forces that develop in childhood to shape the adult; the *behavioral approach,* which emphasizes how people learn from events that reward or punish their behavior; the *humanistic approach,* which emphasizes people's internal drive to develop all their potentials; and the *trait approach,* which emphasizes the various characteristics that both heredity and environment shape in each individual. Although these approaches are sometimes seen as competing or even antagonistic, we feel that each has important insights that contribute to our main task—understanding the individual.

PSYCHODYNAMIC APPROACHES TO PERSONALITY DEVELOPMENT

Psychodynamic approaches to personality have grown out of the theories of Sigmund Freud. Two of Freud's major ideas were that personality is shaped by unconscious motives and conflicts and that people are affected by different motives and conflicts at different times, or stages, of their lives (McAdams, 1990). These two ideas were central to Freud, and they remain central in other psychodynamic approaches to personality. After considering Freud's theories of personality, we will consider some helpful contributions to psychodynamic theory by Erik Erikson. Erikson also discussed motives and conflicts and gave us a picture of psychological growth that nicely supplements Freud's.

Freud's Theory of Personality Structure

Sigmund Freud is a giant in the history of psychology. Freud's thinking has had tremendous impact on our culture, and his 23 volumes of writings touch on virtually every aspect of human experience. Many of Freud's ideas are highly controversial, but we consider his view of development of the major structures of personality during childhood to be useful in thinking about a person's struggle to adjust (Freud, 1940).

The Id and the Emergence of the Ego. According to Freud, the child's personality, or psyche, at birth consists of a single entity. Freud called this entity the **id.** The id behaves instinctively, unconsciously seeking pleasure and satisfaction of bodily needs, such as hunger, sex, and aggression. Unfortunately, the methods the id uses to gain pleasure are not very effective. It relies heavily on what Freud called *primary process,* imagining objects or behaviors that will bring pleasure. We are all familiar with daydreaming—about great achievements, love, food, or sex—but we know that fantasy by itself won't satisfy a person's needs. To get the real satisfaction we require for survival, said Freud, we develop a second entity within the psyche to help the id cope with reality. This entity is called the **ego.**

The ego is the conscious, reality-oriented component of the personality. It perceives how the world works and devises plans for how best to obtain gratification. The ego may observe that it is useless to cry for a feeding until four hours have passed but that then screaming loudly brings results. It may notice that whimpering will lead to being picked up and rocked. Whatever the circumstances, the ego perceives, notices, remembers, plans, and directs action to obtain gratification for the id.

The Oedipus Complex and the Emergence of the Superego. Freud postulated that, at about the age of 3 or 4, children develop feelings of intense love and hostility toward their parents. He felt that boys develop a desire to possess their mothers completely and to sweep their fathers away as rivals for their mothers' affections. He claimed that girls at this age want to eliminate their mothers and have their fathers to themselves. These desires make up Freud's famous *Oedipus complex,* named after the Greek king who unknowingly murdered his father and married his mother. The female's Oedipal wishes are sometimes called the *Electra complex,* referring to Electra's love for her father in the *Oresteia,* the Greek trilogy by Aeschylus.

Ideally, the Oedipus complex is resolved when the child's desire to possess one parent and destroy the other is *repressed* by the ego, that is, driven back into the unconscious, into the id, because of fears of punishment and loss of love. Because these fears are so intense, the Oedipal wishes are completely destroyed. Then the child begins to *identify* with, or emulate, the parent of the same sex, the one he or she previously wanted to eliminate. The child tries to be like that parent because of that parent's success in getting the love of the opposite-sex parent, the one whom the girl or boy desires. By emulating her mother or his father, the child vicariously enjoys the other parent's affections toward that parent.

A key consequence of identifying with the parent of his or her own sex is that the child internalizes that parent's moral standards and ideals. These principles then form a third and separate entity in the psyche called the **superego.** The superego actually contains two parts: the *conscience,* containing prohibitions and restrictions, and the *ego-ideal,* containing aspirations and values to strive for. The superego can be harsh and punitive, causing the ego to feel very guilty if the person behaves inconsistently with its moral dictates.

It seems clear that Martin Luther King, Jr. emerged from the years of the Oedipal conflict with both a firm conscience and an ego-ideal, and that he identified strongly with his father. For example Martin's father was a minister, and the son became one, too. Also, his father was a harsh disciplinarian with clear principles that he would not compromise. On more than one occasion, young Martin watched his father strongly react against the way white people in Georgia treated blacks. One time a white policemen checking his father's driver's license called the elder King "Boy," the term then used for black men by many whites. Martin's father defiantly pointed to his son and told the policeman, "Do you see this child here? That's a *boy* there. I'm a *man.* I'm Reverend King" (Oates, 1982, p. 12). Such defiance was dangerous. Martin admired his father's courage and principles and never forgot the lessons they taught him.

The Ego and Sound Adjustment.   According to Freud, after the Oedipal complex is re-

solved, the three major structures of the personality—the id, the ego, and the superego—are in place. The role of the conscious, rational ego is undoubtedly the most crucial to a person's healthy adjustment. In the healthy person the ego functions as the executive of the personality. It satisfies to a sufficient, but not complete, degree the desires of the id, the prohibitions and exhortations of the superego, and the constraints of reality. The ego has to coordinate these demands and plan effective behavior. It must control our desires and express them in appropriate ways, abide by moral standards, and face the world realistically. These tasks can be difficult and involve many conflicts.

Psychological Defenses.   A strong ego is essential to sound adjustment. According to Freud, the ego has the capacity to create some helpers in handling its complex role. These helpers are the ego's *defense mechanisms.* Freud's theory of ego-defense mechanisms, modified by his daughter, Anna Freud (1946), represent one of his most important contributions (Cramer, 1990; 1996). For convenience, we will organize the defense mechanisms into three categories: the behavior-channeling defenses, the primary reality-distorting defenses, and the secondary reality-distorting defenses.

Behavior-Channeling Defenses.   The three behavior-channeling defense mechanisms are identification, displacement, and sublimation. As we discussed earlier, *identification* involves emulating or imitating another person—usually a parent, an admired friend, an older person in one's profession, or a leader in a group—and trying to be as much like that person as possible. Identification is important in giving us a clear idea of how to behave in various situations; it thus relieves us of much anxiety, conflict, and confusion. Instead of floundering in uncertainty, we follow the example of a trusted other. By identifying with his father, Martin Luther King, Jr. resolved his

Oedipal conflicts and effectively channeled his energies and aspirations for years to come.

Freud regarded identification as one of the healthy defense mechanisms, but there are some pathological instances of it. Inmates in concentration camps have sometimes identified with guards to resolve insecurities and conflicts about how to survive. This action is known as "identification with the aggressor" (Bettelheim, 1958).

Displacement is a defense mechanism used to channel aggression. Consider an employee who is humiliated by her boss in front of other employees or a student who is jilted by his girlfriend. These frustrating circumstances arouse anger and aggressive feelings. But aggressive behavior toward the boss or the girlfriend would be foolhardy: The woman wants to keep her job, and the man wants to keep his relationship. Instead, using displacement, these two injured parties would be likely to redirect, or displace, their anger onto another person or object against whom it is safe to express hostility. The humiliated employee may yell at other drivers on her way home from work, and the jilted student may punch the wall. Such displacement reduces fear of losing control and fear of punishment or retaliation. Displacement most commonly occurs because of the realization of the dangers of directing anger toward the person who aroused it, but it can also occur when moral restraints prevent the expression of aggression. A father may be furious with his children for breaking a window but feel that it's not right to express his aggressive feelings toward them. He could avoid stressful guilt feelings by displacing his anger. In this case, the family dog may be in for trouble.

The third of this group of ego-defenses is *sublimation,* the major technique people use to direct socially unacceptable sexual and aggressive urges into socially acceptable behavior. For example, Freud thought that a surgeon might have channeled aggressive feelings into cutting others in a constructive rather than a harmful way. Through sublima-tion one minimizes anxiety by performing behavior that is socially approved, that will provide some satisfaction of personal needs and impulses, and that is effective in reality. Sublimation is the defense mechanism that usually contributes most positively to an individual's adjustment. It produces effective, socially useful behavior that maintains inner peace and harmony.

These three behavior-channeling defenses are important means of resolving anxiety, and they make, in most instances, a positive contribution to personal adjustment. Sublimation nearly always leads to adaptive and productive behavior. Identification can have positive or negative consequences, depending on the person with whom we identify. If the person is successful and effective by prevailing social standards, then identification with that person will be helpful to one's adjustment to social realities. Displacement is highly tuned to reality and keeps a person out of trouble with those that might cause harm. However, it may lead to destructive action against others who are powerless and in this way have negative consequences for society as a whole. Overall, however, these defenses usually help us to act effectively. The same cannot be said for the reality-distorting defenses.

Primary Reality-Distorting Defenses. One way people minimize anxiety is simply by pushing threatening concerns and the anxiety they cause out of conscious awareness. The most primitive and basic defense mechanisms—repression and denial—perform these tasks. Repression and denial operate on an almost totally unconscious level, seriously distorting both internal and external reality. Repression operates to keep anxiety-producing impulses and guilt feelings out of a person's awareness. Denial operates to ignore or distort reality so that the person is not made anxious by external threats.

We encountered *repression* earlier when we discussed its role in the resolution of the Oedipal complex. Repression usually operates to control sexual and aggressive impulses. It does so when we feel guilty about these feelings or worry that we're losing control of our feelings and impulses. When we say that sexual impulses are repressed, we mean that they are never admitted into a person's awareness. Repression keeps them in the unconscious. Similarly, aggressive feelings that people could never admit, such as hostility toward parents, may be repressed. In addition to repressing basic impulses, people can also repress guilt feelings or feelings of shame. These unpleasant, anxiety-provoking feelings are simply kept out of awareness. In short, as a result of repression, people are not overwhelmed by powerful and frightening impulses on one hand or punishing and debilitating guilt feelings on the other. They are left free to cope with the demands of reality.

Coping with reality is not always so appealing either, especially when there are threatening circumstances to be handled. This is when the defense mechanism of *denial* comes into play. People often simply deny that there is any danger. They ignore warnings and tell themselves that nothing is wrong. One common example of denial is parents denying that their children are having learning or emotional difficulties when it is quite clear that something is wrong and needs correcting. Denying unpleasant facts can mean that harmful behaviors or situations are perpetuated and problems that could be solved are left unattended.

Secondary Reality-Distorting Defenses. Repression and denial push out of consciousness real feelings and real dangers. But the repressed feelings put further pressure on the ego, and sometimes additional techniques come into play to remove further threatening feelings from consciousness. These secondary defense mechanisms usually do the follow-up work of repression or denial (White, 1964).

Projection is one of the most common defense mechanisms. It involves assigning to others traits, impulses, or attitudes that you feel in yourself but can't acknowledge. Projection follows repression, since awareness of the characteristic is first repressed and then projected onto others. A person who feels sexually attracted to someone may project that attraction onto the other person and believe that the other person is seducing him or her. People very often project their own feelings of selfishness or hostility onto others. Thus we see what we think are the worst things about ourselves in other people. The reality-distorting nature of this defense is obvious. A person perceives characteristics in others that simply are not there. While true feelings and tendencies in the self are not admitted, the anxiety they would cause if they were admitted is avoided.

Another secondary defense mechanism is *reaction-formation*. In this case a person who is afraid to admit a certain feeling or attitude about a particular person or situation adopts just the opposite attitude as a way of keeping the true attitude from rising into consciousness and avoiding the anxiety that it would cause. For example, maybe someone you see often really bores you, or you feel envious or resentful of that person. Instead of admitting your true feeling, you tell yourself what great friends the two of you are. Usually the feeling or attitude expressed through reaction-formation seems rigid and exaggerated: The person may overdo the act. Thus, a person who is romantically and sexually attracted to people of the same sex may become vehemently anti-gay and anti-lesbian. A person who feels drawn toward lurid sexual material may react against those tendencies and become a crusader against pornography.

Rationalization is another extremely common defense mechanism. In this case, a person behaves according to his or her impulses but doesn't admit the real reasons. Instead, the person justifies or rationalizes the action by offering some socially acceptable reason for doing it. People who are cruel to their children justify their behavior by saying they are only trying to help the child learn right from wrong. People often rationalize selfishness by saying they think needy people should be taught self-reliance. Hungry people may justify overindulging themselves at fast food restaurants by believing the ad that says "You deserve a break today."

Defense Mechanisms and Adjustment. Our tendency to use psychological defense mechanisms is extremely common. Some defense mechanisms will lead us to take adaptive action, but most of them simply handle anxiety and stress psychologically. They help the ego by warding off feelings of fear, guilt, conflict, frustration, and loss of control.

Defense mechanisms can be abused, but they are absolutely necessary for dealing with the stresses of living. Well-adjusted people use them regularly but do not let them dominate their behavior, perceptions, or feelings. Ego-defenses can safely be used to manage stress and anxiety, but you should remain aware of how they work so that they do not manage you in maladaptive ways.

In their pure form, defense mechanisms operate unconsciously, but people can also reduce anxiety by using conscious variants of the defenses, which involve much less actual distortion of reality (see Kroeber, 1963). For example, people can consciously suppress undesirable impulses rather than unconsciously repressing them. Similarly, they can consciously decide to overcompensate for aggressive feelings by being polite and warm without engaging in an unconscious reaction formation. To the extent that defenses involve unconscious denials and falsifications of reality and inner emotions, it seems that they impede adjustment and personal growth. At the same time, they do provide needed relief. On the whole, it seems that the conscious variants of the defenses, often called **coping mechanisms,** offer the best solution. They interfere less with reality and self-knowledge and can

be used more flexibly than the rather rigid defense mechanisms. The totally unconscious defenses offer stronger protection against anxiety, but they produce more distortion and more rigidity.

Conscious and unconscious defenses can have a strong influence on a person's overall pattern of behavior. Some people develop a set of defenses into a defensive organization that has a pervasive effect on how they act (White, 1964). A boy who was taught as a young child that sexual curiosity and sexual play are immoral may avoid anything that involves sex, project sexuality onto others, and suppress his own sexual strivings. He may feel very uneasy about any affectionate feelings that seem tinged with sexual desire and may find security only by rigidly avoiding even the most innocent sexual behavior. A college student who is terrified of academic failure may throw all her energies into achievement, repress any resentments against pressures to excel, and project competitive behavior onto others. She may even rationalize cheating on exams.

In these two examples, the individuals involved develop a pattern of traits that protect them from feelings of anxiety and guilt. Such patterns are self-sustaining precisely because they are effective in reducing these feelings. Is there any reason to regard such defensive organizations as maladaptive? Perhaps not. We all have defensive patterns of behavior to some extent, and most people function perfectly well with their little rigidities, compulsions, fears, drives, and strivings. They are certainly human, they are sometimes endearing, and they give us individuality and identity. On the other hand, too large a part of our energies can be given over to defensive behaviors. To satisfy defensive needs, one person may be consumed by a need to obtain affection and approval, another may be constantly focused on power issues, and another may always be concerned with rules, regulations, and other safety structures. A major cost of these defensive behaviors can be the inhibition or repression of true feelings and distortion of reality. Fatigue, chronic feelings of dissatisfaction, and insomnia can also result (White, 1964). Still, many people seem locked into these behavior patterns until there is a change for the better initiated by dissatisfaction and desire for a better life, or a change for the worse when the inability to effectively manage increasing anxiety or successful, happy relationships leads to a psychological disorder.

Erikson's Theory of Childhood Development

Martin Luther King emerged from his childhood years as an independent and talented young man. Freud's theories of the id, the ego, and the superego, and his account of the ego-defense mechanisms, don't fully explain this outcome. However, one of Freud's best-known followers, Erik Erikson, has outlined a theory of psychological development that is helpful in understanding how a person with King's qualities might emerge from childhood. Erikson's (1968) theory begins discussing four early stages of childhood development that were originally identified by Freud as the oral, anal, phallic, and latency stages. In this chapter we present Erikson's views of development in those stages. In the next chapter, on adolescence and adulthood, we discuss four adult stages that Erikson added to his theory of psychological development.

We can understand Erikson's theory of early development in terms of a famous statement of Freud's. Asked what made a person healthy, Freud responded, "Love and work" (*Liebe und Arbeit*). Erikson's discussions of the *psychosocial stages* of development can be understood in terms of how a child develops the capacities to love and work.

Erikson believed that the way parents respond to a child's physical, emotional, and social needs is of critical importance. If a child's needs are met in a consistent and caring way, the psychological outcome is likely to be a positive adjustment. If these needs are frustrated or if the child is treated arbitrarily, the outcome is likely to be less than positive. Let us consider Erikson's views of how adjustment is affected by parent–child interaction in the first few years of life.

Trust versus Mistrust.   A child's needs in the earliest months of life are for nourishment and for the physical comfort that comes from cleanliness and warmth. This period Freud called the *oral stage*. The child's needs place great demands on the time, energy, and patience of the parents. For Erikson, the critical question for psychological development is how these needs are met. The child who experiences the parents as dependable and caring will develop a **sense of basic trust.** Basic trust is trust in oneself and in the external world, a sense that "I can rely on the world to provide some satisfaction of my needs, and I can rely on myself to find satisfaction and safety in the world." A child with basic trust is able to have faith that the ego will survive psychic stress. Martin Luther King, Jr. was brought up in an exceptionally supportive family environment that helped establish a sense of trust. He had not only a warm mother and a dependable father but also an extremely supportive and sympathetic grandmother.

Not everyone is so lucky. If parents are neglectful or hostile and do not reliably and warmly meet the child's needs, the child will probably develop a lasting sense of basic mistrust, a sense that the world cannot be counted on and that "I may not be adequate to meet its demands."

Most children don't develop a total sense of trust or a total sense of mistrust, but rather a balance of the two. For the best adjustment, there should probably be a mix of trust and skepticism. People who sense that the world, other people, and they themselves are generally trustworthy, but that there are definite exceptions and one needs to stay alert, will have optimal adjustment. Both the person who thinks that everything is wonderful and pure and the person who is deeply cynical and guarded will have difficulty accepting things as they really are and behaving adaptively.

Autonomy versus Shame and Doubt. At about the age of 18 months, a phase of life that Freud called the *anal stage* typically begins. It is called the anal stage because parents often start toilet training at this age and more generally impose control over the child's increasing desire for freedom. This phase of life can be marked by great conflict. For Erikson, the crucial question is how the parents respond to the child's needs and desires for freedom and in what fashion they teach or impose control. If parents can set clear, reasonable limits, if they can encourage and help the child to do things independently, and if they are consistent in their demands and in their rewards and punishments, the child will develop a **sense of autonomy.** Autonomy begins as a sense of control over the body and its functions, a sense that one has the freedom to act individually within a set of clear limits. A sense of autonomy is very important because it provides a person with the "courage to be an independent individual who can choose and guide his own future" (Erikson, 1968, p. 114).

Parents who impose impossible limits on their children before the children are able to understand or meet them and parents who are inconsistent in their demands will usually instill in their children a sense of shame and doubt. These children will have difficulty learning to control their bodily functions. They will become ashamed of their failures and of themselves in general, and they will question or doubt their abilities to be independent.

Most children will develop a balance between a sense of autonomy and a sense of shame and doubt. Martin Luther King, Jr. developed an unusually strong sense of autonomy. Although he strongly identified with his father, the young King would not always yield to his father's will. For example, he would not let himself cry out loud when his father whipped him. At an early age he told

his father he didn't share all the father's fundamental religious beliefs. After establishing some autonomy from his father, the son eventually became very much like him, but establishing autonomy was a necessary step.

Initiative versus Guilt. As we noted earlier, Freud believed that at about the age of 3 or 4, the Oedipus or Electra complexes begin. Freud called this period the *phallic stage.* At this time, children develop strong attachments to the opposite-sex parent and hostility toward the same-sex parent. For Erikson, the most important feature of this age is that a child's behavior becomes very assertive. At 3 or 4, children can and do get involved in many more things than younger children. When they do, the parents' treatment of sexual curiosity, aggressive impulses, and overall tendency toward action is critical. Within reasonable limits, parents must encourage and guide children's expanding activities and help children develop and appropriately use their emerging skills. Many aggressive energies need to be controlled and suitably channeled.

A child who is guided with clarity and caring will develop a **sense of initiative,** a sense of even greater control than the self-control provided by autonomy, a sense of being able to control objects and other people. A sense of initiative includes a sense of power and a sense of imagination and creative potential in dealing with the environment and people and objects in it. Again, Martin Luther King's own capacities and his supportive upbringing helped develop a strong sense of initiative. From an early age, he was a dominant member of his peer group who initiated and controlled many boyhood activities. King's sense of initiative shaped his activities throughout his long involvement in the civil rights struggles of the 1950s and 1960s.

Children whose initiative isn't nurtured and channeled, who are constantly told no, or who are treated in a harsh and arbitrary fashion will develop a sense of guilt about the many and varied wishes and desires they have in this stage. As in earlier stages, there is a balance of the positive and negative senses.

Industry versus Inferiority. Freud felt that very little happened in the *latency period.* For Erikson, it is a long stage marked by schooling and children's attempts to develop intellectual, athletic, artistic, and social skills. If the increasing demands of authority figures, especially teachers, are accompanied by appropriate care and guidance, children will have a good chance of mastering the tasks that are required of them. Children with inner strength (deriving from favorable psychological balances from the early stages and sufficient physical and intellectual endowments), who also have caring people in the environment to encourage, instruct, and provide needed resources, will develop what Erikson called a **sense of industry:** a feeling of control and power; a sense of being able to do, to finish, to achieve: a sense of being competent and confident. Children who do not meet with suc-

cess in their efforts to do what they want or what others demand will develop a sense of inferiority. This is a feeling of having little worth and of not being a good human being, of being inferior to others or to the demands of the environment. We all have these feelings at some time in our lives, but in many people they predominate and create further psychological problems.

King, Jr. clearly had a strong sense of industry and very little sense of inferiority. His sense of industry built on his previously established senses of trust, autonomy, and initiative. This very favorable psychological development in childhood provided the secure base for King to develop his notable intellectual and interpersonal skills. Trusting himself and feeling independent, he was able to take pleasure in working hard and succeeding at a variety of tasks. His sense of industry persisted from early childhood through his years of college and graduate education to the end of his enormously productive life.

REVIEW QUESTIONS

1. Freud identified three major structures of the psyche: the id, the ego, and the superego. The _____ consists of unconscious instincts, the _____ contains the conscience, and the _____ attempts to manage the _____'s drives, the _____'s dictates, and the demands of reality.

2. In Freud's Oedipus complex, young boys want to possess their _____ and displace their _____.

3. What are the names of the categories of Freud's defense mechanisms that contain the

following defenses: (a) identification, displacement, and sublimation; (b) repression and denial; and (c) projection, reaction-formation, and rationalization.

4. Erikson discussed the crises that take place at each of Freud's stages of development and the psychological balances that are achieved as a result of the child's experience. The crises are trust versus _____, autonomy versus _____ and _____, initiative versus _____, and industry versus _____.

BEHAVIORAL APPROACHES TO PERSONALITY DEVELOPMENT

When Martin Luther King, Jr. first started asking the black citizens of Montgomery to pro-

test the treatment of African Americans in Alabama and throughout the South, he and others planned a one-day boycott of the city busses. As noted earlier, the cooperation with the boycott was much higher than expected.

King's approach was rewarded by the people's reactions. As a result, King grew more insistent in suggesting acts of protest and in emphasizing the importance of nonviolence. Again he was rewarded. People followed his lead. These early successes led King to assume more and more leadership within the civil rights movement.

King's tendency to become more involved in shaping the civil rights movement is highly consistent with the fundamental assumption of the behavioral approach to personality—namely, that behavior is under the control of its consequences. That is, we perform behaviors for which we have been rewarded or reinforced, or for which we expect future reward or reinforcement, and we do not perform behaviors for which we expect either no reinforcement or punishment. King's leadership efforts were rewarded by other people's reactions, and he kept working.

The behavioral approach to personality development is very different from the psychodynamic approach in an important way: The psychodynamic approach views behavior as mainly determined by *internal* events, specifically, unconscious drives and conflicts; the behavioral approach views behavior as determined by *external* events, specifically, rewards and punishments. The behavioral approach has been put forth in an extreme way, called *radical behaviorism*, by J. B. Watson and B. F. Skinner. However, the most influential behavioral approach today is called *cognitive social learning theory*. We will first look at radical behaviorism and then at cognitive social learning theory.

Radical Behaviorism

Radical behaviorism is heavily influenced by a concept known as the *law of effect*. This concept, proposed nearly a century ago by Edward Thorndike (1898), states that behavior that is followed by reward will be "stamped in" and behavior that is followed by punishment will be "stamped out." People learn to perform certain actions on the basis of what follows—reward or punishment. Children will learn to clean up their rooms if that's the only way they can get a smile from their mother in the morning.

The famous psychologist J. B. Watson was highly influenced by the law of effect and other research on conditioning and learning when he stated:

> *Give me a dozen healthy infants, well-formed, and my own specified world to bring them up in and I'll guarantee to take any one of them at random and train him to become any type of specialist I might select—doctor, lawyer, artist, merchant–chief and, yes, even beggarman and thief, regardless of his talents, penchants, tendencies, abilities, vocations and race of his ancestors. (1925, p. 10)*

In making this statement, Watson was arguing that behavior and personality are totally controlled by the environment. It is interesting to note that Martin Luther King, Jr. himself was strongly influenced by Watson's theories. In working on his Ph.D. in theology at Boston University in the early 1950s, he wrote an "Autobiography of Religious Development" that dealt with the development of his own personal religious beliefs in terms of Watson's theories. King traced his economic, political, social, moral, and theological beliefs to the influence of the environment in which he was raised as a child. At least one influential scholar, then, King himself, could understand King's life in terms of Watsonian concepts.

Also deeply influenced by Watson was the psychologist B. F. Skinner, for nearly 50 years the most prominent advocate for radical behaviorism. Skinner is famous for his studies of *operant conditioning*, the procedure whereby the chances of an animal's performing a behavior, such as pressing a bar or pecking at a key, are increased by rewarding the animal after it performs that behavior (Rescorla, 1987). A behavior that is performed because of operant conditioning is called an *operant*; the behavior "operates" on the environment to obtain a reward. In short, Skinner and other

Social Learning and Aggression

An important set of studies by Bandura and his colleagues (Bandura, 1965; Bandura, Ross, & Ross, 1961, 1963) shows the importance of observational learning and vicarious reinforcement. In these studies children watched either a live model or a cartoon model behave aggressively toward a plastic, blow-up clown or "Bobo doll." The model would hit the doll, kick it, throw it, sit on it, and beat it with a hammer, usually making remarks such as "bad doll." After watching the model, the children were given a chance to play with a number of toys, including the Bobo doll.

Do you think children would be influenced by the model's behavior? The results of the studies showed that they definitely were influenced. The children behaved aggressively toward the doll and closely imitated some of the model's specific behavior, such as hitting the doll with a hammer. Clearly, the children had both observed and learned. The fact that children imitated a cartoon model as well as a live model suggests how much their behavior can be influenced by what they see on television.

A number of factors affected how much the children behaved like the model. The model's similarity to the children seemed important. Boys imitated male models more than female models and girls did the opposite. Also, the status of the model was important. Children were more likely to imitate models who had higher status. Another critical factor illustrates the importance of vicarious reinforcement. Children were more likely to imitate aggressive models who were rewarded rather than those who were ignored. The children were least likely to imitate a model who was called a bully and punished.

Clearly, observational learning is an important influence on the acquisition of important behaviors, and vicarious reinforcement affects how much behavior learned through observation is performed.

---

radical behaviorists assume that personality simply reflects the behaviors that people have learned to perform because they were reinforced for doing so.

Cognitive Social Learning Theory

Today most behavioral psychologists believe that learning is more complex than "stamping in" or "stamping out." For example, it has been found that punishment is seldom an effective way to get people or animals to learn (Skinner, 1971). Furthermore, we know that even though reinforcement is a crucial determinant of behavior, it works in subtle and complicated ways. Cognitive social learning theorists have made their most important contributions by exploring precisely how reinforcement does get people to perform certain actions. For instance, they have shown that people can learn behaviors even if they

are not directly reinforced for performing them. A child can learn aggressive behavior simply by observing another person, a *model,* behaving aggressively. This is called *observational learning* (see Lessons from the Laboratory). Reinforcement is still important in this kind of learning because the way we act after observing another person depends in part on whether we see that person rewarded or punished. We are more likely to imitate people if their behavior meets with some kind of success or gratification (Bandura, 1965, 1986). Cognitive social learning theorists use the term *vicarious reinforcement* when people observe others receive reinforcement for their behavior.

Both direct reinforcement and vicarious reinforcement, based on modeling, were important in Martin Luther King's becoming a minister. Martin's strong-willed father wanted his son to follow in his footsteps and rewarded with approval whatever interest young Martin showed in religion. Also, Martin's father was an ideal model since he received reinforcement for preaching. Martin "tingled with excitement" as he watched his father sway audiences with the words of his sermons (Bennett, 1968, p. 17).

The contribution of cognitive social learning theorists to our understanding of how people develop is not limited to the simple concept of observational learning. They have expanded the work of previous behaviorists who argued that people are mechanically influenced by rewards and punishments. Cognitive social learning theorists emphasize the importance of cognitive factors such as perceiving, remembering, thinking, and forming expectancies. For example, how much we imitate a model depends on our estimate of exactly what led him or her to be reinforced, how probable we consider it that we would be reinforced for the same behavior, and our impression of whether or not we have the ability to perform that behavior.

Cognitive social learning theory also emphasizes the ways people make plans and regulate their own behavior (Mischel, 1990) and ways they can motivate themselves through self-regulation (Bandura, 1982). A specific example of self-regulation would be to allow yourself to do something enjoyable, such as watching a favorite television show, only *after* you have finished a homework assignment or written your thank-you notes. This kind of self-management, rather than mere responsiveness to external rewards and punishments, is the kind of psychology emphasized by cognitive social learning theory. Overall, cognitive social learning theory provides a much more complete view of how we can learn to behave than does the old law of effect (see Table 2.1).

A recent development in cognitive social learning theory, one that is closely related to the idea of self-regulation, is the concept of self-efficacy (Bandura, 1982, 1983). People

TABLE 2.1   Person Variables in Social Learning Theory

Social learning theorists have shown that it is not enough to talk about reinforcement and external factors; certain aspects of the person must be considered in order to fully understand behavior. Walter Mischel (1973) has identified five key person variables.

1. *Competencies:* Our mental abilities, such as intelligence and creativity; physical abilities, such as athletic prowess; artistic abilities, such as painting, singing, or dancing.
2. *Encoding strategies and personal constructs:* The ways we categorize information in our environment, especially the groupings or categories we use to classify and judge other people; our concepts about things and people in the world.
3. *Expectancies:* Our expectancies about the consequences of our own behavior, the ways others will behave, and the kinds of behaviors that are most likely to lead to reinforcement.
4. *Values:* What we find satisfying or rewarding; the things that matter to us.
5. *Self-regulatory systems and plans:* Arrangements we make with ourselves to take certain actions and to reward ourselves for doing them. These systems, such as having a snack only after studying for a specified period, are key aspects of self-control.

make judgments about how well they can organize and use their various skills—for example, their intelligence or their ability to get along with people. These judgments about the use of skills lead people to have a certain degree of *perceived self-efficacy*. People with a high degree of perceived self-efficacy are less likely to be fearful in threatening situations and more apt to take action in those situations. Because they feel that their actions will be of some use, they are quicker to take them (Maddux and Rogers, 1983). They don't respond passively. Thus, having a sense of self-efficacy is important in taking the active approach to life that is important for successful adjustment.

Martin Luther King had an unusually high sense of self-efficacy. He faced many threatening situations, including continual assassination threats, throughout his years of active service in the civil rights movement. Despite this, he was able to be act, and to act quickly. He had learned that he could be effective, that he could be that one honest man who could make a difference.

A final important feature of cognitive social learning theory is that it emphasizes each individual's uniqueness. It maintains that each person is different as a result of his or her learning history. It also holds that a person's character will have a certain continuity, or stability, over time because learned patterns of behavior tend to persist until they are replaced by new ones, which takes time and experience. The approach to personality we will consider next provides a thorough consideration of the way time and experience can lead to major changes in personality, particularly through the experience called self-actualization.

HUMANISTIC APPROACHES TO PERSONALITY DEVELOPMENT

The humanistic approach to personality is in part a reaction against perceived shortcomings in the behavioral and psychodynamic approaches. Both those approaches stress the fact that behavior is determined: The psychodynamic approach emphasizes the role of unconscious forces in determining behavior; the behavioral approach emphasizes the role of external rewards and punishments. In contrast, the humanistic perspective emphasizes human free will and the capacity of each individual to determine his or her own destiny. Because it is critical of the other two approaches, the humanistic approach is sometimes called the "third force." Two of the

major exponents of the humanistic approach have been Carl Rogers and Abraham Maslow.

Rogers's Concept of Self-Actualization

Carl Rogers (1951, 1959) emphasized that each person strives toward **self-actualization,** the development of all his or her potentials and capacities. This tendency is also called *self-realization.* Rogers believed that children naturally strive to realize all that they are able to become. However, tendencies toward self-actualization are often compromised by the strong human need for approval. As children we are dependent on our parents to meet this need. However, as we have experienced, parents do not approve just any activity; they only approve certain behaviors, which for the child become *conditions of worth.* Children get approval and feel worthy only when they perform these behaviors. The problem is that the behaviors that meet the conditions of worth may not be the behaviors that lead to self-actualization. For example, a young boy may be drawn to developing his musical potential, but his parents may discourage his interest in music and push him into athletics. As a result of this conflict, children often suppress self-actualizing tendencies in order to get approval from their parents.

Rogers discussed the way people who have lived under stringent parental standards can become more self-actualizing and can build their self-esteem. They must begin to interact with another person, perhaps a psychotherapist, or with other people in general, who will respond to them with unconditional positive regard, caring about them and approving of them as people, even though not necessarily approving of every single behavior they perform. Conditions of worth must be removed. Once this happens, a person can become what Rogers called a *fully functioning person,* one who accepts all his or her various self-actualizing tendencies, even

SELF-ASSESSMENT EXERCISE _____

Measuring Self-Actualization

In recent years a short scale measuring self-actualization has been developed by Jones and Crandall (1986, p. 39). Indicate whether you agree or disagree, definitely or moderately, with each of the following statements. If you tend to agree with the statements without an (N) after them and disagree with the statements with an (N), you are likely to be a highly self-actualized individual.

1. I do not feel ashamed of any of my emotions.
2. I feel I must do what others expect of me. (N)
3. I believe people are essentially good and can be trusted.
4. I feel free to be angry to those I love.
5. It is always necessary that others approve of what I do. (N)
6. I don't accept my own weaknesses. (N)
7. I can like people without having to approve of them.
8. I fear failure. (N)
9. I avoid attempts to analyze and simplify complex domains. (N)
10. It is better to be yourself than to be popular.
11. I have no mission in life to which I feel especially attached. (N)
12. I can express my feelings even when they may result in undesirable consequences.
13. I do not feel responsible to anyone. (N)
14. I am bothered by fears of being inadequate. (N)
15. I am loved because I give love.

Source: A. Jones and R. Crandall, *Personality and Social Psychology Bulletin* (Vol. 12), p. 67, copyright © 1986 by Sage Publications Inc. Reprinted by permission of Sage Publications, Inc.

though many may be inconsistent with the conditions of worth learned in childhood.

Maslow's Hierarchy of Motives

Another important humanistic psychologist, Abraham Maslow, also emphasized the concept of self-actualization. In addition, Maslow showed how the need for self-actualization fits in with other important human motives. Maslow did this through his important concept of the *hierarchy of motives.* Maslow's (1970) hierarchical theory of motivation asserts that many motives underlie human behavior and

that different motives are important at different times and in different situations. People have lower and higher motives (see Table 2.2): once the lower ones, such as the need to breathe or quench one's thirst, are satisfied, people become concerned with satisfying the higher ones, such as self-actualization.

Five kinds of needs form the motivational hierarchy, according to Maslow. First, there are *physiological needs,* such as hunger and thirst. Obviously, if physiological needs are not met, they preempt every other drive and become the main focus of concern. After the physiological needs are *safety needs.* A need

TABLE 2.2 Maslow's Hierarchy of Motives

Self-Actualization
the need to develop all your potentials and become all you are capable of becoming
Esteem Needs
the desire to be competent and to be recognized for your achievements
Belongingness and Love Needs
the needs to be accepted and loved by others and to be part of groups
Safety Needs
the need to feel protected, secure, and out of danger
Physiological Needs
hunger, thirst, the need to breathe, and other bodily needs

Source: Maslow (1970).

for safety is more often seen in children than in adults, although adults show great concern for security and do many things to ensure their safety. Buying insurance policies and seeking secure occupational positions are examples of adult means of satisfying the safety need. Maslow would have agreed with other theorists that people who have been least secure as children will be most worried about safety and security as adults. Their need for safety will be so strong that it can become neurotic and obsessive. Such people may never get beyond a concern for safety. They will always be frightened and unwilling or unable to turn their attention to deeper and more rewarding activities.

Third up the hierarchical ladder of motives are *belongingness and love needs*. These are mainly characterized by the need to be included in groups. They also include the need for affection from parents, peers, lovers, and spouses. People experience the need for love

mainly when there is an absence of it. People who are loved, or who are included in groups and feel liked by others are satisfied and go on to concern themselves with other needs. Maslow believed that people who have satisfied their lower needs but have been frustrated, especially during their formative years, in their needs for love will be insecure about others' feelings and unceasing in their desire to be approved of and liked by others.

The fourth step up the motivational ladder is *esteem needs*. The esteem needs include drives to do well, to achieve, to be effective and competent, and to be self-reliant, independent, and autonomous. In addition, esteem needs include the desire to have one's accomplishments recognized, admired, and respected by others so that one can be dominant and important in relation to others. In short, this is the need to have a positive self-image.

As with any step on the motivational ladder, it is only when the lower physiological, safety, and love needs are met that a person can worry about self-esteem. Also, like the earlier motives, esteem motives are stimulated when there is an absence or deficit of positive self-regard. Martin Luther King's behavior shows the operation of strong esteem motives. He wanted to achieve, to be independent, and to dominate and lead. From his early childhood he consistently demonstrated a desire to succeed, impress, and gain recognition and respect.

The final step in Maslow's hierarchy is the need for *self-actualization*. As mentioned before, this is essentially a need to develop one's potentials and to do as well as one can. It also includes the need to experience the world and people as deeply and richly as possible. One's own needs and worries fade into the background inasmuch as one wants to appreciate as fully as possible what there is in the world and to grow through this appreciation. Self-actualization is a motive entirely different from the other motives beneath it in the hierarchy. The lower needs are all stimulated by a deficit, and the person is strongly driven to get what he or she is missing. For these reasons, Maslow called them **deficiency motives.** On the other hand, self-actualization is what Maslow called a growth motive, or a **being motive,** which represents a general need to develop. There is no specific deficit to fill. People are relaxed. They try to do all they can and to grow. The desire for self-actualization is never really satisfied, because more growth is always possible and there is always more experience to appreciate. Being self-actualized is the highest human potential. The impulse toward self-actualization does not avoid negative states, such as hunger or loneliness; it only seeks and appreciates positive ones.

Maslow has studied a number of well-known individuals who he feels were self-actualized. They include the social worker Jane Addams, the composer Ludwig von Beethoven, American President Thomas Jefferson, and First Lady Eleanor Roosevelt. Maslow felt that they had a number of characteristics in common, characteristics that made them self-actualized. They were accepting of themselves and other people, they were focused on solving problems, they were highly autonomous and less conforming, they were highly creative, they had deeply developed values, and they strongly identified with all humankind.

Review Questions

5. Behavioral approaches to personality emphasize the way personality is shaped by external forces and learning rather than by internal instincts and conflicts. Watson and Skinner emphasized the degree to which behavior is controlled by its _____. Behavior that is _____ is more likely to occur than behavior that is not.

6. Cognitive social learning theorists emphasize the importance of _____, as shown in studies of the imitation of aggression. They also highlight the importance of _____ reinforcement and the person variables such

as competencies, encoding strategies and personal constructs, expectancies, values, and self-regulatory systems and plans.

7. Humanistic theorists emphasize the concept of self-actualization. Rogers believed that organisms strive to develop or actualize their full potential but that social conditions often make it very difficult. Maslow proposed a hierarchy of motivations with _____ on the top. It could be satisfied after the lower needs were satisfied: physiological needs, _____ needs, belongingness and love needs, and _____ needs.

TRAIT APPROACHES TO PERSONALITY DEVELOPMENT

We often hear or read about people describing each other or themselves as having specific traits or characteristics. For example, we just saw that Abraham Maslow talked about self-actualized individuals as having characteristics of autonomy and creativity, etc. Similarly, we might think of our neighbor as extraverted and agreeable, our boss as highly excitable and conscientious, and ourselves as inter-

ested in culture. Why do we think of people in terms of traits? It may be because that is just the way human beings think about personality, or it may be that we think that people have traits because traits really do exist in people.

Many psychologists believe the latter, that traits really exist and that personality is best explained by discovering a person's traits. We could describe how a specific person differs from other people on traits like agreeableness or conscientiousness, or we could describe the individual's unique combination of personal

Introversion and Extraversion at Home

One of the authors has two sons. The older son is highly extraverted and the younger is clearly more introverted. The difference between the two was clearly illustrated one winter when the boys were about 6 and 8 years old and a large number of the extended family gathered for a holiday at our home. The older boy thrived on the action. It was fun for him to talk to all the aunts, uncles, cousins, and grandparents. He wanted to play every game, participate in every conversation, and hear every joke. In the midst of one of the busier, more boisterous afternoons, we noticed that our younger son was missing. After looking around with some concern, we finally found him hiding under his bed, playing happily with some small toys. For him the general turmoil was just too much.

Introverts do not like too much sensory input or stimulation. They prefer quiet to noise and solitude to lots of company. Psychologists are actively working on the hypothesis that introverts have higher levels of cortical stimulation in the brain and easily feel that their circuits are overloaded if too much is going on (Bullock & Gilliland, 1993). Our number two son fit the theory precisely.

---

characteristics or traits. Either way, we describe personality and explain behavior using traits. This trait approach has existed since the time of the ancient Greeks. The Greek physician Hippocrates proposed that there were four personality types based on each individual's bodily fluids. These types were the melancholic, sanguine, choleric, and phlegmatic, each type corresponding to one of the basic elements, earth, air, fire, and water.

Introversion and Extraversion

In modern times, Carl Jung (1971) was the first psychologist to consider types of people and traits. Jung believed that individuals were either introverted or extraverted. *Introverted* people look inward at their own experience. They focus on their own thoughts, feelings, and sensations. They live in their own heads and show much less interest in the world around them. *Extraverts,* on the other hand, are oriented toward the outside world and experiencing what is going on around them. They are focused on external stimulation—people, sights, sounds, and events. They live in the external world and spend less time reflecting on their internal experience (see Lessons from Life).

How do people become introverted or extraverted? The answer is by no means final, but recent research suggests that biological factors, specifically genetics, play a large role in human temperament and whether people tend to be introverted or extraverted. Some of the key studies are done with twins. Studies of identical twins reared apart find some remarkable similarities, showing the potential power of genetic influences (Bouchard, Lykken, McCue, Segal, & Tellegen, 1990). For example, twins, both called Jim, were born in 1940 and separated four weeks after birth. When they were reunited in 1979, some startling similarities were discovered: "They both drove the same model blue Chevrolet, chain-smoked Salems, chewed their fingernails and owned dogs named Toy" (Leo, 1987, p. 63). There were other similarities as well—they vacationed on the same beach in Florida and were very similar on psychological tests measuring sociability and self-control.

Recent studies of temperament in twins have also shown that they can be remarkably similar. Kagan and his colleagues compared identical twins, who have the same genetic make-up, with fraternal twins, who were born at the same time but are not the same genetically. The twins were studied at 14 months, 20 months, and 24 months. Each twin and his or her mother was left in a comfortable room for about an hour, except for two interruptions by strangers with toys. How did the children react to the strangers and the new toys? Some children were notably shy and inhibited; others were clearly outgoing and bold. Furthermore, although many of the twins were similar to each other, identical twins were more similar to each other than fraternal twins. If one identical twin tended to be shy and inhibited, there was a very good chance that the other would be similar. The similarity was not as marked with the fraternal twins (Robinson, Kagan, Reznick, & Corley, 1992).

These studies support the role of heredity but also demonstrate that environment is important. The fact that identical twins are more similar in temperament than fraternal twins shows that biology and genes matter. Yet the behavior of identical twins, who have the same genes, was not identical. It was generally similar, but there were differences. These differences show that the environment and individual experiences, which differ to some extent for each person, also shape personality. Nevertheless, the twin studies give important support to the perspective that biology is important in shaping temperament and personality, particularly characteristics like shyness and sociability or introversion and extraversion.

While Jung felt that individuals were one type or another, either introverts or extraverts, it is interesting that Martin Luther King, Jr. seemed to have elements of both types. From his father he took on expressive, outgoing qualities. From his mother he took on a more reserved, introverted quality. King himself thought carefully about his psychological characteristics and decided that he was an "ambivert—half introvert and half extravert" (Bennett, 1968, p. 18). Like the extravert, he could deal with people and the world around him; like the introvert, he looked inward, re-

lied on inner strength, and was introspective and reflective.

The idea that an individual's personality could be marked by some mix of introversion and extraversion is consistent with more recent psychological studies of traits. Hans Eysenck (1953, 1982) studied traits for several decades and made two important discoveries. First, people vary along a continuum of introversion and extraversion. They can be highly introverted, highly extraverted, or somewhere in between. Second, there is a second basic trait dimension that defines personality. People also vary along a continuum of **stability** shading to neuroticism (referring to stable versus unstable individuals). The stable person is well adjusted, calm, relaxed, and easygoing. The unstable person is neurotic, moody, anxious, restless, and temperamental. As with introversion and extraversion, people can be on one end of the continuum or the other or somewhere in between. Martin Luther King, Jr. was primarily stable, but he sometimes lost control and was capable of marked swings in mood.

If we think of individuals as having some degree of introversion versus extraversion and some degree of stability versus instability in their personalities, we can imagine many different personal qualities that result. These are shown in Figure 2.1. For example, like Martin Luther King, someone who is primarily stable but an "ambivert" would be expected to be calm and have good leadership abilities, as Eysenck suggests. Think about how you would rate yourself or other people you know well on each of these trait dimensions.

The Big Five

Eysenck's work shows two important trait dimensions that distinguish individuals. Are there more than two? The psychologist Raymond Cattell (1950, 1966, 1972, 1973) has been also been studying traits for decades. He proposed that there were 16 key personality traits

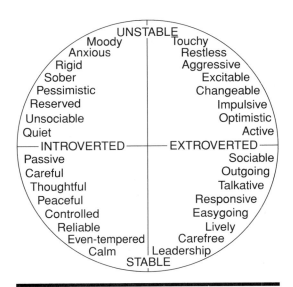

FIGURE   2.1   Eysenck's Dimensions of
Personality
Source: Adapted from Eysenck (1964).

and developed a test called the *Sixteen Personality Factor Questionnaire,* or *16PF.* The traits measured by the 16PF are shown in Table 2.3. You will notice that the introversion–extraversion dimension is represented by items such as *reserved* versus *outgoing* and *shy* versus *venturesome,* and that the stable–unstable or neuroticism dimension is represented by traits such as *stable* versus *emotional* and *relaxed* versus *tense.* In addition, however, there are other traits that are quite different from these two basic dimensions. Again, you should think about how you locate yourself on each of these dimensions.

Although Eysenck's work suggests that there are more than two basic trait dimensions, more recent work suggests that there are fewer than 16. If you look closely at the 16 trait dimensions measured by the 16PF, some of them are similar and do not actually measure distinct traits. For example, *placid* versus *apprehensive, casual* versus *controlled, relaxed* versus *tense,* and *happy-go-lucky* versus *sober*

TABLE 2.3   Cattell's 16 Traits

Terms in parentheses are Cattell's technical names for these traits.

(Sizothymia) Reserved	⟷	Outgoing *(Affectothymia)*
(Low 'g') Less intelligent	⟷	More intelligent *(High 'g')*
(Low ego strength) Emotional	⟷	Stable *(High ego strength)*
(Submissiveness) Humble	⟷	Assertive *(Dominance)*
(Desurgency) Sober	⟷	Happy-go-lucky *(Surgency)*
(Low super-ego) Expedient	⟷	Conscientious *(High super-ego)*
(Threctia) Shy	⟷	Venturesome *(Parmia)*
(Harria) Tough-minded	⟷	Tender-minded *(Premsia)*
(Alaxia) Trusting	⟷	Suspicious *(Protension)*
(Praxternia) Practical	⟷	Imaginative *(Autia)*
(Artlessness) Forthright	⟷	Shrewd *(Shrewdness)*
(Assurance) Placid	⟷	Apprehensive *(Guilt-proneness)*
(Conservatism) Conservative	⟷	Experimenting *(Radicalism)*
(Group adherence) Group-tied	⟷	Self-sufficient *(Self-sufficiency)*
(Low integration) Casual	⟷	Controlled *(High self-concept)*
(Low ergic tension) Relaxed	⟷	Tense *(Ergic tension)*

Source: Adapted from Cattell (1965).

all seem to be getting at the same thing. Statisticians have devised a method called *factor analysis* to identify which dimensions are similar to which other dimensions and how many separate dimensions really exist.

On the basis of scores of studies using factor analysis, psychologists have supported the idea that there are five basic personality traits (McCrae & Costa, 1987; Norman, 1963). These traits are called the *Big Five,* and they include **extraversion, agreeableness, conscientiousness, stability,** and **cultural interest** (cultural interest is also sometimes called *openness, culture,* or *intellect*). The dimensions and some scales measuring them are shown in Table 2.4. Much of the research on the Big Five assumes that people's standings on these traits are stable over time and that they are largely determined biologically. Eysenck (1967) stated: "Personality is determined to a large extent by a person's genes" (p. 20). Consistent with the emphasis on the biological influence on traits is cross-cultural research showing that the five-factor structure of personality traits is found among people in many countries, including Canada, Finland, China, Germany, Japan, and Poland (McRae, Zonderman, Costa, Bond, & Paunonen, 1996; Paunonen, Jackson, Trzebinski, & Forsterling, 1992).

We can learn a great deal about people by their standing on each of the Big Five trait dimensions. Again, think about yourself or some close acquaintances, and decide whether each person is high, low, or in the middle on the five traits. Once you have located the person on each of the five dimensions, you have said a lot about what he or she is like. Martin Luther King, Jr. was high on conscientiousness, cultural interest, and stability, and probably near the middle on extraversion and agreeableness.

Recent research has shown a strong relationship between people's standing on these trait dimensions and their psychological adjustment. For many years we have known that stability, extraversion, and cultural interest are related to happiness and psychological

TABLE 2.4 The Big Five Factors and Scales Commonly Making Up Each Other (After Norman)

Factor 1: Extroversion

Talkative—Silent
Sociable—Reclusive
Adventurous—Cautious

Factor 2: Agreeableness

Good-natured—Irritable
Mild, Gentle—Headstrong
Cooperative—Negativistic
Not Jealous—Jealous

Factor 3: Conscientiousness

Responsible—Undependable
Persevering—Quitting, Fickle
Fussy, Tidy—Careless
Scrupulous—Unscrupulous

Factor 4: Stability

Calm—Anxious
Composed—Excitable
Not hypochondriacal—Hypochondriacal
Poised—Nervous, Tense

Factor 5: Openness

Imaginative—Simple, Direct
Artistically sensitive—Insensitive
Intellectual—Nonreflective, Narrow
Polished, Refined—Boorish

Source: Adapted from Digman & Inouye (1986). Further specification of the five robust factors of personality. *Journal of Personality and Social Psychology, 50,* p. 117. Copyright © 1986 by the American Psychological Association. Adapted with permission.

well-being. A more recent study shows that agreeableness and conscientiousness are also related to life satisfaction and happiness (McCrae & Costa, 1991). This finding reminds us of Freud's statement that happiness is related to love and work (*Liebe und Arbeit*). The person who has the traits needed to love well and work well is significantly more likely achieve a positive adjustment to life.

REVIEW QUESTIONS

8. Jung made the key distinction between the opposing traits of _____ and _____ .

9. Eysenck found that people can be characterized as having some degree of the trait of introversion versus extraversion and some

degree of the trait of _____ versus
_____ .

10. The Big Five traits are _____ ,
_____ , _____ , _____ ,
and _____ .

COMBINING FORCES: WHAT WE LEARN FROM ALL THE APPROACHES

The four perspectives on personality reviewed in this chapter—psychodynamic, behavioral, humanistic, and trait—offer varied accounts of the human personality and human behavior. Although these approaches are often seen as conflicting, we think there is much to be gained by applying the most useful insights of each to understanding adjustment.

What do these theories tell us, and what do they leave unexplained? Trait approaches tell us that our personalities and behavior are shaped by biological predispositions and that introversion–extraversion and stability–neuroticism are major aspects of personality. Behavioral theory makes clear that our behavior is shaped by external events, specifically rewards and punishments in the environment, both as we experience them ourselves and as we observe others encountering the environment. Psychodynamic theories provide a helpful account of the way biological drives interact with the behavior of parents and family dynamics to create a stronger or weaker ego and a more or less well-adjusted personality. Humanistic theories make clear that humans have the drive to develop their many potentials as well as to satisfy biological and social needs.

As much as we have learned, there is a great deal that is not explained, including some key aspects of why some people achieve a strong personality and a healthy adjustment and others do not. One important factor in personality development that is not considered as fully as it might be in the approaches we have discussed is the role of social and cultural forces. In Martin Luther King's case, growing up in the segregated South in the 1930s and 1940s and living as a young adult in Alabama in the 1950s had a major impact on his experience. The segregated South offered many challenges and constraints. To fully understand an African-American man or woman raised in those places and those times, we need to understand those challenges and constraints.

But in addition to acknowledging our need to learn more about the social and cultural environment experienced by people like Dr. King, we also have to acknowledge that we know very little about what enables such individuals to take control of their environment and their lives. Humanistic approaches emphasize that each individual has the potential for achieving self-actualization, but they also tell us that few ever do. What makes a person like Martin Luther King, Jr. develop his potential so fully? All we can say is that some combination of individual strength and determination, a willingness to try to overcome all challenges and setbacks, allowed him not only to adjust to the world but also to change it. Many others have this capacity. Each of you has the capacity to determine how you will react to the challenges and constraints of the environment. By taking risks, assuming responsibility, and asserting leadership, you can find personal happiness and perhaps even social significance. Although they are shaped by both biological inheritance and a lifetime of external forces, much of what happens to individuals is in their hands. Just how people shape their own identities and adjust to the challenges and opportunities of adult life is discussed in the next chapter and throughout the text. Remember, however, that even though the world exerts its pressures, there are different ways to respond to them. Part of our purpose is to equip you to choose the ways that will make your lives most significant.

SUMMARY

1. There are four major approaches to understanding the individual personality: psychodynamic, behavioral, humanistic, and trait.

2. The psychodynamic approach to personality emphasizes internal factors. Behavior is determined by unconscious motives and conflicts related to distinct stages of development.

3. Freud's psychodynamic theory suggests how basic personality structures form in early childhood. The rational ego develops to help the instinctual id satisfy its drives. To resolve intense conflict with the same-sex parent arising from the Oedipal or Electra complex, a child usually forms a strong identification with that parent. The superego develops when a child incorporates the same-sex parent's moral standards and ideals. The defense mechanisms of the ego provide needed support for the ego's complex task of dealing with the id's drives for pleasure, the superego's moral dictates, and the demands of reality. Defense mechanisms can channel behavior or lead people to distort reality.

4. Erikson's psychodynamic theory points out how interactions with others in early childhood give people positive or negative psychological balances that are important throughout life. In the oral stage, a child learns a sense of trust or mistrust; in the anal stage, a sense of autonomy or shame and doubt; in the phallic stage, a sense of initiative or guilt; and in the latency period, a sense of industry or inferiority.

5. The behavioral approach to personality emphasizes external factors. Behavior is determined by reinforcement or expectation of reinforcement from the environment.

6. Radical behaviorism holds that personality reflects behaviors directly controlled by reward and punishment.

7. Cognitive social learning theory, a behavioral approach, emphasizes vicarious reinforcement and observational learning, in which behavior is learned by observing a model. It also stresses the role of cognitive factors, self-regulation of behavior, and individual uniqueness.

8. The humanistic approach to personality emphasizes human free will. Behavior is self determined and motivated by the individual's desire for self-actualization, the development of full potential.

9. Rogers's humanistic theory shows how conditions of worth established by parents can lead to conflict between behavior that will obtain parental approval and behavior that is self-actualizing.

10. Maslow's humanistic hierarchy of motives shows how the need for self-actualization fits in with other important human motives. Physiological needs, safety needs, love and belongingness needs, and esteem needs must be satisfied before people can attempt to actualize their full potential.

11. Trait theorists emphasize the strong influence that genetics has on behavior. Jung identified introverts and extraverts as two basic types of individuals. Eysenck found that introversion–extraversion and stability–neuroticism are two key dimensions of personality.

12. In recent years, trait researchers have emphasized the Big Five personality traits as the key dimensions of personality. These traits are extraversion, agreeableness, conscientiousness, stability, and cultural interest.

CRITICAL THINKING QUESTIONS

1. Do you think your own personality is more shaped by unconscious drives and conflicts or by external reinforcements and models? What about other people you know? Do you tend to explain your own personality in the same way you explain other people's?

2. Do you consider yourself self-actualized? If not, why not? What is keeping you from becoming what Carl Rogers called a fully functioning person?

3. How would you rate yourself on the "Big Five" traits of extraversion, agreeableness, conscientiousness, cultural interest, and stability? Have experiential or biological factors shaped your standing on these traits? Are you similar to your parents?

MATCHING EXERCISE

Match each term with its definition.

a. being motive
b. deficiency motive
c. ego
d. id
e. observational learning
f. self-actualization

g. sense of autonomy
h. sense of basic trust
i. sense of industry
j. sense of initiative
k. superego
l. extraversion

m. stability
n. conscientiousness
o. cultural interest
p. agreeableness

1. Learning that takes place when a person observes a model performing a behavior
2. A trait dimension in the Big Five theory having to do with openness to intellectual and cultural matters
3. A trait dimension in the Big Five theory having to do with being easy to get along with
4. A trait dimension in the Big Five theory having to do with neuroticism
5. The development or realization of all one's potentials
6. A basic feeling of trust in oneself and the environment and the feeling of adequacy in meeting external demands
7. A sense of control over one's body and a feeling that one is free to act independently

8. A trait dimension in the Big Five theory having to do with being mindful, careful, and considerate
9. The motivation to grow and develop
10. Motivation instigated by some psychological deficit experienced as an inner drive to obtain what is missing
11. A trait dimension in the Big Five theory having to do with being open to other people and external stimulation
12. The structure of the psyche that notices, perceives, remembers, and helps the individual cope with reality
13. The structure of the psyche that instinctively and unconsciously seeks pleasure and satisfaction of bodily needs

14. The child's sense of having some control over objects and other people, along with the ability to act creatively
15. The child's sense of control, power, and competence in achieving desired goals
16. The structure of the psyche that contains the parents' morals, ideals, and values

Answers to Matching Exercise

a. 9   b. 10   c. 12   d. 13   e. 1   f. 5   g. 7   h. 6   i. 15   j. 14   k. 16   l. 11   m. 4   n. 8   o. 2   p. 3

ANSWERS TO REVIEW QUESTIONS

1. id, superego, ego, id's, superego's
2. mothers, fathers
3. behavior channeling defenses, primary reality-distorting defenses, secondary reality-distorting defenses
4. mistrust, shame and doubt, quiet, inferiority
5. consequences, reinforced
6. observational learning, vicarious
7. self-actualization, safety, esteem
8. introversion, extraversion
9. stability, instability (or neuroticism)
10. extraversion, agreeableness, conscientiousness, stability, cultural interest

CHAPTER 3

SELF-DISCOVERY IN ADOLESCENCE AND ADULTHOOD

CASE NARRATIVE: ELEANOR ROOSEVELT
SELF-DEFINITION AND CHANGE
ADOLESCENCE
ADULTHOOD
HEALTH AND HAPPINESS IN ADULTHOOD

Eleanor Roosevelt

Eleanor Roosevelt

By the time she was 30, Eleanor Roosevelt seemed headed down the conventional path of dutiful wife and society matron (Lash, 1971; MacLeish, 1965). She faithfully followed the strict social customs of Washington, D.C., and played out the role of the wife of a rising young political star. She was subservient to her husband and to the conservative social traditions of her upbringing. By the time she was 35, however, the world, the United States, and Eleanor Roosevelt were changed forever. In some ways it was an end, but for Roosevelt it was the beginning of a new life of work, commitment, and service which made her one of America's most admired women.

Eleanor Roosevelt was born into a wealthy New York family of established society in 1884. Her early life was materially comfortable but psychologically miserable. Her father Elliot was the younger brother of "Uncle Ted," better known as Theodore Roosevelt, the future President. Eleanor adored her father, but she was separated from him for much of her early childhood. Elliot Roosevelt was an alcoholic who was unable to stick to any life's work. Because he was so unstable, Eleanor's mother shielded the child from Elliot. Unfortunately, Eleanor never felt close to her mother.

Before her marriage to Elliot Roosevelt, Eleanor's mother, Anna Hall, had been known as the most beautiful woman in New York society. Her daughter Eleanor was not beautiful; she was homely, awkward, and shy. One of her aunts called Eleanor the ugly duckling of the family. Her mother dubbed her "Granny" (MacLeish). Eleanor's few moments of happiness were during visits with her beloved father, but these were rare.

When Eleanor was 8 years old, her mother died suddenly. Her father was unable to care for her and could seldom visit. Eleanor went to live with her grandmother Hall. It was a very lonely time. Eleanor once burst into tears and said, "I have no real home." Life became even bleaker the next year when her father died after a riding accident. Mrs. Hall tried to bring Eleanor up to be a fitting member of society, but she was sad and lonely and kept herself apart.

At age 15, Eleanor was sent to school in Europe. Her teacher Marie Souvestre had a great impact on Eleanor's education and development. An outspoken, strong-minded woman who protested the many social injustices of the day with no fear of the consequences, Souvestre cultivated Eleanor's sense of social obligation and duty. The girl's loneliness and unhappiness made her responsive to ideals of helping others. Eleanor was able to act on these ideals in school as she became a well-respected student who could help the younger students adjust and be happy. Leaving school three years later was a particularly sad time for Eleanor because it seemed she had so little to return to at home.

Back in New York after the turn of the century, Eleanor was introduced by her grandmother to New York society. She commented years later, "There was absolutely nothing about me to attract anyone's attention." Of course, there was one person whose attention she did attract—her distant cousin Franklin Delano Roosevelt.

Eleanor and Franklin had met occasionally at clan gatherings and society parties. Franklin was gay, energetic, and magnetic. Many people thought that it was strange that he would be interested in someone as shy and reticent as Eleanor. However, Franklin valued her intelligence, sensitivity, and idealism. He recognized the strength and value of her outlook and realized that Eleanor would help bring out the best in him. Few people realized that their relationship was serious, but Franklin secretly proposed to Eleanor in 1903, when he was 21 and she was 19. They finally married a year and a half later.

In the early years of their marriage, Franklin's mother taught Eleanor how to run a household. Eleanor later described herself as an "entirely dependent person" in those days (Lash). She was an obliging wife and mother, bearing six children in the first eleven years of marriage. By this time Franklin had been called to Washington as Assistant Secretary of the Navy in the Woodrow Wilson administration.

The routine course of life that Eleanor was following was permanently changed in 1917, when the United States entered World War I and a virtual battleground broke out in her marriage. Both events launched Eleanor on a life of independent and constructive work that she never left. When the war started, Eleanor worked in a canteen in a railroad yard serving food and supplies to soldiers on their way to the battlefields in Europe. She also worked with St. Elizabeth's Mental Hospital in Washington, D.C., where many navy personnel with psychological difficulties were hospitalized. Her work with the soldiers and with St. Elizabeth's was highly effective. From it, she gained great satisfaction and great respect from Franklin.

Part of the reason that Eleanor put so much energy into independent work was that her marriage had undergone a crisis that ended forever the possibility of a subservient relationship with Franklin. Stumbling on some letters, she discovered that Franklin had been having an affair with the young and beautiful Lucy Mercer, who was first hired as Eleanor's social secretary. She offered to give Franklin his freedom so he could marry Lucy, but it was clear to them both that a public scandal would ruin Franklin's promising career. He chose not to get divorced, but Eleanor insisted that he and Lucy never see each other again. Eleanor was willing to work with and care for Franklin, but their marriage could never be the same.

As Eleanor and Franklin worked together, his political career shot rapidly upward. In 1920, at the age of 38, he was the Democratic nominee for Vice President. The Republicans won, but FDR seemed positioned to be the next Democratic presidential nominee. Then a year later he contracted polio and his legs were paralyzed. Eleanor wanted him to fight back. She finally succeeded in getting Franklin to try to make a recovery and to re-enter politics. He knew he would always need her help.

Franklin's fight to re-enter politics was successful. He was elected governor of New York in 1928 and President in 1932. Eleanor helped him restore national confidence during the depths of the Depression. She worked unceasingly, traveling for Franklin, writing a regular newspaper column, hosting a radio show, and giving tremendous amounts of time to the poor and needy. She worked hard for racial equality. Sometimes her actions embarrassed Franklin, for they were criticized and ridiculed by the Republicans. But she would not stop, and she pressed Franklin to do what they both knew to be the right thing, even when he feared it might hurt him politically. When Hitler rose to power, Eleanor spoke out against both fascism and communism. She believed in freedom and in America's basic goodness. When World War II started, Eleanor visited soldiers in hospitals in the Pacific, reporting personally on their condition to worried wives and mothers. She became a symbol of strength and goodwill throughout the nation and the world. When Franklin died near the end of the war, Harry Truman, the new President, asked Eleanor, "Is there anything I can do for you?" Typically, she responded, "Is there anything we can do for you? For you are the one in trouble now" (Lash, p. 721).

At first, the death of FDR seemed the end of Eleanor as a public figure, but she had become too much of a national resource to simply go home and grow old. She became part of the United States delegation to the United Nations. She successfully opposed the Soviet Union on humanitarian issues and fought hard to ensure strong and unequivocal U.S. support for the creation of the state of Israel. She was a heroine around the world. The "conscience of the nation," she remained active in its affairs until her death in 1962 at the age of 78.

SELF-DEFINITION AND CHANGE

A key aspect of becoming a healthy, well-adjusted person is the ability to define yourself, discover who you are, and then begin a lifelong process of developing your potentials and abilities. Most people do this most actively during adolescence. Eleanor Roosevelt did as well, but she also made major changes in her self-concept in her early thirties. This change in her identity had a tremendous impact on her behavior and on the people around her.

The self-concept is a very difficult idea to define simply. We can begin by saying that our *self-concepts* are our opinions of ourselves—both what we are and how good we are. That is, we have perceptions of our abilities, our goals and aspirations, what we value and believe in, how we look, how we will behave in life, and what other people think of us. We also have an overall belief or feeling about how worthy we are and whether we feel superior or inferior. This part of the self-concept is known as *self-esteem*. *Self-discovery* is the process of defining the self-concept and making important decisions about what we will do in life, what attitude we take toward ourselves, and what attitude we take toward others.

We would like to emphasize that the period of defining a self-concept or identity is not confined to adolescence. Self-discovery is not a one-time event, as Eleanor Roosevelt's life makes clear. The self is not a single, stable, static entity, like the Rock of Gibraltar or the Pacific Ocean, that we discover once and for all at a single time during the course of life. The self is more like a plant or tree or even a river that grows and changes its course of development. Usually we have a self-concept that is an important and stable part of our lives for a certain period of time. This is often followed by a time of questioning and change, a time when a fresh outlook and redirection are required. Then a somewhat different self-concept may emerge, not completely different from the old, yet altered in some ways. In other words, the self develops, grows, and renews itself. Self-discovery is a lifelong process.

In this chapter, using as an example the extraordinary life of Eleanor Roosevelt, we will consider how identity is defined in adolescence and then changed and reformed again and again throughout life. We want to emphasize the capacity for alteration, improvement, and excitement that is possible at any age. We feel it is critical that people realize that they can remain vital by doing new things and that they can avoid some of the problems of advancing age by thoughtfully renewing themselves.

The process of self-discovery is highly active during adolescence, often a stormy and difficult period of life. Adolescence begins with puberty, with the first feelings of strong and perhaps frightening sexual drives. During this period young men and women must cope with family conflicts about independence and autonomy, with uncertainty about values and morality, with doubts about their ability to cope in the adult world, and with questions about who they are, what role in society they can fill, and in general, what exactly they are good for. Most adolescents make it through these years with their egos and their mental health intact. For some, the result is exhilarating; they find their potentials and inner being. For others, the experience of adolescence is overwhelming. Our first concern in this chapter will be the many challenging aspects of adolescence and their various outcomes.

Although adolescence is important, those who have passed through it know that challenges, opportunities, and self-discovery continue in adulthood. Psychologists have been slow to consider this fully. In recent years, however, psychologists have begun to consider life-span development, or what is sometimes called *cradle-to-grave* or *womb-to-tomb* development. In the second portion of this chapter, we will consider the important psychological developments of adulthood, especially the way the process of self-discovery and renewal continues throughout life.

Our goal in this chapter is to discuss adolescence and adulthood in ways that will help you understand the difficult times that some of you may be going through now and to illustrate some of the possibilities of change and renewal that life offers. The aim is to prepare you for the various changes and stages that people go through during the long course of life and help you realize the opportunities as well as the problems that each stage presents.

ADOLESCENCE

Adolescence begins at sexual maturity, usually around age 11 for girls and 13 for boys. Physical growth is rapid, feelings are strong, and energy levels are high. There is also a questioning and challenging of parents and sometimes the culture or society; there is also generally some fear, uncertainty, and guilt. These powerful needs and feelings must be recognized, understood, and coped with. Somewhere in this sorting-out process, the self is discovered. Let us consider specifically some of the conflicts and emotions that arise during these years.

Conflicts about Independence and Responsibility

With their newfound interests, energies, and strengths, adolescents often expect more freedom and independence from their parents. Although they are still very dependent on their parents to satisfy their basic needs for shelter and nourishment, they often feel that they are old enough to decide how late to stay out at night, how often to date, and, in general, where to be when. Adolescents object to having to notify their parents of their after-school plans and to having their parents evaluate their friends. They feel that they should be able to drive the family car or have their own, that parents are too restrictive, and that adults cramp their style. Parents usually doubt that their children are able to handle as much freedom as they want or to behave completely responsibly without some monitoring of their behavior. These feelings can make home life something of a battleground. Certainly adolescent resentment of adults who have power and privileges that adolescents feel they too deserve contributes to tensions between parents and their adolescent children.

In Eleanor Roosevelt's case, many of these adolescent strivings and resentments were suppressed. She had no parents, and cool and formidable Grandmother Hall was no woman to trifle with. Eleanor did spend three years on her own in a European school. Here she found an impressive older woman, Marie Souvestre, with whom she could identify. When Eleanor returned home, her thinking was largely independent, but her behavior was entirely docile. She could not rebel against her grandmother, and she did what she had to as a young debutante. One reason that she showed so little rebellion, especially given her aversion for society and its customs, was that she had no peer support. No siblings were available to encourage action toward independence. She could be independent in mind but not in behavior. Such a contradiction made life seem absurd and worthless at times.

Uncertainties about Sex

Adolescence begins with sexual maturity, and one of its major challenges is sorting out confusions about sex. The new sex drives are both powerful and frightening, and there is a great deal of uncertainty about which feelings are normal and moral, which will lead to guilt or self-respect, and which kinds of sexual expression will lead to adaptive adjustment in the long run. Our culture tantalizes us with ever-increasing amounts of sexuality in movies, advertisements, books, and television. Many adolescents, however, have no idea how to deal with sex. Some feel guilt and shame over sexual feelings. Probably all worry about AIDS. Some wish that their parents were not so restrictive. Others wish that they had parents who cared and provided guidance. Many struggle with questions of sexual orientation: Am I gay or straight? Peer pressures are enormous in early adolescence, and finding one's way through the tangled issues of sexuality can seem overwhelming.

How do young people deal with these confusions and contradictions? Probably few adolescents know adults with whom they can easily discuss these matters. Although parents can and want to be helpful, often conflicts with their teenage children make it very difficult for parents to know how to help. Few adolescents have the kind of close relationship with a teacher that Eleanor Roosevelt had with Marie Souvestre. As a result, adolescents rely mostly on their peers, who are often no better informed and no more mature, for information and counsel. Norms evolve in adolescent society which most teenagers follow rather than risk rejection. For some, these norms are adaptive; for others, they are not.

In Eleanor Roosevelt's case, sexuality was never successfully integrated into her life. Part of this failure resulted from the strict Victorian moral code under which she was raised, which regarded sexuality as something that must be satisfied in men and tolerated by women; women were supposed neither to deny nor enjoy it. Also, as noted, Eleanor had no peers to consult or follow. Apparently her close relationship with Souvestre did not explore this area. Eleanor did have one short conversation with her grandmother about sex, and she was informed simply that it was a part of marriage that had to be endured. It is no wonder that in her intimate relationship with her husband she was inhibited and submissive. Eleanor recognized her inadequacy as an intimate marital partner and was sensitive about it. She was deeply hurt by FDR's affair with Lucy Mercer, and she was crushed years later when she learned that FDR was with Lucy when he died in Warm Springs, Georgia.

Value Conflict and Change

Part of the struggle for autonomy and independence that goes on during adolescence is a questioning of values. There is frequently a questioning of the religious faith and practice that parents have instilled, or tried to instill, since birth. Adolescents wonder whether they share their parents' beliefs, whether the same ideas make sense to them. Sometimes the questioning of parents' values and beliefs

comes from observing that parents do not really live up to the abstract moral principles they have espoused to their sons and daughters. Also, today's adolescents often doubt whether their parents' experiences and values have any relevance for them. They face a highly technological world, with major changes in the workplace and the availability of jobs. The society and the culture have changed dramatically in the past generation, and many adolescents find little of value to grasp from the older generation.

Part of the reason that there is so much questioning of beliefs, values, and moral behavior is that adolescence is a time of rapid moral as well as physical development. This aspect of personal growth has been explored most extensively by Lawrence Kohlberg (1981, 1984). His ideas and some classic research by Jean Piaget provide an overview of the stages of moral development and the profound changes in conceptions of morality that take place in adolescence.

Stages of Moral Development. The earliest studies of moral development were reported by Piaget in his famous book *The Moral Judgment of the Child* (1932). The ideas in this book were based on Piaget's findings about the way children's intellectual or cognitive abilities mature. Just as Erikson proposed that the personality develops through distinct stages, Piaget argued that cognitive functions such as thinking and reasoning do as well. He showed that children are capable of qualitatively different kinds of thinking as they grow older. It's not simply that they are able to handle a greater quantity of information. For example, young children are unable to view things from other people's point of view or to understand intentions very well. Both Piaget and Kohlberg believe that moral development follows the acquisition of new cognitive capacities. When Piaget discussed morality, he was especially concerned with children's judgments about how severely to punish other children who had caused damage, such as broken dishes or ripped clothing. He felt that the biggest change in these moral judgments came after the age of 9, when children move from the stage of *moral realism* to the stage of *moral relativism*. During the earlier stage of moral realism, children believe in rules very literally. It's almost as if they think of them as objects: A rule is a rule and it must be followed. If children break rules or cause harm, they must be punished according to the magnitude of the harm they cause. For example, children listening to a story about a young girl who breaks dishes assign punishment according to how many dishes she breaks. That is, children punish others according to the seriousness of the consequences of their acts. They give little thought to why someone caused damage or to mitigating circumstances.

During the later stage of moral relativism, or cooperative morality, children realize that rules have no independent meaning or existence other than that which has been given to them by human beings. They become aware that rules and laws are made by people to serve human purposes. They realize further that rules can be changed if change is needed to better serve human needs and that rules can sometimes be broken if it is in the best human interest. During this stage, punishment is not mechanically assigned on the basis of how serious the consequences of action are. Instead, the individual's intention is taken into account. If a child broke some dishes while trying to surprise his or her parents by cleaning up the kitchen, the child is not seen as guilty or deserving of punishment; the intention was a good one. In general, moral judgments are made in a more humanistic way and there is less rigid application of rules. The purpose behind behavior is considered as well as the behavior itself and its consequences.

Kohlberg's scheme of moral development shows some of the same kind of increased human understanding as Piaget's. Rules instilled in childhood are replaced by more carefully thought-out moral principles. Kohlberg investigated moral development using methods similar to those of Piaget. He presented stories about moral dilemmas to subjects who were asked to say what a person in the situation should do and why. In one story a man needed a drug to save his wife from cancer. The druggist who invented the medicine was charging 10 times the cost of making it. The man was unable to borrow more than half the money and could not get the druggist to lower his price. The man got desperate and broke into the store and stole the drug. Subjects are asked whether the man should or should not have stolen the drug and why.

On the basis of subjects' responses to this dilemma, Kohlberg distinguished three major levels of moral development. Within each level there are two separate stages, giving six stages in all (see Table 3.1). As with stages of personality development, a person must go through the stages in order; they cannot be skipped. However, people vary greatly in how fast they progress through the stages and in how far they eventually get. (Many people do not get past stage 4 in Kohlberg's system.) The period of most intense moral development is during adolescence. Between the ages of 10 and 17, some individuals may move all the way from stage 1 to stage 6.

The first two stages of moral development make up the **preconventional level of morality.** Here the child really has no internal morals or values but simply governs his or her behavior on the basis of anticipated rewards and punishments. The first stage, which may last until age 10, is oriented toward the avoidance of punishment. Children may decide not to steal or interrupt their parents so that they won't be punished. The second stage of the preconventional level is oriented more toward reward than punishment. Children may clean up their rooms in order to earn money or tell of their achievements in school to see their parents' delight. During this second stage, the idea of reciprocity also begins to take hold.

TABLE 3.1   Kohlberg's Six Stages of Moral Development

Level I: Preconventional	*Stage 1:* Orientation toward obedience and punishment or reward. Deference to superior power. Goodness or badness is determined by the physical consequences of action.
	Stage 2: Actions are motivated by desire for reward or benefit. People share, but in a pragmatic way, not out of a sense of justice or loyalty.
Level II: Conventional	*Stage 3:* "Good boy, nice girl" orientation. Emphasis on conformity. Behavior that pleases others and is approved by them is good behavior.
	Stage 4: "Law-and-order" orientation. Focus on authority, fixed rules, and the social order. Right behavior consists of maintaining the given social order for its own sake. Respect is earned by performing one's duty.
Level III: Postconventional	*Stage 5:* Social contract, legalistic orientation. Standards that have been agreed upon by the whole society define right action. Emphasis upon legal rules for reaching consensus.
	Stage 6: Emphasis on decisions of conscience and self-chosen, abstract ethical principles such as universal principles of justice, of equality, of human rights, and of respect for the dignity of human beings as individuals.

Source: Kohlberg (1984).

Children realize that if they do something kind to someone else, they are likely to be helped or rewarded in the future. Thus children behave in ways that are likely to lead others to reward them. This second stage characterizes children's actions and morality between ages 10 and 13. Eleanor Roosevelt anticipated little reward during her childhood. She was fearful of her mother's and then her grandmother's criticism. Her behavior was clearly designed to avoid criticism—that is, she followed stage 1 morality, remaining obedient and docile until well into adulthood because of her fear of punishment and rejection.

The next two stages of moral development make up the **conventional morality level.** Here the major concern is conformity to rules and values that have been learned from authorities. The first of these two stages is the one that most 13-year-olds are in. It is marked by "good girl" or "good boy" morality: Children and adolescents are concerned with the approval of parents and other important adults and adopt moral stances that they know conform to family standards. Values are adopted in order to gain the approval of others. A 14-year-old boy might refuse to smoke because his father or a teacher that he admired would be disappointed in him. An adolescent girl might change the way she dresses to gain the approval of an employer she respects. In Eleanor Roosevelt, a good girl morality would have been important in her relationship with Marie Souvestre. Eleanor probably worked hard helping younger students and adopted many of Souvestre's political ideas in order to gain approval. This does not imply that all Eleanor's ideas came from her teacher. Certainly her own inclinations were already consistent with what she learned in school.

The second stage of the conventional morality level, stage 4, is marked by what is sometimes called a *law-and-order* orientation. This stage is most common among people 16 and older, and many people never grow beyond this kind of conventional morality. In this stage people adopt and follow rules and laws that are set by powerful authorities in the culture, such as churches, government, and society as a whole. They learn the rules of these authorities, such as that it is wrong and illegal to steal, and obey them. They do what they think will be regarded as honorable by those in a position to judge. People who do not engage in premarital sexual relations because their religious leaders say it is wrong or who do not exceed the speed limit because it is the state law are following stage 4 conventional morality.

Sometime during the latter part of adolescence, perhaps around 17 years of age, some people move beyond conventional morality into stages 5 and 6 in the Kohlberg scheme. These stages constitute the **postconventional level of morality,** in which people commit themselves to self-accepted moral principles. Few reach this level. While most adults follow one form or another of conventional morality, Eleanor Roosevelt is clearly an example of a person who did adopt self-accepted moral principles.

In stage 5, morality is based on what one perceives as good for people as a whole. It grows out of consensus or agreement on what is in people's best interest and what seems fair and equitable in general. In this stage, morality reflects community welfare: People want the respect of others and want to perceive their choices as rational in light of the interests of all. This seems to be a highly democratic stage in which morals are based on what people can agree on as equals; no authority is allowed to make rules for its followers.

In stage 6, which some individuals reach during late adolescence or early adulthood, people finally adopt internalized, universal ethical principles. They choose these for themselves on the basis of experience and reason. In this stage, people might protest the persecution of minorities or defend or challenge laws on the basis of their own consciences. No longer do they base their morality on gaining rewards, approval, or respect from others. People are only concerned with avoiding self-condemnation and feeling at peace with their own values and their implications.

If their consciences reject values that society seems to have accepted, people in stage 6 often conflict with those who follow conventional morality. They may be condemned by society as they protest society's laws. Thus Henry David Thoreau, who described marching to the "beat of a different drummer," was put in jail for not paying taxes that he considered to be unjust. When he was asked by his friend Ralph Waldo Emerson what he was doing in jail, Thoreau, expecting Emerson to have followed his own conscience as well, replied: "What are you doing out there?" The controversial physician Dr. Jack Kevorkian clearly believes he is doing the right thing in helping terminally ill patients with assisted suicides. His actions severely test conventional legal and moral dictates. Eleanor Roosevelt showed her stage 6 morality when she objected to and successfully opposed the U.S. State Department's policy on the creation of Israel. She thought the department was taking a weak moral stance, and she would not abide by it. It was for these kinds of actions that she was called the "conscience of the nation."

In a Different Voice: Gender and Morality. Kohlberg's studies of moral development have taught us a great deal about human values, but they have raised new issues as well. One criticism of Kohlberg's studies is that the original research was conducted with males only. Even though female values were recorded subsequently, it may be that Kohlberg's studies do a better job of describing the moral principles of men than those of women.

Psychologist Carol Gilligan (1982) wrote an influential book entitled *In a Different Voice: Psychological Theory and Women's Development* in which she argues that men and women do have notably different moral principles. The basic difference is that whereas men's principles are more abstract and more concerned with general standards of justice, men are less concerned with human feelings. Furthermore, men are less interested than women in trying to negotiate problems and to work out a solution that pleases everyone. Women, in contrast, are more concerned with personal feelings, with caring for other people and trying to resolve conflicts between people so that everyone feels respected and reasonably satisfied.

Gilligan argues that men emphasize justice and the belief that "everyone should be treated the same." On the other hand, women emphasize nonviolence, care, compassion, and the belief that "no one should be hurt." Thus we should remember that although there are important stages of moral development, not everyone goes through them in the same way. Just as the sexes can show differences in their moral values and principles, so can individual men and individual women. You might examine the basic principles that underlie your own moral judgments and ask whether they genuinely fit your other values and beliefs and whether they will produce the kind of behavior—and the kind of world—that you would like to see.

REVIEW QUESTIONS

1. Piaget believed that moral development occurs in stages. The biggest changes in moral development, he says, come after the age of 9, when children move from the stage of _____ _____ to the stage of

   _____ _____.

2. Kohlberg distinguished six stages of moral development: three major levels each containing two separate stages. Match each two stages with the major level in which they occur.

   Stage 1: social contract, legalistic orientation

   Stage 2: emphasis on conscience and ethical principles

Stage 1: conformity, "good boy/good girl" orientation

Stage 2: law-and-order, authority orientation

Stage 1: obedience/punishment orientation

Stage 2: actions motivated by desire for reward

a. preconventional
b. conventional
c. postconventional

Uncertainties about Self-Worth

In the highest stage of moral development, Kohlberg found, people base their morality completely on internal standards. They feel good about themselves when they act morally and condemn themselves when they do not. Most people's feelings of worth are only partly determined by their conscience, if conscience plays any role at all. Many other factors determine how we feel about ourselves, what we think we are capable of, and what we think of the persons that we have become. These feelings of self-worth and self-image generate the most important of all the conflicts and uncertainties that need to be sorted out during adolescence. In this section we will consider the major processes of self-conception that affect what we think of ourselves throughout life. These four processes are reflected appraisal, social comparison, attribution, and identification (see Gergen, 1971). None of these processes is tied to any particular act or stage of development. However, all of them are very much in evidence during adolescence as people strive to define themselves. In addition to considering the four processes of self-conception, we will also consider how bias and distortion affect the conclusions we draw about ourselves from these processes.

Reflected Appraisal. Probably the most powerful determinant of our overall estimate of ourselves is the process of reflected appraisal. **Reflected appraisal** is simply the assessment or evaluation that someone else has of us. Our opinions of ourselves are greatly affected by the evaluations of others from early childhood through adulthood. One major step in positive adjustment is being able to become independent, to some degree, of what others think of us and decide for ourselves who we are and what we are worth.

The first person to write systematically about the notion that one's ideas of self derive from what others think was Charles Horton Cooley. In 1922, Cooley discussed how our feelings about ourselves derive from what we imagine others to think of us. Cooley (1922) stated that we feel "ashamed to seem evasive in the presence of the straightforward man, cowardly in the presence of a brave one, gross in the eyes of a refined one, and so on. We always imagine, and in imagining share the judgments of the other mind." The result of

imagining what others think of us, and sharing or accepting their opinion, is a "looking-glass self," a self-image directly reflecting the appraisals of others.

Another social psychologist who wrote about the self-concept was George Herbert Mead (1934). Mead emphasized the importance of "significant others"—parents, teachers, and peers—in the child's development. He suggested that as children we begin to base our self-conceptions on the view of us that is implied in the behavior of significant others. People imply by the way they treat us what they think of us. Then what we think they think of us affects our opinion of ourselves. For example, if the behavior of your parents consistently implies that you are not to be trusted, you will come to feel that you are not a trustworthy person. If your siblings treat you as if you are very skilled, you will come to believe that you are skilled. Parents, siblings, peers, and other significant others have a vast impact on our self-concept through the view of us that their behavior implies. In Eleanor Roosevelt's case, her mother calling her "Granny" and her aunt calling her "ugly duckling" gave Eleanor a negative self-image in her formative years. To some extent she never got over these negative self-evaluations and felt inferior because of them.

Many studies show that even in later years—for example, when we are young adults in college—our opinions of ourselves are affected by the feedback we get from others. A recent study by McNulty and Swann (1994) showed that over a period of several months college students' self-concepts changed in the direction of their roommates' appraisals of them. The students' self-concepts were especially affected by their roommates' appraisals of their academic abilities. A classic study by Videbeck (1960) looked at college students who read poems in a speech class and were given feedback from an expert on oral communication about their adequacy in controlling voice and conveying meaning. The appraisals which the students received were fixed ahead of time to be either positive or negative. The subjects rated themselves on several traits before and after getting the feedback, and the results showed that those who got positive feedback rated themselves more positively at the end than those who got negative feedback.

One important aspect of the results was that subjects changed their opinions of themselves on characteristics that had nothing to do with the specific feedback they received. For example, subjects' opinions of their abilities in social conversation went up or down depending on whether they got good or bad feedback about voice control. This happened even though what the evaluator said had nothing to do with social conversation. Why did this happen? What does it mean?

First, it is hard for people to accept feedback about a specific behavior without letting it affect their overall self-evaluation. Even when someone tries to give us feedback about a single trait, it tends to affect our overall feelings of adequacy and our overall emotional state. A second related point is that our opinion of ourselves does have some consistency to it. We do not have an isolated set of opinions about various aspects of ourselves that are unrelated. If our opinion of one aspect of ourselves is raised or lowered, this affects our opinions about other aspects of our self-concept, all of which are connected and contribute to some extent to our total self-image. These tendencies mean that we are affected by specific feedback from others more than we ought to be from a rational point of view, and more than is good for us emotionally. It is a problem to which we should be alert.

Social Comparison. A second highly important process involved in forming opinions of ourselves is **social comparison** (Festinger, 1954; Gilbert, Giesler, & Morris, 1995). In addition to passively accepting other people's appraisals of us, we also form our own opinion by comparing ourselves to other people. People compare themselves with others on many different traits. When we consider whether we are smart, dull, religious, athletic, lovable, or idealistic, we probably engage in social comparison (Gergen, 1971). For Eleanor Roosevelt, the results of social comparison in adolescence were no more positive than the results of reflected appraisal in childhood. She often compared herself to her vivacious and stunning cousin Alice, President Theodore Roosevelt's daughter, and by comparison felt plain and inept indeed.

When we engage in social comparison, we do not compare ourselves with just anyone. We usually compare ourselves with others who we think should be about as good as we are, inasmuch as they have similar standing on characteristics related to the attribute in question (Goethals & Darley, 1977). For example, if we were evaluating our swimming ability, we would compare ourselves with others of the same age and sex who have had the same amount of training and recent practice. If they are the same on these characteristics, we know that any difference in swimming performance must reflect ability, and we can judge ourselves accordingly. For this reason Eleanor felt compelled to compare herself with her cousin Alice Roosevelt, a female member of the Roosevelt clan who was exactly Eleanor's age.

Comparison with similar others allows very accurate self-appraisal—sometimes too accurate. People don't always like what comparison implies, as Eleanor Roosevelt's example illustrates. As a result, people sometimes compare themselves with others who are worse off so that they can feel better in comparison (Wills, 1981). For example, women who have had breast cancer often compare their situation with that of women who have had worse cases, sometimes even women who have died. A woman who had a lump removed from her breast said, "I had a relatively small amount of surgery. How awful it

SELF-ASSESSMENT EXERCISE_____

Are You a High Self-Monitor?

No matter how firmly people's identity is established, they must respond to the social situation of the moment and present a side of themselves that is appropriate to that situation. However, people vary considerably in how much they change their self-presentation in response to others and to the situation. A self-monitoring scale has been devised to measure how much people alter their behavior in response to others (Snyder, 1987). By answering the questions below, you can see whether you are a high or low self-monitor.

Answer each of the following statements *true* or *false* as it applies to you:

1. I can make impromptu speeches, even on topics about which I have almost no information.

2. When I am uncertain how to act in a social situation, I look to the behavior of others for cues.

3. I am particularly good at making other people like me.

4. Even if I'm not enjoying myself, I often pretend to be having a good time.

5. I can look anyone in the eye and tell a lie with a straight face (if for the right end).

6. I guess I put on a show to impress or entertain people.

7. I would probably make a good actor.

8. I sometimes appear to others to be experiencing deeper emotions than I actually am.

9. In different situations, and with different people, I often act like very different persons.

10. To get along and be liked, I tend to be what people expect me to be rather than anything else.

11. I may deceive people by being friendly when I really dislike them.

12. I am not always the person I appear to be.

In every case a *true* answer represents high self-monitoring.

Source: Adapted from M. Snyder (1986).

must be for women who have had a mastectomy, I just can't imagine. It must be so difficult" (Taylor, 1989, p. 171). Sometimes people deal with the implications of comparing with similar others by denying that they are similar. For example, people tend to deny that they are similar to people who are HIV positive and might have AIDS (Gump & Kulik, 1995; see Chapter 11).

Another way of dealing with the pain of social comparison is to compare with others who are slightly different on related attributes or make excuses for ourselves by perceiving more or less similarity than actually exists. For example, a college student might compare her tennis ability with that of a friend still in high school or her little sister and conclude she has more ability. In fact, the performance difference might simply reflect age. Or we might decide that someone who did better than we did had advantages over us. Eleanor Roosevelt may well have decided that Alice's stable family situation made it easier for her to be cheerful and outgoing.

Even though similarity is very important, we are sometimes affected by social comparison with those who are not very much like us. One clear demonstration of the impact of such social comparison on self-esteem is Morse and Gergen's (1970) Mr. Clean–Mr. Dirty study. In this experiment college students answered an ad for a part-time job at a research institute and reported to a secretary's office to be interviewed. They were asked to complete some questionnaires which included a measure of self-esteem and a measure of self-consistency. After the ratings had been completed, another person, posing as an applicant for the same job, entered the room and filled out the same questionnaires. The appearance of this person was varied to make him a "Mr. Clean" or a "Mr. Dirty." When he was Mr. Clean, he wore a dark business suit, carried an attaché case, opened the case to remove several sharpened pencils, a statistics book, a philosophy text, and a calculator. When he was Mr. Dirty, he wore a smelly sweatshirt with no socks and seemed dazed by the entire procedure. He carried a worn copy of a trashy novel and had to borrow a pencil. After Mr. Clean or Mr. Dirty had been working a while, the subject was given some additional questionnaires to complete that included another form of the self-esteem measure that he had completed before.

The results, which were predicted from social comparison theory, were that subjects who encountered Mr. Clean showed a decrease in self-esteem between the two measures, and subjects who found themselves with Mr. Dirty showed an increase in self-esteem. That is, subjects who think they are competing with the well-organized, well-prepared Mr. Clean feel slightly inferior and

outclassed, and their self-esteem drops, at least temporarily. Those who are up against the seemingly inept Mr. Dirty feel fairly smug and experience a rise in self-esteem. An additional finding of interest is that the subjects who scored high on the self-consistency measure were less affected by social comparison with Mr. Clean or Mr. Dirty. Their self-esteem changed less than did that of the subjects who were low in self-consistency. Perhaps the high self-consistency subjects have a clearer self-concept and thus are unlikely to have their self-concept much affected by brief interactions and short-term social comparisons. Their self-esteem is probably less affected by momentary external events and more determined by inner thought and evaluation. This finding has particular relevance for adolescents, who may not have had the time to form a consistent self-concept. They may be more prone to up and down feelings of self-worth, depending on varying situational influences.

Attribution Processes. Research shows that other important determinants of the self-concept are **attributions,** or inferences we make about our attitudes, emotions, abilities, and motives from our behavior (Bem, 1972; Schlenker, Dlugolecki, & Doherty, 1994). In many cases the kinds of attributions we make about ourselves are very straightforward. We might simply look at our behavior—for example, turning down invitations to parties, avoiding crowded places, and going alone to movies—and infer that we are introverted. Sometimes people make inferences about the strength of their political attitudes by observing whether they are willing to sign a petition, contribute money to a cause, or join a demonstration. Sometimes we know our attitudes fairly well already and guide our behavior according to them; other times we don't have a clear idea of where we stand until something forces us to make a choice. In some cases, we may not like what our behavior implies about us. A very effective advertisement for helping poor children in undeveloped countries proclaims, "You can help this child, or you can turn the page." The ad is effective because most people would ordinarily glance at the ad and turn the page, ignoring both the ad and their own behavior and its implications. By calling attention to the act of turning the page, the ad elicits a good deal of guilt and suggests that you are indifferent, lazy, and uncaring. It's interesting to see how people interpret their behavior in this case.

As is the case with social comparison, attribution can sometimes lead to unpleasant conclusions about the kind of people we are. This is especially true when abilities are involved. Many of our performances are linked to abilities. For example, when we take tests, play games of skill, apply for a job, or even go out on a date, our success depends in part on ability (Weiner, 1979). As is also the case with social comparison, sometimes our attributions are not very objective. We often make the attribution that will preserve our self-esteem or our public image. For example, people often take credit for success but deny responsibility for failure (Greenwald, 1980). This *self-serving bias* shows up when we say that we failed an exam because it was graded unfairly or we won at Monopoly as a result of our skill, ignoring all our lucky rolls of the dice.

Our own interpretations of a wide range of behaviors lead to attributions that build our self-concepts. The fact that these interpretations and attributions are biased in our favor often plays a key role in our psychological well-being. As we shall see in Chapter 6, sometimes people who make fewer self-serving attributions have serious psychological difficulties (Taylor, 1989).

Identification.   Closely related to attribution is the process of identification. In the case of attribution, we considered how people infer specific traits from a behavior or behavior pattern. In the case of **identification**, people adopt an entire pattern of behavior in an attempt to be like someone they admire and then conceive of that behavior pattern as an important aspect of their identity. People may identify with a parent, teacher, charismatic leader or celebrity, or slightly older peer who seems to have been successful. These identifications govern a great deal of their behavior and self-concept. Eleanor Roosevelt strongly identified with Marie Souvestre in terms of social conscience and with her father and grandfather in terms of trying to help the unfortunate. These identifications led to actions that she believed defined who she really was and became an important expression of her values, interests, and motives.

Self-Esteem Motives and Self-Conception Processes.   All the self-conception processes we have discussed thus far involve perception and, to some extent, thinking and reasoning. Psychologists know that a great deal of perception and thinking is irrational and biased, and we discussed some biases in social comparison and attribution. People see what they want to see or what they expect to see. They draw conclusions that serve their own needs (Greenwald, 1980). In no place is bias more pronounced than in the perception of what we care about most—ourselves. It is easy to observe biased self-concept formation in all the self-perception processes we have mentioned.

In the case of reflected appraisal, we can easily distort what others think of us since people seldom state a positive or negative opinion of another person directly. In the case of social comparison, there is room for enormous distortion in the meaning of any comparison outcome (Goethals, Messick, & Allison, 1991; Wood, 1996). If someone sitting next to you in class does better on an exam, there are probably lots of ways that you could convince yourself that her performance in no way implies that she is brighter. You might conclude that she spends all her time in the library and only does well because she works so hard. You might distort the attribution process by deciding that your own performance was poor because of competing demands on your studying time that you couldn't ignore (an old friend from high school came by to visit and you were stuck). In the case of identification, it is easy to imagine ourselves as closer to the ideal we are striving for than is the case. Aspiring singers often think their voices sound more like Reba McEntire's or Garth Brooks' than anyone else does.

The underlying assumption here is that people care about themselves and want to have a positive opinion of themselves. As a consequence, they perceive their behavior and other people's behavior in ways that allow them to maintain a positive self-concept. While this is undoubtedly true, it should not be taken to imply that people always interpret information about themselves positively. As much as people want to believe that they are good and appreciated by others, they fear that this is not true and often make overly negative interpretations of information about the self. Just as there are people who wouldn't recognize an obvious putdown, others, because of anxiety about their worth, insecurity about other people's opinions, or a low self-concept, interpret everything negatively. The most minuscule changes in tone of voice or the most insignificant glance is taken as a sign of displeasure or rejection. Any failure is taken as a sign of incompetence and lack of worth. These fears and insecurities can cause as much distortion and psychological trouble as the need for feelings of self-worth. They can contribute greatly to depression and lack of productivity.

In the course of busy and complex lives, we all fall prey to overjustifying ourselves occasionally and psychologically burning ourselves at the stake at other times. We all go through periods of feeling good and feeling bad about ourselves. This is especially true during adolescence, when parent and peer reactions are highly variable and performance in school, sports, and other domains is constantly being evaluated. It is important to remember that even though we can be more or less accurate in judging how much of a specific ability we have, such as high jumping, our overall worth is not an objective matter. What we feel about ourselves is affected by others' judgments, real and imagined, and by the comparisons and attributions we make. What we finally decide about our worth, however, is determined by us alone. We have considerable choice about feeling good or miserable about ourselves. We have only to exercise that choice. Furthermore, if we can choose positive or negative evaluations, why not choose the positive? Why not accept ourselves? Why not assume that we have worth and value and act on that assumption? It's amazing how beneficial making that choice and following through on it can be. This may seem like self-deception to a certain extent, but it is an important stance you can take in your own life.

Outcomes of Adolescent Conflict and Confusion

As we have noted, adolescence is a time of rapid physical, cognitive, and moral growth. Many have great uncertainties about where all this is taking them. We have seen that there are conflicts about independence, doubts about sex, confusion about values, and uncertainties about self-worth. In short, this is the time of life when people first wonder intensely: Who am I? What am I worth? What shall I do? This is the period when people have their first *identity crisis*, their first struggles with the questions of what they can do and be in the world. What are the outcomes of identity crises? We know most about the answer to this question from Erik Erikson (1968).

Ego-Identity versus Identity Confusion.   For some people the outcome of the identity crisis is a positive balance. They have a greater sense of **ego-identity** or *identity achievement* than of *identity confusion* or *identity diffusion* (Marcia, 1980). They seem to be able to take hold in some way, to gain an overall sense of who they are, what they can do, and how they want to live. Most important, perhaps, they are able to find a place for themselves in society, a job or a career. They feel that they know who they are and that who they are is understood and accepted by others around them. Even more than this, people with a sense of **ego-identity** feel that there is a purpose and meaning in what they have been doing in the past and what they will be doing in the future. They feel that the past and future connect, that there is some coherence in what they are, and that they have things to do in living and becoming. Erikson described this as "an invigorating sense of sameness and continuity" (Erikson, 1968, p. 19).

How do people who have a sense of identity come by it? What makes them so fortunate? Like all other balances, identity rests on what has happened in earlier stages. Erikson proposed that identity has a basis in early childhood (see Chapter 2) in that the sense of basic trust established then forms the foundation for faith, which in turn is an important aspect of a sense of identity. Similarly, autonomy and the early experiencing of the capacity to act alone provide a basis for the young adult's sense of free will, another important part of identity. This sense of free will is extremely important for functioning in a democratic, capitalistic society. Similarly, the earlier sense of initiative extends to a sense of creative potential, and the sense of industry from the latency period contributes to a feeling of being able to behave effectively in the adult world. All of these psychological strengths provide a foundation for the sense of ego-identity.

These foundations are important, but identity still must be achieved by an active process of sorting out, pulling together, and choosing. Erikson (1968) states that identity is based on an integration of past identifications and roles, lifelong motives, needs, and strivings, and the person's skills and modes of coping. From these, a *core self* is identified and a place for that self is made within available social roles. In other words, people decide who they are on the basis of what they have been in the past, what they aspire to, and what they are capable of, and then decide what role they will play in society.

Eleanor Roosevelt achieved a sense of identity after returning to the United States from school in Europe. She was not totally satisfied with her identity, but she did have a clear sense of what she would do and how she would live. She would follow the customs of the established, upper-class society that she knew, even though its parties and dances pained her greatly, and she would make the best of it. She reaffirmed this choice shortly afterward when she became involved with her cousin Franklin, accepted the fact that he loved and needed her, and chose to center her life around being his wife and the mother of his children and helping him in his career as best she could. She knew that he shared some of the humanitarian concerns and political outlooks that she valued, and she thought she could help him further those goals by loving and caring for him. It would be more than 10 years, however, before she would reshape her identity and become an active humanitarian herself.

Of course, not all people are able to achieve a strong sense of ego identity. If they are unable to integrate their aspirations, needs, and skills into social roles and find a place for themselves within the social structure, they will suffer identity diffusion or what Erikson called identity confusion. *Identity diffusion* is the outcome when people try out several identities but none seems to fit (Marcia, 1966). The closely related concept of **identity confusion** consists of role confusion, uncertainty about career choice, or, more generally, what one is going to *do* in society. A person can have identity confusion even if he or she has a job or social role because the role doesn't fit well with his or her personality. The person may feel that the job requires him or her to be too assertive or not assertive enough, places too much emphasis on unimportant or even disliked values, or requires too much time away from other valued activities.

People can also have prized careers at which they excel but still have identity confusion in other ways. They may feel that there is not a good match between their definition of themselves and other people's definitions. People sometimes feel that the world doesn't really understand what is inside them, what they want, and what they value, and that they have no way of communicating this. An example might be a gay man who is afraid to come out of the closet or a mother who really doesn't like child rearing. Without the direction that is provided by having social roles *and* a clear sense of self that is also understood and accepted by others, people will be confused about who they are. They will not have the "invigorating sense of sameness and continuity" that Erikson dubbed such an important part of identity.

REVIEW QUESTIONS

3. Match each definition to the appropriate concept:

   _____ Adoption of a pattern of behavior of someone admired and integration of that pattern into our self-identity
   _____ Our belief about our worth
   _____ The total set of opinions or beliefs we have about ourselves
   _____ Process involving the effect of others' opinions on our estimate of our worth

   a. reflected appraisal
   b. self-concept
   c. self-esteem
   d. identification

4. T or F: Although biases of the self-concept may distort reality to some degree, they are unlikely ever to negatively affect our behavior.

5. T or F: An identity crisis is most likely to occur during middle age.

6. The outcome of an identity crisis may be positive; a person may feel he or she knows who he or she is and have a good sense of ego-identity. However, some people may experience a conflict between how they see themselves and how others see them. Erikson calls this conflict _____ _____.

ADULTHOOD

When the identity crisis is over in late adolescence, people are well on their way to making the transition to adulthood. They face new tasks, challenges, and opportunities in establishing their independent lives. Like childhood and adolescence, the adult years are filled with different problems and possibilities at different times. Erik Erikson has contributed some key insights into some of the issues of adult development. In addition, psychologist Daniel Levinson and his colleagues (1978, 1985, 1986; Roberts & Newton, 1987) have attempted to outline the stages of adult life through which many people pass. This work provides a useful overall picture of how individuals grow during adulthood.

Levinson identifies an alternation of two types of stages in adult development. First, there are several stages marked by *structuring*, that is, choices and commitments to certain aspects of living. These are interspersed with *transition* stages in which earlier commitments are questioned and new decisions made. These new decisions modify what has been built in earlier stages, sometimes with minor adjustments, sometimes with major changes.

In discussing self-discovery and change during adulthood, we will use Levinson's stages to give us an overview of the general trends in adult life. As before, we will also draw on Erikson's insights to look at some specific crises that occur in adulthood. Our discussion will be divided into three chronologically ordered sections: the early adult years, the middle adult years, and the later years.

The Early Adult Years

Levinson's research suggests that the early adult years are marked by two stages of transition, the *early adult transition* and the *age 30 transition,* interspersed with two stages in which young adults try to build structure—*entering the adult world* and *settling down.* We will consider these stages briefly. Finally, we will consider Erikson's insights into a major issue in the early adult years: establishing long-lasting intimate relationships.

Eleanor Roosevelt provides an excellent example of continuing development and change during the early adult years. As we noted at the beginning of the chapter, the course of her life seemed totally determined by the time she was a young adult. Despite the loneliness and insecurity of her childhood, she managed to make peace with her situation in life, find an initial identity, and form an intimate relationship in a reasonably happy marriage. She was married at 20 and by 30 had borne five of six children. The path of her life seemed clear and straight. The pursuit of Franklin's political ambitions promised a great deal of challenge and adventure, but there seemed to be nothing fundamentally different ahead for Eleanor. As it turned out, the next few years were much more filled with crisis, growth, and productive self-discovery than anyone could have imagined.

Levinson's studies of the early adult years provide a good account of the stages during which Eleanor was making these changes, from her late teens to her late thirties.

The Early Adult Transition (Ages 17 to 22). The first stage in Levinson's view of adult development is one of change rather than structuring or commitment. It is called the early adult transition, and its main task is to emerge from the preadult world. It takes place during the college years, and it involves parting with preadult styles of living and old friends to some extent and taking a preliminary step into the adult world. During this stage people start to form an *initial adult identity.* They begin to build an idea of what they would like to be as independent persons. This idea is based on what Levinson calls the *Dream.* The Dream is a vision of what people would like to accomplish in life. It is a "vague sense of self in the world," an "imagined possibility" of adult life that "generates excitement and vitality" (Levinson, 1978, p. 91). For Eleanor Roosevelt, the Dream at this stage was to help her husband succeed in his political career, maybe even to help him do as well as her Uncle Ted.

Entering the Adult World (Ages 22 to 28). People who have formed their Dream during the early adult transition seem prepared to move into the adult world. During this stage they make decisions which form a provisional structure for adult life. Initial choices can provide a strong sense of identity if they fit people's overall personality, especially if they fit the Dream. The more that choices are consistent with the Dream and seem to be advancing it, the more the sense of identity will be experienced.

At this stage a person makes choices in the important areas of occupation, love, values, and lifestyle. Most critical perhaps are choosing an occupation and choosing a marriage partner. Both are significant because of the extent to which they help actualize the Dream. The person whose occupation doesn't fit the Dream will feel a deep sense of alienation from self. A spouse who can share a partner's Dream and help pursue it can contribute greatly to the partner's adjustment. Each must understand and contribute to the other's Dream. After the Dream has been fulfilled, two people can outgrow each other unless there is more to the relationship than one using the other to reach his or her goals.

Another special relationship young people need to establish is with a *mentor,* usually a somewhat older person who is part parent and part friend and peer. The mentor relationship generally lasts two or three years, during which the mentor can provide needed guidance about the adult world, especially one's occupation. Not all mentor relationships are positive, but they have great emotional intensity. They too help make the Dream more concrete and give the young person a tangible model of how to live as an adult.

One of the difficulties of this stage is that people want to explore as many possibilities for adult living as possible, but they must make choices to create a stable structure, even if it is a temporary one. Achieving a balance between these opposing tendencies can be difficult. A person who explores too much might end up with a rootless, unsettled life. A person who does not explore enough can have a deep sense of being locked into a structure which may not be the right one. In any case, during this stage the initial provisional structure of adult life is established. During the next stage it can be modified.

The Age 30 Transition (Ages 28 to 33). The task of this transition is to modify the life structure formed in the previous early adult stage. In making the initial choices required during that stage, one inevitably ignored parts of life that were important. For example, children may not have been planned. Now an attempt is made to review the initial choices to see if it is possible to include some of the important things that have been left out. For some, this transition is fairly smooth and reaffirms most of the choices made upon entering the adult world. Others may experience major changes in direction. There could be divorce or a complete shift in career. Some people feel a deep sense of frustration and profound anxiety about the worth of their lives at this point.

Settling Down (Ages 33 to 40). People eventually complete the age 30 transition period and begin to establish a new life structure. This usually begins at about age 33, as people attempt to form a *niche* for themselves and become successful. They create their own sense of who they are and what they want to be in the adult world. They define their goals for living, or their *project.* Eleanor Roosevelt's project was working to improve social conditions and helping Franklin back to an active life after his paralysis.

This is the stage at which people do the most ladder-climbing in their occupations. They move from being a junior member of their profession to a senior partner with authority and power. At the end of this era is a special substage (ages 36 to 40) in which people make a major effort to achieve eminence in their occupations and to become leading figures. People may well become mentors for others younger than themselves. This is the time when individuals most firmly establish themselves and become dominant members of the adult world. Again, Eleanor Roosevelt did this as she took the lead in her household and began to manage and direct Franklin's recovery and return to politics.

An Early Adult Crisis: Intimacy versus Isolation. One specific task of becoming an adult is that of establishing an intimate relationship and integrating sexuality into that relationship. Levinson noted this task when he discussed finding a spouse who can help build the Dream. According to Erikson, the intimate relationship must be consistent with the identity established in late adolescence and with the Dream being pursued during the early adult transition. Eleanor Roosevelt achieved this task fairly easily. She was engaged to Franklin within about a year of her return to the United States. She seemed to have been fortunate in this aspect of her life because her relationship with Franklin was one of deep love, respect, and intimacy. There was, however, one serious difficulty. That was the sexual side of their relationship, which was not satisfying to either. Integrating the sexual side of love into the total relationship is an important but difficult part of intimacy.

One reason that this integration may be difficult is that many people have grown up feeling that sex is basically immoral. Feeling sexually aroused and behaving sexually can cause a great deal of guilt and anxiety for such people. This is especially true for women who are taught that sex in marriage is normal but before marriage it is taboo. It can be very difficult to make the psychological transition from feeling that sex is wrong and dirty to feeling that it is desirable. So much time has been spent in inhibiting sex and justifying that inhibition that it is hard to make a turnaround. This sudden "green light" makes either the prior inhibitions or the present lack of restraint or both seem slightly absurd and confusing. Of course, some women, like Eleanor Roosevelt, were taught that even in marriage sexuality for women was basically unacceptable. Satisfying men's needs was a duty to be borne.

Men can also find it difficult to handle the lesson that women should not engage in sex before marriage. Depending on their family and culture, some men grow up with the stereotype that women who are not virgins are immoral. These men may not overcome this attitude in their own intimate relations, within or outside marriage, and may find it difficult to accept and feel at ease with the sexual behavior and sexual interest of their partners.

Even if both partners feel that being sexually intimate is good in principle, much may be lost in the translation to practice. Many young people have inadequate knowledge of sex. They find it difficult to communicate openly about sexual feelings with their partners. They are too insecure and self-conscious about their performance or strong sexual drives to be sensitive to the other person. They frequently do not know how to deal with issues such as condom use or other forms of birth control. As a result, awkwardness and failure frequently prevail instead of the relaxed mutual caring and support that is central to the intimate relationship.

For some people intimacy is never achieved. They are unable to participate in a "fusing of identities," or deep caring. Instead of a sense of intimacy, they develop a *sense of isolation* and feel distant from others. They may feel alienated and cynical about humanity in general. These feelings may lead them to avoid others or simply engage in superficial relationships in which they are only concerned with using others to satisfy their own needs. Their sexual relationships are exploitative. They may be reasonably content as individuals, but sharing and caring are absent from their lives.

The Middle Adult Years

Middle age is a time of special importance, when major questions, crises, and reorientations take place. Many people go through *midlife crises,* some mild, some severe, wondering whether their lives have been worthwhile, whether there is any hope of changing life for the better, and whether there is any potential for freshness and vitality in their later years. We will first consider two stages that Levinson has identified as important during these years. Then we will discuss the way Erikson illuminated a key crisis of these years.

The Midlife Transition (Ages 40 to 45). Levinson's studies show that during the stage he calls the midlife transition, people question more deeply than ever what their life has been up to that point. They try to discover its meaning, and they question its significance and the satisfactions it has provided for them. This can be the most traumatic of life stages. After a rather frantic early adulthood during which people have pursued their Dream, formed a family, worked to achieve, and in all these senses "made it," they must now ask: What have I really got? If they feel that they haven't got much, or that too many needs were unmet in the struggle to get to the top, they can experience profound life changes. The midlife adult realizes that any shifts that are to be made in lifestyle had better be made now. Probably not all our needs are met in any of the choices that we make. The midlife transition provides a final opportunity to try to change the life structure to incorporate our unmet needs.

Entering Middle Adulthood (Ages 45 to 50). Levinson also found that the questioning of one's life choices that marks the midlife transition inevitably leads to new choices and thus to changes in life. Sometimes these changes are radical; in other cases they are minor. The new choices may simply reaffirm the old. Whatever degree of change is caused by the new choices, however, some kind of new life structure will have to be formed. The task of entering middle adulthood is to build this new life structure. The new structure may involve spending more time with the family and less on the job, or more time in a position of new responsibility at work and less time in community affairs. New interests may be explored. In some cases these new involvements may build on interests, such as artistic pursuits, which were held briefly in the past, perhaps in the college years. In other cases people plunge into something entirely new. They sometimes change careers, decide to move, or begin a new intimate relationship. Wherever energies go in this stage, it is again a time of choice and commitment rather than questioning and exploring.

One of the changes that many adults make during this stage is adopting what Carl Jung (1960) called the *midlife cultural orientation.* Jung believed that during the first part of life a person's orientation is generally *biological.* There is a concern with gratifying the instincts and with the *expansion* of experience. Young people seek out as many experiences as they can. They strive to enrich themselves by encountering as many new people, places, ideas, and experiences as possible. For the mature person, further expansion and further instinctual gratification are not desirable. Rather, there is an increasing need for simplification, limitation, and intensification. Instead of seeking more experience, the older person wants life to be simpler and calmer, and to enjoy each experience more deeply and intensely. More time is spent reflecting on experiences rather than having new ones right away. Middle adulthood is the time of *spiritual* and *cultural* orientation as opposed to the earlier biological orientation. The trend is toward discovering the meaning of life rather than frantically living it. Unfortunately, Jung notes, "Not a few are wrecked during the transition from the biological to the cultural sphere. Our collective education makes practically no provision for this transitional period. Concerned solely with the education of the young, we disregard the education of the adult" (Jung, 1965, pp. 84–85). That is, middle adulthood may be the time when men and women are most in need of education and guidance and most receptive to it. Their curiosity about the meaning of life puts them in a position to profit immensely from education. This is an extremely important psychological transition that the culture does nothing to provide for, although people who are aware of it can take their own steps to prepare for it.

One of the many activities in which Eleanor Roosevelt became involved during her middle adulthood was a furniture restoration and manufacturing enterprise that was run out of Val-Kill, the house that she designed for herself on FDR's Hyde Park estate. The Dutch term *Val-Kill* meant privacy, and the furniture business meant an involvement in historical and artistic endeavors. Eleanor's involvement in the cultural side of human affairs is a good example of adopting a midlife cultural orientation.

Generativity versus Stagnation in the Middle Years.   A key crisis during the middle adult years concerns the needs of the next generation. Erikson noted that during the early stages of development people are dependent on others. In middle age, however, they develop a concern for others who are dependent on them. This concern, called **generativity** takes the form of a "concern for establishing and guiding the next generation" (Erikson, 1968, p. 138). This can mean having children of one's own and nurturing them, or it can mean living a creative and productive life with the aim of leaving something positive behind, something that will enrich others. It involves being unselfish, unself-centered, and invested in the needs of those who are younger— specific others or the younger generation in general. This rich expansion of caring about others does not always develop. The alternative is *stagnation,* a lack of caring except for oneself, accompanied by boredom, cynicism, and pessimism about the future—one's own and that of humankind. Psychological stagnation can lead parents to the kind of inconsistent and uncaring treatment of children and adolescents that can produce in them the negative balances discussed in Chapter 2.

In Eleanor Roosevelt's life we see a strong balance of generativity. In her middle years she was at her most active. She recognized social problems but never became cynical or pessimistic about the future. She believed that problems could be addressed and solved. She accepted her husband's famous statement that "the only thing we have to fear is fear itself." She felt that if people can overcome

their anxieties and resentments, they make changes and leave the next generation with a better world. Once she adopted the identity of reformer and humanitarian, she worked unceasingly to create that better world.

The Later Years

There is less research on the psychological stages people pass through in later years. This is a serious lack because people are living longer, many are staying healthier, and some are coming out of retirement to work again. The singer Frank Sinatra, a popular performer whose career has lasted nearly 60 years, recently celebrated his eightieth birthday with a highly successful television special. Johnny Kelley continued his inspiring performances in the Boston Marathon until he was well into his eighties. Despite the fact that relatively little has been written on the later years, Levinson and Erikson have given us some relevant insights.

Transition and Restructuring in the Later Years.   Levinson speculated that the alternation of transition stages and structuring stages would continue throughout life. People would choose, structure, re-evaluate, choose again, and so on. This implies a future of continued psychological activity that has the potential to keep life fresh and satisfying. At the same time there is the potential for deep disillusionment if people discover that their life patterns are not satisfying and they are unable to establish new ones. They may feel intensely dissatisfied with their careers but unable to begin new ones, or may regret not having children but find that it is too late to begin a family.

In Eleanor Roosevelt's case, a series of events kept introducing new challenges that made it necessary for her to make new choices or reaffirm old ones. These included World War I, her husband's affair with Lucy Mercer,

Planning for Retirement

One of us had a colleague, whom we'll call Will, who was a workaholic. Until he was in his early seventies, Will juggled three demanding roles, as a scholar, a teacher, and psychotherapist. Will's work was extremely gratifying to him. Many of the people who worked with him were indebted to him for the way he helped them with personal problems, the way he taught them in class, or the way he involved them in research. He left a mark on many of them and enriched their lives. Finally Will decided to retire from the university where he had worked for nearly four decades. He had done enough, and it was time to leave the field to a younger generation of psychologists.

When asked what he planned to do when he retired, Will said "I just don't know." Because so much of his time was spent working, including most evenings and at least a part of every Saturday and Sunday, he had not developed outside interests. While he had a passing interest in sports, literature, and gardening, none of these activities kept his attention for very long. When he retired, his life had an enormous hole in it. He had time on his hands and no place to go.

The effect of the emptiness on Will was dramatic. His health declined rapidly and he seemed unable to find a fulfilling avenue for his energies. Will died within three years of retirement, unable to fight off a series of illnesses. While we'll never know for sure how Will experienced life after retirement, it seemed plain that he was not prepared for the vacuum he found without work.

Clearly, many people thrive on retirement. They have a variety of interests and lots of family and friends to share them with. We all deal with life's changes differently. However, there does seem to be a message here. Preparing for life's transitions is important. Being engaged in a wide range of fulfilling life pursuits helps sustain us when we must close the door on one of those pursuits, especially one as important as a career. Life offers many ways to live fully, and we should try to take advantage of them.

---

his paralysis from polio, his re-entry into politics, his election to the Presidency, World War II, Franklin's death, and her position in the United Nations. Through it all she maintained that no matter what problem she faced or how bad she felt, the only solution was to maintain her faith and to work hard. She tried to be sure she had done all that was possible. With this attitude she kept her life fresh and purposeful until she died.

Integrity versus Despair in Late Adulthood. According to Erikson, people who have done well in the earlier stages of development, have adjusted successfully to life, and have been productive in spite of life's disappointments will be able in old age to fully accept their life cycle as it has been run. They

will accept responsibility for what has happened and not blame family members, other people, or society. In general, such people will have a **sense of integrity.** They will feel at peace with themselves and with others. There will be a feeling of the oneness of individual existence and of life in general.

The emotional opposite of integrity is despair or disgust. Those who failed to develop a sense of integrity will realize that it is too late to make any changes. Whatever they are has been decided already. People who feel that their lives and work have not been worthwhile will face this despair. Old age will lack meaning or happiness. Even at this age, however, one's psychological balance can affect the younger generation positively or negatively. Erikson states: "Healthy children will not fear life if their elders have integrity enough not to fear death" (Erikson, 1963, p. 269).

Eleanor Roosevelt clearly had psychological integrity in her later years. Especially after FDR died, she accepted responsibility for her own life and continued to live it as fully and productively as possible. She was bitter about some of the things that had happened to her and the way others close to her had acted in certain instances, but she chose to forgive and to remain at peace with herself and those around her. She knew her life had been worthwhile.

HEALTH AND HAPPINESS IN ADULTHOOD

One fact that all people have to face as they grow older is the decline in their physical capacities. For most people, this decline first becomes perceptible at about age 30. How rapid and severe is the decline in physical capacity, and how is it related to mental capacity and psychological adjustment?

Health and Happiness in the Early and Middle Adult Years

The decline in physical capacity that begins at around age 30 is very gradual. Many people notice very little loss of vigor or stamina. At about age 50, however, the decline becomes sharper (Troll, 1975). Still, there are wide individual differences. Some people notice fairly dramatic declines in physical capacity; others notice very little. Just as there is great variability among people in the rate of physical decline, there is great variability in psychological response to these losses. People who base their self-esteem and their self-image on physical strength and fitness feel old and less positive about themselves as their bodies begin to decline. On the other hand, people who base their self-esteem on nonphysical characteristics, such as their intelligence, their ability to

get along with people, or their capacity to provide for their families, do not feel old and do not suffer losses of self-esteem (Buhler, 1972).

As people reach middle age, there is a more noticeable decline in physical abilities. Women go through menopause. While about 75 percent of women experience either no symptoms or mild symptoms, up to 60 percent are bothered by hot flashes, feelings of extreme heat or warmth sometimes followed by chills. Men also face increasing signs of growing old. They lose hair, and what remains becomes gray. Their athletic capacity declines noticeably.

These events can be troubling in our youth-oriented culture, but other important events occur during these years that can affect happiness more. For example, most parents experience the last of their children leaving home. How do people react to the empty nest experience? Research suggests that many middle-aged parents actually show increases in happiness after children leave home (White & Edwards, 1990). Even though they may love and miss their children, the increase in personal freedom and the decrease in responsibility can significantly increase happiness and overall well-being.

The Later Adult Years: Meeting and Beating the Aging Process

In old age, health problems and the decline of physical capacity become more serious. People struggle with loss of hearing, they become more far sighted and need reading glasses, and they actually shrink in height. Men lose about 1 inch in height, women 2 inches. The elderly must deal with softer bones and the risk of broken ones; narrowing of the arteries and thus problems related to poor circulation; an increase in blood pressure; and decreased efficiency of the kidneys, lungs, and intestines (Garn, 1975). Half the population over 65 is limited in its daily activities by various health

The Mindbending Effects of Mindset

An astonishing experiment by Langer and her associates demonstrates just how mind-set affects physical and mental aspects of aging (Langer, 1989). Two groups of men between the ages of 75 and 80 were taken off to a five-day retreat at a camp near Boston. Their activities were planned very carefully and focused on either thinking about or actually reliving the year 1959. The first group—the one that simply thought about 1959—spent time in organized discussions of the year 1959, wrote about their lives in 1959, and were told that they might even feel like they did in 1959. The second group was helped to live their five days as if it were actually 1959. Their autobiographies stopped in 1959; they had *Life* and *Saturday Evening Post* magazines from 1959; they were not to mention anything that had happened in the world or in their lives since 1959. Furthermore, they listened to speeches from President Eisenhower, listened to songs and watched TV ads from 1959, watched the 1959 movie classic *Anatomy of a Murder,* and discussed sports heroes of 1959—Bill Russell, Mickey Mantle, and Johnny Unitas. These men, as much as possible, relived 1959.

The results were astounding. Both groups showed some definite changes. In photographs taken after the retreat the men were rated as looking three years younger than in photos taken before. The men's hearing was measurably improved, their hand strength was greater. Even more striking were some of the changes unique to the men who relived 1959. They showed greater joint flexibility; their measured height in a sitting position was taller; their vision in the right eye improved; their manual dexterity was better; and on some specific intelligence test scales, they had higher scores.

---

problems (Hendricks & Hendricks, 1975). As you might expect, physical health is connected to psychological health at this age, and people who face physical limitations in their day-to-day living experience more unhappiness than do people who enjoy continuing good health.

Even though the infirmities of old age pose challenges, there are aspects of the later years that afford special opportunities. It has long been observed that older people take special joy from their grandchildren, and it has been noted that sometimes children identify strongly with their grandparents and sometimes end up being more like their grandparents than their parents. While older people do take pleasure in their grandchildren, it is also clear that they like the freedom that goes with not having the responsibility of taking care of those grandchildren. Research shows that elderly people like having contact with their grandchildren, but they want that contact to last for short periods (Troll, 1971).

Since the number of people over 65 has been growing steadily in the past several decades and will continue to grow, the challenges that this group faces must concern us all. To get a sense of the continuing growth of the population over 65, consider these statistics: When the country was founded in the late 1700s, about 2 percent of the population was over 65. In 1900, that percentage had doubled. Four percent of the population was over 65. In 1981, that number had risen to 11 percent, and it is expected to rise to 20 percent in the year 2030. What can this group do to increase their chances of living happy and productive later years?

Though it is impossible to prevent our eventual death, the way we live the last years of our lives varies tremendously. A key factor in living well-adjusted final years is living them actively and thoughtfully. For example, physical exercise makes a substantial difference in both physical and mental health and can benefit the immune system, at least for a period of time (Simon, 1991). More generally, we should remember the "use it or lose it" principle—when we use a part of our body, and our mind, we keep it functioning and useful much more than if we do not use it.

It is also important to remember that aging is a mind-set, and we can exercise some choice in the way we think about it, as Lessons from the Laboratory (page 73) illustrates. Because age is a state of mind, the way we think about aging and the way we actually live make all the difference in our adjustment, our health, and our happiness. Fortunately, most older adults manage well. Their life satisfaction scores remain high well into their seventies (Gatz & Hurwicz, 1990). Still, there are many life experiences that cannot be controlled. One of the most terrifying is dementia—impairments in thinking, memory, and judgment—especially Alzheimer's disease. We will conclude our review of adulthood with a look at this frightening disorder.

Struggling with Alzheimer's Disease. **Alzheimer's disease,** named for German physician Alios Alzheimer, who discovered the disorder in 1906, is a progressive deterioration of the brain. It is important to realize that Alzheimer's is a disorder; it is not a normal part of aging. However, the number of people affected by Alzheimer's is astonishing. While only 3 percent of people between the ages of 65 and 74 suffer from the disease, 19 percent of those between 75 and 84 and 47 percent of those 85 and over fall victim to it (Evans et al., 1989). At present there are 4 million recognized cases in the United States. It is estimated that there will be 14 million cases in about 40 years (Pendlebury & Solomon, 1996). Alzheimer's disease has been a problem for many years, but it is more in the public eye today because people live longer and prominent individuals, such as former U.S. President Ronald Reagan, have fallen victim to it.

Alzheimer's disease is marked initially by memory loss and attention problems. As the disease progresses, the symptoms get worse. It becomes difficult to express thoughts and feelings, and patients experience a more general loss of mental capacities and ability to function. They may forget what they were saying in the middle of a sentence, have trouble following the plots of stories or movies, or forget why they walked upstairs. Symptoms include anger, general disorientation, and depression. Eventually, in the range of seven to ten years, most Alzheimer's victims die.

There is no known cause or cure for Alzheimer's disease. Suspected causes are infection, genetic vulnerability, changes in neurotransmitters, or aluminum toxicity. There is recent research on drugs that can reduce the symptoms of Alzheimer's disease, and the use of the drug tacrine has been recently approved for use in the United States. However, the drugs are still controversial (Solomon, Knapp, Gracon, Groccia, & Pendlebury, 1996). Some help is available through memory-retraining programs and reality orientation programs (Wilson, 1987; Heston & White, 1991). These programs can help both the victims of the disease and their families stay in touch with their identities and the world around them at least for a period of time.

Conclusion on Aging: Accentuating the Positive

Despite the inevitability of death and the challenges of deterioration and disease, there is great potential for health and happiness in the later adult years. A new approach to understanding the elderly, called the *personal growth model,* emphasizes the freedom and feelings of integrity that older people have in their lives (Kalish, 1982). This approach emphasizes the positive aspects of old age, including the freedom we have already mentioned as well as leisure time and the ability to concentrate on what is important.

Thus while old age presents inevitable physical limitations, happiness and adjustment can be hallmarks of these years. Clearly there are good things to be experienced at any stage of the life cycle.

REVIEW QUESTIONS

7. T or F: According to Erikson, the first specific task of becoming an adult is to establish an intimate relationship.

8. Erikson believed that in the middle years people often develop _____, a concern for guiding the next generation. The alternative is _____, a lack of caring, accompanied by boredom, cynicism, and pessimism.

9. Jung believed that during the first part of life a person's orientation is generally biological and is directed toward expansion of experience. For the older person, there is an increasing need for simplification, limitation, and intensification. This is a time of _____ and _____ orientation.

10. T or F: All people who begin to lose their physical capacities and vigor in middle age feel old and suffer a loss of self-esteem.

SUMMARY

1. A person goes through many changes and faces many problems throughout life. A healthy self-definition, or self-concept, is crucial to dealing with these changes and problems. Most people first form their self-concepts in adolescence.

2. A person's self-concept, or self-theory, is based on reflected appraisal, social comparison, and identification with others.

3. Among the problems and challenges adolescents face are questions about independence, doubts about sex, and value conflicts and changes.

4. Kohlberg identifies changes in morality through which adolescents pass. Adolescents move from a preconventional level of morality, in which moral behavior is based on anticipated punishments and rewards, to a level of conventional morality, in which the emphasis is on conforming to the rules established by authority, and then, in some cases, to a postconventional level of morality, in which moral principles are adopted on the basis of personal experience.

5. People generally resolve the conflicts and confusions of adolescence by forming an ego-identity, a clear sense of who they are and what role they play in society. Some fail to do this and suffer identity confusion, an inability to decide how to live.

6. After identity is formed, a person can develop intimate relationships that include sex. Integrating sexuality into intimate relationships often poses many difficulties.

7. Although identity is first formed during adolescence, it is modified throughout life.

8. Erikson identified generativity and integrity as the positive psychological balances of adulthood, and stagnation and despair as the negative balances.

9. Even though physical capacity declines in old age, many elderly people enjoy the freedom of their later years and maintain high levels of self-esteem. Their capacity to adjust to old age depends significantly on their willingness to live life actively and vigorously.

CRITICAL THINKING QUESTIONS_____

1. What were the most difficult aspects of adolescence for you? In what ways could social institutions such as schools, churches, or municipal governments be structured to help adolescents make the transition into adulthood smoother?

2. What are the elements of your identity? How is it built on your early experiences? Do you think Erikson was right in suggesting that a firm identity is needed before one can become intimate with another person? How could his view be qualified?

3. As you have seen members of your family or your friends retire, or as you have retired yourself, what positive and negative aspects of the retirement transition have you observed? Are there ways our social institutions could be more helpful to people when they retire?

MATCHING EXERCISE_____

Match each term with its definition.

a. cultural orientation
b. ego-identity
c. generativity
d. identity confusion
e. sense of integrity

f. reflected appraisal
g. social comparison
h. identification
i. preconventional level of morality

j. postconventional level of morality
k. Alzheimer's disease

1. At midlife, an interest in spiritual and cultural matters as opposed to the gratification of instincts and to gaining more experience
2. A positive and enduring sense of self and the role one can play in society
3. A sense of peace with oneself and others and the acceptance of responsibility for one's life
4. Lack of a clear sense of self and what one is capable of accomplishing in society
5. A concern for establishing and guiding the next generation
6. The process through which we imagine how other people evaluate us and form our self-concept in response to their appraisals
7. The process of evaluating ourselves by comparing to others
8. The process of forming a self-concept by trying to be as much like another person as possible
9. Morality based on obedience, punishment, and reward
10. A disease associated with aging that involves the progressive deterioration of the brain
11. Morality based on consensus within society or self-chosen ethical principles

Answers to Matching Exercise

a. 1   b. 2   c. 5   d. 4   e. 2   f. 6   g. 7   h. 8   i. 9   j. 11   k. 10

ANSWERS TO REVIEW QUESTIONS_____

1. moral realism, moral relativism
2. c, b, a
3. d, c, b, a
4. false
5. false

6. identity confusion
7. true
8. generativity, stagnation
9. spiritual, cultural
10. false

GENDER

Nancy Lieberman-Cline

Nancy Lieberman-Cline

In 1976, her senior year in high school, Nancy Lieberman wrote in her journal,

> We went 2 hours this morning—I believe they're crazy—yes, the coaches—we ran 3-man weave, 5-man weave, 3 on 2, 2 on 1, 11-man drill, shooting, man defense, zone defense—deny, head on ball, full-court 1 on 1, then "Ladies, let's scrimmage." Scrimmage—I can't breathe or walk. Need some sleep. Next practice session at 2:00. (Lieberman, 1992, p. 58)

"Practice" took place two or three times a day, a grueling regimen for anyone, even one of the best women's basketball players in the United Sates. The setting was the tryouts for the 1976 U.S. Women's Olympic basketball team, and Nancy was one of the hopefuls. Who is Nancy Lieberman, and how did she come to be in a gym in Warrensburg, Missouri, dreaming of being in the Olympics?

Her story began on July 1, 1958, in Brooklyn, New York, when her mother Renee and her father, Jerry, welcomed their second child into the world. Nancy was a big baby, almost 10 pounds, with flaming red hair. Her brother Cliff, two years older, was a quiet and content child while Nancy was very active, climbing on, over, and out of everything, including her playpen. In her early childhood, her parents' marriage fell apart, and they divorced when she was 12. She recalls her parents' conflict, being angry, and becoming rebellious. "I had to know why," she writes, "and I wanted answers to everything" (p. 3). Money was tight, and sometimes the electricity and heat would be turned off because the bills weren't paid. She would wait for visits from her father that never came and then bury her disappointment in hours of tears or in playing basketball.

Indeed, it seemed from an early age that Nancy would rather be out in the street playing ball than almost anything else. Her brother was well behaved and good in his studies, but Nancy had a short attention span and was even known to exit her religious school class by jumping out the window. Cliff became the "book-smart" kid and Nancy became the "street-smart" kid. Even at that age, Nancy was aware that girls and boys were treated differently and that girls' toys and activities were different from boys'. While the other girls played with dolls, she raced around the school yard, running and playing with the boys. One day when she was in the third grade, she watched some older boys play basketball in the school gym. Shortly after that, she saw her first NBA game on television. The constant movement and quick moves of the game mesmerized her, and from then on she was hooked on basketball.

She starting shooting baskets on her own and by the fourth grade was good enough that the boys would let her play without complaining. The playground custom that losers go to the end of the line, winners keep playing made her try very hard to stay in. She also played baseball and football with the neighborhood kids in the family's large yard. Nancy noticed that the boys and girls were pretty much equal in strength and skill when they were kids, but at age 9 she got her first gender-related disappointment. She was told that she couldn't play in Police Athletic League (PAL) baseball because they wouldn't insure girls. She was crushed but continued to play with the same kids in the neighborhood games.

Happily, basketball had fewer barriers, and she played on a boy's 10- to 13-year-old team in the YMCA league. Her first coaches, her first organized team, her first real competition, and the first time she had ever played the game with a net on the basket! She was the tallest on her team, and she played center. She recalls the lesson that these years taught her: "If you proved to the guys that you belonged in their domain of a basketball court, football field, or baseball diamond, you could become a participant instead of just a cheerleader." From the beginning it was Nancy's goal to become a participant.

Becoming a participant, however, meant dealing with other people's judgments and expectations, especially as she became an adolescent: the shoe salesman who didn't want to sell her a pair of Converse basketball shoes because "it's not a shoe for girls," her mother's talk with her in the sixth grade about not playing football any more and giving up her hope of playing sports with boys, and the ever-present "What will the neighbors think?" In the meantime, she continued to be disruptive in school, bought a pet alligator, and in other ways challenged gender stereotypes and her mother's hopes for a ladylike daughter. By the time she was a high school sophomore, she had found a place where she could watch the college stars play, at a Brooklyn playground near her aunt and uncle's home.

One day two of the stars, Brian Winters and Levern Tart, both of whom later played professional basketball, said, "Come on—let's let the girl play," and from then on she was a regular. The guys on the playground accepted her when they realized how earnest she was about the game and saw that she could play. Crossing not only gender lines but also racial and ethnic lines (many of her new buddies were black, and she was, in her words, "a redheaded white Jewish tomboy") was something that came easily to Nancy, who saw herself as a ball-player first and everything else second.

Thriving on the competition, she played day and night. She played in AAU teams all over New York City and began gaining media attention. Her mother joined her brother in becoming a genuine fan of Nancy's and of basketball. By age 16, she had earned a spot on the Pan-American team, playing in Mexico City. There she met and became friends with the other top women basketball players in the country and began to think seriously about college. In her senior year, her high school team made it to the semifinals of the public school championships, and she got over a hundred college scholarship offers. She chose Old Dominion University in Norfolk, Virginia; after a great college career, she went on to play professional basketball. During this time there was a much publicized relationship with tennis pro Martina Navratilova. Today she continues to play basketball. She is married to Tim Cline, and her name is Nancy Lieberman-Cline.

WHAT IS GENDER?

Nancy Lieberman-Cline's story is interesting psychologically for many reasons. It is the story of a girl with a dream who followed it as far as she could. It is the story of a person whose life has been shaped not only by her athletic ability and temperament but also by events in her early environment. Finally, it is the story of someone who challenged certain conceptions of gender, of what it means to be male or female.

In this chapter we are concerned with the psychology of gender. *Gender* is a very commonly used term, but one about which there is a lot of fuzziness. Just what does *gender* mean? That question, however, only leads to more questions. In what ways are males and females really different, and in what ways are they not? How do gender differences arise? How does gender figure into communication, friendships, parenting, and other interpersonal behaviors? What should we make out of gender differences? These and other questions will be addressed in this chapter.

The word *gender* is a confusing one. Formerly it was employed primarily by linguists and grammar teachers to refer to types of pronouns or by foreign language teachers to refer to the category of a noun. In some languages, such as French, nouns have gender: *cat*, or *chat* is considered a masculine noun and referred to as *le chat*, whereas *chair* or *chaise* is a feminine noun and referred to as *la chaise*.

In 1979, Rhoda Unger, a psychologist, suggested that the word *sex* (to differentiate males and females) was being used too loosely by social scientists (Unger, 1979). Specifically, she argued that people were confusing biological sex with all of the social and psychological traits that might be considered masculine or feminine. Is being sensitive an inherently sex-related trait—that is, is it necessarily, or only, linked to whether one is biologically male or female? Is being aggressive? Is wearing pink or playing hockey? No, said Unger. These are human attributes that are also determined by social, cultural, and psychological factors, not just biology. She argued that when we are talking about traits that might be considered masculine or feminine, we should use the word *gender*. *Gender role* is also sometimes used synonymously with *gender*. When we are really talking about biological sex, that is, when we are grouping people on the basis of their chromosomes or their genital structures, Unger argued, we should use the word *sex*. Psychologists and others have adopted this convention. For example, when we are studying differences in activity level between newborn male and female rats, we refer to *sex* differences, but when we are studying differences in play styles among 9-year-old boys and girls, we refer to *gender* differences. The latter is considered preferable because it leaves open for investigation the question of where those differences originate rather than implying that they are the result of biological sex of the child.

Before we move on, we need to clarify a few more terms. **Gender identity** refers to the inner feeling of being male or female. This is nearly always congruent with one's biological sex and develops during childhood as a result of learning and cognitive as well as biological factors. In some people, called *transsexuals*, the inner experience of being male or female is not consistent with their biological sex. Such people feel as though they are women trapped in men's bodies, or men trapped in women's bodies, and may wish to change their physical sex. *Sexual orientation* refers to the preference for the same sex (homosexual) or opposite sex (heterosexual) partner. People who are attracted sexually to partners of both sexes are called bisexuals. (See Chapter 11 for a discussion of sexuality and sexual orientation.) In general, the scientific literature as well as ordinary people's experience reveals that gender role, gender identity, and sexual orientation are not *solely* determined by biological sex nor are they always related to each other in the same ways for each person. For example, a woman may be feminine in her behavior and preferences and feel like a woman yet prefer female partners. A high school girl may be a

tomboy in her dress and choice of activities but still be attracted to boys, and so on.

It was no accident that the use of the word *gender* became popular in the late 1970s. The preceding decade had seen an explosion of interest in topics relating to sex and gender that continues to the present day. Not only psychologists but people in general began to question old assumptions about what it means to be male or female. Traits and activities that were taken for granted as naturally male, such as playing competitive sports, or working at a job outside the home, or naturally female, such as being an elementary school teacher or being in love with babies, were no longer taken for granted. It is interesting that Nancy Lieberman grew up in the middle of this time period. What she did would probably not have been allowed, or even thinkable, a decade earlier. A decade later, it might not have been such an issue with her mother, her neighbors, or her coaches. Today girls who like sports are just as likely to be called simply "girls who like sports" as they are to be called "tomboys."

Making the theoretical distinction between gender and sex, however, leads quickly to more questions. The biggest question in many people's minds is: Are there real differences between males and females? This question can be interpreted in two ways: (1) What differences, if any, have been shown to be reliable, rather than just stereotypes? (2) Of those differences, which ones are biological, which are learned, and which are created by a combination of these factors? The following section addresses the first question in depth.

ARE MALES AND FEMALES REALLY DIFFERENT?

Are males and females really different, in terms of personality traits, physical abilities, and mental abilities? Ask any 100 people, and you'll probably get 80 different answers, with every person being positive that he or she is

Measuring Gender Role:
Feminine, Masculine, or Androgynous? Test Yourself

How well do the following items describe you? For each, rate yourself on the scale from 1 to 7.

	1	2	3	4	5	6	7

Never or almost   Always or almost
never true of me   always true of me

_____ 1. Aggressive

_____ 2. Adaptable

_____ 3. Affectionate

_____ 4. Analytical

_____ 5. Independent

_____ 6. Gentle

_____ 7. Sensitive to the needs of others

_____ 8. Likeable

_____ 9. Happy

_____10. Dominant

_____11. Yielding

_____12. Reliable

These are some items from the *Bem Sex Role Inventory* (BSRI; Bem, 1981), a widely used measure of masculine and feminine personality characteristics. The entire scale contains 60 items, 20 masculine (e.g., items 1, 4, and 5), 20 feminine (e.g., 6, 7, and 11), and 20 neutral filler items. Some people score much higher on the masculine items than the feminine items and are labeled "masculine," while others score much higher on the feminine items and are labeled "feminine" in their sex roles. Still others score high on both and are considered "androgynous." Although the BSRI has been widely used and studied, it is not without its critics. Some (e.g. Spence, 1984) argue that it really measures the more limited traits of instrumentality/self-assertion and expressiveness/interpersonal orientation (Spence, 1984, cited in Robinson, Shaver, Wrightsman, 1991).

right. There are very strong opinions on this topic. Why? Because the answers relate to people's assumptions about human nature, their values, sometimes their religion, and often their upbringing. Moreover, their answers are intimately connected with the choices they have made in their own lives, and we all want to believe we have made good choices. If you believe that men and women are equally capable of taking care of infants, then it becomes a possibility that either parent might take time off from work to care for a newborn, or that as an employer you might be willing to grant maternity leave *or* paternity leave. On the other hand, if you believe that women are better suited to care for infants, it follows that the mother will take the time off from work or leave her job altogether; as an employer, you might be less willing to consider granting paternity leaves. Thus there are social, economic, and political stakes involved in the answers to this question. In this section we will attempt to present answers from the most current research.

Early Studies of Sex Differences

In a frequently cited 1974 study, psychologists Eleanor Maccoby and Carol Jacklin reviewed and summarized all the literature on sex differences. Their conclusions were that many supposed gender differences did not actually exist and that where they did exist, the average difference between men and women was small compared to the variations within each sex. In other words, the differences among men and among women were greater than the differences *between* men and women. They highlighted a few variables on which males and females differed reliably: (1) boys showed better mathematical and spatial ability than girls, (2) girls showed greater verbal ability than boys, and (3) boys proved more aggressive than girls. Their results have made their way into popular beliefs, and many do not question them. However, since the publication of their book, many researchers (Block, 1976; Tieger, 1980; Unger, 1979) have reviewed the same evidence, examined Maccoby and Jacklin's conclusions, and raised criticisms. Some concluded that they had understated the case for sex differences while others concluded that they had overstated it.

Basically, Maccoby and Jacklin counted up the studies that found a gender difference on a certain trait or ability and, if the majority of studies found a difference (in either direction), concluded that there was a gender difference on that variable. Some of the studies were poorly done, and some used very few subjects. A more sophisticated review (Hyde, 1981) of the studies on which these conclusions were based revealed that the gender effect was a very small difference, accounting for less than 5 percent of the overall causes of these variables. For example, genetics, schooling, family environment, early reading opportunities, and other factors were vastly more important in determining who had good verbal ability and who did not than was gender. Hyde and colleagues have also pointed out (Hyde, Fennema, & Lamon, 1990) that these findings differ by group. For example, white males outperform white females slightly on standardized math tests, but among African American and Asian American males and females the differences are even smaller.

Current Status of Sex Differences Research

How have these results fared over time? In math, boys still outperform girls, although the gender gap has become smaller. Interestingly, the gap in math performance is nonexistent in toddlers and in elementary school; it widens in junior high school; by the time they take the SAT, boys score on average 46 points higher than girls. There is an especially high number of boys among the most brilliant math students (Benbow, 1988; Hyde, Fennema, & Lamon, 1990). On visual spatial tasks (remember the puzzles in which you had to rotate objects in space, or mentally unfold a cube?) there are still small but reliable sex differences favoring boys (Burnett, 1986). The difference between boys and girls in verbal skills has shrunk, and the overall conclusion is that verbal abilities no longer can be touted as significantly different (Hyde & Linn, 1988).

A few other differences are worth noting. First, around the world men tend to be bigger than women within the same culture or ethnic group, about 10 percent taller and 30 percent heavier (Doyle, 1985). This does not mean that all men are bigger than all women; indeed we all know men who are shorter than the average woman and women who are taller than the average man. It may surprise you to know that Nancy Lieberman-Cline, though relatively tall for a women (5'-10"), is not taller than the average man. Second, around the world men show more aggression than women. In 1989 in the United States, men committed 88 percent of murders and 87 percent of aggravated assaults. Does this occur simply because North American culture encourages men to be more aggressive than women? It seems not. Similar statistics are found among many diverse peoples and in different time periods: the Bhil people in India; the Belo Horizonte of Brazil; residents of Oxford, England, in the Middle Ages; and the Danish in the time period between 1933 and 1961 (Daly & Wilson, 1988). As we will see shortly, males tend to be more aggressive than females in the animal kingdom as well.

Third, Beall and Sternberg (1993) note that around the world dominance is typically a masculine domain. Positions of social dominance, such as president, chief, CEO, jury foreman, are more likely to be held by men. We note, however, that not only is this changing as more women move into the highest positions in government (for example, in India, England, Norway) but there are also notable exceptions. In some matriarchal societies around the world, women dominate.

Finally, there are sex differences in mating behavior and sexuality. To put it bluntly, men mate with more partners than women. There are many more polygamous societies (in which men take several wives) then there are polyandrous ones (in which women take several husbands). In monogamous societies, men on average have more partners and are more permissive than women. In a recent study (Kenrick, Sadalla, Groth, & Trost, 1990), college students were asked about their criteria for a partner for a hypothetical one-night

stand. The men were much less discriminating in how attractive or intelligent the partner would need to be, whereas the women were highly selective. Buss (1994) argues that across cultures women tend to pair up with men who are older than they are and to be more interested in a partner with resources, whereas men place a higher value on physical attractiveness.

Putting the Facts into Perspective

What are we to make of these facts? Although we have just reviewed a few differences between men and women, there are many more behaviors, skills, and attitudes that are not different. All things considered, males and females are simply more similar than not, and the differences among men and women are greater than the differences between the sexes. We all eat, sleep, talk, think, quarrel, make up, and perform myriad other complex cognitive and social activities. We are motivated, all of us, to some extent by greed, love, need for self-esteem, need for excitement, and need for security. We form friendships, make intimate bonds, reproduce, and find work of some kind.

Why then, does there seem to be such publicity and such interest in U.S. society in sex *differences*? Perhaps there are facets, not of personality traits or abilities but of the everyday lives and experiences of men and women, that fuel this notion. In the next section, we take a look at this question.

ARE U.S. MEN'S AND WOMEN'S LIVES DIFFERENT?

This is a slightly different question than our first one. It concerns not whether men and women are inherently different, but whether, in practical terms, their everyday lives, activities, and outcomes are different. This question focuses on social roles, domestic roles, economic situations, and the like. By necessity it has to be answered within the context of a particular culture; the situation for men and women in the United States, for example, may be very different from that of men and women in Papua, New Guinea, Northern Ireland, or rural India. Here is a brief summary of the findings of psychologists, sociologists, economists, and other social scientists on this question as it relates to U.S. men and women in the 1990s.

Gender, Work, and Pay

Work Outside the Home. First, in the United States, women who work outside the home have lower-paying jobs than men. They make, on average, just over 60 cents for every dollar that men earn. Think of the positions of day-care teacher, elementary school teacher, secretary, nurse, librarian, and the hourly wages or salaries associated with those jobs. Think of the positions of factory worker, school principal, business executive, physician, lawyer, and the salaries associated with those jobs. Now think of the ratio of women to men in these jobs. Some jobs are so sex segregated that they have picked up names like "pink-collar ghetto," which includes teachers, waitresses, bookkeepers, secretaries, and household workers. This situation is changing slowly as more men and more women move into the service industries (food service, retailing), and as women slowly work their way into some professions, such as biology and medicine. Other professions, however, such as physical sciences and engineering, are still overwhelmingly male.

Indeed, recently a lot of attention has been focused on women, or rather the lack of women, in math and physical sciences. Eccles (1989) notes that whereas women received 68 percent of all undergraduate degrees in psychology and sociology and 75 percent of the degrees in education (Vetter & Babco, 1986), they earned only 13 percent of engineering and 27 percent of physical sciences degrees. In colleges and universities, the higher you go up the academic ladder, the greater the disparity in the numbers of men and women. Very few women are tenured professors in the sciences, and even in 1996 there were many major universities with only one woman or none in certain departments. The numbers are even more dramatically lower for minority women.

This pattern seems to begin in high school, where girls tend to limit their math and science courses even though overall they get better grades than boys. Interestingly, in about seventh grade, girls' confidence in their academic abilities (though not their actual abilities) takes a plunge. This is particularly true about their confidence in their math abilities, and holds true even for girls in the most advanced courses in high school. There is also a drop in their assessment of the value of mathematics. When they quit taking math, they are likely to take instead advanced courses in English, foreign language, or social sciences, whereas boys continue to value math and English courses equally (Eccles, 1989). Although these statements represent facts about differences during adolescence, you can see how they also begin to suggest why there are fewer women in math, engineering, and science professions. Eccles proposes that interventions in high school are needed to help girls reevaluate either their abilities in math and science, their beliefs about the value of these subjects, or both. We would add that there are factors well before high school that also shape these kinds of gender differences, as we will see later in the chapter.

Finally, we note that although the *kinds* of jobs that men and women do partially account for differences in pay, they do not fully account for it. Sometimes even when men and women do the same work, or equal work, men still get paid more. This is due in part to sexist assumptions and practices, in part to values that society places on certain jobs, and in part to the behavior and expectations of men and women as workers. For example, the following Lessons from the Laboratory describes some interesting research on male and female college and MBA students' assessments of fair pay.

What Is Your Work Worth?

Consider the following situation. You are assigned to read the admissions folders of 80 first-year college students and predict their future for success based on their ACT math and English scores, high school grades, class rank, and extracurricular activities. You are told to work for 20 minutes and then to pay yourself from some money ($10) that had been left, taking the amount that you think is fair for your work. All your work is anonymous, and the situation is arranged so that no one will know how much you paid yourself. How much would you take? (Note: It might be interesting to compare your answer with your classmates' answers before reading further).

This is exactly the task that Major, McFarlin, and Gagnon (1984) presented to their research subjects (except they used $4 as the amount back then). Their findings? On average, the male subjects paid themselves $3.18, and the women paid themselves $1.95. Men felt they were entitled to more pay for the same work than did women. The researchers then gave new subjects a fixed amount of money ($4) and put them to work on a boring "visual perception" task, counting dots in different patterns. The subjects were told "do as much work as you think is fair for the amount of money we have been able to pay you. The $4 is yours to keep regardless of how long you work on the task or how many sets of dots you count." Again the work was anonymous, but some subjects left on their own (and the experimenter did not know when, the *private* condition) and some had to report to the experimenter when they left (the *public* condition). See Figure 4.1.

How long would you work? On average, the women worked longer than the men. In the private condition, women worked for an average of 50.05 minutes, and men worked for 40.88 minutes. In the public condition, women worked for 67.46 minutes and men worked for 44.18 minutes on average. Women's work was also more thorough and correct.

These findings have been replicated in more recent studies, and several alternative explanations are possible. One of them, which has received much empirical support, rests on the notion of social comparison (Blysma & Major, 1994; Major & Testa, 1989). That is, when people decide what is fair, they tend to rely heavily on comparisons to similar others. What does this mean in terms of the gender gap in wages? To the extent that women compare their pay and make their judgments of entitlement in comparison to other women and tend to disregard information about men's pay, they may be expecting (and getting) relatively less than men.

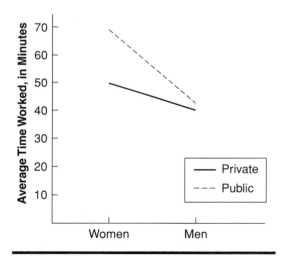

FIGURE 4.1

Work Inside the Home. How about inside the home? Are men's and women's lives different in the area of domestic work? As will be discussed in Chapter 12, many surveys show that women on average are still doing relatively more of the domestic work than men: cooking, cleaning house, shopping, and similar tasks. Today's men do more domestic work (especially child care) than their fathers and grandfathers did, and there are beneficial effects on the children and the family when they do (Collins & Coltrane, 1995). Nonetheless, fathers average only about 2 hours per week for direct child care of preschool children (Coltrane & Ishii-Kuntz, 1992; Russell, 1983). The gap between the amount of domestic work that men and women do narrows somewhat when both are employed outside the home, especially if the wife's job is a high-paying one. However, real imbalances still exist across all socioeconomic classes (Crosby, Pufall, Snyder, O'Connell, & Whalen, 1989).

What about gender and parenting? Do we find differences here? The answer may surprise you. To begin thinking about this question, try a short exercise, if you will. Free associate to the word *fathering*. What words or images come to mind? Now do the same for *mothering*. What words or images come to mind? It would not be surprising if your associations were somewhat different, for strong stereotypes exist about the way men and women behave as parents. Those stereotypes have, in fact, been partially supported by research. Summarizing that research, Lamb (1986) found that fathers tend to be more directive with children, to treat sons and daughters differently, and to play rough-and-tumble games with children, while mothers were less directive, more likely to be verbally encouraging and to be doing housework at the same time as they were interacting with the children. As Collins and Coltrane put it, this is the traditional model, in which "child care is an ongoing and taken-for-granted task for the mother, but a novel and fun distraction for the father" (1995, p. 431).

Some believe (Horn, cited in DeAngelis, 1996) that this model is the result of biological differences between the sexes, but the results of very recent studies suggest that these parenting styles are socially constructed. For example, a study of single fathers (Risman, 1989) found their behaviors and habits to be virtually indistinguishable from "mothering" behaviors. Another observational study, this one of families with two employed parents found that some fathers' and mothers' roles were so interchangeable that the children

sometimes called the mother "Daddy" and the father "Mommy" without even realizing it (Coltrane, 1989, 1990). There is tremendous variability across families in this dimension. Interestingly, there is also tremendous variability in the animal kingdom. Chimpanzee fathers are less involved, whereas marmoset fathers are very involved with their young. When researchers placed male and female adolescent rhesus monkeys in a cage with a baby monkey, the female cared for it; when they removed the female from the cage, the male cared for it (DeAngelis, 1996).

This finding resonates with the findings (Lamb, cited in DeAngelis, 1996) that men and women are both equally competent with a newborn, but by the time the child is a year old mothers have had more experience in child care and appear more competent than fathers. Moreover, fathers and mothers show the same empathic responses to their newborn's cry, but women are more demonstrative about it. These findings provide some clues for how our parenting roles and stereotypes become shaped by our expectations and our habits (DeAngelis, 1996).

Gender and Mental Health

Rates of Disorders among Men and Women. Do men and women suffer at different rates from the kinds of psychological disorders discussed in Chapter 7? For some disorders, no. Schizophrenia occurs at the same rate (about 1 percent) in men and women in the United States and around the world. Manic-depressive illness (bipolar disorder), obsessive-compulsive disorder, and generalized anxiety disorder are also equally likely to occur in men and women. Other disorders, however, show clear sex differences. In infancy and childhood, boys are clearly more vulnerable than girls. Boys are more likely to be miscarried than girls, to have more problematic deliveries and more birth defects. (In fact, throughout the life span males die at higher rates than women, young adult males are more likely to be accident and murder victims, and elderly males die sooner from natural causes.) In school boys are more likely to have reading problems and other learning disabilities, speech problems, and attention deficit disorder (with or without hyperactivity). Autism and mental retardation are also more common among boys. Conduct disorder, which is the forerunner of antisocial personality disorder (discussed in Chapter 7), is also more common in boys (APA, 1994).

It is in adolescence and adulthood that we see the emergence of disorders that are more common among women. Ninety-five percent of those who suffer from anorexia nervosa are women, and about 85 percent of bulimics are women. Depression is two to three times more common in women than in men. Agoraphobia and simple phobias are also more likely to be diagnosed in women. Some disorders are still more prevalent among men: antisocial personality disorder, paranoid personality disorder, and substance abuse and dependence. It is important to note that race and ethnicity intersect with gender differences in mental health. For example, as we mention in Chapter 7, eating disorders have been more prevalent among white teenage girls than among African Americans. Interestingly, there is also evidence of a higher level of weight consciousness and overconcern with body image, and some psychologists believe that white girls are more likely to attempt to use smoking as a form of weight control.

Accounting for Differences.   Think about the psychological disorders that do show a difference in prevalence between men and women. If you are unfamiliar with them, skip ahead and skim those sections in Chapters 6 and 7. Consider their primary features or symptoms. The symptoms of these disorders are exaggerations of gender role traits or stereotypes that are seen in normal men and women. Women in U.S. culture in general show more concern with body image and size than men, and they are more prone to eating disorders. Acting out against others, an exaggeration of aggression and individuality, is seen in the conduct and antisocial personality disorders. Depression, with its passivity and self-blame, is in some ways a caricature of so-called femininity. Clinical psychologists believe that gender roles and the treatment and expectations of men and women in our society are linked to the development of these disorders in individuals who are already vulnerable because of genetic, physiological, or environmental reasons.

Finally, we note that the behaviors that men and women use as coping responses are somewhat different. Women have wider social support networks than men, and they use these networks when they feel down. Women are more likely to attempt suicide, but men are more likely actually to commit suicide. Finally, women are more likely to seek psychological counseling or therapy than men.

REVIEW QUESTIONS

1. _____ is a term used by psychologists when referring to male and female behaviors or characteristics that are presumed to be socially, not just biologically, based, whereas _____ is used when referring solely to the biological distinction between male and female.

2. Current research on gender differences in traits, behaviors or abilities has found stable gender differences in only a few traits and abilities. What are they?

3. Despite the fact that men and women are not so different psychologically, there are ways in which, on average in the United States, their lives differ. List two of these.

4. List three psychological disorders that are diagnosed more frequently in men. List two that are diagnosed more frequently in women.

HOW DOES GENDER DIFFERENTIATION ARISE?

The recognition that there are some differences, even if small and few, between males and females leads quickly to the next question: Where do they come from? How much are they the result of our biology? Of the ways in which we were raised within our families? Of larger social or cultural influences? Hot debates about the answer to these questions rage in many professions and in the general public. Let's first take a look at the biological contributions.

Biological Factors

Sex Determination.   Biological sex is determined during prenatal development by the sex chromosomes. When the egg, which carries an X chromosome, is fertilized by a sperm carrying an X chromosome, the embryo has a female genetic pattern (XX). When the egg is fertilized by a sperm carrying a Y chromosome, the embryo has a male genetic pattern (XY). It will be another six weeks until the reproductive system begins to develop, and all human beings start out with a female pattern of development. Interestingly, the development of female reproductive organs begins spontaneously. Even if the fetus has no ovaries, and thus no female hormones being secreted, female organs will develop. Male reproductive system development, on the other hand, requires that male hormones be produced by the fetus's testes. If something goes awry, even with a genetic male, and this does not happen, a female reproductive system will develop (Money, 1987).

Some rare chromosomal abnormalities shed interesting light on the question of what determines gender. For example, genetic female fetuses (XX) sometimes get exposed to abnormally high levels of androgen, a male hormone. As a result, their external genitalia appear male. They can be labeled and raised successfully as boys. If they received a smaller amount of the androgen prenatally and they have only slightly masculinized external genitalia, they can be given another hormone soon after birth to arrest further biological masculinization and cause the development of female secondary sex characteristics (breasts, body shape) at puberty. These children are raised as "normal" females (Money & Tucker, 1975). These facts show that even the determination of one's sex is a complex process, dependent upon the dynamic interaction of chromosomal, hormonal, and environmental influences.

The Effect of Hormones on Behavior.   Hormonal activity, which resumes at puberty, causes physical changes that have behavioral psychological consequences. For example, the fastest second grader in the gym may well be a girl, but this situation reverses at puberty, when the average boy becomes stronger and bigger than the average girl. What are the consequences of biology for psychological differences between men and women?

Some argue that the relatively higher aggressiveness in males is a result of levels of **testosterone** and androgen and that female hormones help lower aggression. Various animal studies strongly support this hypothesis. In 1849, a scientist removed the testes of a rooster and observed that it no longer crowed, engaged in sex, or behaved aggressively. He then reimplanted one testis in the body of the rooster and again the rooster began crowing and showing normal sexual and aggressive behavior. Because no nerve or other physical connections had been established, he suggested that the behaviors were caused by a chemical produced by the testes and secreted into the circulatory system. The hormone was in fact testosterone, and now such experiments are done by giving animals testosterone and observing its effects on behavior (Becker & Breedlove, 1992).

In humans it has been trickier to make a definite link between higher levels of testosterone in men and higher levels of aggression (Doyle & Paludi, 1995). Clearly, hormones have an influence on behavior, although it is a very complex influence. For example, aggressive behavior itself can alter hormone secretion, and this alteration depends not just on the aggressive experience itself but also on the person's interpretation of it (Monaghan & Glickman, 1992).

Other people argue that biology affects behavior via the female reproductive cycle. The monthly reproductive cycle is said to contribute to moodiness, depression, and irritability as well as other mental and physical discomforts and problems. Both in the public sphere and among scientists there is disagreement about the so-called **premenstrual syndrome** or **PMS.** So many myths and cultural values surround menstruation that most texts spend much effort in talking about what is *not* true about the whole PMS debate. Perhaps they also focus on the debate because the research itself has proved to be inconsistent. Even though a small minority of women do report serious PMS symptoms such as irritability, depression, fatigue, and water retention, most women do not. It has been hard to demonstrate that these symptoms are solely linked to physiology rather than expectations, effects of diet, or stress (Lips, 1988). Nor is there evidence that menstruation itself results in diminished performance on tasks that are important in work or school (Sommer, 1983) despite the *perception* by some women that their performance is lower during this time (Lips, 1988).

The ability to become pregnant, bear children, and nurse them is perhaps the most salient sex difference in conversations about the role of biology on social roles, family life, and psychological traits. A common sex-role stereotype is that women are more nurturing than men. People point to how "naturally" little girls play with dolls, pretending to feed

them, clothing them, putting them to bed, and talking to them. There is the belief that because of the different reproductive roles, there is a mothering instinct that is somehow different from a parenting instinct. Females are supposedly instinctually knowledgable about caring for their young; males are not. As we saw in an earlier section, this is a questionable assumption even among some animals, but especially with humans.

Evolutionary Psychology.   In recent discussions of the role of biology in sex differences, another theory has been raised. The theory is that during evolution certain behaviors or characteristics proved to be useful for survival and that these were selectively encoded in the genes. Sex differences in animals and in humans are accounted for using similar reasoning: If the differences are consistent and universal, they must have served some purpose for the species' survival and are not simply the result of culture or socialization. Proponents of this theory note that among mammals, human and nonhuman, "males tend to be generally more aggressive, more socially dominant, and less discriminating in their choice of sexual partners" (Daly & Wilson, 1983). "Since hamadryas baboons and Ugandan kob antelopes are unlikely to have been influenced by the social conventions displayed on American television," they note, "another explanation of these comparative similarities is called for" (Kenrick & Trost, 1993, p. 156).

Psychologists who tend toward these types of explanation are called *evolutionary psychologists.* For example, David Buss (1988), among others, argues that the male needs to find the most fertile female for reproductive success. Youth and physical attractiveness serve as signals of this. Females, on the other hand, invest a great deal of personal and physical resources in pregnancy and reproduction; thus, they need to find a mate with the best potential as a provider for their young. They therefore look for somewhat older, more powerful, or economically stable men. It is evolutionarily adaptive, he argues, for men to be more promiscuous than women because they increase the likelihood of increasing their progeny by having more partners. Women, on the other hand, are more selective and careful about their mates because being so increases the likelihood that their progeny will survive.

Evolutionary psychology is controversial because it suggests that certain sex and gender differences are biologically fixed and even adaptive. Some worry that it leads to arguments that appear to justify the status quo. Like other theories that cite genetics or instincts as the causes of behavior, it can lead to plausible hypotheses that are impossible to fully test. Evolutionary psychologists argue back (Kenrick & Trost, 1993) that the theory suggests that females are not just the passive pawns of males. Rather, like males, they also evolve in ways that serve them best. Their mate selection strategies are choices, too. These psychologists also argue that genes don't *determine* any behaviors, they just set up predispositions to act in certain ways and furthermore that genes can be influenced by culture. Let us turn, then, to an examination of social and cultural influences on gender and gender differentiation.

Socialization

Sex-Role Socialization in the Home. From the moment a baby is born in our culture, the sex of the baby plays an important role in how people respond to it. When the first child of one of the authors was born, the first statement heard in the birthing room was, "Oh, we've got the wrong color hat." A baby girl had just been born, and the only hat available had blue yarn on it. (The nurse put the blue hat on anyway because the baby's head needed to be kept warm!) Did this one event have any meaning, any implications, any direct effect on the life and outcomes of that little girl? Probably not. But consider the myriad

other ways in which, over a lifetime, the processes of social learning and socialization help shape gender.

Recall from Chapter 2 the definition of *social learning.* The term refers to the ways in which our behavior is shaped or learned via interactions with others. This shaping process happens both directly, through being rewarded or punished, praised or ignored for certain kinds of behaviors, and indirectly, through watching others behave and observing the consequences. All kinds of behaviors are shaped through social learning, including gender-related behaviors.

In some families and some cultures, there are direct or explicit social rules regarding gender. Boys get the blue hats and girls get the pink ones. Girls are allowed or even encouraged to wear dresses and barrettes in their hair; boys are either not allowed to or are discouraged from doing so. In some families girls are required to help with the housework while boys are not. Nancy Lieberman was told directly that she couldn't play in the PAL baseball league because she was a girl, and her mother did her best to help her daughter become more "ladylike." "Why can't you be like other girls? Why do you have to stay out half the night playing basketball? This can't be normal." (Lieberman, 1992, p. 27) summed up her mother's concerns. This kind of sex-role expectation makes it more likely that certain kinds of opportunities will be more available to girls and others to boys. If you are never asked to help with the housework, you won't know how to do it and you won't learn to see it as your responsibility. You will not have the opportunity to be *reinforced* for it, in social learning terms; hence, the behavior will not be strengthened.

In the United States, though we can point easily to examples of sex-role stereotyping, many opportunities are still open to both boys and girls. The most important of these is education. Even though, as we shall see shortly, the educational system is not sex blind, both girls and boys get an early chance at that education. In many countries this is not true. Because of financial constraints or values about educating women or both, girls are sometimes not sent to school but their brothers are, or perhaps the girls are sent for only a few years while the boys continue. This situation sets obvious, severe limits on the choices that women can make later in life.

Social learning takes place not only in direct, explicit ways but also in more indirect ways, sometimes even without our awareness. For example, in an observational study of parents interacting with their toddlers (aged 20 to 24 months), Fagot (1978) found that girls got more positive parental attention for engaging in doll play, asking for help, following their parents around, and watching television, while boys gained positive reactions by engaging in block play. Boys got *negative* reactions when they engaged in doll play and followed their parents around; girls, when they were running, jumping, and climbing. When parents were asked about their childrearing practices, they seemed not to be aware of these differences in practice. On the other hand, some argue that parents are less gender stereotyped in their responses than teachers and others who interact with children because parents respond to the uniqueness of each child, encouraging their children to develop all their strengths. Other researchers (Lytton & Romney, 1991) note that on many dimensions gender does not influence parents' reactions to their children, the exceptions being that they do tend to encourage sex-typed activities for both sons and daughters and to show more warmth toward girls. Lips (1988) reviews findings from observational studies that little girls are talked to more by both parents than boys and talked to more about emotions, although boys are allowed to feel and express anger more than girls. It is not surprising, therefore, that in laboratory studies women tend to outperform men in tasks that require decoding others' emotions and sensitivity to nonverbal cues (Lips, 1988).

Again, there are variations in sex-role socialization by religion, social class, race, and culture, even within the United States. Some research (McBroom, 1981) has shown that there is more sex stereotyping of females in working-class than in middle-class families, and what research there is on African-American families suggests that girls may be socialized more strongly toward employment than they are in white families (Smith, 1982).

Sex-Role Socialization in the Community. In school settings as well, the kinds of attention that boys and girls get from their peers and teachers has been shown to be somewhat different. High-activity play in boys is more rewarded by their peers than is high-activity play in girls (Fagot, 1984a). In another study, boys got more attention for aggressive behaviors and girls for dependent behaviors (Fagot, 1984b). Some studies have shown that boys tend to get called on more than girls, and teachers tend to praise them more for correct answers, or stick with them longer to help them find the correct answers (Sadker & Sadker, 1985). This may be the result of sexist expectations or biases in the classroom, and it may also have to do with subtle classroom dynamics as well (that is, since boys in elementary school are likely to be more fidgety and inattentive than girls, teachers may notice more and favor them when they *are* paying attention).

As in the home, the shaping processes can be very obvious and direct. This is becoming increasingly less so, however, as school administrators and teachers make an effort to create unbiased classrooms. The shaping processes may also be more subtle. Consider the following actual case that occurred not in school but on the playground during after-school soccer.

The children playing were 5 and 6 years old, and it was the first time they had the opportunity to play organized soccer. Needless to say, energy and enthusiasm were higher than skill level or understanding of the game, and the boys and girls were equal in strength and athletic ability. There was, however, one difference. The boys went after the ball more aggressively, running hard after it, using their bodies more to push others out of the way and retain possession of it. The girls were more likely to hang back and let the boys get the ball. The boys were less likely to pass the ball, and when they did, it was to other boys. The coach did not encourage the children to play their position or to pass the ball. This went on for the first two practices (note again: all the children were rank beginners) until the third practice, when it became clear that the coach had divided them into two subteams, an A team and a B team. The A team consisted of all the boys. The B team consisted of all the girls and the youngest boy on the team, who had been having a hard time remembering which goal was his team's and which was the other team's! Further, the A team got put in first, and played longer than the B team, which was sometimes forgotten until the A team got tired. After a few weeks, the girls got discouraged and wanted to quit the team. This is a case in which different kinds of learning opportunities were provided for boys and girls, in part because of the coach's biases and in part because a behavioral difference between boys and girls was interpreted in a manner consistent with those biases.

We see here how the social and physical aspects of the environment were instrumental in molding certain outcomes. The same is true inside the classroom. If all the clothes in the dress-up area are girls' and women's clothes, the boys will tend to wander away from it quickly. If all the active toys in the room are male-oriented sports or masculine action figures, the girls will be less likely to play with them. If the computer games have primarily male characters in them (this is, in fact, the case), boys will tend to play them more than girls. Then, by virtue of the fact that they participate in certain kinds of activities more than

others, boys and girls may develop different kinds of preferences, skills, and beliefs about their abilities. If we look only at adults, it is easy to interpret these differences as natural or biological. Knowledge of socialization processes in childhood, however, sheds a different light on the picture.

Culture Habits and the Media. Earlier, we discussed the role of social learning, specifically the ways in which gender-typed behavior can be shaped directly and indirectly by rewards and punishments, attention or inattention. Social learning, however, also takes place via modeling. As Meyer, Murphy, Cascardi, and Birns (1991) point out, children learn about gender roles by watching what their parents do, and children in two-parent heterosexual families can get the idea on their own that dads do certain things and moms do other things. The following Lessons from Life box illustrates this point with a few anecdotes that reveal young children's notions of gender and its meaning.

Such stories illustrate the powerful effects that modeling, by both parents and other role models, have on gender stereotypes and gender role development. Whether parents, teachers, and other adults intend to or not, and whether they realize it or not, their own habits and behaviors send many messages about gender and gender roles.

The point is that children pick up information from their environments—from the family, school, books, television, newspapers, movies—about gender roles. If they consistently see men in certain roles and women in certain others, they get the idea that those roles are natural or fixed. They form gender schemas (Bem, 1985). **Gender schema** theory asserts that children develop cognitive structures (*schemas*) about gender because the concept is so prevalent in everyday talk around them. The traits that they fit into the categories "male" and "female" depend on their particular social learning histories, but once they

Children's Opinions of Gender and Gender Roles

One of our children, aged 4, who lives in an otherwise fairly nonsex-stereotyped household, noticed his mother looking for a screw driver. He informed her that the tool set belonged only to Daddy and "mommies can't use tools." Asked why, he replied, "Because he's the one that uses it all the time." On another occasion, that same child got into a heated discussion with a friend about whether moms or dads mow the lawn. He had only seen his mother do it, and the friend had only seen his father do it. Both were convinced that lawnmowers "belonged" to a different parent. Another conversation, this one overheard at the breakfast table, revealed a 9-year-old girl announcing that her friend wanted to be the President of the United States when she grew up. Her brother, age 5, informed her, "Girls can't be president." When she replied (in her best "I'm-9-and-I-know-more-than-you" voice) "Oh, yes they can," he said, sticking out his tongue and adding, as evidence, "Well, there's never been a girl President. So there."

form these concepts or expectancies about gender, they use them to analyze and assimilate new information. Moreover, people in general try to act in ways that are consistent with their schemas, particularly schemas that relate to their own identities. A kindergarten boy who likes Winnie-the-Pooh and picks up a shirt with Piglet on it in a clothing store may quickly put it back on the rack when he discovers the tiny bow at the neck and realizes he is in the girls' section. He is behaving in accordance with his developing gender schema. There is evidence, moreover, that by about second or third grade children will consciously seek out information ("Is this a boy's hat or a girl's?") in order to maintain consistency with their own cognitive categories.

Just a few moments of reflection (or browsing in any toy store) reveals how ubiquitous gender-stereotyped messages and images are in the media. From Barbies that say "math is hard" to magazine ads that only use women to sell household products or only men to sell trucks, to ads on Saturday morning cartoon shows, the message is clear. Boys and girls are different. Boys are active, aggressive, bold, adventurous, brave, like frogs and snakes, etc. Girls are passive, helpful, clean, dislike frogs and snakes, and are more interested in domestic activities. Any explanation

of socialization as a cause of gender role development, has to take the powerful influence of cultural modelling into account. This is particularly true in our culture, with its high rates of TV and movie viewing. Much research has demonstrated the sex-stereotyping on television; it is not surprising, therefore, that the more TV children and teenagers watch, the more gender stereotypic are their attitudes (Lips, 1988).

Thus far we have examined biological explanations, evolutionary psychology, and socialization of various kinds as factors in gender development and gender differentiation. Another important theory of how gender identification and gendered behavior develops is psychoanalytic theory.

Psychoanalytic Factors. Recall from Chapter 2 that psychoanalytic (Freudian) theory focuses on the sexual and aggressive drives that are assumed to motivate behavior. As children grow, these drives become channeled toward the opposite-sex parent: Boys desire the mother, and girls the father. At around 3 or 4 years of age, however, children notice anatomical differences between the sexes, or as one wide-eyed preschool boy was overheard saying to his female classmate, "What happened to *yours*?" Psychoanalytic theorists have interpreted these statements and others like them as representing fears concerning castration anxiety. As the theory goes, the boy worries that the jealous father might harm him and thus begins to identify with the father in order to feel less anxious. In identifying with the father, the boy takes on the character-istics, attitudes, and traits of the parent. Among other things, this includes gender role behaviors. The boy who watches his father shaving at the sink and imitates him with the soap is showing signs of identification.

What about girls? Psychoanalytic theory, you will recall, is somewhat fuzzier on this, and that is the source of great controversy about Freud's theory. Girls are said to experi-ence *penis envy* when they notice anatomical differences and initially wish to possess the fa-ther in order to symbolically possess a penis. They soon give this idea up, however, and along with it any impulses they had to iden-tify with or be like the father. Instead, they turn toward a "passive, feminine relationship with the father and the wish for a baby *from* him" (Fast, 1993, p. 175) and begin to identify with the mother. Thus they take on feminine sex-role characteristics by imitating or trying to be like the mother. This process supposedly accounts for the development of sexual orien-tation as well. A classical psychoanalysis of Nancy Lieberman-Cline's personality might suggest the following. Because she lacked a strong father figure, she failed to fully resolve psychosexual conflicts at the Oedipal stage of development. She did not therefore fully iden-tify with her mother. Since identification with the same-sex parent is the underpinning of gender-role identification, she did not de-velop a "feminine" identity. In her autobiogra-phy, Nancy discusses her longing for a father figure and how a series of coaches and men-tors helped fill her partly to fulfill this longing.

From the time it originated, Freud's con-ception of gender development has had its zealous defenders and its critics. Even some of his contemporaries argued that he put too

much emphasis on sex. Alfred Adler, for ex-ample, argued that penis envy was a mis-guided idea; rather, it was the power and the privileges that go along with being male, not their actual physical characteristics, that women envy. Modern researchers have estab-lished the importance of both mothers and fa-thers in children's gender development, yet Freud's theory suggests that the father's role is key and the mother's almost nonexistent (Fast, 1993). His theory does not explain well how boys in fatherless families can grow up to be psychologically healthy, or how homosex-uality develops. It also cannot account for the fact that the majority of children raised by gay or lesbian couples grow up to be heterosexual.

And yet the fact that boys and girls in two-parent heterosexual families are biologi-cally different from one of their parents but similar to the other has been retained in some contemporary psychological theories of gen-der and development. One of these is referred to as **self-in-relation theory** (Miller, 1976; Jor-dan, Kaplan, Miller, Stiver, & Surrey, 1991). Self-in-relation theory points out that at an early age boys realize that they are biologi-cally different from the mother and that this fact (as well as shaping by societal forces) causes boys' personalities to develop in a more differentiated, individualized, and in-dependent fashion. Girls, on the other hand, because of biological similarity to the mother, do not have the same course of development. Rather, their personality and identity develop in connection with others, and throughout life they are more concerned about connectedness and relationships.

Psychologists who follow this line of thinking argue that this leads to different ways of knowing (Belenky, Clinchy, Goldberger, & Tarule, 1986), different types of moral reason-ing (Gilligan, 1977) and different personalities (Jordan et al., 1991). As described in Chapter 2, the basic ideas are that women's ways of thinking are both subjective and objective, in-tuitive and rational, that in contrast to males their moral reasoning is characterized by concern with connection and preserving relationships as much as abstract "rights," and that they are more likely to tend toward interdependence rather than autonomy in their personality traits and motives.

Ironically, much of this research can be criticized on some of the same grounds as psychoanalytic theory. First, empirical support for it is weak. Second, the theorizing tends to focus on observations and studies of only one sex (with Freud it was men; with Belenky et al., and others it was women) and falls into theorizing about how the other sex might differ if they had been directly compared (Crawford, 1989). This theory is also somewhat ethnocentric in its equation of "male" with an individualistic orientation and "female" with a more relational or collectivist orientation. As will be discussed in Chapter 12, both women *and* men in Asian cultures are more collectivist in their orientations than people in U.S. culture. Finally, critics argue that an alternative explanation is that men's and women's psychological differences are really differences attributable to their dominant and subordinate positions in society. If women are really more interconnected with others and concerned with relational issues, is that because of sex or gender or because women *have* to be oriented toward and concerned with others' needs and feelings in order to get along? In other words, we need to pay more attention to the situational contexts, such as the setting or the culture, in which men's and women's behavior is observed (Aries, 1996).

How These Factors Interact

Thus far, we have presented the different factors or accounts of gender differentiation separately. But in actuality they interact in the real world and real lives of men and women. Take pregnancy and childbirth, for example. That is a biological fact, a difference. However, its implications (that is, what it means in the lives of parents) depend on some social values and social practices. Will the father become just as attached to the infant as the mother, and in the same way? That depends on how much time he is able and willing to spend with the baby. Will the father learn to feed, change, and burp the baby, as well as play with it? Again, it depends on whether these behaviors are allowed, reinforced, and modeled by those around him. There are many indications that families are realizing the benefits of both parents being involved in child care; one tangible indication is that fathers have demanded that infant-changing tables in public places are no longer placed only in the women's restrooms!

The relationship between work outside the home, childbearing, and childrearing is another area in which these factors overlap. Across a number of different businesses, women in management positions are more likely than men to face interruptions in work due to childbearing and child-rearing decisions. Men who want to have children and a career in business are more likely to have a spouse at home who will take care of the family while they take care of their career. Women executives are less likely to have a spouse at home and to have more conflicts in trying to balance deadlines, business trips, and other work demands with infants, sick children, and other home demands.

Overall, it is less likely that women with children will move up the ladder with the same success as men with children (Schwartz, 1989). Businesses then get the idea that women are less reliable or achievement oriented, perpetuating old biases about hiring women. Recognition of these facts has led to the suggestion of two career paths for women: the traditional "male" career path or an alternative, which has been nicknamed the "mommy track." The latter would supposedly create a way to balance career and family less stressfully by incorporating job sharing, work at home, and other innovations whereby the worker could retain a position at the same level but not work as many hours in the week and not assume that if there is a brief leave period, they are getting off the work track permanently. If "daddy tracks" and "mommy tracks" both existed, the choices for men—as well as their skills in domestic activities—might broaden. Finally, we should note that it is not only the case that biology affects social and economic roles and choices, but also that these affect biology. Today, many women are delaying childrearing for educational or employment reasons, even into their late thirties and early forties. These delays can cause fertility problems (difficulties in getting pregnant and successfully carrying the baby to term), as those tend to increase with maternal age.

REVIEW QUESTIONS

5. What is the name of the field of psychology concerned with the genetic basis of behavior?

6. Cognitive structures (concepts and expectancies) about the categories of "male" and "female" are called _____.

7. The _____ theory of the development of gender roles rests on concepts such as the Oedipal conflict, penis envy, and eventual identification with the same-sex parent.

GENDER AND SOCIAL INTERACTION

So far, this chapter has been concerned with individual characteristics of men and women (e.g., traits, size, behaviors, work, parenting) and how they compare. Overall, we have seen that the number of significant sex differences is small compared with the public's perception of sex differences. Part of the reason for this discrepancy between the academic wisdom and the folk wisdom on sex differences may be explained by the fact that when men and women interact together, or interact in groups, gender differences show up that were missed when individuals were studied out of their social context (Maccoby, 1990). The following example illustrates this point.

Social Interaction of Girls and Boys

Despite many efforts to create classrooms free of gender bias, people who observe preschool groups of children (ages 3 to 5) during free play are struck by seeming gender differences in play and social interaction. Who is most likely to be in the "block area," making a lot of noise and calling attention to themselves of those within earshot? Who is more likely to be engaged in fine motor activities such as painting or cutting with scissors, or in small groups of more quiet, imaginative play? It may sound sexist, but the observations of parents and teachers—even those who actively seek *not* to promote gender stereotypes—are that it is more likely to be boys in the former type of play and girls in the latter. These observations are born out by a number of observational studies, which find further, that children's play starts to become sex segregated around ages 4–5. Girls and boys are happy to mix in teacher-directed or task-focused activities. But when it comes to free play time, when children choose their own activities and playmates, boys are likely to be playing with boys and girls with girls. This phenomenon continues up until preadolescence, when boys and girls once again begin to take more than a passing interest in each other.

Why? Eleanor Maccoby (1990) has suggested that it is the result of two factors that emerge in the preschool years: (1) boys prefer rough-and-tumble play marked by dominance and competition, and girls are wary, uninterested, or averse to this kind of activity, and (2) girls are less successful at influencing boys than they would like to be. One study, for example, found girls and boys to be on different developmental courses in play styles. Between 3½ and 5½ years of age, girls increased the use of polite requests and suggestions, whereas boys increased their use of demands and became less and less influenced by polite suggestions. These differences may result from the fact that girls mature earlier than boys, from socialization, from modeling, or from other factors. Some say the preference for rough-and-tumble play is partially biologically determined. In any case, girls' influence strategies worked with other girls and with adults but not with boys. Girls, then, in general, avoid joining boys' play groups.

These observations have been used to interpret another interesting gender difference in social interaction styles. It has been found that girls in classrooms stick closer to the teacher than boys. Further studies (e.g., Greeno, 1989) show, however, that this is not true except when when boys are around. When all the children are girls, they tend to play farther from the teacher, and if the teacher moves closer to them, they move in the *opposite* direction. When the group of children is mixed, the girls play together and nearer to the teacher. When the teacher moves, they tend to move closer to the teacher. Boys' locations remain stable regardless of where the teacher is and whether there are girls in the room or not. Another study (Powlishta, 1987) found that when preschool children were competing for a scarce resource (an attractive movie viewer) the boys tended to dominate and got more than their share of time with the toy. (Interestingly, some recent studies on computers in classrooms have also demonstrated that in mixed groups, boys tend to dominate in their use.) When an adult was present, however,

girls and boys had equal access. So perhaps girls stick closer to adults because they sense that some adult intervention, or at least oversight, might be beneficial to them.

Maccoby (1990) suggests that boys' and girls' play styles represent and reinforce two cultures of interaction. When boys and girls do get back together at adolescence, they bring these styles with them. If this is true, then we might expect to see gender differences in interaction styles among adults. This is the topic of the next section.

Social Interaction of Adults

Gender and Communication in Groups. Let's look first at research studies that examine gender and communication among men and women in groups and public social settings. A brief review includes the following findings: Men are less influenced by the other group members' opinions than are women (Eagly, 1987); men are louder and are listened to more (West & Zimmerman, 1985); men are more likely to interrupt, and women to listen and wait for their speaking turn, smile more, and agree more. Aries, reviewing this literature in 1987, concluded that taken together findings suggest that "women work to sustain conversation, are responsive, supportive, and value equality. Their talk is personal. Talk for men is oriented toward solving problems and maintaining dominance and assertiveness. Men are less responsive; their talk is more abstract and less personal" (Aries, 1996, p. 4).

There are several different interpretations of and explanations for these findings. Some time ago, the question of whether there was a **"women's language"** and a "men's language" was raised, and this question remains with us. It was observed (Lakoff, 1975) that women's speech seemed different from men's. Tag questions ("It's cold, *isn't it?*"), qualifiers, hedges, and disclaimers ("I'm not sure, but…") mark uncertainty and deference and are more likely to be found in women's speech. On another note, stop for a moment and think about how people end their sentences. One can say, "The group seemed to be pretty happy with my presentation," with the voice remaining steady and even throughout. Or, one can say "The group seemed to be pretty happy with my presentation?" with the voice rising at the end. This *rising inflection* seems to seek agreement or support rather than to simply assert the idea. It is more common among women speakers than men, and many people don't even realize that they are doing it. Many of these "women's" speech habits can also be interpreted as serving relationship purposes: to keep the conversation going, support the other's participation, encourage disclosure, and otherwise enhance the connections between the people in the relationship.

Others noted that the very words we use have a gender bias toward male dominance built into them. Linguists and psychologists (e.g., Henley, 1989) have argued that our language itself both reflects and helps maintain certain kinds of assumptions about men and women. For example, they note that we have one title for a man (Mr.), which does not reveal his marital status, but three titles for a woman (Mrs., Miss, and Ms.), which reveal either marital status or political stance. There are 220 terms for a sexually promiscuous women compared to 22 for such a man (Stanley, 1977) *Man* is often used as the generic term for people. It's rather curious that Nancy Lieberman's team, which was the *women's* U.S. national team, ran "3-*man* weave," "11-*man* drill," and "*man* defense" drills!

Crawford (1989) argues that this usage affects our thinking in subtle but important ways. If the teacher is always described as "she" and the President as "he," will girls and boys be equally likely to imagine themselves in those roles? If you read a story about "mankind," will men and women be equally likely to assume that it includes them? In one study (Henley, Gruber, & Lerner, 1988), sixth graders read a story with masculine (*he*), feminine (*she*), or unbiased pronouns (*they*), and their self-esteem was measured one week later. The boys showed more positive changes in self-esteem when they had read the story with the masculine pronouns, and the girls had more positive change in self-esteem when they had read the story with the neutral pronouns. In another set of studies (Crawford and English, 1984), females' memory was worse for essays they had read two days earlier if the essays used generic masculine words than gender-neutral ones; this effect was particularly strong for good learners.

Of course, there is much controversy over the policy implications of these ideas. Should college *freshmen* be called *first-year students* instead? Should we say *she* or *he* instead of the generic *he*? *Mail carrier* or *firefighter* instead of *mailman* or *fireman*? Would women be any more likely to head juries if we did not refer to that position as jury *foreman*? Schools, businesses, and local governments are all debating these questions. Some people argue that such changes are unnecessary, while others (e.g., Henley, 1989) argue that such language practices not only reflect current stereotypes but indeed help maintain them as well.

Another interpretation is that the communication style differences between males and females depend on the social context of their interaction rather than something inherently male or female. Indeed, in some studies, in mixed groups women's behavior becomes more like men's, by being more assertive and using more conversationally dominant strategies than they do in all-woman groups (Carli, 1989; Hall & Braunwald, 1981). In other words, women play by the informal rules of the particular social context. This practice is analogous to Nancy Lieberman-Cline's interactional strategies. Nancy wanted to play ball in a serious way, and when she was growing up that meant playing with the boys. Consequently, she adopted their speech and social interaction style—not just a male speech style but the speech style of the males on the basketball courts. She recalls riding the subway to either Brooklyn or Harlem and striding onto playgrounds where she might or might not know the other players. She would walk up to those waiting to play and ask who was next in line. "I'd be throwing an attitude and the guys would just be looking at me. If they didn't say anything, I'd usually announce that I was next, and if they wanted to play they needed to see me. And they'd look at me like, 'I can't believe she's talking to me.' It's no wonder they eventually nicknamed me 'Fire'." This example leads us outside the laboratory to the social contexts of intimate heterosexual relationships.

Gender and Communication in Intimate Relationships: Two Cultures?

What about the interactions of men and women in long-term relationships? Much attention recently has been focused on gender differences in conversational styles between intimates. Books such as *You Just Don't Understand* (Tannen, 1990) have spent weeks on the *New York Times* bestseller list and sold millions of copies. Chapter titles such as "Different Words, Different Worlds," "Put Down That Paper and Talk to Me!: Rapport-talk and Report-talk," and "Living with Asymmetry: Opening Lines of Communication," reveal its simple message: Men's and women's conversational styles and goals are often (but not always) fundamentally different because their psychological goals are fundamentally different. A woman tends to approach the world

> as an individual in a network of connections. In this world, conversations are negotiations for closeness in which people try to seek and give confirmation and support, and to reach consensus. They try to protect themselves from others' attempts to push them away. Life, then, is a community, a struggle to preserve intimacy and avoid isolation. Though there are hierarchies in this world, too, they are hierarchies more of friendship than of power and accomplishment. (Tannen, 1990, p. 25)

A man, on the other hand, according to Tannen, approaches the world

> as in individual in a hierarchical social order in which he [is] either one-up or one-down. In this world, conversations are negotiations in which people try to achieve and maintain the upper hand if they can, and protect themselves from others' attempts to put them down and push them around. Life, then, is a contest, a struggle to preserve independence and avoid failure. (Tannen, 1990, pp. 24–25)

Tannen provides numerous anecdotes and examples likening men's and women's conversations to cross-cultural conversations (or cross-planetary, as the title of a more recent popular book, *Men Are from Mars, Women Are from Venus* [Gray, 1992] suggests). Instead of different dialects, he argues that we speak different *genderlects*. A woman tells her sister that she does not like the way her scar looks after an operation, and the sister's response ("I know, it's like your body has been violated") is comforting. Her husband's response ("You can have plastic surgery to cover up the scar"), however, makes her angry (Gray, 1994, p. 49). She feels that he doesn't understand her feelings, and might even be suggesting that in fact it doesn't look so good. He, on the other hand, thinks he is being helpful by offering a concrete solution. The informal rules of women's conversations include being allowed or even expected to share troubles, to offer emotional support, to avoid boasting, and to express thoughts and feelings. The informal rules of men's conversations include problem solving, expressing few thoughts and feelings, the understanding that boasting is okay, and giving information. In female friendships talk helps people bond, whereas in male friendships activities (jobs, sports, tasks, or talking about them afterward) help people bond. You might see some similar themes here from the discussion of children's play and communication styles. Perhaps the sex-segregation play of youngsters results in certain interactional styles being reinforced and others extinguished, or at least weakened, for boys and girls.

What happens, then, according to this theory, when men and women in close relationships converse? They frequently talk at cross-purposes, disappointing each other or feeling misunderstood and devalued. Tannen argues that this is no one's fault; rather, it reflects simple ignorance of each other's styles and intentions. Her solution is to encourage men and women to recognize that these are style differences (not malevolence!), to try to see things from each other's perspective, and to communicate more directly about their conversational successes and failures.

We have found that this topic raises lively debate among our students. Many offer examples from their own lives that support Tannen's observations. Others give counterexamples and feel that she is stereotyping the sexes. Moreover, researchers (Aries, 1996) have found fault with Tannen's work for exaggerating the differences between men and women, perpetuating the idea that men and women are essentially different, and ignoring the fact that status differences explain many of her observations. Nancy Lieberman-Cline's account of her own relationships and communication styles seems to support both views. On the one hand, she defies the stereotypes and seems to challenge Tannen's assertions about the way females act. Rather than standing around on the playground at recess talking with the other girls, or going to a girlfriend's house for lunch on the weekends, she is shooting baskets. On the other hand, she clearly agrees that there are two kinds of styles and these are gendered. She just happens to choose the active, instrumental, self-assertive, masculine style.

A final concern about Tannen's analysis of men's and women's conversational styles is that it glosses over the fact that a power differential exists between men and women in the larger society. That is, her analyses of these two approaches as "just different styles"

doesn't take into account the societal context in which they occur (Crawford, 1995). It's not, Crawford argues, just two different speech styles but rather that one style (the masculine), in our society, is associated with power and privileges. For better or for worse, the masculine is considered the "better" style to use if one wants to be heard and to influence others, for example, in business or politics.

Gender and Self-Presentation

A magazine survey asked young girls and boys how they thought the sexes were different. Erika, age 12, reported,

> A girl's way of saying that she thinks she is smart is to say "I'm so stupid," and everyone responds, "No, you're not!" She already knows this, but it is a way of getting compliments. Boys, on the other hand, say what they think or would like themselves or others to think. A boy would say, "I'm smart," and his friend would answer, "I'm smarter," and thus a competition would arise. (Snow, 1992, pp. 107–8)

Erika didn't know it, but she was summarizing another topic in social interaction that has been explored in recent years by psychologists and other social scientists. That is, men and women seem to present themselves differently to others when talking about their abilities and achievements. In laboratory studies, after performing some skill or cognitive task, participants are asked to give reports about their performance or abilities. Psychologists have noticed that girls and women, relative to boys and men, tend to underestimate and underevaluate themselves despite the fact that there are no *actual* differences in their performances (e.g., Deaux, 1979; Frey & Ruble, 1987). In addition, when asked to make attributions for their successful performance, males are more likely to cite internal causes such as ability and women to cite external causes such as luck or ease of the task. These differences are not found in every type of situation or on every type of task (some show no sex differences). They are, in fact, more likely to be found in those situations in which the task is considered "masculine," in situations that are competitive, and in situations in which subjects are in the presence of a highly competent other (Lenney, 1977).

One interpretation of this phenomenon is that girls and women are socialized to be less confident. That may be part of the answer, but it is not the complete one. It seems that there are also gender differences in how you choose to present yourself as well. Consider the following scenario. It is early in your first weeks at college. A fellow student whom you do not know knocks on your door and asks you to participate in study of adjustment to college. You agree, and as part of this study you are asked to make a prediction about what your first semester grade point average will be. You either have to look the person in the face and tell him/her what you think you will get (the public condition) or write your prediction on a notecard, anonymously (the private condition).

As it turns out (Daubman, Heatherington, & Ahn, 1992), men and women respond differ-ently. Women's estimates were lower than men's, but only in the public condition. More-over, women gave estimates that actually turned out to be lower than the grade point averages they eventually earned that semester in the public condition, but not in the private condition. Men gave estimates that turned out to be higher than their eventual actual grade point averages in the public condition, but not in the private condition. Thus women seemed to be more concerned with modesty, with not appearing too confident. Let's take it one step farther. What if you believed that the person with whom you were interacting had actually gotten a low grade point average? In this situ-ation, when they had to respond publicly, women's predictions were significantly *lower* than men's, and *lower* than the grades they subsequently earned (Heatherington, Daub-man, Bates, Ahn, Brown, & Preston, 1993). The result suggests that there may be other motives operating in self-presentation for women—in certain kinds of social situations, women be-have more modestly than men to protect the other person's feelings or preserve equality in the relationship.

Review Questions

8. When differences in men's and women's styles of communication in groups have been found, the findings are that _____ tend to use more turn taking and more sup-portive styles, whereas _____ tend to interrupt more and hold the floor longer.

9. What are the ways in which Deborah Tannen's work on the "two cultures of communication" has been criticized?

10. When gender differences in self-presentation are found, do women tend to underestimate or overestimate their performances and abilities?

WHERE DO WE GO FROM HERE?

In this chapter, perhaps more than in any other in this book, the psychological facts and findings about our topic are intermingled with implications for adjustment to everyday life. As we stated at the beginning of the chap-ter, there are high stakes and real-life implica-tions attached to the data on sex differences and the ways in which they are interpreted.

There has been and continues to be an in-teresting tension in this field. In the earlier days of this work, "nonsexist" research and in-terpretations were seen as those that deemphasized sex and gender differences. The more men and women were found to be alike, the reasoning went, the less stereotyping and restricting of women's choices and activities there would be. Interpretations minimized the contributions of biology because biological explanations had in the past been used to constrict the roles of both men and women and to keep women "in their place." Explanations having to do with socialization were preferred because they implied that the status quo could actually be changed by changing practices in homes, schools, media images of men and women, and other social arenas where sex roles are learned. As this strategy was translated into practice, women and girls were implicitly or explicitly given messages about how to succeed and compete in a "man's world" by minimizing sex differences and where possible adopting "masculine" rather than "feminine" gender role traits.

Workshops on assertiveness training for women became very popular, androgyny (behaviors and traits of both sexes) was found to be correlated with the highest levels of health and self-esteem in women, and self-help books and magazines urged androgynous behaviors and activities. There was even a paperback best-seller for women in business and other professions called *Games Mother Never Taught You* (1987). Its premise was that by playing sports and hanging out with all-male groups as boys, men had learned a set of rules and behaviors that were needed to succeed in business. This reasoning is not unlike the findings reviewed in the previous section, but the book focused on the practical. In addition to information about how to behave, it included advice about how to choose clothes that looked the most professional (i.e., masculine): blue or black suits, no big jewelry, low-heeled shoes that wouldn't slow one down when walking with a group of men to meetings, no purses because they impede one's ability to move smoothly through doorways without assistance.

More recently, there has been a turn to include a somewhat different stance. That is, some are now suggesting that we should more readily acknowledge the sex and gender differences that can reliably be shown to exist but that we should also challenge the assumption that the male standard of behavior is the superior one. Gilligan's *In a Different Voice* (1977), Belenky and colleagues' *Women's Ways of Knowing* (1986) and the work of self-in-relation theorists (such as Jordan et al., 1991) are examples of this viewpoint. Men and women *are* different, they argue, for social, cultural and perhaps even some biological reasons. But they also argue that many of society's values, practices, and policies tend to favor men's styles over women's. Assertiveness and individuality are more valued and rewarded in our society than compromise and connection. Self-promotion is rewarded more than modesty. Taking care of others (teaching, household work) pays less than taking care of things (plumbing, banking) or taking care of business. If by changing social practices and values we change this fact of status and hierarchy, then men and women can be themselves (whatever that means) and things can still be fair. This debate (Hare-Mustin & Maracek, 1988; 1990) continues to be a lively one. As you read magazine and newspaper articles as well as academic books and articles, see if you can tell what stance the author is taking on this issue.

What kind of a stance would Nancy Lieberman take in this debate? From her autobiography, it seems that she understood and used both strategies. The former was clearly her first and most dominant strategy. Adopting the language, the moves, the brashness of male players—and rejecting the social habits of girls—helped her to realize her dream of playing competitive basketball, of "keeping the court" (Lieberman, 1992, p. 25), as she puts it. This strategy seemed to her to be necessary. At the same time, no doubt in part because of her and other outstanding women players' impressive abilities and efforts, change also occurred on a broader societal level. High school programs, college scholarships, Olympic competition, summer training camps, good coaches and agents, even enthusiastic audiences have become more available to women athletes. Although inequalities still exist, girls and women who want to play sports at competitive levels today on their own terms have many more opportunities than Nancy did.

SUMMARY

1. The search for sex differences in individual traits and behaviors has revealed fewer differences than our stereotypes would suggest. There are some small differences in spatial abilities and mathematical abilities at the highest levels of performance between males and females, and males tend to be more aggressive than females. Even these conclusions are controversial, however, and the variability among males and among females is greater than the variability between the sexes.

2. Nonetheless, some differences in work, pay, and domestic work habits between men and women exist in the United States. For example, on average men who are employed outside the home make more money than women who are employed outside the home, and women do more domestic work and child care than men.

3. Certain psychological disorders (such as schizophrenia and manic-depression) are equally prevalent among men and women. Others occur more frequently in girls and women (eating disorders, depression) or in boys and men (developmental disorders, conduct and antisocial personality disorders, substance abuse disorders).

4. Biology, evolutionary psychology, socialization, and culture are all important influences on gender differentiation. Each of these factors is complex and controversial and carries political and social implications.

5. Psychoanalytic theory utilizes concepts such as castration anxiety, penis envy, and identification to explain gender differentiation.

6. Gender differences have been found in some social interaction contexts. Males are more conversationally dominant in mixed-sex groups, and this is true in preschools as well as boardrooms. Our language itself is male biased, but the importance of that fact, and the interpretation of the other findings as well, is a source of controversy.

7. When self-preservation differs by sex, women tend to be more modest in presenting their achievements and performances.

8. In intimate relationships, men's and women's styles of interaction and talking are said to be different and to lead to misunderstandings. The extent to which this is true and the causes of these differences are currently being debated.

9. Over time, sex differences have been both emphasized and deemphasized as strategies for equalizing the opportunities for men and women. This situation is reflected not only in the research literature and its interpretation but also in practical suggestions, programs, and policies.

CRITICAL THINKING QUESTIONS

1. Considering what you have learned about gender from reading this chapter as well as from your own experiences, discuss the advantages and disadvantages of single-sex education. Are all-girls' and all-boys' classrooms, or colleges, a good idea? Under what circum-

stances, or at what ages, if any, do you think these would be beneficial?

2. In areas of gender and parenting, we live in a time of great change, opportunity, and confusion. Stereotypes about what it means to be a "good mother" and "good father" are changing. Does "good mothering" and "good fathering" boil down to the same thing, that is, "good parenting"? Or are there some ways in which these roles are, or should be, different?

3. Compare and contrast the customs, rules, and beliefs about gender roles that exist in different cultures or ethnic groups with which you are familiar. This exercise would be particularly interesting to do in a group of people from different backgrounds and perhaps different ages as well.

MATCHING EXERCISE

Match each term with its definition.

a. gender role
b. evolutionary psychology
c. testosterone
d. gender schema

e. gender identity
f. premenstrual syndrome (PMS)
g. identification

h. self-in-relation theory
i. "women's language"

1. A controversial diagnosis that focuses on physical and psychological symptoms presumed to be related to the menstrual cycle
2. Argues that female personality and identity develops in connection with others, thus making concerns with connectedness and relationships particularly salient for women.
3. In psychoanalytic theory, a phenomenon crucial to the child taking on characteristics of the same-sex parent
4. Used by Lakoff to describe a style of speech marked by tag questions, qualifiers, disclaimers, and other signals of uncertainty and deference

5. Term used to denote the combination of traits and behaviors that define "masculine" and "feminine"
6. A male hormone linked to aggressive behaviors in animal studies; its role in human aggression is controversial
7. The subjective or inner feeling that one is male or female; usually congruent with biological sex
8. Concepts or categories about gender that organize thinking and behavior
9. Argues that certain behaviors or characteristics (including some on which males and females differ) proved to be useful for survival and have been selectively encoded in the genes

Answers to Matching Exercise

a. 5   b. 9   c. 6   d. 8   e. 7   f. 1   g. 3   h. 2   i. 4

ANSWERS TO REVIEW QUESTIONS

1. gender, sex
2. aggression, spatial abilities, mathematical performance at the highest levels

3. Men are over-represented in certain occupations and women in others; on average, men get paid more than women for their

work; women do more of the household work than men, even when both spouses work; certain mental disorders are more prevalent in men while others are more prevalent in women. Women also outlive men, on average.

4. More commonly diagnosed in women: anorexia nervosa, bulimia, depression, agoraphobia, simple phobias. More commonly diagnosed in men: antisocial personality disorder, paranoid personality disorder, substance abuse and dependence.

5. evolutionary psychology
6. gender schemas
7. psychoanalytic
8. women, men
9. It exaggerates differences, ignores status, ignores the wider societal context in which men and women communicate.
10. underestimate

CHAPTER 5

IN SICKNESS AND IN HEALTH: STRESS, HEALTH, AND COPING

Gia Carangi

Gia Carangi

Imagine being 18 years old, making nearly $500,000 a year, and being pursued to have your picture on the cover of such prestigious magazines as *Bazaar, Cosmo,* and *Vogue.* Before you leap to trade your life for this position, let us add a few details such as being addicted to heroin by age 18 and being one of the first women to die of AIDS at age 26. This was the tragic fate of Gia Carangi.

Gia grew up in the suburbs of Philadelphia and led a rather normal life in a middle-class family until she was 11 years old. Although her parents often fought, Gia never dreamed that one day she would come home from school to find that her mother had moved out, leaving her to live with her father. Gia felt that her whole world had collapsed. Her mother was her source of strength and support, and now Gia was suddenly without this important relationship. Although her father loved her, he was constantly busy working to develop a chain of hoagie restaurants.

A year later, Gia's mother remarried, and Gia shuffled back and forth between her father's and mother's homes. Both were so busy that they provided Gia little structure or rules. Gia struggled to adjust to this chaotic life. She desperately wanted friends and saw the rock scene as an opportunity to find them. David Bowie was the rage in 1973, so Gia became a Bowie fanatic. She got a Bowie haircut and attended every concert in her area. She thought she had found acceptance and identity as a Bowie "groupie."

But even in this role she was not happy. She quickly graduated from smoking cigarettes to doing drugs and drinking alcohol. By age 14, Gia was a sexual veteran, deciding at this young age that she preferred sexual relations with women. Gia was doing poorly at school and she began to worry about her future. As a lark, she decided to pose for modeling pictures. Despite her tender age, she was strikingly attractive and caught the attention of a number of professional photographers.

She enjoyed modeling and found she could make quick money at it. But her early success brought with it another worry: her weight. By age 15, Gia was going from one diet to another to control her weight. "I remember her eating cereal with wa-

ter on it to try and get skinnier, and she would take an hour to eat it so she wouldn't be hungry" a friend recalled (Fried, 1993, p. 74). After completing high school, Gia moved to New York to model in earnest.

Life in New York was tough for an 18-year-old on her own. Besides frantically going from one photo sitting to another, she was trying to keep up with the fast modeling crowd. Every night brought another party. At first Gia loved the life, but she was soon worn out; nonetheless, she kept it up to be seen with the "right" people. Drugs and alcohol kept her going. While most models take years to make it (if they ever do), Gia landed her first big modeling job after three months. Her agency booked her to model for Italian *Bazaar* at a rate of $750 for a one-day sitting. The next week, she modeled for *Vogue Patterns.* Her ethnic look and flashing eyes catapulted her into high fashion modeling.

Each day seemed to bring a new engagement, and Gia was traveling all over the world for sessions. The famous photographer Scavullo was captivated by Gia. "There is something she had . . . no other girl had it. I never met a girl who had it. She had the perfect body for modeling: perfect eyes, mouth, hair. And to me, the perfect attitude" (Fried, 1993, p. 137).

Gia was commanding phenomenal sums of money for her sittings—up to $10,000—but being the world's image of beauty brought tremendous stress. Everyone wanted to use Gia for her beauty, but she had few close friends. She entered several homosexual relationships, each stormier than the last. Pot and cocaine no longer satisfied her, so she began mainlining heroin. She felt that her life was out of control and she was on a treadmill. Gia confessed,

When you're in demand, and people are saying, "I want you, I want you," it isn't easy to say no.... So you find yourself working a lot—a lot. And if you want to take a day off, because you need a day of rest or to get yourself together and have energy for the next day, it's hard.... When I look in the mirror, I just want to like myself. (Fried, 1993, p. 261)

Gia's addiction to heroin was ruining her life and health. She missed appointments and behaved erratically and unpredictably when she showed up. People had constantly urged her to see a doctor and get help for her drug habit, but Gia was too busy. Now the professional world began to shun her because she could not be counted on. Even make-up could not hide the dark bags under her eyes or the swollen veins in her arm. Her relationship with her mother was also stressful, including an odd mixture of love and rejection.

By age 25, Gia was out of work and broke. She had been through several drug treatment programs, all of which failed. She began to feel sick, and she knew something was wrong with her. The world had been stunned when Rock Hudson died of AIDS on October 2, 1985. AIDS was a new disease, first noticed in the late 1970s, but by the mid-1980s it had claimed several famous actors and people in the fashion world. Most of the victims had been male homosexuals and intravenous drug users. Fearing she had AIDS, Gia checked into a hospital for tests. She wasn't particularly surprised when the tests confirmed that she did. In a few short years, Gia Carangi had fallen from being a wealthy superstar model to being alone, broke, and dying of AIDS. On November 18, 1986, Gia died of AIDS at age 26.

The story of Gia Carangi is tragic. From age 11, her life was one of turmoil and stress although it appeared glamorous and exciting to outsiders. Gia's life was controlled by everyone and everything (drugs, alcohol, AIDS) but herself. Gia's death may be attributed to AIDS, but on closer examination, we can see that Gia's death actually resulted from her behavior and the choices she made. Although Gia's case is extreme at all levels, many of us experience high levels of stress and often feel little control over our lives. This combination, along with failing to take care of ourselves, is a formula that wears us down and chips away at our health. As in the case of Gia, our health, or lack of it, is highly dependent on our behavior and our choices about our lifestyle.

STRESS: THE THIEF OF HEALTH

Most of us have our world of health divided into two neat packages. If we are emotionally distressed, we seek the help of a psychologist or psychiatrist. However, if our problem centers on our physical health, such as having a cold, experiencing high blood pressure, or suffering ulcers, we turn to a medical physician. The physician will seek out the bacteria or virus that has invaded our body and prescribe a medicine to destroy it, or diagnose and remove a diseased organ.

Over the last few decades, however, there has been increasing realization that physical health is closely tied to behavior and psychological well-being. In fact, British psychologist Michael Argyle boldly claimed that "all illnesses have psychological as well as physical causes, and are partly due to stress of various kinds" (Argyle, 1992, p. 224). This point was driven home during World War I, when thousands of soldiers were hospitalized for a variety of symptoms including blindness, extreme nausea, headache, shortness of breath, and rapid heartbeat. They were treated with the standard medicines, but many failed to improve. The source of their problem was not bacteria, not bombs or bullets, but stress. The condition became known as *battle fatigue,* and physicians and psychologists combined efforts to help the soldiers deal effectively with their stress.

Events such as this supported the development of a new field of psychology known as **health psychology,** which examines how behavior affects health and contributes to the recovery from illness. The field is unique in that it draws on resources from many areas of psychology including social psychology, clinical psychology, industrial/organizational psychology, experimental psychology (especially learning, motivation, and emotions), and cognitive psychology. More recently, health psychologists have focused on the important issue of wellness, which is concerned with preventing illness and encouraging happier, more fulfilling lifestyles. Indeed, many

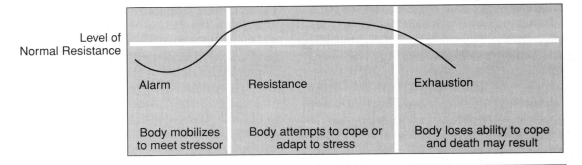

FIGURE 5.1 The General Adaptation Syndrome (GAS)

Source: Adapted from Selye (1974).

organizations have created wellness programs that include exercise, relaxation training, and diet control to enhance the health and work effectiveness of their employees.

Of all the villains in the health equation, **stress** has been identified as one of the most pernicious. Stress is the process by which we respond to environmental and psychological events that are perceived as threatening and challenging (Gatchel & Baum, 1984). Events that give rise to stress are known as *stressors.* Stress itself is not necessarily negative. In fact, the lack of stress can lead us to become bored with and uninvolved in our daily activities. At moderate levels, stress motivates us to adapt, cope, and adjust to our changing situation, but high levels of stress or prolonged stress can rob us of our health, energy, and vitality.

Surprisingly, few events are universal stressors. Rather, stress results from the way we perceive or interpret an event (Lazarus & Folkman, 1987). Consider, for example, two students faced with an upcoming exam. Susan, one of our students, sees the exam as a threat: She assumes that she will probably do badly; she will have to miss several important social events to study for the exam; and her ambition to enter law school will be derailed by a poor grade on the exam. Susan's *appraisal* (interpretation) of the coming exam clearly creates a stressful situation. Alice, on the other

hand, views the upcoming exam as an enjoyable challenge: It will give her a chance to review the class material; she will be able to determine how well she knows the material; and if she makes a good grade on this test, she will be able to relax with her friends afterwards. The exam is not a big stressor for Alice.

Careful research has identified the way our bodies respond to stress and has shown how stress is linked to physical health and functioning. Hans Selye (1976), a Canadian physician, labeled the response pattern to stress as the **general adaptation syndrome (GAS)** (see Figure 5.1). As we examine the stages of the general adaptation syndrome, review your own responses to stress and determine how closely your reactions match the ones listed. During the first phase (*alarm reaction*), the body prepares to meet the stressor. In general, the alarm reaction primes the organism to fight or flee the stressor. Heart rate, breathing, and blood pressure increase, muscles tense, and digestion is slowed. You feel energized, ready to react. At the same time, because the responses are designed to combat the specific stressor, the normal level of resistance to disease is temporarily lowered.

If the stressor persists, the body enters the stage of *resistance,* focusing on adapting to or coping with the stressor. General resistance is increased, but energy level is still high. If the stressor is dealt with or removed, the body returns to a normal level of functioning. However, if the stressor remains, the stage of *exhaustion* begins. The body wears down, and symptoms of the alarm stage may reappear. This stage is like a last, sometimes desperate effort to eliminate the stressor. If it is unsuccessful, the organism may collapse and even die.

The general adaptation syndrome occurs regardless of the nature of the stressor. Stressors may be internal (such as disease) or external (such as loud noise or extreme temperatures). Some stressors are bad (involving distress or harm), but others are good (such as winning a lottery or facing an exciting challenge). It is not the type or the origin of the stressor that determines our body's response. The body reacts to all stressors in a similar way, although our minds respond differently. Indeed, you may recall times when so many good things happened to you that you became ill or exhausted from the excitement. Gia wrote that as her fame increased she felt increasingly stressed and constantly worried about meeting up to the expectations of others. This worry and concern often caused her to be ill and depressed.

The Physiology of Stress

In reviewing your reactions to stress, you may believe that you approach the situation in a calculating way: determining what the problem is, deciding on a sensible course of action, and then acting. This is simply not the case. Throughout your body are complex systems that spring into action when stress arises. One such network is the **autonomic nervous system (ANS),** centered within the brain and composed of an intricate web of nerves connecting the brain to your body's organs (see Figure 5.2). The ANS has two branches that have largely opposite effects. The *sympathetic division* is the "spender" of body energy. When it is stimulated, it sends messages that

increase heartrate, increase breathing, release glucose from the liver, inhibit salivation, and slow digestion. As you might predict, the sympathetic division dominates our bodies during the alarm stage. On the other hand, the *parasympathetic division* of the ANS is the thrifty member of the duo, working to save or replenish the body's energy. It sends messages that slow heart and breathing rates and stimulate digestion and salivation. The parasympathetic division takes command during the exhaustion stage, trying to restore body resources. Though this restoration may be vital for a nearly bankrupt body, it does not help combat the stressor, should the latter still be present at this point.

Working in tandem with the ANS is the endocrine system, consisting of glands that secret hormones directly into the bloodstream (see Figure 5.3). With our focus on stress, we are interested in only certain glands in the endocrine system. When faced with a stressor, the *hypothalamus* releases a hormone known as corticotrophin-releasing hormone (CRH), which in turn stimulates the *pituitary gland* to release adrenocorticotropic hormone (ACTH). This hormone rushes to the *adrenal gland,* exciting it to release epinephrine and norepinephrine. These hormones act on the sympathetic nervous system to increase heart rate, blood pressure, and breathing. In essence, they signal the sympathetic nervous system to start the body on a "spending spree," energizing us to respond to stress. For the most part, these systems spring into action and operate outside our conscious control; we don't decide to "turn on" our endocrine or ANS systems. But these wonderfully complex systems are vital partners in our efforts to respond to and reduce stress.

A third body system, the **immune system,** is important to a consideration of the physiology of stress. When unhealthy cells in the form of bacteria, viruses, or fungi enter our bloodstream, the immune system springs into action. The soldiers of the immune system, white

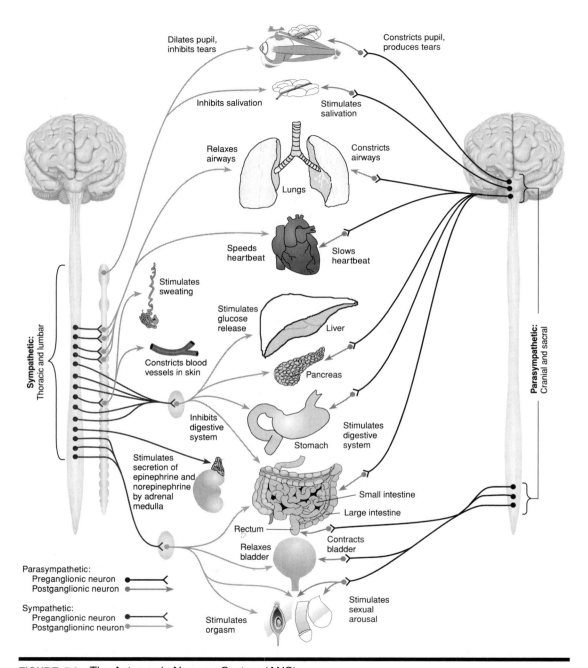

FIGURE 5.2   The Autonomic Nervous System (ANS)

Source: Carlson (1988), *Physiology of Behavior,* 6th edition (Needham, MA: Allyn and Bacon), p. 84.
Used by permission.

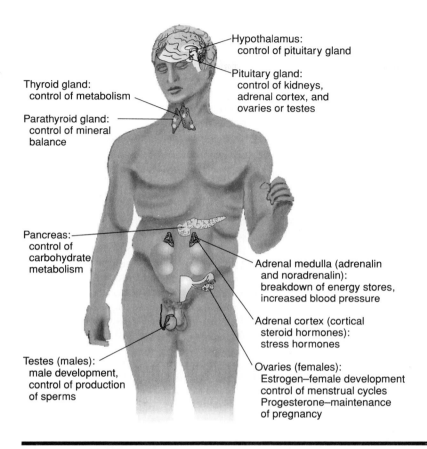

Hypothalamus: control of pituitary gland

Pituitary gland: control of kidneys, adrenal cortex, and ovaries or testes

Thyroid gland: control of metabolism

Parathyroid gland: control of mineral balance

Pancreas: control of carbohydrate metabolism

Adrenal medulla (adrenalin and noradrenalin): breakdown of energy stores, increased blood pressure

Adrenal cortex (cortical steroid hormones): stress hormones

Testes (males): male development, control of production of sperms

Ovaries (females): Estrogen–female development control of menstrual cycles Progesterone–maintenance of pregnancy

FIGURE 5.3 The Endocrine System
Glands of the endocrine system release hormones (chemical messengers) directly into the bloodstream. It is a major coordinating system of body chemistry and exerts great influence on behavior.
Source: Carlson & Buskist (1997), *Psychology: The Science of Behavior*, 5th edition, (Needham, MA: Allyn and Bacon), p. 112. Used by permission.

blood cells (*leukocytes*) attack and destroy these harmful invaders. We stay healthy or quickly recover from illness when our immune system is able to destroy disease-causing organisms. To remain effective, the immune system depends on the regular manufacturing of new leukocytes and the removal of exhausted and used leukocytes. During stress reactions, the hormones released by the endocrine system suppress the functioning of the immune system, making us more susceptible to disease.

Without the rich supply of healthy leukocytes, bacteria and viruses can win the battle for control of our bodies. Therefore, prolonged stress contributes to the likelihood of becoming sick because it cripples the normal functioning of our immune system.

The Causes of Stress

Now that we have met the guardians of our health, let's take a closer look at the villain. If

The Menstrual Cycle and Stress: Fact and Fallacy

Stress and reactions to stress have long been related to the realm of gender differences. Women, in general, have been saddled with the reputation of being moodier and reacting less constructively to stress than men. This position has been used to justify excluding women from critical positions in the workplace. More pointedly, the argument is that women's moods are governed by their menstrual cycle and that during the four days prior to menstruation women are especially moody, unstable, unpredictable, irrational, and quick to respond to stress. This pattern of behaviors and moods, along with a general feeling of physical discomfort and weight gain (due to fluid retention), is known as *premenstrual syndrome (PMS)*.

There is evidence, that women's moods do fluctuate as their hormone levels change. Although nearly 75 percent experience physical or emotional changes during the premenstrual period, only 10 percent have severe enough symptoms to impair normal social or work functioning. Moreover, there is no evidence that academic performance declines during the four-day premenstrual period of time.

Although concerns about performance and the menstrual cycle are largely baseless, there is evidence that women's moods are affected by their hormone levels. Women's moods tend to be most positive during ovulation when estrogen levels are high (Bardwick, 1971). During the period of PMS, there is evidence of an imbalance between estrogen and progesterone levels (Rubinow & Roy-Byrne, 1984). The cramping that occurs during this time in some women is the result of prostaglandins (see the discussion of pain on page 14) that cause the walls of the uterus to contract. When these contractions are violent or unrelieved, cramping is experienced. Although this imbalance of hormones can set the stage for rapid mood swings, attitudes about menstruation often determine the severity of these mood fluctuations and behaviors. For example, one study found that absenteeism from work was more related to expectations and attitudes about PMS than the actual physical discomfort (Gruber & Wildman, 1987).

Though all women undergoing menstruation are subject to these hormone changes, they need not be passive "victims" of their hormone cycles. Exercise has been found to reduce the discomfort in many women. Drugs such as ibuprofen (Advil, Motrin) may relieve cramping by inhibiting the release of prostaglandins (Owen, 1984). Reducing intake of alcohol, fats, and salts may reduce weight gain and lower water retention during the premenstrual period. Women who have severe or prolonged pain should consult a physician. Finally, falling prey to society's attitudes about the relation between menstruation and mood may actually lead to self-fulfilling prophecies and increased difficulties with menstruation. By accepting these attitudes, some women may "psych" themselves into having more frequent and severe problems than are dictated by their physiology. Although there is no denying the hormonal changes that take place during women's cycles, attitudes, and beliefs do influence the impact of these changes.

---

stress always appeared on our life horizon dressed as Darth Vadar, it would be easy to recognize and we could mobilize our forces to combat it. But stress springs from many sources, some quite surprising and apparently benign.

Change.　　When you examine your daily life, you're likely to discover that you are a creature of habit. Your day is generally guided by a regular pattern, even if it is a complex one, and your situation is stable. Now consider how you might respond if you went home tonight and found that your apartment had burned to the ground, or that a rich uncle died and left you a million dollars, or that your steady girlfriend of six years ran away with the exterminator. Even though each of these events is very different from the other, all of them have one thing in common: They represent major change in your life, and each will require dramatic adjustment.

Thomas Holmes and his colleagues (Holmes & Masuda, 1974; Holmes & Rahe, 1967) suggested that major changes in our lives, whether they be positive or negative, create stress. They studied thousands of medical histories and conducted interviews with more than 400 men and women to identify stressful events. The end result was the *Life Events Scale* (see Table 5.1), which lists stressful events and assigns each a stress value. As you can see from the list, each event represents a major change in one's life situation although some are positive changes and others are negative changes. We might locate some of the major stressors in Gia's life on this list, such as her constantly changing family situation when she was young, her success and stardom, and then her being fired from several advertising agencies because of her drug problem and work habits. It is hard to find a year in Gia's life after she was 11 years old that did not include several major life events.

Holmes argued that stress is directly related to major illness. He predicted that people who scored more than 300 points on the *Life Events Scale* during a one-year period were at a high risk of suffering a major illness during the following year. You might try completing the scale—but before you panic, let's consider a few points. Although research has shown a link between stressful events and illness, questions have been raised about the specific values given each event. Do these values accurately reflect the stress associated with a particular event? Second, remember that the scale was introduced in 1967, and events considered stressful at that time might not be so stressful today. For example, dramatic changes in our work environment have made changing jobs more commonplace today than in the early 1960s. Therefore, a change in job may not be as stressful today as in 1965. And we can only smile at the $10,000 mortgage, which was a moderate level in the 1960s, but is very low today. Another sign of the times is that the *Life Event Scale* hardly touches on issues that are more common in

TABLE 5.1   The Life Events Scale

LIFE EVENT	STRESS VALUE
Death of spouse	100
Divorce	73
Marital separation	65
Jail term	63
Death of close family member	63
Personal injury or illness	53
Marriage	50
Fired at work	47
Marital reconciliation	45
Retirement	45
Change in health of family member	44
Pregnancy	40
Sex difficulties	39
Gain of new family member	39
Business readjustment	39
Change in financial state	38
Death of close friend	37
Change to different line of work	36
Change in number of arguments with spouse	35
Mortgage over $10,000	31
Foreclosure of mortgage or loan	30
Change in responsibilities at work	29
Son or daughter leaving home	29
Trouble with in-laws	29
Outstanding personal achievement	28
Wife begins or stops work	26
Begin or end school	26
Change in living conditions	25
Revision of personal habits	24
Trouble with boss	23
Change in work hours or conditions	20
Change in residence	20
Change in schools	20
Change in recreation	19
Change in church activities	19
Change in social activities	18
Mortgage or loan less than $10,000	17
Change in sleeping habits	16
Change in number of family get-togethers	15
Change in eating habits	15
Vacation	13
Christmas	12
Minor violations of the law	11

Source: Reprinted with permission from *Journal of Psychosomatic Research, 11*, T. H. Holmes and R. H. Rahe. The social readjustment rating scale (1967). Elsevier Science Inc.

today's world, such as being the victim of violence, experiencing drug abuse problems, or being involved in a lawsuit. Finally, the scale does not take into account the social support (see page 128) that often follows many major life events for some people. For example, some people receive a great deal of attention and support when ill, whereas others receive little. Illness would, therefore, be more stressful to someone in the latter category.

Minor Hassles. When you completed the scale, you may have scored very low. On reviewing your year, however, you may determine that it was a stressful one. Richard Lazarus (1981; Lazarus & Delongis, 1983) argued that major life events are relatively rare in our lives, but more minor events and changes are common. He identified two categories of minor events. One is *hassles,* which are "irritating, frustrating, or distressing incidents that occur in our everyday transactions with the environment" (Lazarus, 1981, p. 58). Hassles might include failing an exam, ruining your favorite shirt, fighting with your roommate, or having car trouble. On the positive side are *uplifts,* which include feeling healthy, getting a good grade, or visiting a friend.

Lazarus had a group of subjects record the hassles and uplifts they experienced over a year. At the end of the year, these subjects completed the *Life Events Scale.* He examined subjects' physical health and mood during the study and concluded that hassles "turned out to be much better predictors of psychological and physical health than life events" (Lazarus, 1981, p. 62). In other words, it may be the repeated small setbacks that are most troubling in our lives. Interestingly, the uplifts did not offset the negative effects of the hassles. In fact, for women, the uplifts had a temporary negative effect on emotions and mental health. We may understand these results by noting that both hassles and uplifts cause us to change our routine and require us to deal with new circumstances.

Additional research (Caspi, Bolger, & Eckenrode, 1987) found that change is most stressful when experienced against a backdrop of high chronic ecological stress, such as noise, high neighborhood crime, poor housing, and high density. Another intriguing finding in this study was that women who had experienced major life events during the previous year were less bothered by minor life hassles. This finding may suggest that the minor hassles looked very insignificant in comparison to the major life event. Or it is possible that learning to cope with the major life event made it easy to deal with the minor hassles. However, even these reasonable explanations do not explain why the same pattern of behavior was not found for men. Nonetheless, the study suggests that the impact of change is affected by the general situation of our lives at the time of the change.

Before driving the stake through the heart of change, let us just remind you that the lack of change in our lives can also lead to stress. Boredom and monotony are not pleasant. The message, then, is to seek a comfortable degree of change and challenge in our lives and to remember that the way in which we perceive or interpret change is also very important in determining our stress level.

Unpredictability. To demonstrate the importance of predictability, consider two hypothetical college students, John and Bill. Both have been assigned dormitory roommates, and both have enjoyed their roommates. John's roommate informed him that he would be moving at the end of the semester, but Bill's roommate said nothing about moving. On the last day of the semester, both John and Bill return to their rooms to find that their roommates have moved out. Who is most likely to feel stressed?

In the example, Bill's roommate change was unpredictable and should have been the most stressful. Unpredictable events are especially stressful because we cannot prepare or plan for them. When we are faced with an unpredictable environment, we must constantly be prepared to adjust and react. Imagine how you would deal with a situation in which you had no idea what type of weather you might face during the day; the day might begin warm, turn suddenly cold, rain, and turn warm again. You'd have to carry a suitcase of clothing in this case. In a similar way, your body has to keep all its adaptive responses in the ready mode when it is faced with highly unpredictable situations.

One study compared the medical records of air traffic controllers, whose job involves a great deal of unpredictability, with others who had more regular and predictable jobs. The air traffic controllers were more likely to suffer from high blood pressure, anxiety attacks, peptic ulcers, and depression. Even at the height of her fame, Gia faced a very unpredictable world. She often learned in the morning that she had been scheduled for a photo session in the afternoon, and it was not unusual for her agency to tell her the night before that she was to fly to Italy the next morning for a session for the Italian *Vogue*. She could rarely predict where or when she would get a session, so she had to always be ready for whatever might come up.

Lack of Control.   Of all the features in our lives that give rise to stress, lack of control may be the most troublesome (McCaul et al., 1993). The perception that we are pawns of our physical and social environment is very threatening. It implies that we cannot protect ourselves or get our needs met. It suggests that our behavior has little impact on the environment or the people around us. When we feel the loss of control, our first response is to struggle to regain control. However, if we are unsuccessful and control continues to elude our grasp, we may just give up trying. In essence, we have learned that we are helpless, and our surrender to circumstances is termed a state of *learned helplessness* (Seligman, 1975).

It is not surprising that learned helplessness is one of the causes of depression. And learned helplessness often triggers a vicious cycle: We feel that we cannot control our environment, so we stop trying, and this lack of trying ensures that we will have no control.

In many respects, Gia Carangi epitomized this pattern of control. She was stunned by her parents' divorce but learned that she could do nothing to bring them back together. Her life as a model was out of her hands; she was told where to go, when to be there, what to wear, and how to pose. Gia turned to drugs to give her some sense of control over her life, but soon the drugs were controlling her. There were many times when she just gave up, staying in bed all day or running away so no one could find her.

A wide range of studies has linked feelings of lack of control with illness. In one study, some nursing home residents were allowed to control certain aspects of their lives, such as taking care of plants, arranging their furniture, and choosing their meals (Langer & Rodin, 1976). Other residents were well cared for, but they had no control over their environments (a common condition in many nursing homes and hospitals). Residents with control were healthier during the study than residents with no control, and while 15 percent of those residents with control died during the 18-month study, 30 percent of the residents with no control died. Other research has found that victims of crime and natural disasters often report that the most distressing feature of the events is the feeling that they have no control (Normoyle & Lavrokes, 1984).

Goals: Fulfilled and Unfulfilled.   Take a moment to review your life over the past year. What situations did you find particularly stressful? If you are like many students, you will find that stress was associated with goals (Markus & Ruvolo, 1984; Lecci, Okun, & Karloy, 1994). In these studies, students reported that although goals were desirable, they experienced considerable stress in the pursuit of these goals. Regrets, which were unfulfilled goals, were often especially distressing and led to depression. Indeed, older people reported that regrets were especially troublesome because they felt they had less time left in their lives to meet these unfulfilled goals. When we are young, we can tell ourselves that we will eventually take that dream trip or write that popular novel, but as we get older, this optimism fades as the window of remaining time shrinks (Seligman, 1991).

Pain.   Of all the stressors in our surroundings, the one most quickly noticed is probable pain. That splinter in your finger that demands your immediate attention or those aching knees that inform you that you will not jog today are examples of common pain. For many of us, the opportunity to turn off our pain receptors and live a pain-free life might be as attractive as winning the $100 million lottery or becoming a famous actor. Before you curse those aches and pains, consider the fact that pain is a signal that something is wrong, and it motivates us to fix the problem. So even though pain is a stressor that saps energy and demands attention, it is a highly adaptive signal that may save our lives.

Let's place pain under a microscope to see how it functions. Imagine that you place your finger on a hot stove. The injured spot releases a number of chemicals, including *prostaglandins*, that help speed the pain message to your brain. At the same time, blood flow to the area is increased, which also increases the number of disease-fighting white blood cells. When the pain message reaches the brain, neurotransmitters known as *endorphins* are released. These endorphins are similar to morphine, and they act to dampen the pain messages. In this way pain is reduced while your body works to repair the damaged area. At the same time, you respond by avoiding the pain-causing situation; you jerk your finger off the hot burner.

The response to pain demands our attention and uses our body's energy. If the pain passes, we return to normal and begin to rebuild our resources. However, chronic or prolonged pain continues to deplete our resources and makes us more susceptible to illness and fatigue. Therefore, quick and effective response to pain is important to preserving long-term health.

Conflict.   Conflict results when we are required to choose between two or more mutually exclusive goals or courses of action. Some degree of conflict results every time you have to make a decision—the more difficult the decision, the greater the resulting conflict. For example, deciding whether to buy a Mercedes or a Porsche is a difficult decision because it involves a great deal of money, has long-term meaning for you (you'll probably have the car for five years or more), and there is a great deal of information to consider in making the decision. Deciding whether to have pie or cake for dessert will involve less conflict. Conflict is stressful because it demands our attention and involves energy (Radford et al., 1993). In order to understand the energy involved, pay attention to your body's physiological signals the next time you are faced with a difficult decision. Notice the increase in heart rate and breathing rate, the acid feeling in your stomach, and the fatigue that accompany your decision.

Investigators have identified four types of conflict. One is the *approach–approach conflict,* which involves choosing between two attractive alternatives. This type of conflict is relatively easy to resolve because you win regardless of your choice. An example of this situation would be Gia's deciding between two excellent advertising agencies to work with. A second type is the *avoidance–avoidance conflict,* which involves choosing between two negative alternatives. This conflict is difficult to resolve because it results in an unpleasant situation regardless of the alternative. Imagine the condemned person given the choice of dying by a firing squad or hanging! The *approach–avoidance conflict* involves one goal that has both positive and negative features associated with it. Gia faced this situation when deciding to enter a program to kick her drug addiction; she knew the program would cause her pain and struggle (negative), but it could free her from her addiction (positive). Finally, the *double approach–avoidance conflict* arises when you have to choose between two alternatives, each having positive and negative features. Consider, as

an example, choosing between two vacations, one that is exciting but costly, and the other less fun but cheap.

Each of these conflicts involves forces that move us toward one alternative (approach) or away from the alternative (avoidance). The stress associated with these conflicts leads some people to try to delay making decisions. However, this delay may heighten the stress because we continue to ponder the alternatives, and the delay postpones the opportunity to adjust to the eventual decision.

REVIEW QUESTIONS

1. _____ is the field of psychology that studies how behavior affects health and contributes to the recovery from illness.

2. T or F: During the alarm phase (first phase) of the general adaptation syndrome, the normal level of resistance to disease is raised to its highest point.

3. The sympathetic division of the autonomic nervous system

   a. conserves body energy and is most active during the alarm phase of the general adaptation syndrome.

   b. spends body energy and dominates the exhaustion stage of the general adaptation syndrome.

   c. spends energy and dominates the alarm stage of the general adaptation syndrome.

   d. is involved in determining our appraisal of stressors and has little impact on the general adaptation syndrome.

4. _____ are irritating, frustrating, or distressing incidents that occur in everyday life and have been postulated to be at the root of much stress.

5. T or F: Regrets are especially stressful to younger people.

Determining the Impact of Stress

The previous discussion identifies the universal causes of stress. However, people do not experience stress to the same degree, even when faced with the same stressors. Some people seem to be able to calmly deal with the stressor while others feel overwhelmed and panicked. What features affect the way different people will be affected by stress?

Individual Differences. Take a moment to look at the people around you. There are prob-

ably tall people, thin ones, obese folks, people who smile often, and those who speak loudly. People differ, obviously, and just as they differ in physical appearance and personality traits, they also differ in the way they respond to stress. Several years ago, a group of investigators noticed that some people respond to stress by becoming competitive and hostile (Friedman & Rosenman, 1974). These people feel rushed and under pressure, always trying to beat the clock. They are driven to achieve and can turn even a friendly fishing outing into a competitive contest. They find it difficult to share authority or surrender control. They strive for perfection and quickly resort to self-criticism. This collection of behaviors was labeled **type A behavior.**

The initial research suggested that these type A people were prone to suffer coronary heart disease. However, before you decide that you will pursue only the most relaxed lifestyle, without goals or desires to achieve, consider the more recent research in this area. These studies found that there are actually two components in type A behavior (Bluen, Barling, & Burns, 1990). One component, labeled *achievement striving (AS)*, involves taking work seriously, working hard, and striving to reach high goals. People who show high AS behavior are often very successful in work and school, showing high grades and productivity (Schaubroeck & Williams, 1993; Helmreich et al., 1988). High AS is not associated with an increase in illness such as heart disease.

However, the second component of type A behavior (Type A [II]) was related to illness. People who are high on the impatience–irritability (II) component tend to be intolerant of failure or ambiguity, are obsessed with time, and are quick to anger. These people were more likely to suffer heart disease and depression and feel generally dissatisfied with life than people low on the II component (Bluen, Barling, & Burns, 1990). It is generally believed that many of these responses to stress are learned, and that these behaviors reflect differences in interpreting stressful events and reacting to them.

A second personality style that is linked to stress and illness is known as *hardiness.* A study of managers at a large public utility revealed that some managers had high rates of illness while others had low rates, even though both groups had similarly stressful jobs (Kobasa et al., 1979). How can these differences be explained? Extensive questioning of the managers revealed some interesting differences in the way they view their stressful situation. The healthy group viewed stressful situations as challenges rather than threats. They committed themselves to taking action when stress arose rather than being passive observers. And they felt a high degree of control in their lives; they believed their own behavior was important in gaining rewards and avoiding punishment. People high on these three Cs (challenge, commitment, control) were labeled as having a **hardy personality.** Later research also found that these people were willing to seek and accept the support of others in the face of stress. This research can be viewed as showing how individual differences in personality and behavior style affect both how we perceive stressful situations and how we react to them.

Culture.   When we think of all the things that shape our response to stress, we often overlook one important contributor, our culture. Culture is the set of attitudes, values, beliefs and behaviors shared by a group of people and communicated from one generation to the next (Matsumoto, 1996). Culture may be seen as the social stage on which all behaviors occur. We generally don't think about culture because it is always present, usually as a silent partner. But culture can have far-reaching influences on our perception of stress and reactions to it.

To see how culture relates to stress, consider the point that investigators have described cultures along a dimension running from individualistic to collective (Triandis, 1994; Hofstede, 1991; see Chapter 1). Cultures on the individualistic side generally place an emphasis on the individual, viewing individuals as responsible for themselves. Individuals are expected to take care of themselves, and personal privacy and freedom are highly valued. Western societies such as the United States, Great Britain, and Germany are very individualistic. Cultures on the collective side of the dimension emphasize the group. Individuals represent the group, and they often live in extended families. They are expected to support their group (family, tribe), and the group is expected to support the individual. Arab, Asian, and Hispanic societies are generally collective.

These cultural differences lead to many intriguing differences in people's lives, but let us focus for now on their implications for stress. To demonstrate the effect of culture, consider Gia Carangi's problem with drug addiction. In her individualistic culture, this event reflected badly on Gia. Her coworkers and family saw her as weak, and they expected her to do something about *her* problem. The addiction itself was stressful, but added to the problem was Gia's feeling that she was inadequate because she created her problem. If Gia were from a more collective culture, however, her situation would be viewed as unfortunate by her group (her advertising agency and the modeling industry), members of the group would rally to support her and help her get proper treatment as soon as the addiction was evident. Gia might feel bad because her addiction had created a hardship on everyone, but the addiction would not be taken as a personal threat. Therefore, Gia would not be so personally devastated by her addiction. A large study of the relationship between health and culture concluded that culture affects human emotions and physiology, and it influences those events that individuals will experience as stressful (Matsumoto & Fletcher, 1994).

Culture affects other situations, too. For example, in individualistic societies, individuals are often seen as responsible when they become ill (Murphy-Berman & Berman, 1993). The sick individual is expected to seek medical attention to get well. In collective cultures, the health of the individual is viewed as the responsibility of the group (family, tribe). The group is seen as bearing some responsibility for the individual's having become ill, and the group is expected to help heal the individual. This cultural difference is seen in approaches to such illnesses as AIDS. In our Western societies, we often blame the individual for being inflicted with AIDS; he or she engaged in unprotected sexual activity or used drugs (Madey et al., 1993). Because individuals are responsible, there is heated debate about whether society should shoulder the cost of research on AIDS or the treatment of AIDS. As a result of this view, illness is often more stressful in Western individualistic societies than in collective societies.

Class and Economic Conditions. Equality between people is an important principle in many democratic countries, yet it is clear that people live under very different social and economic conditions. These conditions affect a wide range of situations, but one of the clearest impacts is on stress and health. People in lower social and economic classes experience greater stress, have fewer resources to combat stress, and as a consequence have more physical and mental health problems.

Socioeconomic position affects stress in many ways. First, people in lower economic classes must live in areas where they are subjected to more stressors (Vaughn, 1993). These areas have higher crime rates, fewer parks and opportunities for recreation, and more environmental toxins. People in lower socioeconomic classes have less access to medical treatment, and they are less likely to have educational programs that teach about good nutrition and other behaviors that promote good health. Second, people in lower socioeconomic classes have less control over their lives and the stressors in them (El-Sheikh & Klaczynski, 1993). They cannot move out of their neighborhood if it becomes riddled with crime or other stressors. They have little influence over government agencies and businesses, and they have less access to lawyers and other legal agencies to protect them. As we have seen, a lack of control is likely to create a condition of learned helplessness in which people simply stop trying to influence their environment.

The impact of low socioeconomic position is clearly seen in health statistics. For

TABLE 5.2 Illness and Social Class in the United Kingdom

CLASSES[a]	I	II	III	IV	V	VI
Long-standing illness (%)	13.0	16.8	19.2	19.2	26.5	31.7
Limiting long-standing illness (%)	6.5	9.0	10.4	11.3	16.2	20.8
Number of working days lost per year	3	6	6	9	11	18

[a]The higher the number, the lower the social class.
Source: General Household Survey (1980).

example, one study found that British workers in lower economic classes were more likely to have long-standing health problems and miss work because of illness (see Table 5.2) (General Household Survey, 1980). Ethnic minorities in the United States have higher death rates at all ages, and African Americans have higher infant mortality rates than whites (Carcia-Coll, 1990). The highest rates of mental illness are found in poor, African-American, urban communities (Gould, Wunch-Hitzig, & Dohrenwend, 1981). In a real sense, then, socioeconomic condition acts as a filter that influences the degree of stress a person will face and the resources available to deal with these stressors.

STRESS AND HEALTH

If you are like most people, you probably feel that if you could just find a pill to destroy those pesky bacteria and viruses that lurk in your system, you could live a healthy life. Unfortunately, getting and staying healthy is not so easy. In addition to your magic pill, you'd also need a miracle shield to erect around your body to protect it from stress. As we have pointed out, stress is associated with nearly every illness we suffer. And it may be more challenging to protect against stress than disease-causing microbes.

One reason is that stress does not affect everyone's health in the same way. A number of factors including culture, genetics, personality, and learning influence our response to stress. Genetics, for example, predisposes us to suffer certain illnesses. You may be born with a weak heart or a tendency to build up cholesterol in your arteries. Under relaxed conditions, these problems may not hamper you or even be detected. However, if you are faced with severe or prolonged stress, the effect may be to attack these weak areas. As a result, stress may cause one person to suffer cardiac disease, another to suffer cancer, and still another person to experience digestive tract problems.

Culture, too, seems to predispose us to showing certain symptoms in the face of stress. One study compared the responses of Anglo-Americans, Vietnamese-Chinese, and Mexicans to stress (Nishimoto, 1988). People in all these cultures had some common responses, such as having trouble sleeping, feeling restless, and feeling nervous. However, Mexicans typically suffered from headaches and memory problems, while Vietnamese-Chinese reported acid stomach, heart beating hard, and head feeling "full." Anglo-Americans had five symptoms: shortness of breath, headache, heart beating rapidly, hands trembling, and acid stomach. Investigators suggest that our culture teaches us the appropriate responses to stress (Brislin, 1993; Matsumoto, 1996). In some cultures it is acceptable to respond to stress with an upset stomach, whereas in other cultures headaches may prompt the most concern and attention as a response to stress. How often have you heard your parents explain their headaches as caused by stress? Had you grown up in another culture, you might hear your parents attribute their temporary memory lapses to stress. The result is that you would learn the common physiological symptoms your culture allows you to lay at stress's doorstep.

Now let us quickly review some of the specific health problems that research has associated with stress.

Physical Illness

Stress affects our physical health in a number of ways. First, as we pointed out in the previous section, severe or prolonged stress reduces the effectiveness of our immune system, reducing our ability to fight harmful bacteria and viruses. Second, stress increases blood pressure, disrupts digestion, increases fatigue and generally taxes our organs. People confronting frequent stress have been shown to have higher body temperatures than people under lower levels of stress (Cohen, Tyrrell, & Smith, 1993). Finally, we may become so preoccupied with dealing with stressful situations or so depressed by stress that we ignore the body's needs for nourishment and exercise and fail to take the steps necessary to treat illness. These effects increase our chances of suffering a host of illnesses.

Headaches.   Headaches generally have two causes. The most frequent headache is caused by muscle tension, especially in the muscles of the neck, scalp, and forehead. These headaches are often experienced as dull pain and feelings of pressure in the head. A second type of headache, known as *migraine headache,* results from a cycle in which blood vessels are constricted, reducing the flow of blood to the head, followed by a dilation of the vessels, leading to a rapid increase in the flow of blood to the head. Migraine headaches are extremely

painful, often accompanied by an increased sensitivity to light, nausea, vomiting, and even sensory-motor disturbances.

Medications, such as aspirin and ibuprofen, that inhibit the production of prostaglandins can be effective in treating many headaches. In the case of migraine headaches, medication (often including caffeine) that controls the flow of blood by affecting the constriction of the blood vessels is often necessary. Muscle relaxation through the use of medication or therapy techniques such as biofeedback (Blanchard et al., 1990) may be used by people who experience severe or frequent headaches. Although these techniques and medication are helpful, identifying the cause of stress and developing effective ways of coping are often the best means for controlling headaches.

Peptic Ulcers.   Peptic ulcers are lesions or holes that develop in the stomach or upper part of the small intestine. The lesions are caused by an oversecretion of stomach acid, which eats through the lining of the digestive tract. Ulcers are not only painful but also can be fatal. In 1980, an estimated 10,000 people died of ulcers, often due to hemorrhaging caused when the ulcer tore blood vessels. Ulcers are often referred to as the "executive's disease" because it was thought that they were caused by stress associated with making decisions. Further research has found, however, that ulcers are more likely caused by the need to respond quickly over extended periods and uncertainty over whether one has made correct decisions. Although you may not have ulcers, you have probably experienced the feeling of "acid stomach" when you are faced with time pressures and the need to do many things at the same time.

Coronary Heart Disease.   Our behavior and lifestyle play a major role in determining our likelihood of suffering heart disease. A lack of exercise, poor diet (including eating fatty foods and foods high in cholesterol), smoking, and failure to get sufficient rest are behaviors that increase our chances of being a victim of heart disease. Stress associated with work overload and demanding schedules has also been identified as a contributor to heart disease. These activities conspire to raise the blood pressure, taxing the heart and arteries. One study compared the rate of heart disease among people who lived a variety of lifestyles (Triandis et al., 1988). As can be seen in Figure 5.4, U.S. Caucasians had the highest rate of heart disease, whereas Trappist monks who have taken a vow of silence and spend their lives studying and writing had the lowest rate of heart disease. Other studies show the strong influence of culture on heart disease; culture influences our food preferences and the amount of social support we receive (Matsumoto, 1996). For example, rice is a staple diet in Asian cultures, Hindu cultures forbid eating meat, but red meat (beef) is a major part of many people's diet in the United States. A diet that includes a great deal of red meat has been linked to certain types of heart disease.

As you sit on your couch watching television and munching on those fatty barbeque ribs, you can take some comfort in the fact that you can take steps to lower your chances of suffering from heart disease. You can control your diet, you can begin a regular exercise program, and you can stop smoking. With additional effort, you can drop extra pounds and structure your life to reduce your stress. These steps will be very helpful, but they will not completely eliminate your risk of heart attack. There is also the genetic factor; if you are from a family with a history of heart disease, you are at risk (Feist & Brannon, 1988). This finding, however, should not be taken as your ticket to abuse your body. Rather, people with a high risk based on family history should be especially careful to reduce other risk factors.

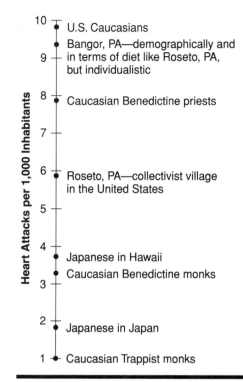

FIGURE 5.4 Heart Attack Rates per 1,000 Inhabitants in Selected Samples
Source: Triandis, Bontempo, Villareal, Asai, & Lucca (1988). Copyright © 1988 by the American Psychological Association. Reprinted by permission of the publisher.

Cancer. The story with cancer is much like that with coronary heart disease; genetic factors may predispose us to the illness, but our behavior contributes to our risk. Evidence that smoking causes cancer is so strong that tobacco products are required to carry a warming notice. Stress, too, is a villain in the cancer story. Over 11 percent of women in the United States will get breast cancer (Derogatis, 1988), but women who feel little control over their lives are the most prone to get cancer (Carver et al., 1993). The stress associated with feeling no control suppresses the immune system, but the story does not end there. Women who feel little

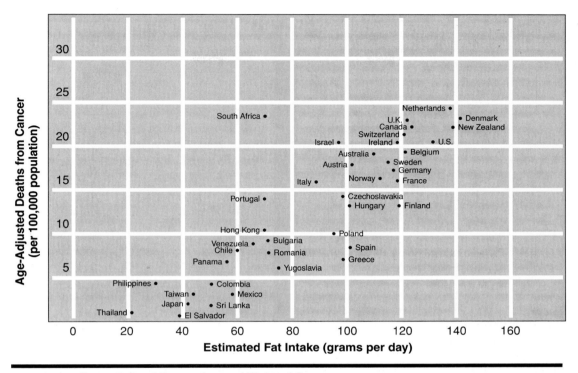

FIGURE 5.5   Cross-Cultural Comparisons of Diet and Cancer
In countries in which individuals have a low daily intake of fat (e.g., Thailand), the rate of breast cancer is low. In countries in which individuals have a high daily intake of fat (e.g., the Netherlands), the rate of breast cancer is high.
Source: From "Diet and Cancer" by Leonard A. Cohen. Copyright © 1987 by Slim Films. All rights reserved.

control over their lives are least likely to engage in health-protective behaviors such as doing monthly breast examinations. Our diet also influences our risk level. High fat diets are associated with higher risk of cancer. A telltale study compared cancer rates in numerous cultures (Cohen, 1987). As can be seen in Figure 5.5, deaths from breast cancer varied greatly across culture. A careful examination of the results shows that breast cancer rates were highest in cultures where people had diets high in fat (such as the Netherlands and Denmark) and lowest in cultures with low-fat diets.

As with so many other illnesses, there are many steps we can take to reduce, but not

eliminate, our risk of getting cancer. Most clearly, avoiding smoking and being in areas where we are victims of secondary smoke (breathing the smoke produced by others who are smoking) will reduce our risk. The newspapers and journals are filled with stories relating certain food products, such as nitrate preservatives, to cancer. At times, it seems that we should avoid eating altogether! More reasonably, we should work on developing a healthier diet, reducing our intake of fatty foods and foods loaded with preservatives. Regular medical checkups are important not only in developing healthy lifestyles but also for detecting the early signs of cancer and enabling us to undertake the necessary treatments if these signs are present. Controlling stress is a vital step we can take. We will discuss some specific ways to control stress later in this chapter, including learning how to relax. The bottom line is that we need not be passive victims of our environment; we can take an active role to promote our health.

6. Which of the following best describes the relationship between type A personality and heart disease?

   a. Type A personality is a good predictor of heart disease.
   b. There are actually two components to type A personality; only the achievement striving dimension is related to heart disease.
   c. There is no relationship between personality and heart disease.
   d. There are actually two components to type A personality, and only the impatience–irritability dimension is related to heart disease.

7. In _____ type cultures, individuals are viewed as responsible for their illness and consequently responsible for "curing" themselves.

8. T or F: Stress is associated only with serious illness involving the heart (coronary disease) and digestion (ulcers) and common illness such as colds are not affected by stress.

9. The most frequent type of headache is caused by _____, but migraine headaches are caused by constricted _____.

10. Stress increases our risk of cancer because it suppresses the _____.

Psychological Disorders

In Chapter 7 we will discuss psychological disorders in more detail. At this point, however, we want to emphasize that many if not all psychological disorders are influenced by stress. In fact, the DSM–IV classification system introduced in 1994 requires that the stressors associated with the onset of a disorder be rated on a 1–6 scale. The system recognizes that stress can lead to a variety of maladaptive behaviors or thinking. The aim of many psychotherapy techniques, including psychoanalysis and cognitive therapies, is to help people correctly recognize the stress that they are experiencing and develop constructive ways to deal with that stress (Dryden, 1992).

COPING WITH STRESS

Given the fact that stress can rob us of physical and mental health, it is important to identify ways to effectively cope with stress. Unfortunately, psychologists have not developed a magic wand that you can wave over your life and banish all stress. However, psychologists have identified ways of dealing with stress to reduce its negative impact. These responses have been placed in two categories (Lazarus, 1993). One is **problem-focused coping,** which involves correctly identifying the causes of stress and taking steps to reduce them. The second is **emotion-focused coping.** This approach includes not becoming preoccupied with stress and not allowing our emotions to be dominated by stress-arousing situations. Within these approaches, there are a number of actions that can help control the impact of stress.

Getting Information

How do you react when you are faced with a stressful situation or on learning that you have a serious illness? Many of us become consumed with dealing with the situation in any way we can. We may become so involved in these efforts that we fail to take the most elemental step: getting information. In the case of a difficult decision, such as choosing between two jobs, we may focus only on the choices we perceive that are available to us. Before making the choice, however, we should gather as much information about the alternatives as we can. We may also want to take a step back and consider whether other options are open to us. For example, one student was making herself sick trying to choose between two jobs that required her to move far away from her family. A friend suggested she inquire if either company had an office close to her hometown. To her surprise, she found that one had recently decided to open an office in her hometown and was looking for people to work in that office. A similar case can be made when illness looms; it is important to get information about the disease and treatment options. In fact, one study found that patients who mistakenly believed that their disease was incurable delayed treatment two and a half times longer than patients with the same disease who believed it was curable (Shafer et al., 1979).

Reappraisal

An old saying maintains that it is not stress itself that is so bad, but rather how bad we think it is. **Reappraisal** involves changing the way we think about stress. For example, in many cases, patients preparing for surgery think about only the bad effects: the pain, the risk, and the long recovery period. In one study, patients were trained to consider both the good and bad sides of surgery. For example, the patients were helped to consider the opportunities that would be open to them after surgery and to think of the positive side of the hospital stay (a chance to rest and get away from the daily stress of outside life). These patients ex-

perienced less pain in surgery and required less pain medication than patients not trained to reappraise their situation (Langer et al., 1975). Another study found that women recovered more quickly from breast cancer if they were trained to see how they could aid their recovery and consider the things they would do after surgery than patients not trained to perceive these sides of the surgery (Carver et al., 1993).

The important point of this work is that we can reduce the negative impact of stress by changing the way we perceive it. This does not mean that we should ignore the negative aspects of a situation. Rather, we should place the stressful event in perspective and consider the ways we can control the situation or profit from it.

Self-Efficacy

Despite her fame and fortune, Gia Carangi had a very bad image of herself. She felt that she could do nothing to take control of her life. Her best approach, she believed, was to find friends and lovers who would help her. As a result, she moved from one homosexual relationship to another, often finding that those closest to her took advantage of her. The perception of control that is helpful for combatting stress involves not only the event, but also the way we see ourselves. Many people see themselves as having little ability to handle stress; they are pawns of fate and situations. Imagine how you might feel when faced with a rough situation, such as breaking up with a girlfriend or boyfriend or failing a test, if you believed you would be unable to handle the consequences. Albert Bandura (1982) suggested that people will be able to deal with stress better if they develop a belief in themselves, a belief in their **self-efficacy,** to use Bandura's term. This belief in self-efficacy becomes a shield that helps us deal with stress; the disappointment of a failed relationship or a poor grade would certainly be reduced if you felt you could handle the crisis and take steps in the future to avoid repeated failures.

According to Bandura, we can be trained (or even train ourselves) to believe in our abilities to handle stress and feel a sense of control over our environment. One program involves performing and succeeding on several tasks that are unrelated to those required in stressful situations. For example, school children who are frustrated with their academic performance may be taught athletic skills or encouraged to develop their artistic talents. Success in these endeavors may raise their self-esteem, allow them to believe in themselves, and prepare them to tackle the frustrating academic subjects.

Social Support

When we are faced with stressful situations, it can be a lonely world. Whether the stress is caused by a personal failure (academic, business, relationship), illness, or simply feeling unhappy with ourselves, there is often a tendency to withdraw from others. The withdrawal may be based on feelings of embarrassment, the perception that no one cares, or the belief that we are worthless and not deserving of help from others. According to a great deal of research, this is exactly the wrong approach to take when faced with stress. Social support, which involves allowing others to help us deal with stress, is important for effectively coping with stress. In fact, it has been shown that both receiving and giving social support is useful in dealing with our stress (Buunk et al., 1993). Social support comes in many packages. In some cases it involves actual material or resources, such as money, shelter, or food. In other cases it may involve information, such as instructions on how to handle a problem or information about job openings. In still other cases social support includes emotional support—a pat on the back, a hug, and knowledge that someone cares. The most effective support is the one that fits the stress we are facing. For ex-

ample, material resources and information will best help us to face controllable stress, while emotional support will be most important when the stress is uncontrollable (Cutrona, 1990).

Social support helps us deal with stress in at least three ways. Support allows us to talk about our problems and fears; expressing our concerns has been shown to reduce stress (Mendolia & Kleck, 1993). Second, social support acts as a buffer against stress by reducing the range of situations that will cause us stress. The skinny youngster need not fear the school bully if he knows that he can count on his four monstrous brothers to come to his aid if the bully threatens him. Finally, the direct aid we receive from others may reduce the duration of stress. You may be terribly distressed if someone steals your stereo and clothing, but this stress will be short-lived if your friends come to you bearing new clothes and a replacement stereo. Overall, the availability of social support enhances self-esteem, feelings of self-efficacy, and may even help bolster the immune system (Baron et al., 1990).

The degree of social support we have is impacted by a number of factors. Women, for example, tend to have stronger support networks than men (Argyle, 1992). Our culture, too, plays a part in determining the level of support. In collective cultures such as those found in Asia, Latin America, and India, social support networks are deeply embedded in the social system (Triandis, 1993). Individuals are integrated into groups such as the family or the tribe, and they can count on support from these groups. In many individualistic societies such as the United States, individuals are expected to be independent. They are not closely tied to groups and therefore have no institutionalized system of support. Finally, the nature of the stressor influences how likely we are to receive social support (Kaniasty & Norris, 1993). For example, dramatic events such as natural disasters or highly publicized situations may bring wide and immediate support,

Surveying the Relation between Social Support and Emotions

This case examines a technique known as a field survey. In this case, people in their natural settings are requested to answer a number of questions, and their responses are examined along the lines of predictions. The study by several Dutch psychologists (Buunk, Doosje, Jans, & Hopstaken, 1993) began with the prediction that people feel better when social support is both given and received (equal) than when it is only given or received. The subjects were 181 employees of a large Dutch psychiatric hospital, 66 percent women and 24 percent men. Subjects responded to three questionnaires. The first asked them to identify the statement that best described their relationship with their superior. They were given five alternatives:

1. I am providing much more help and support to my supervisor than I receive in return.
2. I am providing more help and support than I receive in return.
3. We are both providing the same amount of help and support to one another.
4. My superior is providing more help and support to me than I provide in return.
5. My superior is providing much more help and support to me than I provide in return.

Subjects also completed a 10-item scale measuring the frequency of negative emotions they experienced during work over the past month, Finally, they responded to 15 questions asking them about the stressful aspects of their jobs.

The responses on the three scales were then related to each other. Subjects were categorized as "deprived" if they responded 1 or 2 on the social support scale, "equal" if they responded with a 3, or "advantaged" if they responded with a 4 or 5. As

can be seen in Figure 5.6, subjects experienced the fewest negative emotions at work when the give and take in their social support was equal. The equal situation was even better than the cases in which subjects received more social support than they gave (advantaged). This same pattern of results was found whether subjects viewed their jobs as highly stressful or not very stressful.

The finding is important because it suggests that effective social support is a two-way street, people feel best when they see themselves as giving and receiving equal amounts of support. Simply receiving help from others is not the best situation to be in.

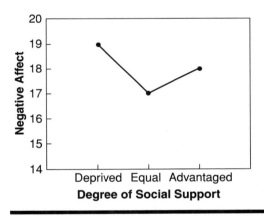

FIGURE 5.6 Reciprocity in the Relationship with a Superior and Negative Affect among Employees of a Psychiatric Hospital

Source: Adapted from B. Buunk et al. (1993). *Journal of Personality and Social Psychology, 65,* 804. Copyright © 1993 by the American Psychological Association. Adapted with permission.

whereas less visible and less dramatic events such as a broken relationship will bring less support. There is also evidence that we are less likely to receive social support when we are perceived as causing our misfortune than as innocent victims. And, as the Lessons from the

Laboratory feature demonstrates, social support works best in both directions.

Gia Carangi obviously tried to deal with her situation by seeking support from others. Unfortunately, she disguised her desire for support by rarely talking about her problems or needs and covering up her advances to others as being based on sexual attraction rather than the desire for close friendship. She also seemed to become involved with people who were so consumed by their own problems that they took from rather than gave to her.

LIFESTYLES THAT PROMOTE HEALTH

Although we may develop a picture of life as being a minefield of illness and stress, the bright side of the picture is that there are a multitude of specific steps we can take to lead happier and healthier lives. We can divide the steps into two categories: the behaviors to avoid and those to adopt. For the most part, there are few surprises in the list. As the world has become more health conscious, we are bombarded by information about the healthy path through life. At the same time, we are subjected to advertisements, peer pressure, and our own desires for quick fixes and an easy lifestyle that entice us to engage in unhealthy behaviors. Despite these conflicting pressures, the bottom line is that each of us is in the position of charting our direction.

Smoking

As we discuss in Chapter 6, smoking cigarettes is one of the don'ts. Nearly 50 million people in the United States smoke cigarettes, including 28 percent of high school seniors (Johnston, O'Malley, & Bachman, 1992). Despite the information about the negative effects of smoking on health, youths often begin smoking early, before they can appreciate the extent of the link. Gia Carangi, unfortunately, is not an exception in today's youth culture; Gia began smoking cigarettes before she was 14.

Smoking causes emphysema and cancer, and it increases the risk of strokes and heart disease, particularly in women who use birth control pills (Zastrow, 1992). It is estimated that between 200,000 and 400,000 people die in the United States each year from smoking (Centers for Disease Control, 1991). Smokers are also more likely than nonsmokers to be plagued by upper respiratory diseases and colds.

The primary message is: If you don't presently smoke, don't begin. If you are a smoker, quit. Quitting can dramatically improve your health even if you have smoked for years. However, quitting is no easy task. Fewer than 20 percent of smokers who try to quit are successful (Hunt & Matarazzo, 1970). Quitting is often accompanied by restlessness, depression, anxiety, and craving. The first step in quitting is to decide you will stop. Next, inform your friends and associates that you are quitting—make a public commitment to quit. Once you've committed yourself, there are a number of steps you can take. If you decide to quit gradually, outline a plan that sets the number of cigarettes you will smoke each day. Buy only the number of cigarettes to meet your goal; don't keep extras around enticing you to backslide. Chew gum, get involved in other activities, such as exercise, and try to distract yourself when you crave a cigarette. Some counselors suggest that you imagine your lungs turning black each time you inhale smoke. Some people may decide to quit cold turkey. If you choose this path, get rid of your cigarettes and lighters, avoid being around people who are smoking, and keep busy with activities that prohibit smoking. Regardless of the path you choose, reward yourself for progress; buy that new shirt, new perfume, or yacht to celebrate progress.

Drug Abuse

In addition to nicotine, there are hundreds of drugs that have been abused. Gia began using marijuana when she was 14, and through her short life she "graduated" from one drug to another. In some cases, the drugs are illegal, so abuse not only destroys health but also places us at risk of being arrested and fined. Drugs such as opium, heroin, cocaine, and marijuana fall into this category. In other cases, the drugs are legal, but their use violates good medical practice or the law

Life-style Changes Can Affect Health and Happiness

I've known Dave since high school. Even then he was a driven man, driven for success. He made straight As since the first grade. He was an Eagle Scout. I remember taking him fishing for the first time. He was a disaster! His line was constantly tangled. He fell out of the boat and nearly drowned because he was wearing boots that weighed about four tons. And worst of all, Dave didn't catch a fish, while I caught a dozen keepers. Dave was humiliated, and I didn't see much of him for the next two weeks. But then he called to invite me fishing. I was somewhat reluctant to go after the last trip, but I agreed to meet him at the lake. When I arrived at sunrise, Dave was already there. But this was a new Dave. He had new fishing gear, a tackle box with the hottest lures, and lightweight clothing (including tight-fitting rubber shoes). Dave assumed command of the boat and took us to a quiet cove. He tied on a carefully chosen lure and cast it with amazing precision so that it quietly entered the water just behind an old stump. It wasn't 20 seconds before he hooked a large bass and deftly guided it to the waiting net. The whole day went this way; it seemed as if Dave caught a hundred fish to my four.

After careful probing, I learned that Dave had spent the two weeks between our trips reading every fishing book available, talking to fishing guides, watching hours of videotapes and television programs on fishing, and practicing casting every night in his backyard. While fishing, Dave was a man possessed, it was him against nature, and he was determined to win. But as bountiful as his catch was, there wasn't a relaxed muscle in Dave's body when we returned home.

This experience characterized much of Dave's life. He graduated at the top of his college and medical school classes. He became a noted neurosurgeon. He bought the biggest house in town, threw the most elaborate parties, and drove the fastest car. He always wore perfectly matched designer clothing that never showed a wrinkle but hid several of his own ripples of fat. At age 38, Dave suffered a serious heart attack.

Two years later, I pulled into a gas station, and to my surprise, a slim version of Dave was sitting at a table in the station playing checkers with three old men. Dave wore a ragged T-shirt, cut-off blue jeans that had a large rip in a crucial location, and old sandals. He bought me a cold drink, and we set up a couple of chairs, strategically located to allow us to watch the world pass by the highway in front of the station.

Dave was happy just to sit as a silent spectator of life, but after prodding from me, he opened up about his life. "My heart attack really caused me to look at my life. I realized that so much of my life was based on habit. I awoke at a particular time, went to work on schedule, smoked two packs a day, went skiing when it snowed and swimming when it was hot, and played golf on Wednesday. Hell, even success was a habit with me. I was like a robot, programmed to act, and quick to get angry if my life went a bit off schedule. I don't even know if I was happy because I never thought about it.

"...When I had my heart attack, I had to change my behavior. At first, I thought I'd just quit living my life by habit, but I realized that it wasn't habit that was necessarily bad, just the behaviors that had become my habits. So I compromised with myself. I'd let myself have habits, but I would ask myself whether or not I wanted a particular habit and whether that habit made me happy. I controlled my habits, rather than let them control me. I stopped smoking and drinking and started cycling every morning. I got in the habit of reading the ingredients on food packages. I think Sally started to wonder about me when I told her I had been at the grocery store for the last two hours! When I started feeling overburdened with the stress at the hospital, I made it a habit to do something relaxing. I'd come to Bill's garage and play checkers, go to a movie, work in the garden, or even go fishing...with an old cane pole and worm! I've lost 40 pounds, and I've got the blood pressure of a 20-year-old, a healthy 20-year-old.

"...I've made it a habit to pay more attention to myself, to how I'm feeling, to what makes me happy. I still carry a heavy load at the hospital, but I enjoy it. I backslide now and then, getting caught up in things. But I try to split my time between being a participant in life and being an observer of life. I think that before, I wanted to get through life as fast as I could. I didn't really enjoy it, and subconsciously I wanted to get it over as quickly as possible. Now I want to enjoy every minute of it, and I think my new habits will add many years to my life."

regulating the proper use of these drugs. Drugs such as amphetamines, barbiturates, sedatives, tranquilizers, and alcohol fall into this category. The use of drugs is as old as humankind, and some drugs, such as alcohol and mescaline, are used in the rituals of some religions. Many of the drugs have medicinal properties, such as reducing pain, that make them valuable for treating certain illnesses. However, the misuse (abuse) of even these helpful drugs is destructive to our health and social well-being. Like nicotine, many of these drugs are addictive, and once people are hooked on the drug, their lives are controlled by the drug or efforts to obtain the drug. In Chapter 7, we discuss in detail many of the commonly abused drugs, so at this point, we want only to point out that the abuse of drugs, often taken initially to combat stress, can turn our lives into a living hell and may prove deadly.

Because they are so addictive, we should avoid any use of these illegal drugs or misuse of the legal drugs. If you are addicted to a drug, immediate attention is necessary. The treatment should begin with a complete medical examination. This should be followed by a treatment program that may involve substitution of a nonaddictive drug such as methadone, medical supervision, psychotherapy, group meetings, and diet regulation. In many cases, these programs take years, and addicts must confront the pain of withdrawal. Although this is not an appealing scenario, it is far preferable to the alternative of life controlled by the drug or an agonizing death.

Safe Sex or No Sex

Chapter 11 examines sexual behavior in some detail; that discussion focuses on positive aspects of sexual behavior such as love, intimacy, and enjoyment. However, a variety of diseases, known as **sexually transmitted diseases (STDs),** are contracted through sexual behavior; these diseases have a profound effect on health. The most common STDs are those caused by bacteria. These include syphilis and gonorrhea, which have a history almost as long as human sexual behavior. In fact, during the late fifteenth century, syphilis was so widespread it affected the outcome of some military battles. These bacterial diseases can create a great deal of pain, sterility, and serious harm to fetuses; untreated syphilis can be fatal. Fortunately these bacterial STDs can be successfully treated with antibiotics, and early treatment is critical for avoiding serious complications.

Other STDs are caused by viruses that are not destroyed with antibiotics of other presently known medications. Herpes genitalis is the most common. Although the disease is painful and incurable, the severity of its outbreak can often be controlled. In the late 1970s, physicians began to notice a strange disease that attacked the victim's immune system and made them unable to fight even relatively benign bacteria. The victims eventually died, often of pneumonia. In 1982, there were 250 cases of this strange disease in the United States; by 1993, the number of cases had mushroomed to over 300,000 (Centers for Disease Control, 1993). At first the disease seemed to be confined to homosexual men and intravenous drug users, but heterosexuals, both male and female, soon joined the ranks of victims. Gia Carangi was the first reported female victim of the disease. Careful study revealed that the disease, **acquired immunodeficiency syndrome** or **AIDS,** is caused by a human immunodeficiency virus (HIV) that destroys the body's immune system and makes the victim unable to fight disease. Because the virus is actually very fragile, dying quickly in open air and other environments, it must directly enter the bloodstream of potential victims to infect them.

There are a limited number of ways in which this transmission can occur. One path is through sharing needles, where one person injects himself or herself with a needle that has recently been used by someone with the HIV virus. This is the path that gave Gia and many other intravenous drug users the disease. Transmission can also occur when infected vaginal fluid (from the female) or semen (from the male) enters another person's blood stream. This path accounts for the high rate of AIDS among homosexual men who practice anal intercourse, which often tears the rectal walls (Laigh & Stall, 1993). Such tears can also occur in heterosexual intercourse, leading to the infection of a partner. A third means of infection is through receiving infected blood through blood transfusions. A fourth involves infants contacting the virus before birth when a mother's infected blood comes in contact with their own. A person can have the HIV virus for 10 years or longer before showing symptoms of AIDS.

AIDS is a frightening disease, threatening to reach epidemic proportions throughout the world, but we can take steps to avoid it. In most cases, it is our behavior that places us at risk (Fisher & Fisher, 1992). Abstinence from sexual intercourse (heterosexual or homosexual) eliminates a major path for the transmission of the HIV virus. However, if you decide to become sexually active, the use of a condom, which prohibits the mingling of body fluids between partners, can close off this path of transmission. Condom use is always advisable, but it is especially important if you have intercourse with a prostitute or anyone who has had multiple partners. It is not enough that the person has not had another partner for a year or so; remember that people can carry the virus for many years without showing any symptoms of AIDS. Indeed, it may be advisable for you and your new partner to get an AIDS test before engaging in unprotected sexual intercourse. These steps may create some inconvenience and embarrassment for you and your partner, but they can save your life.

Diet

A friend of ours recently commented that many people are more careful about the fuel they put in their automobiles than the food they eat. Just as we can destroy our automobiles' engines and catalytic converters if we use incorrect fuel, we can destroy our health by adopting a poor diet. Unfortunately, most of us associate our diets with our physical appearance. Gia Carangi was constantly dieting to lose weight so that she could retain a look considered attractive in modeling. No one can argue that looking attractive is not nice, but our concern with what we eat should not have physical appearance as its main goal. *Some* intake of fat is necessary for health because fats are storage units for many vitamins, they provide energy (especially when prolonged physical activity is necessary), and they insulate our bodies. Bear in mind, however, that fat is readily stored in our bodies, it takes a high activity level to "burn" fat (carbohydrates are more quickly burned for energy), and saturated fats increase the cholesterol levels in our blood. Therefore, fat intake should be kept at low levels to maintain health.

Our diet strongly influences our health. Diets high in fat, refined sugar, and cholesterol and low in fiber increase our risk of heart disease, cancer, and diabetes. In addition, these diets also increase our chances of being obese, and those extra pounds place additional demands on our organs, especially our heart, and make us prone to cardiovascular disease, diabetes, and certain types of cancer.

It is, therefore, very important that we pay attention to what we eat and strive for a healthy diet. As Figure 5.7 shows, a healthy diet includes a proper balance of foods from several groups and avoidance of high levels of fats, oils, and sweets. It is interesting to note that the diet of people in many Western industrialized countries such as the United States is more loaded with these potentially harmful elements than is the diet of people in poorer countries (Triandis, 1993), who eat large amounts of rice, fruit, and high-fiber foods. In general, a nutritious diet should include the

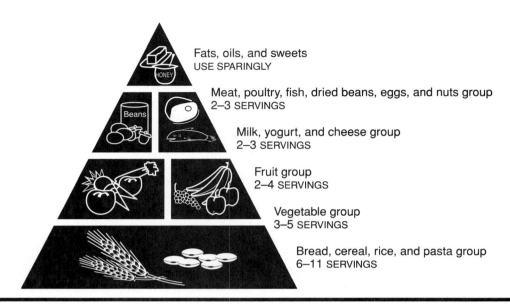

Fats, oils, and sweets
USE SPARINGLY

Meat, poultry, fish, dried beans, eggs, and nuts group
2–3 SERVINGS

Milk, yogurt, and cheese group
2–3 SERVINGS

Fruit group
2–4 SERVINGS

Vegetable group
3–5 SERVINGS

Bread, cereal, rice, and pasta group
6–11 SERVINGS

FIGURE 5.7 Good Nutrition Involves Choosing the Proper Balance of Foods
Source: U.S. Department of Agriculture, U.S. Department of Health and Human Services.

necessary vitamins and minerals; complex carbohydrates, which provide energy to our bodies; and proteins, which are the building blocks for muscles, blood, and bones. Women need to be especially careful to include adequate amounts of calcium (necessary for maintaining bone strength) and iron (required by red blood cells) in their diets. Blood loss during menstruation depletes iron, and child bearing saps calcium.

There are some cruel ironies in our dieting life. One is that so many of the "bad" foods taste good to us. This taste is largely learned, as is shown by the fact that people from other cultures often find these foods distasteful. Second, adding weight is easier for most of us than taking off unwanted pounds. The first step, then, in developing a healthy diet is to start early in life. Learn about the content of foods; packaged foods in the United States are required to feature nutritional descriptions. Learn to interpret the information on these labels, and pay attention

to them in planning your diet. Second, set reasonable goals for yourself. Starving is as unhealthy as overeating. As we discussed in Chapter 6, yo-yo dieting (in which you diet for some time, return to unhealthy eating patterns, and then diet again) is unhealthy and dangerous. Gia learned this the hard way when she became seriously ill after a period of yo-yo dieting. Reduce your calorie intake by substituting low-calorie foods for those higher in calories. Third, exercise; this not only reduces weight but also strengthens muscles, including your heart, and helps replace fat with muscle tissue. As Table 5.3 shows, certain activities burn more calories than others. As we will see in the next section, a sensible exercise program that is designed for your capabilities is useful; overexerting yourself is both painful and dangerous. Although the initial stages of developing a healthy diet may prove challenging, once it is established, maintaining your healthy diet should prove easier.

TABLE 5.3 Calories Expended in One Hour According to Activity and Body Weight

ACTIVITY	BODY WEIGHT (IN POUNDS)				
	100	*125*	*150*	*175*	*200*
Sleeping	40	50	60	70	80
Sitting quietly	60	75	90	105	120
Standing quietly	70	88	105	123	140
Eating	80	100	120	140	160
Driving, housework	95	119	143	166	190
Desk work	100	125	150	175	200
Walking slowly	133	167	200	233	267
Walking rapidly	200	250	300	350	400
Swimming	320	400	480	560	640
Running	400	500	600	700	800

Source: Adapted from J. Rathus and J. Nevid (1992). *Adjustment and Personal Growth*, 5th ed. Fort Worth: Harcourt Brace Jovanovich.

Exercise

Many of Gia Carangi's friends suggested that she develop an exercise program to maintain her health and attractiveness. Her reply was that she was too busy; instead she searched for drugs to maintain her health and figure. The result was disastrous; she was often ill and had no energy to keep up with her breakneck schedule. Proper exercise is vital for both physical and mental health. The most important exercise from a health perspective is *aerobic exercise*, which involves an increase in oxygen consumption over a sustained period of time. Although the term may conjure up images of organized classes going through routines to the beat of rock music, there are many types of aerobic exercise. These include jogging, walking briskly, jumping rope, riding a bicycle, cross-country skiing, and playing basketball or handball as well as participating in aerobic dance or exercise activities. The aim of all these activities is to raise your heart rate, thereby increasing your oxygen consumption, over a period of five minutes or longer.

Regular exercise reduces weight, builds and strengthens muscles, and generally gives us the attractive glow of physical fitness. More important, however, exercise enhances your health. On the physical side, the most widely studied benefit of exercise is reducing the risk of cardiovascular disease, especially heart attack. Regardless of other risk factors, such as smoking and diet, regular exercise burns at least 2,000 calories a week and cuts the risk of heart attack by two-thirds (Sherwood, Light, & Blumenthal, 1989). Figure 5.8 shows the results of a study of 17,000 Harvard graduates over a six to ten year period, which documented that exercise reduces the number of both fatal and nonfatal heart attacks (Paffenbarger et al., 1989). The study also found that subjects who burned at least 2,000 calories a week through exercise lived an average of two years longer than less active subjects. In addition to reducing heart disease, exercise also reduces the risk of hypertension and diabetes and enhances the functioning of the immune system (Antoni et al., 1990). These positive benefits occur because exercise strengthens the heart muscle, reduces the level of low-density lipoprotein ("bad" cholesterol) in the blood, and makes the body a more efficient consumer of oxygen.

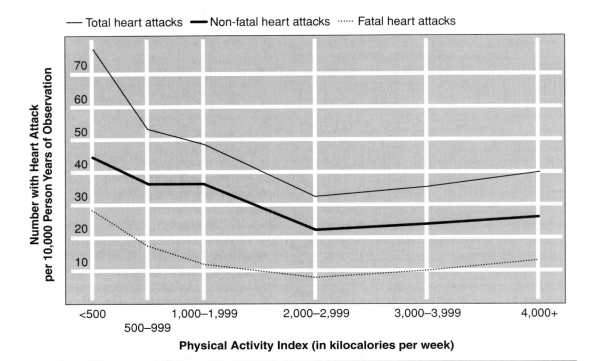

FIGURE 5.8 The Relation between Physical Exercise and Heart Attacks
Age-adjusted first heart attack rates by physical activity index in a 6- to 10-year follow-up of male Harvard alumni.
Source: Pattenbarger et al. (1978). Reprinted by permission.

On the psychological side of health, regular exercise has been found to reduce depression and anxiety and to raise self-esteem (Buffone, 1984). These positive results may be related to the fact that exercise helps people gain a feeling of control over their lives and bodies, improves their physical health, and enhances their physical attractiveness.

Armed with knowledge of the benefits of exercise and the problems associated with a lack of exercise, you may be headed out the door to run in the upcoming marathon race. However, before you do this, let us caution you that *proper* exercise promotes health. You should develop an exercise program that fits your abilities and needs, one that you can maintain on a regular basis. Pain is not glory

when it comes to exercising. In fact, overexercising can lead to health problems, such as injury to joints and muscles and, for women, problems with the menstrual cycle and reduced fertility. (For some tips on developing a proper exercise program, see the accompanying box.)

Sleep and Relaxation

As Gia Carangi's fame as a model skyrocketed, she got more of many things: money, famous friends, attention, and opportunities. However, success came at a price; one cost was that she got less rest and sleep. By her own account she was a person who needed a great deal of sleep and could sleep for 12-hour

Proper Exercise: Avoiding Pain and Getting the Gain

We want to emphasize the importance of developing and maintaining a proper exercise program. You will receive maximum gain from a program that challenges you but does not exceed your limits. Overdoing it will not speed up your benefits, and it may set you back. In developing your program, consider the following points.

1. Start Small.

The younger you are when you begin your program, the more benefits you will get from it. Children should be encouraged to exercise regularly. However, even if you have been a couch potato for most of your life, start your program now. Even people who begin exercise later in life will receive benefits.

Begin your program with moderate and achievable goals. Don't set your sites too high in the beginning; rather set clear goals that build on one another. Setting goals beyond your ability can result in injury and discouragement.

2. Start Smart.

Begin your program by making a careful evaluation of your abilities, risks, and desires. Know yourself! In making your assessment, consider such factors as your age, your weight, your past physical exercise, your diet, your risk behaviors (such as smoking, drug and alcohol use), and your family history of physical difficulties. In most cases, it is advisable to talk over your plans with your physician who can conduct a complete physical examination, and help you plan your program based on your condition. In addition, evaluate your aims and personality. For example, some of us will desire company during our exercise, while others will want solitude. If you desire the companionship of others, choose activities that can be performed in groups, and join an exercise group that is compatible with your social desires and physical abilities.

Besides knowing yourself, know about your chosen activity. Read about the exercise you have chosen and consult experts so you will set reasonable goals and perform the exercise properly. These sources will also help you choose proper equipment and clothing.

3. Play Safe.

We have a colleague who began his exercise program by purchasing a used Nautilus machine. The second time he used it, a bolt snapped, causing him serious injury. The moral of this story is to buy good equipment and keep it in good working order. Likewise, choose a comfortable, safe place to exercise. If you jog, plan your route and study it carefully; you would be well advised to avoid a course that takes you through dangerous neighborhoods or ones that are patrolled by big angry dogs.

4. Stay Smart.

You can make a number of smart moves to enhance the benefit and enjoyment you get from exercising. First, pay attention to the signals from your body. Persistent or sharp pain, aside from normally sore or tired muscles, is a signal to reassess your program. Although it is important to maintain a regular schedule, be sensible and flexible enough to adjust to periodic changes in your physical condition. Skip exercise when you are sick or injured. Keep a diary that charts your progress and identifies activities that are difficult or painful. Your diary should also identify your successes and the benefits (such as sleeping better, having more energy, laughing more, making new friends) you derive from exercise.

5. Have Fun.

Exercise should be enjoyable. If you find that you are not enjoying an activity, consider finding one that does bring you joy. Joy is an important part of being healthy.

---

stretches. Instead, she found herself running from engagement to engagement, partying throughout the night, and having to make early photography appointments. All this

took its toll: Gia often enraged her employers by falling asleep during her sessions or missing sessions because she was too tired to appear. She responded by taking drugs (uppers) to keep her awake, but soon even the best make-up job could not cover up the bags under her eyes.

Proper sleep is critical to good health. Studies show that sleep deprivation leads to irritability, fatigue, poor concentration, and reduced muscle coordination. A lack of sleep inhibits learning and memory, especially for tasks learned the day before (Karni et al., 1992). It is interesting that Gia explained that her absence from several photo sessions occurred because she forgot making the appointments. These lapses in memory were most likely to occur when she was very deprived of sleep. The relationship between sleep and memory has led scientists to suggest that a major function of sleep is to repair and restore the nervous system, especially the neurotransmitters responsible for transporting messages from neuron to neuron (Volk, Schulz, & Yassauridis, 1990).

When we are deprived of sleep, we are apt to fall asleep during the day. To corroborate this statement, look around your classroom in the afternoon. One study found that 60 percent of college students reported falling asleep in afternoon classes sometime during a semester (Carskadon & Roth, 1991). This might be amusing in the classroom but can have serious consequences if it occurs during driving or dangerous work. About 10 percent of automobile crashes result because a driver fell asleep at the wheel (Wellness Letter, 1993). And 59 percent of train engineers report falling asleep at least once while driving the train (Akerstedt, 1991).

Sleep is also important because it gives us a break from dealing with stressful situations. During sleep, our heart rate and blood pressure decrease, and oxygen consumption is reduced. Many of these beneficial effects can also be achieved through *meditation*. There are several types of meditation, including yoga and transcendental meditation. These exercises require finding a quiet place, getting into a comfortable position, and engaging in a simple repetitive mental task, such as repeating a simple phrase. Meditation and other similar relaxation techniques help people gain control over their bodies, reduce physiological arousal, and cope with stress. The important point is that sleep and relaxation exercises allow our bodies and minds to recuperate and temporarily escape the demands of stress.

Working with Your Physician

Much of our discussion of living a healthy life has focused on what you, as an individual, can do. In fact, much of your health is in your hands and affected by your decisions. However, you need not be alone in your quest for wellness. Your physician is an important partner in creating a healthy lifestyle. Unfortunately for Gia, she did not seek medical help or follow medical advice until it was too late. Most of us think of our physician as someone we turn to when we are sick and have clearcut symptoms that interfere with our lives. Indeed, physicians play an important role in helping us deal with illness.

The relationship between doctor and patient has been the focus of a great deal of study. One disturbing finding is that patients follow the advice of their doctors only about 50 percent of the time. Patients often fail to take medication as directed or to make follow-up appointments. Several factors affect whether or not patients will follow their doctor's instructions. For example, they are most likely to comply when their illness is severe and when they believe the procedure or medication will be successful in curing them. They are more likely to follow the instructions when the doctor is warm and shows concern for them as patients (Newhill, 1990). The medical profession has become aware of the importance of the role between doctor and patient, and many medical training programs include instruction in developing positive relationships with patients. From your position as a patient, it is important to choose a physician whom you trust and with whom you feel comfortable and then carefully follow his or her instructions. Don't be afraid to ask for information about your illness and medication, and feel free to seek advice from additional doctors.

Although the role of the physician is generally clear when we are ill, we often overlook the valuable role he or she can play in preventing illness. As one colleague of ours states, "You should make visits to your physician in sickness and in health, till death do you part." Regular check-ups and discussions with your physician can help you identify danger signs before they become serious illness. Your physician can help you develop a lifestyle and diet to avoid illness based on knowledge about your physical condition and history. Knowledge about your family history may allow the physician to be especially vigilant for certain signs of illness and enable him or her to prescribe preventative medication or therapies. In developing a trusting relationship with your physician, it is important to be completely honest. Don't be embarrassed to discuss your lifestyle, your symptoms, your family history, or your fears. Information is often as important as medicine in the journey to health. And when the doctor suggests a certain medication, exercise program, or treatment, follow these instructions or let him or her know the instructions you cannot or will not follow. Work with your physician to develop a prevention plan or treatment.

REVIEW QUESTIONS

11. _____ coping involves dealing with stress by not allowing ourselves to become preoccupied with the stressful event.

12. According to Bandura, belief in self-efficacy

    a. is innate in some individuals.
    b. can be learned.
    c. is more common in young females than older females.
    d. is common in males but rare in females

13. T or F: The most helpful form of social support always involves giving information or advice about how to handle stress.

14. _____ is the most common sexually transmitted disease.

SUMMARY

1. There is increasing evidence that most if not all illness has a psychological and behavioral component. The area of health psychology studies how behavior affects health and contributes to the recovery from illness.

2. Stress is the process by which we respond to environmental and psychological events that we perceive as threatening or challenging. High levels of stress or prolonged stress contribute to illness. Few events are universal stressors. Rather, stress arises from the way we perceive or interpret events. The general adaptation syndrome is a model of how our bodies respond to stress. The autonomic nervous system (ANS) responds to stress. It is divided into two parts, the sympathetic division and the parasympathetic division. The sympathetic system prepares us for action and is activated during the alarm stage. The parasympathetic system works to restore energy. The endocrine system, which involves organs that secrete hormones, is also activated by stress.

3. Common stressors are change, minor life hassles, unpredictable events, lack of control, goals (especially unfulfilled ones), pain, and conflict. Life involves all of these stressors, but they become particularly troublesome when they are numerous or prolonged.

4. A wide variety of factors influence the degree of stress caused by any event. Studies of individual differences show that personality and learning influence the ways people respond to stress. Our culture influences the types of events that we will experience as stressful and the ways we will respond to them. For example, in collective societies, events that threaten the group are viewed as especially stressful. Likewise, an individual who is experiencing stress can generally count on support from the group. People in lower socioeconomic categories experience more stressors and have fewer resources to deal with their stress.

5. Stress has a profound impact on our health. Exactly where that stress will manifest itself is influenced by a wide variety of factors including our genetic composition, culture, personality, and learning. Because stress reduces the ability of our immune system, it has been associated with a number of physical illnesses such as cancer. Stress also increases blood pressure and heart rate and disrupts our digestive system. Because of these effects, stress is a factor in coronary diseases, digestive tract illness such as ulcers, and headaches. In addition to stress, unhealthy lifestyles (including habits such as eating foods high in fat, failing to get adequate exercise, and smoking) increase our chances of suffering from these diseases. Stress also in-creases our chance of experiencing a psychological illness.

6. Psychologists have identified several ways of dealing with stress and reducing its negative impact on our health. Problem-focused coping involves correctly identifying the causes of stress and taking steps to reduce them. Emotion-focused coping includes avoiding becoming preoccupied with stress and not allowing our emotions to be dominated by stress-arousing situations. Specific steps to cope with stress involve gathering information about the stressful event and options for action, changing the way we think about or interpret the stressful event, developing a belief in our self-efficacy, and developing a strong social support network.

7. Despite the risks to our health, there are a wide range of steps we can take to increase our health and guard against illness. One step is to avoid smoking. Smoking is associated with cancer, emphysema, stroke, and heart disease. Another step is to avoid the temptation of using illegal drugs such as opium, heroin, cocaine, and marijuana, and to avoid abuse of legal drugs such as alcohol, sedatives, and tranquilizers. Practicing safe sex (for example, by using a condom) helps to protect us from sexually transmitted diseases such as AIDS, herpes, and syphilis. A good diet, high in fiber and low in fat and cholesterol, is important in promoting health. Aerobic exercise such as skiing, walking, jogging, and even vigorous dancing strengthens muscles, reduces weight, and increases our resistance to disease. Healthy behavior also includes getting enough sleep and relaxation and getting regular medical checkups.

CRITICAL THINKING QUESTIONS

1. Change, minor hassles, unpredictability; lack of control, regrets, pain, and conflict are dimensions that determine the degree of stress caused by a stressor. Consider the events in your life that you view as stressors, and then list those dimensions that characterize each stressor. Based on your list, is the intensity of a stressor determined by the dimensions (if so, which dimensions) or by the number of dimensions that define the stressor?

2. Think about the qualities of collective cultures. What types of situations are likely to cause stress in these collective cultures that would be experienced as less stressful in individualistic cultures? How does culture affect the way people deal with stressful situations?

3. Lazarus (1993) suggested that there are two types of coping with stress: problem-focused coping and emotion-focused coping. List behaviors that would fall under each category in coping with the following stressors: a terminal illness, conflict in a relationship, a critical examination in a class, a physical handicap.

MATCHING EXERCISE

Match each term with its definition.

a. health psychology
b. stress
c. general adaptation syndrome (GAS)
d. autonomic nervous system (ANS)
e. endocrine system
f. immune system
g. type A behavior
h. hardy personality
i. reappraisal
j. self-efficacy
k. social support
l. sexually transmitted diseases (STDs)
m. AIDS
n. problem-focused coping
o. emotion-focused coping

1. A series of glands that secrete hormones directly into the bloodstream
2. The field of psychology that examines how behavior affects health and contributes to the recovery from illness
3. A stage model of the response pattern to stress
4. A response to stress that includes becoming hostile and competitive; has been associated with susceptibility to coronary heart disease
5. The process by which we respond to the environment and psychological events that we perceive as threatening and challenging
6. A system of nerves composed of two divisions (sympathetic and parasympathetic) that regulate glands and organs
7. The system that destroys disease-causing organisms and aids in the recovery from disease
8. A pattern of dealing with stress that involves not becoming preoccupied with stress and not allowing emotions to be dominated by stress-producing events
9. A set of traits characterizing people who have low rates of illness in the face of stress, presumably because they view stress as a challenge rather than a threat
10. A sexually transmitted disease that is caused by a virus that destroys the immune system
11. A pattern of dealing with stress that involves identifying the causes of stress and taking steps to reduce them
12. Diseases that are transmitted through sexual contact
13. An approach to coping with stress that involves changing the way a person interprets events and thinks about stress
14. Help received from others to help us cope with stress
15. Belief that one can successfully deal with stressful events

Answers to Matching Exercise

a. 2   b. 5   c. 3   d. 6   e. 1   f. 7   g. 4   h. 9   i. 13   j. 15   k. 14   l. 12   m. 10   n. 11   o. 8

ANSWERS TO REVIEW QUESTIONS_____

1. health psychology
2. true
3. c
4. minor hassles
5. false
6. d
7. individualistic

8. false
9. muscle tension, blood vessels
10. immune system
11. emotion-focused
12. b
13. false
14. herpes genitalis

STRUGGLING FOR CONTROL

Kurt Cobain

Kurt Cobain

Early in the morning on Friday, April 8, 1994, a Seattle news flash announced that the body of a "white blond male in its mid-20s" had been discovered on the property of Kurt Cobain, lead singer of the popular band, Nirvana. As his friends and fans were soon to discover, the world-famous rock star had taken his own life with a single shotgun blast to the head. Why? How did it happen that this talented young man, who had been called "the poet of this generation" (Guccione, 1994, p. 16), could lose so much control in his life that the only solution apparent to him was to end it? These questions demanded answers, but none was forthcoming.

At the time of his death, it had been quite clear to those close to him that Cobain was highly stressed. He had been missing for five days, his mother told police, and he was suicidal and had a shotgun. Two weeks earlier, his wife, Courtney Love, had called the police when he locked himself in a room with his guns and threatened suicide. Shortly thereafter he was admitted to a drug treatment center. After a few days he escaped and was missing until his death. Later it was learned that during a tour to Rome in early March he had made a serious suicide attempt with pills and alcohol. This incident was covered up by his publicity agents. Even his lyrics, which spoke of suicide being the "bright side," revealed his pain (Arnold, 1994).

Kurt Cobain's short life history sheds some light on how, at age 27, he felt so out of control. He was born in 1967 in an economically depressed, dreary logging town in Washington state. His father was a mechanic and his mother a homemaker. A sister was born 3 years after him, and the family lived together in a trailer park. When Kurt was very young, his world was happy. He was an active and artistic child, often entertaining the family and others with skits, songs, and drawings (Mundy, 1994). He had a sensitive and artistic temperament that seems to have been nurtured and accepted within his immediate family but made it hard for him to handle later events.

When he was 8, his parents divorced, and from then on his life was very unsettled. It was a bitter divorce, which his father protested (Gilmore, 1994). He felt both the anguish of his family and his own

pain and isolation. "Every night at one point I'd go to bed bawling my head off. I used to try to make my head explode by holding my breath, thinking if I blew up my head, they'd be sorry," he recalled in 1993 (Gold, 1994, p. 38). In 1992, his mother told an interviewer that "he became very inward—he just held everything. He became really shy. It [the divorce] just devastated him" (Mundy, 1994, p. 51). He lived with his mother for just a year and then moved in with his father. As he grew into adolescence, he stayed alone often, played guitar, smoked pot, and dreamed of becoming a rock star. Perhaps he sang in part for self-comfort, "clueing in other young isolates in need of a personal shield of sound" (Weisbard, 1994, p. 40). His father remarried, to a woman with two children of her own, further stressing Cobain's already strained relationship with his father. He was kicked out of his father's home and began living here and there—at an aunt and uncle's, back to his father's, in friends' houses, even in cars, and under a bridge—but nowhere he could call home. He dropped out of school, but he continued to play music. In the next few years, he found both a place to call home and a band to play in.

"Home" was the town of Olympia, Washington. Kurt went there with his girlfriend to live and found it to be a very tolerant community of artists, musicians, and college students. The band was Nirvana. At age 18, Cobain cut a homemade tape; just a year later, local bass player Chris Novoselic heard it, recruited him and drummer Dale Crover, and the group Nirvana was born. The success of the group was swift and strong; the boy who as a seventh grader had fantasized about being a "rock god" (Gold, 1994, p. 40) released an album (*Nevermind*) at the age of 24, which sold almost 10 million copies worldwide.

On the outside Kurt Cobain was a loud, angry, provocative performer. On the inside, he was still in pain. Offstage he was shy, solitary, and introspective. His health had never been good—he was frail and sickly as a child—and now he struggled with chronic and severe stomach pain. He developed a heroin habit that he would never fully kick. He began a romance with Courtney Love, leader of the punk rock band Hole, and they married. One author noted that despite their real love for each other, "they knew they had problems. They understood themselves as unloved children, as codependents. They took turns rescuing and protecting each other from exploitation, illness, bad publicity. They said they wanted a better emotional life for their daughter, Francis Bean" (Gaines, 1994, p. 61). It was hard, however, to make this happen. One telling illustration of this is the report that Courtney held Kurt's hand in the delivery room while she was in labor, soothing him through his heroin withdrawal.

Perhaps it was hope for the future, and for a safe, secure home, emotionally, psychologically, and physically, that caused him to try to withdraw from drugs at that particular time. "Now I'm a dad. Everything's changed," he said at one point, talking to Love about their earlier days (Mundy, 1992, p. 52). In any case, both he and Courtney loved their child and struggled for control of their future. Rumors of her heroin use during pregnancy led to a battle with the child welfare authorities for custody of their child (Arnold, 1994). Cobain's drug abuse continued, as did the stomach pain and the stresses of traveling and performing. His hopelessness and despair were expressed in his music and, eventually, in his final act of suicide.

PERCEPTIONS OF THE LOCUS OF CONTROL

Kurt Cobain's tragic story is an example of the way that control—and loss of control—deeply affects our lives. Like all people, Cobain had dreams, hopes, and intentions about what his life would be like. Some of these he met, and there were times when he was happy and healthy. At other times, he could not keep himself from engaging in behaviors and making choices that thwarted his goals and threatened his health. In this chapter we will consider several of the more common psychological problems that reflect a struggle for control. If you stop and think about it, there are many areas of life in which we need to maintain a balance and a sense of control. Eating, sleeping, smoking cigarettes, drinking alcohol, and using drugs are the most obvious ones. We hardly notice these activities when they are in balance, and a normal part of our ongoing lives. But people who struggle for control in these aspects of their lives are acutely aware of them.

Our goal in this chapter is to understand how and why people struggle for control in their lives and sometimes lose it, as Kurt Cobain did. In addition to these topics, we will also examine how and why people lose control in their relationships with other people, and how rape and domestic violence can result. We hope that exploring these problems will help you see how widespread they are, how many of them are related, and how to cope with them most effectively.

Before we consider the range of challenges that people face in the course of living, we want to consider a general psychological factor that is of great importance in the struggle for control. This factor is people's own *perceptions* of the degree of control that they themselves have in determining the quality of their lives.

People differ markedly in their feelings about their capacity to control life situations. Some people feel that they are in control of their own destinies: What happens to them and what they achieve in life, they believe, are the result of their own abilities, attitudes, and actions. In contrast, other people see their lives as being beyond their control: What happens to them is up to external forces. These two types of people are said to have either an *internal* or an *external* locus of control (Rotter, 1966; Rotter, Chance, & Phares, 1972). **Locus of control** refers to a generalized expectancy that your outcomes in life (for example, whether you do well in school, or succeed in romance) are either within your control (*internal*) or controlled by forces outside yourself,

---

The Internal–External Locus of Control Scale

These are some items from the I–E Scale. For each one, choose between a and b.

1. a. Many of the unhappy things in people's lives are largely due to luck.
    b. People's misfortunes result from the mistakes they make.

2. a. One of the major reasons why we have wars is that people don't take enough interest in politics.
    b. There will always be wars, no matter how hard people try to prevent them.

3. a. In the case of the well-prepared student, there is rarely if ever such a thing as an unfair test.
    b. Many times exam questions tend to be so unrelated to course work that studying is really useless.

4. a. No matter how hard you try, some people just don't like you.
    b. People who can't get others to like them don't understand how to get along with others.

5. a. When I make plans, I am almost certain that I can make them work.
    b. It is not always wise to plan too far ahead because many things turn out to be a matter of good or bad fortune anyhow.

Source: J. B. Rotter (1966). Generalized expectancies for internal versus external control of reinforcement. *Psychological Monographs, 80* (whole No. 609). Copyright © 1966 by the American Psychological Association. Adapted with permission.

---

such as fate, luck, or powerful others (*external*). A reliable psychological test measuring whether individuals have an internal or external locus of control has been devised, and some of its items are shown in the box above.

Note that locus of control refers to the person's *perception* of control rather than actual control. Although perceived control and actual control are of course related (a person whose family has lived for generations in poverty may well have a more external locus of control about his or her economic future than one whose family has not), they are not the same. For example, it has been found that women who are depressed tend to believe that their efforts to be friendly and sociable with others are not working even when they are. When asked to rate how the *other* person in an interaction views them, they will report that the other person did not like the conversation even when the other person in fact enjoyed it (Seigel & Alloy, 1990).

Why do psychologists care about perceived locus of control and about control in general? Is this really an important factor in our life and adjustment? The answer is yes: People who can, and who believe they can, control events in their environment will respond to stress, success, and failure differently than those who believe the opposite (Rotter, Chance, & Phares, 1972). When people perceive that they have control over outcomes, they try harder, persist longer in the face of failure, and thus are more likely to be successful. This success in turn feeds back into their perceptions of internal control. When people perceive that they have no effective control over events, especially when outcomes are negative, they become cynical and show helplessness in their behaviors.

In Kurt Cobain's life, suicide was a final desperate act. By all accounts he had felt as though he were on a speeding train that he couldn't stop or get off. We can find plenty of places in his history where the train "picked up speed"—his parents' divorce and his initial drug use, for example. Where might he have gotten off that train? That is, how do problems develop in the area of self-control, and how can they be stopped before they result in desperate acts? In order to answer these questions, we will examine each area in detail.

SELF-CONTROL IN EVERYDAY LIVING

Once we start thinking about the arenas in life in which control is an issue, it seems to pop up everywhere. Many Americans, for example, try to control their eating and their weight, generally in order to lose weight. Some, typically adolescent girls and women, become excessively controlled and restrictive about their eating and develop trouble controlling their weight *loss*. Others have trouble regulating what they eat at all and see-saw from binges, in which they consume massive amounts of food, to purges, in which they attempt to undo the binge by vomiting and using high doses of laxatives. Drinking as well as eating can be an arena in which people lose control. From 10 to 15 million U.S. citizens have trouble controlling the amount of alcohol they consume, to such an extent that even when drinking begins to have negative social and physical consequences, they feel unable to stop. Other drugs, such as cocaine, stimulants, and sleeping pills, can also lead to loss of control, even though, paradoxically, people take them to try to *gain* control over their moods, their ability to stay awake and work, or their ability to fall asleep on schedule.

Like dieting, drugs are used to try to ensure certain outcomes (such as happiness or sleepiness) that are deemed desirable. Unfortunately, they often result in both short- and long-term negative consequences. It is not only with the self that control sometimes presents difficulties. People also struggle for control in relationships and sometimes that struggle for control—to exert control over

others or to maintain control in one's own behaviors—goes awry. Relationship violence, for example, is fraught with issues of control and restraint or the lack thereof. In this chapter, we examine several different arenas in which the usual means of control and the strategies that people use for adjusting to life's pressures begin to slip away.

EATING DISORDERS

In our society, weight, body shape, and even the act of eating have social and psychological as well as nutritional aspects. In an effort to control eating, some people lose control over it and develop an eating disorder. We will discuss the two major eating disorders: anorexia nervosa, and bulimia.

Anorexia Nervosa

Symptoms and Dynamics. "Connie" is an attractive 5-foot 9-inch woman with a medium body frame who weighs only 115 pounds and looks very thin. Connie is often asked—sometimes directly and sometimes indirectly—if she is anorexic. Because there has been so much publicity in recent years about eating disorders, many people are alert to this possibility and make assumptions about people they know.

In this case, however, the assumption is hasty. Why? There are four criteria for diagnosing anorexia. One of them is weight, or more specifically, *"refusal* to maintain body weight, leading to a weight that is 15 percent or more below normal" (American Psychiatric Association, 1994) (Note: Leading fashion models have body weights that are 20 to 25 percent below normal!). The others are an exaggerated fear of putting on weight, despite the fact that one is already underweight, distortions in the way in which one's body weight, size, or shape is perceived, (for example, a person who looks emaciated sees herself as fat), and an unexpected cessation of menstruation for three or more cycles. These criteria make it clear that anorexia is more than just being skinny. The weight is lost deliberately and with a great deal of struggle for control. Punitively denying oneself food when hungry, hoarding or being secretive about food, or forcing oneself into excessive exercise routines are some of the more common symptoms. Moreover, the anorexic person experiences a great deal of inner struggle and turmoil and typically has a harsh, punitive attitude toward herself (Strauss & Ryan, 1987). This painful disorder will affect between 1 and 4 percent of all U.S. women (American Psychiatric Association, 1994) and is most prevalent among female teenagers and college students. Anorexia in men is rare.

The prevalence of anorexia seems to be rising. It is primarily found in the United States, Canada, Europe, and other industrialized countries, and as described in Chapter 7, can be considered a *culture-bound* disorder. Interestingly, as countries become more developed and industrialized, the incidence of anorexia in those countries rises. Anorexia, finally, is a serious disorder not only because of the psychological and social disruption that it brings but also because it can be fatal. Estimates of death from anorexia and related physical complications range from 5 to 18 percent of all diagnosed cases. Christy Heinrich, a U.S. Olympic gymnast, died suddenly in 1994 from a heart attack, one of the more common causes of death in anorexic patients.

Theories about Causes.   How does this disorder develop, and what are its causes? Once it starts, what maintains it? There is no single answer, but there are some clues provided by clinical researchers. Typically, the anorexic girl was slightly overweight as a child and went on a diet "just to lose a little weight," often with the encouragement of her parents. She is also often a "model" child: obedient to her parents, doing very well in school, active in extracurricular activities. In short, she is the opposite of a "troublemaker" in the family.

Expert family therapists (Minuchin, Rosman, & Baker, 1978; Sargent, Liebman, & Silver, 1985; Levine, 1996) have noticed that in the families of anorexic girls, there is an emphasis on order, control, and cohesion. Overt conflict is frowned upon, and extreme closeness, even to the point of enmeshment, is expected. When the daughter in such a family reaches adolescence, the normal drives toward autonomy and rebellion are squelched. The only way in which the daughter feels that she can take control but still be a "good" daughter within this family system is by controlling what she eats. So her body becomes the arena in which the normal adolescent striving for control and self-determination takes place. It is important to note that these generalizations were made by clinicians, based on observations of the families they treated in their clinics. Not every family with an anorexic member will fit this description. In fact, some theories argue that wider forces, such as culture, also play a role in the development of this disorder.

These theories (e.g., Orbach, 1986) also emphasize the role of sexuality and the confining social roles for women in our society. They suggest that although it is normal and even desirable (in terms of reproductive fitness) for body fat to increase in adolescence, some girls feel panicked by this occurrence. The messages in advertising and fashion encourage young girls to have unrealistic expectations about their appearance and to be judgmental about themselves when they don't meet these expectations. Moreover, these theories point out that in many ways, both subtle and explicit, our society equates "thin" with "beautiful, successful, capable, and in control." Thus the young girl may fear a more general loss of control connected with her developing body and may have also sensed that developing into a woman carries with it certain demands and restrictions in our society. These theories suggest that anorexia is a strategy, used consciously or unconsciously, by certain intelligent, ambitious, and frustrated young women to fight the restrictions of society, a dangerous form of self-control. This is a compelling argument, and many anecdotes from young girls themselves can be offered as evidence that weight and body shape are bound up with intense psychological meaning. It does not, however, explain why only some women in our society become anorexic. Other factors (such as family dynamics and individual psychological dynamics) also need to be considered.

Bulimia

Symptoms and Dynamics.   **Bulimia** is an extreme form of weight control that involves binging on large amounts of food, followed by purging via self-induced vomiting, laxative consumption, or vigorous exercise. The purging is an attempt to get rid of food and the accompanying calories. (Incidentally, it is not effective, for most calories are absorbed very quickly.) Many people occasionally overeat, feel guilty, and then skip the next meal or exercise in an attempt to "correct" the overeating. Bulimia is different. The bulimic binge is more than just overeating or having a couple of extra desserts. It typically includes about 3,000 calories worth of foods high in carbohydrates and fats, consumed in one sitting. Moreover, people with full-blown bulimia engage in this behavior recurrently; according to the diagnostic criteria (American Psychiatric Association, 1994), one must have at least two episodes per week of binging and purging for at least three months in order to be diagnosed. As with anorexia, bulimic behavior is accompanied by a great deal of distress and psychological suffering. Bulimia involves a feeling of lack of control over the binging. "Once it starts, it can't be stopped," people report, and they dash from the grocery store back to home, through the food preparation and the eating of all of it, feeling unable to stop until the episode is over. Lack of control also is a precipitating factor for the binge episode itself. In one study (Mitchell, Mitsukami, Eckert, & Pyle, 1985) bulimic patients reported that feeling tense and anxious,

feeling a lack of control over appetite, and even insomnia brought on their binges.

Also like anorexics, bulimics are perpetually concerned—even obsessed—with their body shape and weight. People who suffer from bulimia dwell on their disorder, on their eating, and on their powerlessness. They may become socially isolated because of their behavior and the shame and embarrassment that accompanies it. Depression occurs commonly along with bulimia, and the person may even meet the clinical criteria for a diagnosis of depression. In addition to the psychological disturbance, there are physical disturbances as well. Though their weight is close to normal, bulimics are not healthy. For example, repetitive vomiting causes an imbalance in body chemicals, serious tooth decay, and other physical problems.

Theories about Causes.   Theories about what causes bulimia are somewhat less developed than those about anorexia because research on this disorder is more recent. Bulimics tend to have lower than normal levels of serotonin, a chemical in the brain that has also been linked to depression. The body needs tryptophan (an amino acid) in order to make serotonin, and carbohydrates supply that tryptophan. So perhaps the binging has a biological basis—namely, the body is responding to a low mood state by an increase in carbohydrate consumption. The problem is that the person is then alarmed by the amount of eating she has done and subsequently engages in purging. This purging deprives the body of carbohydrates, creating a craving for serotonin and setting the person up to binge and repeat the cycle (Pirke, 1995).

Other theorists point to the social factors involved in binging. One study (Crandall, 1988) showed how subcultures can have a powerful effect on eating behavior. Crandall measured popularity and binge eating habits in two groups of sorority women. In each sorority, clear standards were found for what was considered a "good" level of binging. In

Taking Control: From "Patients" to Community Activists and Consultants

A psychotherapist in Vancouver, British Columbia (Canada) got a call one day from a woman who lived in a remote area 600 miles north of Vancouver. She had been anorexic for 12 years and there were no mental health services anywhere near her. The therapist felt at a loss about what to do. He described the dilemma to the women in his eating disorders therapy group, and they decided to write to her. Their letters contained descriptions of their own struggles and strategies on how to cope as well as support. She found these letters incredibly helpful, and the group members found themselves feeling empowered by helping her. From this, they formed a grassroots organization, the Vancouver Anti-anorexia/Anti-bulimia League. It now has over 300 members. The league has helped create a forum for advocacy, public education, and community-based healing. For example, they point out public advertising in stores and magazines that promotes waiflike images of women's bodies, they provide education programs for primary and secondary school children, and recovered anorexics visit those who are confined to the hospital to show them that freedom is possible. In doing so, they have reclaimed their own lives and taken back a sense of control, transforming themselves from passive patients to community activists and consultants (Madigan, 1994).

one sorority, the more a woman binged, the more popular she was; in the other, the most popular women were those who binged an "average" amount. By the end of the school year, a sorority member's binge eating was significantly correlated with that of her friends: The more they binged, the more she did; the less they binged, the less she did. As the friendship groups became more cohesive, this correlation increased even more.

Even casual observations in college dining halls reveal that people are not fully comfortable or accepting of their own and others' eating behaviors. Frequent trips to the dessert counter get commented on, some individuals with "too little" on their plates are urged to eat more, while others wait until someone else gets up for seconds before they are comfortable doing so. Other studies have found that it is women who worry the most about these matters and that judgments of "femininity" and social appeal are related to women's eating lightly (Mori, Pliner, & Chaiken, 1987; Basow & Kobrynowicz, 1993).

Surely it would be beneficial for those with clinically diagnosed eating disorders and even those who might be headed in that direction if our society tolerated a wider range of eating habits and body shapes and sizes. In addition to changes in the attitudes of those around them, people who are diagnosed also need professional help for themselves. Antidepressant medications (particularly for bulimics), family therapy (particularly for anorexics), cognitive therapy, and other forms of supportive and insight-oriented psychotherapies (Fairburn, Jones, Peveler, Hope, & O'Connor, 1993) have been shown to be effective in treating eating disorders. Finally, group therapy and self-help groups, in which people with eating disorders help each other are becoming increasingly popular, especially on college campuses. The "Lessons from Life" box describes a unique application of this idea.

SUBSTANCE ABUSE AND DEPENDENCE

Loss of control is sometimes a problem not only with eating but also with drinking. In this section we will take a look at alcoholism and other drug abuse. Note the phrase "alcoholism and *other* drug abuse," which reflects the current thinking among experts that alcohol *is*

1. What are the four criteria for diagnosing anorexia nervosa?

2. People who are bulimic also often have symptoms of, or even meet the diagnostic criteria for, another disorder. What is that disorder?

3. What did the study of friendships and eating habits in two college sororities illustrate?

---

a drug. In fact, in the current classification system for mental disorders, the DSM–IV (see Chapter 7), alcohol and other drugs are listed together in the sections "Substance Abuse" and "Substance Dependence." True, alcohol is more widely used, more readily available, and more socially acceptable than other drugs. Just think of all the advertising of alcohol, references to it in literature and history, and the wide use of it at business, government, and other official functions. Moreover, and importantly, alcohol can be legally obtained by adults. However, physically and psychologically, alcohol is similar to other drugs in the manner in which people become dependent on it and in the difficulties they have in breaking that dependence.

Drug dependence refers to an inability to stop using the substance even when it is having harmful social, psychological, or physical effects. Dependence can be both psychological and physiological. In psychological dependence, one has a compulsive need to take the drug and cannot resist it. In physiological dependence, the body itself is also dependent on the drug. This means that the person needs more and more of it to achieve the same effects—that is, he or she is said to develop **tolerance.**

A person who is physiologically dependent on a drug also will experience **withdrawal** when he or she stops taking the drug. Withdrawal symptoms are unpleasant body sensations such as irritability, anxiety, nausea, and extreme shakiness. Different drugs cause different withdrawal symptoms, from mild to severe.

Alcoholism

As everyone knows, when people lose control of their drinking, either in one episode (a binge) or over time (alcohol dependence) serious problems can result for them and for those around them. One salient problem area is drunk driving. We have recently seen strategies for prevention such as stricter legal punishments for both first offenses and repeat offenders and citizen's action groups such as Mothers Against Drunk Driving (MADD). A recent law passed in Massachusetts makes it illegal for people under 21 to drive if they have been drinking any alcohol at all. The general public, however, is probably less aware of some of the other consequences, both to themselves and others, of drinking that is out of control. In this section we will examine some of those consequences and some of the ways in which alcoholism can be treated.

Effects of Alcoholism. Alcoholism, and its consequences can perhaps best be compared to an octopus. Alcoholism is a disorder of many tentacles, stretching to affect all areas of one's life, including accidents and physical health, reproduction, antisocial behavior, work, love and relationships, and family life. Once alcohol grabs hold of a person—that is, once the drinking becomes a chronic problem—it is very

Measuring Alcohol Dependence

Is alcohol a problem for you? Being as honest as possible, decide how many of the following questions would you answer *yes.*

1. Have you ever awakened in the morning after some drinking and found that you could not remember part of the evening?

2. Does your husband, wife, a parent, or other near relative ever worry or complain about your drinking?

3. Do you ever feel guilty about your drinking?

4. Have you ever been arrested for drunk driving, driving while intoxicated or under the influence of alcoholic beverages? (If yes, how many times?) (2 points each)

5. Have you ever been arrested or taken into custody, even for a few hours, because of other drunk behavior? (If yes, how many times?) (2 points each)

6. Have you ever been told you have liver trouble? Cirrhosis?

7. Have you ever gotten into trouble at work or school because of your drinking?

8. Have you ever neglected your obligations, your family, or your work for two or more days because you were drinking?

These questions are from the *Michigan Alcoholism Screening Test* (Selzer, 1971), a 24-item scale that counselors and other health professionals use. Notice that drinking and driving and other arrests are weighted more heavily; they are highly indicative of a problem. Note also that social and psychological symptoms, not only physical ones, are included in this screening test. This emphasis is consistent with the current definition of drug dependence. If you answered *yes* to any of these questions, you may wish to think more about whether alcohol is a problem for you.

---

hard to get out of its grip. A few facts from the National Institutes on Alcohol and Addictions illustrate this point. For example, alcohol is responsible for 40 to 50 percent of traffic fatalities and up to 64 percent of all fires and burns (NIAAA, 1989). Alcoholism can result in liver damage and eventually in the inability of the liver to repair itself and to rid the body of the ethanol that is in alcoholic drinks. When the liver is damaged, the alcohol goes straight to other body organs, such as the stomach and the brain. This causes conditions such as bleeding ulcers and a type of dementia known as Korsakoff's syndrome. Alcohol abuse and addiction have also been found to be a factor in infertility, sexual dysfunction, and increased risk of miscarriage (NIAAA, 1990). We now know that pregnant women's drinking—even episodic binges—affects the brain of the developing fetus. This may cause the child to be hyperactive and have lowered impulse control, an inability to learn, serious memory problems, and deficits in reasoning ability. There may also be characteristic deformities of the head and face. These symptoms form a syndrome called **fetal alcohol syndrome** (FAS) or in milder cases **fetal alcohol effect** (FAE).

The late Michael Dorris (1989) wrote movingly in *The Broken Cord* about his adopted son Adam who had FAS. Dorris adopted Adam, a 3-year-old Native American boy from South Dakota, in 1971, at a time when fetal alcohol syndrome had not yet been identified. All Dorris knew was that Adam's biological mother had died of alcohol poisoning and that Adam was small for his age and developmentally delayed. At 3, he was not yet toilet trained, spoke only a few words, and had been designated as mentally retarded. Dorris learned, largely on his own, that despite Adam's affectionate and kindhearted personality, he was seriously impaired in his ability to learn, either in school or from experience. The physical and psychological struggles that Adam and his family encountered are a testimony to the devastating effects of alcohol on the developing brain.

Furthermore, approximately half of all homicides involve alcohol. Autopsies show that 20 percent of suicides are completed by people who are legally drunk, and many more by people who have been drinking but are not legally drunk. In college, as well as other settings, there is a strong correlation between alcohol abuse, physical aggression, discipline problems, and property damage. Finally, throughout history as well as currently, there is a well-known relationship between alcohol abuse and rape, incest, and battering.

Alcohol and the Family.   The effects of alcohol abuse and dependence on relationships and family life are substantial. In Chapter 12 we discuss how families are not just collections of people but rather systems in which the behaviors of each member have interlocking, reverberating effects on every other member. Sometimes when one person in the family is a chronic alcoholic, the family reorganizes and adjusts in certain characteristic ways to accommodate that problem.

People who have grown up in such families describe certain common experiences. One is a kind of collective silence and denial of the problem. People pretend not to notice, don't label it or even talk about it, and cover up for the alcoholic person. One recalled a family gathering in which the father literally passed out with his head on his plate of spaghetti. Everyone pretended not to notice; finally, a 10-year-old, afraid that his father would suffocate, lifted his head out of the plate (Collet, 1990). Spouses and children may, each in their own way, try to "make things better."

Some children think that by not making any demands of their own they can keep the peace, so they try desperately to please the parent(s) by trying to be especially well behaved, making good grades in school, and asking little for themselves. Others take on a parental role, watching over the alcoholic parent, taking on household responsibilities that are typically done by the adults, or trying to be "perfect" children in terms of their own achievements. In a sense, these are ways that family members struggle to maintain order, control, and some semblance of normal life in the home. Other family members may give up and follow the alcoholic person into substance abuse. Substance abuse was something that Courtney Love and Kurt Cobain shared and struggled with together. Children of alcoholics have a substantially increased risk of becoming alcoholics themselves. For boys the risk is four times higher and for girls, three times higher, than in the general population (National Institutes on Alcohol and Addictions, 1992).

Treatment of Alcoholism.   Given that alcoholism is such a widespread problem in our society and that it affects so many people other than the alcoholic, getting the drinking under control is imperative. What are the ways in which problem drinking can be treated, and how does that process begin? Every person who has struggled with this problem and every alcohol counselor will agree that the first step is to recognize and admit that there is a problem. Denial of drinking problems, as we discussed earlier, runs deep.

People have many different ways of rationalizing their behavior and convincing themselves that they do not have a problem. Some say, "Well, I never missed a day of work, so I'm not an alcoholic," "I never drink before noon," "I only drink wine," or "I've never had withdrawal symptoms." The fact is that dependence on alcohol is not diagnosed by any single factor such as these but by an inability to stop drinking, even when there are negative social, vocational, physical, or legal consequences. The Michigan Alcohol Screening Test is one instrument (featured in the Self-Assessment Exercise) that counselors and other health professionals can use to screen people for possible alcohol problems.

In addition, here is one quick test that you can take yourself. Pick a date (in the near future) on which you promise yourself that you will cease from any drinking for 3 weeks. Consider how difficult it is for you to even pick a date; are you making excuses about why you couldn't or shouldn't do it on that date? Are you thinking about pushing the date off into the future? Would you have any qualms about telling a friend, so that he or she could be your "witness"? Then go ahead and do the experiment—that is, quit drinking for those three weeks. Ask yourself the following questions: Were you able to do it? How hard or easy was it? Were you tempted to drink, or did you find that you were miserable during that time? And finally, are you being honest with yourself as you assess the results of this little experiment?

People who are heavily dependent on alcohol may have a very hard time being honest with themselves and others about the extent of their problem; alcohol counselors call this "being in denial." As a result, alcoholics are unwilling to seek treatment or to take it seriously if coerced into it. One means of trying to break through this denial is called *intervention*. Intervention is a strategy used after other means of trying to get through to the alcoholic have failed. Concerned family members and friends work with a trained counselor to think about and articulate the ways in which the problem drinking has affected their lives and their concern and caring for their alcoholic family member. When they are all ready, they come together in a group. Sometimes the problem drinker will respond to an invitation to be present; in other cases, the group convenes anyway and confronts the person, who may be unsuspecting. In turn, each gives a prepared, often graphic and detailed statements about the ways in which he or she has been hurt by the person's drinking, the ways in which the alcoholic is perceived as hurting himself or herself, and his or her love and concern for the person.

In the spring of 1994, Courtney Love and 10 friends, including two band members, met to plan such an intervention. They then gathered at Kurt's home to confront him about his drug abuse. Courtney said that she would leave him, and the band said they would break up, unless he entered a drug rehabilitation center (Straus, 1994).

As a part of the intervention, treatment options have been prearranged. It is hoped that this intervention will get through to the person and result in his or her agreement to go immediately to an alcohol treatment facility or to follow some other treatment plan. Cobain did agree to enter a drug treatment center but left there after a short time by climbing over a 6-foot brick wall. He was missing from then until his suicide was discovered. A minority of people on whom an intervention is done still can't accept the reality of their drinking problem, get mad, and walk away from the group. Like Cobain, some who do agree to go to treatment do not follow through with it. However, a larger percentage agree to treatment of one kind or another, and in some cases that response is the beginning of the road to a lifetime of abstinence.

For people who are physically dependent on alcohol, inpatient detoxification programs are also a necessary step in recovery. This is because there are serious physical withdrawal symptoms, such as **delirium tremens (DTs)**. This involves profuse sweating, shaking, and nausea. Disorganized thinking, incoherent speech, and vivid hallucinations (for example, of frightening voices or insects crawling under the skin) are also a component of DTs, and medical treatment is needed. After detoxification, an inpatient treatment program will provide intensive education, support, and counseling, individually and in groups, about alcoholism and recovery. Recovery, however, is a long road, and the bulk of it is done while one is living out in the world and carrying on with everyday life.

Fortunately there are programs to help people who struggle to control their drinking. The most widely used form of outpatient treatment has been the self-help group known as **Alcoholics Anonymous (AA)**. AA was founded in Akron, Ohio, in 1935 by two men who had recovered from problem drinking through spiritual and social support. AA emphasizes social support through group meetings. In many communities, AA meetings can be found every night of the week and provide a place for people to go instead of drinking. In addition to social support, AA works through a 12-step program, which encourages people to acknowledge their lack of control, to seek help from a higher spiritual power, and to begin to make amends with themselves and others for their drinking. The alcoholic works up through the 12 steps, with the goal being total abstinence from drinking. This is a difficult goal to achieve; 90 percent of recovering alcoholics will have at least one relapse. However, recovery is possible, and AA has been effective for many people who stay in it.

In addition to AA, there is a newer self-help group, Rational Recovery, which is based on the premise that people do not have to yield control to a higher power and can control their drinking through careful analysis and challenging of their own thinking patterns associated with stress and drinking. In the later stages of recovery, and after the person has achieved stable sobriety, individual or family counseling can be helpful. As the person attempts to put the pieces of his or her life back together, everyone in the family must adjust to the changes in the family that result from the sobriety. Experienced counselors can help people understand this process and anticipate and cope with its challenges. Self-help groups such as Al-Anon (for family members of alcoholics) and ACOA (for adult children of alcoholics) also address family members' concerns and problems. In sum, there is effective help available for alcoholics, and that help can literally and figuratively save their lives and the lives of those around them.

Other Drugs

Marijuana. Other than alcohol, the drug most commonly used in the United States today (especially by young people) is marijuana. It is the most commonly used illicit drug, and over 5.5 million people report that they smoke it at least weekly (National Institute on Drug Abuse, 1991). Possession of marijuana is illegal, although great controversy surrounds its uses and its status as a controlled substance. In some states, marijuana or its main ingredient, THC, can be prescribed by doctors as an antinausea medication for people undergoing chemotherapy and as a means for treating glaucoma. It is a *psychoactive* drug; that is, it affects the central nervous system. Specifically, it affects sleep and impairs short-term memory, concentration, and motor coordination. Marijuana typically acts as a relaxant; at low doses it induces mild euphoria, silliness, or "placid dreaminess" (McKim, 1991, p. 283). Marijuana's effects depend in part on the user's personality and mood and may exaggerate these (Inaba & Cohen, 1990). At high doses, especially in threatening situations, it may cause feelings of anxiety, foreboding, or mild paranoia.

There is much confusion about the effects of marijuana. This is partly the result of the fact that the THC content of the marijuana sold today is much higher than it was in the 1960s. Then the concentration of THC was 1 to 3 percent; now, it is 8 to 14 percent. Experts today are also more cautious about marijuana's potential ill effects on the body. Research has associated smoking marijuana with an increased risk of lung cancer (one joint or marijuana cigarette has the same amount of tar and other toxic chemicals as 14 to 16 cigarettes), and suppression of immune system functioning (Inaba & Cohen, 1990).

Some heavy users, particularly adolescents, can become psychologically dependent on marijuana and lose their motivation for work, school, and interpersonal relationships. This is called **amotivational syndrome.** Unlike the marijuana of the 1960s, today's marijuana can be physically addicting in that some chronic users report tolerance and withdrawal symptoms associated with its use. The withdrawal symptoms can include headaches, depression, anxiety, sleep problems, craving for the drug, and irritability (Inaba & Cohen, 1990). There is a controversy about whether using marijuana leads to use of harder drugs, such as heroin. Most users of heroin started with marijuana and continue to take it after they begin using other substances. On the other hand, many marijuana smokers never move on to other drugs. Experts suggest that it is not a stepping stone in the physical sense, in that the user needs stronger and stronger drugs to get high. They suggest rather that other aspects of heavy marijuana use—the access to drugs, the opportunity, the friends, and the motivation—may be factors in trying and using other drugs. Recent research suggests that adult marijuana users who are psychologically dependent and wish to decrease

their use can be helped through psychotherapeutic group treatments (Stephens, Roffman, & Simpson, 1994).

Cocaine.   Cocaine, which is extracted from the leaves of the coca plant, has long been used as an anesthetic, stimulant, and a mood enhancer. Sigmund Freud was himself addicted to cocaine, which he used first to combat his depression and later to treat the pain associated with cancer of the jaw. Until 1906 cocaine was used in Coca-Cola and accounted for some of its "uplifting" effects (the only drug left in Coca-Cola now is caffeine, which also has stimulant properties).

Indeed, the cocaine high includes extreme, if fleeting, feelings of arousal and energy, euphoria and well-being, confidence, enhanced sexual experiences, and heightened sensory perception, especially vision. This is a seductive set of experiences for some people, who overlook the negative effects of cocaine. These include overdose, which results in chills, nausea, insomnia, blurred vision, paranoia, and sometimes visual or kinesthetic hallucinations, such as the sensation of bugs crawling under the skin. Death from heart attack is another possible result of an overdose. In addition, after the initial rush, which lasts up to 30 minutes, the down or crash sets in; this includes irritability, nervousness, suspiciousness, lowered mood, and inability to concentrate.

What is the response of addicts to these unpleasant feelings? They take more cocaine because they have learned that the drug removes these symptoms. They become psychologically and, as was recently learned (Davison & Neale, 1994), physically addicted. Cocaine users can become extremely compulsive about the drug, and getting the money to obtain it, to feed this craving, can cost people all of their money, their jobs, and their families. As with any drug addiction, illegal activities and prostitution are the means used by desperate people to obtain money to feed the habit. AIDS is a major problem associated with cocaine addiction through sharing needles, prostitution, or promiscuous and careless sex.

Cocaine was originally "snorted," or sniffed, or injected. In the mid-1980s, a purer form of cocaine, called crack, came out on the streets. Chunks or "rocks" are heated in freebasing pipes, and the vapors are inhaled. It can also be smoked. Taken this way—that is, directly into the lungs—crack reaches the brain much faster (in less than 8 seconds) than when it is injected (which takes up to 30 seconds). Thus it is an almost immediate high (Inaba & Cohen, 1990). Crack cocaine comes in smaller doses and is cheaper than regular cocaine. A whole new segment of the population—namely, poorer people and younger people—began using the drug in larger numbers. More women than before, including pregnant women, use the drug, with serious damage to their babies. All of these factors make cocaine a major social problem as well as a problem for the individuals who are addicted.

Heroin. **Heroin** is an opiate, or narcotic, that is made from the poppy plant. It depresses, or slows down, the functioning of the brain. It provides relief from pain and negative feelings (for example, depression, worry) by sedating the central nervous system. Calming and pleasurable sensations occur because heroin operates on the same receptors in the brain that are sensitive to *endorphins,* the body's natural opiates, or natural painkillers. It is probably no accident, therefore, that Kurt Cobain was particularly dependent on heroin. Other opiate drugs that can be obtained by prescription (codeine, Darvocet, and Percodan) are also sometimes abused.

Heroin produces physiological dependence and leads to serious withdrawal symptoms. Heroin withdrawal symptoms are painful and frightening: anxiety, profuse sweating, rapid breathing, fever, severe aches and cramps, vomiting, and dehydration. Heroin users also develop tolerance to the drug and thus need stronger and stronger doses to get the psychological effects or even to maintain normal bodily functioning. Like cocaine addicts, people who must maintain their heroin addiction often completely disregard the requirements of living and end up mistreating family members and participating in crime to finance their expensive habit. Many people who try to withdraw on their own wind up taking the drug in order to relieve their suffering from the withdrawal. As a result, it is a particularly difficult addiction to cure. Some drug treatment centers try to wean people away from heroin by giving them methadone, a synthetic opiate. Methadone is given daily to block the heroin withdrawal symptoms while counselors work with the person to stop using drugs altogether. As for other drug addictions, counseling for heroin addiction seeks not only to end the substance abuse but also to help the person develop the inner controls, strength, and self-reliance to function without it.

Recently (Leland, 1996), heroin use has increased dramatically in the United States. Disturbing statistics indicate that its use among eighth graders has nearly doubled since 1991; 2.3 percent now report that they have used it. Some experts fear a new wave of heroin addicts is coming and note that the health-care system is not prepared to handle it.

Amphetamines, Barbiturates, and Tranquilizers. Other abused drugs that affect the mood, mind, and body include amphetamines, barbiturates, and tranquilizers. **Amphetamines** (called uppers) are often used as "pep pills" by people to stay awake and are used by entertainers to cope with exhausting schedules and to enhance their performances. Common varieties of amphetamines include Benzedrine, Methedrine (known as speed), and Dexedrine. These drugs cause psychological but not physical dependence, and they can produce uncontrolled and violent behavior if they are used in excess. *Amphetamine psychosis* is the name given to a condition with symptoms similar to schizophrenia, including hallucinations and thought disorder. Amphetamines produce tolerance and can be lethal.

A relatively new form of amphetamine that is a particular problem among young people is methamphetamine hydrochloride, known as crystal meth or ice. Methamphetamine produces feelings of well-being and energy, and people sometimes use it to stay up for several nights in a row for work, study, or social purposes. They can easily become dependent on it, and withdrawal is very difficult. Because methamphetamine is a synthetic drug (that is, it can be made completely in the laboratory out of ingredients that can be legally obtained), it is a particularly difficult one to control (Inaba & Cohen, 1990).

Barbiturates (called *downers*) are frequently prescribed as sleeping pills. In the 1950s and 1960s they were commonly prescribed to control anxiety but have been replaced by "safer" drugs such as Valium. Common varieties of prescription barbiturates include Nembutal, Seconal, and Amytal, also sold on the street with various nicknames that reflect the color of the capsules: yellow jackets, reds or red devils, and blues, respectively (McKim, 1991).

Barbiturates produce a number of effects, depending on the dose (McKim, 1991). Blood pressure drops, and breathing slows; higher doses may result in sedation of many bodily functions and loss of consciousness. Psychologically, they produce effects similar to alcohol when taken in low doses. At higher doses, the user exhibits slurred speech, loss of emotional control, lack of coordination, and sometimes aggressive behavior. Addicts neglect their appearance, lose their ability to think clearly, and are preoccupied with obtaining

the drug. Barbiturates stay in the body for a long time and can cause both physical and psychological withdrawal symptoms, even at low doses, if taken over a long time. Going "cold turkey"—that is, stopping them suddenly—can be fatal. The actress Marilyn Monroe had serious difficulties with Nembutal, taking higher and higher doses and showing many of the common symptoms of barbiturate abuse. These include irritability, reduced effectiveness, and depression. The severe depression caused by barbiturates—and other drugs—became her most serious problem in later years. An overdose can be lethal, and one eventually killed her.

In clinical practice barbiturates have been virtually replaced by a newer group of anti-anxiety drugs, such as Valium, Librium, and Xanax. These are very commonly prescribed medications and, when used correctly and carefully, can help people with various kinds of anxiety disorders. Problems can arise when people begin to overmedicate themselves with these drugs and become psychologically and physically addicted. Withdrawal from Xanax, for example, can be quite difficult and require hospitalization, and withdrawal from Valium is more likely to result in death than is Valium overdose (Inaha & Cohen, 1990). Thus, while they are milder than the traditional barbiturates, they are still very powerful drugs.

The deaths of well-known personalities at early ages—besides Kurt Cobain, figures such as Len Bias, Marilyn Monroe, Elvis Presley, John Belushi, Jimi Hendrix, and Jerry Garcia—illustrate the fact that powerful drugs used in excess are dangerous and that drug dependence is itself a severe threat to the control of one's life.

Why, then, do people abuse drugs in the first place? For Kurt Cobain it was a combination of factors. Cobain himself said (Gold, 1994) that they calmed his stomach pain. Others have asserted that he was clinically depressed, noting that this illness ran in his family and that two of his uncles commited suicide. Drugs (both prescription and illegal drugs) can be a means of escaping or avoiding negative mood states, and that may have been true for Cobain. His family history probably did not provide him with a solid, secure sense of self. Others describe him as insecure and very sensitive, almost vulnerable. His suicide note revealed in part that despite his success he felt like a fake and felt guilty that the "manic roar of the crowd doesn't affect me . . . . Sometimes I feel as if I should have a punch-in time clock before I walk out onstage" (Arnold, 1994, p. 36). And finally, culture and surroundings are a factor in drug use and abuse. Which drugs people use and how they use them (that is, smoking, injecting, and so on) are determined by their availability and the habits of friends and associates. Courtney Love had also been addicted to cocaine, and the entertainment business no doubt shows greater tolerance of drug use and availability than other subcultures do. In fact, there has recently been some public concern and attention by the music industry (*Newsweek*, 1996) about drug addiction. Interestingly, the work hours kept by doctors and nurses and the easy availability of drugs also make them a higher risk group for drug abuse.

Legal Drugs: Caffeine and Nicotine. Some legal drugs also have powerful effects on the central nervous system and therefore on mood and behavior. The two most common are caffeine and nicotine. What exactly do they do to the body and brain? In small doses, caffeine aids in alertness and concentration. High doses or excessive use can result in excitement, insomnia, nervousness, jitteriness, flushed face, gastrointestinal upset, and cardiac arrhythmia. These symptoms can be disturbing, but they pass quickly. However, it is important for people with anxiety disorders, such as a history of panic attacks, to be aware of these effects of caffeine. Caffeine can cause

tolerance and withdrawal although these symptoms are mild compared to those produced by most psychoactive drugs.

Nicotine is a highly addictive substance, as anyone who has tried to break a smoking habit can attest. Nicotine makes people feel more relaxed and calm even though it is a stimulant. Tolerance develops quickly, and withdrawal from the nicotine causes headache, increased appetite, weight gain, and depressed mood. The most obvious effect of withdrawal, however, is anxiety and the craving for a cigarette. People who are denied a cigarette at the time they usually have one experience this intense craving and rush to leave the "no smoking" restaurant or movie theatre so they can have a cigarette. It is now clear that both physical treatments (such as nicotine gum or nicotine patches, which supply a low dose of the drug during withdrawal) and psychological/behavioral treatments are needed to help people overcome this addiction. One book notes succinctly that "tobacco is the most addicting drug there is. Nicotine craving, in fact, may last a lifetime after withdrawal" (Inaba & Cohen, 1990, p. 78).

Quitting is difficult but worth it. Many reliable statistics point out the benefits of quitting smoking, including an increased life expectancy and a healthier life. Those who quit smoking lower their risk of cancer, heart attack, emphysema, and many other respiratory and circulatory problems. They also improve the health of those around them who must breathe the smoke secondhand. These and other facts have led to strong and in some cases highly successful public education efforts. In inner-city African-American communities, for example, the prevalence of smoking is down among teenage girls, whereas it continues to increase in other segments of the population—for example, among low-income white teenage girls. This is a direct result of the community's strong counter-response to the recent cigarette industry advertising that targets women and African Americans. Again we see that societal as well as individual solutions are needed to address the problems that cause people difficulties in living.

4. When a person needs to take more and more of a drug to achieve the same effect, or must keep taking it in order to avoid withdrawal symptoms, we say that a _____ to the drug has developed.

5. Physical withdrawal symptoms from alcohol that include sweating, shaking, and nausea are called _____ _____.

6. Marijuana sold on the street today is _____ (more, less) potent than the marijuana that was sold in the 1960s.

7. Cocaine is a central nervous system _____ (stimulant, depressant?), whereas heroin is a central nervous system _____ (stimulant, depressant).

CONTROL IN PERSONAL RELATIONSHIPS

Thus far, we have been considering self-control problems that involve an individual's physical and psychological well-being. We noted, however, particularly in the case of drug abuse, that these problems also have a major effect on people other than those struggling with the problem, particularly family members. In this section we will consider problems of control that are even more directly interpersonal: acquaintance rape, stranger rape, and domestic abuse—battering of spouses and other intimates.

A man is convicted of assault and battery with a dangerous weapon and attempting to commit murder after assaulting his girlfriend with a box cutter. He is sentenced to a one year jail term and ordered to obtain counseling for batterers. A woman is pursued over three states and eight years by her abusive husband, who finally kills her. In broad daylight, a rapist enters the home of a teenager who is home sick from school and assaults her. Scenes from a horror movie? Unfortunately not. Just a few items from the national news in 1997 and 1998.

Consider these graphic and disturbing individual stories in light of the distressing statistics about relationship violence in the United States. A national study revealed that 15 percent of a sample of college students had been raped (Koss, Dinero, Seibel, & Cox, 1988), and other studies estimate that one in four women will be raped in their lifetime. Among rape victims, stranger rape is not the most common form; in the college student populations estimates are that 50 to 80 percent of rape victims are raped by people they know: acquaintances, casual dates, or steady dates. Women in all life circumstances, including the married and unmarried, the rich and the poor, the young and the elderly, are victims of rape. In addition, wife battering in the United States occurs at a rate of 4 million people per year. Husband battering occurs, but it is less common and less injurious. Homicide among family members and acquaintances is responsible for most homicide deaths.

It is no wonder, then, that violence has become a major domestic issue in the 1990s among politicians and policy makers, educators, religious and community leaders as well as ordinary citizens. In the following sections we will look more closely at the nature and psychological dynamics of violence between individuals. We will focus on rape and domestic abuse in this chapter, while other forms of personal and community violence are discussed in Chapter 13.

Rape

Types and Causes of Rape. What are the causes of rape? Studies of rapists reveal that most men who rape repeat their crimes and that rape is driven by anger and the need for power and control. A majority of rapes stem from the need to wield power over women— to control, conquer, and subdue them. Most of the rapes motivated by needs for power are called **power-expressive rapes,** in which men are actively expressing their felt dominance over women (Groth, Burgess, & Halmstrom, l977). (While rape of men is much less common, it does occur in prisons, where it is also used as a means of asserting dominance and subjugating others.) About half as frequent are **power reassurance rapes,** in which men who feel quite powerless and inadequate are attempting to reassure themselves of their power and adequacy through the subjugation of women. Other rapists—about 40 percent, according to one study (Groth & Birnbuam, 1979)—are motivated by anger; men retaliate against real or imagined mistreatment at the hands of women. Rapes of this type are exceedingly violent. Moreover, Groth and Birnbaum estimate that about 5 percent of rapes involve sadistic anger rather than retaliatory anger. These are committed by pathological sadists who gain sexual pleasure from other people's suffering, often to the point of torturing, mutilating, or murdering them. In some cases, psychological disturbance or a previous history of abuse can be clearly detected in the rapist's background. In other cases, including gang rapes by street buddies, teammates, and fraternity brothers, one also sees the influence of group dynamics such as deindividuation and social contagion, described in Chapter 13.

Alcohol is often a factor in rape, particularly in date and acquaintance rapes among college students. Teenage and college age women are at a higher risk for acquaintance rape than women of other ages. The research on date rape, also called courtship rape, suggests a diversity of causes, which depend on the nature of the relationship (Shotland, 1992). For example, early date rape (occurring after a few dates but before the sexual ground rules are set) seems to be related to (1) misperceptions and miscommunication, that is, males tend to perceive more sexual intent in conversations than females do (Harnish, Abbey, & DeBono, 1992), and (2) men with poor impulse control who become sexually aroused and then frustrated if the activity does not proceed to intercourse. This arousal transfers to anger through a process called **excitation-transfer** (Zillman, 1984). On the other hand, rape within sexually active couples (such as spouses) is more violent and is often associated with battering. Marital rape has only recently begun to be acknowledged and studied; in fact until well into the 1980s it was not even a crime in some states, and in others it was a lesser felony than stranger rape. Very ancient attitudes about wives as their husbands' property and responsible for husbands' sexual gratification underlie these legal facts. They are also seen as factors in explaining the dynamics of rape (Shotland, 1992).

In some cases, rape is also a means of asserting control in the relationship. In one study (Frieze, 1983), 78 percent of women who were raped and beaten by their husbands believed that the husband did it to prove his manhood. Women in these situations sometimes accept the role of victim (that is, stay in the relationship), and it is known that among this group there is a higher than average chance that they were also sexually abused as children (Russell, 1984).

Prevention and Coping. Given the frequency of rape and the variety of its causes, what can women do to control their own lives and protect themselves from rape? An answer to this question must take into account at least two levels. First, on the individual level, the book *Our Bodies, Our Selves* (Boston Women's Health Book Collective, 1979) gives a number of practical suggestions concerning stranger rape. One is communication. Women who share the same apartment building and neighborhoods can organize and work out signals for dealing with danger and other arrangements for getting help. They should make sure their windows and doors are absolutely secure and that more than a key must be used to open them. Entrances and doorways should be well-illuminated. Many women list their telephone numbers in directories using only their first initial. Being aware of situations in which there is too much alcohol flowing and not enough people around whom one trusts is another precautionary measure. When going to her car, a woman should have her key out and ready and check the back seat to make sure no one is concealed there. Of course, all of us need to be cautious about traveling in dark places at night and alone. Many colleges have organized escort services, some staffed by women only and some by both men and women, to provide extra safety.

What if you are actually confronted with a rapist? A study of the effectiveness of various resistance strategies (Ullman & Knight, 1993) used police records and court testimonies of 274 women who were raped or who avoided rape by strangers who were subsequently incarcerated. They found that trying to plead, cry, or reason with the rapist was less effective and resulted in more severe physical and sexual abuse. Screaming, fleeing, and fighting back was more effective in lowering the severity of the sexual abuse, but the authors cautioned that the level of resistance must be very strong to avoid rape.

Obviously, attempts to prevent or control rape are not always successful, and the survivor of rape has a new struggle to face in gaining control over her emotional reactions to the violence done to her and in getting back to

day-to-day living. Rape survivors sometimes experience posttraumatic stress disorder (see Chapter 7), and for those women as well as others, getting help from a supportive counselor can be very important. Relationship difficulties are also sometimes an aftermath, particularly if significant others in the victim's life are having a difficult time handling the fact that she was raped. A frequent emotional struggle for women who have been raped involves self-questioning: Why me? What could or should I have done to stop this? Am I ever going to feel safe again? Unfortunately, a subtle form of violence against women, still prevalent in our society, maintains that "good" women don't get raped and that those who do must have "asked for it" in some way. Other people's need to believe that there is a "just world" (Lerner, 1970) may motivate them to find the victims of misfortune somewhat responsible for their victimization. Such an attitude may be held by women as well as men. Thus, rape survivors must deal not only with the effects of the physical violence but also with damaging attitudes about themselves that prejudices against women have conditioned them and others to feel.

Finally, we note that although the prevention measures described earlier make good common sense, they regretfully put the responsibility on the woman and have the effect of restraining her freedom of movement and spontaneity. Women should not have to be prisoners in their own homes and have their schedules dictated by fear and caution in order to be safe from rape. It is also noted that many of these measures will do nothing to protect against rape by acquaintances, dates, or spouses. Thus, in addition to individual precautions we also need societal changes. Decreasing the incidence of rape requires changing attitudes toward women which are degrading and which regard women as objects. A reduction in the media's glamorization of violence and its tendency to pair images of violence and sex might help in this regard.

People, including young people, need better strategies for communicating with each other about relationship dynamics and sexual expectations. Recently prevention programs in high schools have begun to address the problem of teenage rape and battering of girlfriends, and educational programs that reveal the ways in which advertising and other media link sex and violence have been instituted. A program at the University of Florida called FARE (Fraternity Acquaintance Rape Education), for example, educates men through fraternities and sports teams about date rape (Walsh, 1990, cited in Donat & D'Emilio, 1992).

Our improved understanding of rape and the needs of rape victims is thus slowly being translated into action. There are now rape crisis centers in many communities that, in addition to helping individual women, organize public forums and engage in lobbying and advocacy for the rights of women to be safe. Laws affecting violence against women are slowly improving. The judge who lectures a raped woman on her morality is now likely to shock and anger the public rather than to confirm public opinion. The media representative or researcher who paints a generic picture of the rapist as the mentally disturbed psychopathic stranger is likely to be corrected.

Domestic Violence

The Extent of the Problem. Sometimes it takes a vivid, personal connection to a tragedy (for example, having someone you know killed by a drunk driver) to make people understand the extent of a social problem. With regard to domestic violence, the case of O. J. Simpson and Nicole Brown is surely such a case. O. J. Simpson, football hero at the University of Southern California and later of the Buffalo Bills, winner of the Heisman trophy and many other awards and records, retired from football to become a sports commentator and actor. He was arrested on June 17, 1994, for the fatal stabbing of his ex-wife and a

male friend who was at her house, then tried and found not guilty of the murders. During the trial, however, it was graphically revealed that he had pleaded "no contest" to earlier battering charges. In 1989, Nicole called the police, having been beaten badly on the face and fearful for her life; in addition, she had called 911 on eight other occasions on which he was abusing her. Very little was done to stop the abuse. Some authorities felt that this was the result of Simpson's celebrity status while others pointed out that this is an all-too-common outcome. It is, after all, only recently that the legal community has addressed this problem. Until just a few years ago, a restraining order (under which an abuser can be arrested if he even calls or goes near a victim) could only be obtained if one was married to the abuser.

Statistics provided by the Los Angeles district attorney at the time of the arrest reveal that domestic violence is not a rare problem nor one limited to famous or wealthy people. Rather, 4,000 women in the United States die each year at the hands of their husbands or boyfriends, and another 4 million are beaten every year. Violence between spouses occurs annually in one in six U.S. homes, and approximately one-third of all married women report at least one physically violent episode during their marriage (Straus & Gelles, 1986). Moreover, if there is spouse abuse in a family, there is a 60 percent greater chance (than in nonabusing families) that the children are also being physically or sexually abused (ABC News, June 17, 1995).

When we hear the details of battering cases, the question must arise: How can anyone do this? It has been suggested that cultural and socialization factors need to be taken into account in understanding the roots of the problem. A culture that permits and family socialization that promotes control and degradation of women sets the stage. Gelles and Cornell (1985) note that violence runs in families. "Persons who observed family violence, were victims of violence, or were exposed to high levels of violence in childhood are more likely to be abusers" (Mathias, 1986).

In the actual relationships, there is a great deal of blaming of the woman and rationalizing the act ("Well, she cheated on me"; "She provoked me because the house was a mess again after I warned her I hated it that way"). A common pattern (particularly when the abuse is just beginning) is for the abuser to apologize immediately afterward and leave the home or disappear for a while. Upon his return, the couple does not deal with it, and there is a period of calm until another incident, followed by apologies and promises, and so on. Later in the abusive relationship, the apologies may cease and the home is ruled by denial and terror. The power over the victim may be mental or psychological as well. One woman, battered for 11 years, tried to explain her "imprisonment" (Mathias, 1986): "I thought it was my place to be abused. I sincerely believed that if I had conducted my life differently, if I had been a better wife and not talked back, my husband wouldn't need to abuse me."

This helps explain why the women don't just leave the situation. In addition, it is common for the abuser to isolate the woman from family and friends, follow her, and keep her financially and materially dependent so she cannot leave. We know of one case in a rural area where the husband actually took the car keys every time he left the home and had the phone disconnected. These kinds of facts and a conversation with an abused woman who was only "allowed" out to go to the grocery store prompted one concerned artist to take action. She did a national project to put art pieces about violence and safety information on milk cartons, hoping to reach abused women whose only contact with the outside world was at the grocery store (P. Diggs, personal communication, July 12, 1995).

Some women fear for their lives if they leave the relationship, and often for good reason. Paradoxically, they are also in danger of losing their lives if they do not leave. Thus they perceive that they have very little control over their own safety.

Controlling Domestic Violence. Efforts to help battered women focus on the practical and bureaucratic necessities involved in extricating themselves from an abusive relationship. The most basic is a place to live. Today there are over 1,000 shelters across the United States that offer a haven for battered women and their children. Made safe by 24-hour staffing, the support of other women in the shelter, unpublished locations, and sophisticated security systems, these homes offer crisis intervention, vocational counseling, financial counseling, and help in finding permanent housing. For women who need it, personal counseling, parenting groups, and other services are offered. However, according to Peggy Sissel of the National Coalition against Domestic Violence, the assumption is that they are not mentally ill but victims of a crime, that they need to be listened to and empowered, not rescued or pathologized (Cozzi, 1986). In other words, the battered woman needs to be coached, supported, reminded of her strengths and, if necessary, taught some new skills so that she can regain control over her safety, her happiness, and her future.

In this last section, the issues of control are even more complex, because they take place in the context of relationships. Struggling to control eating by going on a diet may involve others peripherally, but mainly it is a personal struggle for control. With domestic violence, there are two people struggling for control. The victim is struggling to control the relationship or situation in order to protect herself, and the perpetrator is struggling to control the situation to meet his psychological needs. The strongest risk factors that predict whether someone will become a batterer are a history of witnessing parental abuse, low socioeconomic status, alcohol abuse, low assertiveness, and low self-esteem (Hotaling & Sugarman, 1990). In addition, there are some perpetrators who realize that their behavior is out of control, and who—at least at times—struggle to control their own aggression. The most recent treatment innovations include group therapy for batterers who wish to stop the abuse. The therapy is typically educational in focus and tries to help batterers iden-

tify the conditions under which they lose control and substitute other behaviors when they feel angry, hurt, or frustrated. These programs work best when they are highly structured, confrontive (because the batterer tends to blame others and minimize injuries), and paired with legal interventions such as arrest, or court-ordered treatment (Dutton, 1992).

REVIEW QUESTIONS

8. The most common type of rape is _____ (stranger rape or acquaintance rape).

9. Give three reasons why battered women find it difficult to leave their abusers.

10. What are the strongest risk factors that predict whether someone will become a batterer?

We began this chapter by asking about the life and death of Kurt Cobain: What are the ways that people struggle to maintain control in their lives? Clearly, Cobain often lost his struggle for control, but it is not only rock stars and other famous people who face these battles. Given the prevalence of the problems discussed in this chapter, chances are very high that someone you know, or perhaps you yourself, have struggled to gain control over patterns of eating or drinking, over smoking, or over drugs. Chances are also high that you know someone who has struggled with the

problem of rape or domestic violence. Pointing out the fact that these problems are common, however, is not meant to minimize their seriousness. Rather, it is meant to convey the message that we are not alone and that there are periods of time when even basically healthy people struggle for or temporarily lose control. Finally, it should be clear that there are ways to deal with those periods. Individual counseling, self-help groups, and community education and prevention programs can all help in regaining control and getting back to the more satisfying things in life.

SUMMARY

1. The perception of control is an important psychological variable in health and adjustment. An internal locus of control is the generalized expectancy that your behavior matters, that is, that the events and outcomes in your life are linked to your efforts. An external locus of control is the generalized expectancy that important outcomes are determined by luck, chance, fate, or powerful others. Locus of

control expectancies have been shown to be related to a variety of behaviors and choices that people make.

2. The eating disorders anorexia nervosa and bulimia are not simply disorders of weight, although in the former disorder weight can be dangerously low, and in the latter it can fluctuate widely. Rather, eating disorders are psychological disorders that involve disturbances in eating habits, exercise regimen, attitudes toward food and the body, and disturbed emotions. The causes of eating disorders are multifaceted.

3. Alcohol abuse is a form of drug abuse. They share several common features: inability to control the use of the substance (dependence); tolerance; withdrawal symptoms; and disruptions in work, social, and family relationships. Alcohol abuse is associated with a variety of health problems and is a major factor in accidents, suicide, sexual abuse, and other kinds of interpersonal violence. Alcoholism has widespread effects on family members, as well as the individual.

4. Denial is a major roadblock in the treatment of alcoholism, and treatment often begins with breaking through that denial. Alcoholics Anonymous and Rational Recovery are two self-help groups for alcoholic persons; Al-Anon and ACOA (Adult Children of Alcoholics) groups address family members' concerns and problems.

5. In addition to alcohol, there are a wide variety of other psychoactive drugs, both legal and illegal, whose use can cause people to lose control over the substance and their lives. Tobacco use does not lead to the social problems that other drugs do, but it is a major public health problem. Cocaine, a brain stimulant, and heroin, a narcotic, can both result in powerful addictions and the addict's neglect of basic health, work, and family tasks as well as dangerous and criminal activities to support the habit.

6. Marijuana is the most commonly used illegal drug in the United States. Its main ingredient, THC, has some medicinal purposes. It also affects sleep, mood, short-term memory, concentration, and motor coordination.

7. Heroin is an opiate drug which produces pain relief, sedation, and a numbing of emotions by working on the central nervous system in a manner similar to endorphins, the body's natural opiates. Heroin is addictive, producing strong psychological as well as physiological dependence. Withdrawal symptoms are painful and frightening.

8. Violence in interpersonal relationships is a problem in the United States, as statistics on rape and domestic violence can attest. Motivations of rapists can be power assertive or power reassuring, and the motivations of rapists in acquaintance or date rapes may vary according to the nature of the relationship—that is, early dating versus long-term partners. Rape prevention programs involve changing attitudes toward women and helping people clarify their expectations, assumptions, and communication.

9. Domestic violence involves psychological as well as physical maltreatment. Particularly difficult is the sense of loss of control of victims, who have been convinced that they are powerless in the relationship and helpless without the abuser. Domestic violence shelters and other programs seek to help battered women regain a sense of control and competence. Newer group treatments for the batterers involve education, therapy, and self-help programs to enable them to discard abusive behaviors and create new relationship patterns.

CRITICAL THINKING QUESTIONS

1. Eating disorders are most common in the United States and other industrialized Western countries. They are more common in the white community than in the black community in the United States although this is slowly changing as more African-American girls develop the disorder. They are very rare in developing countries in Africa and South Asia. What explanations can you suggest for these facts?

2. Nicotine and alcohol are both addictive substances. Nicotine is known to be harmful to your health, and alcohol can be harmful if used in excess. Both addictions are very costly to society in terms of health care and (in the case of alcohol) violence and accidents. Why, then, do you suppose that these substances are legal and other substances are illegal?

3. In this chapter we have discussed efforts to control one's adjustment and mental health outcomes in control of eating, drinking, and other behaviors. We have generally suggested that having control and perceiving that one has control are desirable goals. Can you think of any situations or life circumstances in which these goals might not be desirable? If so, what kinds of strategies for adjustment might be more beneficial?

MATCHING EXERCISE

Match each term with its definition.

a. locus of control
b. anorexia nervosa
c. bulimia
d. drug dependence
e. delirium tremens (DTs)
f. withdrawal
g. tolerance
h. Alcoholics Anonymous
i. amotivational syndrome
j. heroin
k. amphetamines
l. barbiturates
m. excitation-transfer

1. Eating disorder characterized by refusal to maintain normal body weight, distortion in the way one's body is perceived, exaggerated fear of putting on weight, and cessation of menstruation
2. Term used when heavy marijuana users, especially adolescents, become psychologically dependent on the drug and lose interest and energy for work, school, and relationships
3. An opiate that slows brain functioning, relieves pain and stress, and otherwise mimics the actions of endorphins, the body's "natural opiates"
4. Eating disorder in which body weight may be normal, but there is overconcern with body weight and shape, binging and purging in order to maintain weight, and often depression
5. Psychological and physical symptoms that occur when a person stops taking a drug that he or she is dependent upon. They include shakiness, nausea, anxiety, irritability, and discomfort that may range from mild to very severe
6. A generalized expectancy that outcomes in life are either within our control (internal) or controlled by forces outside ourselves such as fate, luck, or powerful others (external)
7. Stimulant drugs, such as Methedrine ("speed") and Dexedrine, which cause temporary arousal, alertness, and excitement
8. The process by which energy or emotional arousal of one kind (e.g., sexual excitement) can be transformed into another (e.g., anger); discussed as a factor in some kinds of rape
9. Self-help group for people who wish to end their dependence on alcohol, based on a 12-step program
10. Term used to describe the situation when a drug-dependent person needs to keep taking more and more of the substance to achieve the same effects or to avoid withdrawal
11. Also called "tranquilizers" or "sleeping pills," these drugs were commonly prescribed in the 1950s and 1960s to treat anxiety and are also sold as street drugs; they slow breathing, blood pressure, and other physiological processes

12. Drug use that has reached the stage where the user is unable to stop taking the drug even though it is having harmful social, psychological, or physical effects

13. Physical sensations that accompany withdrawal from alcohol, including profuse sweating, shaking, nausea, disorganized thinking, and sometimes hallucinations

Answers to Matching Exercises

a. 6   b. 1   c. 4   d. 12   e. 13   f. 5   g. 10   h. 9   i. 2   j. 3   k. 7   l. 11   m. 8

ANSWERS TO REVIEW QUESTIONS

1. refusal to maintain body weight, leading to weight loss; exaggerated fear of putting on weight; distortions in the way in which one's body is perceived; cessation of menstruation for three or more cycles

2. depression

3. the fact that subcultures can have a powerful effect on eating behaviors

4. tolerance

5. delirium tremens

6. more

7. stimulant, depressant

8. acquaintance rape

9. isolation, self-blame, fear of more harm if they leave

10. a history of witnessing parental abuse, low socioeconomic status, alcohol abuse, low assertiveness, and low self-esteem

PSYCHOLOGICAL DISORDERS

Gould farm, where Maxine Mason lived for a brief time

Maxine Mason

"I'm a doctor, you know," Maxine Mason told a fellow patient. "I don't have a diploma, but I'm a doctor. I'm glad to be a mental patient, because it taught me how to be humble. I use Cover Girl creamy natural makeup. Oral Roberts has been here to visit me. My sister's name is [Trudy], and I like her. My father is five feet two inches, my mother is five feet three inches. They're like Napolean and Josephine, and they're shrinking. Trudy is five feet two. I'm only five foot four and I'm the tallest one in my family. This is the place where *Mad* magazine is published. The Nixons make Noxon metal polish. When I was a little girl, I used to sit and tell stories to myself. When I was older, I turned off the sound on the TV set and made up dialogue to go with the shows I watched. The people in Creedmoor are Hobbits. I dictated the Hobbit stories to Tolkien, and he took them all down. I'm the Hobbit. Ask John Denver. He told me I was. I'm the only person who ever got Ringo Starr angry" (Sheehan, 1982, p. 72).

Maxine had recently been readmitted to Creedmore Psychiatric Center, a large New York State mental hospital, when she spoke these confusing yet fascinating words. She was 29 years old, a daughter, a sister, an intelligent woman with a good sense of humor and some wry and wise insights. She had struggled since age 15 with the disorder called schizophrenia.

There was no indication when Maxine was born, in 1948, that she would develop schizophrenia. Her father was an immigrant from Russia, and her mother's parents had immigrated from the Ukraine; they met in the Lower East Side of New York City. Mr. Mason worked for a bottling company, and Mrs. Mason was a homemaker. A daughter, Trudy, was born first; she was a smart, pretty, easygoing child who began to paint watercolors at age 6. Maxine was born six years later, to her parents' delight. She was thin, with light brown hair, and walked and talked early. In fact, she is remembered by everyone as being a very talkative youngster. Just a few years later, they moved to the middle-class neighborhood in Queens where Maxine grew up.

For Maxine, the family's move proved to be especially difficult, even though she was only four. She had difficulty making friends and being accepted by the children she liked. At times she would wrongly accuse other children of hitting her and at other times she would provoke them. Wearing Trudy's hand-me-downs and being an untidy person added to her woes, as did her parent's strong emphasis on grades in school. The family struggled financially, and there was much bickering and arguing, between the parents and between Trudy and Maxine. In many respects they were much like other families.

In Maxine's case, however, something was different. She seemed to lack an awareness of social conventions or of how she appeared to others when she scratched herself or picked her nose. She was considered odd and was socially rejected in junior high school. Nonetheless, she managed to graduate from junior high school with excellent grades and certificates in several subjects. As she prepared to enter the tenth grade at the prestigious High School of Music and Art, the future seemed brighter. Instead, the next few years held a litany of troubles for Maxine. In the tenth grade, she struggled with long commutes to school, loneliness, a suicidal gesture, and some paranoid thoughts and hallucinations that she shared only with a psychologist. Maxine's first thorough psychiatric evaluation resulted in a "diagnostic impression" of schizophrenia, and she began outpatient therapy. Nonetheless, she finished the school year with an 87 percent average. In the eleventh grade, Maxine continued school and began seeing a young psychologist who helped her to dress and act more appropriately. She made some friends, started to become more independent of her parents, and to act more like a teenager—talking on the phone, listening to Beatles albums, smoking. Her parents disapproved of her new behavior and blamed the therapist for her rebelliousness. In January, Maxine was hit by a car while crossing the street but was not badly injured. In February, she and her friend made an unsuccessful attempt to see the Beatles on their first U.S. tour, and then she went to the airport alone to see them off but couldn't remember how to get home.

It was at this time that Maxine's behavior became unquestionably, and publicly, bizarre. Giggling for no reason, staying up nights in a row, taking several showers a day are perhaps individually not a sign of mental illness. But in addition to these behaviors, Maxine had elaborate delusions involving herself as Cinderella, her mother as the wicked stepmother, her psychologist as the fairy godmother, and Paul McCartney as Prince Charming. She visited some family friends to ask them to adopt her, then started to cry and dance around the living room. Maxine was having her first psychotic break. Subsequently, she would spend long stretches of time in a number of different public and private mental hospitals. At times her "home" was Rockland Psychiatric Center, a huge public institution known in the past for its abuses of patients. At other times, it was Gould Farm in the Berkshire Mountains of Massachusetts, a gentle, open community of patients and staff on a working farm. But her parents' home proved to be a very stressful place for Maxine to live, even for visits. Indeed, once in 1964, riding in an ambulance from one hospital to another, Maxine asked her mother, "Is there no place on earth for me?" (Sheehan, 1982, p. 208)

Everyone hoped that the right medication would cure Maxine's symptoms. During the course of her treatment, she was treated with many different drugs, as well as with electroconvulsive therapy and insulin-coma therapy, multifamily therapy, and outpatient psychotherapy of various kinds. Hers was a very severe case of schizophrenia, and a lasting, satisfactory treatment was not available. Nonetheless, Maxine kept her wit, her sense of humor, and her keen powers of observation about the environments in which she lived.

The final chapter in Maxine's story was written in 1995 (Sheehan, 1995). Maxine Mason died on November 17, 1994 at the Rockland County Psychiatric Center at the age of 46. She died in the middle of the night of a heart attack brought on by a badly bleeding ulcer that no one knew she had. Her life had been a repetition of hospitalizations, discharges, and desperate, bizarre behaviors in the community that led to being rehospitalized once again. There were some bright spots: a new medication, Clozaril, which helped her for a bit, and a brief stint at Fountain House, one of the best community-based programs in the country. In the end, her illness outlasted both of her parents' lives, but not her sister's resolve to stand by her. Trudy Mason graduated from Wheaton College and gradually took over as Maxine's guardian and advocate while pursuing a career in politics and public relations and as an advocate for the mentally ill.

PSYCHOLOGICAL DISORDERS
AND ADJUSTMENT

Maxine Mason's story illuminates the life of a person with a serious and chronic mental disorder. *Mental disorders,* also sometimes called *mental illnesses* or *psychological disorders,* are problems that interfere significantly with people's adjustment and happiness. Some mental disorders, such as anxiety disorders, alcoholism, and depression, are very common in U.S. society: at least 15 percent of the U.S. adult population suffers from an anxiety disorder in any given year, for example (Regier et al., 1993). Others, such as bipolar disorder and schizophrenia, are less common: the prevalence of schizophrenia is about 1 percent (Regier et al., 1993). If this seems like a low and insignificant number, consider the following. The number of people with schizophrenia in the United States alone would fill 25 Rose Bowl stadiums (Weisburd, 1990), and the cost of providing one year of psychiatric hospitalization runs between $100,000 and $150,000 per person. Thus even the less prevalent disorders have a major impact on the health care system as well as on the extent of disability they can cause. Overall, statistics show that nearly 30 percent of adults in the United States will experience a psychological disorder of some kind in any given year (Regier et al., 1993). Thus it is highly likely that you know or will know someone with a psychological disorder.

Our goal in this chapter, then, is to provide an understanding of these disorders, their basic symptoms and their causes. Where appropriate, we will correct some myths about mental illness and give practical suggestions for adjusting to mental illness in the family. We begin with a discussion of the terms *normal* and *abnormal* and the complexities of diagnosis. Sections on schizophrenic disorders, mood disorders, and suicide follow. We then move to a discussion of stress and anxiety in everyday life, psychophysiological disorders, and the range of anxiety disorders. Dissociative disorders such as amnesias and "multiple personality" are examined next. The chapter ends with a focus on personality disorders and how these disorders can be distinguished from ordinary variations among people in traits and styles of interacting with others.

Before we begin, however, a cautionary note is in order.

Medical Student's Disease: A Caution

The term *medical student's disease* originates from the experience of those studying medicine, who find the symptoms of the various disorders uncomfortably familiar and begin to worry that they have the diseases in their textbooks. The more exotic and dangerous the condition, the harder it may be to convince yourself that you do not have it! We have found a similar "condition" among our students, which we call *psychology student's disease:* When they read the list of symptoms, some students begin diagnosing themselves with depression or anxiety. And unlike some exotic diseases, the symptoms may not be so different, qualitatively, from feelings or states we all may have experienced. Many students read, for example, that obsessive-compulsive disorders are marked by recurring thoughts, often of a socially unacceptable nature, that will not go away. They realize that to some extent they have such thoughts and fear they have the disorder and need treatment. We have also noticed that students sometimes fall prey to a variation of psychology student's

disease—that is, they begin to (over)diagnose friends, family members, or roommates! Because it is easy to be wrong, and because people don't appreciate being scrutinized, this kind of diagnosing can be dangerous and should generally be resisted.

On the other hand, we do acknowledge that psychological disorders occur at all ages and in people of all races, ethnicity, occupation, and social class. There is no reason to think that all psychology students are immune from all disorders. So anyone who does experience such concerns, either about oneself or others, especially if they are very strong or persistent, should discuss them with a knowledgeable person such as a teacher or counselor. This will help in evaluating whether there is a basis either for seeking consultation from a mental health professional or for urging someone else to do so. If the worries are not so strong, it should be reassuring to know that both medical student's disease and psychology student's disease are both common and "curable"—by talking about the material with friends or fellow students.

DIAGNOSIS: WHAT IS "NORMAL"? WHAT IS "ABNORMAL"?

Although we frequently use the terms *normal* and *abnormal* in everyday speech, defining exactly what make a person's behavior normal or abnormal can be tricky. A young woman Olympic gymnast who exercises six or more hours a day engages in the singleminded pursuit of one activity, forsaking many social opportunities. She certainly is not *average,* but is she "abnormal"? Probably not in the sense that psychologists and other mental health professionals use that term. A person who wears his hair in a crewcut one month, colors it red the next month, and spends his days reading antigovernment speeches on the street corner is certainly not conforming to society's standards, but is he disordered? Probably not, either.

Dignity and Indignity in Mental Hospitals

Harold was a tall, dignified man in his sixties who had been in the state mental hospital for 30 years. I was a high school volunteer, brought to the place by the fate of geography (my family had moved in down the street), and in a time before various reforms in mental institutions and patients' rights had taken place. For example, Harold's "problem" was that as a young man, he had been caught peeping in a neighbor's window. His family, shocked, had brought him to the hospital, and he had never left.

Harold liked to feed the birds. In the dining hall, he would wait until the end of the meal and then go around politely collecting the leftover bread off of everyone's tray. He stood with it at the huge, steel-mesh grated windows, picking off pieces just small enough to throw through it. Birds would gather, and it was hard to tell who was having a better time, the birds or Harold.

One day it was decided that this was problem behavior. No real reason was given, but one staff member decided it had to stop. So she started following him around the dining hall, reaching out and grabbing the bread off each tray, just ahead of him. This went on for several days until one day at lunchtime, when he did a quick step in front of the staff member and got hold of the bread first. She grabbed to get it back, and the more she struggled for it, the harder he pulled back. Other staff gathered around, ready to intercede, and there was a tense standoff. I then asked him if he would just give it to me. He relaxed as if he were going to, then quickly popped it in his mouth and swallowed it, with a satisfied grin.

Harold had gained a bit of momentary autonomy, perhaps, but not without cost. The other staff did restrain him then, roughly, and put him into the isolation room for the rest of the day for "misbehaving."

This scenario, observed by one of the authors, illustrates how certain harmless behaviors, especially if they occur in the context of a mental hospital, or if they are performed by someone labeled "crazy," can take on negative meanings. Psychiatric diagnoses can be helpful, but they can also sometimes distort our perceptions of the needs and motives of fellow human beings.

To answer the question of whether these people, or any person, is psychologically-disordered, we need to consider whether their behavior or their psychological state is associated with clinically significant "distress (e.g., a painful symptom) or disability (i.e., impairment in one or more important areas of functioning) or with a significantly increased risk of suffering death, pain, disability, or an important loss of freedom" (American Psychiatric Association, 1994, p. xxi). This definition attempts to ensure that people who are merely nonconformists, political dissidents, or culturally different are not diagnosed as being disordered. It comes from a manual called the **DSM–IV** or the *Diagnostic and Statistical Manual of Mental Disorders,* fourth edition, published by the American Psychiatric Association. The DSM–IV includes a list of all the different disorders, their symptoms, prevalence rates, and other important information. This information is quite useful for clinical treatment as well as research, but symptoms must always be considered in light of the context in which the person is living and behaving, as the story in the Lessons from Life box illustrates.

In addition to the standard information, the DSM–IV also includes interesting sections on controversial diagnoses such as premenstrual dysphoric disorder (PMS) and on culture-bound diagnoses that are specific to certain cultures. Anorexia nervosa, a well-known disorder in the United States and other Western industrialized countries, is virtually absent in developing countries. On the other hand, *koro*, a disorder found in South and East Asia but not in the United States, is the sudden and frightening delusion that the penis is withdrawing into the abdomen and may cause death. People suffering from *Susto*, a complaint found in Mexico, Central and South America, and parts of the United States where people have immigrated from those areas, experience sleep and appetite disturbances, sadness, lack of energy and various physical complaints as well as feelings of unworthiness. *Susto* is attributed to "soul loss" following a very frightening event (APA, 1994). The fact that there are controversies over what is normal and what is abnormal and that some disorders are specific to certain cultures shows that diagnosis has social and cultural as well as scientific aspects. One disorder, however, has been found in every culture, and its symptoms show consistency across cultures: schizophrenia.

SCHIZOPHRENIC DISORDERS

Maxine Mason's experiences are characteristic of someone with a severe, chronic case of **schizophrenia,** a major mental illness. Schizophrenia is "major" in terms of its profound effects on afflicted individuals. To appreciate this fact, first consider just a few of the capabilities of human beings. *Perceiving sensory information:* A streak of faint color flies in front of your face at night, and you know it's a moth. *Concentrating:* You can sit in a lecture and (usually!) attend to the professor's voice, not to the hum of the fluorescent lights, the smell of perfume on the person next to you, or the scratch of her pen on the paper. *Thinking:* You can understand this paragraph, relate it to your own experiences, and think abstractly about the meaning of it. *Speech and language:* You can ask your roommate a question and when you open your mouth, the words that come out are the ones that you intended. *Feeling:* You sit and wait for the dentist to start a

root canal procedure, and you feel nervous; you get to the end of watching the film *Apollo 13* and feel exhausted but elated. Your feelings typically match the situation, and generally are not overwhelming. *Relating to others:* You can reach out to others for entertainment, company, information, and support, and give back to others as well.

We tend take these capabilities completely for granted until they are lost. If you have ever lost some *physical* capacity that you previously had, through accident (such as a broken leg), or illness (such as mononucleosis), you know the impact it had on your life, your work or school, your mood, and your relationship with others. Now imagine what it is like to lose the *mental* capacities we just described. Imagine that you can no longer concentrate, focus your attention, regulate your affect or emotional expression appropriately, or make yourself understood to others. Imagine the profound extent of disruption in your life and the lives of those around you. It is this *wide-ranging impairment of complex psychological functions* that defines chronic schizophrenia.

Because of the great personal cost to individuals and to society, much research has focused on the symptoms, causes, and treatments of schizophrenia. Of all the mental disorders, it also holds the most mystery and fear in the minds of the public. Schizophrenia is a complicated disorder that takes several forms, each with its distinct causes and outcomes. Let us look its core characteristics, and then its varieties.

Core Characteristics of Schizophrenia

The most dramatic feature of schizophrenia is periods of psychosis. **Psychosis** is characterized by disordered thought processes, a state of mind in which people are unable to synthesize or make sense of the information that their senses take in: things seem disconnected, like a jumble of words, images, and sounds. E. Fuller Torrey (1983), a noted schizophrenia researcher, asked 100 schizophrenic patients to interpret the proverb, "People who live in glass houses shouldn't throw stones." Their responses ranged from the very concrete, "Well, it could mean exactly like it says 'cause the windows may well be broken," to the confused, "Because if they did, it would break the environment," to the incomprehensible, "Some people are up in the air and some in society and some up in the air." These responses illustrate how a psychotic episode impairs the ability to think clearly and abstractly.

The content of thought is also disordered during psychosis. People may suffer from **delusions,** or false beliefs: that they are Mohammed, Jesus Christ, or an FBI agent; that their enemies are inserting thoughts into their head; that they have killed the neighbor and must hide from the police. During the course of her illness, Maxine Mason believed she was Billy Joel, the Hobbit, an actress, and the fiancee of a number of different rock stars. Delusions are not amenable to reason. When she was told that the Virgin Mary was dead, one delusional patient replied that she was the *reincarnation* of the Virgin Mary.

Another common experience during psychosis is **hallucinations,** or false sensory experiences. The person hears things, sees things, even smells things that aren't there. Most typically, a schizophrenic "hears" voices but cannot distinguish whether the voices are internal or in the external environment. Unfortunately, the voices are often saying disturbing things. One striking example comes from Mark Vonnegut, son of the famous author Kurt Vonnegut. In his memoir *The Eden Express* (1975), Vonnegut describes how his voices convinced him that his father was dead; he went through months of grieving before realizing his father was very much alive. Interestingly, Vonnegut recovered from his illness and went on to medical school.

At times, the schizophrenic person's *emotional* reactions may also be disturbed—they are either inappropriate to the situation (such as laughing at the sight of a funeral procession) or *flat*—that is, showing little emotional expression at all. Obviously, these symptoms are very disturbing both to the people afflicted and those around them. The symptoms of schizophrenia can prevent a person from carrying on the usual life activities of working, going to school, and parenting. It proved impossible for Maxine Mason to finish high school, to maintain her friendships, or even to live on her own in a supervised apartment.

Many people who are schizophrenic also have a tendency to withdraw into themselves, avoiding others and losing the social graces that most people take for granted. The social withdrawal that accompanies the disorder seems to be related in part to the disorder itself and in part to efforts to cope with the other symptoms. It is important to note that a person diagnosed as schizophrenic is not always actively psychotic. There are periods in which the person can think clearly and function successfully. As we will discuss later, finding the correct medication and arranging the best living environment for the person helps prevent relapses and promotes full recovery.

Varieties of Schizophrenia

Experts distinguish between the *Type I* and *Type II* varieties of schizophrenia (Andreasen et al., 1990). In Type I schizophrenia, the abnormal behavior begins later in life (late twenties or later) and comes on more suddenly, often following a highly stressful event. Type I schizophrenics have a relative predominance of psychotic symptoms, less social withdrawal, and less affective disturbance. They typically respond better to medication and show a faster recovery, just as they became disordered more quickly. Approximately one-third of those who have a schizophrenic episode, for example, will recover and never have another. In Type II schizophrenia, the onset is gradual. Often beginning in the late teens and early twenties, the person shows social withdrawal and a progressive deterioration in functioning that finally results in breakdown. No single event causes the gradual decline, although traumatic events, such as Maxine's being hit by the car, can precipitate a psychotic episode. People with a predominance of Type II symptoms are more likely to have a chronic course and to be less responsive to medications; approximately one-third of all people diagnosed with schizophrenia struggle with the disorder for long periods of time, as Maxine did.

Varieties of schizophrenia are also distinguished by their primary behaviors. These include: *paranoid* type, *disorganized* type, *catatonic* type, *undifferentiated* type, and *residual* type (APA, 1994). In the case of *paranoid schizophrenia,* the major symptoms are delusions. These may be delusions of grandeur ("I am actually a princess, with a big estate that was willed to me by my father") or persecutions ("The FBI is after me because I am such an important person"), or both. Delusions are often accompanied by hallucinations and other disturbed thinking. People may act violently against those they think are conspiring against them, although in general people with schizophrenia are actually less dangerous than the stereotyped myths about "mental patients." (People with antisocial personality disorder, for example, are much more likely to show aggression toward others).

In *disorganized schizophrenia,* more extensive personality disintegration occurs and behavior is even more regressed. The person acts silly, with inappropriate laughing and giggling, often speaking, acting and dressing in odd ways. Thinking and behavior are especially fragmented, and even the delusions and hallucinations are not organized into a single theme. In this sense, Maxine Mason's condition seemed to best fit the diagnosis of disorganized schizophrenia. The person with disorganized schizophrenia is more likely to have a continual course of the disorder without remission. Again, this feature fits in Maxine's case.

In *catatonic schizophrenia* there is usually an alternation of periods of total withdrawal, inactivity, and unresponsiveness with periods of wild excitement and activity. In the former, people may adopt strange positions (such as bending one arm up in the air and holding it that way for many hours) or may remain mute for many days. During the agitated states, people need close supervision in order to prevent harm to themselves or others. *Undifferentiated* schizophrenia is diagnosed when hallucinations, delusions, and disorganized thinking are present, but not paranoia, catatonia, or the extreme silliness and fragmentation of the disorganized type.

In contrast, *residual schizophrenia* develops gradually and is marked by withdrawal, lack of interest in normal activities or relationships with others, and apathy. There is also a deterioration in the quality of thoughts and feelings, strange beliefs, and oddities in speech. Milder eccentricities are more prominent than outright psychotic episodes, hallucinations, and delusions.

It is important to distinguish between the different varieties of schizophrenia as they have somewhat different causes and outcomes. We turn now to a study of the complex causes of the schizophrenias.

Causes of Schizophrenia

In recent decades much progress has been made in understanding the factors that contribute both to the development of schizophrenia and recovery from it. It is clear that the disorder has no single, simple cause, but rather several, interacting causes.

Biological Risk. First and foremost, it is clear that schizophrenia is a biologically based disorder of the brain. Abnormally high activity of the neurotransmitter *dopamine* is found in the brains of schizophrenic patients. (*Neurotransmitters* are chemicals that transport messages between neurons in the brain.)

Serotonin, another neurotransmitter, may also be present at abnormally high levels. Not surprisingly, drugs that decrease the activity of those neurotransmitters are successful in treating the symptoms of schizophrenia. Other patients, particularly those with more chronic forms of the disorder, show actual physical abnormalities of the brain, such as degeneration of brain tissue and enlarged *ventricles*, the fluid-filled spaces inside the brain (Andreasen et al., 1990). Such abnormalities may be caused by genetic factors, prenatal viruses, or birth complications.

Genetics play a role, too, in that having a close relative with schizophrenia increases one's chances of having the disorder. For example, whereas the overall prevalence of schizophrenia is 1 percent in the United States, the risk is closer to 13 percent if a parent has had the disorder (Gottesman, 1991). However, the exact role that genetics plays— that is, which chromosomes are involved and how—remains unclear. Even people with close relatives who are schizophrenic are more likely *not* to get the disorder than they are to get it. A certain set of genes are believed to put a person at special **risk** for the disorder, which may be brought out by *environmental factors and stressors.*

Environmental Factors and Stressors. Early theories of schizophrenia emphasized the role of the family in bringing on the disorder. In particular, it was thought that psychopathology in the parents and highly disturbed communication patterns drove the children to this disorder. The theories tended to blame mothers in particular and were based on little or poor research evidence. It is now known that families do not cause the disorder. The only reliable information about families and schizophrenia, however, is that once a person is treated and leaves the hospital, relapse is more likely if the person returns to family (or other, such as a group home) environments in which there is a high level of expressed emo-

tion. **Expressed emotion** is constituted by criticism, hostility, and emotional overinvolvement in the way that family members talk about each other (Leff, 1976; Left & Vaughn, 1985). A scene from Maxine Mason's story illustrates a high level of expressed emotion. When Maxine was home from the hospital on a holiday visit, her mother asked her if she was experiencing any side effects of her medication. Maxine misunderstood and thought her mother was accusing her of not taking her medication. Grabbing and twisting her mother's arm and shouting, "Don't you dare talk to me about my medication. I know what it is and when to take it." This drew Trudy in. "You twisted your mother's arthritic arm, you blimp," she said, leading to an escalating war of angry and hurtful words. This culminated later that day when Mrs. Mason said accusingly to Maxine, "Can't you leave Creedmoor there when you come home?" Maxine lifted her fist menacingly and retorted, "I don't bring Creedmoor home, I come home to it" (Sheehan, 1982, p. 145). When there are many interactions of this type, a family is considered high in expressed emotion.

Recall that the core of schizophrenia is an inability to cope with stimulation from the environment or with emotional disturbances. Thus it makes sense that a family environment high in expressed emotion would be especially difficult for the schizophrenic person. The best environment for recovery is one that is not overstimulating, in which communication is clear and supportive and in which the person can be engaged in some kind of productive activity and relate to others at his or her own pace. Advancements in the treatment of people with schizophrenia include vocational programs that allow progression in work as recovery occurs, "clubhouse" programs for social support in which members regain the self-control and dignity of their former lives, and supported housing in which the person has as much autonomy as possible while having the "safety net" of a counselor/advocate nearby. Perhaps this combination of programs, instituted early enough, would have made a difference in the ending to Maxine's story. The days in which patients were kept locked up for years in huge, isolated institutions are gone. And as the public becomes more educated about the disorder, the stigma and fear of it are, hopefully, being replaced with sympathy and a commitment to finding the causes and even better treatments.

Because this disorder can be especially difficult for families, and because there is a history of mistaken ideas about the family's role in schizophrenia, we close with a personal note to readers. If you have friends or family members with schizophrenia, the following facts may be helpful. First, we reiterate the fact that families do not *cause* schizophrenia. Rereading that section of the chapter will convince you that there are clear biological abnormalities associated with this disorder and that factors such as poor parenting and family stress are not causal. It is true that cer-

tain kinds of family environments can impede recovery from the disorder, and in those cases counseling for the entire family or alternative living arrangements may be helpful. Besides frequent new advances in medications, there are other helpful treatments. For all families, psychoeducational family therapy (Anderson, Reiss, & Hogarty, 1986) may be helpful in educating family members about the disorder, providing support and consultation. These types of therapy enlist families as allies in the treatment process. Another important resource is the National Alliance for the Mentally Ill (NAMI), an advocacy and support group composed of families and friends of people with mental illness. Both patients and family members have reported that this group was invaluable in helping them cope with the very real stresses of living with a person with mental illness. There are NAMI chapters in most cities that can be located by contacting your local mental health agency or the national office.

REVIEW QUESTIONS

1. _____ is an example of a culture-bound disorder that is found in the U.S., while _____ is another culture-bound disorder that is found in China.

2. The _____ is the current classification system for mental disorders.

3. The _____ disorders are characterized by periods of psychosis, disturbances in emotion and social relations.

4. Traditional antipsychotic medications, such as Thorazine and other medications that were given to Maxine Mason, _____ (increase or decrease?) the action of dopamine, a neurotransmitter, lending support to the dopamine hypothesis about the cause of schizophrenia.

5. Expressed emotion and other family or environmental factors predict _____ in schizophrenia.

MOOD OR AFFECTIVE DISORDERS

The mood disorders are also often called **affective disorders.** These include the *depressive disorders* and the *bipolar disorders* (commonly

referred to as *manic-depressive disorders*). While they are sometimes accompanied by psychotic states and are severe or chronic enough to be considered major mental illnesses, in general they are more easily treated and therefore typically not as debilitating as the schizophrenias. The DSM–IV also distinguishes milder forms of the mood disorders such as *dysthymia* (a low-level, but continuing low mood state) and *cyclothymic disorder* (fluctuating moods states which are not as extreme as in bipolar disorder).

We will first discuss depression and then bipolar disorder.

Major Depressive Disorder

Symptoms of Depression. In general, a person who is clinically depressed has very strong and persistent experiences of feeling down or "blue." A feeling of sadness and dejection is often accompanied by lack of energy, lethargy, and weariness. In addition, the depressed person experiences negative thoughts, such as dwelling on inadequacies, failures, and disappointments in life. There may also be physical symptoms of depression, such as lack of appetite, sleeping too much and/or waking up early in the morning and not being able to fall back to sleep, and lack of sex drive. These feelings and behaviors are all within the normal range of experience if they are mild and shortlived. But the person who is clinically depressed—that is, who would be diagnosed as having a **major depressive disorder**—experiences these symptoms to an extreme and for an extended period of time. The person feels so low that he or she may not be able to work, attend school, or even get out of bed and get dressed in the morning. Crying spells, morose ideas to the exclusion of any positive thoughts or feelings, weight loss, and an overwhelming feeling of helplessness and despair take over. The following Self-Assessment exercise shows some of the items from the *Beck Depression Inventory,* a screening test for depressive symptoms that is commonly used in clinical and research settings.

Novelist William Styron, who wrote about his experience with depression in a book called *Darkness Visible,* movingly explains this state: "My thought processes were being engulfed by a toxic and unnameable tide that obliterated any enjoyable response to the living world.... I was feeling in my mind a sensation close to, but indescribably different from, actual pain.... For myself, the pain is most closely connected to drowning or suffocation" (1990, pp. 16–17).

In a minority of depressed patients (about 15 percent) the negative thinking reaches psychotic proportions. People may believe that they are so unworthy that they *are* the devil, or they may hear voices blaming, berating, or urging them to die. Suicide is a serious risk in all people, psychotic or not, suffering from major depression. It will be discussed shortly.

Causes of Depression

Depression is caused by a combination of biological and environmental factors. Research has shown that depression runs in families (although this link is weaker than in schizophrenia) and that some depressed people have abnormalities in the neurotransmitters norepinephrine and serotonin. The medications that provide relief for depressed persons work on these neurotransmitters. Recent research also suggests that for some people the biological effects of seasonal changes can bring on a type of depression, **seasonal affective disorder (SAD).** Seasonal affective disorder is a type of depression that worsens in the winter months and improves in summer. We know that there is a complex interplay between hormones, moods, and energy levels. One hormone, melatonin, is secreted when our surroundings are dark and has the effect of lowering energy levels. Most people experience a natural slowing down during the shorter days of winter; for people with SAD, however, this process is exaggerated and they become tired, depressed, and sleepy. Treatment using special lights provides relief for many people with this condition (Rosenthal & Blehar, 1989).

Measuring Depression

The following are two items from the *Beck Depression Inventory* (Beck, 1978), a widely used self-report measure of depression. Respondents circle the number for each item that corresponds to how they are feeling at the time. In addition to these items, others ask about recent experiences such as loss of interest in others, pessimistic thoughts, suicidal thoughts, appetite, and ability to initiate work. The scores are averaged across all the items and differentiate nondepressed from moderately depressed, and moderately from severely depressed, persons. A high score alone does not indicate a clinical diagnosis of depression because this is only a screening test. However, if several symptoms of depression last for two weeks or if a person with *any* score has suicidal thoughts, he or she needs to seek counseling.

(Sadness Item)

0   I do not feel sad.

1   I feel blue or sad.

2a   I am sad or blue all of the time and I can't snap out of it.

2b   I am so sad or unhappy that it is quite painful.

3   I am so sad or unhappy that I can't stand it.

(Sleep Loss Item)

0   I can sleep as well as usual.

1   I wake up more tired in the morning than I used to.

2   I wake up 1–2 hours earlier than usual and find it hard to get back to sleep.

3   I wake up early every day and can't get more than 5 hours of sleep.

In addition to biological factors, certain environmental and psychological factors also put people at risk for depression. A low level of positive events and social contacts (Lewinsohn, 1975) in one's life has been associated with depression, as has the major loss of a loved one, particularly early in life (Brown & Harris, 1978). Another factor that puts people at risk for depression is cognitive. Some people have a negative thinking style (Beck, 1967, 1991). They "see the glass as half empty, rather than half full," and use a faulty logic that sustains this thinking style. For example, they magnify negative events (my friend passed by without speaking; that must mean she's dropping me as a friend) and minimize positive ones (my friend spoke to me; that must have been a fluke); they also overgeneralize (I failed this quiz; I'll never get into law school) and personalize (the house next door is for sale; maybe the owner doesn't like living next to me) events in their life.

Another way in which thinking styles can help contribute to depression derives from the ways in which people make attributions about the causes of events (Abramson, Seligman, & Teasdale, 1978; Seligman et al., 1979). People who believe that negative events in

"What Did You Think of the Earthquake?"

An unexpected event, the Loma Prieta earthquake in the San Francisco area in 1989, provided some quick-thinking Stanford University researchers with a natural experiment. Early in the fall semester, Nolen-Hoeksema and Morrow (1991) had given student volunteers some questionnaires measuring mood and response styles. Specifically, they measured the students' (self-reported) tendencies toward "ruminative" response styles (focusing and dwelling on problems or negative emotional states without taking any action) versus "distracting" response styles (trying to use pleasant or neutral activities to distract oneself from problems or negative emotional states). After the earthquake hit in October, their question was, "Will response style and/or preexisting depression predict people's responses to the earthquake?"

Ten days after the earthquake, they measured the mood of the subjects again and also asked them how much damage they witnessed and how much time they had ruminated about the earthquake. Then, seven weeks after the quake, they measured the students' mood again.

The results were highly interesting. First, those students who had a ruminative response style as measured before the earthquake were more likely than those with a less ruminative style to be depressed, both at ten days and at seven weeks after the earthquake. People who reported ruminating more about the quake itself were also more likely to be depressed at the seven-week follow-up. Taking the students' mood in the beginning of the semester and the amount of damage they witnessed into account, these results were still viable. Something about the rumination itself was associated with continuing bad moods.

But what? Nolen-Hoeksema (1991) speculates that (1) perhaps thinking about a negative event leads to thinking about other negative events, producing a kind of snowballing of negative thoughts that in turn produces low mood, or (2) perhaps rumination interferes with engaging in constructive problem solving about the negative event.

---

their life (such as being turned down for a date) are the result of their own global, stable, internal characteristics (I'm a boring person, everything about me is boring, I will always be boring) but that the positive events are the result of luck or chance are more likely to become depressed. They feel incapable of controlling the events in their lives and quit trying. One study showed that students who make these kinds of attributions at the beginning of the school year are more likely than students with positive thinking styles to become depressed over the school year, even when both group experienced academic failure (Zullow & Seligman, 1985). The Lessons from the Laboratory box illustrates how thinking style is a risk factor for depression, even in situations which are out of one's control.

The fact that more women than men become depressed is consistent with some of the causes for depression that we have just discussed. Perhaps women are less likely than men to receive the kinds of positive social reinforcements, in terms of recognition for job performance, respect of others, and other areas. Indeed, researchers have shown that women who have three or more young children and do not work outside the home (Brown & Harris, 1978), and who have marriages in which there is high conflict and little emotional intimacy (Coyne, Kahn, & Gotlib, 1987) are especially likely to become depressed.

Women may also be more likely than men to be raised to feel a lack of control over their lives. Other research done in psychology laboratories has shown that women are more likely than men to attribute their successes on various tasks to chance and their failures to their own inabilities (Berg, Stephan, & Dodson, 1981). If these kinds of attributions are more common in general in women than in men, it makes sense that more women than men become depressed. Finally, it may be that women express their low mood states differently than men, being more likely to show outward signs of depression.

Bipolar Disorder

In **bipolar disorder,** or manic-depressive disorder, the low mood state of depression alternates with a high mood state of mania. People in manic states feel as though they are on top of the world; they have an exaggerated sense of their own abilities and feel highly energetic, attractive, and animated. The manic person sleeps little, undertakes grand schemes and projects, and talks and jokes quickly. As with depression, this behavior can reach psychotic proportions in which ideas become jumbled together and speech becomes so disorganized that it loses any coherence. There may be delusions of grandeur. These roller-coaster mood states may alternate across several months or may switch every several days. The latter effect, called *rapid cycling,* is more severe and more debilitating.

Interestingly, the list of famous and creative people who have had depression or manic-depression is a long one. It includes royalty and political leaders (Abraham Lincoln, Winston Churchill, Queen Victoria), writers (Lord Byron, Virginia Woolf, Sylvia Plath, Vachel Lindsay, Jack London, Ernest Hemingway), artists (Van Gogh), and many composers (Handel, Berlioz, Schumann, Mahler) (Jamison, 1993). George Frideric Handel wrote *The Messiah* in 23 days, during which he never left his house and had all his meals brought to him. After writing the Hallelujah chorus section, he called to his manservant with tears in his eyes and exclaimed "I think I did see all heaven before me and the great God Him-

self" (Welch, n.d.). Is there a genetic link between creativity and affective disorders? Researchers are currently investigating this hypothesis. They do find higher levels of creativity in the relatives of people with manic-depressive illness, and high levels of mood disorders in the family histories of highly creative people. Genealogies of the families of writers and thinkers like William James and Earnest Hemingway reveal that manic-depressive illness ran throughout their families (Jamison, 1993).

Bipolar disorders have a strong genetic component. In general, less than 1 percent of the U.S. population will get the disorder in their lifetime. But people with an immediate family member with the disorder have a 4 to 20 times higher chance than the general population of developing the disorder. (Note: The chances of such a person *not* getting the disorder, however, are still higher than the chances of getting it. Having a relative with the disorder by no means implies that you will get it.) Researchers believe that there is probably some genetically related abnormality in the brain's chemistry. It is thought that biochemical abnormalities involving interactions of the neurotransmitters norepinephrine, serotonin, and dopamine (Goodwin & Jamison, 1990) play a role in this disorder.

It is not surprising, then, that the most effective treatment is a chemical one: lithium. *Lithium* is a naturally occurring element; given as a medication, it evens out both the manic and depressive moods and lets most people with this disorder function normally. The early and accurate diagnosis of manic-depressive illness is very important for two reasons. First, without proper treatment, the disorder can be highly disturbing to oneself and one's family and friends. Alcohol and suicide are two of the desperate measures to which people turn for relief if they are not properly diagnosed and treated. On the other hand, with early and appropriate treatment, the prognosis is very good. Second, as people experience repeated episodes of mania and depression, the cycling tends to become more rapid and the course of the disorder more chronic. Because suicide is linked with affective disorders, we discuss it briefly before moving on to the anxiety disorders.

Suicide

Suicide is one of those subjects in adjustment and mental health that is hard to talk about, and therefore often overlooked, even among professionals. Because there are legal, religious and moral taboos in our society against taking one's own life, and because it is a hard subject to research, suicide takes on a sense of mystery. In this section we examine some of the myths and facts about suicide as well as some issues relating to its prevention.

First, we wish to acknowledge that not all suicides are the result of mental illness. Some people who deliberately take their lives are making clear, conscious choices. Such was the case of one of our elementary school teachers, a woman in her late sixties who had taken care of her first husband as he suffered and then died of cancer. When she learned that she had terminal cancer, she shot herself, in part, her friends believed, to spare her second husband, as well as herself, from what was to come. There is of course disagreement in our society about the morality of such acts, as can be seen in the controversy surrounding Dr. Jack Kevorkian, the Michigan doctor who "assists" ill people in commiting suicide.

But here we are concerned with suicide from a psychological perspective. Who commits suicide, and why? In what ways does the act accompany mental illnesses and other problems in adjustment? First, a general answer to the question, "Who commits suicide?" is: those who have *given up hope* that their lives could be better, that there could be any escape to their current suffering. This group includes of course, people suffering from depressive disorders and bipolar disorders. Depressed

people, it should be noted, are most at risk *not* at the depths of their depression (when they lack the energy to do anything), but rather as the depression begins to lift, when they still feel miserable but a little more energized. People suffering from chronic schizophrenia, alcoholism, and other drug abuse are also more likely than the average person to commit suicide. People who are *alone*, who do not have family and friends to remind them of the joys and responsibilities of living and to help prevent them from sinking into hopelessness, are also more at risk. Divorced people have the highest rate of suicide, followed by widowed, then single, then married people. Married people with children have the lowest rate of all (Comer, 1992). Perhaps, despite the fact that they too have stressors in their life, the responsibility and the knowledge that they are needed makes suicide a less acceptable option for married people. *Stressful events*, while not a cause of suicide alone, often precipitate suicide. In the summer of 1993, Vince Foster, a White House legal counsel and good friend of President and Mrs. Clinton, shot himself without warning. Though he was a highly accomplished person and was married with children, he had been under a great deal of job stress. Heavy responsibilities, his workaholic habits, and his alleged involvement in the Whitewater scandal were all weighing on him at the time of his suicide.

Finally, the role of *alcohol* in suicide cannot be overlooked. About 20 percent of those who die from suicide are found on autopsy to have been legally intoxicated (Comer, 1992). Alcohol not only impairs judgment but also lowers inhibitions, making it less likely that the person will stop his own actions before it is too late.

How do psychologists and other mental health professionals assess the risk of suicide in an individual person? Indeed, what factors might you consider if you are worried that someone that you know is at risk? The following behaviors are warning signs: talking or hinting about suicide, previous suicide attempts, giving away one's possessions or putting one's affairs in order. Recent losses or major stresses along with heavy alcohol and other drug use raise the cause for concern, especially when the person is engaging in some of the behaviors just described. It is a fact that the vast majority of people who commit suicide can, and at some level want, to be helped. Therefore, recognizing the warning signs and helping the person to get counseling before the attempt is very important.

STRESS AND ANXIETY DISORDERS

Thus far our discussion has focused on the major mental illnesses. Chances are good that you know someone who has experienced one or more of these problems, but they are not everyday occurrences. Stress and anxiety, on the other hand, are more ubiquitous in everyday life. In this section we will discuss the origins of stress and how continued stress and anxiety can lead to physical and psychological disorders.

Everyday Stress and Anxiety

Stress and anxiety are closely related, but separable, phenomena. A few definitions will help keep them straight. *Stress* exists when we perceive a demand in the environment that threatens our well-being and that needs to be met or coped with. Whether a particular event (finding nothing in the refrigerator for dinner) will be stressful or not depends in part on the person's coping abilities and resources. For example, a 10-year-old child whose parents are home, a young unemployed mother with no money and three children, and a single working person who lives next to a deli will have different resources for coping with this event and therefore different perceptions of how stressful it is. *Anxiety* is an emotion we sometimes feel in facing stress. We become anxious when we feel uncertain about how to cope with the stress, when we doubt that we

have the capacity to do so, or when we feel certain the stress will overwhelm us. For example, consider your professor's announcing a pop quiz that will count for half of your final course grade, consider your airplane's suddenly losing altitude, or consider a middle-of-the-night phone call from a family member that begins, "I have some bad news." We also feel anxious in certain situations that remind us of threatening or traumatic experiences we had in the past.

As described in detail in Chapter 5, the experience of stress and anxiety is accompanied by certain physical symptoms and sensations. These may be adaptive in the short term, by preparing us to take action when confronted with danger, for example. But when the stressor or threat is mental and when the stress is prolonged over a period of time, these physical consequences can take at high toll. As described in Chapter 5, stress-related illnesses and diseases, exhaustion, and decreases in immune system functioning are some ways in which stress effects its toll.

Consider, for example, the case of Caroline, a college student who is very concerned about her future medical career. Caroline perceives that she must do well in college the whole time she is there if she wants to get into medical school. Her courses are demanding and seem to take more time to prepare for than she has. She gets highly nervous before exams, worries about her performance in the near and distant future, and subjectively feels highly stressed. Caroline continues to study hard and is making decent grades, but her coping behavior doesn't remove the demand and the threat of failure. She may get an *A* this week, but she needs another one next week as well. The pressure is constant. How well is Caroline prepared to meet these stresses in the environment? If she is able to do well in her classes, has some social support, gets some relaxation and exercise, she will probably handle the challenge. But if her coping mechanisms or personal resources are not enough to meet the demands of the environment, she may not. If the pressure produces long-term emotional and physiological responses, damage to the internal organs, such as stomach ulcers or high blood pressure, can occur. Continued emotionally produced physiological responding is what causes **psychosomatic disorders**. They are called *psychosomatic* because while they affect certain body organs (the *somatic* part of the term), they are caused by the psychological perception of threat and the reaction to it (the *psycho* part of the term).

Contrary to the myth that psychosomatic disorders are "all in your head," real damage to organs of the body results from these conditions. The psychosomatic disorders are not contained in the DSM–IV because the symptoms are expressed medically. We mention them again here, however, to illustrate how mental states can influence physical states. Conversely, as we will see throughout this chapter, many mental disorders are related to physical factors.

Anxiety Disorders

Anxiety disorders are diagnosed when stress, fears, or worries become so intense that the person begins to have difficulty functioning. What kinds of difficulties in functioning? It depends on the type of anxiety disorder, as the following cases illustrate.

Obsessive-Compulsive Disorder. In one case, a man with obsessive-compulsive disorder fears that dirt picked up outside the house will contaminate and harm him and his family if brought into the house. Everyone is required to go through a half-hour cleansing ritual, changing their shoes and clothing in the entranceway before entering the house. He himself spends a total of two hours during the day washing his hands and showering until the skin on his hands is red and raw from scrubbing. He feels depressed and helpless to withstand the impulse to wash. In this case, the person had both **obsessions,** or specific intrusive thoughts that are not wanted,

and **compulsions,** the irresistible urge to perform some behavior. Some people have only obsessions. Note that this use of the term *obsessions* is quite different from informally labeling strong preferences or habits as obsessions, as in, "He is obsessed with exercise," or "She is obsessed with studying."

Agoraphobia. A middle-aged woman with **agoraphobia** is fearful of leaving her home. She avoids traveling, especially to places (such as movie theatres, offices, and restaurants) in which she might have a panic attack and not be able to escape to "safety." Eventually, she refuses to leave the house altogether, becomes very dependent on others, depressed, and develops an addiction to Valium, a prescription drug used to treat anxiety. Agoraphobia, which literally means "fear of the marketplace" is often linked with panic disorder.

Panic Disorder. *Panic disorder* is a condition in which people suddenly feel their heart beating fast, feel breathless, dizzy, and incredibly afraid. People commonly report that they feel as if they are going to have a heart attack or even die, and that they are convinced that something catastrophic is happening. Panic disorder and agoraphobia can occur together, and they can also occur separately, without each other.

Posttraumatic Stress Disorder. In a case of posttraumatic stress disorder (PTSD) a young soldier just home from heavy combat finds himself having vivid flashbacks and dreams of combat, avoiding any reminders of it, being very "jumpy" at loud noises and sometimes even reaching for his gun when startled. Emotionally, he feels numb and cannot relate to other people or enjoy normal life activities. PTSD can last long after the war is over, and also occurs in victims of sudden and catastrophic peacetime traumas, such as earthquakes, rape, and hostage situations. Some symptoms of PTSD occur in children as well, both directly (such as children exposed to

---

Phobias: A Short List

There are long lists of phobias, some common and others rare and obscure, indicating the large and varied number of things people have been afraid of over the years. Here is a partial list of the many human phobias identified so far:

Aerophobia: fear of flying
Ailurophobia: fear of cats
Amaxophobia: fear of cars and driving
Anthrophibia: fear of human beings
Aquaphobia: fear of water
Arachnophobia: fear of spiders
Brontophobia: fear of thunder
Claustrophobia: fear of closed spaces
Cynophobia: fear of dogs

Dementophobia: fear of insanity
Gephyrophobia: fear of bridges
Herpetophobia: fear of reptiles
Mikrophobia: fear of germs
Murophobia: fear of mice
Numerophobia: fear of numbers
Nyctophobia: fear of darkness
Ochlophobia: fear of crowds
Ornithophobia: fear of birds
Phonophobia: fear of speaking aloud
Pyrophobia: fear of fire
Thanatophobia: fear of death
Trichophobia: fear of hair
Xenophobia: fear of strangers

---

recent conflicts in Bosnia, or to neighborhood violence in U.S. cities) and indirectly (such as children of survivors of catastrophic events such as the Nazi holocaust).

Simple Phobias. *Phobias* are another category of anxiety disorders. The majority of phobias are limited in scope (such as fear of snakes, dental work, or flying) and do not interfere with a person's everyday functioning. Therefore, they are often not diagnosed. Moreover, many people without phobias are afraid or slightly nervous about snakes, dental work, or flying. It was noted that following the crash of TWA flight 800 off the coast of Long Island in 1996, air travel dropped sharply for a while. People with disabling phobias, in contrast, are so fearful that not only occasional decisions, but also their everyday life, health, and happiness are affected. There are cases of dental phobics whose teeth and gums become diseased because they refuse to go to the dentist, people who panic and stop their cars at the entrance to bridges, and people who cannot visit city buildings if it means they have to ride in an elevator. There are several general classifications of phobias. The *simple phobias* include fears of specific objects

or events, as in the examples just cited and in the accompanying box.

Social Phobias. A *social phobia* is diagnosed if the person's fear centers around being embarrassed in public situations. These people may fear speaking, writing, or eating in front of others and studiously avoid all such situations. One woman, phobic about inadvertently burping in public, became hyperattentive to every sensation in her stomach, leaving public places quickly at the slightest inkling that she might burp. Situations such as concerts and church services were excruciating for her and she avoided them whenever she could. Interestingly, phobias may and often do occur in combination with other anxiety disorders.

Generalized Anxiety Disorder. *Generalized anxiety disorder* is diagnosed when the person is in a chronic state of unrealistic rumination and worry, thinking ahead to all the possible troubles that might occur and fretting about many things that pose no immediate danger. The person with this disorder is hypervigilant ("on alert"), jumpy, and restless. Physical symptoms such as breathlessness, heart palpitations, stomach problems, and sweating are also common. If this sounds like a very uncomfortable state to you, you are right. Generalized anxiety disorder, like the other anxiety disorders, is particularly uncomfortable because it affects the person's functioning in several spheres: emotional, cognitive, and physical. However, as in most anxiety disorders, the person may be able to get by on a day-to-day basis. That is, while the disorder impairs optimal adjustment and happiness, there is not a complete breakdown of functioning or loss of contact with reality, as with the major mental illnesses. Another feature that all the anxiety disorders have in common is that the anxiety is consciously experienced; the person is (very!) aware of being anxious or fearful. As we will see later, this feature distinguishes the anxiety disorders from the dissociative disorders.

Causes of Anxiety Disorders

The answer to this question is complicated. First, each of the anxiety disorders has somewhat different causes. Second, there is controversy about the causes of some. Let us look broadly at those causes about which most mental health professionals agree. For phobias of various kinds, a *behavioral* explanation works well. That is, fears can be classically conditioned. For example, a child who was previously unafraid of deer becomes extremely phobic of deer after getting in the way of a frightened doe and being trampled. That fear may generalize to other large, four-legged animals. Naturally, the child may avoid any contact with such creatures and this effect has the paradoxical effect of maintaining the fear. If the child had subsequent contact with deer, chances are she would learn that nothing bad would happen and the fear would be extinguished. But in the absence of that contact, the fear remains strong. This is true also for people with agoraphobia; because they avoid the fear-provoking situations, the fear is never extinguished. Treatments in which the person is supported during gradual exposure to the fear-producing situation are often effective, as we will see in the next chapter.

For other anxiety disorders, the underlying *meaning* of the anxiety is a factor. Veterans and other people with PTSD may need to acknowledge and come to terms with the horrors of their experience in order to find some relief. A person with a social phobia may need to understand how the stringent expectations of her parents for proper behavior are a factor in her anxiety about being embarrassed by her own behavior. Finally, some anxiety disorders seem to be at least partly caused by physical factors, or by a combination of physical and cognitive factors. People with obsessive-compulsive disorder are also likely to be depressed and may have an abnormality with the neurotransmitter serotonin. People with panic disorder seem to have some biochemical abnormalities in the brain that make them overreactive to their own internal sensations. They are quick to sense, for example, that their heart is beating quickly, interpret this symptom as a possible heart attack, and thereby increase their panic.

REVIEW QUESTIONS

6. The symptoms of _____ involves very low mood, lack of energy, and disturbances in sleep, appetite and sexual drive as well as negative thinking.

7. _____ involves alternating states of very low and very high (manic) mood states.

8. Anxiety disorders range from _____, a fear of public situations in which one might be embarrassed, to _____, a more chronic, diffuse state of worry, rumination, and anxiety.

DISSOCIATIVE DISORDERS

In the set of disorders we have just been discussing, anxiety is typically very obvious. Traumatic situations are not only remembered, but relived or anticipated with fear and worry. In contrast, sometimes an event is so traumatic and the person's psychological defenses so inadequate to cope with it that the event is walled off from the person's conscious awareness, resulting in a dissociative disorder.

In the **dissociative disorders,** one or more aspects of the self or personality are dissociated or split off from other parts. Mild and fleeting dissociative experiences are actually not uncommon in everyday life. For example, have you ever had the experience of driving somewhere—say, from home to a friend's house—and once you arrived having no memory of having driven there because your attention was focused on something else during the drive? Or have you ever been concentrating so deeply on a book that you weren't aware of someone right next to you calling for you to listen to them? Of course you were "seeing" the road during the drive and "hearing" the other person's voice, but the awareness of that was lost because of your ability to split your attention. These kinds of states, as well as the related state of hypnosis, are of interest to psychologists because they help us understand how the mind works. Sometimes, however, the splitting of awareness becomes so deep and so prolonged that it prevents the person from functioning well. Then the person is diagnosed with a dissociative disorder.

Dissociative Amnesia

One kind of dissociative disorder is called *dissociative amnesia,* or psychologically caused forgetting. Usually following some intense anxiety or trauma, people temporarily forget who they are, where they live, and, in extreme cases, everything about themselves and their past. This dissociation from one's very identity seems to serve a protective function;

when the trauma is so great (such as seeing a loved one killed) that the normal defenses are overwhelmed, dissociation occurs. In rare cases, the amnesia is accompanied by travel to a different place. Then it is diagnosed as *dissociative fugue.* Comer (1992, p. 577) reports a case in 1980 in which "a Florida park ranger found a woman naked and starving in a shallow grave. Unaware of her identity and in an apparent fugue state, she was hospitalized as 'Jane Doe.' Five months later, the woman was recognized on *Good Morning America* by her mother. She was thirty-four years old and had been missing for seven years."

Dissociative Identity Disorder

A particularly devastating type of trauma is prolonged sexual abuse in childhood, especially when there is also physical violence involved. Not only are children too young to protect themselves or escape from the situation, but their psychological defenses are not strong enough to withstand the abuse. Some of these children also have the ability to put themselves in a kind of trance state. They report being able to tune out the abuse or "be somewhere else," a kind of self-hypnotic ability. This ability helps them to psychologically escape the trauma, and it becomes a defensive coping mechanism. While they do this consciously at first, the splitting off later becomes unconscious and occurs without their intention. The mind thus creates "other" personalities to help them cope. That is, they develop *dissociative identity disorder* (commonly called "multiple personalities"). The other personalities are, of course, only walled-off parts of one's own personality and one's own past. They are not distinct "people" living inside one's body, as Hollywood portrays them; rather, they hold the memories that are too painful for the person afflicted to be consciously aware of. Also, these personalities "possess" abilities and characteristics that the original personality does not have and which in certain situations are needed for physical and mental survival. This survival strategy is illustrated by the case of Sybil (Schreiber, 1973), whose treatment is described in the next chapter.

"Sybil," a rather depleted, fearful person, had 16 different personalties, including Vicky (who was attractive, sophisticated, and self-assured), Peggy Lou (assertive, energetic, often angry, and spunky), Marcia Lynn (a very emotional writer and painter), and Mike (one of the two male personalities, a builder). The "alter personalities," in a sense, took care of her by keeping very painful childhood memories encapsulated and by allowing the expression of emotions or traits that were too anxiety provoking for her to acknowledge as her own.

PERSONALITY DISORDERS

We turn now to a different set of disorders that are less dramatic, perhaps, then dissociative disorders but which nonetheless present serious challenges for adjustment. A **personality disorder** is diagnosed when the individual has a longstanding and inflexible set of personality traits or inner experiences that cause significant distress or impairment. Such persons are not psychotic and may perform work tasks adequately, but they have great difficulty in interpersonal relationships, often making others and themselves miserable. To appreciate personality disorders, it is first necessary to understand what constitutes a well-adjusted personality. Fundamentally, the well-adjusted personality requires a good solid sense of *self*. What, then, is the role of the self in adjustment?

The Importance of the Self in Adjustment

The *self* has always been of great interest to psychologists, philosophers, and others concerned with human existence (see Chapter 3). In childhood the sense of self undergoes great change and development. In response to repeated interactions with parents and others and even interactions with the physical environment, children develop a sense of who they are and what their capabilities are and are not. The tiny baby has no sense of himself separate from his caretaker, but by age 2 he knows not only that he is a separate being but that he has a will and some control in the world. Two-year-olds delight in saying "no," or dumping bowls of spaghetti over their heads, not to exasperate their parents but to assert their own identities. This behavior is to be expected in normal development. The parents' task is to help the child learn the rules of society without totally suppressing the child's own needs and interests. Warm, consistent parents who set limits and also accept the child as a unique individual help the child develop a solid sense of self. Indeed, psychologist Margaret Mahler (1979) and others argued that all of normal development from birth through adolescence, indeed the ongoing task of healthy adults, is to find a balance between asserting autonomy or independence and seeking connection with others. Human beings need both. To the extent that their early development has given them a strong sense of self, they will manage this balance well as adults and be able to relate to others. Unfortunately, some adults do not manage this balance well. Their personalities do not allow them to have satisfying or adaptive relationships with others, and they may be diagnosed as having a personality disorder.

Types of Personality Disorders

The DSM–IV (1994) distinguishes eleven different types of personality disorders and groups them into three rough clusters on the basis of their primary features, as shown in Figure 7.1.

Cluster A includes disorders in which the person shows odd or eccentric behavior, such as the *paranoid* and *schizoid* diagnoses. Cluster

CLUSTER A

The cluster A disorders are characterized by odd or eccentric behaviors.

- paranoid personality disorder
- schizoid personality disorder
- schizotypal personality disorder

CLUSTER B

The cluster B disorders are characterized by emotional, dramatic, or erratic behaviors.

- antisocial personality disorder
- borderline personality disorder
- histrionic personality disorder
- narcissistic personality disorder

CLUSTER C

The cluster C disorders are characterized by anxious or fearful behaviors.

- avoidant personality disorder
- dependent personality disorder
- obsessive-compulsive personality disorder

FIGURE 7.1   Personality Disorders
Source: DSM–IV Casebook (1994).

B includes disorders in which behavior is erratic, emotional, and dramatic, such as the *antisocial* and *borderline* diagnoses. Gary Gilmore, whose family history and resulting troubles are mentioned in Chapter 12, had an *antisocial personality disorder.* Cluster C includes disorders in which the person is extremely fearful or anxious, such as the *avoidant* and *obsessive-compulsive disorders.* Note that obsessive-compulsive disorder, as described in the section on anxiety disorders, and obsessive-compulsive *Personality* Disorder are two different disorders, as will be made clear shortly. Unfortunately, their names are almost identical.

To illustrate the range of personality disorders, we will examine one disorder from each cluster in detail.

Schizoid Personality Disorder (from Cluster A). Consider the following case, called "Man's Best Friend" described by Spitzer and colleagues (1989, pp. 249–250).

The Case. The patient was a retired policeman, aged 50, who had a long and difficult bereavement over the death of his dog. When he sought treatment for his sadness, sleep difficulties, and lack of concentration, it was found that he "lives alone, and has for many years had virtually no conversational contacts with other human beings beyond a 'Hello' or 'How are you?' He prefers to be by himself, finds talk a waste of time, and feels awkward when people try to initiate a relationship. He is employed as a security guard, but is known by fellow workers as a 'cold fish' and a 'loner.' They no longer even notice or tease him, especially since he never seemed to notice or care about their teasing anyway" (p. 249). He has virtually no relationships, felt very little emotion when both his parents died, and does not mind at all having no other family contact. He is aware that he is different from others and is puzzled by others' emotionality.

Analysis. Is John's extended grief over the loss of his dog normal bereavement, or does it indicate a disorder? His social history and current behavior (few to no close relationships, little experience of emotion, but no other odd or eccentric behaviors) led the psychotherapist to a diagnosis of schizoid personality disorder. This term is a label for the pattern of behavior described above. According to the DSM–IV (1994, p. 641), there are two criteria for this diagnosis. The first is a "pervasive pattern of detachment from social relationships and a restricted range of emotions in interpersonal settings," as seen in few close friends, no desire for them, few interests or activities, emotional distance, and coldness. The second criterion is that these symptoms do not occur only in the presence of another disorder, such as schizophrenia. This criterion is important because it underscores the fact that personality disorders are longstanding and do not change with the circumstances, contexts, or problems in people's lives.

Little is known about the causes of schizoid personality disorder, although it seems to begin with being isolated, socially awkward, and having academic difficulties in childhood and adolescence (APA, 1994). John entered supportive individual therapy and after his therapist moved away the next year, called the therapist regularly for the next several years. Though he did not talk long, the contact seemed to be important for him. He got another dog, but very little else changed in his life.

Borderline Personality Disorder (from Cluster B).

It is interesting to compare the case of John with the following case, called "Empty Shell" (Spitzer et al., 1994, pp. 236–238).

The Case. The patient was a 23-year-old woman who worked as a veterinary assistant and lived alone. She was admitted to the hospital for the first time following a two-week period in which she felt panicky, as if she were in a trance and removed from her body. She heard voices telling her to jump off a bridge and had been slashing her wrists and drinking heavily. The therapist described her as cooperative but frightened and disheveled on her admission to the hospital. She herself reported feeling like "an empty shell that is transparent to everyone."

Indeed, her personal history was one in which developing a secure sense of her self and identity was difficult. After her parents were divorced when she was 3, she lived with her grandmother and mother, who had a serious drinking problem. At age 6 she was sent to boarding school for a year and a half and then was withdrawn suddenly by her mother. When she was 8, her grandmother died, but she did not grieve openly for her. When she was 9, her mother was hospitalized with schizophrenia, and later she lived with different relatives. She dated, but her relationships with men were stormy and possessive. Living with roommates was unsuccessful because she easily became jealous of their relationships with others and made manipulative efforts to keep them loyal to her. Although she had been a good student and held a steady job, she found herself bothered by feelings of loneliness and inadequacy, and was frequently anxious and depressed.

Analysis. The most recent episode of troubles for this patient started 3 months prior to her admission to the hospital, when she found out that her mother was pregnant. She began drinking heavily and engaging in one-night stands. However, her history also included a longstanding pattern of unstable mood and identity, unsatisfying interpersonal relationships, self-damaging behavior, and chronic feelings of loneliness and emptiness. These are a few of the criteria for diagnosing **borderline personality disorder.** Others include desperate behaviors designed to prevent abandonment, impulsivity (in drugs, sex, eating, reckless driving), self-mutilating or suicidal behavior or threats, chronic feelings of emptiness, and intense, uncontrollable anger. Crises in relationships are, as you might imagine, a hallmark of borderline personality disorder.

Treatment, unfortunately, did not have a very satisfactory outcome. After her hospitalization, she had psychotherapy twice a week. The therapist described their relationship as tenuous, and the patient as alternating between wanting special favors and support and criticizing the therapy and wanting to drop out. After three months, she became involved with a new boyfriend and stopped therapy, complaining that the therapist didn't care enough for her. People with borderline personality disorder often alternate between loving and hating, pursuing and distancing in their relationships, including their therapeutic relationships. While the diagnosis of this disorder is not always reliable, the clinical picture is one that practicing therapists strongly feel represents a distinct disorder. Controversy, research, and theorizing about the causes of this disorder have all increased dramatically in recent years.

Obsessive-Compulsive Personality Disorder (from Cluster C).

Finally, the case of "The Workaholic" (Spitzer et al., 1994, pp. 147–148) illustrates the more anxiety-laden personality disorders found in Cluster C. This person meets the criteria for a diagnosis of **obsessive-compulsive personality disorder.** Note that despite the similarity in the name of this disorder and the anxiety disorder called obsessive-compulsive disorder (OCD) that we discussed earlier, these diagnoses are distinct. People with OCD are typically highly anxious people, but their anxiety focuses on their obsessions and compulsions. They typically have good relationships with others and tend to be married and employed in jobs where they function well and get along with others. In contrast, according to the DSM–IV diagnostic criteria, people with obsessive-compulsive *personality* disorder tend to be emotionally cold, rigid in their habits and their relationships. Perfectionism, overconcern with details, being indecisive but stubborn, excessively devoted to work, and stinginess are other characteristics of the personality disorder. This set of personality traits is maladaptive, causing pain and concern to family, friends, and colleagues as well as to the person.

The Case.   In this case the patient was a 45-year-old lawyer who sought outpatient counseling at his wife's insistence. She complained that he was emotionally cold, rigid, bullying, sexually uninterested, and worked to an extreme, while he saw nothing wrong at all at home. Indeed, he described his wife as a "suitable mate." He did, however, admit to work problems. Essentially, he was a perfectionist and a stickler for details, to the extent that he could not keep up with his own work and was highly critical of the work of others. The case history indicates that he had had two or three secretaries a year for the last 15 years because he was so difficult to work for. He became impatient and furious if others, including colleagues and the family, refused to follow his plans. Even on vacation and at games such as tennis, he could not relax. He was highly competitive and a poor loser.

Analysis.   The patient's difficulties began in his adolescence, when as the son of two upwardly mobile, hardworking parents, he never felt that he worked hard enough. This patient, fortunately, had enough caring for his family that he began psychotherapy and was seen on and off for several years. He made some progress in learning to relax and play more, and began to spend frequent weekends with his family at a vacation house. He felt happier and more relaxed and his relationships with his children, at least, improved.

Together, these cases illustrate some of the characteristics of personality disorders. In a sense, they are all exaggerations of "normal" personality traits. Everyone knows people who are a little shy, a little possessive and demanding in relationships, or a little perfectionistic. Certainly, there is room for tolerance of personality differences without labeling those that are annoying to you as "disordered." (Note: This should be taken as a reminder about psychology student's disease!) Rather, it is when these traits are strong enough to be disruptive in social and work relationships that they are labeled as personality disorders. Thus the distinction between personality disorders and normal personality traits is more of a quantitative than a qualitative one. It is still somewhat unclear, however, *how* dysfunctional a person needs to be in order to be diagnosed as having a disorder, and there are ongoing debates about various diagnostic categories. As we discussed at the beginning of the chapter, diagnosis of psychological disorders is a dynamic scientific enterprise. That is, diagnosis changes with new research findings, with new clinical observations, and with new insights that come from the study of mental illness across cultures.

By this time, it should be clear that *mental illness* is a deceptively simple term for a varied set of disorders. Some of these disorders can be highly debilitating at times, whereas others are not so debilitating and, in fact, may be quite invisible to outside observers. Some, such as bipolar disorder, have very clear and strong biological causes. Others, such as the personality disorders, seem to stem from disturbances in early interpersonal relationships. But even in these disorders a single cause is not usually sufficient to fully explain the causes of the disorder. A person who is genetically at risk for bipolar disorder will be more likely to become ill and remain so if there are many stressors in her life. A person whose early relationships are disturbed *and* who is shy and retiring by nature will be more likely to develop one of the "avoidant" type of personality disorders than one of the "dramatic" types of personality disorders. As with other areas in the psychology of adjustment, optimum happiness depends on a combination of the person's characteristics and the nature of the environment. A good fit between skills, abilities, and temperament on one hand and the demands and opportunities of the environment on the other facilitates adjustment.

SUMMARY

1. Diagnosis of mental disorders requires that the person be significantly distressed or disabled by his or her psychological state or symptoms rather than just different from other people. Diagnosis, and the nature of mental disorder itself, is influenced by scientific, social, and cultural factors.

2. Schizophrenia is a major mental illness characterized by periods of psychosis, disturbed emotions, and social withdrawal. The hallmarks of psychosis are inability to synthesize information and think logically, delusions (false beliefs), and hallucinations (false sensory experiences).

3. Varieties of schizophrenia include Type I and Type II as well as the paranoid, disorganized, catatonic, undifferentiated, and residual types. Each has somewhat different symptoms, causes, and prognosis.

4. Schizophrenia is caused by a combination of genetic and biochemical risk factors and is exacerbated by environments which are high in expressed emotion and other kinds of overstimulation.

5. Major depressive disorder is characterized by extreme sadness, lethargy, negative thinking, lack of appetite, and sleep disturbances. In bipolar disorder, this depressed state alternates with periods of mania in which the person is euphoric, talks and moves quickly, has extremely positive beliefs about themselves and their ability. In some cases of either unipolar or bipolar disorder, there may be psychotic episodes as well as affective disturbances.

6. People with affective disorders are at higher risk for suicide, particularly if they also abuse drugs or alcohol, have suffered recent losses, or are alone. Most people who commit suicide want to be helped, and there are warning signs that can alert potential helpers.

7. Stress and anxiety occur in everyday life. When they are extreme, they can result in psychophysiological disorders, in which the organs of the body are affected, or anxiety disorders.

8. The anxiety disorders include obsessive-compulsive disorder, agoraphobia (with or without panic disorder), posttraumatic stress disorder, simple phobias, social phobias, and generalized anxiety disorder. Each has distinct features and causes but all are associated with the conscious experience of anxiety—physically, emotionally, and cognitively.

9. In the dissociative disorders, overwhelming anxiety is dealt with by splitting off memories, conscious awareness, and aspects of the personality. They occur when a person with an ability to split his or her awareness is subjected to highly traumatic events. The dissociative disorders include dissociative amnesia, dissociative fugue, and dissociative identity disorder ("multiple personalities").

10. Personality disorders are characterized by a longstanding, rigid set of personality traits that causes significant distress or impairment, especially in the ability to sustain satisfying relationships with others. There are a variety of personality disorders, including those in which behavior is odd or eccentric, those in which behavior is erratic, emotional, and dramatic, and those in which behavior is marked by fear, anxiety and social withdrawal.

CRITICAL THINKING QUESTIONS

1. Mental illness is still associated with a good deal of public fear, shame, and stigma. This is particularly true of schizophrenia and bipolar disorder. Why do you think these reactions exist? Is it something about the afflicted person's behavior, about the observer's own fears or needs, about our societal values and attitudes, or some combination of these factors? Perhaps your own observations of the reactions of others to mental illness among family or friends will provide some clues.

2. Ethical aspects of psychological disorders and their treatment are very important but often neglected in our thinking. Where do you stand on the following ethical questions, and why? Should a person with bipolar disorder be forced to take lithium, even if he or she "enjoys" the manic phases? Should potential employers or schools or spouse be told about a history of major mental illness? If not, why? If so, under what circumstances and when should they be told?

3. Both anxiety disorders and depression are more common today in the United States than they were in previous generations. What kinds of hypotheses might you make about why this is so? How could you test your hypotheses?

MATCHING EXERCISE

Match each term with its definition.

a. hallucinations
b. delusions
c. culture-bound syndromes
d. dopamine, serotonin
e. expressed emotion
f. seasonal affective disorder

g. bipolar disorder
h. psychosomatic disorder
i. obsessions
j. compulsions
k. agoraphobia
l. dissociative disorder
m. borderline personality disorder

n. obsessive-compulsive personality disorder
o. schizoid personality disorder

1. False sensory experiences, seeing or hearing things that are not real, which sometimes accompany psychotic episodes
2. Disorder characterized by overconcern with details and order, stinginess, and inflexibility in interpersonal relationships
3. Also known as manic-depression, a type of mood disorder characterized by wide swings in mood
4. Intrusive, unwarranted and bothersome thoughts that are difficult to control
5. An anxiety disorder that includes fear of being out in crowds, on roads, or to leave home at all
6. A characteristic of family communication that helps predict relapse in schizophrenia
7. Disorders in which consciousness or identity are split
8. A disorder characterized by instability and crises in relationships, self-damaging behavior, chronic feelings of loneliness and emptiness, and instability of identity and mood
9. Neurotransmitters thought to be important in schizophrenia and in the mood disorders
10. Disorders in some organ or physical process in the body, related to stress
11. Disorders, such as anorexia nervosa and *susto*, that are found only in certain places and not others
12. A type of affective disorder related to disturbances in the way the body copes with lack of light in the winter months
13. Behaviors that are repeated over and over, often having to do with cleaning, washing, or checking, in order to decrease anxiety
14. Disorder characterized by an extreme lack of social relationships, lack of interest in them, restricted range of emotions, emotional coldness and distance
15. False beliefs that sometimes accompany psychotic episodes

Answers to Matching Exercise

a. 1   b. 15   c. 11   d. 9   e. 6   f. 12   g. 3   h. 10   i. 4   j. 13   k. 5   l. 7   m. 8   n. 2   o. 14

ANSWERS TO REVIEW QUESTIONS

1. anorexia nervosa, *koro*
2. *Diagnostic and Statistical Manual of Mental Disorders* or DSM–IV
3. schizophrenic
4. decrease
5. relapse

6. major depressive disorder

7. bipolar disorder

8. social phobia, generalized anxiety disorder

9. quantitative

10. borderline personality disorder

11. dissociative fugue

CHAPTER 8

PSYCHOTHERAPY

Sally Field as Sybil

Sybil

Sybil Dorsett climbed out of the taxi cab, paid the driver, and walked slowly into the office building of Dr. Cornelia Wilbur. In the foyer leading to the office, the door stood open so that patients did not have to knock. Sybil entered a cozy waiting room, and Dr. Wilbur came out to usher her in to the sunny consulting room. It had been nearly ten years since they last saw each other. And although Sybil had no way of knowing it at that moment, it was the beginning of an extraordinary journey that would take the next eleven years and change her life immeasurably (Schreiber, 1973).

What Sybil did know on that day was that she was in serious need of help. For several years now, she had been feeling like she was at the end of her rope. Sybil was a teacher, and as long as she was in the classroom, things seemed to be okay. At other times, however, strange and confusing things happened to her without forewarning. She would "lose" chunks of time, even days. She recalled later that "people she had never seen before would insist they knew her. She would go on a picnic and have a vague sense of having been there before. She would begin a painting and return to the studio to find that it had been completed by someone else—in a style not hers. Sleep was a nightmare . . . many were the occasions of waking up without going to sleep, of going to sleep to wake up not the next morning, but at some unrecognizable time" (Schreiber, 1973, p. 57). While Sybil's problem was unusual (dissociative identity disorder, or multiple personalities; see Chapter 7) her response—seeking help from a psychotherapist—was not.

Sybil sought help from Dr. Wilbur because she had met the psychiatrist ten years earlier and had been hopeful then about getting some help from her. The circumstances under which she met, and then lost track of, Dr. Wilbur were very disturbing. At that time, Sybil was living in her parents' home in Omaha, Nebraska. She was 22 and had been sent home from college because her nervous symptoms had become so severe. Summoning up all her nerve (her parents disapproved of psychotherapy), Sybil had asked to see a psychiatrist and had two appointments with Dr. Wilbur. She trusted

and liked her, and began to think that she could share with Dr. Wilbur the many things, some vague and some quite clear, that were troubling her. When Sybil got sick on the day of her third appointment, Sybil's mother pretended, in front of Sybil, to call and cancel the appointment. She told Sybil that Dr. Wilbur said nothing about rescheduling it. In fact, Mrs. Dorsett never made the call. Dr. Wilbur moved out of the area soon after that, and Sybil believed that the psychiatrist had abandoned her. Then, three years later, to Sybil's great distress, Mrs. Dorsett confessed that she had never made the call.

This is what Sybil was thinking about as she walked into Dr. Wilbur's office ten years later. She was hoping that Dr. Wilbur would forgive her for dropping out of treatment and that somehow she would be able to truly understand Sybil's inner thoughts, feelings, and behavior. And, like all psychotherapy clients, Sybil was hoping for some relief from her problems.

In their first appointment, Sybil gave a mild-mannered, superficial, clipped summary of her life over the last ten years. She didn't mention the problems she was having because she was too nervous to bring them up. She showed no emotion, even when she talked about the fellow school-teacher who had asked her to marry him. On her part, Dr. Wilbur listened carefully, not only to what Sybil was saying, but also to what she was *not* saying. She noticed that Sybil's pupils were dilated from anxiety and that her body language spoke of tension and fear. She didn't press for more but asked at the end what Sybil would like from her. Sybil asked to begin psychoanalysis, and Dr. Wilbur agreed to see her once a week for an indefinite period of time.

In the practice of psychotherapy, one always has to expect the unexpected. Revelations, confessions, changes of mood, heart, and mind are all part of the process of self-discovery toward which the therapist helps guide the client. So it was that three months into the therapy the case took a surprising turn. Sybil had come in with a letter from her boyfriend, but when she reached into her purse to show it to Dr. Wilbur, she found that it was torn in half and had no memory of doing this. Panicking, she realized that "*it* had happened again—this terrible thing that happened to time. It had followed her here, to the haven of the doctor's office...." Just then, she jumped up from her chair, her face contorted with anger and fear, ripping up the other letters in her purse. She clenched her fist, yelling, "Men are all alike. You just can't trust 'em. You really can't" (Schreiber, 1973, p. 65). Then she headed to the window, pounding on it with her fist, and before Dr. Wilbur could stop her, smashed her fist through it. After that, while Dr. Wilbur tended her hand, Sybil became meek, plaintive, and vulnerable in her behavior. She talked in a small childlike voice and identified herself as Peggy Baldwin.

Dr. Wilbur was mystified and intrigued. She explained to Sybil that she had been in a dissociative state called a *fugue,* in which a person's consciousness shifts suddenly, with attempted physical flight from the situation, usually with amnesia for the event. (Beyond that, however, Dr. Wilbur could not yet explain what was going on. Very little was known then about dissociative identity disorder.) In the meantime, however, she needed to find a way to do effective psychotherapy with Sybil. The treatment unfolded through stages, each building on the previous gains that had been made. First, Dr. Wilbur established a good working alliance with Sybil. She then got to know all the personalities and gained their trust. She did this by being nonjudgmental, calm, and empathetic. That is not to say that Dr. Wilbur was accepting of any and all behavior. At times, when it was necessary to set limits in order to protect Sybil, she did so. She also educated Sybil about her disorder, helping her to understand that her consciousness changed or shifted when either external events or her own inner memories were too anxiety provoking. Then, when Sybil was ready and the opportunities presented themselves, Dr. Wilbur began to help Sybil uncover the original childhood traumas that were at the root of the dissociation. Here, as with other psychotherapy interventions, timing was crucial. Bringing out too much information too soon can overwhelm clients' defenses; too little can delay progress in therapy. Dr. Wilbur's training and experience as well as her growing understanding of Sybil as a unique person helped guide these decisions.

For example, Dr. Wilbur used an opening in a conversation with "Vicky," one of Sybil's personalities, to make gains in uncovering the trauma. "Music hurts," Vicky had stated; "it hurts way inside because it is beautiful, and it makes both Sybil and Peggy Lou sad. They're sad because they're alone and nobody cares. When they hear music, they feel more alone than ever" (Schreiber, 1973, p. 112). Dr. Wilbur hypothesized to herself that perhaps this related to the original trauma, which involved lack of nurturance. She asked why, to which Vicky replied, "It's like love." Dr. Wilbur used this opportunity to ask, directly but gently, "Was there something about love that hurt?" "There was," said Vicki.

At this point in the therapy, Sybil trusted Dr. Wilbur. This was the beginning of the unraveling of a story which for Sybil had remained unconscious—a story of emotional, physical, and sexual cruelty inflicted by her mother. At first, only some of the other personalities would or could remember and talk about the trauma. Dr. Wilbur, sometimes with Sybil and sometimes without her, actually sought—and found—external corroboration of some of the traumatic events.

This breakthrough gave them the courage to continue with the unorthodox and sometimes painful process of helping a strengthened Sybil to reclaim some of the memories. At times she was overwhelmed with feelings of anger, hatred, and loss. There were times when she was suicidal. Through these times Dr. Wilbur stood by her and protected her as necessary, sometimes seeing her very frequently. As the original trauma was worked through, Sybil became stronger psychologically. The need for the protective or defensive functions of the other personalities was reduced, and they started to fade. Just as Sybil was able to reclaim her memories, she was also able to reclaim the personality characteristics, skills, and talents of the personalities. The depleted, meek, anxious Sybil began to reclaim Peggy Lou's joy for life and interest in art and Vicky's assertiveness. Slowly these different aspects of herself became reintegrated back into the original personality, Sybil. She resumed her painting and later landed a job as a professor. The treatment ended by mutual consent eleven years after it had begun.

WHAT IS PSYCHOTHERAPY?

The fascinating story of Dr. Wilbur's work with Sybil offers some revealing glimpses into the process of psychotherapy and raises many questions. Just what is psychotherapy? How does it differ from other kinds of close relationships? Is Sybil's story a "typical" one, and if not, how does it differ from others' stories of psychotherapy? As this chapter unfolds, it will become clear that there are many different forms of psychotherapies, all with their own underlying assumptions about the nature of change and their own set of techniques or interventions. We will discuss several of these psychotherapies in depth and identify which are most effective for particular kinds of disorders. Having some knowledge and appreciation of the process of therapy is important for two reasons. First, psychotherapy is such a widely discussed part of North American society that it is important to be well informed on the field. Although many people espouse opinions about psychological treatment, few have actually experienced it. Because opinions about therapy are often extreme and controversial, it is doubly important to have knowledge of the basic processes and basic varieties of treatment.

Second, being well informed is important from the consumer's perspective. Chances are that you or someone close to you will one day consider getting some counseling or therapy. You may then want to think about whether any form of help should be sought at all and if so, what kind. Knowing the range of therapies available and what each can accomplish will help you to make this decision. We have found that these two perspectives—the intellectual and the practical—are mutually important. That is, practical decisions about psychotherapy and other forms of treatment can and must be informed by an understanding of the theories and research on psychotherapy. At the same time, the intellectual or academic perspective is useless if it is not grounded in real people's experiences in psychotherapy. Thus, as we proceed through this chapter, we include actual examples of therapy sessions. We invite you to take an inside look at the different types of psychotherapies, and to think for yourself about them.

Psychotherapy has been defined as "the art of change and healing through personal interaction" (Strong & Claiborn, 1982, p. 1). Its focus is on changing a client's behavior, emotions, or cognitions. Change takes place in a collaborative relationship between the therapist and one or more client(s). In individual therapy, the participants are just two; in couples and family therapy, two or more clients are treated together, and the therapist's focus is not only on the individual but also on the interactions among the individuals. The most typical medium of psychotherapy is language. Indeed, it was first called the "talking cure" by Josef Breuer, an early psychoanalyst and contemporary of Freud's. But psychotherapy and healing also take place via other avenues—play therapy, dance and movement therapy, music therapy, and art therapy, for example.

It should be clear from this description that psychotherapy is a type of social interaction. How is it different, then, from other relationships—say, between two friends? First, in psychotherapy the energies and expertise of one person, the therapist, are focused on the concerns of the other, the client. The client is a consumer who pays the therapist for his or her help. In this sense it is a more asymmetrical or unbalanced relationship than the typical friendship. Second, the psychotherapist is trained, and is ethically required, to give the welfare of the client the highest priority in the relationship. That means that the therapist does not use the client to meet his or her own needs for self-esteem, advice, friendship, dating, and the like. In a friendship, in contrast, both people can expect to get a number of their own needs met. By maintaining a professional distance, the therapist is better able to challenge, support, question, interpret, and make other interventions that are necessary for the therapy to work. Friends and family who attempt to behave like therapists may be seen as impolite, nosy, or presumptuous and may thus damage the original relationship if they try to take on a therapeutic relationship with the troubled person.

This is not to say that friendships and other close relationships cannot be valuable in helping us adjust to life's challenges. Indeed, active empathy for other human beings is a quality well worth developing, and there is a great deal that each of us can do to affect others positively and help them with their difficulties. More than anything else, helping others requires caring, listening, and a genuine desire to be helpful as well as a fundamental awareness of what an untrained person can and can't do. We believe that concern about others, as well as mutual caring and support, are of great importance and enhance our collective well-being in a complex and stressful world. Indeed, as discussed in Chapter 5, social support has been shown to buffer the negative effects of stressful events. At times, however, it is clear that we or others need professional help as well as support from family and friends. What are the forms that such help might take?

TYPES OF PSYCHOTHERAPY

If you include all the minor variations, over 200 types of therapy have been developed and used at one time or another in our culture. If the core assumptions and major techniques of each of these treatments is clearly examined, however, that number can be reduced considerably. In this section we consider some of the major types of psychotherapy currently used in North America: psychodynamic psychotherapies (including psychoanalytic psychotherapy and short-term psychodynamic therapies), behavioral and cognitive therapies, experiential psychotherapies, and group therapies. Psychotherapy in general has been found to be effec-

tive in helping people change (see the accompanying Lessons from the Laboratory) and that no one therapy is superior overall to another. Because some are more effective for specific problems than others, however, it is important to understand their differences. Finally, we will examine some biological approaches to treatment.

Psychodynamic Therapies

Sybil's treatment is an example of **psychodynamic psychotherapy.** Dr. Wilbur's core assumption was that Sybil had experienced severe trauma early in her life and that her symptoms were a means of coping with that trauma while keeping it unconscious in order to protect her ego from overwhelming anxiety and pain. One assumption that all the psychodynamic therapies share is the belief that an improvement in behavior and personal adjustment will occur if a person's underlying personality structure and inner dynamics can be changed for the better. This transformation is accomplished through gaining insight into the origins of one's difficulties and the reasons for one's actions. They also share the assumption that unconscious motives and distortions of reality can be illuminated or controlled once they are fully exposed to view. This theory is based on the further assumption that unconscious conflicts that were unresolved in earlier development (typically childhood, as described in Chapter 2) are the source of anxiety, depression, and disordered behaviors and emotions of many kinds. The principal goal is to make more and more hidden psychological contents in the person conscious, known, and understood—to leave less and less unconscious. Freud's famous statement of this goal is: "Where there is id, there shall ego be"—that is, what was once unconscious becomes conscious. Psychodynamic psychotherapy is also concerned, where appropriate, with releasing the stranglehold of the superego on the ego. Some individuals

Does Psychotherapy Work?

Research on the effectiveness of psychotherapy has a long, rich history (Eysenck, 1952; to Smith, Glass, & Miller, 1980; Lipsey & Wilson, 1993). Typically, psychotherapy is studied by having experts compare the outcomes of people treated in psychotherapy to a comparison or "control" group of some kind.

Then along came a very different kind of study, this time from *Consumer Reports!* Yes, just as you would rate your car, or your VCR, the magazine, with consultation from psychologist Martin Seligman (1995), asked consumers to rate their therapists ("Mental Health: Does Therapy Help?" *Consumer Reports,* November 1995).

The survey, included as a supplement in the 1994 *Consumer Reports* annual questionnaire, had 26 questions about use of and satisfaction with mental health professionals as well as additional questions about whether people had sought help for psychological problems from others (e.g., physicians, self-help groups) and their satisfaction with those alternative services. The questions included items about what kind of therapist had been used, for what problems, therapist competence, how much therapy did or did not help, satisfaction, and reasons for termination. An "Effectiveness Score" ranging from 0–300 was computed for each respondent by combining the answers to these questions.

Of the 2,900 respondents who had consulted a mental health professional, 37 percent had used a psychologist, 22 percent had used a psychiatrist, and 14 percent had used a clinical social worker. The remaining (9%) saw marriage counselors or some other helper. The respondents were typically middle class, highly educated, and about evenly split between men and women.

Overall, treatment usually helped people to feel better and the longer the therapy, the higher the reported effectiveness. Psychotherapy alone and psychotherapy plus medication worked about equally well in the eyes of the consumers who responded, and the different types of mental health professionals (psychiatrist, psychologist, social worker) were equally effective from their perspective. Among self-help strategies, Alcoholics Anonymous was rated especially high by those who had used it. Seligman (1995, p. 974) argues that this study shows evidence that "people have fewer symptoms and a better life after therapy than they did before" and that asking the consumers what they think of psychotherapy is good idea. Others worry that the findings are biased because those who were happy with their treatment were more likely to respond and that the therapy was rated retrospectively. What do you think?

---

have internalized too many rules and strictures, and their conscience is too repressive.

Psychodynamic is a general term applied to a number of therapies that make these core assumptions. Here we consider two therapies that illustrate the variety of ways that self-knowledge and growth are attempted through psychodynamic methods.

Freudian Psychoanalysis. Once again we start with Sigmund Freud. It was Freud who pioneered psychological treatment, and many psychotherapies represent some kind of modification of his methods. Classical *Freudian*

psychoanalysis is the longest and most complex of all therapies. It emphasizes discovering unconscious wishes, fears, and defenses that originated in childhood but that affect the personality in the present. Psychoanalysis attempts to explore all the significant emotional experiences that occurred in a person's early life and to connect the effects of these experiences with present functioning.

In Freudian therapy a client meets with his or her therapist several times a week for years. Therapy consists of continual exploration of the unconscious in the hope that knowing and accepting what is hidden will give the person more control and happiness. This exploration is done through language: The therapist listens very carefully and deeply to what the client says and does not say, as well as to how the client phrases things and behaves nonverbally. Doing this helps the therapist to analyze the person's defenses and conflicts and to form hypotheses that guide future questions and interpretations. In classical psychoanalysis the therapist does a lot of listening, as Dr. Wilbur did, and typically does not give advice, share personal information, or directly prescribe a course of action for the client to take. In this respect Dr. Wilbur was atypical in a number of ways. She was sometimes directive with Sybil, and she did sometimes express affection for Sybil, even called her "dear" in a mothering kind of way. She also spoke with Sybil's father to confirm her suspicions about the abuse, something an analyst would not typically do. Dr. Wilbur modified her treatment in response to her assessment of Sybil's unique needs. "Her conviction that straight psychoanalysis was the treatment of choice in the Dorsett case remained firm, yet she was willing to experiment as long as there was no threat to her patient or the treatment situation" (Schreiber, 1973, p. 383).

What is it, then, that classical psychoanalysts actually *do*, besides listen? Some of their primary tools are free association, hypnosis, and dream analysis. All of these provide material for interpretation, which is one of the primary interventions of the analyst.

Free Association.   The primary tool for uncovering unconscious material is **free association.** The client is asked to sit or lie in a comfortable position, often with eyes closed or the therapist out of view, and say whatever comes into his or her mind. The client simply talks and is required to hold nothing back, no matter how silly, cruel, obscene, or ridiculous it may seem. Try doing this out loud for a minute and see how difficult free associating

can be! It is assumed that this relaxed, unguarded process will allow ideas that are usually kept hidden from awareness to emerge into consciousness and that the ego ceases its censoring of unconscious material once the person is involved in free association.

Hypnosis.   Some Freudian therapists use hypnosis. *Hypnosis* is an induced psychological state of deep relaxation and suggestibility. Many people, but not all, can be trained to enter a hypnotic trance state. Note that hypnosis can be used for purposes other than psychotherapy, such as pain control in childbirth or habit breaking (such as stopping smoking). When it is used in therapy, however, the purpose of hypnosis is to help clients access feelings and memories. People can have experiences under hypnosis that are unusual, including thinking over past events with less inhibition than normal and reporting things that are usually hidden, even from their own awareness. It is true that recent research (Loftus, 1979; Loftus & Klinger, 1992) shows that people can be led into "remembering" events that did not happen. Good clinicians and interviewers are careful not to do this.

In the case of Sybil, hypnosis proved to be useful in bringing each of the selves forward in time so that they could be integrated back into one personality. Working with Ruthie, a 2-year-old personality of Sybil's, Dr. Wilbur suggested, under hypnosis, "In ten minutes I'm going to say it is five minutes of seven. Between now and that time, you are going to grow up one whole year. It's going to be all right, Ruthie. You're going to grow up, and later all the others are going to grow up too. Would you like to?" (Schreiber, 1973, p. 385). Dr. Wilbur was aware that this age progression would not work as a simple suggestion; it would only work if the traumas and conflicts were also being resolved. Here hypnosis was used as an aid or adjunct to other interventions. It is interesting that Freud's work originally used hypnosis as the primary road to the unconscious. He soon discovered, however, that not everyone could be hypnotized, and he began to favor free association and dream analysis as the means of accessing the unconscious.

Dream Analysis.   During free association and hypnosis the censoring functions of the ego are disarmed to a great extent. As a result, much unconscious material can be brought into awareness and reported through these methods. Another time that the ego's censoring functions are relaxed is during sleep. According to psychoanalytic theory, unconscious wishes and fears make themselves known in dreams. For this reason Freud dubbed dreams the "royal road to the unconscious" and employed **dream analysis** as a way of gaining access to hidden content. However, Freudian theory holds that the ego doesn't completely lift censorship during dreaming and thus the unconscious material is rarely expressed in direct form even in dreams.

For example, one woman in analysis had a dream about opening a boutique to which her sister came and bought a dress on sale. This is called the *manifest content* of the dream, or what is directly obvious or revealed. Psychoanalysts believe, however, that there is another level of meaning, called the *latent content,* that is, unconscious or hidden. For example, this dream was interpreted as indirectly expressing the woman's guilt for not having been generous with her sister in the past and a wish to make up for her behavior by giving her sister presents. Other dreams seem more obvious in their meaning. A new teacher had a dream just before the school year started and just after she had picked up her orange Volkswagen beetle from the repair shop. She dreamed that she walked into her class and the students would not come to order; rather, they ignored her and kept talking and moving about the room. She then climbed on top of the car, which was placed near the blackboard, and shouted until the students came to order. That is the manifest content of the dream. Can you interpret this dream or guess what the latent content, the hidden meaning, might be?

Issues in Interpreting Associations and Dreams. Eliciting unconscious material is only the beginning of the long process of psychoanalysis. Eventually the therapist must offer further interpretations that help clients understand their unconscious wishes, fears, and conflicts. While the analyst is always privately interpreting the client's language and other behavior, he or she does not offer these interpretations frequently or give direct advice. Rather, the analyst proceeds slowly. Why? Because there is natural **resistance** on the part of the client to uncovering hidden material. Interpretations, memories, and other beginnings of insight produce anxiety. When clients begin to "clam up," when they become defensive or argumentative, when they miss or cancel appointments, this can be a sign of resistance. The psychoanalyst must be extremely sensitive in knowing how and when to interpret and how to overcome resistance so the client can genuinely and fully become self-aware.

Also important in psychoanalysis is the emotional relationship between the therapist and the client. Underlying conflicts are not resolved in a vacuum, but rather in the context of this new relationship. This brings us to another important aspect of psychoanalysis, the transference. **Transference** occurs when the client projects attitudes toward significant people in his or her life, especially parents, onto the therapist and begins acting toward the therapist as he or she acted, or *wished* to act, toward these significant others from the past. Transference occurs because of the deep emotional relationship that develops between client and therapist and needs to be carefully understood by the client before therapy can succeed. Transference is useful to analysts because it often reveals repressed feelings about other people, as when a client repeatedly accuses the therapist of being too demanding of him (just as his father was). This provides an opportunity for "working through" feelings and an opportunity for the client to become less conflicted about his own and others' expectations for himself.

Interpretations can sometimes be tricky, however, as some critics of psychoanalysis point out. For example, suppose that the therapist in the last example *was* being too demanding of the client. If the client raised this issue, and if it were wrongly interpreted simply as the client's own transference, then the therapist could avoid dealing genuinely with that important—and potentially damaging—aspect of their relationship. Clearly, a delicate and skillful interpretation of the transference is needed. Therapists must strive to ensure that their own moods and psychological issues (called *countertransference*) are not interfering with the treatment. Only a small minority of clients these days are treated with classical psychoanalysis because the time and expense involved are prohibitive and other methods have been shown to work just as well. Many psychotherapists practice a shorter version of the classical technique, which we will now examine.

Short-term Psychodynamic Psychotherapy. What characterizes **short-term psychodynamic therapy?** First, the therapist believes in the importance of psychoanalytic concepts such as unconscious motivations, the role of conflicts, and the role of childhood events and relationships in current problems. The therapist also uses interpretations and clarifications. However, this therapy differs from Freudian analysis in that it is time limited, typically anywhere from 12 sessions to a year. Also, it is focused; rather than attempting a reconstruction of the entire personality, the treatment focuses only on one or more major problems. This means that the therapist is more active in the sessions and works more quickly to help the client resolve the core conflicts (Crits-Cristoph & Barber, 1991). This kind of therapy features several different styles or approaches.

Here is an excerpt from an actual case. In this case, a 23-year-old client asked the therapist for a prescription for an antihistamine. Her father, who was a doctor, had once given the prescription to her for a bad cold.

PATIENT: I seem to have that cold again, and the medicine my father gave me seems to help. Could you give me a prescription for...

THERAPIST: (*interrupting*) Can we talk first about your feelings for my giving you...

PATIENT: (*interrupting*) Oh if you don't want to give it to me, I can have my old prescription filled at my pharmacy.

THERAPIST: It is not a question of wanting or not wanting, but rather that I'm interested in your putting me in your father's position. We know that you had very strong and mixed feelings about your father, so I wonder if you have the same feelings for me?

PATIENT: Is that important?

THERAPIST: What do you think?

PATIENT: I don't know.

THERAPIST: Well, let's look at it this way. Your father played a very important role in your childhood. This we discussed already.

PATIENT: That's true.

THERAPIST: Furthermore, there were those boyfriends of yours who had certain characteristics and physical attributes which reminded you of your father, and which you described here last week.

PATIENT: Yes.

THERAPIST: Well, I was just wondering, then, if I also had the same attributes in common with your father.

PATIENT: You are both MDs.

THERAPIST: Precisely.

PATIENT: I see...there is something in all this.

THERAPIST: Carry on.

PATIENT: My roommate is also in therapy with a psychologist. She and I have talked several times about her treatment, and I remember thinking that I would have preferred to have a therapist who was also a physician. When I was assigned to you, I asked whether you were an MD or not. I was pleased when the secretary confirmed that you were. My father is a GP, but he has great respect for psychiatrists.

THERAPIST: So there is a clear connection in your mind between your father and your feelings for me.

PATIENT: I hadn't thought of it in this connection before, but there is an element of

truth in what you say. (Sifneos, 1987, p. 94–95)

Here we see the therapist interpreting the transference. He sees psychological meaning in what others may see as a "meaningless" request—for a prescription for cold medicine. By pointing this out, he is encouraging the development of the transference. If the patient can come to see him as like her father in some ways, that relationship can then be a platform for a "corrective emotional experience" (Alexander & French, 1946). In other words, unresolved issues that she has with her father can be worked out in the therapy relationship.

REVIEW QUESTIONS

1. _____ is the art of change and healing through personal interaction.

2. What general type of therapy focuses on resolving unconscious conflicts that are presumed to underlie symptoms of depression, anxiety, or other problems?

3. The type of psychodynamic therapy that involves deep and long exploration of unconscious processes and unresolved childhood

conflicts via tools such as free association, interpretation, dream analysis, and transference is called _____, whereas the type that employs interpretation and transference but is briefer, more limited in scope, and more active on the therapist's part is called _____.

4. What is it called when the patient projects attitudes or feelings about significant people in his/her life (usually parents) onto the analyst?

Behavioral Therapies

The **behavioral therapies** grew out of dissatisfaction with some aspects of Freudian ideas and practice, and their underlying assumptions are very different from those of psychodynamic therapies. First, they assume that a person's maladaptive behaviors and feelings have been learned and are maintained by external reinforcers. If a young adult is demanding and thoughtless of others, for example, the therapist would look for how those behaviors were reinforced (perhaps by others giving into him or her) in childhood and in the present.

For these behaviors to be changed, new and more adaptive responses have to be learned and reinforced. This process of learning and reinforcement enables people to respond differently and more adaptively than before.

A second difference between psychodynamic therapies and behavior therapies is that the behavior therapies work directly with the problematic behavior itself rather than with the underlying personality structure. They don't concern themselves directly with unconscious conflicts or wishes. Moreover, the problem behavior is mutually and openly defined by the therapist and the client together—for example, they might agree on a goal of helping the person to increase his assertiveness with coworkers. Before considering the specific therapeutic techniques of behavioral therapies, we need to review the principles of conditioning on which they are based.

Principles of Classical Conditioning. Classical, or respondent, conditioning was first discovered in Russia in the early part of this century by the great physiologist Ivan Pavlov, who received a Nobel Prize for his work in 1904. In **classical conditioning,** an animal or person is conditioned to make a response to a *stimulus* that previously didn't evoke that response. This is accomplished by consistent pairing of the new stimulus (*conditioned stimulus*) with another stimulus (*unconditioned stimulus*) that naturally elicits the response. Pavlov's classic demonstration of this phenomenon showed that a dog would salivate to a bell if that bell had been rung consistently just before the dog was given meat powder, which naturally elicits salivation. A common example in humans occurs with thunder and lightning. Lightning usually precedes thunder. The sound of thunder is enough to elicit a startle reaction from most people, but a flash of lightning by itself isn't. However, since thunder so often follows lightning in just a few seconds—because nature has paired the two—lightning gains the power to elicit the startle reaction because of its association with thunder.

This kind of association or *pairing* is important in leading to the positive or negative attitudes and emotions we have about many objects, events, and people in our everyday life. Especially common, as pointed out in Chapter 7, is learning to fear perfectly innocent objects because of their pairing or association with other, more sinister objects or situations. For example, an infant whose father accidentally pinches his finger in the door may develop an extreme fear of doors.

Behavior therapies, as we will see, are often directed at reducing fears of these benign objects and situations.

Principles of Operant Conditioning. Operant conditioning is closely associated with the name of B. F. Skinner. Skinner (1938, 1958) and others have researched this phenomenon extensively and written volumes about its implications though the idea itself is extremely simple. The basic premise of **operant conditioning** is that behavior is under the control of its consequences and that, if positive consequences follow a behavior, the tendency to perform the behavior is increased. Such a positive consequence is called a *reinforcer;* it strengthens the behavior. A toddler whose older sister laughs whenever he spills his apple juice on the floor will begin to spill it more and more. This behavior, which is under the control of the reinforcer (laughter), is called an *operant;* it is a behavior that has been learned or conditioned on the basis of reinforcement. Similarly, a child who cleans up his or her room in anticipation of a parent's smile or of being allowed to go outside is emitting an operant. Unfortunately, many behaviors that are highly maladaptive are nevertheless repeated because of some kind of reinforcer. Examples include children's behavior problems, alcohol and other drug abuse, even self-injurious behavior in retarded persons. In the last instance, for example, a severely mentally retarded person in an unstimulating environment may bang his head as a means of self-stimulation.

A behavior therapist using operant conditioning principles in treatment would attempt to remove or change the reinforcers that strengthen the client's maladaptive behaviors or might provide reinforcement for other, adaptive behaviors, especially those that can replace maladaptive ones. In the previous example, the mentally retarded person might be taught how to bounce a ball through a process called *shaping,* in which small food rewards are given as each new step is performed (e.g., first holding the ball, then holding and dropping it, then holding, dropping, and catching it again). The hope is that the stimulation provided by playing with the ball will become reinforcing in and of itself, and that the head-banging behavior will diminish as ball playing increases. We will see how this therapy can work in the sections that follow.

An important learning phenomenon involved in both classical and operant conditioning should be mentioned here because of its importance in behavior therapy. This is the phenomenon of *extinction*. A conditioned response will gradually be extinguished—that is, cease to occur—if it isn't paired with the unconditioned stimulus or reinforcer. In classical conditioning the dog will stop salivating at the sound of bell if the meat powder is never given again after the bell. In operant conditioning, the operant behavior will be extinguished if it is no longer followed by the reinforcer; a child will cease to whine if the parents never again attend to the whining. When these conditioned responses stop being emitted, extinction is said to have occurred. This process sounds so simple. Why, then, is it so hard to extinguish certain behaviors, such as whining? The answer is, because in the world outside the laboratory it is hard to be consistent in never reinforcing the behavior. Moreover, once the behavior is conditioned, if it is reinforced only occasionally it will actually become more resistant to extinction! Another reason why maladaptive behaviors don't extinguish easily is that people avoid putting themselves in the fear-provoking situation. A person who is fearful of dogs will lose his fear if exposed to a number of harmless dogs over time. If he totally avoids dogs, however, there is no opportunity for the fear to extinguish.

Techniques of Behavior Therapy.   The principles of conditioning have wide application to the challenge of changing or modifying maladaptive behavior. We will consider several specific techniques, each based on some combination of classical or operant conditioning.

Systematic Desensitization.   Perhaps the most widely used form of behavior therapy is a technique developed by Wolpe (1958) called *systematic desensitization.* It is most applicable to treating phobias and other kinds of anxiety disorders. The first step in systematic desensitization is to teach the client a new response, *relaxation,* that is incompatible with feeling frightened. The client is instructed in how to breathe deeply and slowly, and then how to progressively tense and relax all of the large muscle groups in the body. The therapist provides relaxing images and suggestions such as, "Imagine the tension flowing from your shoulders," and "Let your feet feel totally relaxed and heavy, resting on the floor." As the client gets more adept at relaxing, the therapist requires, and then reinforces, progressively improved approximations toward total relaxation. The goal is to get the client to recognize and be able to attain a relaxed state at will.

The next step in systematic desensitization is for the client to construct a list of about eight or ten situations, beginning with those that are hardly frightening at all and ending with the scariest circumstance possible. For a person with a social phobia, the list might begin with a nonthreatening situation, such as watching a funny movie at home, then anonymously and in a dark theater; to watching a movie in which someone is talking to two others in a small room; all the way up to giving a speech oneself in a crowded lecture hall. This list is called a *hierarchy.* The client is told to relax and to imagine the least frightening situation in the hierarchy. This continues until a scene is imagined that begins to make the client feel anxious. At that point, the client is told to stop imagining the scene, get totally relaxed again, and, when he or she is ready, try again until the anxiety-provoking situation can finally be imagined fully with complete relaxation. As soon as this goal is accomplished at the current step on the hierarchy, the client moves up to the next step.

This procedure is called *counterconditioning* because the client is learning to pair a new response, relaxation, with a situation that previously only produced anxiety. This pairing extinguishes the anxious feeling because it is impossible to simultaneously experience anxiety (which is controlled by the sympathetic branch of the autonomic nervous system) and relaxation (which is controlled by the parasympathetic branch of the autonomic nervous system; these systems are discussed in Chapter 5). This procedure is widely and successfully used for the treatment of phobias, including simple phobias, social phobias, agoraphobia, and even obsessive-compulsive disorder. For agoraphobia, *in vivo desensitization* is sometimes used instead; in this procedure the client is actually exposed to the anxiety-producing situations, perhaps beginning with standing at the front door of home and ending with a trip to a crowded mall. The therapist accompanies the client, helping him or her to follow these steps and providing support. As we will see shortly, certain medications are often used to supplement behavioral treatment of the more complex anxiety disorders such as agoraphobia and obsessive-compulsive disorder.

Implosion and Flooding. In the behavioral treatments just described, exposure to the feared stimuli is gradual, and work up to the most feared situations. In contrast, implosion (Stampfl, 1967) requires immediate exposure to the feared stimulus; the client is asked to think as vividly as possible of the most frightening situation imaginable and to feel fully and deeply the dread of this situation (*implosion*). A person who is phobic of dogs is told to think as vividly as possible about being in a kennel in which all the cages are open and the dogs are running out. In *flooding* the person is actually put into the feared situation, in

this case the kennel. The idea is that if the client continues to do this, he or she will see that no negative harmful consequences follow the frightening stimulus, and the fear or anxiety response will be extinguished. This process takes place consciously as well as automatically; that is, the body "unlearns" the classically conditioned response. Dogs no longer elicit the phobic person's increased heartrate, sweating, and other bodily changes characteristic of fear.

Teaching New Behaviors. For certain types of problems and disorders, the difficulty lies in not having a repertoire of behaviors to cope successfully in different life situations. That is, the task is not to extinguish or modify behaviors they already have, but to shape new ones. Some people lack assertiveness, whereas others lack social skills and cause offense by their inappropriate behaviors. Thus other forms of behavior therapy have been developed for getting the client to perform effective behaviors in situations that ordinarily cause debilitating anxiety, depression, or rejection by others. *Role playing* is generally used to teach these new behaviors. After helping the client to relax, the therapist acts out the effective behavior in an imaginary situation to give the client a model to imitate; then the client has to role-play the effective behavior him or herself. The therapist gives feedback and acts as a coach, using approval to shape and reinforce the client's role playing until the client is able to perform the desired behavior effectively. Finally, the client attempts the new adaptive behavior in a real situation, reporting back to the therapist.

One form of this technique is *assertiveness training*. People who are afraid to express their opinions or to protest being manipulated, or people who lack the knowledge or ability to assert themselves appropriately, can be helped through assertiveness training. This form of therapy can be used with anyone, although it is most widely used with women as a means of overcoming traditional conditioning that encourages them to be submissive and to suppress feelings of resentment or anger, which in turn can lead to depression and interpersonal difficulties. Skilled trainers work with clients through lengthy and detailed role playing, demonstrating how to be assertive and shaping the client's behavior until the client can behave flexibly and effectively. Assertiveness is not the same as ineffective or inappropriate *aggression,* and clients who successfully complete assertiveness training are able to operate more successfully and happily in life situations. In assertiveness training, as in many other behavioral therapies, the therapist may also urge clients to examine the *cognitions,* or thoughts, that underlie their unassertiveness. Does the client believe that to be a good person, everyone has to like her all the time? The therapist may help clients to challenge these assumptions (we'll be discussing the concept of challenging unconscious assumptions in more detail shortly) as well as to change her behaviors.

Overall, there is much research demonstrating the effectiveness of behavior therapies for problems such as phobias and other anxieties, marital conflict, child behavior problems, and shaping daily living skills and socially appropriate behavior in mentally retarded persons. Moreover, because behavioral techniques can be successfully taught to parents and teachers, they are also widely used to help solve behavior problems in homes and schools.

Cognitive Therapies

Cognitive therapies expand on the behavior therapies by adding to them an important component: the role of thinking and beliefs in maintaining disordered behaviors and psychological distress. Cognitive behavior therapists—or cognitive therapists, as they are sometimes called—emphasize our beliefs and our interpretation of experience. They also consider how our faulty information processing about ourselves and our relationships can lead to self-defeating or irrational behaviors or attitudes.

Perhaps an example will help illustrate this idea. Imagine that you have just entered a crowded party at the home of an acquaintance. You are alone. You greet the host, and he does not reply. Now consider some of the possible interpretations you could make about this behavior: that the host didn't hear you, that he wishes you hadn't come to the party, that he is ignoring you because there is someone across the room he'd rather talk with, or that he is a snob. Each of these beliefs carries with it certain implications for what your next behavior will be as well as for the current status of your self-esteem. The goal of cognitive behavior therapy is to help clients closely examine their beliefs, to look at the world more rationally, and to entertain alternative beliefs so that they can choose more effective, appropriate, and satisfying behaviors.

Beck's Cognitive Therapy. One of the most widely used approaches to cognitive therapy is Aaron Beck's cognitive therapy (Beck, 1976; Beck, Rush, Shaw, & Emery, 1979), which is particularly effective in treating depression and anxiety. After establishing a collaborative therapeutic relationship with the client, the cognitive therapist's first step is to analyze the faulty thinking patterns that accompany the feeling of depression or anxiety. In Beck's theory, depressed people tend to think in certain ways that help sustain their depression, as described in Chapter 7. Say, for example, the therapist notices that the client has "negative automatic thoughts." The therapist would then work with the client to help him recognize these thinking patterns, as in the following excerpt:

THERAPIST: So settle back in a comfortable position, close your eyes to shut out distractions, and let yourself relax.... Now

I'd like you to imagine being back in that situation as realistically as you can. It's Thursday morning, the mail has just come, and you're flipping through it. Imagine the room just the way it was on Thursday, the mail in your hands, the whole situation. How do you feel as you imagine that?

CLIENT: I'm starting to feel depressed like I did then.

THERAPIST: What thoughts are running through your head?

CLIENT: I'm thinking about the bills.

THERAPIST: What I'd like you to do is try to quote the thoughts as much as possible in the same words as when they ran through your head because sometimes the wording can make a big difference.

CLIENT: "Look at all these bills! I'll never be able to pay them off. How's Jack ever going to go to college?"

THERAPIST: Ok, stop imagining and open your eyes. Do you think those thoughts might have something to do with your getting more depressed right then? (Freeman, Pretzer, Fleming, & Simon, 1990, p. 94)

The therapist then went on to explain how those kinds of automatic negative thoughts helped sustain the client's depressed mood. He led the client in an exercise to help him challenge those negative thoughts and substitute others:

THERAPIST: How do you think you would have felt if instead of thinking "I'll never be able to pay them off," you'd been thinking, "These damn bills are a pain. It's a good thing I've got unemployment and some money in the bank?"

CLIENT: I'd probably have felt better.

THERAPIST: Which would have been closer to the truth?

CLIENT: That they're a pain. (Freeman et al., 1990, pp. 94–95)

This excerpt gives a flavor of the style of Beck's cognitive therapy. Besides working with the client during the session, cognitive therapists often give homework assignments to help clients discover and change their negative thinking patterns. Behavioral techniques are also sometimes used. For example, with a client who was very depressed and inactive (which itself lowers mood), the therapist might use reinforcement principles—perhaps with the help of family members—to try to get the client to engage in more activities. This combination of cognitive and behavioral techniques can be quite effective for both depressive and anxiety disorders.

Ellis's Rational-Emotive Therapy. Another prominent cognitive behavior therapy is known as **rational-emotive therapy** (RET). Its founder and major proponent is Albert Ellis (1962, 1979). The major assumption underlying RET is that some people have irrational or unrealistic beliefs, usually learned from their parents and reinforced by society, that cause them great misery and lead to self-defeating behavior. Specifically, Ellis's *ABC model* argues that it not just antecedent events (*A*), such as failing a test, that cause negative consequences (*C*), such as depression, but the intervening evaluative judgments or beliefs (*B*) that are the problem. One of the beliefs that cause trouble for people is their belief that they must be competent and skillful in all situations in order to have worth. A person who received a low grade on an exam might conclude that he is a worthless person, leading to consequences such as depression and hopeless behaviors. The accompanying box shows some of the other irrational beliefs that Ellis has described.

The rational-emotive therapist tries to show the client that these beliefs are irrational and debilitating and tries to get the person to change them. In changing these beliefs, the therapist plays a much more active and directive role than does the Freudian therapist. At

Irrational Ideas (Rational-Emotive Therapy)

Here are some examples of the kinds of irrational beliefs that Albert Ellis has described. When people subscribe, even implicitly, to such beliefs, maladaptive emotions and behaviors develop.

1. It is a crucial for every important person you know to love or approve of you.
2. If you are concerned about something that might be dangerous, it is important to focus on the danger aspect.
3. Avoiding, rather than facing, difficulties or problems works better.
4. What happened in the past fixes (determines) the future.
5. It is catastrophic if the "perfect" solution for a problem is not found.
6. Happiness or good outcomes are not under your own control.

Source: Ellis (1962).

times the therapist sounds like a teacher or a coach; the emphasis is on the present and on how a person can change for the better—in this case by realizing and changing the debilitating beliefs. Let's consider an example of rational-emotive therapy to get an idea of how it actually works.

ELLIS: Well, I understand…that you have the problem of feeling intellectually inferior, is that correct?

PATIENT: Yes, I've always felt that that's been very important to me, and I've felt that I…I always doubt that I have what it takes intellectually, yes.

ELLIS: Well, let's suppose you haven't. Let's just suppose for the sake of discussion that you really are inferior to some degree, and you're not up to your fellow—your old peers from childhood or your present peers. Now what is so catastrophic about that, if it were true?

PATIENT: Well, this is a fear, I'm not…if they found out then, if I can't keep my job teaching, then I…

ELLIS: You've done pretty well in keeping your job. You're not that concerned about your job…You're saying you don't respect yourself, if you act effectively as a teacher. Right?

PATIENT: Yes, I wouldn't respect myself.

ELLIS: Why not?

PATIENT: Well, it wouldn't be right to say that I'm teaching when…if I haven't got the qualifications, if I'm not capable to do the job.

ELLIS: Let's assume you're a lousy teacher. Now why are you tying up your performance? Lousy teacher, we're assuming now. You are a lousy teacher and may always be a lousy teacher. Why are you tying that aspect of you up with your total self? I am a slob because my teaching is slobbish. Now do you see any inconsistency with that conclusion?

PATIENT: Yeah, but it still feels that it would be a terrible thing that if I should be a teacher and not really have the stuff to do it.

ELLIS: Why? Why is it terrible? It's unfortunate. Why is it terrible? Who said so? Where is the evidence?

PATIENT: Well, everybody says so. I feel that way about the other teachers too. If they don't…

ELLIS: You're a moralist. You blame human beings for being [imperfect].

PATIENT: You mean I'm expecting too much of them?…I got to believe it's okay to be mediocre?

ELLIS: That it's a pain in the ass to be mediocre. But I in total am not a louse for having a mediocre performance. Not good, so your performance would be deplorable, sad, frustrating, if you were mediocre. But you are not your performance.

PATIENT: But people judge me on...

ELLIS: That's right. They're just as nutty as you are, and they think if this guy is no good in teaching...then he is no good as a whole. Are they correct in that kind of thinking? Is this a good generalization, from the evidence?

PATIENT: I never thought of it.

ELLIS: That's right. That's what I'm trying to get you to think of.

PATIENT: You mean if they don't like me I should say that's tough, that it doesn't matter?

ELLIS: That's exactly right. Not that "It doesn't matter at all because I would like them to like me," but "I don't *need* them to like me." (Hersher, 1970, p. 64–72)

This excerpt gives some flavor of what Ellis tries to do in therapy. Elsewhere in this interview he tries to make the point that the client's performance is probably negatively affected by constantly evaluating himself and that if he stopped berating himself he would enjoy teaching more and do better. Ellis makes the point that students need to be taught and that the client should work on ways of doing the best he can and improving, without worrying about what others think or becoming undone by his own evaluative concerns.

REVIEW QUESTIONS

5. Classical conditioning is also referred to as _____ conditioning and involves the repeated pairing of an unconditioned stimulus with the conditioned stimulus.

6. Systematic desensitization is a behavioral therapy technique based on _____ (classical, operant) conditioning, whereas shaping is a behavioral therapy technique based on _____ (classical, operant) conditioning.

7. _____ therapies are concerned with the role of distorted thinking and beliefs as causes of psychological disorders and seek to help clients modify those beliefs.

8. One such therapy, called _____, focuses on helping people to recognize and change such faulty thinking patterns as "automatic thoughts," whereas another type, called _____, focuses on strongly challenging irrational beliefs.

Experiential Therapies

The word *experiential* refers to experiencing, and is used here in the sense of *emotional* experiencing. The **experiential therapies** are concerned with helping people get in touch with their feelings and discovering their true selves. They differ from the behavioral and cognitive behavioral therapies in their emphasis on feelings and their focus on the inner world of the patient rather than just observable behavior or cognitions. Experiential ther-

apies differ from the psychoanalytic and psychodynamic therapies in their deemphasis on unresolved childhood conflicts, deemphasis on interpretation, and even in their fundamental philosophy about human nature. That is, experiential therapists believe that people have a natural tendency toward growth and positive behaviors rather than toward the instincts of the id. It is only the demands, restrictions, and self-denying influences of society that cause people to become disordered. If a child's own needs, feelings, and thoughts are not respected by parents and other significant adults and adults instead tell the child how to feel or how to think, the child will come to deny and mistrust herself. She will take on the "correct" behavior or beliefs, creating *incongruence* with her inner self. Low self-confidence, anxiety, depression, and other psychological disorders can result.

The clearest statement of this philosophy was made by Carl Rogers (Rogers & Sanford, 1989, Rogers, 1951), who developed and modified his approach, called client-centered therapy, for over three decades. Some more detail about this therapy should illustrate its unique characteristics.

Client-Centered Therapy.   Rogers is the person who first began using the term *client* instead of *patient,* and his **client-centered,** or **nondirective, therapy** the client rather than the therapist is the active participant who does most of the talking. Rogers believed that the client must learn to trust his or her own feelings and take the lead. Therapy will be successful only to the extent that the client is talking about what is really on his or her mind. The therapist does not challenge the client (as in RET), nor does the therapist make interpretations (as in psychoanalytic therapy); both of these behaviors would undermine the client's competence. Indeed, according to client-centered therapy, too many authority figures in the client's life have already tried to tell him or her what to think and feel. Instead, the therapist's role is to provide a safe, nonthreatening atmosphere in which the client can explore his or her true feelings. Often nondirective therapists do little other than listen intently and articulate what clients are groping to say so that clients can more vividly and directly experience their own feelings and learn to accept and reflect on their own inner worlds. They believe that client insight is more powerful for having come from within.

Rogers' belief was that people are sometimes not accepted for who they are; rather, other people often place *conditions of worth* upon them, such as only accepting a child if she lives up to parental expectations that she will be a good student or withholding love from a child who sometimes expresses angry feelings toward them. As a result, the person's real self becomes estranged from his or her ideal self. The *ideal self* is what we think we need to be in order to be acceptable to ourselves and others, whereas the *real self* is our honest assessment of our characteristics and abilities. A large discrepancy between the ideal self and the real self can cause anxiety, depression, or disordered attempts to cope with those feelings, according to client-centered theory. The client-centered therapist aims to help the person get in touch with and accept his or her real self, and throw off the conditions of worth.

Rogers believed that the therapeutic relationship was the critical ingredient in helping the client accomplish this goal. He proposed that three personal characteristics of the therapist were critical in successful therapy: congruence, empathic understanding, and unconditional positive regard. **Congruence** refers to genuineness in dealing with the client; it means being absolutely honest. The key here is that what the therapist says must match his or her inner feelings. If the therapist feels anger, she must make that plain; if he is skeptical, he must show that. Whatever the therapist's feelings and attitudes, they must be expressed genuinely to the client. In Roger's words, the therapist must be "dependably real." This is important in establishing dependability and trustworthiness, two crucial elements in the therapeutic relationship. In addition, Rogers points out, it isn't sufficient merely to be congruent and real; the therapist must also be expressive enough and communicative enough to make his or her congruence felt by the client. When clients understand that the therapist can express real emotions and still be accepted and acceptable as a human being, they feel more able to do the same. This realization counteracts the client's earlier experience with authority figures that acceptance is contingent on having the "correct" feelings or behaviors that might be incongruent with one's actual feelings.

A second critical characteristic of the successful helper is **empathic understanding.** This is not the same as sympathy or feeling sorry for the client. Rather, empathic understanding means being able to see the world from the client's point of view, to understand what the client understands, see what the client sees, and feel what the client feels. The therapist must be able to keep these feelings and perceptions separate from his or her own, yet be able to see into the client's inner world, even to the point of being able to make clear to the client things the client presently only sees dimly. Again, expressiveness is important. The therapist must be able to communicate that he or she does understand and can feel what is going on inside the patient. **Unconditional positive regard,** mentioned earlier, refers to warm caring for the client as a human being, with no strings attached. The therapist must be willing to accept all that the client is as a human being—good or bad, desirable or undesirable. Rogers believed that positive regard, warm acceptance, and caring must be present no matter how much the therapist may not like specific behaviors or attitudes of the client. Again, the unconditional nature of this attitude helps establish trust.

Rogers and others systematically studied psychotherapy and provided support for the importance of these characteristics. In other kinds of therapies as well, the nature of the therapeutic relationship—the bonds between the therapist and client—has also been correlated with successful outcomes. Thus Rogers' contributions have extended far beyond his own type of therapy.

Process-Experiential Therapy. Over the years, others have extended and modified Rogers' ideas, creating some other forms of experiential therapies. A recent and exciting development in experiential therapy is called *process-experiential* (also sometimes referred to as *emotion-focused*) *therapy*, developed by Leslie Greenberg, Jeremy Safran, and colleagues. This therapy has been used successfully with individuals and with couples having relationship problems. It focuses on affective change events as the curative element of therapy. *Affective change events* are periods during a therapy session that involve the "processing or expression of some form of emotional experience on the clients' part" (Safran & Greenberg, 1991, p. 4). For example, the therapist in the following case is helping the client to reexperience the emotion that accompanied a difficult situation:

CLIENT: There was something that happened last week. I don't really understand it. It was kind of weird. I went to a sort of party. I do volunteer work with this kid and it was her family. And I went there on my own to this get-together and I just hated it. Like ... I ... It's probably just the way I was feeling....

THERAPIST: So, somehow, um ... what you feel puzzled about at this point is being there and feeling uncomfortable, or...

CLIENT: It happens once in a while. I just sort of.... It sort of overwhelms me. Like I feel kind of ... um ... (short pause) Like a big weight is on me kind of. It's weird. It's a really weird thing. I'm not.... It's not even really depression. It's (short pause) It's just like ... I don't know. I can't explain it. Maybe it's because I was tired or something. But afterwards when I remember ... like feeling this when I went home. Sort of strange and I don't really understand it.

THERAPIST: So it's the feeling of being really heavy and bogged down that's strange for you?

CLIENT: Yeah. It was weird. It's just sort of um.... Well, probably I was overtired for one thing.

THERAPIST: I wonder if we could go back to that situation? (*Client:* OK.) And um, sort of recreate it and see if we can get a sense of ... of um ... what was happening for you. You went over in the evening.... (Safran & Greenberg, 1991, p. 214)

In this case, the client was able to fully re-experience the emotional state and think about it with the therapist. She realized that the "heavy feeling" comes over her in situations in which she is doing something she doesn't like but feels powerless to change or get out of the situation.

How does it help to "get in touch with your emotions," so to speak? The theory proposes that there are a number of ways that it helps. First, simply being aware of your emotions can enhance your adjustment. The person who finally realizes he is angry can now begin to figure out why and what to do about it. Second, he will also become more aware of the effects of his emotion on those around him. He will also be more aware of the importance and meaning (for him) of certain situations that make him angry, better able to concentrate on other tasks rather than devoting so much energy to the emotion, and better able to work with the therapist to change his emotional responding. In simple terms, he will be able to think more clearly and to relate to others more productively. Emotion-focused therapy is an important new development because it brings together a focus on both cognitions and emotions while preserving Rogers' focus on the client's own experience. Moreover, it has been well studied and there is good research evidence that it works (Greenberg & Safran, 1987; Safran & Greenberg, 1991).

Group Therapies

As the preceding discussion suggested, sometimes the best way to help people is not in individual therapy but in groups of two or more. There is a marked trend today in the United States toward helping people in groups, both therapist-led groups and the self-help groups that were described in Chapters 6 and 7. One advantage of group therapy is that more people can get help in a shorter time in groups than in individual therapy. Thus, group therapy is more efficient as long as the particular problem lends itself to group treatment. Another advantage of group treatment is that it emphasizes interpersonal relations, an aspect of living that many people feel is most important and most worth improving. People in groups want to become more fully aware of how others see them, of how they can grow and how they can help others. A group can be a good place to practice skills of relating to others in an atmosphere that is honest but supportive.

There are many different theoretical approaches to group therapy: psychodynamic, behavioral, and cognitive group therapies, Gestalt group therapies, and psychoeducational group therapies, among others. There are groups designed around particular problems (e.g., eating disorders groups, anxiety disorders groups), around particular life circumstances (e.g., young single parents, separation and divorce), and around specific goals (e.g., enhancing the interaction of a work unit). Still other forms of group therapy are defined by the relationships of the people in them. A good example is family therapy, which we consider in Chapter 12. We will briefly describe two different forms of group therapy here and then discuss some of the factors that account for the success of group psychotherapies in general.

Gestalt Group Therapy.   One approach to group therapy is Fritz Perls' (1969) *Gestalt therapy*, which grew out of Freudian principles but took on a highly distinctive humanistic flavor. Gestalt therapy emphasizes personal integration and taking responsibility for one's own life. (The word *Gestalt* means whole or complete.) It recognizes that the past is important in influencing what we are like today but emphasizes that people must live in the here and now. To become whole, we must thoroughly experience and accept all that is inside us in as vivid and active a way as possible. We must "take care of unfinished business"—such as conflicts and compulsions from the past—by living responsibly in the present. Instead of blaming others, we must make an active commitment to becoming more honest, aware, and decisive on our own.

Gestalt therapy groups are designed to help people meet these goals by means of various exercises and role-playing techniques. People may act out the *top dog* role, playing the moralistic part of the personality, or they may play the *underdog*, the aspect of the self that has low self-esteem. There is also the *hot seat* technique, whereby the group members focus on an individual and give that person honest feedback about how they view him or her. This helps people see parts of themselves they might have been unaware of. Often people are asked to reenact past conflicts to make themselves more aware of their inner feeling, but the objective is always to "take care" of this "unfinished business" and then put it aside. The emphasis in Gestalt therapy is on the present and the future, on living fully and taking responsibility for one's own growth and development.

Psychoeducational Group Therapy. Psychoeducational group therapy is a specific form of group therapy that was developed and has proven to be very effective for people with schizophrenia and their families (Anderson, Reiss, & Hogarty, 1986; Goldstein & Miklowitz, 1995). In this therapy, multiple families are treated together. As a group they learn about the nature and causes of schizophrenia as well as the advantages and limitations of the most current forms of treatment for schizophrenia. They also share with each other the difficulties and challenges of living with a schizophrenic family member as well as the solutions to specific situations that each of them has found. Families get emotional support, direct guidance and advice, affirmation of the very real challenges of living with chronic mental illness, and inspiration from the solutions that others have found. Group members learn

from each other as well as from the mental health professionals who run the group. At the same time, the mental health professionals learn from the family—what things are really like at home, what strengths the family brings to the treatment situation, and what area the family may need further help with. As discussed in Chapter 7, the rate of relapse in schizophrenia is rather high, even for people who are on medication. The family environment that the schizophrenic returns to when he or she leaves the hospital is a crucial factor in the likelihood of future relapse. Thus, by working with family groups, the clinician helps both the patient as well as the family. In the words of one woman whose husband had been ill for 21 years, "If only somebody had offered us this kind of help before, life would have been so much better" (Anderson, Reiss, & Hogarty, 1986, p. 1).

Psychoeducational group therapy has also been recently used with families in which one member is depressed (Anderson, Griffin et al., 1986) and is being adapted for other uses as well, such as with families of children with attention deficit disorder. Psychoeducational group therapy is also consistent with a general trend in mental health treatment to treat clients and families as *consumers* of services and as co-collaborators in their own treatment rather than as sick and helpless.

What Makes Group Therapy Effective? Given the diversity of group therapies, an interesting question arises: Do they have any common factors that account for their success? Regardless of the leader's orientation or style, are there core factors that make group therapy work? A well-known expert on groups, Irving Yalom, argues that there are, and he has described a number of these factors. For illustration, we include three. One is *universality*, the understanding that one's problems are not unique, which can provide a sense of relief, support, and normalizing of one's problems. *Catharsis*, or releasing emotions, can be another benefit of telling one's story in groups because there are many others to hear and react to it. Finally, group members themselves frequently cite *group cohesiveness* as an important curative factor. The experience of belonging to a small close group in which people are committed to trust, honesty, and mutually helping each other can be a powerful one. Not only do people gain knowledge from others, they also feel empowered by helping others (Yalom, 1985). The therapist's role in group therapy is also important (Dies, 1995). The therapist helps keep the group members on track and on task, bringing the work back to the goals that the members have each set for themselves. In addition, therapists, by virtue of their training and their role, can be somewhat more confrontive and direct with group members and can help the group handle anger and other strong emotions that arise.

BIOLOGICAL AND PHYSICAL THERAPIES

In addition to the psychotherapies or "talk therapies," biological or physical treatments are effective for certain kinds of disorders. The most widely used biological or physical therapies include psychotropic medication, electroconvulsive therapy (ECT), and phototherapy or light therapy. In some cases these therapies are effective on their own, although in many cases a combination of both biological therapy and psychotherapy is the most effective treatment. Some specific illustrations provide evidence for this statement.

Psychotropic Medication

First and foremost, for the major mental illnesses such as the schizophrenias and bipolar disorder (manic-depression) medication is almost always needed. Those who have schizophrenia have found, as has much research, that the antipsychotic medications help reduce the recurrence of psychotic episodes, particularly hallucinations and delusions.

The brand names of some of these medications include Haldol, Mellaril, and Thorazine. Newer antipsychotic medications, such as Clozaril, have been found to help people who did not respond to the older medications and to reduce some of the affective or emotional symptoms of the disorder as well. Each of these medications has its own adverse or *side effects*. Moreover, a medication that works, and works with a minimum of side effects for one person may not work for another or may cause worse side effects. Thus every individual, with his or her doctor, needs to consider the pros and cons of each medication; sometimes more than one medication needs to be tried until the best one is found. But the bottom line is that antipsychotic medications have drastically improved the prognosis for schizophrenia and the quality of life for those who suffer from it. People who used to spend years locked in mental institutions are now able to live in the community, if they have the right medication and adequate social supports and supportive therapy. Unfortunately, those programs are not numerous enough, nor are they sufficiently funded, to provide for the changing needs of people with chronic mental illness. Also, modern families are often not able and sometimes not willing to care for a person who is seriously disabled by mental illness. The numerous homeless mentally ill people that live on our city streets are a sign of the fact that the delivery of services for severe mental illness falls short of the need despite the fact that treatments exist. The accompanying box describes how this problem exists, with some interesting differences, in other countries.

For bipolar disorder, the effects of medication are even more dramatic. The vast majority of people with bipolar disorder can control their moods and their psychotic episodes with the drug lithium. A simple element that seems to even out both the highs of mania and the lows of depression, lithium can allow people to live normal lives. The most

Cross-Cultural Views of the Homeless Mentally Ill

The United States is not the only country in which mentally ill people sometimes live on the streets. For example, in the West African country of Cote D'Ivoire (Ivory Coast) those who cannot be cared for by the family or village, or by one of the few hospitals, also take to the streets There are some interesting differences, however, in how the mentally ill are viewed across these two cultures. In the Ivory Coast and surrounding countries, many people believe that psychosis is caused by possession and that the mentally ill are the victims of sorcery. Even in the modern city of Abidjan where a few psychiatrists who use psychotropic medicines and psychotherapy practice, there is also another sector of care, the traditional healers. Traditional healers are believed to have special powers and techniques passed down to them through older family members who were healers. They use rituals, dream analysis, shells and other special objects, potions, and prayer as techniques. A traditional healer might recommend that a troubled person light a candle and meditate upon some topic before going to bed to facilitate therapeutic dreaming, or make some kind of "sacrifice." While this treatment may seem unusual in U.S. society, it makes sense within the context of a more spiritual culture, one in which many things in life are unpredictable and fate and symbolic protections against fate are routinely used (Dr. Souleymane Barry, July 31, 1996, personal communication).

---

important thing about this medication is that the diagnosis of bipolar disorder needs to be made early and the medication given as early as possible in the course of the illness. The longer people wait to start it, and the more they go off and on it, the worse the disorder becomes and the harder it is to treat.

An excellent testimony to timely and accurate use of medication is the memoir *An Unquiet Mind*, by Kay Jamison (1995). Dr. Jamison, a psychologist and international authority on bipolar disorder, has bipolar disorder herself. She recalls:

> Because my illness seemed at first to be an extension of myself—that is to say, of my ordinarily changeable moods, energies, and enthusiasms ... and because I thought I ought to be able to handle my increasingly violent mood swings by myself, for the first ten years I did not seek any kind of treatment. Even after my condition became a medical emergency, I still intermittently resisted the medications that both my training and clinical research expertise told me were the only sensible way to deal with the illness I had.... Medications not only cut into these fast-flowing, high-flying times [i.e., her manic states], they also brought with them seemingly intolerable side effects. It took me far too long to realize that lost years and relationships cannot be recovered, that damage done to oneself and others cannot always be put right again, and that freedom from the control imposed by medication loses its meaning when the only alternatives are death and insanity. (1995, pp. 6–7)

Interestingly, despite the fact that bipolar disorder is probably the most clearly biological of the mental disorders and the most responsive to medication, Dr. Jamison also stresses the importance of psychotherapy and of supportive family and friends in recovery from the disorder.

Medication can also be helpful in treating other disorders as well. Depressed persons often benefit from taking antidepressant medication in combination with individual or couples therapy. The recent antidepressant medication Prozac has received much publicity, some based on fact and some not. The fact is that this medication has successfully relieved the depression of many people who either did not respond to other, older antidepressants or could not tolerate their side effects. Prozac does not cause people to become suicidal or violent toward others. Some researchers argue (Kramer, 1993) that the drug causes personality changes, making people less inhibited, more outgoing, and more confident. Some people who have taken it report such changes, but it is hard to disentangle these changes from the effects of feeling free from depression. Prozac also seems to be helpful, as an adjunct to therapy, for people suffering from obsessive-compulsive disorder and bulimia. (Both of these disorders are known to include a strong element of depression). Anti-anxiety medications such as Valium and Xanax (not to be confused with the ulcer medication Zantac) can also help people with anxiety disorders to relax enough to make the most out of their behavioral psychotherapy. New medications, and new uses for existing medications, are constantly being developed. For example, Paxil, which is in the same family of drugs as Prozac, has just been approved for treating panic disorder and obsessive-compulsive disorder ("FDA approves Paxil," 1996). As with any drugs, psychotropic medications need to be carefully prescribed and monitored, and the patient needs to collaborate with the psychiatrist in evaluating adverse side effects as well as the benefits of the medication.

Electroconvulsive Therapy (ECT)

There has been endless public fascination with another physical treatment, *electroconvulsive therapy,* or *ECT.* This is sometimes used in cases of severe depression because it works to lift the depression more quickly than antidepressant medications, which can take two to three weeks to be fully effective. What exactly happens in ECT? First the patient is given, by injection, a muscle relaxant to prevent seizure activity of the muscles during the ECT. (The therapeutic effects of ECT are derived from inducing a seizure of electrical activity in the brain, but convulsions in the body, especially in the arms and legs, is not needed and can put the person at risk for broken limbs.) The patient is also given an anesthetic so that he or she is unconscious when the procedure is done. Next, an electri-

cal current is passed through the head between two electrodes, one on each side of the head. The amount and duration of the current is carefully controlled and monitored by a machine. This current causes the firing of many neurons in the brain, including (it is hypothesized) those which use certain neurotransmitters which are implicated as being deficient in depressed persons. Because of the muscle relaxant, full body seizures are prevented and a slight twitching of the toes is the only outward side of the storm of activity in the central nervous system. Unlike the image of ECT created by movies such as *One Flew Over the Cuckoo's Nest,* this is a relatively safe procedure (it carries about the same risks as having a general anesthetic). The only side effect seems to be brief memory loss for the time period just before the treatment, although in a few cases some people claim that long-term memory loss has occurred.

Other Physical Therapies

Finally, there are other physical treatments and habits which can also be helpful in treating psychological disorders. For instance, as described in Chapter 7, some people who suffer from seasonal affective disorders are helped by phototherapy. *Phototherapy* is the use of a very bright special light at home, typically early in the morning. Acupuncture has been used successfully in the treatment of anxiety and substance abuse. Severe vitamin deficiencies, lead poisoning, and other environmental toxins can lead to intellectual and psychological dysfunction. Thus, identifying and correcting these situations is also a means of treatment. Finally, recent reports indicate that the benefits of exercise enhance outcome in psychotherapy. Exercise improves mood, reduces body tension, and counteracts the effects of stress. Psychologists speculate that exercise may also serve, particularly for depressed people, to provide a sense of accomplishment and a nonthreatening way to interact with other people (DeAngelis, 1996).

CHANGE AND HEALING ACROSS TIME AND CULTURES

In the United States, we tend to think in terms of *biopsychosocial* causes for unhappiness and mental disturbances. Psychotherapies, medications, and the use of groups follow logically from these perceived causes. In other countries, however, as in some cultures within United States society, environmental and spiritual elements can also be important in change and healing practices. We end this chapter with a story that illustrates, how, in the context of Native American culture, alternative healing practices can work.

Traditional Healing in Native American Culture: A Story

The story is told by Carl Hammerschlag (1988), a psychiatrist trained at Yale University in traditional psychoanalytic methods. Through his own background and life experiences, however, Hammerschlag came to believe that social problems are a big force in people's unhappiness. When he graduated, he moved to the Southwest to practice community psychiatry with the Indian Health Service.

One day, driving from a remote Navajo reservation town, he picked up a young Navajo woman named Mary, who was hitchhiking. She was angry and spoke with him bitterly about how the White Man had destroyed the local country and way of life. She seemed very unhappy with herself and her current life as well. Dr. Hammerschlag was surprised when she called his office two weeks later and asked to speak with him; they continued to meet for two years.

Mary's story was a sad one. Her father had been an alcoholic, and her mother became one, too, out of despair. When her father died of an alcohol-related accident and her mother continued to drink alone, Mary and her 11 siblings had been separated and sent to off-reservation homes. Mary was 4 years old at the time. Her earliest memories of her adoptive white family were of picnics and church and of feeling different; she thought that her own skin would turn whiter as she grew up. By age 13, she had what might be diagnosed as a conduct disorder problem: She was sullen and defiant at home and at school, angry about feeling abandoned by her birth mother (she had absolutely no contact with her birth family), and angry at being adopted by her white mother. She declared that she wanted to attend an Indian boarding school, and her family and social worker agreed. There she was a star student, but this achievement only complicated her identity problems because she stood out as more well educated and more privileged than most of her classmates. Mary organized a chapter of a militant Indian organization, graduated, joined a commune, and eventually searched for her biological family on their reservation.

What happened next was very important: She found her family, and there was disappointment. Her mother was very old, suffered from the effects of alcoholism, and could not recognize or remember Mary. She learned that all of her siblings had been returned to the reservation after just a short while in foster care. But there was also fulfillment. Her siblings welcomed Mary joyfully and prepared a traditional welcoming home ceremony for her, which helped heal the rift and offered a sense of home and belonging. Her sister helped her learn her own part in the ritual, which was run by the medicine man and included prayers and a sand painting illustrating a tribal legend about a lost child who was returned in another form. For everyone, Mary recalled, "the air was charged with feeling."

As Hammerschlag wrote, "Navajo medicine men and women use ritual to help restore mental and physical health. They do not reject Western medical or psychological concepts—they only see them as limited. They see the universe as filled with many enormously powerful forces, all of which hold the potential for good and evil. If, for some reason, the

Testing Yourself

What is your "alliance" with your therapist?

Below are some items from the *Integrative Psychotherapy Alliance Scales* (IPAS; Pinsof & Catherall, 1986). If you have ever been in psychotherapy or counseling, think about that experience as you answer these items. If you have not, imagine a helping relationship that you have had with a friend or family member as you read the questions.

	1	2	3	4	5	6	7
Completely Agree							Completely Disagree

The therapist (counselor, helper) does not understand me.	1 2 3 4 5 6 7
The therapist understands the goals I have for my important relationships.	1 2 3 4 5 6 7
I trust the therapist.	1 2 3 4 5 6 7
The therapist has the skills and ability to help me.	1 2 3 4 5 6 7
The therapist and I are not in agreement about the goals of this therapy.	1 2 3 4 5 6 7

balance between good and evil is upset, people get sick. You have to keep in balance if you want to stay healthy" (1988, p. 45). Hammerschlag noted that the ceremony helped Mary to find a way to still be Navajo *and* be well educated, have material possessions that were not common on the reservation, and even live off the reservation. She connected all the parts of herself together, found some peace, and became a health professional who now works among her people.

Implications for Understanding Psychotherapy

This story illustrates the fact that many and diverse forms of healing and therapy can be effective. Effectiveness depends in part on how well the therapy fits into the local cultural and social context. In addition, effective therapies share some common elements: a strong trust in the therapist or helper, a sense of shared collaboration or **working alliance** (Horvath & Greenberg, 1994), and faith that the procedure itself will be effective (Frank, 1961). (The self-assessment exercise above illustrates how the working alliance can be measured; this measure is commonly used in psychotherapy research to study the factors that promote a good alliance.) All of these elements were present, we should note, in the relationship between Sybil and Dr. Wilbur. They sustained Sybil's committment to the therapy, even when it was very difficult. Without this kind of alliance, dropping out of treatment prematurely and unsuccessful outcomes are more likely.

The entire IPAS has 27 items and is used to measure the *client's* view of the working alliances. Why the client's view, rather than the therapist's? Because research has shown that there is a significant correlation between how strong the *client* feels the alliance is and the eventual success (or failure) of the therapy.

LESSONS FROM LIFE

Because of a Bee

A professional colleague once related this story about his work as a psychotherapist. He had been seeing a woman client for almost two years, and the therapy was coming to a close. It had been very successful, and both the client and therapist were quite satisfied with the treatment outcome. In the last session, the therapist asked the client to describe what most seemed to her to account for the successful outcome.

In response, she asked, "Do you remember that time the bee flew in the window?" He did, with considerable embarrassment. He was not only al-

lergic to, but also deathly afraid of bees, and he had dived under the desk while she shooed it out the window. He recounted this to his client, who interrupted him to reveal, "That was the turning point for me in the therapy." "Before that," she continued, "I couldn't fully relate to you because you seemed to have it perfectly together. But after that, I saw that even though you were very successful, you still had fears and vulnerabilities. I could relate to you as a person. I felt then like there was hope for me, and I really started to work in our sessions."

Those who perceived mutual agreement about the tasks and goals of therapy and who felt a strong emotional bond or trust with the therapist had better outcomes than those who did not. The *relationship* is a key ingredient of successful therapy (Horvath, 1995).

This is not to say that these "common factors"—trust, faith in the procedures, and a strong alliance—are the *only* ingredients of successful therapy, or that every therapy is effective for every problem. Even though *overall* the major therapies are roughly equivalent in terms of their effectiveness (Smith, Glass, & Miller, 1980) they are not equally interchangeable. Indeed, there are also some specific factors that account for therapeutic effectiveness—that is, there is now good evidence that some specific therapies work better than others for certain problems. For problems like Sybil's, for example, the insight-oriented psychodynamic therapies are more appropriate than the behavior therapies. On the other hand, psychodynamic therapies are not the treatment of choice for schizophrenia and may even be harmful. Medication, supportive counseling, and psychoeducational groups are the preferred treatments for schizophrenia. Behavioral therapies work especially well for phobias and certain other anxiety disor-

ders but are inadequate for treating the personality disorders. One exception, however, is an effective cognitive-behavioral treatment for borderline personality disorder (Linehan & Kehrer, 1993). Thus, the effectiveness of the different psychotherapies is based on both common and specific factors.

Finally, as noted, therapy also takes place in a cultural context and personal context. For this reason, when people are choosing a therapist or trying to decide if their current therapist is good for them, their choice should be based not only on the therapist's credentials (i.e., good training and experience) but also on whether they feel comfortable in the relationship with the therapist. Does the therapist seem to truly understand you and your situation? Does the therapist share your values, or, if not, is he or she respectful of them? Do the interventions or techniques being used make sense to you? These kinds of questions can help guide personal decisions when you or your friends and family seek help from a mental health professional. As the Lessons from Life box above illustrates, the psychotherapy relationship is a highly personal, individualized one; sometimes even therapists cannot predict fully the effects of certain interventions on the therapeutic relationship.

This story illustrates the fact that the psychotherapy relationship is, above all, a relationship between people. Training, treatment manuals, and research findings can help guide the therapist's interventions, but they cannot prescribe exactly how each therapist and client should establish a warm trusting, working relationship. That is up to the individuals involved, and that is where therapy becomes an art as well as a science.

REVIEW QUESTIONS

9. Client-centered therapy, which was developed by _____, rests on the assumption that people have natural instincts toward growth and health but that these can be thwarted by "conditions of worth" that others have created.

10. The client-centered therapist believes that successful therapy requires three key ingredients. What are they?

11. The type of therapy that helps clients to process or express an emotional experience and to understand the meaning of it is called _____.

12. Three of the factors that account for the success of group therapy, according to Yalom, are _____, _____, and _____.

13. Of the biological therapies, both phototherapy and electroconvulsive therapy are sometimes used to treat _____ (what disorder?).

SUMMARY

1. Psychotherapy is a form of treatment for psychological problems that involves two or more people in sustained social interaction. The medium of psychotherapy is usually language, but it can also be art, music or dance.

2. There are many different types of psychotherapy, each with its own core assumptions and techniques.

3. Psychodynamic therapies focus on the analysis of unconscious conflicts and feelings via free association, the development of a transference relationship, and interpretation. Dream analysis and hypnosis can also be used. Through these processes, clients gain insight and have "corrective emotional experiences."

4. Behavior and cognitive behavioral therapies focus on modifying overt behavior using principles of conditioning and reinforcement. Systematic desensitization, flooding, assertiveness training, and role playing are behavioral techniques. Cognitive behavioral therapies also attempt to modify the specific beliefs and the logic that people use in forming beliefs about themselves and significant events in their lives.

5. Experiential therapies focus on emotion and the client's experience in the here and now. They emphasize the relationship among emotion, cognition, and mental health. Client-centered therapy and emotion-focused therapy are two of the different varieties of experiential therapy.

6. Group therapies also take many forms, such as Gestalt and psychoeducational group therapy. Curative elements in group therapies include universality, catharsis, and group cohesiveness.

7. Medications and electroconvulsive therapies are two varieties of physical treatment that have proven very helpful for certain disorders. They are particularly effective in the treatment of schizophrenia, bipolar disorder, and depression and are used as adjuncts to psychotherapy for the treatment of other disorders as well.

8. Change and healing takes many forms across cultures. Psychological, biological, environmental, and spiritual factors account for change. Common ingredients in all successful therapies are a faith in the process itself and a good working alliance with the therapist or helper.

9. Self-help and self-control strategies, many of them based on behavioral principles, are effective strategies for maximizing mental health and happiness.

CRITICAL THINKING QUESTIONS

1. There are many different kinds of psychotherapy and, as discussed in the chapter, they vary in terms of their assumptions and techniques. Think about the different therapies as if you were a client trying to choose one, and then as if you were a therapist trying to decide which to practice. Which would you choose, and why?

2. Like any treatments, psychotropic drugs and other biological therapies such as ECT have risks and side effects as well as benefits. Whose place should it be to weigh those benefits and risks, and arrive at a final decision about treatment? Should the patient's, the family's, or the mental health professional's decision be the most important? Under what circumstances might your position on this question change?

3. When researchers study the question, "Does psychotherapy work?" they must first come up with a definition or criterion for successful outcomes. A complete "cure" (that is, problems never recur)? Adjustment to life's roles and tasks? Happiness? Family and friends' opinions that the patient is easier to live with? Can you think of other criteria? Discuss the advantages and disadvantages of each.

MATCHING EXERCISE

Match each term with its definition.

a. psychodynamic psychotherapies
b. Freudian psychoanalysis
c. free association
d. transference
e. classical conditioning

f. operant conditioning
g. rational-emotive therapy
h. client-centered therapy
i. unconditional positive regard

j. psychoeducational group therapy
k. working alliance

1. A tool for accessing the unconscious, in which the patient says whatever comes into his or her mind, without censoring it
2. A type of cognitive therapy, devised by Albert Ellis, that seeks to help clients shed irrational beliefs
3. A type of conditioning in which a previously neutral stimulus elicits a response by means of consistent pairing with an unconditioned stimulus

4. Total acceptance of the client as a person, without conditions of worth, by the client-centered therapist
5. The sense of collaboration between therapist and client, involving agreement on the tasks and techniques of therapy as well as emotional bonds, or trust
6. The client's projection of feelings or wishes about significant figures such as parents onto the therapist

7. Therapies that tend to be shorter than traditional Freudian analysis but that retain the use of interpretation, transference, and other techniques based on insight into unconscious motives and resolution of inner conflicts

8. A treatment that combines education and support for families of people with schizophrenia and other mental illnesses

9. A type of humanistic therapy pioneered by Carl Rogers

10. Long-term therapy that emphasizes the resolution of unconscious conflicts from childhood through the use of free association, hypnosis, dream analysis, interpretation and other techniques

11. A type of conditioning in which a behavior or response is strengthened when it is consistently followed by positive consequences, or reinforcers

Answers to Matching Exercise

a. 7   b. 10   c. 1   d. 6   e. 3   f. 11   g. 2   h. 9   i. 4   j. 8   k. 5

ANSWERS TO REVIEW QUESTIONS

1. psychotherapy
2. psychodynamic
3. Freudian psychoanalysis, short-term psychodynamic psychotherapy
4. transference
5. respondent
6. classical; operant
7. cognitive
8. Beck's cognitive therapy, Ellis's rational-emotive therapy

9. Carl Rogers
10. empathy, congruence, and unconditional positive regard
11. process-experiential psychotherapy, or emotion-focused therapy
12. universality, catharsis, and group cohesiveness
13. depression, or, in the case of phototherapy, a specific form of depression called seasonal affective disorder

CHAPTER 9

GETTING TO KNOW
AND LIKE OTHERS

CASE NARRATIVE: SHERLOCK HOLMES AND DR. WATSON
PERCEIVING OTHERS
INTERPERSONAL ATTRACTION: WHO WE LIKE AND WHY

Jeremy Brett and Edward Hardwicke as Sherlock Holmes and Dr. Watson

Sherlock Holmes and Dr. Watson

John Watson contemplated his fate as he stood sipping a drink in the Criterion Bar. The wounds he had received in the Afghan wars gave him a dull ache. He had little money and few friends in London, and he was not sure what his next step should be. Shaken from his deep thoughts by a tap on the shoulder, he turned to find an old acquaintance who had once worked for him in the hospital. As the two talked over old times, Watson admitted that he had no place to live and was short of funds. The friend mused, "That's a strange thing, you're the second man today who has used that expression to me." He told of a man who was right now working in the chemistry laboratory of a hospital, who had an apartment but needed someone to go in halves on the rent.

"By Jove!" shouted Watson, "If he really wants someone to share the rooms and expense, I am the very man for him." The friend admitted that Watson might find this man a bit unusual, but Watson insisted that he needed the room. So off they went, soon finding themselves in a chemistry laboratory in the bowels of St. Bartholomew's Hospital. There, seated on a stool peering over a tiny flame, was a tall man who sprang to his feet shouting, "I've found it! I've found it! I have found a reagent which is precipitated by hemoglobin, and by nothing else." The two strangers were quickly introduced: "Dr. Watson, meet Mr. Sherlock Holmes."

Watson and Holmes talked for several minutes, quickly realizing that they had many interests in common, including a background in science and a desire for privacy, and both were pipe smokers. They agreed to share the apartment and made an appointment to meet the next day to examine the accommodations. Thus began a friendship between two fictitious characters that was to delight mystery readers for the next century.

As the weeks went by, Watson became increasingly interested in Holmes. Like Watson, Holmes had few friends. Although he was not schooled in medicine, Holmes had a wealth of knowledge of medicine and the other sciences. Watson was fascinated by the unusual array of people who visited Holmes, talked in low voices with him, and scurried away with a kernel of infor-

mation or advice. What most interested Watson, however, was Holmes's uncanny powers of reasoning. Holmes often bragged of his abilities and talked about how he could put these abilities to use in solving crimes.

One day Watson was looking out the window at a man across the street. He mused, "I wonder what that fellow is looking for?" Holmes immediately responded, "You mean the retired sergeant of the Marines?" Somewhat annoyed, Watson thought that there was no way that Holmes could know about this man in such detail, but he thought there was no way to verify Holmes's guess. To his surprise, the man crossed the street and knocked on their door. He had a letter for Sherlock Holmes, but Watson was not going to let the opportunity pass to test Holmes's deduction. "May I ask, my lad, what your trade may be?" To Watson's surprise the man reported that he was a retired sergeant in the Royal Marine Light Infantry. As Holmes read the letter, Watson wracked his brain to figure out how Holmes could have known about the courier. Later Holmes mentioned what seemed obvious to him: The man's anchor tattoo, his military carriage and regulation side whiskers, his air of command, and the way he swung his cane.

The letter from Inspector Gregson of Scotland Yard stated that a murder victim had just been found and the circumstances were so unusual that he requested Holmes's help in solving the mystery. Without delay, Holmes invited Watson to go with him to the murder scene. He felt that Watson's medical experience might help in solving the crime, and he wanted to use Watson to sound out his ideas about the case.

On arriving at the scene of the crime, Watson and Holmes found a corpse stretched on the floor with an expression of horror and hatred on his face. No wound was visible, but there were pools of blood on the floor. Written in blood on the wall was the word *RACHE,* the German term for revenge. How had the man died? Who had killed him, and why?

Over the next few days the two sleuths worked feverishly to unravel the mystery. Watson often asked questions and Holmes supplied the answers. The grisly crime took on more ominous tones when the secretary of the victim was found murdered in his room in Liverpool, the word *RACHE* again scrawled in blood on the wall. Thus began the story of *The Study in Scarlet*, a tale of revenge and lost love that had its beginnings in the remote deserts of Utah.

Their success and the shared experiences of the case led to a lasting bond of friendship between Watson and Holmes. What began as a chance meeting between two men short of funds and in need of a place to stay ended in a close relationship. The two continued to combine their talents over the years to solve some of the most creative mysteries that could be devised by author Sir Arthur Conan Doyle. A century after the publication of the original Sherlock Holmes novels and stories, the world is still enjoying the combined talents of Sherlock Holmes and Dr. John Watson, M.D. (Doyle, 1930).

PERCEIVING OTHERS

All of us meet and become acquainted with other people daily, just as Holmes and Watson met in the chemistry lab many years ago. One of the first aspects of getting acquainted and then becoming friends is perceiving other people and trying to understand them. As John Donne wrote, "No man is an island," and the well-adjusted person needs to understand how to perceive and evaluate other people. In this chapter we consider not only how we perceive others but also how we misperceive them, what leads us to like them and what leads them to like us. Let's first consider how we perceive other people and the ways our impressions of others affect our interactions with them.

Our perceptions of others are crucial determinants of personal interaction. We respond to people as we perceive them to be, not as they really are. Whether we think a person is friendly, intelligent, or sincere makes a vast difference in how we treat that person. Because our impressions of others are so important in determining how we relate to them and because we are so deeply interested in other people, it seems very important that we judge them accurately. In many cases, perhaps, we are accurate, but human beings are extraordinarily complex and there are many ways in which our impressions can be biased (Funder, 1995).

When our impressions are biased, there is trouble in store. Sometimes that trouble is a problem for us. For example, if we believe that a crooked real estate agent is honest, we can easily be swindled. In the case of Holmes and Watson, Watson was in for some discomfort when it turned out that Holmes was not the orderly and even-tempered companion he predicted. In other cases, our misperceptions can lead to unfair and perhaps harmful treatment of others. Jurors in a trial like that of O. J. Simpson commit a serious injustice if they help condemn an innocent person—or fail to convict a murderer. Thus, anything we can do to minimize bias and inaccuracy in forming impressions is important. It can protect our own well-being as well as that of others. Getting the facts straight about other people is critical to making the proper decisions about them and treating them fairly in a free and democratic society.

We also believe that perceiving others accurately is important for effective behavior. Erroneous impressions can contribute to self-defeating action and poor personal adjustment to the world as it really is. Perceiving the world accurately—including, of course, other people in it—is a mark of the healthy personality. Therefore, our aim in this section is to outline the basic processes of **person perception** and to show how our impressions can go awry. We hope you will become more aware of the ways in which your judgments can be in error and use this awareness to guard against bias.

The Process of Forming Impressions

The overall process of perceiving others can be separated into two related phases. First, we make inferences about a person's specific traits. Second, we resolve conflicting data we may have about a person into an organized and coherent impression.

There are many ways we make inferences about people's traits. The key process here is interpreting another person's behavior and drawing conclusions about why that person acted in a specific manner. On the basis of our interpretations, we may be able to attribute one or more traits to the person (Fiske & Taylor, 1991). This process of *attribution* is often exceedingly difficult. For example, John Watson had to make inferences about Sherlock Holmes's truly odd combination of knowledge and ignorance. Holmes knew very little chemistry yet was well acquainted with most poisons. He didn't read the newspapers thoroughly but knew the details of nearly every crime committed over many years. It took some time for Watson to infer that Holmes was a consulting detective and that he had learned what was needed for his profession. Making inferences on the basis of behavior can be extraordinarily complex. Of course, not all traits are inferred from behavior. Sometimes we make snap judgments about other people on the basis of their appearance or their nonverbal communication. Sometimes simply knowing one trait allows us to infer others on the basis of our "implicit personality theory," that is, our idea of what traits go with what other traits (Schneider, 1973).

In addition to attributing traits to people, we have to integrate information related to several traits. Often this information is contradictory. Sometimes we may have information that suggests that a person is friendly, but

someone else may tell us that the person is unfriendly or cruel. Or we may see a person act in a clumsy fashion in one situation but later perform with skill and grace. How do we resolve these discrepancies?

Because people are complex, we have several ways of organizing all the information we have about them. We inevitably take shortcuts and make summary judgments, but we have to integrate our impressions in some way or else be overwhelmed with information. The ways we do organize our impressions are often sound. But there is room for considerable error because of the complexity of the information and the strength of our own motives. As we will see, bias is pervasive in people's perceptions of each other and affects both our inferences about others' specific traits and our overall picture of them.

Inferring Traits: Attribution Processes

Among the most complex and important of the person perception processes are those involving attributions about the causes of behavior. Making attributions that explain why a person did something is very common. Whenever a person makes a statement about a political issue, succeeds or fails at a task, or treats another with respect or neglect, we are likely to ask why. What is the reason for the person acting that way? We don't make attributions only about other people's behavior; we do the same for our own behavior as well. We may wonder, "Why am I so scared?" or "Why did I do so poorly on that exam?" (see Chapter 2).

Answering these questions correctly—that is, making accurate attributions—is extremely important. Just as we base our actions toward others on our interpretations of their behavior, we also make decisions about our own future actions on the basis of self-attributions. For example, if we attribute our failure on a test to low ability in a certain subject, we may not study that subject anymore. If the reason for the failure was actually inadequate effort, not studying would be a serious mistake. In this section we will talk about the rational principles of attribution, and in the next section we will show some of the many ways that attributions can be biased. We hope that once you are aware of these attributional errors you will be less likely to make them.

The starting point for discussing attribution is Fritz Heider's (1944) distinction between internal and external causes of behavior. Heider pointed out that when observers watch another person act, they try to judge the extent to which the behavior reflects either underlying personality traits and dispositions or external and situational pressure. In other words, is some trait of the person causing his or her behavior, or is his or her behavior attributable to external forces in the environment? In Sherlock Holmes's cases he frequently asked why a person committed a crime. Was the person violent or dishonest, or was there something in the case that led the person to commit a crime that did not reflect his or her true personal traits? As in a story where Holmes let a murderer escape because he was avenging the killing of the woman he loved by a swindler, Holmes often decided that crimes could be excused because of circumstances. Although we can use logical processes to attribute people's behavior to internal traits or external influence, often we don't. Research shows that people are often sloppy and lazy in collecting data needed for accurate impressions and that many motives get in the way of objectivity in even the simplest situations (Jones, 1990).

Attribution Biases

There are several important biases in the way we make attributions. We will consider two of the most common: the correspondence bias and the actor–observer bias (see Table 9.1).

The ***correspondence bias*** refers to our tendency to ignore situational constraints and

TABLE 9.1 Biases in Attribution

1. *Correspondence bias:* Also called the fundamental attribution error, the tendency to disregard situational or external factors that are plausible causes of a person's behavior

2. *Actor–observer bias:* The tendency for people to attribute their own behavior to external, situational factors and other people's behavior to internal, personal characteristics

perceive that a person's behavior corresponds directly to an underlying personal trait or disposition. If an employee at the bank is unfriendly, we might assume that her unfriendly behavior corresponds to an unfriendly personality, forgetting that she may be tired or that her superiors may require that she maintain a formal and seemingly unfriendly manner in dealing with customers. In many such cases, the person's behavior occupies so much of our attention that it "engulfs the field," and we fail to pay enough attention to external constraints. Then we infer that the person must have a trait corresponding to the behavior. Our tendency to spontaneously make trait attributions of this kind is very strong (Uleman, Newman, & Moskowitz, 1996).

One demonstration of this tendency was found in a study by Napolitan and Goethals (1979). Subjects had a discussion with a female "consultant" who was actually a confederate of the experimenter, trained to act either very friendly or distinctly unfriendly. In some cases subjects thought the consultant's behavior was spontaneous, and in other cases they were told that she was practicing a friendly or unfriendly role as part of her training as a consultant and that she was thus forced to be friendly or unfriendly. Subjects who encountered forced friendly behavior thought the woman was just as friendly as did subjects who thought her friendliness was freely chosen. Similarly, subjects who knew the woman was forced to be unfriendly thought her to be just as unfriendly as did subjects who thought her unfriendliness was her own. That is, even when they were forewarned, subjects totally ignored the constraints on the woman's behavior and believed her to be as friendly or unfriendly as she behaved on that occasion.

This study provides a dramatic example of our tendency to ignore the causes of behavior and take behavior too much at face value. It suggests that people are lazy in forming impressions of others and won't think about the reasons for other people's behavior unless they are forced to by inconsistent information.

In general, people don't give enough consideration to the external constraints that may be forcing others to act in particular ways. People do behave differently in different situations, and their present behavior may have more to do with the situation than with their personality. One way to try to change other people's behavior is to try to change the situation you create for them with your own behavior. You will probably have better luck trying to change the social situation that you create for others than in trying to change their personalities. In general, be aware of the external constraints that are acting on another person, and remember them when judging an unfriendly police officer or a friendly salesperson. To some extent, their behavior is forced upon them by their jobs (see the accompanying Lessons from the Laboratory).

A second key bias in attribution, closely related to the correspondence bias, is called the *actor–observer bias* (Jones & Nisbett, 1971). While people tend to ignore the constraints on other people's behavior and attribute others' actions to personal dispositions, they do not do the same for themselves. When people are actors rather than observers and judge their own behavior, they tend to explain it in terms of situational constraints (Karasawa, 1995). That is, a person is likely to see his or her own behavior as responsive to external pressures

and as appropriate to the situation. An observer, however, is likely to attribute that same behavior to the person's personality traits.

There is much evidence for the difference in the way we make attributions about ourselves and others. One study by Nisbett, Caputo, Legant, and Marecek (1973) showed that when subjects were asked to explain why they chose a particular major or why they were dating a particular person, they gave as reasons the interest of the subject matter or the attractiveness of the person. That is, they saw their behavior as natural responses to objects and people in the environment. Subjects were also asked to explain why a friend made these same choices. When explaining the friend's choices, they tended toward explanations of the friend's needs, interests, and traits. That is, they believed that their own behavior reflected the intrinsic desirability of the choices but that the friend's actions reflected the kind of person she or he was.

These differences in attribution raise the question of who is correct, the person acting or the observer. Most evidence seems to suggest that the actor is correct. We are usually accurate when we explain our own behavior in terms of the situation. We are less apt to be correct when we explain someone else's behavior in terms of traits. People are not as stable as we assume when we make trait attributions. They are adaptive, complex, changing, and inconsistent. People are indeed hard to pigeonhole, and we should resist the tendency to ignore constraints and to infer traits. Greater accuracy and possibly greater appreciation of others will result from being sensitive to the obstacles and constraints in other people's environments and the complexity and richness of their inner lives. Before you make an attribution or judgment about someone else, consider how comfortable you would feel having it applied to you and ask how fair and accurate it is, given the facts. The golden rule can very usefully be applied in person perception.

Culture and Cause

The research on the correspondence bias has emphasized people's tendency to let behavior "engulf the field" and to explain other people's behavior using internal or dispositional causes: If a person behaves in an angry way, we assume it's because he or she is a hostile, angry person. When someone is helpful, it's because he or she is a cooperative, considerate person. Is the tendency to make dispositional attributions a cultural universal, or do people in different cultures perceive causality differently?

Anthropologists have long noted that situational explanations for behavior are much more common in many other cultures, especially those with a *collectivist* orientation, where the group is important, rather than an *individualist* orientation, which emphasizes the importance of the individual (Hofstede, 1980; Triandis, 1993). For example, among some of the native peoples of North America, internal events are not used to explain behavior. This orientation is captured in the statement "We see the face but do not know what is in the heart" (Selby, 1975, p. 21): The external behavior, in other words, does not reveal internal dispositions. Rather, it reflects the force of the situation and the environment. If a tendency toward explaining behavior in terms of situational or environmental causes is characteristic of people

from collectivist cultures, should we find different causal attributions for behavior in a collectivist culture such as China versus attributions for behavior in a society like the United States?

Recent research suggests that Chinese and American students do in fact make very different attributions (Morris & Peng, 1994). Although the two student groups make similar attributions for physical events, such as a collision between two objects, Chinese students made more situational attributions for social events, such as the movements of a group of fish. Further, an analysis of crime reporting in English-language and Chinese-language newspapers were very different, with the English-language newspapers using more dispositional explanations of the same crimes. Finally, Chinese people responding to surveys gave more situational explanations of recent murders than American respondents and were more likely to talk about how the situation could have been changed to avoid the murder (Morris & Peng, 1994).

Correspondence bias is an important aspect of the way people in Western cultures explain behavior. People in collectivist societies do not discount behavior to the same degree; they emphasize the situation instead.

Resolving Discrepancies

Consider how you integrate information that is clearly at odds with your first impression of a person. We often have contradictory information about other people, and we need to be aware of the processes we use every day to resolve the inconsistencies and form coherent impressions of others.

One way we achieve coherent assessments of others is by insulating ourselves from information that violates our impressions: We perceive the facts as conforming to our own initial expectations. Our expectations form a **schema,** a mental image or model that works

on new information to make it fit the original expectations (Fiske & Taylor, 1991). This tendency is shown clearly in an experiment by Harold Kelley (1950). In this study students in an economics class were told that they would have a guest speaker during the hour and that some information would be given about him beforehand so that people would be able to get to know him quickly and be able to evaluate him at the end of the class. Half the students were given the following description:

> *Mr. _____ is a graduate student in the Department of Economics and Social Science. He has had three semesters of teaching experience in*

psychology. This is his first semester teaching this course. He is 26 years old and married. People who know him consider him to be a rather cold person, industrious, critical, practical, and determined.

Kelley gave the other half of the students in the class the same description except that "very warm" was substituted for "rather cold." After the class period, students evaluated the instructor. Students who had been given the "cold" description rated the instructor as more self-centered, formal, proud, unpopular, humorless, irritable, and ruthless than did people who had been given the "warm" description. Subjects, in other words, saw exactly what they expected. The single adjective, *warm* or *cold*, created an expectancy that biased subjects' impressions of everything the instructor did during the entire class period. Kelley's study shows how easy it is to distort the facts to fit your biases and to see what you are expecting to see.

The Kelley warm/cold study demonstrates how biased our impressions can be, but it doesn't tell the whole story about resolving inconsistent information. Sometimes a perceiver's data about another person are more directly contradictory than was the case in the Kelley study. The major question then is whether the perceiver's final impression of a person will be more influenced by initial impressions or by the latest information. We can imagine Sherlock Holmes thinking of a criminal as a truly despicable individual and then changing his mind as he got more information. Or we can imagine that his initial impression is reinforced when he learns about other crimes the person committed in the past. What usually happens in cases like this?

REVIEW QUESTIONS

1. T or F: Perhaps the most important requirement of effective social interaction is that we accurately perceive the actions and intentions of others.

2. Because people's actions are often ambiguous and their intentions often vague, a key aspect of perceiving others is to interpret their actions and draw conclusions about their intentions. This is known as the process of _____ .

3. Judging that a person's behavior is caused by an underlying disposition or personality trait is called a(n) _____ attribution, while a judgment that the behavior is caused by situational or environmental influences is called a(n) _____ attribution.

4. In a study, Harold Kelley (1950) substituted the trait terms *warm* or *cold* into his description of a person who was to speak to his class. His finding that these central traits could differentially influence the subsequent impression that the class formed of this speaker is an example of how we perceive behavior to fit our _____ .

Primacy Effects

When people's impressions are more influenced by early information than by later information we refer to a **primacy effect**. When their impressions are more influenced by the most recent information they have about another person, we speak of a **recency effect**. Studies of primacy versus recency show that the most common results are primacy effects.

Let's consider a specific example. Suppose you are watching someone perform. Would you be more impressed if that person's early performance was superb and then got worse, or would you be more impressed if the early performance was weak but got much stronger at the end? In one study on this question subjects and a female confederate tried to solve 30 very difficult problems drawn from intelligence tests allegedly "designed to discriminate at the very highest levels of ability" (Jones, Rock, Shaver, Goethals, & Ward, 1968). The test contained items of this type: "Quality is to benevolence as judgment is to what? Praise, endearment, criticism, or malevolence?" *"Tim, tan; rib, rid; rat, raw; hip,...hid, hit, his,* or *him?"* (The first item is actually insoluble and has no correct answer. The second has a correct answer and is left as an exercise for the reader.*)

The confederate met with one subject at a time. All subjects were given false feedback indicating that they had gotten 10 problems correct in random order. The confederate always got 15 problems correct, but she did so in different orders. With some subjects, the confederate got seven of the first eight problems correct but then started to do less and less well toward the end. With other subjects she started off poorly but got better and finished with seven of the last eight correct. The question was whether subjects would perceive the confederate as more intelligent when she had started off well or when she had a strong finish.

Jones and his colleagues predicted a recency effect, essentially a "What's she done lately?" phenomenon, whereby subjects would think that the person who had done well at the end had demonstrated the most definitive mastery of the test. The results, however, showed a strong primacy effect. Subjects thought the woman was much smarter when she had done well at the beginning. The explanation seemed to be that subjects jumped quickly to a conclusion about the confederate's intelligence on the basis of the first few trials. Then they explained away later discrepant performances in terms of external or unstable factors. For example, subjects who saw the woman do well at the beginning believed that her early performance proved she was brilliant and that she must have gotten bored or careless at the end. Those who saw her do well at the end concluded that the later problems were a bit easier for her and that she was trying extra hard.

We see, then, that people are willing to make quick judgments about others but are less willing to change those impressions in the face of contradictory information. They rather glibly attribute any later discrepant behavior to external causes and maintain their original perceptions. Kelley's warm/cold study showed that we often interpret other people's behavior in ways that fit our expectations. These studies show that this effect happens even when a person's behavior is inconsistent with our expectations. In other words, it's difficult to get people to change their minds about someone after they've formed an initial impression.

Recency and Overcompensation Effects

Although studies showing primacy effects are legion, there are certainly circumstances in which recency effects appear. For example, if subjects are asked to delay making any judgment until the end, primacy effects disappear and recency effects sometimes occur. Still, primacy effects prevail, indicating that people have interpreted later information to fit their initial expectancies. There is one important kind of exception, however, that actually results in another kind of bias. This is the **overcompensation effect** shown in studies by Elaine Walster and her colleagues (Walster & Prestholdt, 1966; Walster, Walster, Abrahams, & Brown, 1966).

In these studies subjects are given information that leads them to form a first impression of someone else. Usually the impression is that the person is very kind or very cruel.

---

*The correct answer is *hit.* In the first pair of words the two last letters are one letter apart, in the second pair two letters apart, and so forth.

Then subjects are given later information that explains away the initial behavior and indicates unequivocally that the person actually has the opposite disposition. Under these circumstances, subjects do change their minds. There is no primacy effect; instead, people overcompensate for their original erroneous assumptions. For example, if the later information shows the person to be kind, subjects who had received the initial, misleading information think that the person is more kind, generous, and altruistic than do subjects who had never formed the erroneous impression in the first place. That is, subjects first led to think that the person was cruel and then shown that he or she is kind rate the person more favorably than do those who were only shown that the person is kind. It is as if subjects overreact to their mistakes and compensate for them by going too far in the opposite direction once they realize that they were wrong.

There are probably many examples of overcompensation effects in everyday life, especially in college situations in which people meet in an environment that is new for everybody, with lots of room for erroneous first impressions. For instance, suppose that on your first day of school you meet someone who seems dazed by the whole experience and panicked by her classes. You might conclude that she is unintelligent and will probably flunk out of school. If it turns out that she gets very high grades, you might overcompensate and think that she is extremely brilliant. You might attribute more intelligence to her than to someone who did equally well but whom you didn't misjudge in the first place.

In short, people's original impressions seem to set traps for them. Research shows that the more people are able to resist premature judgments, and the more they are able to tolerate the ambiguity of not drawing definitive conclusions, the more accurate their impressions of others will be in the long run. But this kind of self-restraint is difficult. Our natural tendency is to make immediate confident pronouncements about others—which is unfair to both the perceiver and the perceived.

The Consequences of Being Wrong

We have pointed out that inaccurate impressions can lead to inappropriate behavior. Erroneous perceptions about someone being likable or unlikable, intelligent or unintelligent can lead to action that is in the worst interests of both the perceiver and the perceived. One interesting but disturbing consequence of such errors is that they sometimes lead to behavior that makes the error come true. Sometimes inaccurate impressions become what are called **self-fulfilling prophecies.** A self-fulfilling prophecy has been defined by Robert Merton (1957) as a prediction that is false but that produces behavior that makes it come true. A hypothetical example is the incorrect prophecy in a small city that the bank is about to fail. The bank is sound, but panic causes all the depositors to withdraw their money, which does make the bank go broke. A real example in times of high inflation is that people are worried that inflation will continue and that it will be impossible for them to buy a house if it does. Consequently many people buy houses immediately, which causes inflation to continue or get worse.

Self-fulfilling prophecies are also common in interpersonal behavior. For example, if people form an initially negative impression of someone, they may avoid interaction with that person, which makes it impossible for the perception to be corrected by new information. Newcomb (1961) has referred to this as the "autistic hostility" phenomenon. The opposite can work as well. If you decide that another person is friendly and likable, you will treat her or him in a way that is most likely to lead that person to behave in a friendly way.

One startling demonstration of the self-fulfilling prophecy was reported in a study by Rosenthal and Jacobson entitled "Pygmalion in the Classroom" (1968). Rosenthal and Jacobson wanted to know whether the self-fulfilling prophecy might operate among teachers of elementary school children in ways that would have grave consequences for the pupils. Suppose a teacher expected that a student would do poorly and that another would do well. Could this expectation affect the teacher's behavior in some way that might ultimately confirm the expectation? Perhaps teachers would give more help and more sustained attention to students they thought to be talented and ignore students they considered less capable? To examine this possibility, the researchers tested children at an elementary school and told their teachers that some of these children, who were actually selected randomly, were "late bloomers." The researchers said that the tests had shown that these children had a great deal of intellectual potential, which would start developing in the near future. At the end of the year all the children were retested. The ones who had been designated late bloomers actually showed greater increases in intelligence scores than did other children. Rosenthal and Jacobson suggested that these effects were achieved because teachers who thought that specific children had exceptional potential gave them extra encouragement, dismissed their shortcomings as temporary, and fostered a good climate for their intellectual development (Rosenthal, 1973).

Although the Pygmalion study didn't look at the effects of negative expectations, it's not unreasonable to believe that teachers who expect pupils to do poorly might be less helpful and supportive to such students. In some cases the negative expectations might be based on ethnic stereotypes. A prejudiced white teacher, for example, might expect a black child not to be intelligent. The teacher's behavior might then actually retard the pupil's development.

Self-fulfilling prophecies can be important in many aspects of interpersonal behavior outside classrooms. For example, often the expectation that another person is highly at-

tractive can be self-fulfilling. In one study male subjects were led to believe that a woman whom they were talking to on the telephone was attractive. The men talked to the woman in a lively, enthusiastic way. Not surprisingly, she responded in a relaxed, engaging way that led other subjects who heard the conversation to think she really was attractive. When the men talking to the woman believed she was unattractive, they spoke without much enthusiasm, and the woman responded in a tense, uneasy manner. In this case, other subjects hearing the conversation thought she was probably unattractive (Snyder, Tanke, & Berscheid, 1977). As this study suggests, in many situations we bring expectations that affect our behavior and the way others respond. Sometimes their responses fulfill our expectations (Jussim, Eccles, & Madon, 1996).

In general, it is important to be aware that our perceptions and the behavior they lead to have a profound effect on the way others act toward us. To a significant degree, "what you see is what you get." No matter what their internal predispositions, the more favorably we treat others, the more favorably they are likely to treat us in return. While we don't want to make ourselves vulnerable to people who would exploit us, it seems to make sense to foster good will and caring in relationships as much as possible regardless of our initial expectations. It's hard to see why this would not be a good approach to other people.

Table 9.2 reviews the common biases found in impression formation.

Accurate Perceptions and Personal Adjustment

We began this chapter by noting a strong relationship between personal adjustment and person perception. Accurate perception contributes immeasurably to adaptive action in the world as it is and to good interpersonal relationships. In our review of impression

TABLE 9.2 Common Biases in Impression Formation

1. *Primacy effect:* The general tendency to base our impressions on the earliest information we have about a person and to explain away inconsistent information as reflecting external or temporary causes

2. *Overcompensation effect:* The tendency to overcorrect for an original incorrect perception in order to see a person as more in line with later information than we would have without the mistaken first impression (e.g., seeing a person as smarter than we would have if we hadn't seen him or her as unintelligent at first)

3. *Self-fulfilling prophecy:* Making predictions about other people and then behaving so as to make our predictions come true (e.g., predicting that someone is unfriendly and then not talking to that person, with the result that the person acts unfriendly)

formation processes, we have seen that error is more common than accuracy. Forming correct impressions is difficult because people are complex and in many ways fundamentally inconsistent. This, of course, is part of being human, and it is what makes humanity rich and fascinating.

Although being accurate in our perceptions can be difficult, there are a few things that can help. First, we should try to be as sensitive as possible to the external forces that contribute to other people's behavior. A reasonable goal is to try to be as sensitive to the constraints on other people's behavior as we are to the constraints on our own. Second, we should avoid jumping to conclusions on the basis of behavior, hearsay, or stereotypes. A lot of evidence shows that the simple effort of waiting for a little more information is rewarded with increased accuracy. Sometimes a quick decision is required because of the need for action, but most often there is no penalty attached to patience and caution. Third, remember that a great deal of what a person does—and, in the final analysis, is—depends on how we treat her or him. Little is lost and much is gained by hoping for the best in others and doing all we can to cultivate the best. Without being naive, we can do much to call forth the better impulses in others. So why not?

REVIEW QUESTIONS

5. The order in which we receive information about a person is very important to the overall impression that we form. When the initial information received has the strongest influence on the final impression, this is a demonstration of a _____ effect.

6. Changing an erroneous first impression in the face of overwhelmingly contradictory evidence often results in a new impression that is too strong in the opposite direction. This is known as _____.

7. One of the consequences of forming an inaccurate impression of someone is that it can produce behavior that makes the impression come true. This is called a _____.

8. T or F: Although the process of forming correct impressions of people is complex, the fact is that most of our perceptions are accurate, not erroneous.

9. Which of the following is *not* recommended as a way of countering erroneous perceptions?

   a. Be aware of external constraints on behavior.
   b. Avoid stereotypes.
   c. Look for the best in others as a way of cultivating the best response.
   d. Learn to trust your initial impression; it is often the most accurate.

SELF-ASSESSMENT EXERCISE

How Much Do You Like Others?

A questionnaire designed to measure liking and loving has been developed to try to distinguish the two concepts (Rubin, 1970). Liking is generally viewed as a tendency to evaluate another person in a positive way. The following are a number of dimensions that have been found to measure liking. Think of some people you know and rate them on these dimensions using a scale of 1 (lowest rating or statement does not describe person) to 10 (highest rating or statement fits person well). When you add your ratings, you should find that your highest ratings were given to those people you liked the most.

1. Shows good judgment   _____

2. Others react favorably to him or her   _____

3. Unusually well adjusted   _____

4. Exceptionally mature   _____

5. Is sort of person I would like to be   _____

6. Easily gains admiration   _____

7. Could easily handle a responsible job   _____

Source: Adapted from Z. Rubin (1970).

INTERPERSONAL ATTRACTION: WHO WE LIKE AND WHY

Though it is important to understand how we form impressions, accurate and inaccurate, of other people, it is equally important to understand the variables that help determine whom we'll be attracted to. People often take interpersonal attraction for granted; they rarely think about why they are attracted to one person and not to another. To demonstrate this, you might try approaching a friend and asking, "Why do you like me?" Chances are the friend will be surprised by the question and will probably hem and haw, trying to find an answer. It is unlikely that your friend will have given much thought to the specific reasons for his or her attraction.

The basis for interpersonal attraction can be very important to understand. Often people complain that they have difficulty making new friends. They attempt to get others to like them but feel thwarted in this effort. Or they wonder why one person is attracted to them even when they think they have done little to invite this attention. People are also concerned when they lose friends. This is particularly true for couples who have dated for some time and then move apart, vowing to write each other faithfully. Generally, the writing becomes more and more infrequent and the relationship deteriorates.

Interestingly, we are often more aware of why we dislike someone than we are of why we like him or her. Attraction may sneak up on us. If we probe, however, we can identify many of the factors that lead to attraction.

Physical Proximity

Watson and Holmes were total strangers to each other when they met and decided to share an apartment. That decision ensured that they would be in constant contact with each other. Their contact increased because

Proximity and Attraction

One of the highest compliments one of the authors ever received was many years ago in graduate school. Housing was tight around the university and there was a wide range of people living closely together in large numbers. We were married and lived in a small apartment complex. We had to walk by the doors of ten of our neighbors to get to ours. Naturally, as time went on, we became more and more familiar to the many people who lived behind those doors. The group was quite varied. There were undergraduates, medical students, hospital workers, families with children, and a few other graduate students. We were all from different backgrounds, ethnic groups, and economic situations. At first we just nodded and tried to smile. But gradually the ice was broken and people actually began to have conversations, help each other bake cakes, and even invite the neighbors to small block parties.

We realized something important had happened when, during a cookout, one of the hospital workers, with a beer in hand, and feeling in a festive mood, solemnly admitted to me, "You may be a graduate student, but you're a human being." Somehow proximity had overcome a lot of dissimilarities and created liking and a genuine friendship. The "mere exposure effect" had worked its wonders, and familiarity had bred content (Zajonc, 1968). Contact doesn't always lead to liking, but in the typical case, if given a chance, it will.

they both shared an interest in solving the crimes that came their way.

Could a seemingly simple variable such as physical **proximity** affect interpersonal attraction? Research over the last 35 years suggests that it can have strong effects; in fact, in many cases proximity is a prerequisite to attraction. Festinger, Schachter, and Back (1950) studied friendship patterns that emerged in a married student apartment complex. Couples were randomly assigned to apartments, and few knew each other before moving into the complex. After some time the residents were asked whom they saw socially. The closer together people lived, the more likely they were to see each other on a social basis. Couples who lived on the same floor were more likely to be friends than were couples living on different floors.

In another interesting study, Segal (1974) investigated friendship patterns among Maryland state police trainees. She found that the closer together the first letters of the trainees' surnames were, the more likely it was they would be friends. It turned out that the train-

ees were assigned to seats in the classroom by alphabetical order. Hence, the closer together the first letters of their last names were, the closer they sat together in class. In a study of married men and women, Clarke (1952) found that over half the couples in Columbus, Ohio lived within 16 blocks of one another at the time of their first date.

This evidence clearly suggests that physical proximity can lead to interpersonal attraction. We like the people who are physically close to us. Unless some prior dislike is present, we may be able to get others to like us by simply being physically close to them. Taking this a step further, it has also been shown (Brehm, 1992) that even the anticipation that we will be interacting with someone can boost our attraction for that person, as the accompanying Lessons from Life illustrates.

Why should proximity lead to liking? There are a number of possible reasons. First, it has been shown repeatedly that we like things (and people) with which we are familiar, and we dislike those things that are strange to us. A young child will generally smile with happiness upon seeing a familiar face, but the same young child may burst into tears when a stranger approaches.

Zajonc (1968) reports that familiarity leads to attraction, even with adults. In studies of what he called the "mere exposure effect," Zajonc showed subjects a series of photographs; some of the photographs were shown often in the series, while others were shown less frequently. People whose pictures had been seen often were rated as more likable than were people whose pictures had been seen infrequently. These results support the idea that "to know him (her) is to love him (her)." Researchers (Moreland & Zajonc, 1982) also found that people assume that others familiar to them are also similar to them; as we will soon see, similarity leads to attraction.

Another possible explanation for the relationship between proximity and attraction is that people who are around us are often in the position of giving us rewards. Watson not only helped Holmes solve the mysteries, he also boosted Holmes' self-esteem by praising the detective. As we will see in the next section, we like people who reward us and are generally repelled by those who punish us.

Finally, we may become attracted to people with whom we interact as a means of self-preservation and preserving the quality of our life. Many of us who have had to share a room or apartment with someone we disliked can appreciate the problems that may arise. Life becomes a constant struggle if we know we must go home to someone whose very sight manages to upset us. Thus, if we know we must interact with someone on a regular basis, it is to our own advantage that we manage to like that person.

Before you jump to the conclusion that making yourself attractive simply means that you should make yourself constantly present, there are a few other eye-opening statistics. Berscheid and Walster (1978) cite an FBI report that one-third of all murders and most aggravated assaults occur within the family unit or between neighbors. Another report shows that robberies often occur between family members or within neighborhoods.

These and similar statistics suggest that proximity does not always lead to attraction. Being close to another person simply intensifies the relationship. That is, if two people have a basis for attraction, spending lots of time together will increase the chances of attraction. If two people are likely to frustrate or repel one another, however, closeness will increase the chances of that happening.

Regardless of the exact effects of proximity, one point should be clear: Proximity is an important ingredient for fostering attraction. The research on attraction does not support the popular saying, "Absence makes the heart grow fonder." While short periods of absence may lead to increased attraction, long absences reduce interpersonal attraction ("Out of sight, out of mind"). This is an important point to remember, because some people feel guilty or shallow when they find their attraction for another dwindling after long absences. This process is part of human nature and is neither shallow nor unusual.

Receiving Rewards

Most of us would like to view our personal relationships as being based on some spark that does not apply to our other day-to-day interactions. We may choose a grocery store because it has the freshest meats and vegetables and we get "the most for our money" by shopping there. But we like to think something more is involved in the way we choose our friends. A number of psychologists (Kelley & Thibaut, 1978; Lott & Lott, 1974) have argued against such an idealistic view of friendship. They say we can better understand our social relationships if we view them on a cost-and-rewards basis. They propose a social exchange theory to help predict who we'll be attracted to.

Simply put, *social exchange theory* suggests that in every relationship there are costs and rewards. For example, our interactions with others "cost" us time and effort: We may have to expend money or other material goods in the relationship, and being in one interaction costs us the freedom to engage in another interaction at the same time. On the other hand, we get certain "rewards" for our interactions—love, status, money, services, material goods, or information. Our outcome from an action is the difference between the rewards and the costs. If the costs are greater than the rewards, our outcome is negative. If the rewards are greater than the costs, our outcome is positive. One of the basic positions of social exchange theory is that we are attracted to relationships that earn us the greatest positive outcome (Cate & Lloyd, 1988).

This may seem like a crass way to view social relationships, but it does point out that we want to be with people who will reward us. For example, it has been suggested (Levinger, 1983) that many people consider the gains and losses in deciding who to marry. While social exchange theory may seem to equate the way we choose friends with the way we choose grocery stores or toothpaste, there is an important difference to remember. The economics of interpersonal relationships are not measured in dollars and cents. Rewards in relationships can come in many forms, and what is valuable to a person at one time may not be so valuable at another time.

Aronson and Linder (1965) demonstrated this latter point in a clever experiment. They had a subject hold a series of seven brief conversations with another person. The subject didn't know that this person was a confederate working for the experimenter. Between each of the seven conversations the subject was given the opportunity to "overhear" the confederate talking to the experimenter. The topic of their conversations was the confederate's evaluation of the subject. Unknown to the subject, the conversations were preplanned and the sequence of positive rewards in them was varied. In the positive–positive condition, some

subjects heard the confederate begin by making positive statements about the subject and continue making these positive statements throughout the series of conversations. In the negative–negative condition, the confederate began making derogatory statements about the subject and continued making these statements throughout. In the negative–positive condition, the confederate began making negative statements about the subject, but the remarks became increasingly positive as the series of conversations continued. In the positive–negative condition, the subject heard the confederate make positive statements about her but the statements subsequently became increasingly negative. After the subject had "overheard" the series of conversations, the experimenter asked her to rate how much she was attracted to the other person.

In what condition do you think the subject most liked the other person? The subject most liked the confederate when she began with negative comments but switched to positive ones. Interestingly, the number of positive statements (reward) was smaller in this condition than in the positive–positive condition. Also, it can be seen that the confederate was liked least when she began with positive statements but later switched to negative ones. Aronson and Linder call this process the *gain–loss phenomenon of attraction*. Supposedly, a need for positive reward was created when the confederate began with negative statements. When she then switched to positive statements, she was fulfilling the subject's need. In the positive–positive condition, the subject did not have such a strong need for positive reward.

The results of the Aronson and Linder study make the point that the value of a reward in a relationship is determined by many things, among them the needs of the person being rewarded, any previous interaction between the two people, and other possible relationships the person could choose to be in. This study also shows that we will not necessarily win friends by indiscriminantly giving others rewards. It is important that we be sensitive to the situation and the needs of others in deciding what value others will place on our actions.

Before leaving the topic of rewards, we want to offer encouragement to the individual who may feel that he or she has nothing particularly rewarding to offer that "special person." Is such an individual doomed to a life of unpopularity? According to Lott and Lott (1974), there is hope for such a person because we are attracted not only to people who directly reward us, but also to those who are associated with rewards.

For example, Griffitt and Gray (1969) administered either a reward or a punishment to a subject when a bystander was present. Even though the bystander had nothing to do with the reward or the punishment, subjects tended to like him when they had been rewarded and dislike him when they had been punished. Thus simply being present when others are rewarded may increase our attractiveness to them.

With this in mind, we might ask whether the mere presence of Watson when Holmes solved so many of the crimes influenced the relationship between the two men. According to the research, we could assume that Holmes came to like Watson more simply because he was present when Holmes was rewarded by solving a mystery. This effect should be found even when Watson did nothing to help Holmes reach the solution.

Rewarding Others: The Two-Way Street to Attraction

It is easy to understand why we would be attracted to people who reward us. We can see why Watson became increasingly valuable to Holmes when he helped Holmes solve crimes or sang Holmes's praises. But let's take this reasoning a step farther. Imagine yourself in a relationship where another person constantly does things for you. He or she sends you gifts, does your homework, cooks your meals, and constantly compliments you. It sounds nice at first, but on further consideration you might become uneasy with this lopsided relationship. As the rewards kept coming, you would likely find yourself wanting to do something in return for this wonderful friend.

In fact, if you consider the relationship you have with your friends, you will find that they are based on *reciprocity*; each of you rewards the other. You feel better if the relationship seems to have equity (see Chapter 10). They invite you to their home for dinner, and you reciprocate by inviting them to your home at a later occasion. In an interesting survey of elderly women, Rook (1987) found that most satisfying relationships occurred when two friends could reward each other. Relationships where only one person provided support (emotional or material) were not found satisfying by either party; the woman receiving the lopsided support felt inadequate and lonely. We bolster our esteem by being able to do things for others. Hence, in friendships, giving as well as taking is important for attraction. One exception to this rule seems to be the case of family members. In Rook's survey, the elderly women reported being very satisfied with a relationship in which they received a great deal from their adult children even when the women had little opportunity to reciprocate. This suggests that our relationship with family members may be guided by different rules than our relationships with friends. And there may be other so-called "communal" relationships where reciprocity matters less, at least for a time (Clark & Mills, 1979). In communal relationships we trust the relationship to be fair and valuable over a long period of time and we don't keep a running scorecard. We don't worry if we've been doing most of the giving in recent days and weeks. However, in many less intimate "exchange" relationships, reciprocity matters. Returning to Holmes and Watson, we can speculate that their relationship flourished because each man was able to help the other solve crimes. Because each man could contribute as well as receive help and praise, each felt good about himself as well as his partner.

Before leaving this topic, let us consider another reason why giving may lead us to be attracted to the object of our favors.

Cognitive dissonance theory hypothesizes that individuals attempt to keep their attitudes consistent with their behavior (Aronson, 1992; Festinger, 1957). It's consistent for an individual to like someone for whom he or she has done a favor. A dissonant relationship between attitudes and behavior would result if the individual were to say, "I did a favor for someone I dislike." Thus, dissonance theory suggests that we like people *because* we do favors for them. The theory also hypothesizes that the bigger the favor is, the more we should grow to like the other person. The reason for this tendency is what is called *effort justification:* It is more dissonant to dislike someone for whom we've done a large favor than to dislike someone for whom we've done a small favor. Thus we like those things (and people) for whom we have suffered (Aronson, Wilson, & Akert, 1997).

Jecker and Landy (1969) demonstrated this relationship between favors and liking in interpersonal attraction. They had subjects perform a concept formation task. The experimenter behaved in a rude, unfriendly manner toward the subjects. In the course of the experiment, the subjects won either 60 cents or $3. After the experiment was over, the experimenter told subjects he was "running out of money" and requested that they give him back the money. Most subjects did return the money they had legitimately won. Later the subjects were asked to rate how much they liked the experimenter. The subjects who had returned $3 liked the experimenter more than did those who had returned only 60 cents. The former group had done a larger favor for the experimenter than the latter group had.

Similarities: Likes Attract and Opposites Repel

In their first meeting Holmes and Watson carefully probed each other, finding out their similarities and dissimilarities. In a brief time they discovered that they both smoked a pipe, had an interest in chemistry and medicine, liked quiet and were often moody, and enjoyed violin music. On finding out how similar they were to each other, Holmes laughed, "I think we may consider the thing as settled—that is, if the rooms are agreeable to you" (Doyle, 1930, p. 19). As the two sleuths came to know each other better, they found many other similarities that bound them together.

The fact that similarity can serve as the basis for attraction has been clearly demonstrated by psychologists. In a classic study at the University of Michigan, 17 new male transfer students were placed in a dormitory. Before arriving on campus, the students completed a questionnaire measuring their attitudes on a variety of issues. Interaction between these students and the development of friendships were closely studied over the year. Although the students were initially strangers, those who had similar attitudes (as measured by the questionnaire) formed close friendships with each other. In addition, students who liked the same others became close friends themselves (Newcomb, 1961).

In short, research has shown that *similarity* leads to *attraction*. This rule seems to hold almost regardless of the dimension on which the similarity occurs. While the **similarity-attraction** effect seems to be strongest in the area of attitudes, research has also shown that we are attracted to people who come from backgrounds similar to our own, who are in a similar economic bracket, who have similar abilities, and who even have similar physical characteristics. For example, short people are often attracted to short people (Byrne, Clore, & Smeaton, 1986).

There are two additional points related to the similarity–attraction relationship. First, we tend to believe that people we like or find attractive are similar to us. According to this finding, you are likely to believe that the student sitting next to you who seems attractive and friendly holds attitudes similar to your own. Second, while we are drawn to similarity, we are also put off by dissimilarity (Rosenbaum, 1986). According to the "repulsion hypothesis," we find dissimilar others unattractive and will avoid interacting with them.

Having made this strong case for the importance of similarity, let us raise a caution lest you be tempted to rush out and reevaluate your relationships. Similarity is clearly not the only dimension that leads to interpersonal attraction, and there are qualifying aspects to the relationship between similarity and attraction. For example, the importance of the dimension on which the similarity occurs influences attraction. We are more attracted to others who are similar to us on important dimensions than to those who are similar on less important dimensions. For example, if you have very strong interests in politics, you will be more attracted to someone who holds similar political attitudes than to someone who holds similar attitudes about a less important topic, such as whether Coke or Pepsi makes a better soda.

The dimension that is important may vary from one individual to another, however. For example, Touhey (1972) asked subjects for their attitudes about religion and sex. Then, under the guise of a computer dating format, he matched some couples by religious attitudes and others by sexual attitudes. He also mismatched other couples on these dimensions. After the couples had been on their dates, he measured how much they liked each other. Although he found greater attraction in matched than in mismatched couples, he found that males were more attracted to females who had similar attitudes about sex than to females who had similar attitudes about religion. On the

other hand, females were more attracted to males who had similar attitudes about religion than to those who had similar attitudes about sex. It seems that in this case sexual attitudes were more important for males, whereas attitudes about religion were more important for females. Thus one way to enhance our attractiveness to another person is to accentuate our similarity to the other, especially on important dimensions.

Knowing the similarity–attraction relationship exists is only half the battle; it is also important to understand why it exists. Why should you be attracted to someone who holds attitudes similar to yours or who drives an automobile similar to yours? There seem to be a number of reasons for this relationship. First, we often assume that others who are similar to us will like us. Since we enjoy being liked, we are attracted to those we expect to like us. Another reason is that similar others often validate our opinions or actions, and this validation may be very rewarding. Finding that another person also believes the moon is made of Swiss cheese suggests that our similar belief is not so odd. On the other hand, finding that another has very different political views may make us question our own attitudes in this area. A third reason is that we expect to enjoy the company of others who have similar interests and abilities. This expectation can affect the way we behave and thus become a self-fulfilling prophecy.

While similarity often leads to attraction, we also find cases in which individuals are attracted to others who are different from them. We have all probably seen instances in which an older person marries a younger person or a relatively meek individual has an overbearing spouse. We probably all have friends who have backgrounds or interests different from our own. In many cases, these examples of **complementarity** exist when individuals are able to satisfy each other's needs. For example, an older man may be attracted to a younger woman because she satisfies his need to view himself as still possessing youth and being attractive to younger people. On the other hand, the older man may fulfill the security or stability needs of his younger friend. Thus, while the similarity–attraction relationship will be found in most cases, the complementarity–attraction phenomenon may be found when individuals' personal needs are better satisfied by the coupling of opposites (Winch, 1958).

Physical Attractiveness

One of the lessons that most of us were taught as children is that "you can't judge a book by its cover." Most of us were probably also cautioned that "beauty is only skin deep." The major thrust of this advice is that we shouldn't let an individual's looks determine our attraction for that person. Most of us would probably agree that physical attractiveness *should not* be a major factor in interpersonal attraction. In light of this, it is staggering that Americans spend over $3 billion a year on "beauty aids." In fact, some people spend more on such beauty aids than they do on food! A walk through the local drugstore reveals such marvels as false eyelashes, hair dyes, wigs, hair sprays, perfumes, aftershave lotions, deodorants, vitamins to inhibit acne, special soaps to wash away pimples and give "soft skin," lipstick, blush, and almost every conceivable color of "paint" to be put on the face or the eyelids. In the grocery store we are offered diet foods to slim our bodies or other foods to "put on weight in the right places." If we are wealthy enough, we can have our doctors "lift our faces," remove excess fat from our midsections, transplant hair, or add silicone to increase the size of our busts. In essence, despite cautions from the wise, Americans are preoccupied with beauty.

Can beauty buy attraction? Can skinny Bob get more friends by building his muscles and wearing tailored clothes? Can shy Sue gain popularity by dying her hair blonde, painting her face, and wearing contact lenses instead of glasses? Surprisingly, the answer to these questions seems to be yes: Physical beauty does lead to interpersonal attraction. This is especially true in the case of women attracting men. Men in cultures around the world show a strong preference for attractive women. Women, on the other hand, attach more importance to a man's earning potential and capacity to provide for them (Buss, 1989; Kenrick, 1994).

Physical attractiveness has a number of effects on our social interactions and perceptions. Overall, we are attracted to physically attractive people, but the effects of this concern with appearances are much greater than simply making us want to be with those who are beautiful or handsome. Research shows that physically attractive people are rated as being more sensitive, kind, exciting, sociable, and poised than are unattractive people (Eagly, Ashmore, Makhijani, & Longo, 1991). The view that "good-looking is good" has a number of effects on behavior (Berscheid, 1985). For example, research suggests that for many crimes an attractive defendant will be given a less severe sentence than an unattractive defendant (Landy & Aronson, 1969). Even children rate the misdeeds of attractive people as being less "bad" than the same misdeeds committed by an unattractive person. The work of an attractive person is rated as being better than the same work performed by an unattractive person (Landy & Sigall, 1974). Given a choice between two equally qualified applicants, interviewers are more likely to choose the attractive person than the unattractive person for the job (Dipboye, Arvey, & Terpstra, 1977).

Physical attractiveness has an interesting effect on *heterosexual behavior*. Research has shown that people *desire* to date the most attractive person possible. But when given the opportunity actually to *choose* a date, people tend to choose someone of attractiveness nearly equal to their own (Berscheid, Dion, Walser, & Walser, 1971). They follow a *match-*

ing principle. It seems that while people desire a very attractive partner, they temper their actual choices with realism. They're afraid of being rejected by people who are much better looking than they are and therefore choose a person whose looks are about on par with their own and thus who is less likely to reject them.

This overwhelming emphasis on attractiveness gives us reason to pause. Why should physical appearance be the key that opens so many doors? There seem to be a number of reasons for our preoccupation with physical appearance. First, research suggests that attractiveness "rubs off" on others. For example, it has been found that people are rated by observers as being more attractive when they are seen with an attractive partner than when they are seen with an unattractive partner (Kernis & Wheeler, 1981). Individuals develop their own self-concept by the friends they have. It has been shown that being a member of a peer group enhances the self-esteem of adolescents and the more popular the peer group, the greater the enhancement of self-esteem (Brown & Lohr, 1987) In other words, attractiveness seems to have a *halo effect:* Our own status is enhanced if we are seen associating with attractive people.

Second, people tend to see themselves as being more similar to attractive people than to unattractive people. In one study (Marks, Miller, & Maruyama, 1981), subjects were shown a number of pictures and asked to rate how similar they were to the people in the pictures. There was a tendency for the subjects to report themselves as being similar to the more attractive people. As we discussed earlier, a strong relationship exists between similarity and attraction.

Third, attractive people may well be more socially skilled and have more pleasing personalities. In other words, there may be some truth to the relationship between physical attractiveness and "goodness." This relationship may be easier to understand if we think

of the lives of an attractive child and an unattractive child. The attractive child is likely to be the center of attention (Hatfield & Sprecher, 1986). His or her parents are likely to buy that child nice clothing and place him or her in social situations. Through being "shown off," the child will have numerous opportunities to interact with others, develop social skills, and develop a positive self-image. On the other hand, the parents of the unattractive child may not give that child the same opportunities. He or she will not be pushed to center stage and "shown off" to the same extent as the attractive child is. So this child's self-concept and social skills will not develop in the same way as those of the attractive child.

Finally, when we meet other people, one of the very first things we notice is their physical appearance. Holmes made a point of carefully examining each person he met and developed a habit of attempting to learn as much as possible through this examination. Our physical appearance is our calling card. On this basis, others form their first impressions of us. They may be enticed to interact with us or compelled to seek refuge depending on what they see. In this sense, physical appearance influences who will interact with us and what the tone of that interaction may be.

The research on physical attractiveness suggests at least two important points. First, if you are looking for a formula to increase your attractiveness to others, one factor to consider is your physical appearance. Unfortunately, people do judge the book by its cover, and the way you look will influence how much people like you. There is some agreement on what characteristics are physically attractive. Tall men seem to be viewed as more attractive than short men. In general men prefer women with medium-sized legs and breasts (Wiggins et al., 1978). Smiling, eye contact, and straight posture are considered physically attractive in both men and women. Beyond these general characteristics, however, there is little agreement about what is physically attractive

(Alicke, Smith, & Klotz, 1986). So we can't make a list of steps you should take to become certifiably "beautiful" or "handsome."

The second point is that we should be careful not to be "blinded by what we see." Our judgments about individuals and their actions are affected by their physical attractiveness even when this is an irrelevant factor. Unfair and unwise judgments often result. Hence, we must be careful to determine that we are using relevant variables to judge people and to guide our attraction to them.

Self Esteem

We have examined a number of variables that influence who will be attractive to us. For the most part these variables could be divided into Situations (proximity) and Actions/Characteristics of the other person (reward, similarity, favors, and physical attractiveness). But just as beauty is often in the eye of the beholder, so too are the seeds of attraction. That is, our own characteristics influence who will be attracted to us and when we are most likely to be attracted to other people.

When Watson arrived in London in Doyle's first Sherlock Holmes story, he was feeling very low. He had little money, few friends, and no plans for his future, and his wounds pained him. He needed a friend and jumped at the chance to meet Sherlock Holmes. We might imagine that the Watson–Holmes team would have been less plausible if Watson had returned to London with a full purse, a lucrative job, and an eager group of friends and relatives. In reviewing your own life, you, too, may find that some of your closest friendships blossomed during a period when you were feeling down and were experiencing self-doubts.

There is wide recognition, both in scientific psychology and in "folk" psychology, that our **self-esteem** affects our attraction to others: We are more apt to reciprocate another

person's liking when our self-esteem is low than when it is high (Walster, 1965). Many a parent has cautioned a child against rushing into a new relationship immediately after ending an old one. The concern is that being "on the rebound" is likely to lead to taking the first person who comes along rather than to being patient and exercising good judgment in choosing an object for one's affections.

This fear is well founded. Walster (1965) found that women whose self-esteem had been lowered were more attracted to a handsome male who asked them out than were females whose self-esteem was high. In another study, Walster et al. (1973) found that individuals who had high self-esteem were more demanding and expected more from their dates than was true of individuals who had lower self-esteem. It seems that people with lower self-esteem have a greater need to be accepted by others. Hence people with low self-esteem are likely to seek out others who will reward them and to be very accepting of anyone who does offer rewards and acceptance. As we pointed out earlier, our needs define what we view as a reward. Thus a friendly smile or word is more likely to be seen as rewarding by a person with low self-esteem who has great need for acceptance than by a person with high self-esteem who does not have this strong need.

In spite of the fact that the person with high self-esteem has a less strong need for rewards from others, such an individual often faces a difficult problem. People with high self-esteem often have some degree of high status in the social world. When others give them praise, they wonder whether the praise is genuine or if the praiser is simply trying to get something in return? Because the person with high self-esteem and high social status does have something that others want, it is very likely that the praise is simply an attempt at **ingratiation** (Jones, 1964), not an expression of the other's true beliefs. Individuals with low social status do not face this dilemma; they have little that others want, so there is no need to be concerned about attempts at ingratiation. Thus people with low self-esteem are more likely to accept another's praise as genuine than are people with high self-esteem.

This discussion should alert us to the need to work for a better understanding in our own lives of our reasons for being attracted to others. Are we simply attracted to someone because of our own temporary need to bolster our self-esteem? Are we so suspicious of ingratiation that we automatically reject praise and thereby erect walls that inhibit our relationships? It is important for us to understand how our self-esteem can affect our relationships, and it is also important that we not let our own self-esteem be the only factor guiding these relationships.

Playing Hard to Get

Groucho Marx used to joke, "Any club that would have me is not worth belonging to." Some people seem to adopt this point of view in their personal relationships: "Anyone who's attracted to me, I'm not attracted to." Advice based on this kind of attitude was given to most of us by our parents or other coaches when we began to seek out social relationships. In most cases, we were cautioned, "Don't appear too eager," or "Play hard to get."

As it turns out, there is no clear evidence that this is a good strategy. Walster, Walster, Piliaurin, and Schmitt (1973) designed a number of studies where a woman acted either "hard" or "easy" to get. The situations ranged from dates to interactions between a prostitute and her client. The conclusion was that playing hard to get did not increase attractiveness. However, men were most attracted to women who were hard to get for others but easy to get for themselves. A woman who always played hard to get was rejected as being unattainable, and a woman who was always easy to get was

viewed as undiscriminating. But a woman who rejected everybody else was seen by the man she accepted as being choosy and showing good taste. It seems that we are attracted to people who treat us as if we are "special." These data may explain why exclusive relationships are so important to many of us. In an exclusive relationship, someone is telling us that we are special by rejecting all others.

Interpersonal Attraction: Some Conclusions

We can learn a number of lessons from what we know about attraction. The first is that we are attracted to others for a variety of reasons and that they are attracted to us for an equally wide variety of reasons. Often we may get confused by our liking for a person. We may say to ourselves, "I can't understand why I like that person. We're so different." However, we have seen that similarity is only one of many reasons why we like people. An understanding of the reasons for attraction may make us more accepting of our attraction to others and their attraction to us.

Another point to remember is that there are some aspects of ourselves or some types of behavior that we can emphasize to increase our desirability for others. For example, we should be aware of the needs of others and know that they will want more reinforcement at some times than at others. This is not to say that we should invent or manufacture kindness when we don't feel it. Genuineness and openness in interpersonal relations should be an overriding goal. However, it is important to be sensitive to the needs of the other person in a relationship while working to achieve this authenticity.

Finally, this discussion may shed some light on the reasons why we aren't attracted to others or they aren't attracted to us. At times we may be in a position where we feel we are doing everything possible to attract another person, but it isn't "working." We may interpret this rejection as a reflection of our own worth and abilities, which may have serious negative consequences for our self-esteem. We should remember, however, that the interpersonal attraction process is many-faceted and determined by the characteristics of both individuals in the interaction, by the nature of the present situation, and by the past histories and needs of the participants. So to assume the blame for the failure of a relationship is unwise and clearly not in line with what we have learned about interpersonal attraction.

REVIEW QUESTIONS

10. T or F: The most attractive relationships are those that allow us to contribute as well as receive.

11. Liking those who are familiar to us and who are in a position to reward us may be reasons why _____ often leads to attraction.

12. The theory that views social relationships in terms of the costs and rewards is called _____.

13. Aronson and Linder (1965) found in their experiment that subjects were most attracted to the confederate when he or she heard the confederate begin with negative statements about the subject but end with positive statements. Subjects were least attracted to the confederate when the reverse occurred. Aronson and Linder called this process the _____ of attraction.

14. The theory that predicts we will be attracted to those for whom we do large favors is called _____.

15. One reason why physical attractiveness leads to interpersonal attraction is that people see themselves as being more _____ to attractive people than to unattractive people.

16. Attraction to others because of strong needs for rewards is **more** likely to be found in those with low _____.

17. A person with high self-esteem may be likely to suspect someone who praises him or her of _____.

18. T or F: Walster and her colleagues found that males were most attracted to women who were hard to get for others but easy to get for themselves.

SUMMARY

1. The process of perceiving others can be separated into two phases: making inferences about a person's specific traits and resolving various and often conflicting data about a person into a coherent overall impression.

2. People infer others' traits by observing behavior and deciding whether it is indicative of an underlying personal characteristic or is a reflection of environmental contingencies. Many biases are involved in trait attribution, including strong tendencies to pay too little attention to situational forces that affect people's actions.

3. Combining trait information into an overall impression is a complex process. Often the overall impression is highly influenced by what the observer sees as a person's central traits, such as whether the person is emotionally warm or cold.

4. When later information about a person is inconsistent with perceiver's initial impressions, there are three possible results. Most often there is a primacy effect, in which people force later information to fit their original impression—even, if necessary, seeing the later behavior as reflecting temporary moods or situational pressures. Sometimes people are strongly affected by the later information and show recency effects, in which their impression of a person is more heavily affected by the later information than by the earlier. There are also overcompensation effects, in which people overcorrect for initial mistaken impressions.

5. Our impressions of people are biased in many ways. We often see what we expect to see. Often our false impressions have a significant impact on the people we are perceiving. Behavior toward them that is based on our false impressions may cause them to behave in ways that are consistent with our impressions.

6. We are attracted to certain people for a number of reasons.

7. Physical proximity increases a person's attractiveness to us. We tend to like people we are physically close to and spend a lot of time with. Proximity increases the intensity of a relationship.

8. We are attracted to relationships we expect to have the greatest positive outcome. Social exchange theory views relationships in economic terms: that is, people weigh the possible costs and rewards of a relationship to determine its likely outcome.

9. We are often attracted to people for whom we do favors and expend effort. Cogni-

tive dissonance theory explains this phenomenon in terms of people's desire to keep their feelings consistent with their behavior. Being able to contribute to a relationship enhances our self-esteem and increases our satisfaction with a relationship.

10. Similarity can lead to attraction between people. Research shows that we tend to be attracted to people who are similar to us in attitudes, background, physical characteristics, economic condition, and experience. Sometimes we're attracted to people who are different from us because they complement us and satisfy our needs.

11. We tend to be attracted to good-looking people and to equate physical attractiveness with sensitivity, kindness, being exciting, and being sociable.

12. We are more likely to be attracted to others when our self-esteem is low than when our self-esteem is high. At such times we tend to be attracted to people with high self-esteem. People with high self-esteem, and therefore high social status, often face the dilemma of deciding whether others' interest and kindness is genuine or aimed at ingratiating the high-status person.

13. We are often attracted to people who seem hard to get for others but easy to get for ourselves.

CRITICAL THINKING QUESTIONS

1. Can you think of times when your judgment of another person has been biased by a primacy effect? Did you judge that person to be unfriendly and ignore or dismiss later friendly behavior? Has your judgment been a self-fulfilling prophecy? Were you reserved when talking to that person and thereby turn his or her openness into a anxious silence that seemed to be unfriendly?

2. How important is similarity in creating your friends? Are there aspects of attraction

that have led you to like people who were very different from you? Do you think you should be more open to liking people who are different? How could you make that happen?

3. Do you find yourself trying to ingratiate yourself to your teachers, your supervisors, or your friend's parents? When does it work? How do you feel about yourself when you ingratiate? When you present yourself very positively, do you sometimes believe your own act? Why or why not?

MATCHING EXERCISE

Match each term with its definition.

a. overcompensation effect
b. primacy effect
c. recency effect
d. self-fulfilling prophecy

e. complementarity
f. ingratiation
g. cognitive dissonance
h. self-esteem

i. proximity
j. similarity and attraction
k. social exchange theory

1. The theory that views social relationships in economic terms such as inputs, costs, and outcomes
2. One person's geographical closeness to another person; an important factor in influencing interpersonal attraction
3. The finding that people are attracted to others who have attitudes, appearance, background, or desires in common
4. The degree to which one likes and respects oneself
5. A feeling of discomfort resulting from inconsistent thoughts
6. Having opposite but congruent needs
7. Attempts by an individual to enhance his or her image in the eyes of another by expressing attitudes that he or she thinks the other person wants to hear
8. A prophecy or prediction that may not be inevitable but that leads to behavior that makes it come true
9. A tendency to correct for an initial incorrect impression and overemphasize the most recent information
10. An impression of another that is most heavily influenced by the earliest information about the person
11. The heavy influence of the most recent information about another person in the creation of one's impression of that person

Answers to Matching Exercise

a. 9   b. 10   c. 11   d. 8   e. 6   f. 7   g. 5   h. 4   i. 2   j. 3   k. 1

ANSWERS TO REVIEW QUESTIONS

1. true
2. attribution
3. internal, external
4. expectations
5. primacy
6. overcompensation
7. self-fulfilling prophecy
8. false
9. d
10. true
11. proximity
12. social exchange theory
13. gain–loss phenomenon
14. cognitive dissonance theory
15. similar
16. self-esteem
17. ingratiation
18. true

BECOMING INTIMATE

Ekaterina Gordeeva and Sergei Grinkov

Ekaterina Gordeeva and Sergei Grinkov

When Dr. Schwartzberg told Katya that Sergei had died, she asked to see him. "We went into the room," said Schwartzberg. "She spoke a few words to him in Russian. It seemed very tender. She caressed his face. She kissed him. I left her alone with him" (Wulf, 1995, p. 89). And so on November 20, 1995, Katya (the beautiful figure skater Ekaterina Gordeeva) said goodbye to her husband and skating partner, Sergei Grinkov. Grinkov had died of a heart attack after collapsing during a morning practice in Lake Placid, New York. He was 28 years old. He left Katya, his 24-year-old wife and partner, and their daughter, 3-year-old Daria. The small, close circle of champion skaters and the larger world of their supporters mourned Sergei's passing. It ended the storybook romance of Grinkov and Gordeeva, known among friends as G & G, and deprived skating enthusiasts of the sport's greatest pair.

Grinkov and Gordeeva burst onto the international athletic scene in 1986. That year, when Gordeeva was just 14, G & G were world champions. Two years later, they won their first gold medal at the Olympic Games in Calgary. By that time they had already been skating together for six years. They began when Katya was 10 and Sergei was 14. Paired together by Russian authorities under the old Soviet Union sports system in 1982, the two worked hard to rise to the top of the skating world.

Initially there was no romance between the two. When she was young, Katya seemed rather plain. The older, mature Grinkov took no romantic interest in his junior partner. At Calgary, their act portrayed them as older brother and younger sister. She was the 90-pound sprite, the centerpiece of their act. He was the foundation from which she could do her jumps and spins. They could skate perfectly together and flawlessly perform their signature quadruple twist. "The two of them were just one," noted skating producer Jirina Ribbens (Starr, 1995, p. 71).

As she matured, the 90-pound Gordeeva blossomed into a beautiful young woman. Katya had harbored romantic feelings for Sergei for several years, but he was involved with other women and did not reciprocate. Finally, he noticed her as a woman and not just a coworker. Then things moved quickly. Tom Collins, organizer of the Tour of World Champions, said "You could see it happen. It was all very sweet.... At first she was like this little rag doll that he threw around in the air, but she sure grew up" (Montville, 1995, p. 36). The couple fell in love shortly after Calgary and married in 1991 in their native Moscow. In 1992, Daria was born. Two years later, they won their second gold medal in the Olympic Games in Lillehammer, Norway; despite a few glitches, their performance was so electric that they could not be denied the championship. U.S. Olympics coach John Nicks noted that "the change in their relationship into a loving, caring, mature union changed their skating for the better" (Wulf, 1995, p. 89). A few months later, Katya was named one of "The 50 Most Beautiful People in the World" by *People* magazine.

For the year preceding Sergei's death, G & G had been living in the United States and traveling together on tours with other members of the skating elite. They lived an idyllic life of traveling and working together in high style. When they went on tour, Gordeeva's mother took care of Daria. A few months before Grinkov's collapse, Katya said, "I am very happy we can travel together. I think it's the best thing that we can get and be in this life." Silver medalist Paul Wylie said "Their eyes never left each other during" their performances. "No one else does that in pairs skating.... For them it was natural. You could see how much they loved each other.... We all wish we could find that kind of feeling, that perfect nuclear life. So few people actually do" (Montville, 1995, p. 36).

After they had shown the world how magical a love can be, Sergei and Katya's storybook romance came to an abrupt end. One skater said, "They had everything. He was the perfect husband; they had the perfect career, the perfect marriage." Katya was the one to say, "Maybe it was too perfect." But skater Scott Hamilton noted that "the only flaw in G & G's program is that it wasn't long enough" (Wulf, 1995, p. 89). Grinkov and Gordeeva were lucky to have found each other, and we were lucky to have seen them. Tragically, it was all too brief.

WHAT IS LOVE?

In lots of ways, G & G's romance seems like a fairytale, though a sad one. Their championship skating partnership, Sergei's discovery that his partner had become a stunningly beautiful young woman, their all-consuming mutual love, and his tragic death all appeal to our ideals about romantic love. But like many couples, they did not live "happily ever after." Love and intimacy provide moments of great pleasure and great pain and involve work as well as hearts and flowers. In this chapter we will examine love and intimate relationships, considering their satisfactions and their problems, and try to point out some of the important aspects of a loving bond between two people.

First of all, what is love? It is clear that there are many kinds of love, and that they vary greatly from one culture to another (Brehm, 1992). Recently psychologists have argued that adult love stems from very basic motives for interpersonal attachment that probably grow out of infants' attachment to their mothers (Baumeister & Leary, 1995; Bowlby, 1969; Shaver, Hazan, & Bradshaw, 1988). According to this view, human beings have a deeply rooted need to establish and maintain strong and long-lasting interpersonal relationships.

One way to define love in present-day North American culture is to distinguish it from liking. Zick Rubin (1973) has shown that liking is based in large part on feelings of respect, high regard, and similarity but it is also defined by more emotional reactions. As relationships develop, we often wonder, "Do I love this person or just 'like them very much'?" Often couples will engage in lengthy discussions, attempting to decide whether they love each other or are simply very attracted to each other. Often a crisis is reached when one partner says that he or she is truly in love with the other, whereupon the question "How do you know you love me?" arises. This question may bring the partners to the realiza-

tion that they don't really know what love is, or at least that they can't put it into words.

People shouldn't feel alone when they wonder whether or not they know what love is. One dictionary lists 24 definitions of "love." In Western history love has been defined numerous ways, including madness and torment, a game, a noble quest, as being doomed, and as not involving sex. Most psychologists begin with Rubin's (1973) definition. In this view there are three components. The first is **caring,** the feeling that the other person's satisfactions and well-being are as important as your own. The second component is **attachment,** or the need to be with the other person and to be approved of by that person. The final component, **intimacy,** involves close and confidential communication.

In an effort to identify love more clearly, Rubin developed two scales, one to measure love and the other to measure liking. To determine if his scale did discriminate between these two concepts, Rubin asked each person in a dating couple to fill out the two scales in reference to his or her partner. He then asked the subjects to complete the same two scales with reference to a same-sex friend. The results indicated that while friends and lovers were both well liked, only lovers scored high on the love scale.

Further work on love has focused on passionate or romantic love in particular (Hatfield, 1988). The self-assessment exercise on page 256 measures how romantic you are. Passionate, romantic love is defined as a state of intense absorption in another person, longing for the partner, physiological arousal and feelings of ecstasy at having attained the other person's love, and a sense of complete fulfillment as a result of having the relationship. This is the kind of feeling that Katya Gordeeva seemed to reveal when she looked at Sergei Grinkov. Former pairs champion Jo Starbuck said "she would look at him with this I'm-so-in-love-with-you look that would just make your heart sing." (Wulf, 1995, p. 89).

How Romantic Are You?

Charles Hobart (1958) developed a questionnaire to measure how romantic people were during courtship. One of his findings was that men had higher romanticism scores than women. You can get your own romanticism score by indicating whether you agree or disagree with each of the following statements. Agree answers to numbers 3, 5, 6, 7, 8, and 11 and disagree answers to 1, 2, 4, 9, 10, and 12 indicate romanticism. How do you score?

1. Lovers ought to expect a certain amount of disillusionment after marriage.

2. True love should be suppressed in cases where its existence conflicts with the prevailing standards of morality.

3. To be truly in love is to be in love forever.

4. The sweetly feminine "clinging vine" girl cannot compare with the capable and sympathetic girl as a sweetheart.

5. As long as they at least love each other, two people should have no trouble getting along together in marriage.

6. A girl should expect her sweetheart to be chivalrous on all occasions.

7. A person should marry whomever he or she loves regardless of social position.

8. Lovers should freely confess everything of personal significance to each other.

9. Economic security should be carefully considered before selecting a marriage partner.

10. Most of us could sincerely love any one of several people equally well.

11. A lover without jealousy is hardly to be desired.

12. One should not marry against the serious advice of one's parents.

There are three conditions that, taken together, give rise to feelings of passionate, romantic love (Walster & Walster, 1978). First, there must be a culturally based expectation of falling in love. Certainly in our lifetime the romantic ideal is alive and well, and we expect to fall in love in a romantic way (Dion & Dion, 1988). G & G's relationship seemed to be a perfect example of such love. Their devotion and total absorption was obvious for all to see. The second condition for falling in love is that the right person must come along to fulfill our ex-pectation of the romantic ideal. Having the expectation of falling in love and finding the right person leads many people to experience the feeling of "love at first sight." Katya Gordeeva seemed to have this feeling for Sergei from a very early age, though it took him longer to reciprocate. As soon as we meet someone who fits our ideal image we experience love. Half of all adult men and women report that they have experienced love at first sight (Berscheid & Walster, 1974). In one of their big hit songs, the English band the Beat-

Love at First Sight

Do you believe in a love at first sight? This is an area where lessons from life and lessons from the laboratory seem to conflict. One of us remembers well the first time he saw his wife at a party. There was a definite reaction. She looked awfully good, and it wasn't long before love had blossomed. We also heard an interesting account from the U.S. Olympic marathon champion in 1984, Joan Benoit Samuelson. She told us about first meeting her husband, Scott. She describes it this way in her book: "I saw him right away—he is so tall that I can always find him in a crowd. I can't say it was love at first sight because I know how complicated love is; there was something there, though" (Benoit, 1987, p. 90).

We have the expectation of falling in love quickly because the idea of love at first sight is very much alive in the culture. But is it real? As we noted, some psychologists have reported that approximately 50 percent of adult men and women claim they experienced love at first sight (Berscheid & Walster, 1974). However, other studies have reported only 8 percent of men and 5 percent of women feeling "strong physical attraction" within a few days of first meeting (Rubin, 1973). So it's hard to know whether to believe in love at first sight. For some individuals, life experiences clearly support the reality of love at first sight. And that includes one of us. But it may be rarer than those who are so sure of it actually think. Clearly, whether love at first sight is real for you will depend on the lessons you learn from your own life.

les asked, "Do you believe in a love at first sight?" For many people, the answer is yes (see the Lessons from Life box above).

The third and final condition for feeling passionate, romantic love is physiological arousal, that may come from a range of emotions, or even from exercise, that is *interpreted* as love. Studies of emotion show that physiological arousal can be experienced as one of several emotions, depending on the cues in the environment (Zillman, 1996). Several studies show that arousal from other sources can be labeled as love and lead people to experience passionate feelings for potential romantic partners they encounter. In one study (Dutton & Aron, 1974) male subjects were interviewed after walking across a rickety, scary bridge or over a very solid one. The interviewer was an attractive female. The male subjects showed more romantic interest in her if they were physiologically aroused from crossing the dangerous bridge.

Romantic passion is strong and intense. It preoccupies us during the time we experience it. We have constant fantasies about our loved one. But this powerful emotion often quickly diminishes in intensity. Then feelings of closeness and of commitment must develop if a relationship is to last. Feelings of closeness and commitment are central to what is called companionate love, sometimes referred to as the warm afterglow of romantic passion (Berscheid, 1985). **Companionate love** is the intimacy or closeness we feel for those whom our lives are intertwined and to whom we are committed. The lover may seem more like a friend, and the attachment is peaceful and tender. In some relationships, the feelings of passion and romance remain alongside the feelings of intimacy and commitment. Then psychologists speak of **consummate love** (Sternberg, 1986), a love that has all the characteristics of the ideal love. The marriage of Grinkov and Gordeeva has these qualities, in part because they were able to work together as well as share a personal relationship. There were clearly some doubters who felt that they couldn't both work together and love together at the same time. One of Sergei's coaches said, "At the beginning, everyone laughed. They showed them all" (Montville, 1995, p. 36). Let's consider some important aspects of love and then some of the stages of intimate relationships that may lead to companionate or consummate love.

Love and Sex

The relationship between love and sex usually becomes an issue when people try to define love (see Chapter 11). Often love and sex are talked about as if they're the same thing. Indeed, the phrase "making love" is often used to denote sexual intercourse, as Bob Dylan observed in his song, "Love Is Just a Four Letter Word."

Sexual attraction and sexual relations do play an important part in love. As Rubin (1973) points out, intimacy is a component of love, and sexual intercourse is an aspect of intimacy. Reproductive and sexual drives are basic to humans, so partners may fulfill each other's needs through the act of sexual intercourse (Buss, 1988). Thus tenderness and intimacy can be expressed through sexual behavior, and interpersonal needs can be filled through sexual union.

Clearly sexual behavior can be viewed as one component of love. But it's important not to identify sexual behavior as being love, or even an expression of love. Love isn't a necessary prerequisite for sex. People may have sex because it's a physical pleasure or to express simple affection or momentary elation. And there are also less positive reasons for people's sexual behavior. As pointed out in Chapter 12, some use sexual behavior to express dominance or to assuage feelings of inadequacy. Others engage in sexual behavior because they feel that they must do so to be accepted by others or because they feel peer pressure because "everyone else is doing it," (Thornton, 1989).

Sexual intercourse is an act of interpersonal union. The meaning of the act is based on the context in which it's performed. If two people have sex to fulfill the needs of *both* of them in a caring and tender atmosphere, and if both partners have freely chosen to be sexual with each other, sex can increase interpersonal intimacy and foster love. Like other aspects of an intimate relationship, a good sexual relationship requires patience and caring. The caring component of sexual behavior involves a consideration of the other's needs and the genuine desire to satisfy the other person's needs in addition to your own. If the partners aren't aware of each other's needs, or don't care about them, and engage in sexual behavior for self-gratification only, sexual behavior can inhibit a love relationship.

Learning to Love

It may come as a surprise to some, but research suggests that love isn't an emotion that comes naturally to everyone. Unfortunately, because of their life experience, some people don't have the ability to love. Harry Harlow identified five stages of loving relationships (1971). The first is *parental love,* the love of a father or mother for a child. *Infant love,* the love of the infant for its parent, is the second stage. Next is *peer love,* which is the love of a child or preadolescent for another child or preadolescent. The fourth stage is *age-mate passion,* which is sexual love, and the final stage is *parental love,* or the love of an adult male for his family. According to Harlow, our experiences at each stage prepare us for the next stage. For example, "age-mate experience is fundamental to the development of normal and natural heterosexual love" (1971, p. 4). If we are deprived of love at an early stage, we will have difficulty experiencing love at the later stages.

In a dramatic series of experiments with monkeys, Harlow demonstrated how crucial the early experience of love is to the ability to feel and express love later in life. Harlow removed some infant monkeys from their mothers shortly after birth. They were raised in isolation without maternal love, although they were adequately cared for and fed by their human handler. Three months, six months, and two years later, these monkeys were introduced to other monkeys of their age and the interactions were observed. Harlow found that the isolated monkeys couldn't form friendships or play with their age mates. The longer the period of isolation had been, the more impoverished were the monkey's relationships. The isolated monkeys were also unable to engage in sexual behavior and were not receptive to the sexual advances of other monkeys. In some cases, Harlow impregnated female isolated monkeys in an effort to study whether they could develop a loving relationship with their offspring. The results were most startling: These mothers not only failed to feed and care for their infants, but they treated them brutally. The infants would have been killed had the experimenters not removed them from the care of their own mothers. Thus the failure of these isolated monkeys to experience love at the early stages of their development prevented them from being able to express peer love, age-mate passion, or maternal love at later stages in their lives.

Erich Fromm (1956) also points out that early experiences are important for the development of love. Fromm states that we must learn to love ourselves before we can love others. In loving ourselves we learn to foster our own growth and happiness, and we can then transfer this learning into the loving of others. According to Fromm, without learning these lessons we can't truly know how to care about the happiness of others.

The important lesson to be learned from these theories is that our ability to love others is strongly affected by our own early experiences. Someone who is raised in an emotionally impoverished environment in which love is absent will have difficulty loving others later in life. We must learn how to love by experiencing love from others and practicing loving ourselves. People who have not had these opportunities may require therapy to help them "learn to love."

A true loving relationship takes time to develop. Each partner must learn about the other. Each must understand the needs of the other and learn how he or she can fulfill those needs. To do this, two people must work to develop open and honest communication with each other. The love relationship will continue to grow as long as the partners trust each other enough to disclose their emotions, hopes, aspirations, inadequacies, and feelings about each other. To the extent that this honest communication can be achieved, each person in the relationship will be able to experience personal growth. To reach these goals takes time.

A love relationship is complex and often delicate. In addition to learning to understand each other, the partners must learn to accept each other as individuals who are likely to have different needs and desires. One of the dilemmas that often makes love relationships fragile and leads to misunderstanding between partners is the conflict between feelings of dependency on the relationship and desire for independence (Berscheid & Walster, 1978). As the love relationship grows, each partner becomes more giving and at the same time receives more and more need fulfillment. On one hand, it's great to have your needs satisfied by someone you love. On the other hand, this satisfaction itself often causes people to feel increasingly dependent on the relationship. Feeling dependent can be frightening, since it may seem to threaten the independence people desire. The result of this conflict is that people may be afraid of falling in love or may begin to feel strong ambivalence about their intimate relationship.

These feelings are common in most love relationships, and it's important to discuss them. Too many times one of the partners may sense this ambivalence in the other and interpret it as a sign of rejection. This interpretation then leads that person to withdraw from the relationship, and the love and trust is quickly destroyed. To avoid this problem, individuals in relationships must respect and even encourage each other's independence. There must be room for individual growth within the relationship and a willingness to openly explore each other's feelings of ambivalence without immediately assuming that they are signs of rejection.

Thus love is an emotion that grows slowly into its mature forms, and it is one that requires practice and constant nurturing.

With proper attention, it can lead to tremendous happiness and satisfaction for the partners and result in a relationship that blends dependence and independence in a way that encourages both individual growth and growth of the relationship itself: The development of a loving relationship depends on the willingness of the partners to be truly accepting of each other and to discuss their feelings honestly.

Review Questions

1. Although both love and liking may involve feelings of respect and perceptions of similarity, love is distinguished from liking by its strong _____ reaction.

2. Rubin believes that love consists of three components: caring, _____, and _____.

3. Several conditions together give rise to feelings of passionate love: the expectation of falling in love, meeting someone who fulfills our expectation of the romantic ideal, and _____ _____ that is interpreted as love.

4. Mature or _____ love is the warm afterglow of passionate love, the affection we feel for those with whom our lives are intertwined.

5. T or F: Harlow found that even isolated monkeys who did not experience nurturing were instinctively able to express age-mate passion and maternal love later in life.

FORMING AND MAINTAINING A RELATIONSHIP

How do people decide whom they want to form a relationship with from among all those who are initially available? How did Sergei Grinkov finally decide that his young and petite partner was the one that he was drawn to? And after a relationship begins, how does it blossom into an intimate relationship? How are intimate relationships maintained? How did Grinkov and Gordeeva handle the complex roles of husband and wife, parents, coworkers, and new immigrants to a strange country? Once people are married, how likely is it that they will stay married, and what are some of the things that pull marriages and other intimate relationships apart? In the rest of this chapter we will look at the major as-

pects of building an intimate relationship. The value of understanding intimate relationships is probably obvious. Since they are such an important part of living and psychological adjustment, it is crucial that we explore them as fully as possible. Establishing intimate relationships is one of the most important steps in achieving happiness and successful personal adjustment. We hope the information in this chapter will be useful to you in understanding how relationships work and how they can be improved.

In discussing the development of relationships we will consider a series of stages in relationship development and some of the events that occur in each stage. There are four such stages: sampling, bargaining, commitment, and institutionalization (Backman, 1981; Thibaut & Kelley, 1959). We will describe them briefly now and then explain more fully in the next sections.

Sampling refers to the process of looking over the possibilities and then deciding on a person with whom to attempt to form a relationship. It involves a quick "forecasting" of how satisfying a relationship with various people might be. It is based on a small amount of information, usually just watching or looking at other people, or possibly conversing with them at a superficial level (Murstein, 1986).

The second stage of a relationship is called **bargaining.** This is the stage in which the relationship is actually built. During this phase people try to "negotiate" or work out mutually satisfying ways of interacting, although no formal bargaining actually takes place. This is the stage where two people get to know each other well and try to pattern a successful way of being together.

If the bargaining or building process is successful, two people might decide to make a **commitment** to each other. This may mean being best friends who can count on one another to spend time together and engage in mutually satisfying activities, or it may mean living together as exclusive partners in a complete adult relationship. A relationship in the commitment phase is clearly an intimate one.

The final stage of relationship development, **institutionalization,** is simply an extension of the commitment stage. In this final stage there is some formalization of the commitment. This may involve marriage, as in the case of G & G, or some other ritual or ceremony that more or less formally recognizes the relationship as highly intimate and committed. We will consider each of these stages, with special emphasis on the process of initiating and building a relationship.

INITIATING A RELATIONSHIP: SAMPLING

Sampling, the initiating stage of a relationship, usually occurs when one person enters a crowded room, perhaps at a party, and looks at the other people in the room and decides who to approach and talk to or, after some initial conversation, who to try to contact later. Sampling can occur at parties, dances, and singles bars as well as in offices, buses, churches, and classrooms. We are all aware of this possibility and govern our behavior accordingly. We try to present ourselves in a positive light and make a good first impression on other people. Thus sampling generally takes place in the context of self-presentation (Goffman, 1959; Leary, 1995).

We all try to control other people's impressions of us so that we can influence to some extent how they treat us. We usually do this by trying to present ourselves in a positive way (Baumeister & Hutton, 1987). Often in a first-impression situation, people give what are called **idealized performances,** acting as if they support and conform to ideal standards of good conduct more than they actually do (Goffman, 1959). For example, you might dress up for an interview with a corporate recruiter and say things to try to make the recruiter think that your lifestyle and attitudes are more in accord with corporate philosophy than is really the case. People also often display magazines and books in their living rooms that may suggest better taste than they really have.

We are probably more aware of others presenting themselves in an idealized way than we are of doing it ourselves. But there is an overwhelming tendency in human interaction not to challenge or contradict other people's idealized performances. We act so that open contradiction seldom occurs (Goffman, 1955). Instead, we act as if we accept other people's presented or "projected" selves. If they claim they run six miles every morning, we commend them even if we doubt that it's true. This doesn't mean that we really agree with the image another person tries to project. We simply appear to accept and believe in someone's idealized performance. We suppress our true feelings and go along with the other person's act. In this way a working agreement is achieved, and people can conduct their business easily. Goffman claims that societies everywhere regulate people to behave in this way so that interaction can proceed smoothly, without fear of embarrassment or challenge.

Although we seldom openly challenge other people's idealized performances, we do make private judgments about how honest and straightforward they seem to be and to what extent they are inflating themselves and pretending to be something they aren't. We admire the person who seems to behave according to honest feelings and shows others exactly who he or she is.

Problems in the Sampling Stage

We face several problems during the sampling phase of interaction and in moving past it into more meaningful relationships. We've already discussed how "putting up a good front" can squelch possibilities for genuine intimacy. Ritualized self-presentation patterns make interaction very superficial. When two people pass each other and say "Hi. How are you?" and "Fine, thanks. How are you?" they learn very little about each other. We often present only the part of ourselves that is "appropriate" to the situation and reveal very little of a personal nature. Under these circumstances, it can be very difficult to forecast accurately how much value any future interaction might have. We're forced to choose potential candidates for future relationships largely on the basis of appearance and first impressions. Furthermore, it can be very difficult to move a relationship beyond this superficial chat. If people are to develop relationships beyond formalities, they must open up a little more. This involves taking risks, but such risks are necessary if relationships are to grow.

Some of the difficulties in the sampling stage of a relationship were conveniently bypassed for Katya and Sergei. Because they had been paired as skaters by Soviet authorities at a very young age, they knew each other well for several years before romantic issues entered the picture. Katya decided earlier in their relationship that Sergei was the person with whom she wanted to have a romantic relationship. Sergei sampled more widely. But both of them knew each other well when the relationship finally blossomed.

Another serious problem in this early stage of relationship development can be *shyness*. Studies by Zimbardo (1990) and his colleagues show that shyness is a very common obstacle to forming relationships. Forty percent of the populations that Zimbardo studied in large surveys considered themselves to be shy, and more than 80 percent said that they had been shy at one time. Shyness, or "people phobia," as Zimbardo refers to it, manifests itself in physiological reactions (increased heart pounding and blushing), various thoughts and feelings (self-consciousness and concern about others' impressions), and overt behaviors such as being silent and avoiding eye contact. Shyness is so unpleasant that it can prevent people from interacting with others and cause them to suffer some serious losses as the result of diminished interpersonal contact.

The vast majority of people find great rewards in being with other people. People who are shy are less likely to develop relationships and more likely to miss out on these rewards and satisfactions. They are also less likely than others to have close friends to draw on for social support in times of stress or crisis. Shy people may also have more difficulty in accurately appraising themselves, especially in appraising the seriousness of their shyness-related problems, because they have few people with whom they can compare themselves. In short, because their relationships and interactions with others are limited, they lack the rewards, support, and comparison information that normally come from others.

Measures Related to Shyness

Psychologist Arnold Buss (1980) developed questionnaires designed to measure public self-consciousness and social anxiety. People who agree with the public self-consciousness statements tend to be concerned about their appearance and the impression they make on other people. These people also tend to have higher scores on social anxiety, a more direct measure of how shy, how easily embarrassed, and how anxious with other people someone is. You can get some idea of your own public self-consciousness and social anxiety by seeing how many of the statements in each group below you agree with.

Public self-consciousness

1. I'm concerned about what other people think of me.
2. I usually worry about making a good impression.
3. I'm concerned about the way I present myself.
4. I'm self-conscious about the way I look.
5. I'm usually aware of my appearance.
6. One of the last things I do before leaving my house is look in the mirror.
7. I'm concerned about my style of doing things.

Social anxiety

1. It takes me time to get over my shyness in new situations.
2. I get embarrassed easily.
3. Large groups make me nervous.
4. I find it hard to talk to strangers.
5. I feel anxious when I speak in front of a group.
6. I have trouble working when someone is watching me.

Source: Adapted from A. H. Buss (1980).

What are the consequences of losing contact with others in these ways? Not surprisingly, there are indications that the personal adjustment of shy people suffers. They are more socially anxious, show more signs of being anxious, show memory lapses in stressful situations, and are more easily influenced by others. They even have difficulties in their sexual adjustment. Zimbardo reports that shy people have fewer sexual contacts than non-shy people do and that they enjoy less those sexual contacts they do have. Shy people also show more dissatisfaction with their jobs and tend to feel "passed over."

Although shyness can be a serious problem in starting relationships and in interaction generally, it is a difficulty that can be overcome. Zimbardo reports that in his shyness clinic people are helped by various treatments. Some are helped to practice social skills such as smiling or making eye contact, some are helped to control anxiety through the use of relaxation techniques, and some are helped to improve their self-concepts through self-acceptance.

BUILDING A RELATIONSHIP: BARGAINING

After you've made an initial judgment on the basis of sampling whom it might be worthwhile to get to know better, the relationship can begin in earnest. The postsampling phase may start with a telephone call suggesting that you and the other person might enjoy playing tennis or skiing together, or simply initiating a more than casual conversation on the dance floor. It will usually be clear to both people that the relationship is entering a new stage.

Once the conversation, date, game, or stroll has started and it's clear that both of you are interested in exploring the possibility of some kind of mutually satisfying relationship, bargaining can truly begin. This is the stage where people begin to "negotiate" with each other about what kind of relationship they might have. Each of you will have interests to promote, things you want from the relationship and that you will try to get, with the hope that some sort of accommodation can be reached that is satisfactory to both. Usually you will want the other person to behave in certain ways, and he or she will also have preferences about how you act. These preferred behaviors may involve working on certain tasks, adopting particular beliefs, solving difficult problems, or being attentive to important needs, including needs for companionship, protection, warmth, feeding, sex, and self-actualization. For Grinkov and Gordeeva, a careful separation of roles in their personal and professional lives needed to be worked out. On the personal side, Sergei seems to have been the one in charge. He was older and controlled the pace of their relationship. On the professional side, Katya was in charge. She spoke for the pair, partly because she had better command of English than Sergei did (Montville, 1995).

We can see, in short, that each person in a relationship has things he or she wants from the other. The question, then, is how much each person will want to behave in the way the other prefers. Both people will probably be willing to do some things and unwilling to do others. The issue is whether a mutually satisfactory pattern of interaction, a successful accommodation, can be reached. Can the two of you work it out?

Self-Disclosure

One of the most important aspects of trying to work out a successful accommodation and building a rewarding relationship is **self-disclosure.** This means talking to the other person about your thoughts and feelings, your aspirations and dreams, your fears and doubts. It may even involve talking about things you're ashamed of. Only through honest self-disclosure can people really learn about each other's needs and wishes for being together and begin to build a truly intimate relationship. Through this process people discover who their partners really are and come to love and respect them for who they are. Self-disclosure is a critical part of relationship building. It is closely related to the quality of relationships and to an individual's degree of personal adjustment.

Self-Disclosure and Personal Adjustment. One of the most important findings about self-disclosure is that it has a great impact on the self-disclosing person (Derlega & Berg, 1987). When people can confide in others and freely discuss their worries and concerns, there are clear improvements in physical health (Pennebaker, Colder, & Sharp, 1990). The ability to talk about oneself to another person is also a sign of psychological health and good adjustment. Openness to other people greatly facilitates self-actualization and growth (Jourard, 1971). In fact, hiding oneself from others stunts our growth in a number of ways.

One result of keeping information about ourselves from others is that we never get feedback from them. We don't learn what others think of our thoughts, feelings, and actions. Also, as we will see later, people who don't disclose information about themselves to others, who are unwilling to talk about their own personal matters, aren't likely to be taken into the confidence of others. They will be cut off from intimate interpersonal contact. Thus they aren't likely to learn what others are really like and what they care deeply about. Most important, Jourard suggests that not talking about ourselves to others leads us to become less and less in touch with ourselves. A lack of awareness of our own inner lives sets in, and our self-concepts weaken and get lost (Chaikin & Derlega, 1976).

Another problem is that an unwillingness to talk about oneself, and to talk honestly, means that one is, in effect, hiding important parts of oneself from others. This means that what one does present to others is partially a facade. Presenting a facade makes interaction stressful. Other people become a source of threat. Being with others is painful if we are unwilling to talk personally with them. Many psychologists advocate the necessity of self-disclosure and strongly urge people to become more "transparent" to others (e.g., Mowrer, 1971). In general, they believe that self-disclosure and feedback increase the public area of a person's life and that this contributes to effective personal adjustment.

Being able to share deep personal feelings in an intimate relationship is undoubtedly important. Still, just how open and self-disclosing we should be in a particular situation needs to be judged carefully. There are very strong social norms about how much self-disclosure is appropriate. People who violate this norm are thought to be "weird" and are not liked. Those who disclose too much too soon, the "plungers," make others feel very uncomfortable and are strongly avoided (Luft, 1969). Recent research makes clear that there needs to be a balance of self-disclosure and respect for privacy in a successful, intimate relationship (Baxter, 1988).

Psychologically healthy people follow self-disclosure norms, revealing a great deal to a few significant others with whom they are intimate or who are helping or counseling them, and a medium amount to others in general (Cozby, 1973). They are sensitive to a given situation and can accommodate themselves to the needs of others. They are open, but they don't rush things. They don't seem to be desperate for contact, approval, or information about others. They don't ask more of others in terms of disclosure than others are willing to give, and they don't tell others more about themselves than others would want to hear.

Determinants of Self-Disclosure. Many studies have indicated that self-disclosure is reciprocal (Derlega & Berg, 1987; Jourard & Friedman, 1970; Rubin, 1973; Cozby, 1972). That is, the more one person discloses about herself or himself to another, the more the second person will disclose in return. This finding has been demonstrated repeatedly (see Chaikin & Derlega, 1976), and it is clear that the best predictor of how self-disclosing one person is being with another is how self-disclosing the other has just been. It has even been shown that when others reveal too much, we don't like them as well as we do when they reveal the normative amount, but we still disclose more to them, closely following the reciprocity principle.

Reciprocity is a powerful determinant of self-disclosure, but it is by no means the only one. As we indicated before, people try hard to disclose the normative, or "appropriate," amount of information about themselves, depending on the situation. If someone else's self-disclosure seems too personal, we will probably compromise between the wish to reciprocate and the wish to act appropriately. The more others disclose to us, the more we will disclose to them in return, but this doesn't mean that we will exactly match their level of self-disclosure. The appropriateness norm can exert a restraining force. Thus we might disclose a great deal to people who tell us about their love affairs, but perhaps not reveal the details of our own intimate relationships.

Another restraining force on self-disclosure is fear of the possible negative consequences of revealing too much. We may feel that we will be ridiculed or rejected for some of our thoughts and feelings, or that information we have shared may not be held in confidence or may be used against us in some way. Trust is therefore a key factor in determining how much we will disclose about ourselves to others. If we can count on people not to exploit our confidences, we're likely to tell them a good deal, especially if they've indicated that they trust us by making their own self-disclosures. How much we trust another person is affected by two things, how trustworthy they seem compared to other people and how much *basic trust*, in the Eriksonian sense, we have in our own psychological outlook (see Chapter 2). In short, self-disclosure is affected by how much others disclose, norms of appropriateness, and our degree of trust in another person.

Self-Disclosure and the Quality of Relationships.   Self-disclosure has a great impact on relationships and in turn is very much affected by the quality of a relationship (Miller, 1990). For example, Altman and Haythorn (1965) suggest that as relationships become more intimate, there is an increase in both the number of topics that are mutually disclosed and the depth with which any one of them is discussed. Thus both the breadth and depth of self-disclosure are greater in intimate relationships.

While studies indicate that self-disclosure is greatest in highly intimate relationships, research also indicates that strangers often disclose a great deal to each other. Georg Simmel wrote: "The stranger often receives the most surprising openness—confidences which sometimes have the character of a con-

fessional and which would be carefully withheld from a more closely related person" (1950, p. 404). Toffler (1970) quotes a college student who remarked about her behavior in Fort Lauderdale during spring vacation, "You're not worried about what you do or say here because, frankly, you'll never see these people again" (p. 96). These observations suggest that we'll open up to strangers about highly personal matters because we don't need to trust them. We simply have to be sure we'll never see them again. This underscores the fact that, in ordinary relationships, fear of being vulnerable to manipulation as a result of having revealed too much is a powerful inhibitor of self-disclosure.

While most research and theory have focused on intimacy as a factor related to self-disclosure, it has also been shown that status is an important determinant of who discloses what to whom. Erving Goffman (1967) provides an illustration: "In American business organizations the boss may thoughtfully ask the elevator man how his children are, but this entrance into another's life may be blocked to the elevator man, who can appreciate the concern but not return it" (p. 64). That is, those who have high status are allowed to intrude into the lives of those of lower status and ask for self-disclosures. Those with low status would be regarded as impertinent if they asked similar questions. By obtaining information about others, high-status people put themselves in a powerful position; by not reciprocating, they indicate that they don't consider themselves to be at the same level as others. Thus they reinforce the difference in status and power.

Gender Differences in Self-Disclosure.   Studies of intimate self-disclosure have consistently shown that women disclose more than men do (Dindia & Allen, 1992; Hill & Stull, 1987; see the accompanying Lessons from the Laboratory). Men disclose very little in general, and individual males who reveal deep

Gender and Self-Disclosure

Many studies have made it clear that girls and women disclose more than boys and men. Recent research has shifted the focus away from who discloses to the question of to whom do people disclose (Pegalis, Shaffer, Bazzini, & Greenier, 1994). Are people more likely to disclose to a man or a woman? One study tested the hypothesis that both men and women disclose more to women than to men (Shaffer, Pegalis, & Bazzini, 1996). It also explored the idea that the tendency of men to disclose more to women than to men would be most apparent when the men expected to interact with the women in the future. The reasoning behind these hypotheses was that both men and women view women as more sympathetic to disclosure than men and that men would only chose to disclose to women more than men if they could imagine developing a long-term intimate relationship with them. The basic idea was when men think there is the possibility of developing a deeper relationship with a woman, they try to live up to the general cultural expectation that in a male-female couple the man should be the one to initiate a longer-term relationship with the woman.

To test this hypothesis, male and female college students were asked to carry on a series of exchanges of personal information with another person who was either male or female. In addition, the students believed either that they would or would not have future interactions with the other man or woman. The other person in this study was a confederate and data were carefully collected on how intimately and how emotionally the students disclosed personal information.

The findings of the study fit the predictions. Women were more disclosing with another woman than with a man. Men generally tended to disclose more to a woman than another man as well, but this finding was qualified. First, as predicted, men only disclosed more to a woman than to a man when they expected to have future interactions with the woman. And as predicted, men who anticipated future interaction with the woman attempted to steer the conversation around to more personal topics. They seemed to want to take control of a relationship that might have the potential for intimacy.

Finally, it should be noted that the finding that men disclosed more to women with whom they anticipated future interaction was much more pronounced among men who endorsed traditional gender roles. They are the ones who take seriously the idea that men should take control of the development of a potentially intimate relationship.

---

personal feelings are often regarded as weak and inadequate. Jourard believes that men pay dearly for adhering to norms dictating low self-disclosure; he contends that keeping their feelings inside imposes "an added burden of stress" on men. Men do sometimes disclose their innermost feelings, usually to a woman, most often a girlfriend or wife. Writing from a feminist perspective, Henley (1977) notes that this pattern is bad for men, because it reinforces the severe limits on appropriate channels for male self-disclosure and emotional release, and that it is also bad for women, because it keeps them in the subordinate position of having to serve as "emotional service stations" for use at male convenience. Whether you are a man or a woman, you might consider how your self-disclosure patterns are limited by cultural norms (Wheeler, Reis, & Bond, 1989).

In summary, research on self-disclosure shows that many people find the intimate exchange of personal information very rewarding. They are willing to take the risks that are often involved. We seem more attracted by the high rewards that can come from self-disclosure than we are repelled by the vulnerability it creates. The reason for this is that self-disclosure involves the highly satisfying experience of self-expression and acceptance by others. When we reveal ourselves to others, there is a good chance that we can show them what we are really like, what really concerns us and makes us feel good or bad, and that they will appreciate and accept who we are. There is no more rewarding experience than having other people interested in listening to us, in sharing and validating our concerns, and in showing their affection and trust by disclosing themselves in return. This kind of sharing of personal feelings and concerns, and the affection and trust that go along with it, is the core of intimacy. It is tremendously self-validating. It feels exhilarating. It can contribute greatly to personal adjustment. It is this kind of communication and interaction that people strive for in intimate relationships.

EVALUATING A RELATIONSHIP

Disclosing oneself to another person is one of the most important aspects of intimacy. When one's self is understood and accepted in an intimate relationship, there can be no greater reward for the effort required to build and maintain an honest, trusting bond with another person. Still, there is more to relationships than self-disclosure. People do many other things together: they run, play tennis, watch television, play backgammon or bridge, go dancing, discuss books and movies, debate politics or religion. This sharing of activities, particularly their professional pairs skating career, was clearly important for Sergei Grinkov and Katya Gordeeva. Such shared interests are very important in a relationship because they have a large impact on two people's total evaluation of their relationship. People who are relating directly to each other, through self-disclosure and sex, *and* two people who together are enjoying things outside themselves, such as children, hiking, or the movies, have a great deal going for their relationship. Enjoying the other person, enjoying that person's enjoyment of you, and enjoying external things together are all important.

Given the pleasure they find in various mutual activities, how do people decide how satisfied they are with their overall relationship? What keeps people in a relationship with each other?

Satisfaction and Dependence in Relationships

Very few relationships are completely satisfying in every way to both people involved. The two of you may have great affection for each other and lots of things in common while still disagreeing about certain tastes, interests, and patterns of relating. No one relationship can satisfy all a person's needs for human interaction. An overall sense of satisfaction seems to be one thing that keeps couples together. Sometimes, however, people choose to stay in relationships that are basically unsatisfying to them or break up with lovers they get along with very well. Thibaut and Kelley (1959) outlined some principles that help explain how we evaluate our intimate relationships and why we choose to sustain or end them.

Satisfaction. Satisfaction in a relationship, according to Thibaut and Kelley, depends first on what is called the outcome level. The **outcome level (OL)** is defined as the average level of pleasure or gratification a person gets from interactions in the relationship, as determined by the rewards minus the costs that are experienced in the relationship. Each time you interact with another person, there will be some rewarding or pleasant aspects of the interaction, such as recognition or interesting conversation, and some costly, painful, or unpleasant features, such as disappointment, embarrassment, or effort. Thus each interaction will have a net positive or negative degree of rewards–costs, or gratification. The average amount of gratification, positive or negative, that you receive from all the interactions in the relationship determines the outcome level.

The outcome level is crucial in determining how happy you are in your relationships, but it doesn't tell the whole story. The other critical factor is what Thibaut and Kelley called the comparison level. The **comparison level (CL)** is the baseline, or neutral point, to which you compare outcomes to determine your satisfaction. It is based in part on outcomes you have experienced in the past and in part on outcomes you observe other people receiving. Your comparison level creates expectations for the outcomes you will receive in any given relationship. You expect high outcomes, or gratification, if you have a high CL, and low outcomes, or a certain degree of misery, if you have a low CL (Brehm, 1992).

When your outcomes in a relationship are above your CL, you will feel satisfied; when they are below your CL, you will feel dissatisfied. For example, if the outcomes in your relationship with a person you've been dating casually for the past two weeks are greater than the outcomes you have had in similar relationships in the past and the outcome levels other people around you seem to be having with their dates, and are therefore greater than you expect, you will feel relatively satisfied with your new relationship.

Dependence. If you're satisfied spending time with the person you've been dating—that is, if your OL is above your CL—chances are that you will remain in that relationship. But your degree of satisfaction isn't the only determinant of whether or not you continue a relationship. As just noted, sometimes people remain in relationships where they are unhappy and leave relationships they enjoy a great deal. Their degree of dependence on the relationship helps explain why this happens. Dependence is determined by the difference between your outcome level and what Thibaut and Kelley called the comparison level for alternatives. The **comparison level for alternatives,** or **Clalt,** is simply the level of outcomes that one could get in the next best available re-

lationship. It is assumed that the Clalt is the lowest level of outcomes a person will accept in a relationship. If your outcomes in a relationship are lower than your Clalt, you will move to the next best available relationship.

If a person has an outcome level in a relationship that is much higher than his or her Clalt, he or she is very dependent on that relationship; if the relationship were to dissolve, the person would have to move to an alternative in which the outcome would be much lower. You are in a much better position if you have a high Clalt, one nearly as high as your outcome level. Then you aren't dependent on your current relationship. If that relationship should end, you would still have another appealing option, one that is almost as satisfying. Because you aren't dependent on the relationship, it's hard for your partner to exert much control over your behavior. You are much more susceptible to control by the other person's rewards and punishments when your Clalt is low.

Talking about dependency and control in a relationship seems somewhat crass, but it's an important, if unspoken, aspect of relationships that should be recognized for your own benefit.

Kinds of Relationships. In light of what we have said about outcome levels, comparison levels, and comparison levels for alternatives, we can distinguish three kinds of relationships with varying degrees of satisfaction and dependence. First, we can assume that in all relationships the OL will be above the Clalt; otherwise the person would leave for the alternative relationship. Given this assumption, one kind of relationship would be one in which both the outcome level (OL) and the comparison level for alternatives (Clalt) are above the comparison level (CL). Here people are in a good position because they are satisfied but not dependent. They have an alternative relationship where outcomes are still above the CL (see Figure 10.1). Sergei

Outcome Level	=	Rewards – Costs
Satisfaction	=	Outcome Level – Comparison Level
Dependence	=	Outcome Level – Comparison Level for Alternatives
Commitment	=	Satisfaction + Dependence + Investments

FIGURE 10.1   Satisfaction, Dependence, and Commitment in Relationships
Source: Adapted from Brehm & Kassin (1996).

Grinkov was in this position before he married Katya. He had a good relationship with her, but lots of other potential relationships. A somewhat less desirable kind of relationship would be one where your CL is below your OL but above your Clalt. You have satisfactory outcomes, but no alternative relationship with acceptable alternatives. You are in a dependent position. Finally, people may have the misfortune to be in relationships where their OL is below their CL, but they can't change because their Clalt is still lower. This is called a nonvoluntary relationship. An example might be a person in an unhappy marriage with no alternative available. A worker who is getting paid very little but can't do even that well anywhere else is dependent on his or her company and in a nonvoluntary relationship with it.

Equity in Relationships

Another very important aspect of a relationship is how fairly two people treat each other and how much happiness each partner gets out of the interaction relative to what he or she puts into it. Psychologists have done much research on the question of fairness in relationships and have developed what is known as *equity theory*. There are several different versions of equity theory, but they agree that behaving equitably is desirable, that people will attempt to be fair, according to their own standards, in their dealings with others, and that they will be distressed when they perceive their relationships to be unfair.

For many years psychologists assumed that people would feel distressed regardless of whether the fairness is to their advantage or disadvantage (Walster, Walster, & Berscheid, 1978). However, recent research suggests that people are more upset by unfairness that works to their disadvantage than to their advantage (Brehm, 1992). Thus neither partner in a marriage where one is getting more than the other will be happy, but the one who is getting less will be notably more distressed.

Perceiving Equity.   What determines whether a relationship is perceived as equitable? The answer can be best stated as:

$$\frac{OA}{IA} = \frac{OB}{IB}$$

where O refers to outcomes, I refers to inputs, and A and B are persons (Walster et al., 1978). If either person perceives that this formula holds—that the ratio of what one of them is getting relative to what he or she is putting in is equal to the other person's outcome-to-input ratio—then the relationship will be perceived as equitable. For example, if two people are both working equally hard in a relationship and are making equal sacrifices (equal inputs) and each is deriving as much satisfaction from it as the other (equal outcomes), the formula holds and the relationship is equitable. Another possibility is that one person contributes more to the relationship but also gets more benefit from it. The formula would also hold in this case. An instance of this might be seen in the relationship between two roommates. One works hard to arrange their room for a party and the other spends most of the time in the library and makes minimal contributions. If the first partner is given more say about who comes to the party and what music is played, the equity formula holds, and both roommates probably feel that justice has been done.

Responses to Inequity.   When people perceive themselves to be in an inequitable relationship, they will feel distress and take steps to change the situation (Walster et al., 1978). There are several ways to do this. One is simply to alter one's perceptions of one's own or the other person's inputs or outcomes so that *psychological equity* is restored. A second method is to change inputs or outcomes to restore *actual equity*. Walster and colleagues predict that people will choose between restoring psychological versus actual equity depending on which method most simply and completely eliminates unfairness. In some cases it might be easy for the people involved actually to change their inputs or outcomes. For example, two people who are living together might make an adjustment in how much work each of them does around the apartment if they recognize an inequity in the division of household tasks. In other cases, however, there may be little anyone can do to restore actual equity. Then the predictable result is distortion of reality through reliance on psychological equity.

Consider the case of a business executive in an industrial setting who feels that it's unfair how little workers are paid, given how much they contribute to the success of the company. At the same time she realizes that there is nothing she can do that will have any real impact on company policy. Equity theory holds that the executive will feel distressed and seek some kind of psychological relief. Usually, the relief takes the form of distorting the situation so that it is perceived as fair. In

the case of the executive, she may decide that the workers really contribute very little to company success compared to the "brains" at the top and that their wages are really very high, given their low level of education and sophistication. Ironically, the executive's initial concern about a social injustice causes her to convince herself that there is no injustice after all.

Very often people who are on the advantaged end of an unfair relationship use psychological distortion to convince themselves that equity actually exists. This is relatively easy, and it allows them to maintain their favored position. How does the person who is disadvantaged respond? He or she should be doubly distressed: first, that an inequity exists, and second, that he or she is getting the short end of it. Much to the dismay and frustration of social reformers, however, people in this position often use psychological distortion just as much as those whom the inequity favors. If they believe they can do nothing about the inequity, denying reality and viewing what exists as fair and satisfying can be the best way of feeling happy. Of course, an unwillingness to perceive unfairness perpetuates the unfairness.

Sometimes restoring neither perceived nor actual equity is possible. Then the only way to change the situation may be to end the relationship. In fact, research suggests that married couples are more likely to have extramarital affairs if they perceive their relationships to be inequitable (Walster, Walster, & Traupmann, 1978). Having an affair does not necessarily mean ending a marriage, but it probably means supplementing what may be a bad relationship with a more satisfying one. There is also evidence that concerns about equity can lead directly to divorce. Among newlyweds, those who feel involved in unfair relationships were more likely to think of getting divorced. Interestingly, among wives, there was more distress if they felt that the unfairness worked to their advantage. Among husbands, the opposite was true. They were more distressed, as is typical of other relationships, when unfairness worked to their disadvantage. Appar- ently, women but not men were upset by getting more than they felt they deserved (Hatfield, Utne, & Traupmann, 1979).

6. Thibaut and Kelley identified four stages of relationship development. In the _____ stage, people look over the possibilities for relationships and decide with whom to have a relationship.

7. In initiating a relationship, we may try to present ourselves in a more positive way than we normally act. Goffman called these initial presentations _____ _____.

8. T or F: Although it may be experienced as an unpleasant emotional response, shyness is not a major obstacle to forming relationships.

9. If a person's outcome level (level of gratification) in a relationship is higher than his or her comparison level of outcomes, then the person is likely to be _____ with the relationship.

10. A person whose inputs into a relationship are equivalent to his or her outcomes is likely to perceive the relationship as _____. Someone whose outcomes are greater than his or her inputs may use _____ to reduce the psychological tension created by the unbalanced relationship.

MAKING A COMMITMENT

Strong relationships are built on mutual acceptance, mutual satisfactory outcomes, and a style of living and working within the relationship that both people feel is fair. Once two people feel they have a strong, satisfying relationship, they may decide they want to make a commitment to each other to strengthen and extend the relationship further. What is involved when we take the important step of making a commitment in a relationship? How do we move beyond bargaining? And what makes a commitment work or not work? For all of us, commitment is a serious decision, and we can make mistakes. Let's see how people make commitments, and how their commitments are likely to work out.

Deciding to Make a Commitment

It's not entirely clear how and when commitment begins. At some time and in some way two people in a relationship decide that their satisfaction or happiness with each other is significantly greater than in their relationships with other people, and they agree to begin a relatively long-lasting, more intimate relationship that to some extent excludes other close relationships. They agree to depend on each other for satisfaction of important needs, including companionship, love, and sex. The commitment may or may not involve a decision to live together. The most important element in their commitment is the decision to become more intimate and to forego intimate relationships with others. Once they fell in love, this decision came quickly for Grinkov and Gordeeva. They committed to each other off the ice as fully as they committed to each other on it.

Commitment is based on the conviction that you'll get more happiness with one special person than you would get with others. Beyond that, commitments can vary tremendously in how lasting partners expect them to be. Most are based on faith that the relationship can be enduring. Some people hold this conviction rather casually, willing to remain committed as long as they feel satisfied with the way things are going, but frankly acknowledging that at any time either partner may become unhappy or bored or may find a better relationship. For others, commitment and faith in the longevity of a relationship include a determination to see that the relationship does last. For them, and for all of us with such determination, there's a lot of work ahead.

Freedom and Commitment

Making an agreement with another person to enter into a deeper, more exclusive, and lasting relationship is a crucially important life decision that must be made freely and with careful thought. In many cases you may find yourself under various pressures to enter into a commitment that you aren't sure is good for you. Sometimes parents push their children into making commitments, worried that they'll lose a good relationship. Sometimes friends push you to become more committed so that your relationship will be as exclusive as theirs. Most common perhaps is the situation where one person in a relationship feels committed and wants the other to make an equal commitment. It often happens that one person is sure of the high value of the relationship sooner than the other and wants the other person to feel equally strongly. This perception can easily lead to pushing the other person. The person who is pushed may react negatively and lose interest or may be pressured into a commitment. Either of these outcomes is regrettable. We can't emphasize enough that a commitment that isn't truly felt is unlikely to last. Any agreement to form an exclusive relationship must be based on a clear individual decision that is made freely.

Although a commitment must be made privately and freely, it's also true that once a commitment is made privately, public behaviors afterward can serve to strengthen it further. After two people have decided to live together, for example, they may have to exert a lot of energy to move, they may have to break off or at least "simmer down" other relationships, and they may even have to change jobs. In other cases a decision to have sexual relations for the first time may follow a decision about commitment. All the behaviors that one engages in after a commitment to another person are justified because of the commitment, and they strengthen the commitment (Aronson, 1992). People who have taken action following a commitment will work hard to maintain their relationship.

Just as a commitment is usually weaker and less enduring if it's made under pressure, so a commitment that is made in defiance of pressure from parents or peers can be very strong (Darley & Cooper, 1972). Parental disapproval of a relationship can in time undermine it, but at least initially the perception that one was willing to defy parental pressure and perhaps forego parental support for a relationship demonstrates the depth of one's love and can greatly strengthen a commitment. Rubin (1973) has referred to this as the "Romeo and Juliet effect," after the two young lovers in Shakespeare's play whose commitment was deepened by the knowledge that they risked the wrath of their families by being together. In sum, a commitment is likely to be strongest when it is arrived at freely and when it is cemented by taking action as a result of the commitment.

An interesting new perspective on commitment has been suggested by Brehm and Kassin (1996), who extended the ideas we discussed earlier about satisfaction and dependence in relationships. You may recall satisfaction in a relationship is determined by the difference between the outcome level (OL) and the comparison level (CL). On the other hand, dependence in a relationship is determined by the difference between the outcome level (OL) and the comparison level for alternatives (Clalt). If the OL is much higher than the Clalt, then dependence is high. If the OL is only slightly higher than the Clalt, dependence is low. Brehm and Kassin (1996) suggest that commitment can be measured adding "investments" to the levels of satisfaction and dependence in a relationship. Investments include the time, energy, money, and resources that people have put into relationships, especially if they are not recoverable. Thus people feel committed to a relationship based on how satisfied they are with it, how dependent they are on it, and how much they have invested in it. G & G were highly committed to their marriage because they experienced a very high level of satisfaction in it and because they had invested a great deal in it. However, they were not dependent on it. They did have other alternatives. Figure 10.1 summarizes the various relationships between satisfaction, dependence, and commitments.

MARRIAGE, ENDURING RELATIONSHIPS, AND DIVORCE

For many people commitment to an exclusive, intimate relationship is closely followed by a decision to formalize and make public their commitment in some way that is sanctioned by the society as a whole. This final stage of relationship development is often referred to as *institutionalization* (Thibaut and Kelley, 1959). For most relationships between adult men and women in many societies, this means marriage. In the United States, about 90 percent of young adults will marry (Norton & Moorman, 1987). Although this represents a slight decline from the 95 percent figure of a few decades ago, it is the overwhelming choice. Sergei and Grinkov chose this option because of their commitment to each other and their desire to have children within a married family. For many other people, however, whether or not to marry can be an agonizing decision. Even though marriage can be terminated, many people view it as the biggest decision and commitment of their

lives. They realize that while courtship was fun and living together worked well perhaps, marriage means entering uncharted waters. It has its own satisfactions and its own stresses. What studies have shown about the joys and sorrows of wedlock is relevant information for anyone contemplating this major step.

Sources of Gratification in Marriage

People get married for many reasons. We live in a culture in which marriage is encouraged and rewarded with social approval and economic advantages. Throughout our lives we develop ideas about what lies ahead in marriage and what its rewards are. As a result of these expectations we generally look forward to getting married, thinking of the pleasures of having a family, being financially secure, and developing a stable home life. However, two kinds of expectations are essential to having a happy marriage. First, having realistic expectations about the stresses of marriage is key. It is not a rose garden. Many people have unrealistic expectations based on the fairytale image that marriages such as G & G's reinforce. Even when a highly publicized, storybook marriage like that of Prince Charles and Princess Diana dissolves almost before our very eyes, people still hold on to the idealized image (Seccombe, 1991). Second, having agreements about what role each partner in the couple will play is critical. There is a great deal of work in a marriage. Being thoughtful and flexible, and communicating clearly and caringly, is of great importance (Buehlman, Gottman, & Katz, 1992).

What people find rewarding in marriage can be very different from their expectations. A recent study revealed that the most important factors in marital satisfaction for married women are love, respect, and friendship (Tavris & Jayarante, 1976). Sexual compatibility is a distant fourth, and shared interests and having children are much lower than that. People enjoy being together, loving and respecting each other, and being loved and respected in turn. Sex is important, but the more basic psychological factors that are basic to intimacy, and that are known to enhance sexual pleasure, lie at the core of marriage. These are the things that give people meaning and pleasure in living. They hold people together. When it becomes impossible to have respect for one's partner, difficult to be a friend, and hard to love, unhappiness is inevitable. Unfortunately, love, respect, and friendship between two people are fragile and can be lost as a result of other stresses of living. Once they are lost, most people find these feelings impossible to recover. Let's consider how this can happen.

Stresses in Marriage

One of the most positive and exhilarating aspects of living is building an intimate relationship with another person. It's a joy to learn what someone else is all about, to have that person care about you, and to enjoy a relationship of total openness and acceptance that includes the powerful attractions of sex. Usually a relationship is built before marriage. After marriage, people must stop working on building the relationship to some degree and use it as a foundation from which other aspects of living can be built. These include pursuing careers, perhaps raising a family, and finding satisfying ways of enjoying leisure time. Relationship building can still go on, and must go on, but the focus on living turns to other things after the early, exciting formative period. Sometimes a great deal of stress is involved in this shift in energy and attention from building the relationship itself to using the relationship as a foundation for solving other problems and coping with other aspects of life.

As committed couples spend more and more time and energy on work, getting things done, and making decisions, they have less time to talk about their feelings and their personal needs. Problems aren't solved immediately, resentments aren't aired, and new concerns aren't fully discussed. Couples sometimes feel a pulling apart, a loss of the closeness they used to have. They can feel great disappointment, almost betrayal, about this change in their relationship and wonder whether it's worth the effort to keep the marriage together. They may find that while they are still compatible as lovers and even as friends and intimate partners, they don't do well as coworkers. They can't agree on how money should be spent or how jobs in the household should be divided or how they should spend leisure time. The love that seemed so much greater than all these small problems isn't given as much attention as before, and it becomes less and less effective as a foundation for the rest of living. In other words, the success people have as intimate partners may not translate into being good partners for dealing with the external world. Even those who do succeed in being good married partners can expect to feel these stresses.

One of the key determinants of marital satisfaction and success is the way people think about the inevitable stresses and strains that arise in the relationship. Not surprisingly, in light of what we discussed in Chapter 9, the attributions that people make for problems are critical. When either husbands or wives attribute marital problems or the negative behavior of their spouses to internal, stable, and global characteristics of their partners, such as an intention to harm the relationship, the marriage is likely to become less satisfying over time (Karney, Bradbury, Fincham, & Sullivan, 1994). For example, if a husband or wife can attribute an angry outburst to the spouse's having a bad day or dealing with too much pressure at work, then the incident will be forgotten. If it is attributed to continuing ill will, serious problems and discontents are much more likely to arise or persist. Although it isn't clear why people would make such destructive attributions, it is probably the case that distressed, depressed, or discontent individuals are much more likely to make the negative attributions that undermine the quality of a marriage.

When, and if, children come, the pleasure or pain that exists in a marriage can increase sharply. Typically, couples are less satisfied with their marriages and less happy with life overall when they are raising children. Many studies show that marital satisfaction rises after children leave home (Brubaker, 1990). This finding calls to mind the old joke that life begins when "the dog dies and the kids leave home." However, couples vary considerably in how they cope with the stress of childbearing and childrearing. When people have a basically solid marriage and agree well about how to cope with reality's demands as well as each other's needs, they have a good foundation from which to face the challenges of childrearing. In this case the result is usually very positive. The child becomes a source of real joy and satisfaction to the couple, and their relationship can be enhanced. When people have a marriage that is already strained, having a child is likely to strain it even further, perhaps to the breaking point. This result is an unhappy one for the parents, and especially so for the child. Sometimes whether the child will be a positive or negative addition to the marriage can be forecast before it arrives. Physicians note that women often look their best or their worst during pregnancy (Nevin, 1970). If they are happy and looking forward to the child, there is an unmistakable bloom and look of joy. If they are frightened or resentful about having a baby, they look tired, depressed, and strained. Such women are not in a position to enjoy raising a child, even with an enthusiastic husband.

In sum, living together as married and strongly committed partners in the struggle with the demands of the world is a challenge.

Some people find that meeting the world's challenges is easier in the context of a happy marriage. They also find that solving the problems of living together strengthens their relationship. Others find that coping with life's stresses pulls them apart. They find that their success in dealing with the world is reduced because of worries about their relationship and that worries about their job, home, and children reduce the quality of their relationship. Being successful inside and outside marriage is difficult and requires a great deal of patience and hard work. A positive outlook and genuine caring about one's spouse makes it easier to find the strength to work hard at these challenges and increases the chances for success.

Enduring Relationships

Getting married is an extremely common event in our society today. Although both men and women are waiting longer and longer before they get married, still 90 percent of the American population gets married at least once. Thus, institutionalization of relationships happens very frequently. However, the dissolution of marriages is highly frequent as well. The divorce rate has been increasing dramatically over the past several decades. In 1960, 25 percent of all marriages ended in divorce. That figure was up to 33 percent in 1974, and over 50 percent by 1980. In one recent year there were more divorces than marriages in California, the largest state in the union. Since 1980, the divorce rate has declined slightly, but most estimates put it at about 50 percent at present. Although many people do get divorced, they are by no means cured of the marriage habit. Seventy-five percent of women and 80 percent of men who are divorced get married again within three years.

In the faces of these stresses and strains, let's consider what can keep a love relationship alive and how we can nurture companionate love. First, it is clear that both parties in a relationship must work to make the relationship stable (Attridge, Berscheid, & Simpson, 1995). Several key factors promote the ease, harmony, and peacefulness of companionate love. It takes successful communication, avoiding the kind of ambiguity and confusion we saw in Chapter 9, and attaining the kind of self-disclosure and honesty we discussed earlier in this chapter. It also takes equality. There has to be give and take in relationships. Both partners must have times when they are dominant, times when they are submissive, and times when they are on an equal footing. Over time, this alternation in each person being one-up and one-down should make possible an equality in the division of labor and the decision-making power in the relationship. A relationship can become stagnant and sour without such a balance of power.

A recent study of enduring relationships has identified other factors that are important in satisfying, long-term marriages, specifically, those that last more than 15 years (Lauer & Lauer, 1985). First, people who have long-lasting marriages basically like their spouses. They tend to say that their spouse is their best friend, that they like their spouse as a person, and that their spouse has become more interesting over the years. Thus basic liking is ter-

ribly important. You should ask whether you really *like* the person for whom you might feel passionately. Will you enjoy each other once the passion has gone?

Second, commitment and the desire to succeed is important. People in enduring relationships are willing to work hard to make the marriage last. They have to take the long-term perspective and be willing to work through the trouble spots. Sometimes that simply means being stubborn and refusing to quit when things seem bleak. One has to have faith that things can get better and that the struggle is worth it.

Third, learning to control anger is important. Sometimes people can say destructive things when they are frustrated and aroused, and often they regret those things. Even though some people argue that it's best to express your feelings and clear the air, the data indicate it's best to wait until the turbulence has passed. Expressing anger simply leads to an escalation of hostility. Being willing to swallow your frustrations and anger can be beneficial to the relationship in the long run.

In short, a variety of factors contribute to enduring and satisfying relationships. Good communication, respect, hard work, flexibility, patience, equality, and caring are all important.

REVIEW QUESTIONS

11. The process in which people in a relationship decide to depend on each other for satisfaction of their needs and to somewhat limit their intimate relationships with other people is called _____.

12. In our society, commitment to an exclusive, intimate relationship is often followed by _____ in the form of marriage.

13. T or F: Although differences in a marriage may strain the relationship, having a child inevitably eases the pressures and enhances the relationship.

SUMMARY

1. Liking is based on perceived similarity between two people and high regard or respect. Love may include these characteristics, but it is also defined by deep emotional attachment, caring, and intimacy.

2. Passionate, romantic love is marked by intense absorption and preoccupation with the loved one, physiological arousal, and feelings of fulfillment and momentary ecstasy. To experience romantic passion, people must have a cultural expectation of it, must meet the right person, and must interpret arousal felt while with that person as passionate, romantic love.

3. Companionate love is the affection we feel for those with whom our lives are intertwined. Romantic passion becomes companionate love when a relationship grows and endures over time.

4. Sexual intercourse may be a component of love when people are truly caring and concerned about their partners' needs. It is important to distinguish between love and physical passion. Passion is often a fleeting experience, while love is an emotion that will continue to grow if properly nurtured.

5. People must learn to love. Early family experiences may determine whether or not a person can develop a mature loving relationship. We must love ourselves before we can love others.

6. Love is based on people's ability to accept and respect each other and be concerned for each other's needs. It's important for people to define their own needs clearly and to be aware of the needs of their partners. A loving relationship will grow and develop to the extent that two people engage in open and honest communication with each other.

7. A sense of ambivalence often pervades love relationships. On the one hand, people develop a dependency on the relationship; on the other hand, they want to retain their independence.

8. Relationships move through various stages of development: sampling, bargaining, commitment, and institutionalization.

9. The sampling stage involves a superficial presentation of personal characteristics as people attempt to communicate a positive image to others. The self-presentations of others are seldom challenged. During this initial stage of interaction, people try to cut through the facades and make an accurate forecast of how much potential there is for good relationship with various people.

10. During the bargaining stage, people attempt to build a strong and satisfying relationship. One of the most important aspects of this stage is self-disclosure, opening yourself up to another person and sharing your deepest thoughts and feelings. Telling others about yourself needs to be based on trust. When trust exists and self-disclosure occurs, the quality of your own personal adjustment is enhanced and relationships grow more intimate and satisfying.

11. People evaluate their relationships before making lasting commitments. Satisfaction in a relationship depends first on the rewards, or outcomes, of the relationship. People's overall evaluation of their relationship is affected not only by their outcomes, but also by how much satisfaction they expect from the relationship. If a person has a high baseline, or comparison level, he or she will be less satisfied by certain outcomes than will a person who expects less.

12. Satisfaction is often linked to dependence. Dependence on a relationship is determined by the availability of alternatives. When a person has other possibilities that are almost as satisfying as his or her present relationship, the person isn't dependent and thus has more power in the relationship.

13. Equity is another factor that must be considered when evaluating relationships. People are usually disturbed to be in an inequitable relationship and take steps to correct a situation they perceive as unfair. Sometimes they will actually change their inputs or outcomes or those of the other person, but other times they will simply convince themselves that the inequity doesn't exist.

14. During the commitment stage of relationship development, two people agree to begin a relatively long-lasting, more intimate relationship that to some extent excludes other close relationships. This commitment must be made freely by both partners, or the commitment is unlikely to last.

15. A committed relationship becomes institutionalized when the partners decide to formalize their commitment in some way that is sanctioned by their society as a whole. This can, but doesn't have to, involve formal marriage.

16. The vast majority of people in our society get married once they have made a commitment to each other. Nearly half of these marriages end in divorce. People find it easy and exciting to build a positive relationship, but often they aren't able to maintain caring and intimacy when they have to work with their partners to deal with the challenging aspects of everyday living. Enduring relationships depend on liking and respect, a commitment to making the relationship work, and a willingness to control the expression of anger and frustration.

CRITICAL THINKING QUESTIONS

1. How much do you think social exchange or economic issues, such as equity, play a role in relationships? Do you find yourself keeping score in your own relationships? Do you worry that you are putting in more than you are getting out? Do you have a better or worse deal than your partner? Should we try to get away from such crass concerns? Can we?

2. Is it important for you to have an enduring long-term relationship, such as a marriage that does not end in divorce? If so, what are the most important things you can do in a relationship to make them endure? Many marriages end in divorce, and in most cases we can assume that the partners intended to stay married. Could those marriages have been saved? Would it have been worth it?

MATCHING EXERCISE

Match each term with its definition.

a. attachment
b. bargaining
c. caring
d. commitment
e. comparison level
f. comparison level for alternatives
g. idealized performance
h. institutionalization
i. intimacy
j. outcome level
k. sampling

1. In Thibaut and Kelley's theory of the stages of relationships, the stage in which people negotiate or work out mutually satisfying ways of interacting while trying to build a relationship

2. In Thibaut and Kelley's theory of the stages of relationships, the stage in which people decide to be special or exclusive partners in a relationship

3. The standard by which the outcome level of interactions in a relationship is evaluated; it is based on all the outcomes a person knows about through his or her own or another's experiences

4. The lowest level of outcomes a person will accept in a relationship; it is the level of outcomes in the next best available relationship
5. In Thibaut and Kelley's theory of the stages of relationships, the stage in which there is some formalization of the commitment
6. The average level of outcomes that is experienced in a relationship
7. In Thibaut and Kelley's theory of the stages of relationships, the process of looking over the possibilities and then deciding on a person with whom to attempt to form a relationship
8. The feeling that another person's satisfactions and well-being are as important as your own
9. The need to be with another person and to be approved of by that person
10. Close and confidential communication along with deep caring
11. Acting as if you support and conform to ideal standards of good conduct more than you actually do

Answers to Matching Exercise

a. 9   b. 1   c. 8   d. 2   e. 3   f. 4   g. 11   h. 5   i. 10   j. 6   k. 7

ANSWERS TO REVIEW QUESTIONS

1. emotional
2. attachment, intimacy
3. physiological arousal
4. companionate
5. false
6. sampling
7. idealized performances
8. false
9. satisfied
10. equitable, distortion
11. commitment
12. institutionalization
13. false

CHAPTER 11

HUMAN SEXUALITY

Madonna

Madonna

Early in the fall of 1992, *Sex* hit the bookstores. The volume cost $49.95 and was marked clearly FOR ADULTS ONLY. *Sex* was the latest attempt by singer, actress, and all-around performer Madonna to market her image, her story, and herself. *Sex* celebrated a wide variety of sexual practices, including bisexuality, sadomasochism, and exhibitionism. Since bursting onto the international entertainment scene in 1983, Madonna had shocked and delighted millions. But *Sex* was her boldest departure. Despite the fact that this heavy book of varied nude photographs and political commentary received generally poor reviews, it once again sent Madonna's earnings skyrocketing. A review in the *New Yorker* magazine was entitled "Madonna's Anticlimax." Still the beat went on.

Madonna was born in Pontiac, Michigan in 1959. Her given name was Madonna Louise Veronica Ciccone. The third of six children in a staunchly Roman Catholic home, Madonna had her life change dramatically when at the age of 5 she lost her mother to cancer. Shortly thereafter, her father married a woman who had formerly been the family's housekeeper. Although Madonna's father supported her as she grew up and during her early career, after her mother's death life at home was never as secure or happy as it had been when her mother was alive.

Like many young women trying to make a living as an artist and entertainer, Madonna headed for New York City. Her break came at the age of 21, when she was discovered dancing in the club called, ironically, *21*. Her first two albums, "Madonna," released in 1983, and "Like a Virgin," released in 1984, were instant hits. Madonna became an overnight success on the record charts and on MTV. By 1985 Madonna's career was soaring. She and other performers such as Cyndi Lauper were attracting attention outside the usual youth markets and began to appear on the covers of national magazines such as *Time* and *Newsweek*.

At about this time Madonna was also making a successful breakthrough into another form of entertainment, the movies. Her role in the 1985 film *Desperately Seeking Susan* proved that she was a screen property to be reckoned with and that she could succeed in a comedy role. While not all of her films did equally well, her roles in *Dick Tracy* (1990) and *Evita* (1997) established Madonna as a formidable Hollywood talent.

As Madonna's career rose to new levels and diversified, she became a greater focus of media attention, not all of it favorable. Controversy surrounded her lifestyle and opinions as well as her work. Madonna's performances, which were never tame, became more and more sexually explicit. They were highlighted with erotic dress, partial nudity, and simulated sex. Furthermore, her outspoken statements about sexuality generated heated discussion among supporters and detractors. For example, on one of her videos she said, "I'm getting a hard-on" while watching two male dancers French kiss. In 1990, MTV banned Madonna's video "Justify My Love" because of its sexual explicitness. Her documentary film *Madonna: Truth or Dare*, based on her Blond Ambition tour in 1991, generated furor when Madonna was filmed performing simulated oral sex on a bottle of mineral water.

In short, Madonna has been controversial. But her performances and her statements have been important in current discussions of sexual identity and sexual behavior. She strives to bring the "sexual underground" to the mainstream, and she has succeeded. For example, Madonna has been outspoken in her bisexuality. In an interview she said that she got "aroused by the idea of a woman making love to me while either a man or another woman watches" (Johnson, 1991, p. 46). As a result, Madonna has been admired by gay men and women. She personally likes gays and has supported a variety of AIDS projects. The fact that her closest brother, Christopher, is gay has had an influence on her views.

Madonna's life has changed with the recent birth of a child. After affairs with several men, including *Dick Tracy* costar Warren Beaty and a failed marriage to actor Sean Penn, she decided that she wanted to have a child of her own, without marrying the child's father. As in many other cases, she did what she wanted.

We do not know whether Madonna will continue to have the impact she has had for the past fifteen years as a singer, dancer, performer, and disturber of conventional morality. We do know that her bold and controversial videos, books, and songs have been a part of modern North American culture's attempts to rethink sex, identity, family, and morality at the end of the twentieth century. She has made a contribution, for better or worse.

SEXUAL BEHAVIOR: THEN AND NOW

The sexual culture that Madonna grew up in and helped shape is far different than the one her parents experienced. Sexual behavior wasn't an accepted topic of discussion in the 1950s, except in veiled suggestions in the gossip columns, and it certainly wasn't a topic taught in schools and openly portrayed in newspapers, radio, and television. Women were expected to be virgins until they got married, when their husbands, who were expected to be sexual experts, would "show them the ropes." The double standard for males' and females' sexual conduct was clear, but the players had very little knowledge about sexual behavior itself. "Learning" occurred through guarded half-informed discussions with same-sex friends or through clumsy experimentation with opposite-sex partners. The hushed nature of the topic was portrayed in movies that were designed to stimulate the imagination through suggestion but keep the audience ignorant of the behavior itself.

In the 1960s, a so-called "Sexual Revolution" began, and the rules of sexual behavior began changing (Thornton, 1989). For one thing, the sexual desires of women were acknowledged. Sexual behavior is no longer viewed as the woman's "giving away" of something to the eager male. Women, and not only women like Madonna, may now be the initiators. It's now widely accepted that women desire and enjoy sex as much as men do.

But even though the rules regarding sexual behavior have changed, people's knowledge of sexual behavior is still woefully lacking. Children's knowledge of sexual behavior is more likely to come from friends than from school or parents. With peers as the main source of information, it is hardly surprising that children are misinformed or make unwise choices about sexual behavior.

Unfortunately, ignorance is not necessarily bliss when it comes to sexual behavior. As you will see, with proper knowledge and sensitivity, sexual behavior can be a source of great pleasure that enhances our intimacy with ourselves and others. Without this knowledge, it can be a source of constant confusion and anxiety. Whether we understand it or not, our sexuality plays a major role in the personal adjustment process. In this chapter we hope to unravel some of the mysteries of sexual behavior.

THE HUMAN SEXUAL RESPONSE

Not until the early 1960s did laboratory research by William Masters and Virginia Johnson begin to uncover some of the mystery of the human sexual response. Because of the sensitivity of the issue, Masters and Johnson began their research by recruiting male and female prostitutes. They soon found that the prostitutes weren't good subjects with which to work, and they recruited 694 other subjects from the local population. They took careful readings while the subjects engaged in a wide variety of sexual behaviors, including masturbation and sexual intercourse. The results of their research have presented us with the most complete picture of the human sexual response currently available.

Before we examine the findings of Masters and Johnson, two cautions should be expressed. First, just as with the size and shape of the genitals, there is a wide variety in people's sexual responsiveness. Research presents a general picture, but it also shows the wonderful variety of people's responses. We aren't machines made from the same mold and programmed to follow the exact same pattern. The second caution is against overanalyzing our own behavior. One of the most maddening experiences is to watch a good movie with a friend (or ex-friend) who insists on analyzing every part of the movie, the acting, and the stage setting. This boorish individual can suddenly dampen our enjoyment of the movie. So, too, can we ruin our own pleasure of a sexual experience if we become too intent on analyzing every feeling and physical change that occurs. By doing this, we may become inhibited and lose the spontaneity that is so vital for enjoying our sexual experiences. Thus knowledge may remove confusion and misunderstanding, but misuse of this knowledge may have unfortunate consequences.

Masters and Johnson (1966) identified four phases in the sexual response. Interestingly, they found that both males and females experience these phases and that their responses during these phases are similar in many cases.

The *excitement phase* begins whenever a man or a woman becomes aroused sexually as a result of being caressed by another person or by imagining, reading about, observing, anticipating, or discussing sexual behavior. During this phase the heartrate increases and breathing becomes deeper and faster. In males there is an erection of the penis and in females the breasts and clitoris swell and vaginal lubrication occurs. The vaginal secretions play two important roles. First, they lubricate the vagina to make penetration by the penis easier. Second, they neutralize the vagina's natural acidity, which would kill the sperm. This excitement phase can last from slightly more than a minute to several hours, depending on the circumstances.

The genitals aren't the only areas of the body whose stimulation results in sexual arousal. In both males and females, light stimulation of the lips, ears, and neck can lead to sexual arousal. Gentle touching of the nipples of the breast also produces sexual arousal in many males and females. In many cultures, including our own, the size and shape of the female breasts are associated with attractiveness and sexual arousal. The size of the female breast is determined by heredity, and no difference in function of the breasts is associated with size: Small breasts produce as much milk for a nursing baby as do large ones. Nor is breast size related to responsiveness to sexual stimulation.

Another, and in many respects the most important, erogenous zone is the mind. As we will discuss later in this chapter, our minds may conjure up an almost endless variety of sexual fantasies that are capable of arousing us or enhancing sexual arousal we are already experiencing. Females have reported being able to reach orgasm solely through the use of fantasy (Stock & Greer, 1982).

Just as our thoughts can stimulate us to arousal, they can also play a more villainous role of ensuring that almost no amount of stimulation will arouse us or allow us to enjoy sexual experiences. As we will see in the section on sexual dysfunction, feelings of guilt, fear, or embarrassment can turn our sexuality into a nightmare.

When arousal increases even more, the *plateau phase* is reached. Even greater swelling of the penis and secretion in the vagina occur. The clitoris retracts under a fold of skin where it can't receive direct stimulation; it is so sensitive during this stage that direct stimulation could be experienced as painful. The male testes also retract, moving up in the scrotum. During this phase, the testes increase in size, sometimes as much as 100 percent. There may be a *sex flush,* or reddening of the skin and an increase in muscle tension throughout the body. As arousal increases, there is a feeling of losing control and of the inevitability of reaching the sexual climax called **orgasm.**

When the *orgasm phase* is reached, people experience very intense pleasure and release from tension. In men there are rhythmic contractions of the muscles in and around the pe-

Learning about Sex

All of us remember from our own lives either the jolting experience of learning about some aspect of sex ourselves, or the amusing but moving experience of watching our children cope with its mysteries. One of us had a 3-year-old son who saw a stallion urinating and said of its penis, "Oh boy! I hope mine gets that big." He was fascinated with the idea of "shooting" urine with a large penis. Another of us recalls learning from an older sister at age 8 that sexual intercourse was necessary for procreation and being astounded, and somewhat horrified, that our parents had sex once for each time they had a child. And another recalls a young daughter saying she would never have children because she had learned that a woman had to kiss a man's penis in order to get pregnant. She was disgusted at the prospect.

For many young people, sex is a strange and emotionally charged part of life. Some are excited by or curious about its prospects and promises, others are frightened or disgusted. Many parents find that this is a very difficult topic to discuss with their children. At the same time, so many children get misinformation through the usual informal channels of communication that their parents wish that they could learn the truth, at the right time and place. For some parents, sex education in the schools is a blessing—it relieves them of the responsibility of teaching the hard lessons. But other parents feel that sex is a private family matter that should not be discussed publicly in the community at large.

It seems that our society does not handle the matter of sex education either very gracefully or very effectively. How might we do it better? Perhaps you can make a contribution to thinking this problem through.

---

nis and ejaculation of semen. In women there are muscular contractions around the vagina and pulsation of the uterus. In both men and women the contractions occur every eight-tenths of a second and last for varying lengths of time. For both men and women, the first five or six contractions are the most pleasurable. During orgasm the heartrate may double, muscles may go into intense spasms, and the person may emit uncontrollable cries.

In the *resolution phase* the body gradually returns to normal. In the female the vaginal muscles relax and the clitoris reemerges from its protective fold of skin. Women may be stimulated back to orgasm at any time during the resolution phase; women often experience the succeeding orgasms more intensely than the initial orgasm. Unlike females, males have a *refractory period* during the resolution phase; during this period they are unresponsive to sexual stimulation. The length of the refractory period varies from male to male and is influenced by a number of factors, including age

and health. During the resolution phase, the penis and testes return to their unstimulated state. Both males and females experience the resolution phase as relaxing and pleasant.

Comparing Male and Female Sexual Response

As we have pointed out, there are many similarities between male and female sexual responses. Similar changes occur in breathing, heartrate, and muscle tension. Both males and females may show a sex flush, although it is more common in females. Enlargement of the genitals occurs in both sexes. There is also some evidence that males and females experience, or at least describe, orgasm in similar ways. In an interesting study, Vance and Wagner (1976) asked male and female subjects to write descriptions of their orgasms. These descriptions were then examined by a group of judges (medical students, gynecologists, and clinical psychologists), who were asked to identify which descriptions were written by males and which were written by females. These experts were unable to match correctly the description with the sex of the author.

While there are many similarities between male and female sexual response, there are also differences. Males have one orgasm, while females show considerable variability. Women may experience no orgasms, one orgasm, or multiple orgasms during intercourse. The orgasm for the male is generally similar in strength and duration from one time to the next. A woman, on the other hand, may show considerable variation in strength and duration of orgasm. Although there are

many individual differences in the pattern of sexual responses, females show considerably more variability. Significant variation occurs among women in the number of orgasms they experience and in their responses during the resolution phase. Also, as we will discuss later in the chapter, there are differences in the stimuli that arouse males and females and in their speed of arousal. Males generally become aroused more quickly than females. This difference may account for some of the complaints by females that their sexual encounters are often too brief to be fully satisfying (Hite, 1976).

REVIEW QUESTIONS

1. Masters and Johnson have identified four phases of sexual arousal. The phase characterized by a sex flush and an increase in muscle tension is called the _____ phase.

2. The period of time after orgasm when men are relatively unresponsive to sexual stimulation is called the _____.

3. T or F: Men and women tend to describe their orgasms in similar ways.

SEXUAL BEHAVIOR: WHAT, WHEN, AND HOW OFTEN

Madonna's book *Sex* suggests that for her, almost anything goes. She suggests she enjoys having sex with a man or a woman, or both at once, or acting out almost any sexual idea that comes to mind. Is her openness to so many different kinds of sex with so many different partners unusual? How do other people in our culture feel about sex? What do they do?

Fifty years ago, it was extremely difficult to answer this question with any certainty. There was virtually no research on the sexual behavior of North Americans. It's ironic, but until 1948 we knew more about the sexual behavior of the Trobriand Islanders and the Sa-

moans than we did about the sexual activities of people in Canada and the United States. Anthropologists such as Bronislaw Malinowski and Margaret Mead had studied and published books on the sexual behavior of tribal and island peoples in far-off lands. Not until 1948 did Alfred Kinsey and his associates shock the country by publishing the results of a survey on the sexual behavior of men in the United States. This book was followed in 1953 by a publication on the sexual behavior of women. Kinsey and his associates conducted interviews with over 18,000 men and women, asking them questions about all aspects of their sexual experiences. This work began to give us insight into the sexual behavior of people during the 1940s and early 1950s.

More recently, other surveys (Hite, 1976; Hunt, 1974) have been conducted, and it is now not unusual to see magazines conducting their own surveys. Results from these surveys allow us to examine how sexual behavior has changed (or not changed) in the half-century since the pioneering work of Alfred Kinsey. As we review some of these findings, one point will be particularly striking. Whereas reports about the frequency of some behaviors show some change over time, in many other cases there seems to have been little change in sexual behavior in 50 years despite the obvious change in expressed attitudes. As we review these findings, it is important to keep in mind that these results rely on the self-reports of people questioned. It's difficult to carefully check their accuracy or to be sure that the people who were interviewed or completed questionnaires were truly representative of the population as a whole. With this caution in mind, let's examine some specific behaviors.

Sexual Fantasy

One of the most common sexual behaviors is to fantasize about sexual experiences. A *sexual fantasy* is a thought or daydream that is sexually exciting (Schultz, 1984). Kinsey reported that 84 percent of the males and 69 percent of the females in his study reported being sometimes aroused by sexual fantasies.

Sexual fantasies serve many purposes. First, they can excite and arouse a person. One study found that men with active fantasy lives reported the highest level of general sexual arousal (Giambra & Martin, 1977). Men are most likely to use fantasy as a means of becoming aroused, whereas women tend to fantasize after becoming aroused (Daley, 1975). Second, fantasies can enrich and add excitement to sexual behavior. Third, sexual fantasies may be used to rehearse or plan anticipated sexual contacts. Madonna's reveries about having sex with another woman while someone else looks on are good examples of using fantasies to enhance sexuality. Fourth, sexual fantasies may provide relief from boredom. Many people state that they often fantasize during dull situations such as lectures (Maier, 1984).

People show a great deal of variety in the topics of their sexual fantasies. Overall, men's fantasies often involve themes of aggression or power, whereas women's fantasies tend to be more romantic and focused on intimacy. Though the specifics of fantasies may vary widely, Hunt (1974) found some common themes: The most common male fantasies involved having intercourse with a stranger or having sex with more than one opposite-sex person at a time. Females most often fantasized about doing things they wouldn't do in reality or about having intercourse with a stranger.

Masturbation

The first and most common sexual experience for most people is **masturbation,** the self-manipulation of one's genitals to orgasm. Kinsey found that more than 90 percent of males and 60 percent of females had masturbated. Males begin masturbating at an earlier age and engage in this behavior more frequently than do females. The frequency of masturbation is greatest during adolescence, although 72 percent of married men and 68 percent of married women over the age of 30 engage in masturbation (Hunt, 1974).

Given these figures, it is amazing to consider the bad reputation that masturbation has acquired and the great lengths that parents have gone to in trying to prevent their children from masturbating. Kinsey (1948) summed up the conventional horror story about masturbation: "Every conceivable ill, from pimples to insanity, including stooped shoulders, loss of weight, fatigue, insomnia, general weakness, neurasthenia, loss of manly mindedness, genital cancer, and the rest was ascribed to masturbation" (p. 513). In the early part of the century, the United States Patent Office issued a patent for a device that would ring a bell in the parents' bedroom when the child's bed moved in a pattern suggestive of masturbation. It may seem difficult to comprehend why people could become so upset about a seemingly benign act. Clark Hyde (1986) offers some insight into this by examining sexuality in a religious context. He points out that Old Testament view of sexuality is basically positive, but that it also stresses intimacy and the relationship between two people. He reasons that the Old Testament was written during a time when the Jews were a group of nomadic tribes concerned with their survival. This survival demanded that there be enough children to keep the tribe viable, and hence sexual behavior for reproduction was stressed. Masturbation, as a solitary nonreproductive act, was viewed in a dim light. Even recently, surveys have found as high as 50 percent of respondents agree with statements asserting that masturbation is wrong (Levitt & Klassen, 1973). An interesting aside on this result is the finding that people tend to be most disturbed by portrayals of their own sex masturbating; males surveyed were most upset with depictions of males masturbating, and females were most upset with portrayals of females masturbating (Hatfield, Sprecher, & Traupman, 1978).

Despite these historical concerns, there is no evidence to suggest any physical harm resulting from masturbation (McMullen & Rosen, 1979). In fact, masturbation may be recommended by sex therapists in treating sexual dysfunctions (Maier, 1984). Although masturbation itself isn't harmful, the guilt and anxiety instilled in children by attempts to prevent masturbation may be traumatic. Since masturbation is often the person's first sexual behavior, insensitive attempts to repress and punish it may shape the individual's perception of all sexual behavior; sexual behavior, in general, may come to be viewed as something that is wrong and must be performed in secrecy. In this light it is interesting to note how explicitly Madonna is trying to make mastur-

bation seem normal. In breaking out of her staunchly Roman Catholic background, she's trying to make masturbation a natural and acceptable form of sexual behavior.

Premarital Intercourse

The Kinsey data collected during the late 1940s and early 1950s suggest that premarital sex before age 20 was unusual for women of that time. Kinsey found that only 20 percent of the women he interviewed had engaged in sexual intercourse before their twentieth birthdays. On the other hand, over 70 percent of the males reported having intercourse before their twentieth birthdays. Kinsey also found differences between males and females when they were asked whether or not they had ever engaged in premarital sex: More than twice as many men as women answered in the affirmative. As these figures show, a double standard clearly existed during that time.

Times have changed with regard to the incidence of premarital sex, especially for women. In the early 1970s, two-thirds of the women surveyed by Hunt (1974) had engaged in premarital intercourse. The rate was also up for men, but not as dramatically. The figures are even more striking when we examine the responses of people between the ages of 18 and 24. Hunt found that 95 percent of the men and 81 percent of the women had engaged in premarital intercourse. Two conclusions are suggested by these results: (1) a greater percentage of people (especially of women) were engaging in premarital sexual intercourse in the 1970s than was the case one or two generations earlier, and (2) the double standard seems to be dying, since the difference between the percentage of men and of women engaging in premarital sex is rapidly decreasing. One additional point of interest is that both males and females engaged in sexual intercourse at younger ages in the 1980s than they did even 20 years before (Reed & Weinberg, 1984). Another is that recent figures may seriously underestimate the prevalence of premarital sex. Not only are people having sex at a younger age, but people are delaying marriage now for a longer time than at any other period in the past century (*Washington Post,* 1996). People are delaying marriage, but there are no data to suggest they are delaying sex.

Even though a majority of unmarried adults in our society today have had sexual relationships, it isn't true that these people lead wild sexual lives with an endless stream of partners. Quite the contrary. On the average, women who have engaged in premarital intercourse have done so with two partners, and over half of the women reported having done so with only one partner whom they later married (Hunt, 1974). The average male surveyed had had six premarital sex partners.

In addition to a difference in the number of premarital sex partners, there also seems to be a difference in the way males and females react to their first experience of sexual intercourse. Males express positive feelings twice as frequently as do females (Sorenson, 1973). Males view their loss of virginity as a triumph, whereas some females experience guilt and anxiety at this critical life event. Women, unlike men, may also experience physical pain during their first intercourse; one study found that 30 percent of the women surveyed had experienced severe pain, while an additional 50 percent experienced brief or moderate pain (Oliven, 1974).

Women, however, tend to attach less significance to their first act of intercourse than do men. Women's reaction has been labeled the Peggy Lee syndrome (named after the song "Is That All There Is?") because the experience does not meet their romanticized expectations. One study (Weiss, 1983) found that college women, recalling their first sexual experience, rated it an average of 3.9 on a pleasure scale (1 = didn't experience pleasure at all, 10 = strongly experienced pleasure). In most cases, negative emotional reactions and physical pain disappear quickly, and women express satisfaction with later sexual intercourse.

Before leaving the subject of premarital sexual intercourse, let's examine how this behavior affects, or doesn't affect, a relationship. Many young women are taught that men will lose interest if they become sexually involved with them. A group of investigators (Peplau, Rubin, & Hill, 1977) conducted an in-depth study of 200 dating couples in Boston. Eighty-two percent of the couples had had sexual intercourse with their current partners; approximately half of this group had done so within one month of their first date. Thus we can define three groups based on sexual experience: those who abstained from sexual intercourse, those who experienced it early in the relationship, and those who experienced it later. When the investigators examined the relationships two years later, they found that experience with sexual behavior didn't affect the long-term success of the relationship; overall, 20 percent of the couples had married, 34 percent had continued to date, and 46 percent had broken up. Thus engaging in premarital intercourse with one's partner will neither increase the chances of the relationship succeeding nor harm the chances of success.

Marital Intercourse

Western cultures attempt to regulate sexual behavior through the institution of marriage. Sexual intercourse between married people is universally accepted and expected, although some societies have rules governing the nature and frequency of marital intercourse. The association between marriage and intercourse is so strong in our society that until recently people could force their marriage partners to have sex without fear of being prosecuted for rape.

Studies (Kinsey, Pomeroy, & Martin, 1948; Hunt, 1974) have found that married couples have sex on the average of two to four times a week. However, the frequency of marital intercourse has changed over the last 30 years, and it is affected by age. Overall, married partners now have sex more than they did 30 years ago. This difference is found regardless of the age of the individuals (Hunt, 1974).

Surveys (Thornton, 1977; Levin & Levin, 1975) show a positive relationship between frequency of intercourse and satisfaction with the marriage: The more often couples have sexual intercourse, the more likely they are to report being satisfied with their marriages. We can't take these results to mean that frequent sex makes for better marriages. It may well be the other way around: that satisfaction with a marriage may lead to more frequent intercourse. However, the results do indicate that the two are related. In addition, other research suggests that both having sex and arguing are related to marital satisfaction, and that the positive ratio of having sex more than arguing is strongly correlated to marital satisfaction (Howard & Dawes, 1976).

Today's more open attitudes about sex also are influencing the sexual behavior of married couples. Compared to Kinsey's survey in 1903, Hunt (1974) found that foreplay is longer for today's married couples (12 minutes versus 1 minute) and that the duration of intercourse (measured by the time for the male to reach orgasm) has significantly increased. Married couples are also more likely to use a variety of positions and to engage in oral–genital techniques than were couples at the time of the Kinsey report. The world in which the sexual versatility of Madonna is open to discussion in the mass media is also, not surprisingly, one where married people feel comfortable experimenting freely. Also, the stereotype that sex becomes dull as the marriage wears on is generally not supported. In fact, many people reported enjoying sex after years of marriage; they reported better communication and understanding of their partner's desires.

Extramarital Sex

Extramarital sexual relationships are considered wrong in many societies. One study found that over 61 percent of societies had rules against extramarital sexual relationships; in 16 percent of the societies these rules applied only to women (Ford & Beach, 1951). A survey of attitudes of people in the United States found that 72 percent of respondents believed that extramarital sex is "always wrong" (Levitt & Klassen, 1973). Despite these attitudes, Kinsey (1953) found that 50 percent of males and 25 percent of females had experienced extramarital sex. More recent research (Thompson, 1983) found that although the percentage of males having extramarital affairs has remained fairly stable, 40 percent of the females reported having extramarital affairs. The frequency of extramarital affairs decreases with age for males but tends to increase up to age 40 for females. Another trend is that wives who hold full-time jobs outside the home are more likely to have affairs than are housewives. One reason for this figure may be that women who work outside the home have more opportunity to meet a variety of men.

With such strong attitudes against extramarital relationships, we may ask why they occur. In some cases, the cause may be dissatisfaction with marital sex. In other cases, the individual may wish to punish his or her spouse. A third reason is insecurity; the person may feel the need to prove that he or she is still attractive to others. A fourth reason may be a desire to find excitement and escape boredom.

We seem to have a morbid curiosity about extramarital affairs. Stories about Madonna's love life while married to Sean Penn, and stories about many other recently married public figures, such as singer Michael Jackson, dominate magazine covers at the grocery checkout lines. Although news items about these affairs may conjure up images of excitement and romance, the facts tend to portray a different picture. People tend to find extramarital affairs less satisfying than marital sex. For example, in one survey two-thirds of the husbands rated their marital intercourse as "very pleasurable," while less than 50 percent of the men who had had extramarital affairs rated this intercourse as "very pleasurable" (Hunt, 1974). Guilt, fear of being discovered, and the secrecy surrounding extramarital affairs distract from the pleasure and intimacy.

Homosexuality

A great deal of attention has recently been focused on **homosexuality,** or sexual relationships between individuals of the same sex. Bill Clinton began his Presidency on day one in 1993 by dealing with the issue of gays in the military, finally adopting the compromise "don't ask, don't tell" policy. Stories today about homosexuals "coming out of the closet" and about fights in states and municipalities for and against "gay rights" are now common. And Madonna has certainly brought issues of sexual orientation into the mainstream, as we have seen. But homosexuality is nothing new. We can assume it is as old as **heterosexuality,** or sex between males and females. Homosexual relationships were common among the ancient Greeks. Both Plato and Socrates wrote about homosexuality and may have engaged in homosexual behavior. The term *lesbian* (female homosexual) originated in ancient Greece. Sappho, one of the great poets of antiquity, ran a school for girls in the sixth century B.C.E. and fell in love with some of her students. She lived on the Greek island of Lesbos and was therefore called a Lesbian. Homosexuality was also widely accepted by the ancient Romans: Julius Caesar has been described as "every woman's man and every man's woman" (Leisor, 1979).

But attitudes and behavior change with culture. The advent of Christianity was accompanied by condemnation of homosexual behavior. Augustine (354–430 C.E.) described homosexuality as a crime against nature, and by the fourth century homosexuals were being burned at the stake. Negative attitudes toward homosexuality continued into recent times. A survey in the United States in 1977 found that 72 percent of white Americans felt that homosexual relations were "always wrong" (Lief, 1977). Although tolerance is definitely higher today, studies continue to show strong traces of **homophobia,** or negative reactions to homosexuals, especially gay men (Williams & Jacoby, 1989).

While these results paint a very unaccepting picture of homosexuality, there is another side to the coin. For example, the attitudes expressed by Americans aren't found in other Western cultures; only 11.8 percent of a sample of Danes and 5.4 percent of a Dutch sample believed that homosexuality was vulgar and obscene. In 1973, the American Psychiatric Association decided that it was inaccurate to describe homosexuality as a "psychological disorder."

Just as there may be confusion about attitudes toward homosexuality, there is also misunderstanding about the definition of homosexuality and homosexual behavior. Kinsey argued that there is no clear line dividing homosexuals and heterosexuals. Rather, sexual orientation should be viewed as a continuum running from exclusively heterosexual to exclusively homosexual (see Figure 11.1). In support of this position, Kinsey found that only about 2 percent of the males and 1 percent of the females he surveyed described themselves as exclusively homosexual in orientation. But almost a quarter of the men and 15 to 20 percent of the females reported some homosexual experience in their lives.

Another misconception about homosexual relationships is that they are solely based on sex. Actually, the frequency of sexual relations is about the same in homosexual relationships as it is in heterosexual relationships (Bell & Weinberg, 1978). Many homosexuals, like heterosexuals, enter relationships in search of mutual love and intimacy; sexual gratification is of secondary importance. In fact, a significant proportion of homosexuals

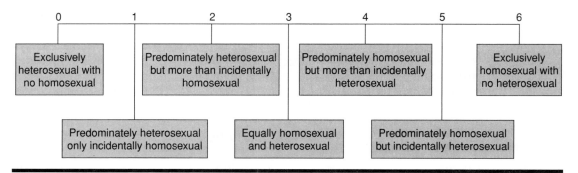

FIGURE 11.1   Range of Sexual Orientations[a]

Source: Adapted from Kinsey et al. (1948), p. 638, taken from Maier (1984) p. 361.

[a]Note that there is no sharp line of distinction between homosexual and heterosexual orientation.

form lasting relationships similar to those of married heterosexual couples and remain sexually faithful to their partner. In one study of 16 such couples, investigators found that the couples had been together an average of 8.9 years and that some relationships had lasted over 30 years (McWhirter & Mattison, 1984). These couples had set up homes and had clear rules about who performed the various duties around the house. They experienced conflicts and disagreements about their relationship similar to those experienced by married heterosexual couples. And obviously the growing concern about AIDS (see p. 305) is leading to an increase in number of both heterosexual and homosexual couples establishing monogamous relationships. This should not be taken to mean that all homosexuals form lasting couple relationships. Like heterosexuals, a number of homosexuals remain "single" and engage in sexual activity with a number of partners.

Numerous theories have been advanced to explain the causes of homosexuality. Some argue that the cause is genetic or biological (LeVay & Hamer, 1994). For example, one study found that a part of the brain associated with sexual orientation was twice as large in heterosexual men as homosexual men (LeVay, 1993). Similarly, a study of twins showed that

52 percent of the identical twins of male homosexuals are also homosexual compared to only 22 percent of the fraternal twins of male homosexuals, implying a genetic link (Bailey & Pillar, 1991; Bailey & Martin, 1995).

Other theory and research emphasize early family life and social experience, or a combination of social and biological influences. One theory (Storms, 1981) links physiological changes with homosexual social development. According to this theory, a person is more likely to develop a homosexual orientation if his or her sex drive develops at an early stage in life, when most friends are of the same sex. At later stages of adolescence, people develop many friendships with opposite-sex others; if the sex drive develops at that stage, sexual desires will be associated with people of the opposite sex. The most recent theory, called the "exotic becomes erotic" model, suggests that sexual orientation is influenced by the gender of one's early childhood playmates. Little boys who play with little girls rather than other boys will find those other boys strange, exotic and alluring when they reach puberty and will become sexually attracted to them. Similarly, girls who play with little boys will find young women alluring when they reach adolescence and become lesbians (Bem, 1996). Considering all the research, it seems clear that biological and genetic factors play a strong role but that experiential factors contribute as well.

Although there is disagreement about the causes of homosexual orientation, some agreement exists about the adjustment of homosexuals. At one time, it was common to view homosexuals as emotionally disturbed people who turned to homosexual relationships because they couldn't adjust to the heterosexual world. This doesn't seem to be the case. Most homosexuals tend to have steady relationships and wide circles of friends, to be satisfied with their jobs, and to describe themselves as being "pretty happy" (Bell & Weinberg, 1978). Some, however, report being less accepting of themselves; some have psychosomatic illnesses and have contemplated suicide. It's difficult to know the exact cause of these feelings, but they may well be the result of the stresses experienced by nonheterosexual people in a predominantly heterosexual society.

Sex and the Elderly

For the most part, people in our society view sex as an activity for the younger generation. In one study that asked college students to complete the sentence "Sex for most old people...," most responded with the terms "unimportant," "past," or "negligible" (Golde & Kogan, 1959).

These perceptions to the contrary, however, a significant proportion of the elderly remain sexually active; surveys indicate that about two out of three men and women remain sexually active into their seventies (Cox, 1986), although the frequency of sexual intercourse does decline. In a survey of men and women between 65 and 97 years old, averaging 74, 40 percent were sexually active (Clements, 1996). There is also an indication that the more frequently and regularly a woman engaged in sexual behavior (intercourse and masturbation), the fewer problems she experienced in sexual activity during her later years (Masters & Johnson, 1966).

Although many elderly people continue to have very satisfying sexual lives, there are physiological changes that affect sexual behavior. In men, testosterone production declines gradually over the years, requiring longer periods of stimulation to achieve erection, and manual stimulation of the penis may be required. The refractory period for older men is usually longer than that for young men. However, older men are typically capable of maintaining their erections for longer periods of time than are young men and hence may engage in coitus for a longer period of time.

Aging women undergo more physiological changes than do aging men. At **menopause,** which generally occurs between the ages of 45 and 55, menstruation ceases and a woman is no longer capable of reproduction. Menopause is sometimes marked by a general hormonal imbalance. The vaginal walls become less elastic and lubrication of the vagina is slower and less complete. Menopause may also be accompanied by headaches, dizziness, and hot flashes, which are sudden waves of heat from the waist up. However, women have the same physical capacity to have an orgasm at age 80 as they do at age 30. Hormone replacement therapy and the use of lubricants may be employed to deal with the discomforts caused by intercourse.

Sexual expression among the aged is affected by a number of factors in addition to these physiological changes. One factor is physical health. Not only are the aged more likely to suffer from periodic illnesses that curtail their sexual behavior, but the aged may have a harder time regaining normal sexual functioning after periods of abstinence. A second important factor is a common notion in our society that sexual behavior in older persons is unusual or even ridiculous. Some elderly people accept this propaganda, and even those who don't are often reluctant to discuss their sexual problems, even with doctors. Thus these and other factors work against the aged engaging in active sex lives, even though they are very capable of doing so.

FACTORS AFFECTING THE JOY OF SEX

The sexual behavior of most animals is controlled by hormones and instinct. The goal of animals' heterosexual intercourse is reproduction. Humans, however, have been freed from the straightjacket of hormones and instinct. We may engage in sexual behavior for pleasure and intimacy, as well as reproduction. Our sexual activities are limited more by our imaginations than by our hormonal attributes. This freedom can add exciting and pleasing dimensions to our lives. For some of us, however, it may create a living hell, dominated by anxiety and insecurity. The choice in most cases is our own, but it can be strongly affected by others. For this reason, it's important that we understand our bodies and our sexual responses and develop a sensitivity to others. A wide variety of factors will influence whether or not we will enjoy our sexuality or dread it.

Expectations

Sex is glorified in our society. Madonna's books, videos, and tours have added to that celebration. Reading love novels leads us to expect ecstasy and pure pleasure every time we engage in sexual behavior. Watching movies leads us to believe that people are natural-born lovers; all that is needed for a satisfying sexual encounter is two willing people. The movies rarely show the star having trouble achieving an erection or experiencing pain during intercourse.

These unrealistic expectations may create problems in enjoying our actual sexual experiences. On one hand, we may be disappointed with a relationship if our early sexual experience does not meet our expectations: "This can't be love because the bands didn't play and whistles didn't blow when we had sex." On the other hand, we may worry about our own adequacy if we don't perform as expected: "There must be something wrong with me because I didn't have an orgasm" (or "I could only wait 5 seconds before having an orgasm"). It is important to realize that our sexual experiences and performance will vary: sometimes great and sometimes not so great. The art of making love is something that must be learned and our expectations about it must be realistic to avoid confusion, disappointment, and self-doubt.

Communication

Most of us wouldn't hesitate to complain if we were in a room that was too hot or if someone standing on our toes was causing us pain. We are quick to say what movies we enjoyed and what food we don't like. Too often, however, we're reluctant to communicate our feelings about our sexual experiences. Some people are embarrassed to discuss the sexual activities that give them pleasure or to tell their partners about the actions that cause pain or discomfort. It's not unusual for a person to fake an orgasm to make his or her partner think a "successful" encounter has occurred. The lack of communication turns sex into a guessing game: Sexual partners must guess what the other person is willing to do and enjoys. Open communication about feelings, both positive and negative, will go a long way toward making sexual behavior more enjoyable for those involved.

Exploration

Some people approach sexual behavior much as they do their jobs; sexual performance is something to be measured by criteria such as efficiency and speed. Sexual behavior is taken to mean simply sexual intercourse. But intercourse is only one of the sexual activities people can enjoy together. Sexual behavior offers people the opportunity to experience a deep sense of intimacy. It's an opportunity to explore another person's body and to experience the exciting sensations that result from touching and being touched. Thus *foreplay*, the activities used to heighten sexual arousal before intercourse, may be as satisfying and enjoyable as intercourse itself. Taking the time to enjoy exploration and experience physical intimacy heightens the pleasure of sexual relationships.

Setting

The setting is important to having a satisfying sexual experience. Variety may instill new excitement in the relationship, but both people should be comfortable with the chosen time and place. Hurried encounters in unappealing spots turn the relationship into a frantic race against time and discovery. They can also result in guilt and in feelings that sex is wrong or something to be hidden.

Alcohol and Drugs

Many people believe that alcohol and drugs enhance sexual pleasure. In one study 60 percent of those surveyed reported that they enjoyed sex more after drinking (Athanasiou, Shaver, & Lauris, 1970). But before you reach for the bottle, consider the following points.

First, alcohol is a depressant; it reduces sensation and in large amounts can even result in men's inability to have erections. Given this fact, it has been argued that the positive effects of alcohol on sexual behavior result because alcohol reduces inhibitions and feelings of guilt. It seems, however, that the alcohol itself doesn't accomplish this. Wilson and Lawson (1978) divided male subjects into groups. They gave one group a mixture of vodka and tonic and another group only tonic, although those men were led to believe they were drinking alcohol. A third group was given vodka but was led to believe it was only tonic. The groups were then shown an erotic film, and their arousal was measured. The greatest arousal was found in the men who drank only tonic but believed they were drinking vodka.

The least arousal resulted in the men who drank vodka but believed it was only tonic. Thus it may be our *belief* that we aren't responsible for behavior when drinking, and not the alcohol itself, that reduces inhibitions and heightens sexual enjoyment.

The effect of drugs on sexual satisfaction hasn't been well studied. There is some indication that heroin decreases sexual desire but that small amounts of cocaine and marijuana increase sensitivity to touch and enjoyment of sex. However, long-term use of even these latter drugs can have negative effects, such as lowered sperm production and retarded ejaculation (Maier, 1984).

BIRTH CONTROL

Of the over 3 million births that occur each year in the United States, there are 700,000 unwanted pregnancies in teenaged girls. One out of four teenaged girls will become pregnant before the age of eighteen (Kassin, 1995). Failure to use contraception is a major cause. According to findings from anonymous questionnaires, 63 percent of women and 57 percent of men did not use contraceptives the first time they had sex (Darling, Davidson, & Passarello, 1992). Fewer than one-third of college students who acknowledge being sexually active use contraceptives regularly (Byrne, 1982). One study found that college women were using less effective contraceptive methods today than they did five years earlier, despite being more sexually active (Gerrard, 1982).

While the terms *birth control* and *contraception* are often used interchangeably, there are differences between the two. **Birth control** involves any method used to prevent the birth of children; these include abstinence, contraception, sterilization, and abortion. **Contraception** on the other hand, refers to methods used to prevent conception. Concern about birth control dates back over 4,000 years. Women in ancient Egypt used a contraceptive made of crocodile dung and honey that they inserted into their vaginas before intercourse.

TABLE 11.1 Methods of Birth Control

METHOD	THEORETICAL FAILURE RATE (PERCENT)	MAJOR ADVANTAGES	MAJOR DISADVANTAGES
Withdrawal	9	No preplanning or artificiality	Frustration or lack of fulfullment
Rhythm	13	Acceptable to Roman Catholic Church	Anxiety; difficulties with periods of abstinence
Condom	3	Protection against diseases; ease of use	Reduced sensitivity of penis; interruption of sexual activity
Spermacide	3	Ease of use; added lubrication	Allergic reactions in some women
Diaphragm	3	May hold menstrual flow	Allergic reactions in some women; inconvenience
IUD	1–3	Little attention required after insertion; possible after-the-fact effectiveness	Side effects, including bleeding and possible infections
Oral contraceptive	1	Ease of use; relief of some menstrual problems	Side effects, especially in very young women, women over 35, and smokers
Female sterilization	Close to 0	Permanent effectiveness	Restoration of fertility not always possible
Male sterilization	Close to 0	Simple procedure; permanent effectiveness	Restoration of fertility unlikely
Induced abortion	—	After-the-fact procedure	Health risks; moral implications

Source: Adapted from Maier (1984), p. 27.

In earlier times, contraception and birth control were considered by many to be mainly the woman's concern. Today we are coming to realize that contraception and birth control are the responsibility of both the woman and the man. These topics should be discussed openly by both partners and a mutual decision should be reached.

There are a wide variety of contraceptives available. As can be seen in Table 11.1, contraceptives work in a variety of ways. In some cases, the aid of a physician is necessary to obtain or fit the contraceptive, but in other cases the contraceptive can be obtained from birth control centers and drugstores. Table 11.1 also shows that, used properly, many of the contraceptives are highly effective. The difference between the theoretical failure rate and the actual failure rate is the result of improper use of the contraceptive.

Given the availability and effectiveness of contraceptives, it's somewhat surprising to find figures showing that many people don't use contraceptives. It has been suggested (Byrne, 1982) that the decision to use contraceptives occurs in five steps: acquiring information, admitting the likelihood of engaging in sexual intercourse, obtaining contraceptives, discussing contraceptives with the sexual partner, and practicing contraception. A number of factors may break this chain of events and lead people not to use contraceptives.

First, some people have difficulty admitting that they are likely to engage in sexual intercourse. Inserting a diaphragm or buying a condom may seem too "premeditated" to them. Planning for sexual behavior and obtaining contraceptives may seem to remove the spontaneity and romance from sexual activity. Unfortunately, the romance for people with this attitude may be quickly replaced with the anxiety over an unwanted pregnancy.

A second factor is that some people are embarrassed about discussing contraceptives with their sexual partners, doctors, or birth control counselors. As we pointed out earlier, sex for many people is something that may be engaged in but not talked about. This view is often reinforced by movies and novels. After all, how often does a movie portray two people discussing contraceptives before engaging in sexual intercourse?

Finally, failure to use contraceptives may be an intentional act. People may feel that they can save a dying relationship by an unexpected pregnancy. Thus many factors may inhibit the use of contraceptives.

Before leaving this topic, let's examine one method of birth control that is presently the center of much controversy: induced abortion. *Abortion* terminates pregnancy by removing the immature fetus from the uterus. Abortions were used by the Chinese over 4,000 years ago and have been fairly common in most societies since then. Abortion was legal in the United States until the 1860s. However, during the 1860s laws were passed making abortion illegal. The intent of these laws was largely to protect women from procedures that were dangerous at that time. The laws weren't very effective, however; almost 25 percent of the women interviewed by Kinsey (1953) had had an illegal abortion by the time they reached midlife. In 1973, the U.S. Supreme Court declared that state laws prohibiting abortion were unconstitutional. Women now have the right to have abortions during the first three months of pregnancy; abortions between the third and sixth month are permitted with the consultation of a doctor; abortions after the sixth month (when the fetus has a chance of surviving outside the mother) are permitted only when there is a serious threat to the mother's health.

The issue of abortion is a very emotional one and has been the center of a heated controversy since the Supreme Court's ruling. *Pro-abortion,* or *pro-choice,* advocates argue that women should be able to control their own bodies; a woman should be able to determine whether or not she wishes to carry a fetus. Pro-choice advocates also argue that abortion may be preferable to forcing a mother or a couple to cope with an unwanted child. On the other hand, anti-abortion, or "pro-life," advocates argue that life begins at conception, not at birth. According to this view, abortion is a form of murder and the rights of the unborn child should be protected. This is clearly a tough issue to deal with, and one that isn't likely to be resolved easily. The question of abortion has become increasingly complicated by advancing medical techniques that can sustain the life of an immature fetus outside the womb. At present, people must rely on their own values and judgments in deciding the role that abortion should play in their own birth control efforts.

PORNOGRAPHY

Madonna's book *Sex* walks the borderline between cutting edge, artistic erotica, and pornography. Supreme Court Justice Potter

Stewart once said that it was difficult to define pornography, but he knew when he saw it. But many people find that after seeing *Sex* they don't know whether it should be regarded as pornography, art, or just silliness. We clearly live in a society that is characterized by openness in depicting sexually explicit material in television, films, art, and literature. Madonna has encouraged and pushed the boundaries of that openness. She and others have created a storm of controversy, conflict, and confusion. We can begin to understand some of the issues better by offering some definitions, despite the Supreme Court's reluctance.

Pornography is sexually arousing art, literature, or films (Hyde, 1986). At one extreme on the continuum is *obscenity*, which is pornography that is offensive by accepted standards of decency; this material is generally very explicit, often involves aggression, and tends to portray sex in a foul or lewd manner. Obscenity is a legal term that is applied to pornographic material found to violate community standards by the courts. **Erotica,** on the other hand, is sexually arousing material that is not degrading to women, men, or children; it rarely involves violence and generally portrays sexual activity between consenting partners. As you can imagine, one of the first grounds where conflict arises is how material is classified. What may appear obscene and offensive to you may be viewed as erotica by the person sitting next to you. Who is to determine what is obscenity and what is erotica? The courts have been involved in many battles on just this issue and have yet to come up with clear guidelines for making this distinction.

We might question why this should be an issue at all; shouldn't producers of pornography be happy to stay within fairly defined and conservative guidelines? The answer to this question is clearly negative; pornography is a big business with big profits. It is estimated that the industry grosses between $2.5 and $3 billion a year. Hard-core pornography is cheap to produce and can reap enormous

returns. For example, *Deep Throat*, one of the first widely viewed full-length hard-core pornographic films, cost $24,000 to make, but by 1982 it had yielded a profit of $25,000,000 ("Video Turns Big Profit for Porn Products," 1982). Clearly, there is an audience for pornography and a handsome return on it.

Hence, we can phrase our earlier question differently: Rather than worrying about the distinctions between pornographic material, why not adopt a policy that "anything goes"? Let the people who want it have it, and those who do not want it don't have to look. Opponents of this position include a curious set of allies, among them fundamentalist religious groups and feminists. Among the points they make, one is that pornography undermines basic moral and family values of our society. Another is that people may be forced into pornography for the profit of others; this is especially a concern in the case of children (the kiddie porn industry is a $1-billion-a-year business and over 1 million children a year are involved in commercial sex) (Hyde, 1986). Finally, pornography degrades women and portrays them as sex objects. Sex is often coupled with violence against women, and pornography glorifies an unequal power relationship between men and women.

At the base of much of the concern about pornography is how it affects the consumers. Some argue that it has no negative effects and may even provide a safe release for sexual tension. Others argue that pornography promotes sexual crimes and violence. Though we do not have a complete picture of the effects of pornography, research is beginning to give us some indication of the influence of pornography.

We might expect pornography to have a marked effect on sexual behavior. However, this does not appear to be the case. For example, Bryant (1985) surveyed adolescents after their first contact with X-rated magazines and films. Although two-thirds of the males and nearly half of the females surveyed expressed a desire to imitate what they had seen, less than 25 percent of the males and 15 percent of the females actually attempted to carry out their desires. On a larger scale, researchers had the opportunity to examine the effects of pornography when the Danish Parliament legalized the sale of explicit sexual material to anyone over age 16. There was a fear that this act would result in an increase in sexually related crimes. Instead, there was a decrease in the number of child molestation and homosexual offenses; the number of rapes was unaffected. Other countries (West Germany and Japan) that have legalized pornography have also found either a decrease or no effect on sex crimes (Baron & Byrne, 1981).

While these studies suggest that we need not be concerned about the effect of pornography on sexual behavior or sex crimes, there is growing evidence that pornography increases aggressive behavior, especially that toward women (Malamuth, 1984). It also seems that pornography reduces anxiety about performing aggressive acts and lowers concerns about women as victims of violence. These findings should not surprise us, given that much of hard-core pornography mixes sex and violence; rape and other sadistic activities are favorite topics of this pornography. Still other research suggests that viewing pornography reduces the positive emotions associated with

sexual behavior and encourages consumers to associate such negative feelings as anger and rage with sexual behavior (see the accompanying Lessons from the Laboratory).

Given the evidence that pornography can lead to increased aggression, the next question that arises is: What should be done about pornography? A simple solution might be to ban it or closely regulate what behaviors can be shown in pornographic material. This solution may be tempting, but it has two important problems. The first is that this action threatens our rights to freedom of expression; this freedom is vital if we are to maintain our democratic society. Second, numerous studies (Worchel & Arnold, 1973) have shown that censorship actually increases the attractiveness of the censored material. Other possible solutions include warnings such as those now placed on cigarette packages that tell consumers what is contained in pornography and what its effects are likely to be. In addition, it is important to educate people about the ways in which pornography degrades certain groups and to distinguish clearly between hard-core pornography and erotica. Indeed, the issues are complex and difficult, but understanding them is the first major step in being able to deal with them in a reasonable and constructive manner.

REVIEW QUESTIONS

4. Despite its generally taboo reputation, the first and most common sexual experience for most people is _____.

5. T or F: The long-term success of a relationship is decreased for couples who engage in premarital intercourse.

6. Which of the following is (are) true regarding marital intercourse?

   a. Married partners are more likely to engage in coitus today than they did 30 years ago.
   b. Frequency of intercourse declines with age.

   c. There is a positive relationship between frequency of marital intercourse and overall satisfaction with the marriage.
   d. Only a and c are true.
   e. All the above are true.

7. T or F: Obscenity is sexually arousing material that is not degrading to women, men, or children and rarely involves violence.

8. T or F: Abstinence, sterilization, and abortion are all forms of contraception.

9. The minor surgical procedure used to sterilize males is called _____.

Pornography and Aggression toward Women

One of the most controversial social policy questions today concerns the effect of pornography. Does pornography lead men to be violent toward women? Two presidential commissions addressing this issue in the 1970s and 1980s reached different conclusions. The 1970 Presidential Commission on Obscenity and Pornography concluded that pornography, by itself, did not contribute to violence toward women. However, the Meese Commission, convened under President Ronald Reagan, concluded in 1985 that pornography did have such an effect. What do psychologists now believe? The answer is complicated, but there appears to be a consensus.

First, most psychologists believe that mild forms of erotica such as nudes from *Playboy* magazine do not adversely affect attitudes toward women or contribute to violence toward women. However, the picture is different for forms of pornography that include violence. This is especially true of R-rated, easily available "slasher movies" that depict violent actions against women made to appear as sexually enticing, for example, shooting a woman who had been masturbating in a bath tub with a nail gun (Donnerstein, Linz, & Penrod, 1987).

Research suggests that the link between violent pornography and aggression can be complex. In one study male subjects watched one of four films: a neutral film from a talk show; an erotic but nonviolent film showing a couple having consensual sex; or one of two violent films in which two men assaulted and had sex with a woman. In one version of the violent film the woman clearly suffered throughout the assault. In the other she gradually came to enjoy the violent sex and became a willing participant. After seeing one of these four films, half the subjects were insulted and angered by a woman confederate and half were not. Later, subjects had a chance to retaliate against the woman confederate.

The results are shown in Table 11.2. There was little aggression toward the woman following the talk show film or the nonviolent erotic film, and it did not make any difference whether the subjects were insulted. When subjects saw the violent film in which the woman came to enjoy the sexual assault, they were aggressive whether or not they had been assaulted. It seems that the message that women like violence came through to the subjects. However, when the subjects saw the violent film in which the woman suffered throughout the assault, they increased their aggression if they were angry but not when they had not been insulted. The woman's suffering led the men who had not been insulted to restrain their aggression. But the angry men were influenced toward aggression toward the insulting confederate even if the woman in the film had suffered (Donnerstein & Berkowitz, 1981).

More recent evidence that violent pornography may lead to aggressive behavior, including sexually aggressive and coercive behavior such as rape, comes from a study that found that men's self-reported exposure to violent pornography is correlated with their sexually aggressive behavior (Demare, Lips, & Briere, 1993). Although this result may reflect the fact that men who are sexually

TABLE 11.2 Degree of Aggression Shown toward Female Confederate by Angered and Nonangered Male Subjects after Watching Various Films

	FILM			
SUBJECTS	*Neutral Talk Show*	*Nonviolent, Erotic*	*Violent, Woman Enjoys*	*Violent, Woman Suffers*
Nonangered	Low	Low	High	Low
Angered	Low	Low	High	High

Source: Based on Donnerstein & Berkowitz (1981).

aggressive are drawn to violent pornography rather than the possibility that violent pornography directly contributes to sexual aggression, the re-

sults are further warning that violent pornography can lead to aggression.

SEXUAL DYSFUNCTIONS

Throughout this chapter, we've attempted to dispel the common belief that people are "born lovers." We don't suddenly wake up one morning to discover that we've been transformed into well-functioning sexual machines. A number of factors—including physical health, learning, emotions, and experience—must be combined to teach us the art of love. Even people most experienced with sexual behavior find that their enjoyment and sexual performance vary from time to time. Sometimes sex may be exciting and fulfilling; other times nothing seems to go right. Most people experience periodic problems with their sexual behavior. In many cases, these may be caused by fatigue, alcohol, drugs, distractions, or worry. Although periodic problems with sexual behavior may be frustrating, they should be expected and not cause great concern.

For some people, however, sexual problems are frequent or long lasting. In these cases, we refer to the problems as **sexual dysfunctions.** There are numerous causes of these dysfunctions. Some are the result of physical or organic problems such as illness, hormonal imbalance or the side effects of surgery. Some are the result of learning or, more correctly, the failure to learn satisfying and fulfilling sexual behaviors. Still others are the result of emotions associated with sexual behavior such as fear or embarrassment.

Sexual dysfunctions may be particularly devastating to a person for a number of reasons. One is the great emphasis our society places on sexual performance; we can often accept the fact that someone is not a great athlete or musician, but everyone is expected to be able to perform sexually. Therefore sexual dysfunction may destroy a person's self-

esteem. Second, the dysfunction affects not only the individual, but also relationships with other people. Frustration over the lack of sexual fulfillment can be at the root of discord and distress between partners. It's also possible that this discord and distress may be the root of the sexual dysfunction. Finally, until recently, people suffering sexual dysfunctions lived in a lonely hell. It was difficult for them to talk about their problem and hard for them to find someone who could effectively treat them.

Erectile Dysfunction (Impotence)

One of the most common sexual dysfunctions in males is *erectile disfunction,* or impotence. This problem involves the failure to have or maintain an erection long enough to have sexual intercourse. *Primary erectile dysfunction* (which rarely occurs) refers to cases where the man has never had an erection long enough to have sexual intercourse. The more common type is *secondary erectile dysfunction,* which results when a man who has previously functioned normally can no longer maintain an erection. In some cases, this dysfunction results from the failure to engage in effective foreplay before attempting sexual intercourse. In other cases the problem may stem from emotions such as fear, guilt, shame, or disgust. Unfortunately, the problem often perpetuates itself. For example, a man may experience difficulty maintaining an erection at one time. Although the cause of this failure may be fatigue, he may become very concerned about his ability to perform sexually. At the next opportunity to engage in sexual intercourse his fear may surface and further inhibit erection. A third cause of secondary impotence is physical. In one study (Spark, White & Connolly, 1980), physicians examined 105 impotent men and found physical causes in 70 of the cases.

Premature Ejaculation

Premature ejaculation involves a man's inability to delay ejaculation long enough "to penetrate and satisfy his partner at least fifty percent of the time" (Masters & Johnson, 1970). Clearly this definition is based not only on the man's behavior, but also on how easily his partner is satisfied. In most cases, however, ejaculation occurs as soon as the penis penetrates the vagina. One of the main causes of this dysfunction is learned behavior. The man's early experience with sexual intercourse may have taught him that sex is a behavior that should be rushed; he may have a history of trying to hurry intercourse in order to avoid being detected or "caught in the act." This habit may have carried over into other situations in which there was no need to hurry sexual behavior. Another cause may be the man's attitude toward women. One study (Masters & Johnson, 1970) found that many premature ejaculators held women in low regard and didn't consider the woman's satisfaction to be of importance in sexual intercourse.

Retarded Ejaculation

Retarded ejaculation is the opposite of premature ejaculation. In this case the man finds it difficult or impossible to ejaculate during intercourse. In some cases the problem may result from diseases that attack the nervous system or from injury or surgical error that affects the nervous system. But in most cases the problem is psychological. At the extreme of this category is the man's fear that ejaculation is an indication that he is losing control. On the other hand, the most common inhibi-

tions involve the man's fear of impregnating his partner or the loss of feelings of attraction for her. Sometimes hostility toward the partner may result in the man's determination not to "give her part of himself."

Orgasmic Dysfunction

The inability to experience an orgasm even when there is a normal sexual interest and drive is referred to as *orgasmic dysfunction*. *Primary orgasmic dysfunction* involves cases where the woman has never experienced an orgasm. According to one survey (Hunt, 1974), about 10 percent of the women who responded stated that they had never had an orgasm. *Secondary* or *situational orgasmic dysfunction* involves cases where the woman has had orgasms but is not having them at the present time. The causes of this problem are quite debatable. It could be argued that the man, not the woman, is the cause of the woman's orgasmic dysfunction. The man's lack of tenderness, lack of interest in foreplay, or rush to satisfy himself may be the root of this problem for many women. In other cases, the dysfunction may be associated with the woman's inhibitions about experiencing strong sexual feelings. Other feelings that inhibit orgasm include fear of abandonment, hostility or ambivalence toward the partner, and concern about losing control.

Vaginismus

Vaginismus is a relatively rare dysfunction that results when the muscles surrounding the vagina involuntarily constrict to inhibit penetration by the penis or to make penetration extremely painful. Like the other dysfunctions, the cause is often psychological. In some cases, the woman may have extreme fear about vaginal penetration. For other women, the cause can be traced to painful ex-

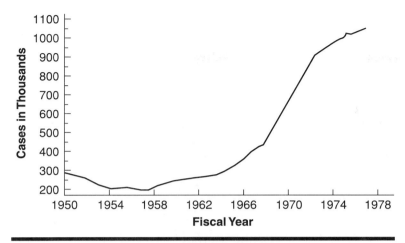

FIGURE 11.2   Number of reported gonorrhea cases in the United States, 1950–1978.

Source: From Maier (1984), p. 474.

periences associated with penetration, such as rape or an unpleasant pelvic examination.

SEXUALLY TRANSMITTED DISEASES

The causes of sexual dysfunctions are largely psychological. On the other hand, a number of diseases that have physical causes are transmitted through sexual contact. These diseases were once known collectively as *venereal disease* (VD) but are now referred to as *sexually transmitted disease (STD)*. These diseases have been recognized for a long time and have in fact had an impact on history. During the late fifteenth century, syphilis became so widespread that it influenced the outcome of some important military battles. It is important to diagnose and treat these diseases as early as possible because they can have disastrous physical effects, including death. Gynecologists specialize in female disease, and urologists often treat male diseases. Although there are a number of different sexually transmitted diseases, we will list some of the most common.

Gonorrhea

Gonorrhea is the most prevalent STD today; in fact, of all the communicable diseases, only the common cold is found more frequently in the United States. Gonorrhea is also the oldest known STD; its symptoms are described in the Old Testament. As can be seen in Figure 11.2, the number of cases of gonorrhea has increased dramatically over the last few years. In 1976, there were a million reported cases in the United States and it is estimated that four times that many cases went unreported.

The cause of gonorrhea is a bacterium transmitted through sexual contact. Ten percent of males and 80 percent of females who have gonorrhea show no symptoms. When symptoms do appear, they are more easily recognizable in males than in females. In males, the symptoms may include a burning sensation when urinating, urine that contains pus or blood, and a mucous discharge that seeps from the tip of the penis. If treatment is neglected, urination becomes more painful and the penis becomes sore. In extreme cases sterility can result. Females may also discharge pus, but it is often in such small amounts that it is not noticed. If the disease attacks the urethra, urination may be painful. If it isn't treated, the bacteria may move up the uterus during menstruation and settle in the fallopian tubes. When this happens, pelvic pain may result and in some cases menstruation will become painful and irregular. If it is not treated, scar tissue will develop in the fallopian tubes, causing sterility.

The treatment of gonorrhea is relatively simple. Two large injections of penicillin will generally cure the disease.

Syphilis

Although there are records of *syphilis* dating back well before Columbus, the exact cause of the disease wasn't identified until 1905. Syphilis is caused by spiral-shaped bacteria and can be diagnosed by a blood test. It is the fourth most common communicable disease in the United States. The first sign of syphilis is a chancre—a painless round sore with hard, raised edges. In males, the chancre appears on the penis or the scrotum. In females, it occurs most frequently on internal sex organs, where it is often unnoticed. The chancre usually appears within two to four weeks of exposure to syphilis and disappears within three to six weeks.

The disappearance of the chancre doesn't mean the disease is cured; it simply means that the bacteria have entered the bloodstream. The next symptoms are usually a rash and a low-grade fever, which begin six months after the appearance of the chancre. These symptoms last anywhere between a few months to a year, and they too disappear on their own. At this point, the disease enters the latent stage, where the bacteria burrow into the blood vessels, central nervous system, and bones. In the last stage of syphilis, which may not develop for several years, cardiovas-

cular or neurological problems may occur and the result can be death or psychosis.

Although syphilis is a terrible disease, the treatment is often relatively simple. Antibiotics such as penicillin and tetracycline generally kill the bacteria. The longer the individual has had the disease, however, the greater the doses of the antibiotics must be. Therefore, early detection and treatment of syphilis are very important. Also, in recent years strains of syphilis have emerged that are resistant to antibiotics. Great care should be taken to prevent it.

Genital Herpes

Genital herpes is caused by a virus similar to the one that causes cold sores in the mouth. This disease was rare in the United States before 1965, but its rate of incidence has increased so rapidly that it is now the second most common sexually transmitted disease. Genital herpes causes small blisters on the genitals that can be quite painful. The disease goes through repeated phases of being active and then dormant. An active phase lasts two to four weeks, and it is during this time that the virus can be transmitted to others. Often an active phase is triggered by fatigue or stress.

The problems associated with herpes are greater than the discomfort resulting in the active stage. In rare cases, the herpes virus can attack the fetus of an infected woman, causing a spontaneous abortion or infecting the brain of the infant after birth. A more likely possibility is that the baby can become infected during birth. For this reason, deliveries are performed by caesarean section if the mother is experiencing an active stage of herpes. There has also been some suggestion that herpes may be associated with cancer (Kessler, 1979).

Unlike the bacterial STDs, there is as yet no cure for herpes. The symptoms may be treated and the pain reduced, but no drug has been discovered that will kill the herpes virus.

Chlamydia and Urethritis

Chlamydia or *chlamydial infection* is becoming an extremely common sexually transmitted disease. Many women with the infection are symptom free, but some experience lower abdominal pain, inflammation, and vaginal discharge. Among men a chlamydial infection manifests itself as *urethritis*, an inflammation of the urethra. It is similar to gonorrhea but is caused by different bacteria and is more difficult to identify than gonorrhea. The symptoms are also similar to gonorrhea: a thin, clear discharge from the penis and pain during urination. The incidence of urethritis has been rapidly increasing over the years, and it is now more common among college students than gonorrhea is. The disease can be treated with antibiotics like tetracycline; unlike with gonorrhea, however, penicillin is not effective. This makes a correct diagnosis very important.

AIDS

Today when anyone talks about sexually transmitted diseases, the one that immediately comes to mind is **acquired immune deficiency syndrome (AIDS)**. In 1981, a Los Angeles physician began noticing a condition in gay men that destroyed their resistance to disease and ultimately ended in death. Careful research has found that this disease is caused by a virus similar to the virus that causes leukemia. The virus itself is not a killer; rather, it destroys the body's natural immune system. The individual then becomes susceptible to a host of diseases, especially pneumonia and a rare form of cancer, that cause death in a matter of months or a few years.

AIDS is transmitted by semen or blood. Over 70 percent of diagnosed AIDS victims are gay or bisexual men; it is believed that in these cases AIDS is transmitted by anal intercourse, which creates small lesions in tissues allowing the exchange of body fluids. Very recently, it has been shown that even oral sex can spread AIDS, so oral sex is no longer regarded as "safe sex." AIDS has also been found in intravenous drug users and people who have received transfusions with AIDS tainted blood. More recently, there has been an increasing number of exclusively heterosexuals diagnosed as having AIDS.

While AIDS is still rather rare, the numbers are frightening. Statistics from the U.S. Centers for Disease Control and Prevention show that in 1987 there were 21,000 cases reported in this country. That figure jumped to 42,000 in 1990 and 103,000 in 1993. There was some reduction in 1994, but the trend is generally upward. Furthermore, AIDS is fatal; half of those diagnosed as having AIDS have already died. In 1993 and 1994 combined, there were 71,000 deaths from AIDS. At present there is no cure for AIDS. Researchers throughout the world are searching for a cure, but none has yet been discovered.

AIDS or the fear of AIDS has already created major changes in our society. Many employers, including the army, have undertaken testing their employees for the AIDS antibodies; those found to have these antibodies may be denied employment. The fear of AIDS has led many gays to reduce their number of sexual partners and to alter their sexual activities. Legal questions have been raised concerning the rights of people with AIDS or AIDS antibodies to attend public schools or hold jobs. We are now seeing television stations airing ads for latex condoms that are effective in stopping the spread of AIDS. Clearly, we are only beginning to see the effects of AIDS. The hope is that safer sex practices will control the spread of AIDS and that researchers can develop a cure for or a vaccine against the AIDS virus.

10. The male sexual disorder characterized by an inability to *maintain* an erection once achieved in order to have intercourse is called _____ _____ dysfunction.

11. A female sexual dysfunction that results when the muscles surrounding the vagina involuntarily constrict to prevent penile penetration or to make penetration extremely painful is called _____.

12. Many, if not most, of the sexual dysfunctions are simply the result of _____.

13. Today in the United States the most prevalent sexually transmitted disease is _____.

14. Syphilis and gonorrhea are caused by bacteria; genital herpes and AIDS are caused by a _____.

15. The sexually transmitted disease that is most likely to be misdiagnosed as gonorrhea is _____.

16. T or F: AIDS is the most common sexually transmitted disease today.

SUMMARY

1. Despite the more liberal attitudes about sexual behavior today, many people are still very uninformed about sexuality.

2. Fantasy is an important part of sexual arousal; many people become sexually aroused by simply fantasizing or imagining sexual events or actions.

3. There are many similarities in the sexual responses of males and females. The first phase is the excitement phase, where sexual arousal may begin by touching, imagining sexual activity, or observing sexual stimuli. The second phase is the plateau phase, where physiological responses such as heartrate and breathing increase and swelling occurs in the penis and the vagina. The orgasm phase is experienced as a highly pleasurable release from tension. In men there are rhythmic contractions of the penis and ejaculation of semen. In women there are muscular contractions in the vagina and pulsations of the uterus. In the resolution phase the body gradually returns to normal, muscles relax, and there is often a calm feeling. Women may be stimulated back to orgasm during the resolution phase, but men enter a refractory phase, where they are unresponsive to sexual stimulation.

4. One of the first large surveys on sexual behavior in the United States was published by Alfred Kinsey in 1948.

5. One common sexual behavior is sexual fantasy, which is a thought or daydream that is sexually exciting.

6. The first and most common sexual experience for most people is masturbation, which is the self-manipulation of one's genitals to orgasm. The frequency of masturbation is highest during adolescence, but a majority of married people engage in masturbation. Although masturbation has long been considered an evil behavior by many people, there is no evidence that it is harmful, and it is used by many sex therapists in treating sexual dysfunctions.

7. While more people engage in premarital intercourse today than 50 years ago, the percentage of women who engage in this behavior has increased most dramatically. The frequency of men and women who have had premarital intercourse is becoming more similar, but women typically have had premarital sex with only two partners, while the average male has had six partners.

8. Married couples engage in sex on the average of two to four times a week; the frequency of coitus decreases with age, although many older couples continue to have active and satisfying sex lives.

9. Despite the fact that a majority of people believe that extramarital sexual relationships are wrong, half of the males and 40 percent of the females in a recent survey reported having had extramarital affairs. The likelihood of a male having an extramarital affair decreases with age, but the likelihood of a female engaging in extramarital sexual behavior increases with age up to age 40.

10. Homosexuality involves a sexual relationship between individuals of the same sex. Although in 1948 only about 2 percent of males and 1 percent of females in this country reported themselves as being exclusively homosexual, Kinsey found that almost 25 percent of males and 20 percent of females reported some homosexual experience in their lives. There are numerous theories about the factors that lead to homosexual preferences. Most now focus on hormonal and genetic factors, but some argue that early childhood experiences influence sexual orientation.

11. Contrary to some beliefs, about two-thirds of men and women remain sexually active into their seventies, although the frequency of sexual intercourse declines. Although both men and women experience physiological changes as they grow older, they are still capable of active and satisfying sexual lives.

12. Sexual behavior will be enjoyed more fully if people have realistic expectations, openly communicate with their partners, take the time to explore their partners' bodies and experience the sensations of touching, and choose a comfortable setting.

13. While alcohol and certain drugs may reduce inhibitions, they can also act as depressants and can work against full enjoyment of sexual behavior.

14. Birth control involves any method used to prevent the birth of children; contracep-

tion is one method of birth control. There are numerous types of contraceptives. Despite the easy availability of contraceptives today, there is evidence suggesting that college students are using less effective contraceptive methods today than they did five years ago.

15. Induced abortion has been used as a means of birth control for centuries, but it has become the center of a heated controversy between pro-choice and pro-life advocates in the United States.

16. Pornography is sexually arousing art, literature, or films. Hard-core pornography that falls into the category of obscenity often portrays violence such as rape and is degrading, especially to women. Although pornography does not have lasting effects on sexual behavior, research has found that pornography promotes violence.

17. Sexual dysfunctions refer to sexual difficulties that are frequent or long lasting. There are many causes, including physical or organic problems, failure to learn satisfying sexual behavior, and attitudes or emotions such as guilt. The more common sexual dysfunctions include erectile dysfunction, premature ejaculation, and retarded ejaculation in men and orgasmic dysfunction and vaginismus in women.

18. Sexually transmitted diseases are physical diseases that are transmitted through sexual contact. The most common is gonorrhea. Gonorrhea, syphilis, and nonspecific urethritis are caused by bacteria; genital herpes is caused by a virus. Early diagnosis of sexually transmitted diseases is important for treatment and to prevent their spread. The bacterial diseases can be treated with antibiotics, but at present there is no known cure for genital herpes. AIDS results from a virus (HIV) transmitted through blood and semen. It has no known cure and it is rapidly spreading. Although most victims are gay men, there are increasing numbers of heterosexual victims.

CRITICAL THINKING QUESTIONS

1. Why is extramarital sex so common? Do you think society should be stronger in condemning extramarital sex, or should we just accept extramarital sex as a natural part of life?

2. In what ways, if any, do you think pornography should be controlled? Would your controls draw a distinction between violent pornography and erotica that contained no violence?

3. Do you think that you learned about sexuality in a healthy and illuminating way? What recommendations would you make for families or social institutions, perhaps the church, school, or the medical profession, to convey better information to young people about sex?

MATCHING EXERCISE

Match each term with its definition.

a. AIDS
b. birth control
c. contraception
d. erotica

e. homosexuality
f. masturbation
g. menopause
h. orgasm

i. pornography
j. sexual dysfunction
k. sexually transmitted diseases

1. An intense physical and emotional experience often experienced at the climax of an act such as intercourse or masturbation
2. Method of birth control used to prevent conception
3. Sexual relations between individuals of the same sex
4. Physical diseases that are transmitted through sexual contact
5. Any method used to prevent the birth of children
6. Time in a woman's life when menstruation ceases and she is no longer capable of reproduction

7. Sexual problems that are frequent or long lasting
8. Self-manipulation of one's genitals to orgasm
9. Acquired immune deficiency that destroys resistance to disease
10. Sexually arousing material that rarely involves violence and is not degrading to women, men, or children
11. Sexually arousing art, literature, or films

Answers to Matching Exercise

a. 9   b. 5   c. 2   d. 10   e. 3   f. 8   g. 6   h. 1   i. 11   j. 7   k. 4

ANSWERS TO REVIEW QUESTIONS

1. plateau
2. refractory period
3. true

4. masturbation
5. false
6. e

7. false

8. false

9. vasectomy

10. secondary erectile

11. vaginismus

12. misinformation

13. gonorrhea

14. virus

15. nonspecific urethritis

16. false

CHAPTER 12

LIVING IN FAMILIES

The Kennedys

The Kennedys

The motorcade of John F. Kennedy, newly elected president of the United States, was just passing the stands where Joseph P. Kennedy, his father, and Rose Kennedy, his mother, were seated along with other members of their large family. Eunice Kennedy, Jack's sister recalled (Deane, 1992) that in that instant her father did a most unusual thing. He nodded and tipped his hat to Jack, his son, the President. As the first sign of any deference that she had seen her father—a very strong authority figure—make to any one of his children, it seemed so out of place to her. At the very same time, Jack rose to stand up in the convertible and tipped *his* hat to his father. Behind these simple parallel acts lay a great deal of meaning and a long history of family events.

The patriarch of the family was Joseph Kennedy, Sr., born 1888 in East Boston. Joseph Kennedy's father was a liquor dealer and political ward boss, the highest status an Irish-American could attain in those times. Joseph Kennedy was a smart, eager, confident boy who went to prestigious schools, including Harvard University, and was remembered for his competitiveness. Still, being Irish and Catholic, he was not considered acceptable for the "best" social clubs at Harvard. This insult and similar issues would haunt him and his family as they strove to be accepted by what his wife Rose called the "nice" people. Indeed, some consider Joseph Kennedy's humble beginnings as well as his personality to have fueled a driving ambition for wealth and power. There is no doubt that the senior Kennedy was very ambitious. By age 25, he was a bank president; by age 49, the American ambassador to Great Britain. In the interim, he married a "catch," Rose Fitzgerald, daughter of the influential mayor of Boston, John F. ("Honey Fitz") Fitzgerald.

The family settled in a Boston suburb, where Rose devoted her life to the home and children while Joe worked in New York, garnering wealth and power, sometimes by dubious means. In six years they had five children: Joseph, Jr.; John, named for his grandfather and called "Jack"; Rosemary, who was later diagnosed as mentally retarded; Kathleen; and Eunice. These were fol-lowed by Patricia, Robert, Jean, and finally Teddy, the youngest. The family had moved to Hyannisport, on Cape Cod. There were maids, tutors and other staff brought in for their care and education. There was sailing, boarding schools, and family games of touch football and other sports. They were an attractive, energetic, photogenic group, and the myth of the glamorous Kennedy clan began to grow.

But what was life like inside the Kennedy clan? Some historians and family friends described Joe Kennedy as a warm and affectionate father who kept a close hand in family life, while others describe him as domineering, unfaithful to his wife, and mentally abusive. Rose was less affectionate with her children. She was strictly religious and very demanding that the children's behavior and appearances be "proper." The marriage of Rose and Joe, Sr. was not close. Joe kept his family life compartmentalized from his other worlds of making money, power brokering, and womanizing, and Rose traveled frequently in Europe. One historian (Hamilton, 1992) noted that Rose never visited Jack while he was in boarding school, although she traveled frequently during that time period, and linked her emotional distance from the children to the emotional coldness that she felt from her husband.

Although they were a "clan" to the outside world, the Kennedy children were diverse in their personalities and roles. Their relationships with each other were shaped by their own temperaments and talents as well as by their father's ambitions and by world events. Joe, Jr. was a dutiful student and his father's favorite. His father's hope that he would become president was dashed when Joe, Jr. was killed in action in World War II. Their father's political ambitions then turned to Jack, an unlikely candidate in many ways. As the second son, he struggled unsuccessfully to keep up with his older brother. As a child, he was sickly, and as an adolescent and young adult he was the happy-go-lucky one, the risk taker, known in college more for his social life than for his studies. Rosemary, as a teenager, became difficult for the family to handle. When she was a young woman, the decision was made to have doctors give her a prefrontal lobotomy. This was a new operation at the time, and the procedure involved cutting parts of the brain of people who were retarded or mentally ill. The family hoped the operation would make her life easier, but it left her even more mentally disabled and she was sent to live in an institution, a secret that was never talked about publicly until after Joe, Sr. died. Kathleen, a vivacious, popular girl nicknamed "Kick," worked in London for the Red Cross during World War II as a young woman, then fell in love with, and married a Protestant man. Her marriage caused a family crisis. Rose was horrified and considered it "a blow to the family prestige," cabling Kathleen that she was "heartbroken." (Hamilton, 1992, p. 648). Kathleen was 24 when she married, the only one of the Kennedy girls to be married before they were 30.

These details about the four oldest children illustrate the complex picture that historians paint of the Kennedy family. On the one hand, a wealthy, successful, fun-loving family; on the other hand, a complex group of different individuals, all with their own interests, pressures and strains. Plus two parents with strong domineering personalities, a sense of striving and competing, a sense of being "outsiders" socially, and, even in the early years, a hint of tragedy hanging over them.

The Kennedy children grew up and started families of their own while remaining very close to their family of origin. Jack, still wielding power, money, and influence with his father, rose to Congress and then to the presidency, beating more experienced opponents along the way. He was a glamorous, charming candidate whose appeal and popularity were buoyed by the charm of his wife.

Jacqueline Bouvier was an elegant, educated young reporter of 24 when she met Jack, then 37. They brought two young children to the White House. Jack, like his father, appreciated the power of images that photographs and the new medium of television could provide, and the nation watched charming pictures of his own children cavorting in the White House. His father had always told the children, "You must remember, it's not who you are, but who people think you are" (Deane, 1992).

Indeed, their adult lives echoed some old family themes. When JFK was president, his younger brother Robert was Attorney General and his brother's closest advisor. "In a crisis," said John, "family members are the only ones you can count on." When JFK was assassinated Rose was stoic as Bobby, devastated, assumed the role of caretaker of the family, his own eight children as well as Jackie's and his parents. Bobby's own subsequent bid for the presidency was again heavily influenced by his father as well as by his own dreams and values, which by that time had become significantly different from his father's. Sadly, he was assassinated shortly after winning the California primary, in 1968. Ted Kennedy would go on to become the family caretaker and a distinguished senator from Massachusetts. Like many youngest children, Teddy had been open, optimistic, and cheerful. But his adulthood was darkened by the deaths of his siblings as well as his own personal difficulties. Joseph, Sr. died in 1969, having been mute and incapacitated from a stroke for eight years previously. Rose died at age 104, having campaigned into her eighties for her sons. There are sixteen Kennedy grandchildren, some in public service, whose own family stories are still being written.

WHAT IS A FAMILY?

The Kennedy family history is intertwined with national history. Three of its sons were national political figures, and the Kennedy name is associated with programs such as the Peace Corps and legislation to secure the rights of and provide services for retarded citizens. The history of the Vietnam War, the Cold War, and the civil rights movement all included Kennedys as major figures. In this sense, they are unlike most ordinary families.

In many other senses, however, we see in the Kennedy family the same dynamics and elements in all families. Events in the world, such as World War II, and prejudice against immigrants, shaped their collective and individual lives as they have shaped many families'. As in ordinary families, the fears and strivings of the Kennedy parents were not theirs alone but got visited upon the children in the form of do's and dont's, pressures, and opportunities. The family, whether it is "famous" or not, is a complex entity with many interesting facets. Children delight and also disappoint their parents. Birth order and sibling rivalries help shape the future of individual family members. Relationships between people change as the family grows older; those who were taken care of as children later become the caretakers.

In this chapter we examine the family from a psychological perspective, with a particular focus on how families influence the adjustment of the individual person. We first tackle the task of defining "family," which itself raises interesting issues. Following this, we ask, "What makes a happy family?" and discuss the characteristics of families that function well and those that do not. Since families grow and change with their members, we then describe the family life cycle and the different challenges and opportunities throughout the family life cycle. The chapter moves to discussions of divorce and remarriage as normal family transitions and ends with a section on resources for families who need help coping with transitions and crises.

The Stereotype

Before we can discuss living in families, we must first provide a definition. Just what is a "family?" That question is perhaps harder now to answer than it was in the generation in which John F. Kennedy and his siblings grew up. It's even harder to answer than it was twenty years ago. The U.S. Census bureau defines a **family** as a household in which two or more people related by marriage, birth, or adoption live together.

The stereotype of the traditional family includes a mother, father, and two or more children, who live in their own home, perhaps with a sport utility vehicle, a dog, and a cat.

The father goes to work and the mother stays home and runs the household. There are at least two generations living in the house, but there may be more, such as a grandparent. This was the post–World War II suburban family reflected in 1950s television shows (and their reruns!) such as *Leave It to Beaver* and *Ozzie and Harriet. The Cosby Show,* and *Roseanne* might be seen as modern versions of that image. They depict slightly more diverse families in terms of race, social class, and the mother's work status, but still hold to the "mom-dad-and-biological kids" definition of the family.

The Reality

Upon closer inspection, however, we find that this definition does not fully fit modern U.S. families, who are much more diverse. According to the Census Bureau in 1992, the most common family was married couples without children (28 percent), followed closely by married couples with children (27 percent). (Compare the last figure with 1970, in which 39 percent of households were married couples with children.) Interestingly, in the 1992 report, almost the same percentage of households were comprised of people living alone (25 percent); this is because younger people are putting off marriage longer, and the elderly are living longer. Single mothers with children comprise 7.4 percent of households and single fathers with children, 1.3 percent of households (*Statistical Abstracts of the United States,* 1992). Both of these have increased since the 1960s.

So has the frequency of births to single women. In the U.S. in 1989, 27 percent of all births were to unmarried women, compared to only 5 percent in 1960 (Ahlburg & DeVita, 1992). What are the characteristics of the single mothers? (Collins & Coltrane, 1995). It used to be that they were primarily teenagers, but presently a majority (one-third) of all nonmarried births are to women over 20. This trend is more pronounced among black mothers (two-thirds are unmarried) and Hispanic mothers (one-third are unmarried) than among white mothers (one-fifth) are unmarried, although it is rising in all groups.

What about those families with married couples? Are they really less likely to stay married than in the 1950s, as the popular belief holds? The answer is "Yes, but..." The most commonly quoted statistic is that today one in two marriages will eventually end in divorce. The "but" part of the answer, however, is that the divorce rate has actually fallen and stabilized after it peaked in the early 1980s. Still, 75 percent of black children and 40 percent of white children live in families in which there is a divorce or separation before age 16: these households are single parent households for an average of five years. (Bumpass & Sweet, 1989). Thus at present 25 percent of all children live in single parent households.

Another demographic change in families is that people are having fewer children than they did in the 1950s, when many men came home from service in World War II, anticipating family life in peacetime and giving rise to the "baby boom." Again, however, the average number of children per family reached an all-time low in the 1980s and is climbing back up slightly. The average family in the 1950s had "3.7" children, in 1976, "1.7" children and today, "2.1" children.

Even families with two parents cannot be assumed to fit the stereotype described earlier. First, of those families with children, both parents are likely to be working either full or part time. The stereotyped 1950s family in which only the father works outside the home fits fewer than 20 percent of today's families (Collins & Coltrane, 1995). Second, a two-parent family in the 1990's may also be headed by gay and lesbian couples with children. Whereas previously there were a small number of such families with children and those children were usually from previous marriages, there is now a growing number of gay and lesbian families with children through adoption or birth via surrogate mothers, artificial insemination, and the like. Lesbians are more likely to be mothers (one in three is a mother) than gay men are to be fathers (about one in ten) (Collins & Coltrane, 1995). Another common family configuration is a cohabitating (nonmarried) couple with children; about one in three such couples of opposite sex have children. This form of family life has become both increasingly common (though it is still small compared to married families) and increasingly accepted in the United States (Collins & Coltrane, 1995).

To summarize all of these facts, the reality is that in the United States today there are many different kinds of families. Contrary to some reports, the family as an institution is not "dead." People are still marrying, making committed relationships, and having children. They are just doing it in somewhat different configurations than they did in earlier times. In fact, the general public has a fairly inclusive definition of the family. In a poll, 74 percent of Americans defined a family not by whether they were related, but by whether they were group of people who loved and cared for one another (Seligman, 1989). Psychologists point out (Edwards, 1995) that these "nontraditional families" face the same tasks and many of the same problems of "traditional" families: communication, money-management, childrearing issues, sex, and resolving conflicts. All families have the common task of providing a safe and nurturing place for individuals to grow and develop, at all stages of life. Having a "happy family"—however one defines family—is a goal of many people. In the next section we address the question of what makes families happy or unhappy, healthy or unhealthy. As we will see, these are not distinct categories but occur rather on a continuum from the most happy and healthy to the least so.

Family Habits

Although Tolstoy (1918) might disagree, all happy families are not alike, at least in the habits and everyday concrete details of their family life. Indeed, American families vary widely in their norms or customs, in part because in the United States people come from many cultural backgrounds.

How would you rate the family in which you grew up on these items? Take the following quiz and compare your answer with those of your friends and classmates. The differences and similarities should make for an interesting discussion.

True or False?

1. In our family, everyone sits down to dinner together every night.

2. Cursing is common in our family, but no one takes it personally.

3. Great respect and deference is shown to the elders in our family, even if one disagrees privately with them.

4. In our house, people typically leave the doors to their rooms open.

5. The mother is the one who has the final say about family matters.

6. The father is the one who has final say about family matters.

7. All decisions in our family are made by majority vote.

8. The television is often playing during mealtime in my family.

9. Everyone who is working outside the home, including teenagers, contributes financially to the family accounts.

10. It would be a source of conflict in my family if people practiced different religions.

11. Pets are not a part of our family life.

WHAT MAKES A "HAPPY" FAMILY?

In the the beginning of the Russian novel *Anna Karenina,* (Tolstoy, 1918), Leo Tolstoy wrote "All happy families are alike; every unhappy family is unhappy in its own way." If this is true, then we all—parents, children, and young adults about to start new families of their own—would like to know *how* happy families are alike. When people are fortunate enough to be able to claim, sincerely, "I come from a happy family," others want to know what their family was like, and what their parents did, that made it a happy family. Many variables need to be considered in trying to define a "happy" or a "healthy" family. These include the cohesiveness of the family (whether it "feels" and "acts" like a close group rather than a collection of distant individuals), the ability of the family to let individual members grow and develop, the psychological health of its members, the mood tone in the family, affection and intimacy, and how well the family interacts with the larger community surrounding it.

Optimal Families

The Beavers Systems Model (Beavers, 1982; Beavers & Hampson, 1990) provides a way of thinking about successful families that incorporates many of these variables. Let's examine first their general description of the *optimal family.*

Characteristics of Optimal Families. First, optimal (Beavers & Hampson, 1990) family members realize that they are interdependent on one another; that each of them can satisfy their needs and help satisfy the others' needs through their relationships. No one is only a "taker" or only a "giver" in the family. Optimal families also have clear boundaries. For example, the parents do not draw children into their conflicts, and they set appropriate boundaries around parent and child subsystems. "This is between me and your father, not you" and "Because parents have to set some rules, that's why" are responses that children don't always like to hear but that ultimately help define clear family roles.

This is not to say that optimal families do not talk to each other and explain their thoughts, feelings, and behaviors; indeed, clear communication is another hallmark of the such families. Clear family communication allows the members to experience empathy. Family members are able to relate to each other's feelings and emotions rather than being cold and distant. There is a happy intimacy. Finally, optimally healthy families have the ability to accept change, growth, and loss as inevitable and natural aspects of family life. Having a set of transcendent values or beliefs, whether traditional, religious, or unique, helps the family to sustain a sense of meaningful connection even as it allows individual members autonomy to grow and develop. Shared beliefs such as "We are a family that looks out for each other," "We are a family that helps others in need," or "We are an athletic family" help strengthen family identity. Even assumptions or family beliefs that are not conscious or explicit help bind the family together as a unit (Reiss, 1981).

Cultural and Ethnic Variations. It is important to note here that there are cultural and ethnic variations in optimal family life, variations that depend on the particular values in the larger group to which the family belongs. Families in Japan, for example, place less emphasis on the independence and separateness of the individuals and more emphasis on connections with the extended family group. This is illustrated in the names that children are given. For example, family name comes first to give it priority over the individual's name: "Bill Smith" becomes "Smith Bill." People address each other according to their social rank in the family, such as "younger sister," or "elder brother." Expectations of what is considered proper, loyal, and loving family behavior differ from those in Western countries, which are more likely to emphasize independence and autonomy. Even within the United States there is variation based on culture, gender, and local values in what is considered happy or healthy family behavior (see the Lessons from the Laboratory box). Moreover, family functioning is influenced by the intersection of cultures when they meet (Koss-Chioino & Canive, 1995). Szapocznik, Kurtines, and Fernandez (1980) have observed clinically that conflict in Cuban-American families increases as the children become more acculturated to American lifestyles and values, which disrupts the traditional hierarchy of authority within the family. Similarly, placing values and expectations of family need above individual need get disrupted in Mexican immigrant families as the members become more individualistic about their personal resources; consequently the balance between control and support is also disrupted (Mirowsky & Ross, 1987).

In addition, please note that we are not suggesting that families who do not show all of these ideal characteristics all of the time are dysfunctional. Rather, such families may be functional and healthy and raise competent children but with somewhat more tension,

Using Research to Study Family Health

Many family variables can potentially affect the competence of children in families. How and where do family researchers begin to study them? A study by Brody, Stoneman, and Flor (1996), called "Parental Religiosity, Family Process, and Youth Competence in Rural, Two-Parent African-American Families" provides an illustration of how important questions about families can be studied in a meaningful way.

The *first step* is to formulate research questions. Past findings, theory, and clinical or practical knowledge of families are all sources of research questions. Brody and colleagues focused on youth competence in rural African-American families. Since previous research found that religiousness can ease adjustment to stressful life events and since the church is often a central and cohesive force in the African-American community, they asked: Is parental religiousity associated with youth competence? And if so, what are the family processes the provide the link between religiosity and youth competence?

The *second step* is to measure these variables. They used self-report questionnaires and tests to measure religiosity and various aspects of family functioning (conflict, cohesion) and youth competence (self-control, academic competence,

and the absence of behavior problems). They also videotaped the family's interaction twice, once while they played a board game and the other time while they discussed the question of why *they* thought some children from the community "make it" in life and some do not.

The *third step* is to use statistical methods to analysis all the data. In this study some complex statistical techniques were used to determine the relationships among these variables while controlling for the effects of family income.

The findings? Higher levels of religiosity were correlated with family cohesion and less parental conflict, which were in turn related to fewer youth behavior problems. They concluded that "formal religiosity enhances norms that govern close interpersonal relationships, regardless of family financial resources (Brody, Stoneman, & Flor, 1996, p. 703). Also, religiosity was indirectly related to academic competence in that it was correlated with youth self-regulation, which in turn was correlated with academic competence. Brody and colleagues also noted that future research was needed to determine how generalizable the results were to urban African-American families and to white families.

---

conflict, and discouragement. Perhaps there is a parent in the family who is somewhat stressed or depressed. Perhaps there is a young adult who never quite lived up to the parents' expectations and experiences guilt and anxiety over this, even though she is successful in her own way. Perhaps one person feels somewhat constricted by the closeness of the family, whereas other people long for more closeness. Most families fit this middle ground. The Kennedy family did, too.

In fact, the Beavers model (Beavers & Hampson, 1990) allows for a range of family health or competence, from optimal to "severely dysfunctional." In between these extremes, in descending order of health, are "adequate" families," "midrange" families, "borderline" families, and then the "severely dysfunctional" families. A brief look at the characteristics of these types of families will provide a feel for the distinctions between them.

Adequate Families

In *adequate families* (Beavers & Hampson, 1990) there is still a good deal of health, with fairly clear boundaries and communication between parents and children and among the members of these subsystems. Their negotiations with each other are fraught with some pain, conflict, or ambivalence, but there are periods of warmth and sharing as glue to hold them together emotionally. Beavers and Hampson's (1990) research has shown that sex roles and other roles are more stereotyped and rigid in these families than in optimal families. People are more stuck in their assigned jobs and privileges and there is some discomfort on the part of individuals who wish to break out of these roles, and conflict when they attempt to. The parents are committed to parenting and work at it. The children in adequate families are unlikely to develop behavioral problems or psychiatric disturbances. On this last dimension, the Kennedy family seemed to be in the adequate range. Both parents clearly cared about their children and put their energy into raising the children, albeit in different ways. On other dimensions, as we will discuss shortly, the Kennedy family seemed to be more of a "midrange" family.

Midrange Families

Moving down the continuum of family competence, other families are considered **midrange** (Beavers, 1982; Beavers & Hampson, 1990) in their functioning. In this type of family, there are a few more problems than in the families previously discussed. The members of midrange families experience some pain and unhappiness, largely because they have not learned how to be close and intimate with each other without being controlling and domineering, or how to give each other enough independence without being distant. There is evidence that this balance was sometimes a source of tension in the Kennedy family. For example, even as young adults, the Kennedy children were regularly watched by private detectives hired by their father. Ambassador Kennedy also investigated their friends' backgrounds, moves that made some of them seek distance from the family in various ways. For Kathleen, it was physical dis-

tance, seen in her move to England; for others, it was emotional distance.

There are also power struggles in midrange families, which may be expressed in open competition and arguing or in hidden conflict. Even more personality stereotyping occurs, forcing individuals into set roles, which are then difficult to grow out of, such as: "Joe, Jr. is the ambitious one; Jack is the partier." In midrange families there is often a troubled, or distant relationship between the parents, was seen in the Kennedy family. The family's many strengths and possibilities were somewhat darkened by the distant relationship between Joe and Rose. Also, there may be coalitions between one parent and a child (or children) against the other parent. When children hear their parents talk negatively about each other, for example, it puts them in a very uncomfortable position. First, they feel sad to hear negative things about a parent, even if that parent does have faults. Second, they feel divided loyalties and confusion. They wonder if they should agree with the parent who is complaining about the other, or should they disagree or defend the parent who is being criticized? Should they keep this information to themselves, or tell the other parent? If this kind of situation continues in the family, children may form unhealthy alliances (e.g., Dad and daughter against mother) or learn to play their parents against each other to get what they want. While this may be satisfying to the child in the short run (e.g., she plays both parents against each other to get her curfew raised), it is damaging in the long run because the child develops a cynical, untrusting attitude toward adults.

As you might imagine, the children in such families are less interested in spending their free time at home and are more likely than other children to spend their time elsewhere as they grow into adolescence. If and when they get into trouble there, the parents are likely to have some trouble in working together to set limits and rules, express affection, and do all of those things that strengthen the child's sense of security and trust. Family therapy or counseling at this point can be very helpful. While the children in midrange families typically do not grow up to be seriously disordered adults, they are more likely to experience problems in school, at work, and getting along with others. They may become adults who seek psychological help for problems such as depression, excessive anxiety, and problems having happy relationships with others. Others may have some trouble following society's rules. Overall, however, they do not have major psychiatric problems or present a major threat to others around them.

Borderline Families

In **borderline families** (Beavers & Hampson, 1990), there are far fewer satisfactions than pleasures. The marital relationship is very weak, with one member very dominant and controlling and the other submissive and passive. There are either overt coalitions of one parent and children against the other parent or covert but destructive coalitions. There is significant conflict. In some families this takes the form of shouting, hostile attacks, and blaming others. In others this takes a more internalized form, in which verbal expressions of angry, control, and rebellion are not allowed. Instead, family members "retreat and protect themselves through patterned rituals and attempts at individuation or attention-seeking" (Beavers & Hampson, 1990, p. 51). Individual psychological problems of various kinds are more likely to occur in some borderline families. In addition, this kind of environment is a breeding ground for the kinds of psychological disorders that are associated with serious disturbances in the ability to sustain satisfying relationships outside of the family, e.g., borderline personality disorder (see Chapter 7).

Severely Dysfunctional Families

Finally, there are those families who can be considered *severely dysfunctional* (Beavers & Hampson, 1990). The following are some characteristics of these families.

Characteristics of Severely Dysfunctional Families. Like borderline families, these families also feature weak parental coalition and an emotional atmosphere that not only lacks warmth and affection but is also highly cynical, angry, resentful, and depressed. It is almost as if the family has given up—on each other, on themselves, and on their interests and goals. Moreover, there is a serious lack of effective communication. The members find it difficult to share a focus of conversation and to answer each other directly. For example, a son might say, "I heard you and Dad yelling last night" and the mother might say, "Oh, was the cat out?" Sometimes families with severe communication difficulties do not even seem to make sense when they speak. Their communication also may reflect a family environment that is overly close or emotional overinvolvement (Leff & Vaughn, 1985). In such families, there are few boundaries between people: "I'm cold; put on your sweater" is the classic example. Or people may speak for each other and make decisions for each other long after it is developmentally appropriate to do so. One study of a 29-year-old psychiatric hospital patient marked overinvolvement. In the mother's words, "Geraldine's always been at home with me, and she's always willing to do anything for me. I wouldn't want her to get a job; there's so much for me to do, and she's a help".... "She's not interested in marriage, no. I don't really want her to marry, I would miss her. Anyway, marriages aren't very happy, are they? No, I'm happy to have her home: She would never listen to anybody else if not to me" (Leff & Vaughn, 1985, p. 55). Children are expected to remain close and loyal to the family, but those that do often do so at the expense of their adjustment to the larger world or their own mental health.

Rather than too much closeness, some other severely dysfunctional families show none at all. Parents come and go, children run away and return; harsh punishment, cold words, and rejection are common. There is little expression of caring and no consistent rewards or punishments. Children who grow up in such families are at risk for becoming delinquent youths and antisocial adults who pose a threat to others. Having a conscience and a sense of morality requires that one has had a close emotional connection with a caregiver in childhood (see Chapter 2). These early relationships give human beings a basis for forming connections with other people later in life. Sadly, some children never have a chance for this. A dramatic example of this is provided in the family story of Gary Gilmore, as told by his brother, Mikal Gilmore (1994) in a book called *Shot in the Heart.* The family of three boys, a mother, and a father who was there on and off, was characterized by physical and emotional cruelty. This environment turned brother against brother, and eventually, against others as well. Both older boys went on to a lifetime of antisocial and violent acts. In Gary's case, the cycle ended in the senseless murder of a young clerk and in his own conviction and execution.

Specific Issues in Family Dysfunction: Child Abuse.   Child abuse represents a specific issue in dysfunctional family life. Not all families with serious problems abuse their children. However, when child abuse does occur, it is a sign that there is a serious problem in the family. Physical child abuse is the intentional use of force (striking, punching, beating with objects) on a child, typically with the purpose of hurting the child. It may be called "discipline" by the parent, but it goes beyond the occasional spanking. Child sexual abuse is sexual contact between a child and adult for

the sexual gratification of the adult. It is not the kind of exploratory "sex play" that is common in many siblings close to the same age.

Unfortunately, close to 2 million children in the United States are physically abused every year, and 2,000–4,000 of the cases end in the child's death (Comer, 1992). Some studies estimate that one of every four U.S. women have had sexual contact with a relative during their childhood (Russel, 1984). Although this figure has recently been contested, most studies indicate that it is a major mental health problem (Trepper & Niedner, 1995). Contrary to the stereotype of the "dirty old man offering candy," the vast majority of sexual abuse occurs with someone the child knows. Statistically, a stepfather, brother, or father is most likely to abuse a girl. Reports of sexual abuse of boys are less common, but authorities feel that boys are victims more often than the statistics show. Families in which there are high levels of stress, substance abuse, and social isolation are at particular risk (Trepper & Niedner, 1995). There is an usually high incidence of sexual abuse in the childhood histories of abusers; one-third of the fathers and stepfathers and over half of the mothers were found to have been abused themselves in one study (Faller, 1989). However, the majority of adult abusers were not abused themselves as children (Kaufman & Zigler, 1987).

Both physical abuse and sexual abuse of children teach exactly the opposite of what the family is supposed to teach a child. Physical abuse teaches that the way to handle anger or frustration is to hit someone, that power and force are the best means to social ends, and the child is "bad." Sexual abuse teaches that the child is merely an object of other people, to be used by powerful others. It is often done in great secrecy, and its disclosure is often accompanied by shame and fear, which reinforces that child's sense of himself or herself as "bad." Sexual abuse can rob children of their self-esteem, their chance to learn in school, and their ability to form satisfying relationships with others both as children and as adults. Because children experience the other adults in their life, such as the mother if the perpetrator is a father, as unable or unwilling to take care of them, it also interferes with those other important relationships. Both kinds of abuse rob children of a sense of control over their lives and bodies, and perhaps most important, of the ability to trust. From the child's point of view, if one is betrayed by the very person who is supposed to protect one, who can be trusted? Indeed, difficulties in trusting others can be a longstanding problem for incest survivors. Finally, physical violence and sexual abuse combined are an especially devastating combination. For some of these children, the only means of coping is to dissociate, or "space out," by putting themselves in a kind of trance; this is the precursor to dissociative identity disorder, discussed in Chapter 7.

We hope it is clear that these severely dysfunctional families represent extremes of family functioning. Although all families experience troubles now and then, most children grow up to be happy and healthy. Perhaps the most important characteristic of a healthy family is its ability to change and grow as the members within it grow and develop. Like the hermit crab, which sheds its shell and finds a larger one as its body grows, the family must change, too. The ways of expressing affection and anger; the nature of the rules, restrictions, and privileges; the family jobs and even people's rooms are all different in your family now than they were when you were 3 years old. And they will continue to change throughout your life. Because of this change and development, psychologists refer to the family itself as having a life cycle (Duvall, 1977). The family life cycle depends, in part, on the physical growth and development of its members. As we will see, other factors such as poverty, national policies, and gender, also have an impact on the family life cycle.

REVIEW QUESTIONS

1. What are some ways in which the families of today differ demographically from the families of the 1970s?

2. The Beavers Systems Model suggests that there is a continuum of family competence.

What are the different types of families, in order from the most healthy to the least?

3. Child sexual abuse is more likely to be perpetrated by _____ (strangers, relatives).

THE FAMILY LIFE CYCLE: HOW FAMILIES GROW WITH THEIR MEMBERS

Families have a **life cycle** and go through stages, just as their members do. Duvall (1977) divided these stages according to the entry and departure of various family members, and others have followed his lead. These include family therapists Betty Carter and Monica McGoldrick (1989), whose work also incorporates a focus on changes in the family life cycle and on gender. They discuss several key stages in the family life cycle: being a new couple, becoming parents for the first time and having young children, being a family with adolescents, launching young adult children and the transition back to being a couple, and finally, being a family in retirement and later life (Duvall, 1977). They note that there are, of course, variations on this sequence. In

some families children are born before the
parents have had a chance to live as a couple
together. In other families, children are born
to single mothers. Some children are born
very early in parents' lives, so that the parents
may also be grandparents at age 40, while in
other families the parents are new parents at
age 40 and may still be launching children
well into their own retirement. Despite the
family variations created by life circumstances and individual choices, however, for
all families, and at every stage of the family
life cycle, there are changes to adjust to, new
challenges to be met, and new opportunities
for satisfying relationships. In this section we
examine these stages in turn, with concrete
examples from everyday life that illustrate
family dynamics.

The New Couple

It is interesting that this stage of the family life
cycle is viewed by many people as the most
romantic, yet the early years of marriage account for the highest rates of divorce (Collins
& Coltrane, 1995). When a couple get married
or begin living together, they also begin a long
process of learning—learning about each
other's habits and values, negotiating everything from how to handle money, religion,
work and free time to which relatives to visit
on which holidays. Habits and assumptions
that are taken for granted in one's own family
may be different from those in the partner's
family (McGoldrick, 1989). All couples can remember arguments when they were newly
together that seem silly later; some actual
examples from clinical experience include
whether it's better to drink water or milk with
meals, whether mayonnaise or mustard is
better on sandwiches, whether it's best to set
the alarm early so that you can hit the snooze
button several times before getting up versus
setting the alarm for the waking time so that
the last minutes of sleep are not disturbed by
the buzzing alarm. These are among the more

trivial examples of differences, and they are
easier to resolve than the larger issues, such as
those involving work, independence, values,
and children.

If the new couple come from different
ethnic or cultural backgrounds, they will find
other interesting (sometimes amusing and
sometimes not) situations that need to be ne-
gotiated. One Jewish couple whose families
came from different parts of the world (one
from Europe and the other from the Middle
East) discovered that in her family it was an
honor to name an infant after a living relative
(and almost an insult if you did not) whereas
in his family it was considered bad luck (and
almost a curse) to name an infant after a living
relative.

The nature and timing of the new couple
stage is more variable than it used to be. People are waiting longer to get married. There is
some evidence (Glick, 1984) that this delay
may be beneficial. Women who marry very
young (before age 20) are twice as likely to get
divorced as those who marry after 20; women
who marry after age 30 are actually less likely
to get divorced. Also, more people are living
with one or more persons before they get married. These facts mean that marriage is less of
a major turning point in the life cycle (for
example, fewer young people are moving
directly out of their parents' home into marriage). However, it still carries with it added
meaning and added adjustments even if the
couple has been living together.

If the couple is a gay or lesbian couple,
there are additional adjustments besides those
already discussed (McGoldrick, 1989). These
include the decisions about when, whether,
and with whom to reveal their relationship;
dealing with the possible disapproval of parents and society; and defining their identity as
an adult couple within their extended families
and circle of friends. Some researchers find
that like the unmarried adult child, lesbians
tend to be perceived as late adolescents even if
they are in a committed relationship (Krestan

& Bepko, 1980). Life transitions in heterosexuals, such as marriage, are often marked by rituals that help legitimize the new stage of life. These rituals are more likely to be missing in the life cycle of people in nontraditional relationships, and sometimes new rituals need to be established (McGoldrick, 1989). Moreover, the state in which they live may not legally recognize their relationship or their rights to the same financial and insurance advantages of marriage. Their families may hesitate to include them both in family gatherings or may balk at introducing the partner to the extended family at gatherings. These issues and decisions, large and small, shape the identity of the new couple and their family.

Marriage or a committed relationship also brings with it adjustments to other new relationships, with each other's parents, siblings, and extended families. The first question many people in newly committed couples have is what to call the other's parents. "Mrs G.," which was okay before the wedding, may seem too formal, but "Shirley" may seem too familiar and "Mom" may seem strangely intimate. These choices are a reflection of the recognition that one's role in the relationships is changing and an uncertainty about how it will evolve. With luck, that uncertainty is also full of hope and promise.

The Family with Young Children

Not all families include children, as some couples are childless by choice and others are unable to have children. If and when children are added to the family, however, a new set of developmental tasks arises. If there are two parents in the home, the couple must now learn how to relate to each other as mother and father while struggling to find the time and energy to continue to relate to each other as a couple and to maintain a sense of their own personal identities (Bradt, 1989). If the personalities of the people or their life circumstances do not permit this, the couple may

grow farther and farther apart, as with Rose and Joe Kennedy, Sr. For single parents, the challenge of maintaining relationships with other adults is multiplied and may be accompanied by loneliness if the parent does not have loyal family or friends nearby for social support. It is very easy, and often necessary, to focus on the needs of the baby or children rather than on oneself or one's spouse. The time that one used to spend listening to and talking with one's spouse, going out with friends, pursuing professional and recreational interests, even keeping the house clean, seems to disappear into thin air. The physical demands of simply feeding, changing, and putting a new baby to sleep are constant; add to this the time spent playing with the baby and keeping some semblance of order in the house. As the baby grows, less time is spent in physical care taking but more in interacting with and keeping the child safe as he or she becomes a more active and mobile person. It is clear to see how adding children represents a major, perhaps the most profound, change to a family.

Adjustments in the Couples Relationship. Family experts agree on two things. First, this period marks a drop in marital satisfaction. One study found that couples with young children rated their marital satisfaction lower during this stage of the family life cycle than during any other, and this is particularly true for women (Belsky, Perry-Jenkins, & Crouter, 1985). (Another study found that although the drop started here, its very lowest point was in the later teen years (Collins & Coltrane, 1995).) Second, those couples who have established a strong sense of intimacy before the child arrives survive it best. Couples who have managed to do this respond better to the challenges of parenthood and are able to balancing out the increased tensions pleasurable experiences as well.

Fathers of today spend considerably more time interacting with their children in both caretaking and playing than did the fathers of the 1950s (Collins & Coltrane, 1995). (In fact, by all accounts, Joe Kennedy, Sr. was unusual for his generation in the close attention he paid to the everyday lives and habits of his children.) And there is great variation across families, and across cultures, in how much men and women share in the work at home. Perhaps the most important variable in this, at least in the United States, is whether both parents or just one is working outside the home. However, studies have found that in the average family with young children, even when both people work full time outside the home, women do more of the domestic work (housework and child care) than their husbands and live-in boyfriends. In an interview study of working parents, Hochschild (1989) found that the mothers were more likely than fathers to work a "second shift" at home in addition to their "first shift" jobs. By the "second shift" she was referring to the hours that the women put in, after their normal workday outside the home, on cooking, cleaning, grocery shopping, laundry, child care, and other domestic duties. When the fathers shared more in domestic chores, both parents reported that they felt stressed by not having enough time to "do it all," but women especially reported feeling pulled in many directions and drained of energy. Some women report that this is a factor in their decision to leave the workforce when their children are small, and psychologists have worried about the negative effects of "role-strain" on working parents, especially mothers (Clay, 1995). On the other hand, there is solid evidence that wives employed outside the home have higher self-esteem and are less likely to be depressed than mothers of small children who are full-time homemakers and that working women with husbands who share child-care responsibilities have a lower than average chance of depression (Ross & Mirowsky, 1987; Collins & Coltrane, 1995).

Adjustments in Other Relationships.   In addition to transformations in the couples' relationship and household routines, the addition of a new child causes transformations in extended family relationships. Parents are no longer the "kids" in the family; rather, their own parents are likely to be fussing and showering attention on the baby. This can make the new parents feel somewhat neglected and wistful of the times when they were the focus of attention, even if it wasn't that long ago when they wished that their parents would be less attentive. Young single mothers who are still teenagers can find this loss of attention especially difficult. New babies can also bring a change in the extended family's closeness. Some families draw closer once grandchildren are born, and it becomes time for reconciling old conflicts; in others, the nuclear family draws further away from the family of origin and into itself.

Within the family, adding new children shifts the nature of sibling relationships as well. The oldest is the first to adjust, and often does so ambivalently, to the birth of the second child. There is an old joke about a 9-year-old new brother who, when asked what if anything he would like to change about the new baby, replied, "His address." One little boy stated suddenly, while looking into the bassinet at his new sister, "Let's take her back to the hospital where we got her." This attitude may alternate with adoration and disinterest. From then on, over many years as children and even as adults, the siblings compete and cooperate, play and fight and make up (see the accompanying Lessons from Life).

Through interactions with each other as well as with parents, siblings learn many social skills, and develop their own personalities. Did Jack Kennedy's position as the middle child have an effect on his personality? Possibly. His own political talents and ambitions were certainly secondary to Joe's in his father's eyes until after Joe's untimely death.

Siblings: Can't Live with Them, Can't Live Without Them

Do you have favorite family stories about your interactions with your brothers and sisters? Or have you heard some of your parents' stories?

Family psychologists believe that such stories, along with all their embellishments and contested details, reveal the psychological dynamics between siblings. The following story is told by Kevin, an adult with children of his own, as a significant one about his family.

Kevin was 10 years old, and his twin brothers, Dan and David, were 8½ years old. Kevin's most prized possession was a baseball that his aunt had caught during a Pittsburgh Pirates game and given to him. Even better, it was autographed by Roberto Clemente, arguably one of the greatest right field-

ers in baseball history and a Hall of Fame member. The ball sat on his dresser.

One day when Kevin was not home, Dan and David needed a ball to play with. They took the ball and used it for hours. When they were done, they discovered that the autograph had rubbed off! Fearful of Kevin's reaction, they panicked and threw it in a pile of burning leaves. Not only was the autograph destroyed, but so was the ball!

What do you make of this story? Kevin considers it to be a fine example of how having not one but two younger siblings close in age can be a trial. Happily, however, they are all good friends as adults.

Generalizations about birth order, however, must be tempered by a number of other important variables, including ethnicity and social class, the spacing of the children, their gender, and their own temperaments and abilities (Toman, 1988). For example, the role of the "oldest girl" is different from the role of the "oldest boy" is traditional families. The Kennedy girls in JFK's generation were not deliberately groomed for political and career achievements, although their parents were concerned with their religious and social lives.

Policies and Practices of Society. Any discussion of family life with children would be incomplete without some mention of the major ways in which the policies and practices of the larger society affect the family. Moreover, socioeconomic status interacts with these policies and has a strong effect on family life. As described in Chapter 4, today in the United States there are many families in which both parents work outside the home. For example, 70 percent of women with children aged 6–13 and more than half of all women with chil-

dren under 3 are in the labor force (Bradt, 1989). (These statistics assume that fathers are working.) Yet the United States is unique among industrialized countries in not having paid parental leave or a national child care policy. In Sweden, one parent in every family gets six months of paid leave after the birth or adoption of each child. This permits infants to be cared for in their homes. Parents' jobs, and therefore their economic security, remain safe from disruptions caused by birth. In the United States a "family leave policy" requires employers to grant up to three months of *unpaid* leave, but many families either cannot afford to take this, or fear that the costs to their future status at work will be too high.

These social and economic facts present many decisions and adjustments for the family with young children. How will the early months of infancy be handled? Will the mother or the father take a leave, or leave work altogether, to care for the infant? If the parent is single and not well educated, she may find that she cannot afford to work (the day care is too expensive, the job is part time and doesn't provide health insurance) but also cannot afford *not* to work, and thus is forced onto "welfare." Many single working mothers in the United States live near the poverty line because their pay is low; they are at risk for layoffs, and child care expenses leave them with no savings (Eisenberg, 1995). Poverty puts a different spin on this stage of the family life cycle, as it does on all stages (Fulmer, 1988).

The Family with Adolescent Children

While the major task of the family with young children is to protect and nurture them, the major task of the family with adolescents is to begin to prepare them for independence and the transition to adulthood (Preto, 1989). Actually, that preparation will have (ideally) begun long ago, during childhood, when the family imparts a solid sense of security, confidence and values that is the basis for successful adulthood.

Issues and Challenges.   During adolescence, the issues of separation and independence become much more central, as described in Chapter 3. The young person is suspended between childhood and adulthood, and for both him/her and the family, this can be both exciting and scary.

Since adolescents typically beg for and demand autonomy while their parents are typically more cautious about granting it, conflict is also an inevitable and natural element of family life at this stage. However, whether the conflict is managable or whether it spirals out of control depends on a number of factors. One important factor is the kinds of beliefs that family members hold about each other's behaviors. In every family, people will sometimes behave in ways that the others find annoying, and sometimes in ways that others find pleasing. But different families will have different attributions or beliefs about causes of each others' behaviors. The most beneficial be-

liefs seem to be those that attribute the positive behaviors, but not the negative behaviors, to internal and stable characteristics of the family member (Bradbury & Fincham, 1990). High-conflict families are more likely than low-conflict families to attribute the adolescent's negative behaviors to his or her personality (e.g., he's a "bad apple") rather than to their relationship (e.g., "we rub each other the wrong way") or other external circumstances (e.g., "he's having a hard time in his new school") (Mas, Alexander, & Turner, 1991).

Other factors in how well families weather the adolescence of their members are whether the family has effective problem-solving skills, whether they have established good communication habits, and whether they have flexible and appropriate expectations about the adolescent's behavior. For example, some parents have developed the mistaken belief that if the adolescent does not always mind his parents, he will turn out to be a delinquent, or that if she gets her ears pierced for multiple earrings, she is a drug addict; some adolescents have developed the mistaken idea that their future life will be ruined if their parents do not lift particular restrictions. (Vincent-Roehling & Robin, 1986). These ideas can lead to defensive and unreasonably extreme behaviors, which elicit similar behaviors from the other persons, creating a vicious cycle. Unhealthy coalitions or alliances in the family, as discussed earlier, can also make this stage of the family life cycle more difficult because they prevent the parents from working together as a team (Robin, Koepke, & Moye, 1990).

Despite the focus on independence in adolescence, all family members still need and want closeness. Thus the other task for families in this stage of their life cycle is to find mutually agreeable ways to still maintain closeness. Hugs that, during childhood, communicated family closeness may no longer be comfortable and are perhaps replaced for a time by good-natured teasing, family jokes, or warm looks. Sometimes just the presence of each other can communicate closeness to adolescents, and adolescents who might never admit it openly feel cared about when a parent attends their school events or sports matches.

Launching Adolescents.   At the later stages of adolescence, the family's task is that of launching children and moving on (McCollough & Rutenberg, 1989). Historically in the United States, this was done around the time of high school graduation or marriage, in the late teens or early twenties. Today's adolescents are financially dependent on their parents for a longer period of time, often through the college years especially in middle- and upper-middle-class families. Some grown children are now moving back into their parents' home following college, a financial setback, or a divorce.

Various writers (e.g., Preto, 1989) have noted that ethnicity has an effect on how families handle closeness and separation at adolescence. For example, while traditional Portugese families expect their late adolescents to get a job and help financially, the youth are expected to live at home and be loyal socially and emotionally to their parents until they marry (Moitoza, 1982). British-American families tend to promote earlier separation (McGill & Pearce, 1982), while Italian and Hispanic families are more likely to struggle to keep their adolescents close to home. Indeed, one of the authors was consulted by two families, both living in the same East Coast state, with opposite perspectives on their children's leaving home. One was a traditional first-generation Italian family that was in conflict over their 19-year-old daughter's desire to move out of their house and into her own apartment. She was unmarried, and this was considered an unacceptable option as well as a source of worry about her psychological state. The other family was a suburban family whose ancestors were originally from England but who had lived in the United States for many generations. The parents were concerned that something was psychologically wrong with their 19-year-old son because he did *not* want to move out on his own or to go to college! Thus the standards and expectations about family life differ even within the same geographic area.

Since life expectancies are longer than ever, there is a significant period of life without children in the house, the so-called *empty nest* effect. Contrary to popular beliefs (and, often, the fears of the children who are leaving home), after a slight period of adjustment the psychological well-being of the parents improves. This is especially true for mothers (Glenn, 1975; Harkins, 1978). Both parents now have more time to take stock of their lives and relationships, and change of all kinds is more likely than it was when their energies were bound up in the parenting of adolescents. For example, new careers or jobs may be embarked on, singleminded pursuit of careers may be lessened in favor of deepening their relationship, and domestic duties may be divided up less strictly according to sex roles (McCollough & Rutenberg, 1989).

One challenge increasingly common during this phase, and even before, is that of caring for elderly parents. The current generation of adults has been called the *sandwich generation;* even while they are still taking care of their own children, they may also need to be taking care of their parents. The Kennedy clan became responsible for their own large number of children, many of them fatherless, at the same time that they were caring for their incapacitated father and their aging mother. They were fortunate to have the resources to afford nurses and other help. In other families, these events are also accompanied by great financial and physical care hardships.

The Family in Later Life

Despite the pessimistic stereotypes in our society about old age being a lonely and alone time, devoid of family and close relationships, the family in later life continues to be very important (Walsh, 1989). Here are some facts that support this claim. Of people 65 and over, 70 percent are grandparents and one-third are great-grandparents (Streib & Beck, 1981). Being a grandparent, and having a grandparent, can be among the most satisfying of family relationships. Grandparents have the opportunity to express the same warmth, love, and affection that parents feel, but without as much obligation for setting rules and teaching responsibility. Children often experience their grandparents as more easygoing, perhaps willing to bend some of the rules, and as having more time to just play, talk, or teach. There is a growing phenomenon, especially in families in which there is early pregnancy and/or poverty, of grandparents actually taking over the parenting functions. This can allow children to stay in the home when the only alternative is foster care, and many children have warm memories of being raised by their grandparents. It does, however, put extra burdens on the grandparents as they age.

Older family members are also in closer proximity to other family members than one might think. Seventy percent live with other family members, and most who do not say that a relative could be there in minutes if needed. Those who do live in their own homes, often by preference, maintain intimacy by phone, visits, and mutual support bonds. Only 3 percent are totally isolated from their children, and 4 percent live in institutions (Walsh, 1989). Nonetheless, as discussed in Chapter 3, old age brings with it serious adjustments, notably to declining health and physical capabilities and the loss of spouses and friends. Going to the grocery store alone may become impossible, one's house may need to be rearranged to make stair climbing less necessary, help will be needed in other cases to maintain the home. The decision about whether and when to move from one's home is a very difficult one, and family members may disagree on when that should happen, and where the older family member(s) should live. Choices about which child the aging parent will live with or whether a retirement community or nursing home is the best setting for the elderly parent can bring up old tensions. Likewise, however, successfully resolving these family crises can bring family members even closer together.

Obviously, these changes require all family members to make psychological adjustments. Many adults, for example, experience discomfort as their role shifts from being the "child" to being the "caretaker" of the elderly parent. Old issues of authority and control, closeness or distance, even sibling rivalry, may resurface during this period and need to be worked out.

OTHER FAMILY TRANSITIONS

The stages or transitions in the life of a family just described are developmental stages. That is, they result from the natural changes in families that happen as their members grow up and grow older. There is another very common transition in families, however, which is caused less by developmental influences and more by a complex set of other influences: divorce.

Divorce

Divorce is common in our society; approximately 50 percent of marriage will end in divorce (Collins & Coltrane, 1995). Despite the fact that many people experience divorce, it is rarely an easy period in the family's life. It is a major transition in families that affects changes in living arrangements, family finances, roles, and relationships in many ways (Peck & Manocherian, 1989). Divorce typically involves a difficult and painful set of events, but it also offers a new chance for happier personal and family life (Bray & Hetherington, 1993). In this section, we will examine some of the changes that accompany marital separation and divorce and some of the factors that promote healthier adjustment in divorced families.

Psychologists have studied divorced and remarried families intensively to discover how divorce affects the family in the short term and the long term. A longitudinal study done by Hetherington (1993) and her colleagues found that in the short term (the first two years after the divorce), divorced families experience a number of negative stresses. Mothers reported struggling with an overload of tasks, feeling that the household was more disorganized, being lonely, and having childrearing problems. Stress about childrearing was higher in mothers of young boys and mothers of adolescents (whether they were boys or girls).

A major stress is finances because after divorce the woman's household income tends to decrease dramatically while the the man's household income rises slightly, even though in 90 percent of families the children live with the mother. In the study just described, the average income of divorced mothers (including child support payments) was only half of the fathers' income, at two years after the divorce and even at eleven years after the divorce (Hetherington, 1993). This is because the mothers were less likely to have had full-time, high-paying jobs before divorce than were fathers. Even if both parents were working, the family expenses such as housing and day care still have to be paid after the divorce, but typically by one person's income rather than two. While the old saying "Money doesn't make you happy" may be true, it is certainly a major factor in the stresses of divorce. For example, think about how money affects where the family lives, the neighborhood, the schools that the children attend, the number of jobs and the hours that the divorced parent must work, and recreation that the family can afford. The more the divorce affects family income, the more changes there will be in all

these areas. Money can also "buy time" (e.g., occasional babysitting) to give some relief and support to single parents, thus helping their parenting and, in turn, the children's adjustment to the divorce.

The adjustment of children to divorce is a gradual process, with young children showing more anxious, demanding, aggressive, and unruly behavior in the first two year or two after the divorce compared with children from intact families. After two years, there were no differences in girls from divorced versus nondivorced families. The boys in divorced families had improved, but on average even eleven years later they were still showing more behavior problems in school and home than boys from the nondivorced families (Hetherington, 1993).

Given these facts, is divorce "worth it?" That question is currently being hotly debated, and the answer seems to be "yes" for some people and "no" for others. The Hetherington study found that as early as two years after the divorce the mothers felt happier in their new situation than they had been in their final year of marriage. Women whose marriages had included a lot of conflict were actually physically and mentally healthier than women who were still in unhappy, high-conflict marriages. This is also interesting because research has shown that the *children's* problems seem to be more related to the high conflict in the dissolving marriage than the divorce itself or the absence of the father. This finding fits with the fact that children who lose a parent because of death generally have fewer problems than children from divorced families (Hetherington, 1972). The study also found that a small group of the divorced mothers, despite the challenges, wound up excelling in their work, in social relations, and in parenting. They had much higher self-esteem than a comparable group of nondivorced mothers. Thus while some people suffer long-term consequences of divorce, some are actually better off.

What promotes or impedes the adjustment to divorce? What can families do to make the best out of this transition? The first and most important thing is for the parents to find a way to cooperate on childrearing: to demonstrate that the love, strong guidance, and involvement of each of them as parents will not be lost when the marriage breaks up. Parents must struggle not to allow their conflicts with each other to spill over onto the children and to avoid putting the children in the middle or forcing them to take sides (Maccoby, Buchanan, Mnookin, & Dornbusch, 1993). They each need to find ways to be a parent even though they no longer live in the same house. Families can and do manage this whether the children live with the mother or father or have some shared living arrangements. Interestingly, a study of "deadbeat dads" (noncustodial fathers who do not pay child support) has shown than an important factor in the noncustodial parent's staying involved is whether he or she felt some control over the child's upbringing. Those parents who felt they had some control, and who were fully employed, remained highly involved with their children (Braver, Wolchik, Sandler, Sheets, Fogas, & Bay, 1993).

A second important consideration is the timing of new marital and "live-in" relationships. There is some evidence that adolescence is a particularly difficult time for remarriage and that adjustment of children is not as satisfactory if a parent's remarriage occurs close to or at adolescence, or on the heels of a divorce. The next section examines remarriage in more detail.

Remarriage

Divorce is one transition in families that usually leads to another because, as stated earlier, the divorced person is likely to remarry. The remarried family, often called the *stepfamily*, has been the subject of mostly negative stereotypes in our society. Consider, for example, all the fairy tales that include an "evil stepmother" (McGoldrick & Carter, 1989). In this section we consider the nature of remarried families, and how they differ—in positive, negative, or simply neutral ways—from other families.

Remarriage is a more complicated situation than a first marriage. Remarriage is the joining together not just of the married couple but of several families with histories and habits of their own. In the remarried household there are two such families, but in close proximity are usually two other families (the families of the former spouses). Take the case of Karen, age 43, and Wayne, age 49, who met through their work. Karen had been previously married to James, whom she divorced two years before she and Robert met. They did not have children. She was and still is on friendly terms with Jim's family as well as her own large family of four brothers, mother, stepfather, and relatives. Robert is widowed; his wife, Mary, died eight years before he met Karen. He has two children, Lauren, 15, and Keisha, 17. The family has close ties with both his extended family and his first wife's extended family.

Consider the many questions and issues that arise for the new family unit of Karen, Robert, Lauren, and Keisha. Should the children call their stepmother "Karen" or "Mom"? What should be her relationship with them: friend, housemate, mother, or some combination? How can the family members resolve their differences without taking sides and competing for each other's time and affections? Which relatives, if any, should they visit on holidays? These are a few of the many questions that have come up in this family, which is a fairly simple remarried family. (Consider the extra questions involved if there had been multiples marriages or divorce, children between Karen and James, and the like.) These questions reflect the special tasks facing remarried families: respecting the bonds that the original family members have, distributing household responsibilities and privileges, negotiating the raising of children from the original and the new family, and establishing new family habits and rituals (McGoldrick & Carter, 1989).

Some research supports the view that this is a more difficult set of tasks than those facing intact families. Remarried families are somewhat less cohesive or tight knit, more stressful, and more likely to have problems in family relationships and children's behavior when the remarriage involves adolescent children. This may be because (Cherlin, 1981) society provides no clear guidelines on what stepfamily relationships should be like, because supports for stepfamilies are lacking, and because of the trauma of divorce that preceded the remarriage. On the other hand, the majority of the remarried families studied are still within the "normal" range and the couples are just as satisfied in their relationships as people in their

first marriages. They are also more likely than couples in first marriages to be open in communication, more practical than romantic, more willing to discuss conflict, and more equal in sharing childrearing and housekeeping duties (Bray & Hetherington, 1993).

Working out the remarriage transition takes time, approximately three to five years—and longer if there are adolescents in the family (Dahl, Cowgill, & Asmundsson, 1987). The families in one study had some advice for other remarried families (Dahl, cited in McGoldrick & Carter, 1989, p. 403). This included: (1) "Go slow. Settle your old marriage (divorce) before you start new one." (2) "Help children maintain relationships with their biological parents." (3) "Stepparents should try for mutual courtesy, but not expect a stepchild's love," and (4) "Communicate, negotiate, compromise, and accept what cannot be changed."

REVIEW QUESTIONS

4. What are the stages in the traditional family life cycle?

5. The adjustment of children of divorce is enhanced when there is _____, _____, and _____.

6. How many years does full adjustment to stepfamily life typically take?

Knowing that families have life cycles of their own and that different challenges and opportunities present themselves as the family grows can be helpful in adjusting to those changes. Especially with regard to transitions such as launching adolescent children, divorce, and remarriage, a little bit of information can help. Information allows people to understand that what they are experiencing is not "abnormal." Information can also provide support, and it can help inform the many decisions they need to make. At other times,

however, families need help beyond what can be found in books.

WHEN FAMILIES NEED HELP

Self-Help

Traditionally, and still today, families who are in distress and need help turn to the people around them in the community. The most common source of support is the extended family. For example, a mother feeling overwhelmed and depressed by the full-time care of small children might be greatly relieved by having two days to herself while the children visit at their aunt and uncle's house. A teenager in conflict with his father might be helped by a talk with his grandfather, while the grandfather in turn is helped by being needed. One study (Dornbusch et al., 1985) found that having an extended family member in the household such as a grandmother or aunt helped single mothers retain control and guidance longer over their teenage sons and daughters; without the extended family members, the teenagers, especially the boys, were less likely to listen to their mothers' advice or even discuss important matters with her. Interestingly, the presence of a stepfather seemed to *increase* boys' rebelliousness.

Other common sources of help for families include clergy (priests, rabbis, ministers), the family doctor, and school counselors. In addition, there is a range of self-help groups, such as Parents Anonymous (for parents who abuse their children physically or fear they are at risk for doing so), Compassionate Friends (for parents who have lost a child to death), Resolve (for people who are experiencing infertility), and support groups for people who are taking care of family members with Alzheimer's disease and other forms of dementia. These groups can be very helpful in providing emotional support from other people who understand the problems firsthand, as well as sharing information and resources.

Because our society has recently begun to realize that many family problems can be *prevented* by well-designed social service programs, a number of these services are also available. In most communities, for example, there are prenatal and early infancy programs in which young parents and their children are visited by nurses or social workers. Family life support programs are newer and are designed to prevent homelessness by offering financial counseling, domestic skills, parenting

groups, and other services that families may need to maintain a home. Battered women's shelters are common now in most cities. While they help women and children who have already been abused in their families, they also prevent homelessness, prevent the children from getting trapped in long-term abusive situations, and prevent children being removed from their mothers because of the home situation. These are just a few examples of the kinds of services available to help families.

Family Therapy

For families who need more focused counseling, there is also a special type of psychotherapy, called family therapy, in which the whole family is counseled as a group. Family therapy is a rapidly growing field, and there is now good evidence that it can be effective in helping families solve a variety of problems (Pinsof, 1995). What is family therapy, and how does it work? The following description and case study provide some answers to these questions.

Goals and Types of Family Therapy. **Family therapy** is based on the assumption that families operate as living systems, as networks of interdependent elements (people) in which the whole is more than the sum of its individual parts. For example, when the last child leaves home or when a grandmother comes to live with the family, that is not a simple subtraction or addition of one person. Rather, that change causes a shifting and realignment of other relationships in the family. When the last child leaves home, the parents have more time alone with each other, which may increase intimacy or expose conflicts that were previously masked by focusing attention on the child. The parents will thus have to work out these conflicts and find new ways of interacting. When an elderly grandparent joins the home, the parent's authority may be challenged by the grandparent's advice and the children may attempt to make an ally of the grandparent in family discussions. Family members may even change their physical space in the home, as a vacated bedroom is taken over by a younger sibling or two children bunk together to create an extra room for the grandparent. All of these changes require adjustments in roles and relationships.

Sometimes those adjustments are painful for families and are conflict ridden. Other events and situations that sometimes cause difficult adjustments are marital conflict, divorce, adolescence, and physical illness of a family member. Moreover, sometimes one or more family members experience unhappiness or begin acting in disordered ways. This behavior can affect the entire family as well as the individual.

For all these circumstances, family therapists believe that it is most beneficial to understand and treat such behaviors in the context of the family. Thus the entire family (everyone who lives in the house or who is considered by the family to be a member) is invited to therapy together. The family therapist asks each person for his or her opinions about the problem and to state what he or she would like to see changed or improved during the therapy. The therapist also observes the family's behavior. How clearly are they communicating? Are there topics or issues that they are evading? Do they seem to be divided into alliances or "camps"? Do they seem to be "stuck" in nonfunctional patterns of interacting (e.g., dad corrects daughter's misbehavior, daughter starts to cry, mother defends daughter, parents begin to argue, and the focus on the daughter is lost)? Are they "stuck" in rigid beliefs about each other or about the problem? Who is the most supportive of the person who is identified as having the problem? What are their strengths (e.g., a sense of humor, loyalty to each other, a strong

marriage) that may be utilized later in treatment? These kinds of questions, and their answers, provide the therapist with hypotheses about the problem and ideas about possible solutions.

Case Illustration of Family Therapy. The specific solutions, and the techniques that the therapist uses to reach those solutions, depends on the specific type of family therapy that he or she practices and on the nature of the family's problems. There are several different approaches to doing family therapy (Kaslow & Celano, 1995). Here is a case, "Maria, On Her Own at Age Fifteen," which illustrates a Structural Family Therapy approach. Structural Family Therapy (Minuchin, 1974; Minuchin & Fishman, 1981), as we will discuss later, focuses on how the family's own structure and organization relates to their individual and collective well-being. This particular case was conducted by the expert therapist and author Charles Fishman (Fishman, 1988).

The Family.   The family came to see Dr. Fishman because of concerns about their 15-year-old daughter, Maria. Maria stood out in the family both because she was a "strikingly beautiful" girl and because she was the one who challenged the parents the most. Several months earlier, Maria had flatly refused to follow her parents' rules, had run away from home, and was now living with a boy in a poor area of the city. The family, a "prominent" one, included two younger sisters aged 9 and 12 and an older brother, 17.

The Family Dynamics.   In the early part of the therapy, Dr. Fishman made an assessment of the *family dynamics*—that is, the ways in which they related to each other psychologically. He noted that Maria's father was himself depressed over work problems and was taking medication for his depression. Her mother, who was the more worried of the two, was feeling the loss of having the children need her less and was distressed that she could not foresee any employment opportunities at the time. Their marriage was distant and sexual intimacy was very infrequent.

He observed that the family members were highly intelligent and educated and they dealt with conflicts in a very intellectual, cut-and-dried manner. If Maria didn't obey the rules, they warned, she would simply have to go. Maria left at that point. There was little negotiation or discussion because this was a family who avoided any potential for open conflict. Yet earlier they had been somewhat lax about rules and had given her perhaps too much leeway. Moreover, the parents seemed to undermine each other, even in the therapy room, as Dr. Fishman began to work with them. (*Undermining* means that one parent implicitly or explicitly interferes with the other's parenting efforts.) As the case history reads, "The parents in this family were no longer a couple, but merely two individuals in crisis. Their marital evolution had stopped as each spouse withdrew into him- or herself. The adolescent's acting up was the only thing that brought them together; in this sense, her running away can be seen as constructive. The job of the therapist was to help rework the system so that the parents would have more than their troublesome daughter to hold them together" and so that the daughter would have something "to run *back* to" (Fishman, 1988, p. 66).

The Therapist's Interventions and the Family's Response.   Early on, the therapist worked with the parents on establishing negotiation between themselves and with their daughter. He served as a coach and a consultant as the parents struggled to discuss with each other how they could set limits for their daughter, and he reminded them that as the parents they needed to work together to set those limits, gradually and consistently. At times it was

necessary for him to challenge them, to increase the intensity in the sessions in order to counter the family's avoidance of conflict, and to help all of them be more clear and sincere in their communications.

The Outcome.   Maria did come home to live and stayed there until she graduated from high school. The therapy continued to help the family create a caring atmosphere in which family members could voice their opinions and thoroughly discuss matters of importance, and in which the parents worked together as a team. With her parents' blessing, Maria went to college in a distant city. Dr. Fishman's summary was that the therapy had helped to empower the parents—that is, they gained the confidence to assert their authority as parents and the belief that what their efforts could, and would, work. He also felt that the therapy had helped to strengthen the family system emotionally so as to withstand and grow past the challenges of adolescence. Eventually, the father was able to go off his medication and end his own therapy and the couple started a business together. This case is a good illustration of how everyone in the family, directed by an experienced therapist, can be a potential resource in helping create a happier family life.

As with many families, the growth and change of individual members had caused a need for changes in the ways in which they related to one other. As with many families, the parents really cared about their children and everyone felt strong bonds with each other, despite the fact that there was a lot of tension and conflict at times. Some families work through these times on their own, while others need the help of people outside the family. The ultimate goal of all families, however, as stated at the beginning of this chapter, is to provide a safe and nurturing place where each family member can grow throughout the life cycle.

SUMMARY

1. The definition of family has changed and expanded over the last few generations in the United States. There are now more single-parent families, more families in which both parents work, more families without children, and more gay and lesbian families. All of these families share the common task of providing a safe and nurturing place for individuals to grow and develop at all stages of life.

2. Family health and happiness exists on a continuum from optimal through severely dysfunctional. Optimal families have a good balance among interdependence and independence, emotional closeness and empathy, clear communication, and shared beliefs.

3. Many families are not quite optimal in their functioning but still raise fundamentally healthy children. These midrange families experience more conflict and struggle because the balance between intimacy and independence is not perfect. They may stereotype members and there may be unhealthy alliances or other difficulties.

4. Dysfunctional families are not well organized enough to provide a safe growth environment for its members. There may be a high level of conflict, emotional distance, lack of socialization, extreme interdependence, or some combination of these two factors.

5. Family life is also shaped by culture, ethnicity, economics, religion, and world events. There is variation across countries and cultures in what are considered "normal" or "good" family habits, values, and choices.

6. The family has a life cycle of its own, which is linked to the physical growth and development of its members. Stages of the traditional life cycle include the new couple, the family with young children, the family with adolescent children, the family launching young adults, and the family in later life.

7. Divorce and remarriage represent other transitions in family life. These transitions can be stressful, especially in the first few years, but may lead to more satisfying family situations as well. Children's adjustment to divorce is enhanced when parents cooperate in child-rearing, regardless of their living situation.

8. Families who experience stress may benefit from help within the extended family, the community, or a self-help group. Family therapy is a specialized form of psychotherapy in which the whole family is treated together in order to resolve conflicts and help family members over difficult transitions and problems.

CRITICAL THINKING QUESTIONS

1. Consider families you know that include children and that are two-parent, single-parent, or remarried families. In what ways are the children's everyday lives similar, and in what ways different, across these different types of families? How might these family structures help shape the children's personalities, habits, or choices as they grow up?

2. What are some of the advantages and disadvantages for families in which the children are born when their parents are young (e.g., in

their twenties) versus when their parents are older (e.g., in their forties)? What was the case in your family? *If* you think you may have children, *when* do you think would be the ideal time, and why?

3. Research has shown that stepfamilies take up to five years to fully adapt and adjust to the blending of two families. Why do you think it takes that long? Do you think the ages of the children make a difference in how long it takes? If so, explain how and why.

MATCHING EXERCISE

Match each term with its definition.

a. optimal family
b. midrange family
c. severely dysfunctional family
d. child sexual abuse

e. family life cycle
f. family leave policy
g. sandwich generation
h. "second shift"
i. empty nest

j. remarried family
k. self-help
l. family therapy

1. Term used in Beavers Systems Model of family functioning to describe extremely disorganized, enmeshed, antisocial, or unhappy families; individual members are likely to have behavioral or psychological problems
2. Refers to the possible dynamics and feelings in the family system whose children have recently grown and moved out of the house
3. The stages of growth and change through which a family progresses
4. The clinical treatment of an entire family when there is conflict or psychological problems in one or more members
5. Refers to a U.S. government policy that parents be given up to three months of unpaid leave from their jobs to take care for new children or sick family members
6. Sexual contact between a child and an adult for the sexual gratification of the adult
7. The growing number of adults in the U.S. who are taking care of both young children and aging parents at the same time

8. Term used in Beavers Systems Model of family functioning to describe families who have clear boundaries, high intimacy, low conflict, and good communication, and in general very good psychological health
9. Families in which there has previously been divorce or death of a previous spouse; also called "stepfamilies"
10. Term used in Beavers Systems Model of family functioning to describe families in which there is some tension, conflict, problems in managing independence and closeness, stereotyping, but whose members get along in society
11. Refers to the finding that women who work outside the home still tend to do more of the domestic work than their working husbands
12. The use of family members, community members, or groups of people with similar problems for support and guidance

Answers to Matching Exercise

a. 8   b. 10   c. 1   d. 6   e. 3   f. 5   g. 7   h. 11   i. 2   j. 9   k. 12   l. 4

ANSWERS TO REVIEW QUESTIONS

1. Compared to the 1970s, there are now fewer "married with kids" families, more single-parent households, and more single people.

2. optimal, adequate, midrange, borderline, and severely dysfunctional families

3. relatives

4. the new couple, the family with young children, the family with adolescent children, the family in retirement and later life; each stage provides new challenges and opportunities for adjustment

5. low overt conflict, cooperation by the divorced parents in childrearing, less financial stress

6. three to five years

CHAPTER 13

COMING TOGETHER: THE PSYCHOLOGY OF GROUP BEHAVIOR

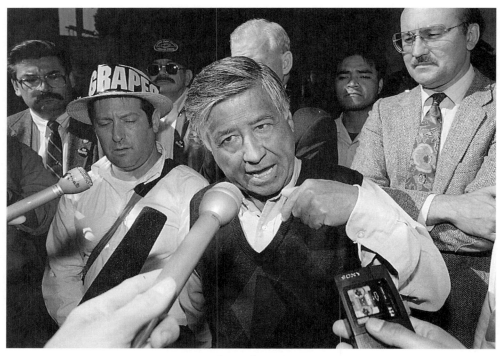

Cesar Chavez

Cesar Chavez

Fate sometimes plays strange tricks on people. As a young boy, Cesar Chavez lived on his family's prosperous farm. He saw the migrant workers come into his valley during harvest time and wondered about their lives as nomads. Now Cesar was learning firsthand about the life of a migrant farmworker. A combination of the Great Depression and drought caused his family to lose the farm. At the age of 10, Cesar joined the hordes of migrant farmworkers who moved up and down California searching for work. Picking grapes and lettuce from sunup to sundown was backbreaking labor. Wages ranged from 15 to 40 cents an hour. Shacks, provided by the growers, often had no indoor plumbing.

Cesar learned that the farmworkers were completely at the mercy of the growers. They were paid what the growers wanted to pay, they lived where the growers wanted them to live, and they had jobs only when the growers wanted to give them jobs. A worker who complained would be without a job; there were plenty of migrant laborers anxious for work. A single worker could do little to change the system. And the National Labor Relations Act of 1935, which gave employees in other industries the right to organize, had excluded farmworkers.

But the plight of farmworkers didn't go unnoticed. Numerous groups tried to organize the migrant laborers to demand their rights. One of these organizers was Fred Ross. One day in 1951 he approached Cesar and outlined a plan to organize the farmworkers. Cesar was suspicious of this Anglo, but he agreed to get a group of workers together to meet with Fred Ross. The group of 20 Chicano workers who gathered at Cesar's house secretly planned to destroy the foolish dream of Fred Ross. They felt that this Anglo, like the growers, only wanted to use the Mexican Americans for his own benefit.

To the workers' surprise, Ross greeted the group in Spanish, "Buenos tardes, amigos." He continued to speak in Spanish and drew the workers into the discussion. Ross outlined how the migrants could influence their own lives if they organized and voted in elections.

After the meeting Chavez approached Ross and told him, "I want to know more about leadership,

Mr. Ross. I want to know how it can come from me, the Chicano, and how I can work with you, and the outfit you work for" (Terzian & Cramer, 1970, p. 44). So Cesar became a volunteer. He traveled the agricultural valleys of California helping Mexican-American farmworkers register to vote. Chavez began holding meetings with the farmworkers who were uneasy about the new ideas he offered.

Cesar Chavez was successful in getting many of the workers to register to vote. But he saw that more was needed. As individuals the workers could do very little to make themselves heard, but together they could have an impact. They needed to form a union so the growers would listen to them. In 1962 he began to recruit members into the National Farm Workers Association. Each member would have to pay monthly dues of $3.50. Chavez knew this was a large sum of money to the poor migrants, but he believed that "each worker should feel he has a stake in our association." He also knew that people wouldn't join the association unless it met their needs. He put the dues in a bank and set up a credit union from which the workers could borrow during hard times.

With the aid of many NFWA members, Cesar began to define goals for the association. One goal was to get a minimum wage of $1.25 an hour for farmworkers. A second goal was to improve farmworkers' housing. The grape-growing region of the San Joaquin Valley was chosen as the target of a strike protesting unfair wages and poor working conditions. The large grape growers, such as Gallo, Christian Brothers, and Almaden, controlled the valley and the jobs. With harvest time fast approaching, the NFWA set up picket lines in front of the entrances to the vineyards in the valley. The growers answered the threat by importing workers from other areas of California and from Mexico. Tensions were high and there were a number of violent encounters between the growers and strikers. Chavez worked tirelessly; he had read books about Gandhi, and he pushed for a plan of nonviolence.

Chavez quickly realized that there was more to a strike than simply marching in front of the vineyards. The strikers had to be fed, and their needs had to be taken care of. Volunteers from all over the country came to the NFWA's aid; many of the first volunteers were college students. A grocery in Los Angeles donated 100 dozen eggs a week, and a meat packer delivered 40 pounds of hamburger meat each Saturday to strikers' headquarters in the San Joaquin Valley.

As the months passed, Chavez made impassioned speeches on television and testified before a Senate subcommittee. The NFWA members worked together to gain support; each member had a job. Some manned the picket lines; some cooked food and carried supplies to the picket lines; some gave speeches and searched for donations.

Despite the organization, the patience of the workers began to wear thin as the strike dragged on. New action was needed to keep the strike going. The workers decided to march from the valley to Sacramento, the state capital a 300-mile trip.

The march would dramatize the demands of the workers and gain national attention. The NFWA used the march to ask people across the country to boycott California grapes until the growers paid fair wages. A group of 200 NFWA members gathered to make the march. As they passed though small towns, they were greeted by groups of well wishers.

The ranks of marchers grew, dwindled, and then grew again as the trek continued. When the group was 50 miles from Sacramento, the happy news reached them. One of the growers had agreed to negotiate with the NFWA and guarantee minimum wages for the workers. The marchers leaped in the air and danced on their sore, blistered feet—they had won. It was only a matter of time before the other growers agreed to the conditions of fair labor practices.

JOINING WITH OTHERS

Cesar Chavez's example is important because it demonstrates the importance of groups in everyday life. It might seem unusual that a chapter on groups is included in text on personal adjustment. But think about your life for a moment. If you review your daily behavior, you should find that much of it involves groups. We live in groups, worship in groups, play in groups, work in groups, attend school in groups, and eat in groups. The adjustment process, therefore, is largely involved with the task of adjusting to groups. For many of us, a basic dilemma is how to fit into groups and be accepted without sacrificing our personal privacy and independence. To achieve a comfortable balance in this domain, it is important to understand how groups function. And it is to this topic that we now turn our attention.

Cesar Chavez was successful in his effort to improve the conditions of farmworkers because he was able to organize the workers. As a group, the farmworkers could accomplish far more than could any single individual worker, even someone as forceful as Chavez. But every worker who joined the NFWA did not do so because of a strong belief that the group would actually have much impact on living conditions and wages. In fact, most of the workers had little faith in the power of the NFWA, and some were even unaware of all the demands the association was making. Why, then, did so many workers join the group?

In answering this question, consider your own life. If you are like most people, you probably belong to five to eight groups at any one time. Your membership in some of your groups, such as your family, was not a matter of choice. But with most of your other groups, such as social groups, athletic teams, church groups, and study groups, your membership was a matter of choice. Why did you join these groups?

A Need to Belong

Poets and philosophers alike suggest that humans are "social animals"; in other words, they have a basic need to belong to groups. Abraham Maslow (1954, 1970), in fact, developed a hierarchy of human needs in which he listed the *need to belong* after only physiological needs (eating, drinking, warmth) and safety needs. It seems that many prison systems recognize the desire of people to be with others, because one of the harshest forms of punishment for inmates who break rules is social isolation or solitary confinement. But labeling us as social animals does not explain why we join some groups, but not others, and why we are more likely to join groups at some times rather than others.

Rewards and Goal Achievement

In many cases we join groups because we expect to get something from them. You may work for a company because it offered you the highest salary. You may join a certain fraternity or sorority because it has the best parties, the nicest house, or the most interesting people. We gain prestige and respect by holding membership in some group. In situations like those faced by the farmworkers, forming a group was the only way to *achieve the goal* of better living conditions and wages. The group was powerful; the individuals on their own were powerless. In other situations, we need the group to engage in a particular activity. You could not play baseball or bridge by yourself. Therefore, we choose many groups because they offer us rewards and allow us to achieve goals.

Social Support

Being a part of a unit often makes us feel comfortable and gives us a sense of well-being. Our groups offer us a ready source of people who will listen to our problems and come to our aid. Psychologists call this function *social support* and this support plays a vital role in our lives. Research shows that people with a strong network of social support are better able to cope with stress and better able to adjust to the demands of life (Major et al., 1990; Rook, 1987). In fact, one study found that when spouses of cancer patients had strong social support networks, their immune system functioned better and they were less prone to illness (Baron et al., 1990). In another case, Israeli soldiers in the 1982 Israel-Lebanon war were less likely to experience devastating combat stress if they viewed their platoon as a source of social support (Solomon, Mukulincer, & Hobfoll 1986).

Information and Evaluation

Cesar Chavez felt that he was not receiving fair wages for his work and that his living conditions were not good. But was he alone in these feelings? Was he simply a malcontent, or was he correct in his beliefs? Looking at your own situation, you probably ask similar questions about yourself and your life each day. Are you a good student or simply average? Are your beliefs in areas such as religion and politics reasonable or unusual and off base? At an even more basic level, how do you decide whether you are friendly, attractive, or athletic?

For the answer to many questions, we can look to physical reality. Chavez, for example, could look at his paycheck each month to determine how much money he was making. You can get on a scale to determine how much you weigh. Your friend can tally up the number of strokes she needed to complete 18 holes of golf. But the answer to many other questions cannot be found in physical reality. Was Chavez receiving a fair wage? Does the fact that you tip the scales at 280 pounds mean you are fat? Does a round of golf at 84 mean your friend is a good golfer? The answer to these and hundreds of other questions lies in **social reality,** the actions, attitudes, characteristics, and behaviors of other people.

According to **social comparison theory** (see Chapter 3), we determine many things about ourselves by comparing with others (Festinger, 1954; Suls & Wills, 1990). For example, if you want to decide whether you are a good student, you not only look at your grade point average, but you compare that average to that of other students. When Chavez wanted to decide whether living condition of the farm workers was truly substandard, he compared that condition with that of other laborers. At this point you might take a moment to consider all the areas in your own life that you evaluate by using social reality as a comparison standard. Chances are you will be surprised by the number of areas involved in social comparison. One reason that we are attracted to groups, then, is that we can make social comparisons.

If this were the end of the story, social comparison theory might help explain why we join groups, but it could not help much in explaining why we choose certain groups. As you might expect there is more to the theory. First, it suggests that comparing with any person will not help us much; we want to make comparisons with people who are *similar* to us. For example, if you want to evaluate your grade point average, you will want to compare with students who have your same major at your university or college. In Chavez's case, he wanted to compare his situation with that of other laborers; comparisons with bank presidents or prison inmates would not have told him much. Therefore, if we want to use groups as a source of social comparison, we will be attracted to groups of people who are similar to us. However, in making our social comparisons we are often motivated to compare with others who may be just a bit inferior to us. This **self-serving bias** results in downward comparisons because we want to appear positive in our self-evaluations.

The Foundation of Self-Identity

To illustrate one of the most important reasons we join groups, ask any of your friends a seemingly simple question: "Who are you?" After a nervous giggle or two, they will probably identify themselves by describing their family, their school, the clubs to which they belong, their religion, their political party, and so on. Each of these descriptions has one

thing in common: It is rooted in a group membership.

Many psychologists argue that much of our self identity is rooted in the groups to which we belong (Tajfel, 1982; Turner, Oakes, Haslam, & McGarty, 1994). According to *social identity theory* we all have a desire to hold a positive self concept (Tajfel & Turner, 1986). Because so much of our identity is defined by the groups to which we belong, we strive to be members of "good" groups and avoid membership in groups that do not have good reputations. When we think of our own groups, we focus on the positive aspects of these groups. Similarly, when we consider groups to which we do not belong, we emphasize their negative points. In an interesting demonstration of this point, (Hastorf & Cantril, 1954) interviewed Dartmouth and Princeton students after they watched films of a particularly rough football game between the two schools. The students were asked to record the number of infractions that occurred during the game and to comment on the play of each team. Dartmouth students felt that their team had played more fairly and cleanly then the Princeton team, and Princeton students viewed the Princeton team as more fair. These differences even showed up when the students recorded infractions committed during the game. As Figure 13.1 shows, whereas Dartmouth students saw an equal number of infractions for both sides, Princeton students stated that the Dartmouth players committed twice as many infractions as the Princeton players. These differences were found despite the fact that all the students watched the same films.

By seeing our own group as good and other groups as inferior, we enhance our self-identity. In many cases, this desire to be a part of the best groups can lead to unimportant biases and errors in judgment. Moreover, as we will see later in this chapter, the desire to elevate our groups can also become the foundation for destructive prejudice and discrimination.

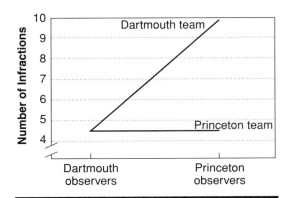

FIGURE 13.1 The Number of Infractions Recorded by Dartmouth and Princeton Students While Watching the Film of a Dartmouth/Princeton Game.
Source: Hastorf & Cantril (1954).

SELF VERSUS GROUP: THE ULTIMATE DILEMMA

As we have seen, groups play a vital role in our lives and adjustment to our world. We are all members of groups and spend much of our lives in group activities. But as we all know, being a member of a group has certain consequences. One of the more troublesome costs of being a group member is that we must sacrifice a bit of our independence. We must consider the wants and needs of other group members when we act. We may be called on to make personal sacrifices for the good of the group. The group will often receive recognition and rewards for our personal achievements. For example, Cesar Chavez spent much of his lifetime working for the goals of the NFWA. Even though many members of the association did not make the same sacrifices of time and effort, they all benefited equally from the ultimate settlement with the growers.

In each of our groups we will constantly be faced with the pull between individual recognition and personal gain, on one side and group gain on the other (Brewer, 1991). If each person in a group works only for personal gain, the group will fall apart. However, if the group fails to give individuals recognition, the members will become dissatisfied and leave the group. This conflict between individual and group needs has been labeled the *social dilemma.* A wonderful illustration of this dilemma has been described as the Tragedy of the Commons (Hardin, 1968). Early New England towns were built around a common pasture that was used by all the residents for grazing their cattle. This plan kept the cattle herds safe from Indian raids and thieves who would steal the cattle if they grazed on open range. However, the common pasture could only accommodate a certain number of cattle or it would become overgrazed and barren. Therefore, each farmer was allowed a limited number of cattle of his own. In theory, all went well. But many farmers concluded that they could add one or two more cows without being noticed or causing injury to the pasture. By adding that extra cow or two, the farmer would personally prosper. Each farmer might have been correct in his thinking *if* he were the only one who added the extra cow. However, many of the farmers had the same thoughts; as each added his extra cow, the pasture was overgrazed and ruined.

We find this pattern of behavior in many aspects of our lives. Driving down the highway, we may think that it will not hurt if we throw out that candy wrapper or bottle. But clearly, if everyone on the highway thinks the same way, it will not be long before the highway looks like a trash pit. As a member of a social organization, you may believe that it will not affect your group much if you spend a few extra dollars from the treasury on a gift or dinner for yourself. Indeed, you may deserve this extra reward. But if each member of the organization feels the same way, the funds in the treasury will soon be depleted.

Social dilemmas are very difficult to resolve because individuals do not immediately see the effect of individual action on the

Teamwork is the Key to a Good Team

Psychologists who research groups are often called upon to work in a number of settings including business, sports, and the military. Several years ago, one of the authors was asked to work with a college football team that had suffered one of its worst seasons in its recent history. The team's problems began when they recruited one of the best college players in the country. Dave Thomas was one of the most talented receivers in football. He was fast, had great moves, and had two hands that seemed to stick to the football like they had glue. As one of the most sought-after high school football players in the United States, Dave seemed to have everything going for him, except one. He knew he was good and felt he should be given special recognition.

Dave's troubles began when he started playing for his college team. He announced his presence by demanding the largest room in the dorm and decorating it with his high school newspaper clippings. On the field, he made spectacular catches, but his behavior after the catch was even more spectacular. He danced in a wide circle and turned somersaults back to the huddle. He announced in a television interview, "I'm going to make this team the nation's best of the decade." At first his coaches and teammates found him amusing, passing his behavior off as the immature actions of a freshman. But they soon began to resent Dave and the attention he received. His coaches tried to talk with him, going so far as to forbid his after-catch antics and keeping him away from the press. But Dave didn't get the message, and he began to skip practice because, he announced, "My game is already 'on.'"

The team won the first three games, but after that things began to fall apart. The players began to shun Dave off the field. They avoided him at mealtimes, he wasn't invited to their parties, and they played pranks on him such as putting worms in his shoes. On the field, things were even worse. The quarterback avoided giving Dave the ball and when he got it, the other players refused to block for him. Fights broke out between Dave and the other players, as each blamed the other for the team's losses.

So the team that had been picked to finish in the top 10 finished the season with a 5 win–8 loss record. The team was unable to use its talent because the members spent so much time fighting among themselves. The trouble on the team spilled over into other domains of college life. Players were unhappy, and their grades suffered.

At the end of the season the coach sought this author's advice. He began by talking with several of the players. Everyone was quick to point a finger at others who they believed were responsible for the team's failure. Many of the players blamed Dave for the problem, but others blamed the coaches for failing to deal with the problem. The coaches felt that this was a player problem that should have been handled by the players. Dave, who was ready to quit the team, blamed everyone but himself.

A team meeting was held where people were encouraged to express their feelings. The tone of the meeting began very hostile, and the finger pointing continued. At one point, however, Dave made a particularly revealing statement: "I was really nervous coming to college and leaving my parents. I guess I tried to hide behind my past success to secure my place on the team. I even thought I overdid it at times, but soon it seemed like I couldn't change if I wanted to. I was labeled a loudmouthed hot shot and everyone expected me to act the part. So I did." Dave's statement was surprising to many of the players. Few realized that he had been nervous coming to college because he acted so self-confident. Others were surprised to learn that Dave felt the group expected him to continue the very behaviors they hated.

After several meetings, the team realized several points about groups and the way their team functioned. They saw how one member could strongly influence the mood of the whole group. They began to recognize how roles were developed in the group and how unspoken expectations affected player's behaviors. They discussed the role of leadership and examined why the team had not developed a way to openly communicate about problems. They also realized how problems with one group (the team) impacted their behaviors in many other groups. The team vowed to work to-gether and to pay more attention to what was happening within their group.

As is so often the case, the events of the next season took an ironic turn. During the first game, Dave Thomas suffered a season-ending injury. He spent the remainder of the season on the bench, cheering his team on and becoming the team jokester. The team had a good, but not great, season. And all agreed they could have won the national championship if Dave had not been hurt.

---

group. For this reason many groups have stiff penalties for members who violate even minor group rules (Sato, 1987), while other groups attempt to increase members' identification with and concern for their group (Lynn & Oldenquist, 1986). Throughout the life of the group, there is a constant tension between the need for individual recognition and gain and group needs, and this tension is often a major reason for people's leaving the group and, in extreme cases, for group disintegration.

Deindividuation: Getting Lost in the Group

Although groups must protect against each individual's "doing his or her own thing," there is a danger in not allowing room for personal uniqueness and freedom. For example, the farmworkers were a large group. Most were Hispanic, and most wore similar types of clothing. When they gathered together at a large rally, it was often hard to distinguish one worker from another. In a sense, the workers lost their individual identities and assumed the identity of the group. A similar thing happens when we attend a football game or a rock concert. In these cases, we become part of a sea of humanity; to the observer, we aren't Bob or Susan, but only an indistinguishable part of the crowd. In psychological terms, we become *deindividuated*.

Deindividuation, or losing our personal identity and assuming the group's identity, occurs in many groups. Zimbardo (1970) identified several factors that lead us to feel deindividuated in groups. The larger the group, the more likely we will feel deindividuated. We are most likely to lose individuality in groups in which members are relatively anonymous and similarity of dress is required. Deindividuation is most common in groups where individuals don't feel responsible for their actions. It's very clear that these factors were present in the NFWA meetings and that members felt deindividuated; the NFWA was large, and the members often worked together. The workers were relatively anonymous to outsiders and to the growers and they felt that "the association" would assume responsibility for many of their actions.

The results of deindividuation are startling. On a personal level we may lose pride in ourselves and our behavior. We receive little personal recognition or credit for outstanding behavior, so why strive for excellence? We also lose concern for social evaluation, and as a result we feel less inhibited—less guilty, ashamed, or fearful—about performing socially unacceptable behaviors (Prentice-Dunn & Rogers, 1989).

Zimbardo (1971) presented a frightening demonstration of the effects of deindividuation on an individual's behavior. He set up a mock prison in the basement of the psychology building at Stanford University. The prison contained a number of barred cells with just room enough for three bare beds in each. There was also a guard room where his prison "guards" could observe the inmates. Zimbardo hired 24 carefully selected male students, whom he described as "mature, emotionally stable, normal, intelligent college students from middle-class homes through-out the United States and Canada". Half the students were arbitrarily assigned to the prison group, and the other half were instructed to take the role of guards.

The prisoners were given white dresslike garments to wear and numbers to be used instead of their names. At night each inmate slept with a chain around one leg. The guards were also given uniforms: khaki pants and shirts and dark sunglasses that hid their eyes. These procedures were aimed at deindividuating both groups by effacing individual identities and substituting the class identity of prisoner or guard. Zimbardo expected to observe and record the behavior in his prison over a two-week period. The guards were given complete control of the prison and the "inmates"; Zimbardo served as the prison warden.

What happened as a result of deindividuating these normal college students and placing them in clearly defined groups? Zimbardo (1971) reports with disbelief and horror that the deindividuating situation "undid (temporarily) a lifetime of learning; human values were suspended, self-concepts were challenged, and the ugliest, most base, pathologic side of human nature surfaced". The inmates became "servile, dehumanized robots" who thought only of their own survival and hated their guards. Many of the guards became tyrannical and brutalized the inmates. The situation became so bad that the experiment had to be terminated in six days instead of the two weeks originally planned!

Most of us will never be in a group that deindividuates us to the extent of the Zimbardo "prison." The important point, however, is that the factors that led to deindividuation in that experiment exist in many groups. We must, therefore, be aware of what those factors are and how they are likely to affect our own feelings and behaviors. The conditions in many groups invite us to sacrifice our uniqueness and become submerged in the group.

Too often we unwittingly accept this invitation and allow ourselves to become deindividuated. In a large crowd, for example, we may scream obscenities, knowing that we can't be identified or held responsible for these actions. The result are often disturbing to us and to observers. An understanding of the deindividuation process should better enable you to determine how much of yourself you will "give" to the group and how much individual identity you will retain. To remain totally aloof from the group is clearly as poor a solution as to become totally submerged in it. A wiser course of action is to understand the forces that push for deindividuation and to be prepared to give into them only to the degree with which you are comfortable.

Culture and the Importance of Groups

Most of us grow up hearing messages that urge us to strive to achieve highest level we can achieve and "to stand out" from the crowd. We accept that we are responsible for our own actions and that we should reward based on our behavior. We accept the position that people who work harder than others should receive greater pay and that when problems or accidents occur, it is proper to find out who is to blame. We live in a society that values individual rights and places great emphasis on individuals. Although we may study in groups or play on sport teams, we are comfortable with the system that grades individuals separately or keeps individual records of performance. Most of us look forward to the day we can move away from our family to "make it on our own." As a result, our society has been referred to as an **individualistic culture** (Triandis, 1994).

However, all societies are not based on these principles. In many other societies (Asian, Arab, Eastern European, Latin American) the group rather than the individual is the most important unit (see Chapter 1). In these societies, known as **collective cultures,** individuals learn not to "stand out" in the group because they will embarrass other group members. Individuals achieve not so much to advance their own position, but to help their group (their family, tribe, work group). A person's failure hurts not only the individual, it also brings shame to that person's group. The group supports the individual and the individual supports the group. Individuals in collective cultures are more comfortable when the group is rewarded for performance than when a single individual is rewarded. Children often do not move away from the family when they grow up. Rather, they continue to live at home, raising their own family within the larger family unit.

The cultural approach to groups and individuals has wide-ranging effects on personal behavior. Most interesting from our present perspective is the impact of culture on social identity. Research has shown that individuals from collective cultures are more likely to describe themselves in group terms than are people from individualistic cultures (see Chapter 1; Bochner, 1994; Diener, Diener, & Diener, 1995). For example, when asked to describe themselves, people from collective cultures are likely to mention their family ("I am the third son in the Wong family"), their school ("I am a student at Wilson University"), their work group ("I work as a manager at IBM"), and other groups. People from individualistic cultures often give personal traits (friendly, smart, tall, honor student) when asked the same question. Likewise, people from individualistic cultures often spend considerable effort to develop their independence from the group, whereas those from collective cultures strive to remain embedded in the group.

One approach is not necessarily better than the other. However, it is important to recognize how culture can affect our behavior in groups and the role of groups in our identity. Because we rarely think of culture, its influence can be very subtle and easily overlooked.

Cesar Chavez, for example, was Hispanic, a culture that is more strongly collective than the Anglo culture. His cultural background set the stage for him to willingly make personal sacrifices for his group (farm laborers, in this case). Given the fact that we will interact with increasing frequency with people from other cultures, we should keep in mind how culture influences our own behavior and perceptions as well as those of others with whom we come in contact. Cultural differences also have interesting implications for how groups deal with group members. For example, Sanchez-Ku and her colleagues (1996) argue that because people in Western individualistic cultures are trained to be independent and to strive for personal excellence, groups must socialize members to be more cooperative and considerate of others. In collective cultures, however, individuals are reared to be socially responsive, so the task of groups is to encourage members to strive to reach their potential rather than holding back in order to avoid recognition.

THE STRUCTURE OF GROUPS

Given that we all belong to groups and that they have an important influence on our lives, we should understand how groups are structured. A careful look at groups will show that members don't behave in a haphazard or random fashion; their behavior follows prescribed patterns and conforms to identifiable rules.

Norms

The first type of rule applies to everyone. The NFWA adopted the rule of nonviolence in confronting the growers. All members, from leaders such as Cesar Chavez to the newest member, were expected to avoid violent encounters with the growers.

Such guidelines for group behavior are called norms. **Norms** are rules that govern specific behaviors, and they usually apply to all members of the group: "Norms specify what must, or must not, be done when" (Steiner, 1972). Norms are often unwritten, as can be seen in the NFWA example and in family settings. It may be interesting for you to consider the groups to which you belong and to list the "unwritten laws" of these groups.

In some cases, however, norms are explicitly written. Laws are an example of written norms. Thus, the law setting the speed limit at 65 miles per hour is a norm that applies (or is intended to apply) to everyone in the state that sets this law, regardless of age, occupation, sex, or type of automobile driven.

Roles

A second set of guidelines that influences the behavior of group members is roles. **Roles** define the obligations and expectations for an individual in a particular position within a group. In the NFWA, Cesar Chavez had the role of leader. Because he occupied this role, he was expected to develop a successful plan for getting higher wages, to take care of the daily needs of the other members, and to represent the united farmworkers to the nation. In addition to these expectations, Chavez had benefits the other member didn't have. He could draw a salary from the NFWA. He didn't have to march on the picket lines. These expectations and benefits existed for Chavez only because of his role in the NFWA.

A system of roles can be found in most groups. In families, the roles of father, mother, eldest child, and youngest child can be identified. Each of these positions entails a specific set of privileges, obligations, and expectations. In university and college departments, there are the roles of chairperson, professor, associate professor, assistant professor, lecturer, and teaching assistant. Again, each role has specific obligations and expectations.

Roles and norms are developed so that the group can function in an orderly fashion. A group member who knows the roles and

norms of his or her group can predict how other group members will act. If the norms prevail and role expectations are fulfilled, maintenance of the group is assured. Norms and roles play a vital part in group life because they structure the group, ensure the predictability of members' behavior, and ensure that the group will be maintained and continue to function.

Role Conflict

Groups develop roles and norms so they can function smoothly. But we must remember that we belong to many groups at once. At times, the demands of our role in a group may conflict with the demands of our role in another group. When this happens we experience **role conflict** (see Chapter 14; Forsyth, 1990). For example, Cesar Chavez was the leader of the National Farm Workers Association; this role demanded that he take care of the association members and that he travel and gain support for the association. Chavez was also a husband and the father of eight children; his role in the family demanded that he help support his family and spend time with his wife and children. So the roles of NFWA leader and father in a family placed conflicting demands on Chavez.

Another area where the issues of role conflict has been raised lies in the role of women in today's world. The traditional role for women was that of the homemaker responsible for keeping the home and raising the children. Many women, however, prefer to apply their skills and abilities in working outside the home. Twenty years ago, women who had this desire faced an uncompromising world that told them the conflict between the roles of mother and working woman couldn't be reconciled. Women were often led to believe that they must choose one role or the other. Today, however, we realize that this isn't the case.

The adaptation that has been made so that women, like men, can have both a family and career indicates how to deal with potential role conflict. On one hand, adjustments have been made in both family roles and work-place roles. In many families, taking care of children and keeping house are no longer the sole responsibility of the woman; the requirements of the roles have been changed to allow both wife and husband to work outside the home. Sensitive employers have also adjusted job requirements for both men and women to accommodate these changes in the family group. Thus, one way to deal with role conflict is to change the requirements of the roles in groups. A second way to deal with potential role conflict is to choose groups that present a minimum of conflict. In this case, couples talk about their desires for dual careers, and the choice of a mate is often influenced by considering whether both partners' desires can be met in their relationship. Similarly, decisions about jobs and careers are also influenced by the roles people expect to play in the family. Finally, many people have accepted the fact that in satisfying their desires they will experience some degree of conflict. Couples expect and openly discuss the conflicts. Adjustments and sacrifices are sometimes made. For example, working couples may realize that the demands of their jobs make it impossible for them to prepare fancy meals at home every night. In such a case, the couple may eat out more often or plan meals that can be cooked more quickly.

Given the number of groups to which we belong, there is probably no way to avoid role conflict completely. But we can identify the roles that we will be required to fulfill in a certain group and consider whether or not these roles will conflict with the roles required by other groups. We should also explore the possibility that the roles we play in various groups can be modified so that they mesh together more easily. If it's impossible to avoid a role conflict, we will have to decide whether membership in the group is worth the conflict and tension that will be created. While there is

no clear formula for making this decision, simply knowing the potential for role conflict should make us better able to choose our groups wisely.

The Changing Nature of Groups and Members

Before leaving the issue of group structure, we should make one more point: Groups are in a constant state of change. Consider the groups to which you belong and you will probably find that the present condition of those groups is very different from when you joined the groups. Clearly, the National Farm Workers Association underwent a great deal of change. As a fledgling unit, its main concern was attracting and organizing its members. It had a loose organization, but it paid close attention to the needs of each member. As the NFWA tackled the growers, it developed a clearer set of norms and rule, a tighter organization, and a focus. As the association grew, subgroups and committees formed and its agenda became broader.

Psychologists have long observed that groups develop through different cycles or stages (Tuckerman, 1965; Mullen, Rozell, & Johnson, 1996; Worchel, Coutant-Sassic, & Grossman, 1992). These stages influence the structure and the focus of the group and impact each member. For example, Worchel, Grossman, and Coutant-Sassic (1994) observed work groups over a six-week period. They found that groups often begin by focusing on establishing their *identity*. During this period group members often adopt a name for their group, they make a clear distinction between member and nonmember, rule and structure are defined, and a strong emphasis is placed on loyalty and conformity. Following this period, groups turn to issues affecting *group productivity*. Members set goals for the group, identify individuals who have special knowledge or ability, and focus their efforts on "getting the job done." During the state of group

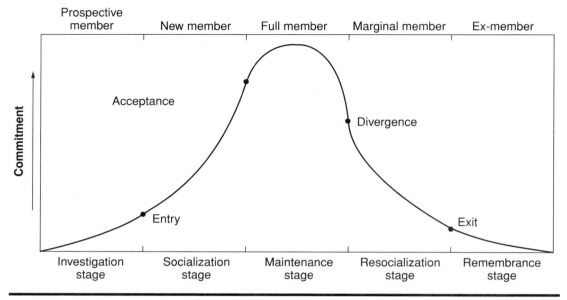

FIGURE 13.2 Stages of Membership in Groups

productivity, the needs of the individual are often overlooked in favor of the needs of the group. Later in the life of the group, however, members become concerned with *individuality*. Individuals demand to be recognized for their special contributions and members want individual rewards. They also desire greater personal freedom. Finally, the group begins a period of *decay* in which unhappy members leave the group to join other groups. Those who remain push the group to change its focus, its leadership, and its structure. The period of decay leads the group to reconsider its identity, and the cycle of group development and change begins anew.

This picture of groups as constantly changing units is important because it impacts a wide range of behaviors. For example, one study found that minorities could be most influential in a group during its latter stages (individuality and decay). During the earlier stages of group identity and productivity, minorities who expressed deviant opin-

ions were ignored or punished (Worchel, Grossman, & Coutant-Sassic, 1994). It has also been found that groups tend to be most open to accepting new members during certain stages of development, whereas they may refuse new members at other stages (Moreland & Levine, 1989; Worchel et al., 1992).

And just as groups go through stages of development, group members also change. As Figure 13.2. shows, the stages of group membership influence both the concerns of members and their commitment to the group. For example, a new member is most likely to be concerned with learning the rules of the group and being accepted. He or she will be highly committed to the group and willing to sacrifice individual needs for acceptance. The marginal member, on the other hand, will be less committed to the group as he or she seeks out opportunities for membership in other groups. The marginal member may also be interested in finding the faults and weaknesses in the group in order to justify leaving the group.

As you can see, both groups and members are constantly changing. Adjustment to the group requires that we be sensitive to these changes in the group and our role in the group. We cannot simply adopt a rigid way of behaving and expect that it will always "work" in the group. We shouldn't be surprised to find that we are sometimes happy with the group and its focus, whereas at other times we are not as comfortable or feel less central to our group. We need not always change our desires and wants to fit the group. Doing this means we lose a sense of self and our personal needs. We must, however, realize that the group will go through change and that this change is natural and inevitable.

Leaving the group simply because it does not meet our momentary needs is no more adaptive than frantically clinging to membership in a group that we realize will never be satisfying for us. It is important that we understand the cyclical nature of groups and members, recognize the constant tension between groups needs and individual recognition, and make decisions about group membership and behavior that will allow us to contribute to our groups and gain personal satisfaction and fulfillment.

With this information in mind, let's turn our attention to examining how groups influence us and, in turn, how we influence groups.

REVIEW QUESTIONS

1. Social comparison theory predicts that we will be attracted to groups of people who are similar to us or slightly inferior. However, social identity theory suggests we will want to join the _____ groups in order to raise our social identity.

2. The social dilemma revolves around the conflict between _____ needs and _____ needs.

3. Which of the following is not associated with deindividuation?

   a. reduced pride and concern with personal behavior
   b. less restraint against performing socially unacceptable behavior
   c. reduced feelings of personal guilt
   d. greater embarrassment when our behavior does not meet our standards

4. David was uncomfortable in groups because he was concerned that his personal achievement would not be recognized. He often wore brightly colored clothing to stand out and he "played up" to his supervisor at work to get recommended for a promotion. David most likely lived in a _____ culture.

5. T or F: Norms and roles help provide predictability in groups.

TO INFLUENCE...

The members of the National Farm Workers Association agreed that they wanted higher wages and better working conditions. But they were divided about how to achieve these goals. Cesar Chavez wanted to use nonviolent methods such as strikes and boycotts.

Others such as Emilio Hernandez wanted a more aggressive approach: "What kind of men are we to sit back and wait? Our grandfathers fought with Pancho Villa—they were men, not afraid to fight, not afraid to die. Would they not be ashamed to see us denying our manhood—our *machismo?*" (Terzian & Cramer, 1970, p. 138). Given this split, how was Chavez able to get the members to follow the nonviolent course of action? How was he able to convince them to give up their jobs and suffer the hardships of the long strike?

Social Power

If we examine our lives, we find that our behavior is often influenced by other people. You may struggle out of bed and hurry to work because your boss has threatened to fire you if you're late. When you get into your car, you buckle your seatbelt because you heard a traffic safety official speak about the importance of using seatbelts. The outfit you're wearing to work is very similar to one your favorite movie star had on in a show you saw last month.

In each of these cases, your behavior has been influenced by others, but the basis for the influence is different in each case. In fact, psychologists have identified six types of social power that can be used to influence our behavior (French & Raven, 1959; Aries, 1976).

Coercive Power. One of the most common types of power is *coercive power,* which involves the use of threats or punishments. Coercive power is easy to use and often enhances the self-esteem of the person using it (Kipnis, 1992). Many people find a certain satisfaction in feeling that they are strong enough to get others to carry out behaviors simply by threatening them. But there are drawbacks to using threats and punishment to influence others. First, the recipient of the threat or punishment will be motivated to leave the relationship as soon as an opportunity presents itself. Clearly, you wouldn't want to be around a person who was always threatening you to get you to change your behavior. Second, coercive power works only as long as the more powerful person is present and watching.

Reward Power.   *Reward power* involves giving positive reinforcement to produce change.

The reward can be material goods, money, or simple praise or status. For example, a friend offering $50 if you would stop smoking for a week involves the use of reward power. Unlike coercive power, reward power motivates people to stay in relationships that influence their behavior. Although surveillance is required for the effective use of reward power, the degree of surveillance isn't as high as the needed to use coercive power. The disadvantage of reward power is that it may be costly to the person using the power; he or she might have to give up money or other material goods, or expend time and effort, to influence the behavior of others.

Expert Power. People have *expert power* when we see them as having special knowledge about something. Expert power is generally limited to the area in which the individual has expertise. For example, you may stop smoking or lose weight because your doctor tells you it will be good for your health. But it's less likely that you'll run down to the store and buy polo shirts because your doctor tells you they're great. The use of expert power doesn't require surveillance by the powerful person.

Legitimate Power. As the leader of the NFWA, Cesar Chavez had *legitimate power* because of the role he occupied. Many roles—personnel manager, club president, parent, professor—carry power within the role. People feel that they should follow the demands of those bearing legitimate power. Like expert power, legitimate power is limited, however. Its domain is only within a single group. For example, your professor has legitimate power to influence your behavior in class, but he or she doesn't have the power to influence your behavior within your family.

Informational Power.   There is an old saying that "knowledge is power." We listen to people we see as having knowledge or special information about something. This *infora-*

tional power is somewhat different from expert power because the knowledge may not necessarily make the person an expert. If you are on a jury, you will be influenced by someone who has eyewitness information about a crime; this person isn't an expert, but his or her information gives the witness power. The limitation of information power is that the powerful person loses power once others have the information. In the preceding case, the witness loses power once he or she has given the jury the information.

Referent Power.   Many people in the NFWA admired Cesar Chavez for his courage and ability. One young boy admired him so much he began to dress like Chavez and adopt his mannerisms. People we like and admire have *referent power* over us. They can influence our behavior because we want to be like them. Referent power doesn't require surveillance, nor does the powerful person have to change his or her behavior to use this power.

The Corrupting Influence of Power.   When we talk of power, the eyes of many people light up. For many of us, the ultimate dream is to have the power to influence others to do whatever we want them to do. What a good life this would be! And this power would make better people of us. Or would it? Another old saying holds that "absolute power corrupts absolutely." History provides many examples that support this statement. It isn't hard to think of the names of dozens of people whose power brought them corruption and ruin.

A number of explanations are possible for this unfortunate outcome. First, having power and being able to influence others makes people think they are better than the nonpowerful others. Power tends to inflate people's self-esteem, and they begin to see themselves as more important than others. Second, people with power often think they can do no wrong. Few people will risk challenging a powerful person. Third, power

tends to separate the powerful from the nonpowerful. Powerful people may lose the ability to be sensitive to the needs of less powerful others. Cesar Chavez seemed well aware of this possible outcome; he continued to live with the farmworkers, and he refused to take a large salary for his efforts. In this way he continued his close contact with the workers and was able to see the world through their eyes. Chavez's actions provide a valuable lesson on how we can avoid the pitfalls of power. It is important to seek out the company of less powerful people and to invite open communication with them.

Leadership

When we think of power, we also think of leadership. A **leader** is a person who influences other group members. In essence, leadership involves the exercise of power. People have always questioned what special qualities make a leader. Why did Cesar Chavez, rather than one of the thousands of other farmworkers, become the leader of NFWA?

As it turns out, this is a very difficult question to answer. One set of theories suggest that leaders have some special traits or characteristics that make them leaders. Many businesses and industries have adopted this approach and have developed tests to identify who will be a leader. Unfortunately, hundreds of studies on leadership have failed to identify clearly traits that make a person a leader. There is some indication that leaders tend to be more intelligent, assertive, vocal, and taller than others in the group. However, for the most part, there is often little clear difference between leaders and the people who follow them.

A second set of theories argues that it is the situation that makes a person a leader. In other words, leaders are people who happen to be in the right place at the right time, and anyone who happened to be in the situation would have become the leader. Using this approach, we might argue that Cesar Chavez became a leader of the farmworkers movement because he happened to be the person who was approached by Fred Ross to help organize the first meetings. There is some evidence that the situation does influence who will be a leader. For example, studies have shown that people who are seated at the head (as opposed to along the sides) of a rectangular table tend to be more influential (Lecuyer, 1976). Other studies have found that seniority affects leadership; people who have been with the group the longest tend to emerge as leaders (Insko et al., 1980).

The specific needs of the group also help determine who will be its leader. Cesar Chavez may have become leader of the National Farm Workers Association because the workers needed someone who could organize and give forceful speeches. As the needs of a group change, the person who leads may also change. In a study of U.S. presidents, it was found that presidents whose personal motives matched those motives of their contemporary society had the greatest public appeal (Winter, 1987).

But even if we accept these situational influences, they don't present the whole picture. Why is it, we might ask, that given the same situation, one person becomes a leader and another does not? There were many members of the NFWA who had been with the movement from its beginning. Why did Cesar Chavez emerge and remain the leader?

Thus, neither the trait nor the situational theory can completely explain why some people become leaders. The better answer probably lies somewhere in between these extreme theories (Hollander, 1985). Who will lead a group is a function of personal characteristics of both leader and followers and of the specific characteristics of the situation. People with certain traits and abilities will emerge as leaders in certain situations.

This point has been supported by research into what type of person is likely to be an effective leader (Fiedler, 1978). This work has shown that someone who is highly task oriented and has concerns about getting the job done at all costs will be an effective leader in groups that are either very organized or very disorganized (see p. 355). When the group is only moderately well organized, a person who has strong concerns about the feelings and well-being of the members will be the most effective leader. The bottom line, therefore, is that both the situation and the characteristics of the people in a group determine who the group's leader will be and how well he or she will lead.

Overall, research has supported this interaction theory of leadership (Scriesheim, Tepper, & Tetrault, 1994). One of the important implications of this theory is that we should choose leaders whose characteristics match a particular situation.

Other approaches to leadership study leader behavior (Yukl, 1982). According to these researchers, leaders do the following:

1. Initiate ideas
2. Take responsibility
3. Develop vision
4. Organize and structure groups
5. Reward and punish subordinates
6. Set goals
7. Stand up for and support subordinates
8. Make decisions
9. Solve problems
10. Generate enthusiasm
11. Communicate

The behavioral approach is important because it suggests that if we know the behaviors that characterize leaders, we can create leader training programs (Aamodt, 1996). The study of leadership continues at a furious pace because of the importance for groups of selecting and training good leaders.

Obedience: I Was Only Following Orders

Our discussion of power and leadership has concerned influencing group members.

SELF-ASSESSMENT EXERCISE

What Type of Leader Are You?

Leaders are people who influence the activities of other group members. There are, however, many ways to use this influence. Some leaders tend to be task oriented; their main concern is getting the job done and seeing that a goal is reached. Other leaders tend to be relationship oriented; their main concern is the feelings of other group members. Answer the following scale as instructed. Then add up your score. It has been suggested that low scores represent leaders who are task oriented in their approach. Which are you?

Think of the person with whom you can work least well. He or she may be someone you work with now or someone you knew in the past. This person does not have to be the one you like least well but should be the person with whom you had the most difficulty in getting a job done. Describe this person.

Confident	8 7 6 5 4 3 2 1	Not confident
Close	8 7 6 5 4 3 2 1	Distant
Hardworking	8 7 6 5 4 3 2 1	Not Hardworking
Warm	8 7 6 5 4 3 2 1	Cold
Ambitious	8 7 6 5 4 3 2 1	Not ambitious
Happy	8 7 6 5 4 3 2 1	Sad
Productive	8 7 6 5 4 3 2 1	Not productive
Sociable	8 7 6 5 4 3 2 1	Not sociable
Dependable	8 7 6 5 4 3 2 1	Not dependable
Relaxed	8 7 6 5 4 3 2 1	Tense
Creative	8 7 6 5 4 3 2 1	Not creative
Satisfied	8 7 6 5 4 3 2 1	Not satisfied
Intelligent	8 7 6 5 4 3 2 1	Not intelligent
Friendly	8 7 6 5 4 3 2 1	Not friendly
Calm	8 7 6 5 4 3 2 1	Nervous
Pleasant	8 7 6 5 4 3 2 1	Not pleasant

Source: F. Fiedler (1964). A contingency model of leadership effectiveness. In L. Berkowitz (Ed.), *Advances in Experimental Social Psychology.* New York: Academic Press, pp. 149–190.

Obedience, the ultimate level of being influenced, means following the direct orders of a more powerful person. Cesar Chavez gave clear instructions to those working directly with him. They followed his orders by being models of nonviolent protest. The outcome of their obedience was positive; others followed their example and the workers won higher wages and better working conditions.

Unfortunately, there are other cases where following the leader has led to tragic results. As the end of World War II, Allied forces in Germany uncovered scores of concentration camps that quickly yielded their grisly secret. During the war, the Nazis had sent political prisoners and members of persecuted religious and ethnic groups to be "processed." In all, over 6 million men, women, and children were tortured and killed in these camps. How could anyone knowingly send innocent people to such horrible deaths? After the war, many of the Nazis who had operated these camps were put on trial and the world learned their rationale for their actions. In nearly every case, the executioners argued that they were "merely following orders" and hence were not responsible for their actions.

Such horrible and frightening outcomes of obedience to authority raise a general question about the extent to which group members will blindly follow the orders of their leaders. It was this question that Stanley Milgram (1963; 1965) attempted to answer through a series of controversial experiments.

As the experiment described in the Lessons from the Laboratory box on page 358 shows, Milgram found that ordinary people would often follow the orders of an authority figure even when their behavior involved giving painful shock to an innocent and protesting target.

A number of other studies provided additional examples of people's tendency to obey orders. For example, Hofling, Brotzman, Dalrymple, Graves, and Pierce (1966) telephoned nurses in a hospital and ordered them to administer a drug at double the maximum recommended dose to a patient. In their telephone conversations, they used the name of a doctor who was unfamiliar to the nurses. All but one of the 22 nurses who were telephoned intended to follow the order, even though it was against hospital policy and could have been dangerous for the patient. (The nurses were stopped before they could administer the drugs.)

What is this strange power that is contained in a command? Why will people perform behaviors on the basis of a simple order that they would never perform on their own? When Milgram questioned his subjects about why they followed the experimenter's orders, they reported that they believed the experimenter was taking responsibility for their behavior. Because he gave the orders, the experimenter was responsible for the outcome. This trap of denying responsibility for our actions is a dangerous one, but it is easy to fall into. Remember our discussion about deindividuation on page 345; here we saw that people will perform unusual and sometimes violent behaviors when they believe the group is responsible for their behaviors. Our belief that a leader is responsible for our behavior may also cause us to perform acts that we later regret and feel ashamed of. It's important to keep in mind that we control our own behavior and that no one else is responsible for our actions. Knowing this should make us less willing to do something blindly because someone has ordered it. Certainly there may be negative consequences to disobeying an order from a high-status person, but these consequences are usually much less negative than are those that follow when we perform a behavior we know to be wrong. For this, we must eventually assume the responsibility.

It is not only the lack of responsibility that pushes us to follow orders. Herbert Kelman and Lee Hamilton (1989) carefully analyzed several "crimes of obedience" such as the Mai Lai massacre and the extermination policies of Nazi Germany. They found that some people follow orders because of *ideological zeal*, the belief that they are doing the right thing for a good cause. Others get *personal satisfaction* such as the feeling of power, while still others hope *to gain rewards or personal advancement* by following orders. Finally, we return to the issue of roles. In many cases, the *role* people find themselves in dictates that they follow orders. A private should follow the orders of superiors, a nurse should follow the orders of doctors, a student should follow the instructions of the professor, and the child should follow the parent's commands. Thus, you can see that there are many forces that combine to move us to follow the orders of our leaders.

CONFORMITY: POWER IN NUMBERS

It is not only the leader of groups who exercises influence over us. We often watch to see what the other members are doing, and even when we think they are wrong we change our behavior to be in step with them. The other group members don't have to order us to follow their example, but we often believe that we'd better follow if "we know what's good for us." *Conformity* occurs when we change our actions or attitudes to be more like those of other group members as a result of real or imagined group pressures, despite personal feelings to the contrary.

Conformity can actually occur at two levels. *Public compliance* occurs when we change our public or observed behavior but maintain contrary attitudes. For example, you might exhibit public compliance if you participated in smoking with your friends even though you didn't like the taste of cigarettes and knew they were harmful to your health. *Private acceptance* involves change in both our public behavior and private attitudes as a result of group pressure. In this example, private acceptance would occur if you came to believe after smoking with your friends that smoking was not bad for your health and cigarettes tasted like candy. The distinction is an important one, because public compliance is only likely to occur when we are in the presence of the group, while behaviors involving private acceptance will occur even when we are alone.

Another important distinction concerns the foundation for the group's power. Consider a farmworker who wants higher wages and better living conditions for his family. However, he does not know the best way to achieve these goals, so he looks to a group such as the NFWA to help him identify a course of action. In this case, the group (NFWA) has the power to influence the farmworker because of the information it possess; it has *information influence*. Now consider the same farmworker who believes that he can best achieve his goals through a violent confrontation with the growers. However, he wants to be part of the NFWA and believes that if he violates the organization's norm of nonviolence, he will be punished or expelled from the group. *Normative influence* occurs when we conform because we fear punishment or rejection.

Thus, groups influence the individual through the information they can provide and through the threat that they will reject the individual if he or she doesn't conform. In most cases both effects operate simultaneously to pressure the individual to conform. When you consider your own behavior in relation to a group, try to identify the influences to which you're reacting. Are you truly trying to obtain information from the group, or are you more concerned with being accepted by it? In most cases, you are more likely to show private acceptance if your conformity is based on informational influence rather than on normative influence (Argyle, 1991).

A Study of Obedience

In order to grasp the impact of Stanley Milgram's (1963; 1965) procedure, put yourself in the place of a subject who has volunteered for a psychological experiment. When you arrive at the experimental room, you meet a nice middle-aged man who has also signed up for the experiment. You chat until the experimenter arrives and informs you both that the experiment involves the effect of punishment on learning. You draw straws to determine who will be the "learner" and who will be the "teacher": You draw the "teacher" straw. The experimenter then explains that the teacher will ask the learner a series of questions and administer shock each time the learner gives an incorrect answer. The learner is then led into another room and hooked up with electrodes.

The experimenter returns and shows you the shock machine. There are a series of levers labeled from 15 volts to 450 volts; over the lower levers is the label "SLIGHT SHOCK," and over the upper levers the label reads "DANGER: SEVERE SHOCK." The final 450-volt level is marked "XXX." The experimenter tells you to begin reading the list of questions to the learner and to shock the learner for each incorrect answer given. You are to increase your level of shock by one lever after each incorrect answer; the first shock will be 15 volts, the next will be 30 volts, and so on.

You begin reading the questions, and each time the listener gives an incorrect answer, you administer the next level of shock. At 90 volts, the learner lets out a cry of pain. At 150 volts, the learner cries out again and begs to be released from the experiment. At 180 volts the learner bangs on the wall and cries that he can't stand the pain. At 300 volts, the learner refuses to answer any more questions and begs to have the experiment stopped. From this point on, there is no further response from the learner, but the experimenter instructs you to continue administering shocks anyhow.

What would you do in this situation? In Milgram's study, which was run at Yale University, the subjects were 20 to 50 years old; 40 percent held unskilled jobs, 40 percent held white-collar jobs, and 20 percent were professionals. Of the 40 subjects in the study, 26 (65 percent) followed orders to the end and administered 450 volts to the learner. Amazingly, not a single subject stopped the experiment before delivering 300 volts. Fortunately, the "learner" wasn't really receiving shock, but was actually an experimental accomplice who had been trained to make particular mistakes. The important point, however, is that the subjects thought that the learner was really receiving shock.

The results of the Milgram study are quite disturbing. They suggest that a majority of people are unwilling or unable to resist the orders of someone of higher status. The results of this study should make all of us question our ability to refuse to obey the leaders of groups. You may believe that you would never follow orders that you felt were morally wrong, but are you sure of this? Milgram described his experiment to 14 Yale seniors and to a group of psychiatrists. He then asked them to predict how many of the subjects would follow orders to deliver the 450 volts. They predicted that less than 2 percent would obey orders to the end. Clearly, most of us don't believe that we or our friends would blindly follow orders to hurt another person. Yet the results of Milgram's research suggest that we may indeed do just that.

Conformity: Who and When?

If you look back over your own history in various groups, you'll find that there were times when you went along with the group and other times when you didn't. Studies examining conformity have indeed found that there are conditions under which people are more likely to give in to group pressures.

If we look first at the *characteristics of the individual*, we find that people are most likely to conform when they (1) are strongly attracted to the group, (2) have a low status in the group and don't feel completely accepted by it, (3) expect future interactions with the group members, and (4) are new members in the group (see Forsyth, 1990; Worchel et al., 1992). Individuals who don't feel competent to perform the group's current task are most prone to conform to group norms. This description fits many of the outsiders who came to California to help the farmworkers. These people wanted very much to help the striking workers and believed they would be interacting with the workers for some time. In most cases, these outsiders didn't feel that they belonged in the workers' group; many of the workers were Hispanic, while the outsiders were mostly Anglo. In addition, the outsiders didn't know what to expect.

Before leaving the issue of individual characteristics, we should examine the effect of *gender* on conformity. Perhaps no other characteristic has received so much attention and has been the center of so much debate. Much of the early research suggested that women were more likely to conform than were men. However, research has shown that the gender difference is smaller than was once believed (Eagly & Wood, 1985). Further, the difference that does exist may be the result of status rather than gender. That is, in groups made up of members of both sexes, men are often in higher-status roles.

There is also evidence that women conform because of their concern with group cohesion, whereas men are more often focused on task issues. In other words, women conform to avoid group conflict and maintain harmony. Interestingly, there is also evidence that people in collective cultures are more likely to conform to groups that are important to them in order to avoid group conflict (Bond, 1996). Individuals in more individualistic cultures show less concern for group climate and more concern for task requirements.

The *characteristics of the group* also help determine group members' conformity. Asch (1956) found that people are much more likely to conform to a unanimous group than to one that has dissenters. Even one group member who openly refuses to go along with the group is enough to reduce drastically the amount of conformity. This finding may explain why many groups are quick to punish a person who tries to deviate from the group. In history, we find cases like the Spanish Inquisition and the Salem witch trials, where deviants were publicly tortured and killed. Clearly, the effect of these punishments was to demonstrate to others that deviation from the norm wouldn't be tolerated. From the group's point of view, allowing one deviant to exist can be very dangerous to the life of the group.

Finally, research has shown that conformity is greater on ambiguous *tasks* than on tasks where the correct answer is clear. Of course, this doesn't mean that people don't conform even when they know the correct answer; we have already seen that they do. But group members are more likely to conform when they don't know the correct position.

An important point that shouldn't be overlooked is that conformity is often a positive behavior. In our society we are taught that conformity is a herd instinct engaged in only by fools and those too weak in character to "hold their own." However, some conformity is absolutely necessary for the order and survival of the group. Imagine a society where no one conformed. Even the most simple tasks, such as driving to school, would be dangerous because you could not predict whether an oncoming driver would stop for a red light. Neither blind conformity nor blind deviance is a positive course of action. Rather, you should understand the pressures that motivate you to conform and determine for yourself whether or not a particular situation is one in which conforming feels comfortable.

You should also be aware of the possible reaction of the group should you decide not to conform. Taking all this information into account, you will be in a better position to control your own behavior and to make a wise decision about your course of action.

MINORITY INFLUENCE: THE POWER OF THE FEW

Just when you thought you would be safe if you could resist the powerful leaders and majority in your groups, we must open up a new concern—the influence of the minority. It is relatively clear that group activities are most heavily influenced by the leaders and the majority (Zimbardo & Leippe, 1991). In fact, it has been shown that group members often focus their attention on information that is known by most group members, ignoring information that is known by only a few (Stasser, 1992). But the minority is not totally powerless.

There is growing evidence that minorities can exert important influence on their groups if they are willing to run the risk of expressing their opinions. Minorities can become influential to the extent that they make themselves *visible* and *create tension and conflict* in groups (Moscovici, 1994). The success of minorities is largely determined by the way they present their position. Several investigations have found that minorities must take a clear and consistent stand and hold their position even in the face of pressure to change from the group (Nemeth, 1994; Papastamos & Mugny, 1989). By doing this, the minority often forces group members to consider the deviant position. Interestingly, the influence of the minority takes place over time rather than immediately, as does majority influence. And the impact of the minority is most evident in the private views of group members (Nemeth, 1989). The minority influ-

ences us, not because we fear retaliation from them, but because their consistent stand leads us to reconsider issues that we had previously ignored. We may not necessarily adopt the exact position of the minority, but the process of reconsideration may lead us to arrive at new and creative solutions to problems. In a sense, the minority frees us from the pressure of the majority.

WHY GROUPS CAN MAKE BAD DECISIONS: GROUPTHINK

From our discussion of the influence process that occur in groups, we might think that groups should make good decisions. Groups are generally composed of people with a variety of perspectives and sources of information. Although the majority usually is able to influence the group, the minority can also exert influence to get members to consider different points. Although this view seems logical, it is not always the case that groups make better decisions than single individuals. One reason for this situation concerns the influence pressures that work in many groups.

Thinking about your experience in groups, you may be able to recall times when those group made bad decisions and overlooked obvious flaws in a plan. This is not unusual. Irving Janis (1972; 1982) examined disastrous decisions made by presidents and their advisors such as the Bay of Pigs invasion and U.S. involvement in Vietnam. Janis suggests that a condition be labeled as *groupthink* led to these bad decisions. Groupthink occurs when groups think they are invulnerable and cannot do wrong. The members want to avoid conflict and strong pressures for conformity. Groupthink occurs when there is a strong leader that the members do not want to challenge. These conditions lead the members to adopt a position quickly without carefully considering alternatives or the flaws in the decision. Janis suggests that one way to avoid groupthink is to have the group allow—in fact, encourage—minorities to express their opinions.

It is interesting to see that the meetings of the NFWA were characterized by open discussion and much disagreement. During the early days, Chavez often refrained from ex-pressing his opinion until many of the other members had spoken. While this style of meeting often led to periods of discomfort, it created an atmosphere in which the minority could be heard. Quite possibly, these open meetings helped the association craft the successful plan that won vast concessions from the growers.

6. Your professor decides that everyone in class will listen to lectures without taking notes. Although you really want to take notes, you refrain from doing so. In this case, your professor is using _____ power to influence your behavior in the classroom.

7. T or F: Research on leadership has been able to identify several traits that "make" people good leaders.

8. According to interaction theories of leadership, people become leaders as a result of both _____ and _____ .

9. T or F: Laboratory research on obedience suggests that blind obedience is largely confined to stressful real-life situations.

10. _____ influence is most likely to lead to public compliance, whereas _____ influence may create private acceptance.

INTERGROUP RELATIONS: FROM WITHIN TO BETWEEN

To this point our focus has been on events that occur within a group. As a group member, however, you will find that some, if not much, of your activity involves interacting with members of *outgroups*, groups to which you do not belong. Indeed, Chavez and other members of the NFWA spent much time dealing with members of other unions, politicians, and the growers. The NFWA took its case to the people of the United States, encouraging them to boycott grapes and lettuce. While pressures within groups bind the members together, there are forces at play between and among groups that create tension and separate groups. And, as we will see, while these forces may be subtle, they can be very destructive.

Earlier in this chapter, we suggested that the groups to which we belong (our ingroups) form an important part of our self-identity. This seemingly simple statement has some very complex implications. Because most of us desire to have a positive self-concept, we want the groups to which we belong to be positive. This desire leads us to join attractive groups. But as we have seen, our self-serving bias also motivates us to do everything possible to enhance the condition of our own groups and depreciate the condition of our own groups and depreciate the condition of outgroups. Research has shown that (1) we tend to view the products of our own group as good and those of outgroups as inferior (Hinkle & Schopler, 1986), and (2) when given the opportunity to distribute rewards, we give higher payment to members of our own group than to members of outgroups even when they interact with members of our own group (Tajfel, 1970). And this is not the end of the story. Several studies have shown that we view our groups as composed of diverse and varied members, while we see the members of outgroups as being very similar to each other (Quattrone & Jones, 1980; Linville, 1982). One reason for this effect is that we interact more frequently with the members of our own group and consequently become aware of their differences. This simple perceptual bias may seem harmless, but consider the consequences. If you believe that members of outgroups are all the same, you need only interact with one of them to determine the characteristics of all of them. This belief not only results in reduced contact with outgroup members, but it encourages you to form stereotypes of outgroups based on very little contact.

Thus, there is real danger in the forces unwittingly set into motion by group membership. It is important that we understand and recognize these forces because they so easily give rise to conflict between groups. Our popular literature abounds with examples of this conflict. For example, you may have little difficulty describing the students of a rival university in a few terms. "Those folks" are rich party animals, not very smart, conservative, and snobbish. However, if you are asked to describe at your university, you may protest, saying that they are very different, some are conservative while others are liberal, some are athletic while others prefer to study, and so on.

Jonathan Swift's *Gulliver's Travels* describes vicious conflict between the "big enders" and the "little enders": Individuals became members of one of these two groups depending on which end (big end or little end) they cracked their hard-boiled eggs. Dr. Seuss (1984) picked up this theme in his children's book, *The Butter Battle Book,* which tells the story of a bitter conflict between the Yooks and Zooks that led them to develop ultimate weapons of destruction. The sole difference between the two groups was that one ate their bread with the buttered side up while the other ate bread with the buttered side down. The message here is that intergroup conflict that may be based solely on group membership has a tendency to expand and escalate.

Prejudice and Discrimination

The forces set into motion by group membership contribute to another type of intergroup behavior: prejudice and discrimination. Cesar Chavez was very aware of these issues in his fight with the growers. Most of the members of the NFWA were Hispanic or Mexican nationals. Not only did they fight their unfair treatment because of their low-status jobs, but they also had to combat extreme hostility aimed at them because of their ethnic group. Chavez received death threats because of his ethnic identity. Some people sided with the growers because of their dislike of Hispanics, and others openly stated that the laborers deserved their fate because of their ethnic group.

Prejudice is an unjustified negative *attitude* toward an individual based solely on the person's membership in a group (Brewer & Kramer, 1985). Our prejudices are generally founded on **stereotypes,** which are simplified generalizations about the characteristics of a group. Stereotypes not only involve general traits that are assigned to groups, they also include our view of how similar the group members are to each other and how important or central specific traits are to the group (Worchel & Rothgerber, 1997). These stereotypes are notoriously difficult to change because we interpret and remember events in ways that support these stereotypes. For example, if we examine the conditions of the farm laborers, we might be appalled by the low salaries, hard work, and poor living conditions. However, if we have a stereotype that Hispanics are lazy and dirty, we might interpret the farm workers' strike as evidence that the workers did not want to work to better their condition, they simply wanted to get something given to them for nothing. While prejudice and stereotypes are conditions of our minds, **discrimination** is negative, often aggressive, *behavior* aimed at the target of prejudice.

As we saw in the earlier section, simply being a member of a group can set the stage for prejudice and discrimination by leading us to elevate our ingroup and reduce contact with outgroup members. But we are not necessarily prejudiced against all outgroups. Our *sociocultural conditions* influence which groups will become the objects of our prejudice; we learn prejudice. As we grow up, we observe powerful others, such as our parents and politicians, express negative opinions about certain groups. We see certain groups constantly portrayed in a negative light on television or in the newspapers. We adopt these negative attitudes, and when we express them, we find others rewarding us and approving of our behavior (Pettigrew, 1959). As you might expect, if learning plays such a central role in forming our prejudice, the object of prejudice and discrimination is different from one culture to the next. In our own society, we find common prejudices against groups such as blacks, Hispanics, Jews, Asians, and women. In modern-day Germany, prejudice exists against Turks and Italians; in Thailand there are negative feelings toward Chinese; and in Iraq and Turkey the objects of prejudice are the Kurds.

Groups are not randomly chosen within cultures as the objects of discrimination and prejudice. Often there is a perception that these groups are a real threat, hence the name *realistic conflict* theory (Kinder & Sears, 1981). Scarce resources, such as land or jobs, may be perceived to be threatened. In the southern United States, for example, blacks were tradi-

tionally viewed as being in direct competition with whites for jobs. Prejudice and discrimination also increase during difficult economic times like depressions or recessions (Hepworth & West, 1998). During these periods, resources and opportunities are scarce and there is realistic competition between people and groups. A second source of threat that underlies prejudice is the perception that a group is a menace to basic values or traditions (McConahay, 1986). Because religion is so much a part of the lives of many people, they may feel threatened when a group has different religious beliefs or practices. These differences may be viewed as questioning the validity of their beliefs.

Finally, there is some evidence that certain types of people are more prone to adopt prejudiced attitudes. Early work after World War II identified a personality type known as the *authoritarian personality* that seemed to characterize many people who were prejudiced against Jews and other ethnic groups (Adorno et al., 1954). People with this personality tended to come from homes where discipline was severe and threatening and the parents had very high aspirations for their children. While people with the authoritarian personality tended to idolize their parents and see no wrong in them, below the surface they seethed with anger against the parents. These people had a strong need for order and structure and a blind respect for authority.

As you can see, numerous factors contribute to developing prejudice and discrimination. Despite the fact that these attitudes and behaviors are destructive, they are highly resistant to change and no place in the world is completely free from them.

Reducing Conflict, Prejudice, and Discrimination

All is not lost, however, because there are steps that can be taken to reduce these negative attitudes and behaviors. Simple education and learning about other groups can help, but as we have seen, we are prone to distort information. Hence, information alone is not the answer.

An additional factor is how easy it is to identify groups. Groups that are readily identifiable are often the target of prejudice. A group may be distinguished because of some physical characteristic such as color or dress, and we often quickly lump together people who seem to share a common feature and develop prejudice toward the whole group. However, the short-sightedness of this approach is not only evident in the attempt to apply general traits to a large group, but in the fact that these "groups" often represent widely different peoples. For example, prejudiced individuals are often quick to identify all people from India, Africa, many Arab countries, the Caribbean Islands, and the United States as being black. Therefore, while ease of identifying a group often influences which group will be singled out as the target of prejudice, the process of identifying a group is often as flawed as the traits assigned to the group.

We tend to avoid groups and people who are the object of our conflict and prejudice. One way to reduce prejudice is to reverse this tendency and increase contact. But not all types of contact will help. Imagine that you are prejudiced against Hispanics and that you get a job dealing with parole violators among the farm workers. Your job brings you into contact with many Hispanics, but you have contact with only those who have broken the law and you are always in a position of high status and authority. Instead of reducing your prejudice, this type of contact might reinforce it. Research has shown that having *equal status* with the object of prejudice can reduce these attitudes (Worchel, 1986; Ben-Ari & Amir, 1988). Equal status involves being with members of the outgroup who have power and

ability equal to yours and who can contribute to your interaction goals.

A second method involves *cooperation.* In an interesting study on boys at summer camp, investigators found that hostility between groups was reduced when the two groups worked together to solve common problems (Sherif et al., 1961). For example, in one case, a truck bringing water to the camp became stuck and it took the efforts of both groups to move the truck. After a series of cooperative efforts, the boys from the two groups began to like each other. Further research showed that intergroup hostility was reduced most effectively when the cooperative efforts ended in success and allowed the two groups to share attractive rewards (Worchel et al., 1979). In an interesting twist on this theme, students in an elementary school were placed into mixed racial groups. Each group had to solve a problem, but the solution required each child in the groups to contribute the unique information that he or she had (Aronson & Bridgemen, 1979). This approach was similar to putting together a jigsaw puzzle in which each person has some of the pieces; only if everyone contributes can the puzzle by completed.

Finally, there is some evidence that experiencing prejudice can reduce prejudice. A third-grade teacher in Riceville, Iowa announced to her class that blue-eyed people are smarter, cleaner, and more civilized than brown-eyed people. The teacher let the blue-eyed children sit in the front of the room and gave them extra privileges. The blue-eyed children went through the day feeling superior and the brown-eyed kids felt lousy. The blue-eyed children refused to associate with the brown-eyed children and teased the "inferior" brown-eyes. But the next morning, the teacher announced that she had made a mistake and that it was the brown-eyed people who were really the superior folks. And, as you might expect, the pattern of discrimination and prejudice reversed itself and the blue-eyed kids became the victims. The following day, the teacher told the kids that there was, in fact, no superior group and that she wanted them to see how easily prejudice developed. They discussed their feelings. Research on this method suggests that it can lead to a reduction in prejudice and discrimination (Weiner & Wright, 1973).

A third approach involves changing people's perceptions of the group, *recategorization* in scientific terms (Brewer & Miller, 1988; Gaertner et al., 1990). Researchers have found that prejudice and discrimination can be reduced by changing how people define groups. By emphasizing common bonds between groups and encouraging people to redefine group boundaries, the tendency to depreciate others is reduced. When we look at the striking farmworkers, there is a tendency to see them as largely a group of Hispanic people protesting their work conditions. This perception sets up two groups, the Hispanic farmworkers and us, and gives us an outgroup as a target for prejudice and discrimination. Now let's change our thinking a bit. We can view the farmworkers as North Americans (like us) or as parents concerned about supporting their families (also like us). Viewed in this way, it is no longer an us-them situation and there is no outgroup as the target of discrimination.

Each of these methods, alone or in combination, can affect the level of prejudice and discrimination. But each is difficult to implement because of our tendency to hold tight to our prejudices and stereotypes and avoid the object of these negative feelings.

Groups and Conflict: A Final Comment

We have painted an often dark picture of groups and the dynamics of group behavior.

Indeed, groups can have a negative effect on our behavior. We may follow orders of leaders to carry out hurtful and destructive acts. We may conform to the group even though we know it is wrong. As group members, we are motivated to discriminate and complete with outgroups. All of this is true.

However, before indicting groups and group conflict, let's not forget the other side of the coin. We can achieve goals with the aid of groups that we could never achieve on our own. Groups can be a source of comfort, support, security, and information.

Likewise, conflict between groups is not necessarily negative. Conflict helps identify problems and motivates us to find new solutions. The conflict between the farmworkers and growers identified problems and forced each side to consider both sides of the issue. Conflict, in this case and in many others, brings parties together and allows them to exchange information and points of view. Conflict brings about social change (Simmel, 1955). And intergroup conflict unites members within each group. Simmel (1955) states, "One unites in order to fight." This was certainly the effect of conflict in Chavez's case. As it pushed its fight against the growers, the NFWA saw its ranks grow. Laborers put aside their differences and united in a common cause to force the growers to give higher salaries and better living conditions.

The forces set into motion by group membership and intergroup conflict are thus neither all good nor all bad. We would not want to avoid group membership, nor should all group conflict be avoided. What is important is that we work to enhance the positive forces while being aware of the pitfalls. If we understand the dynamics of group and intergroup behavior, we can work to manage these forces to the benefit of all.

11. T or F: There is a tendency to view our own groups as being composed of more diverse members than outgroups, especially late in the group's existence.

12. _____ is an unjustified negative attitude toward an individual based on his or her membership in a group, while _____ involves negative behavior.

13. T or F: Actual competition between groups for limited resources is not a foundation for prejudice.

14. _____ is the most effective contact for reducing prejudice between groups.

15. Which of the following is not a good means for reducing prejudice and conflict between groups?

   a. getting the groups to cooperate together on a common project
   b. avoiding contact between the groups
   c. encouraging the members to recategorize their perceptions of the groups to emphasize common boundaries
   d. creating opportunities for equal-status contact

SUMMARY

1. We join groups for many reasons. Groups give us rewards and help us achieve goals; they serve as a source of social support; they are a source of information and allow us to compare ourselves with others; they often make up an important part of our identity, our social identity. According to social comparison theory, we are most attracted to groups of people similar to us. However, social identity theory suggests that we want to join the best groups possible to enhance our self-identity.

2. Joining a groups gives us certain benefits, but it also requires that we sacrifice some of our independence. The conflict between individual needs and group needs is the basis for the social dilemma. Because of the attraction of working toward individual goals, many groups have stiff penalties for members who fail to contribute to the group goals.

3. Deindividuation occurs when individuals lose their sense of responsibility for their actions and become submerged in the group. In such cases, individuals are not guided by common norms or rules of behavior and they become more likely to engage in socially unacceptable behaviors and have less feelings of guilt.

4. The role of the group is an important issue that distinguishes individualistic and collective cultures. People in individualistic cultures strive for independence and personal recognition, whereas people in collective cultures often behave so as not to "stand out" and embarrass other group members.

5. Groups generally have clear structure and boundaries. Norms are general rules that apply to all group members. Roles define the obligations and responsibilities of people in specific positions. Because we belong to many groups at the same time, we may face role conflict, which involves competing demands from the different groups.

6. Groups seem to develop through predictable stages. One model suggests group begin by focusing on group identity, then move to productivity issues, followed by concerns for individual recognition, and then decaying as some group members leave the group. In addition, group members go through stages or

phases in the group from perspective member to ex-member.

7. Power involves the potential to influence others, and six types of power have been identified: coercive, reward, expert, legitimate, informational and referent. Coercive power is easy to use but separates the power figure from the less powerful. Referent power is the broadest type of power, and it does not require surveillance.

8. Leadership involves the exercise of power. Leaders are the people who influence groups. Some theories suggest that certain traits make people leaders, but other theories suggest the situation determines who will be the leader. More recent theories suggest that a combination of personal characteristics and situation determines who will be a leader.

9. Obedience involves following the orders of a more powerful person. People follow orders because they hold the leader responsible for their behavior, the desire to gain rewards or personal advancement, ideological zeal, personal satisfaction, and the role requirements of follower. Blind obedience can have negative consequences.

10. Conformity occurs when we change our actions or attitudes to be more like those of other group members as a result of real or imagined group pressure, despite personal feelings to the contrary. Conformity may involve only public behaviors (public compliance), or it may also involve only public behaviors (public compliance), or it may also involve changing of private attitudes (private acceptance). Groups influence members be-

havior because of the information they possess (informational influence) and the threat of rejecting members who do not conform (normative influence). Individual, task, and group factors will influence the degree of conformity. Although the research suggests that we are most often influenced by the majority, there is also evidence that minorities who take clear and unyielding positions may have influence, especially over an extended period of time.

11. Because groups are the core of our social identities and we strive for positive identities, we are motivated to join the best possible groups and we often discriminate about outgroups. There is also a tendency to see our own groups are more terogeneous than outgroups and to see our group's products as being better than those of outgroups. Prejudice is a negative attitude toward an individual based on his or her membership in a group, while discrimination is negative behavior that is guided by prejudice. Learning, clear distinguishing characteristics of a group, actual conflict between groups, and our own personality influence the development of prejudice and discrimination. Prejudice is often difficult to reduce because of our tendency to avoid contact with members of the outgroup or to seek information that supports our prejudice. However, research has shown that prejudice can be reduced by equal-status contact between the two groups, cooperation on joint projects, and recategorization of our perceptions of group boundaries.

CRITICAL THINKING QUESTIONS

1. Consider for the moment the differences between individualistic and collective cultures as they involve group behavior. Individualistic cultures stress independence, whereas collective cultures stress fitting in the group. This difference has broad implications for

groups. For example, groups in individualistic cultures will need to bring forces on individuals to support group goals, while groups in collective cultures will need to find ways to encourage members to perform as well as possible. Carrying this point further, describe how groups in individualistic and collective cultures might differ.

2. We have a tendency to speak in absolutes. For example, we might argue that conformity is bad or that obedience will have negative consequences. Certainly we can find examples to support these positions. However, think about the difficulties you would face if no one conformed to laws or social norms, and obedience to the directives of leaders never occurred. Given this picture, how would you modify these absolute statements? How, too, would you instruct your children about conformity and obedience?

3. Most of us hate to admit our prejudices toward people from other groups. Think honestly about your own prejudices toward a particular group. How did they develop? How much of the foundation is based on your personal experience with members of the outgroup? Now outline a program that you might undertake to reduce your prejudice toward this group.

MATCHING EXERCISE

Match each term with its definition.

a. self-serving bias
b. collective culture
c. social dilemma
d. role conflict

e. groupthink
f. norms
g. prejudice
h. discrimination

i. stereotype
j. realistic conflict theory
k. deindividuation

1. Conflict that results when an individual must choose between options that benefit the self or those that benefit the group
2. Situation that results when the demands of a person's role in two groups are in conflict
3. Situation that exists when groups are cohesive and feel invulnerable, often resulting in poor decision making by the group
4. Loss of individuality that occurs when the individual becomes submerged in the group and feels relatively anonymous
5. Tendency for social comparisons to be made with people who are less accomplished on the specific dimension

6. Rules that govern specific behaviors and apply to all group members
7. Negative, often aggressive, behavior aimed at the target of prejudice
8. Theory that suggests that one cause of prejudice is conflict between groups for scarce resources
9. Cultures that stress the importance of the group over that of the individual
10. Simplified generalizations about the characteristics of a group
11. An unjustified negative attitude toward an individual based solely on the person's membership in a group

Answers to Matching Exercise

a. 5   b. 9   c. 1   d. 2   e. 3   f. 6   g. 11   h. 7   i. 10   j. 8   k. 4

ANSWERS TO REVIEW QUESTIONS_____

1. best
2. individual, group
3. d
4. individualistic
5. true
6. legitimate
7. false
8. traits, situations

9. false
10. normative, informational
11. true
12. prejudice, discrimination
13. false
14. equal status
15. b

WORKING

James Herriot

James Herriot

A universal *rite of passage* for young people in college is deciding what they would like to be "when they grow up" and finding a job in their chosen field. A popular set of books which later became a television series described the trials and triumphs of a young veterinarian, James Herriot, in the 1930s. After slaving away for five years in vet school, Herriot faced a dismal job market. Farming was in a sad state, and the tractor had replaced the draught horse. In a situation not so different from today, technology had reduced the demand for certain jobs, such as veterinarian.

Herriot describes how he answered an advertisement for a position in Darrowby, a small town in Yorkshire Dales. When he arrived for the interview, he was met by Siegfried Farnon, who gave him a quick tour of the clinic and living quarters. Then rather than sitting down and describing the job, Siegfried bundled James into his old Hillman auto and whisked him to an isolated farm. There in the barn was Mr. Sharpe's cow, in terrible pain from a blocked udder. Anxious to demonstrate his ability, James volunteered to treat the cow. He gently worked the Hudson instrument into the teat to clear the blockage. The next thing he knew, he "was sitting gasping in the dung channel with the neat imprint of a cloven hoof on my shirt front, just over the solar plexus (Herriot, 1972, p. 28)." Siegfried and Mr. Sharpe burst into laughter, and Mr. Sharpe bellowed, "I'm sorry, young man, but I owt to 'ave told you that this is a very friendly cow. She allus likes to shake hands."

Later that evening, Siegfried told James about the job, and to James' surprise he was immediately offered the job. This seemed to be too good to be true, and James quickly accepted the offer. The first few years proved to be a great challenge. The farmers in Yorkshire Dales were reluctant to accept a new upstart veterinarian, and they adopted a "show me" attitude. James found that the actual practice of veterinary medicine was very different from what he had learned in textbooks. Few cases were routine, and many required him to improvise. He quickly learned that he not only had to treat his patients' ailments, but he also had to deal with their owners, who were quick to offer their own diagnoses or suggest the "proper" procedure for treatment. Each case was a test where James had to prove himself.

OUR JOBS AND OUR LIVES

James Herriot's books about his life as a veterinarian are fascinating. The appeal of his life doesn't come from the fact that Herriot was a superman who performed incredible feats that made the front page of the newspaper. His story is similar to what most of us could write about our lives and our work. Taken together, however, Herriot's experiences teach many lessons.

One of the most important lessons is the important role that people's work plays in their lives. When we think about our jobs, two things usually come to mind: *money* and *time*. Clearly, the money earned from employment plays a major role in our lives: It enables us to feed and clothe ourselves; it helps determine our standard of living, what kind of home we have, the type of car we drive, and the number of vacations we take. Holding a job outside the home also influences how we spend much of our time during the day. Most of us will work at least 40 years of our lives at a job. Assuming that we work an average of 40 hours a week, we will spend over 80,000 hours on our jobs. That's a long time, and it's easy to see that our careers will occupy a large part of our attention.

But James Herriot's story shows that our jobs will play a role in our lives even larger than determining how our time is spent and how much money we have. James's job *determined where he lived*. In taking the one job that was open to him, he had to move to a small town in an area he had never even visited. For many of us, our jobs will determine where we live. We may have to leave the place where we now live to find the type of work we desire.

Our jobs may also influence our *daily routine*. Many of us will work the five-days-a-week, 9-to-5 schedule, but others won't. James Herriot worked weekends and many nights. Regardless of our particular schedules, the requirements of our jobs may well determine when we can shop, go out dancing or to the movies, and take our vacations.

Herriot's books are filled with tales about people. The striking part of these stories is that almost all the people he describes he met through his job. They were people who came to the clinic, people whose farms he visited to work on their animals, other vets he met at conventions, or people he met on his way to and from cases he was working on. He even met his future wife when he was called to a farm to work on a sick bull. The same story will hold true for most of us. Our jobs will determine *whom we come into contact with* and who will be our friends. As we pointed out in Chapter 9, proximity and similarity are two important factors that influence who will be attractive to us. It is important to recognize the influence on our lives played by the type of work we choose and the place in which we work. So our personal adjustment process must include adjustment to our work and work setting.

WHY WORK?

Given that a career can take over so much of our lives, a natural question to ask is: Why put ourselves through all the effort to have an occupation? Why did James Herriot spend so many years in school learning his profession and then accept a position that required him to work long hours under some very bad conditions? The first answer that comes to mind is money. We work to live. This is certainly true,

but it doesn't present the whole picture. In one study, workers were asked what they would do if they had a million dollars (Rubin, 1979). Although some said they would change their jobs, almost all reported they would continue to work. Thus survival is only one of the reasons that we work; there are many other reasons as well.

Independence.   Working fulfills our need for independence. Having a job and an income allows us to achieve independence from our parents. We can support ourselves, set up our own households, and start our own families if we desire. This independence represents freedom; having a job allows us to make basic choices within the limits of our income.

Identity.   If someone asked who James Herriot was, people familiar with his books would reply that he was a veterinarian. For many of us, as for Herriot, our occupation becomes a part of our identity. Like our family, hometown, or university, our occupation is one bit of information that makes us unique from many other people and helps define who we are. In fact, some people choose a career based on the identity they want to assume. For example, someone who wants to be seen as rugged and tough may choose a career that portrays this image, such as truck driving, ranching, or athletics.

Self-esteem.   Despite the fact that he actually earned little money, James Herriot felt that his work was important. Not only was he helping other people in his hometown, but each time he cured a sick or injured animal he was demonstrating his skills to himself. Herriot's work was like a stage on which he could demonstrate his abilities to others and to himself. Work helps give many of us a sense of self-worth. It bolsters our self-esteem by helping us gain a sense of competency.

Self-actualization.   Maslow's (1954) concept of **self-actualization** means, in a nutshell, that a person is able to develop his or her potential, to use personal abilities in creative ways. Herriot speaks with pride of one of his most difficult cases. A poor family's prize heifer had an abscess in her throat and was slowly dying. Herriot knew of no technique that had been developed to treat this problem. For days he thought of the problem as the cow became weaker. In desperation he developed a new technique. The technique worked, and the cow was saved! Herriot's pride knew no bounds: He had created something new; he had used his skills to the best of his ability. So it is that in many cases our work gives us the opportunity to use our skills, to do the best job we can, and, sometimes, to do it in a new, creative way.

As we can see, although working is crucial to our survival, we work to satisfy needs broader than food, clothing, and shelter. We can define **work** as some disciplined activity that gives us a feeling of personal accomplishment and that makes a contribution to our society. An **occupation** or a **job** is the specific form our choice of work takes. You may have chosen educating children as the work you'd like to do, but you could accomplish this work by raising your own children as a full-time occupation or by taking a job as a teacher, writer of children's literature, or secretary of your state's department of education. Almost any job will enable us to earn enough money to survive. It is important to choose a form of work that will also enable us to satisfy our desires for independence, identity, self-esteem, and creativity.

CHOOSING A CAREER

The Decision Process

By the time you entered college, you were probably sick of being asked, "What are you going to be when you grow up?" It seems that in our society we begin asking this question of children almost as soon as they learn to talk. In

fact, a child may have an easier time answering this question than a young adult does. When you're at the point of actually choosing a career, the question has real meaning.

It may interest you to learn that the difficulties you experience in choosing a career are not universal. In some collective societies (see Chapter 13), the decision about an individuals career is not based only on his or her desires. Rather, the group (family, village, tribe) determines what jobs it needs performed and which family member will undertake this job (Triandis, 1994). For example, the family business may need an accountant to help run the business. The family may, therefore, decide that one of its young members will go to college to become an accountant. In the Basque country of northern Spain, the tradition among farming families is that the oldest son will inherit the farm and become a farmer. In these societies, the individual is obligated to choose the career that will help the family. Therefore, the individuals do not agonize over making a career choice, though they may not be particularly happy with the choice that is made for them.

In more individualistic societies such as the United States, however, we are able to choose the career that we desire. We are, in fact, generally expected to choose a line of work that will make us independent from our family. On one hand, this freedom allows us to pursue a *career* that fits our desires. On the other hand, the responsibility of making this decision may seem daunting and frightening. How are we to know at age 20 or so the type of work that will be fulfilling for the next 40 years? What happens if we make the "wrong" choice? As we will see, there are many sources that can help us in making this decision, and a career decision is not final. Many people change careers during their lifetime.

Even with this apparent failsafe, the decision about what to be "when we grow up" is a difficult and important one, and not a decision that most of us make overnight. In fact, research suggests that in early childhood we begin laying the groundwork for choosing our careers (Ginsberg, 1966). This research identifies stages we go through in making the decision. The *fantasy stage* begins when we are very young and lasts until approximately the age of 11. During this stage, children assume that they can be whatever they want to be. They spend a great deal of time thinking about various occupations and playing at jobs. You might remember some of the happy moments of your childhood when you "were" a doctor, movie star, firefighter, or astronaut.

Between ages 11 and 17, young people enter the *tentative stage*. During this period they realize that they must soon make a decision about the occupation they will enter. They begin to examine their interests, abilities, and values and search for occupations that will best fit these characteristics.

During the *realistic stage* from age 17 on, people begin to realize that no one job may fit all their desires and their choice may have to be a compromise. People look at the rewards offered by jobs and weigh these against the training required for the job and the effort required in the occupation. Choices become narrowed and more realistic.

Aids to Making an Informed Decision

James Herriot began veterinary school in the early 1930s. Compared to the present, his decision about an occupation was simple. Today the variety in types of jobs is almost unbelievable. In fact, the government publishes the *Dictionary of Occupational Titles,* which lists over 20,000 jobs, and new jobs are being added each year. Given the number of possibilities, how can anyone make the "right" choice?

Before examining some of the aids we can use in making a decision, we should stress some important points. First, there is no one "right" job for any of us. Many different occupations could fulfill each of our needs. The aim is to find a job or occupation, not *the* job,

that will make us happy. Second, as we grow older, our needs and desires change. An occupation we choose when we are in our twenties may not fulfill our needs when we are in our forties. So it's important to realize that we will be faced with making decision about our occupation throughout our lives. No decision is irreversible. But the decision about our first job is a very important one because it will serve as the foundation for decisions throughout our lives.

Counselors and Tests.   Many high schools and most colleges and universities have job or *guidance counselors.* These people are trained to help students choose an occupation. Their work doesn't involve telling you what you should be. Rather, the counselors attempt to identify your interests, values, attitudes, and abilities.

Often counselors will suggest that students take tests aimed at identifying their abilities and interests. *Ability tests* measure reasoning, memory, mechanical, math, and psychomotor abilities. Entrance examinations for many professional schools include a wide range of ability questions. For example, a student wishing to enter some dental schools may be given a psychomotor test where he or she is asked to carve a figure out of a block of soap. *Interest tests* compare the individual's interests with those of successful people in a wide variety of occupations. The assumption behind these tests is that a person is more likely to be happy if his or her basic interests are similar to those of people already in the field.

Armed with the results of the tests and with a record of the person's background, the counselor then conducts an interview with the individual. In the interview, the counselor further pinpoints the person's values and desires and discusses the results of the tests. The counselor and student discuss a number of different occupations, and the counselor outlines what is required to enter each of these professions.

Parents. Parents can be either one of the most helpful resources or one of the greatest hindrances for a person attempting to decide on a career. Parents who understand the anxiety and uncertainty that accompany making a decision about a career can supply a supportive environment. They can lend a sympathetic ear and help their children "talk through" their feelings about their career options. They can help arrange interviews with people who work in different professions. They can discourage their children from making premature or uneducated decisions.

Unfortunately, some parents become roadblocks in their children's quest for a career. Parents hold values about what occupations are good and bad, and they may feel that they "know what is best" for their children. They may try to force their children to adopt their values and deny them the independence to make their own choices. Often parents attempt to guide their children because they care about them and want them to have a better life than they themselves had. In other cases, parents try to live their own lives again through their children. A frustrated father who wanted to be a doctor or an unfulfilled mother who wanted to be a business executive may push his or her children in these directions.

Attempts by parents to determine their children's careers can have two disastrous consequences. On one hand, children may follow the parents' advice only to find out many years later that they have made a bad decision. Not only will the children be unhappy, they will also resent their parents for causing their misfortune. On the other hand, the children may experience reactance (Brehm & Brehm, 1981). **Reactance** results when a person feels that his or her freedom is being threatened. As a consequence, the threatened freedom becomes more attractive, and the person engages in the threatened free behavior simply to demonstrate that he or she has freedom. In the case of parental interference, telling children that they must not enter a certain occupation may boomerang; the forbidden occupation may begin to look more attractive. A child may choose that occupation simply to defy his or her parents and proclaim his or her freedom of choice.

Internships and Summer Jobs. There is an old saying that "experience is the best teacher." In the case of career choices, this saying suggests that the more experience you have with different jobs, the better able you'll be to make a wise career choice. Summer jobs, volunteer work, and internships give you the chance to get firsthand experience with specific jobs before you make a career choice. In many cases, colleges and universities have arrangements with local businesses that allow students to work on an internship basis during the school year.

These internships may be in the police department, courts, hospitals, law offices, local industries, or even on farms. Students have the opportunity to learn about jobs and can gain course credit for their work. Summer jobs and volunteer work also offer this kind of hands-on experience that allows students to learn about careers. A semester or summer of work clearly won't present the whole picture, but what you learn can be combined with what you've gained from tests and talks with guidance counselors, parents, and people in those professions. Applicants can often get information about internships, and summer jobs from school placement offices and counselors.

Getting the Job

James Herriot was surprised by his first meeting with Siegfried Farnon. He had expected Siegfried to quiz him about his understanding of veterinary medicine and carefully probe his background. Instead, Siegfried hustled James off to see a number of cases. Siegfried watched with a mixture of amusement and careful attention when James was kicked by the "friendly" cow at one of the first stops. Later in the pub Siegfried explained the method behind his unorthodox interview; he told James that he could see from his record that James knew veterinary medicine. What Siegfried wanted to find out was how James could adapt to the specific conditions of his practice. How would he react to being embarrassed by the cow incident? How would he react to the variety of clients he would have to work for?

In this approach, Siegfried was expressing one of the major concerns of employers in their decision about who to hire. Performing well on a job is not only determined by having the right skills; a person must be able to apply these skills and adapt to the work conditions. Psychologists (Muchinsky, 1993) talk about the importance of a **person–environment fit;** we will encounter this term again in Chapter 15, but for our purposes here, we are focusing on the need to ensure that the worker and the job are suited for each other. For example, one study found that students who are not very sociable perform better in lecture sections, whereas more sociable students perform better in classes arranged around discussion groups (Pervin, 1968). One type of student is not necessarily smarter than the other; rather, the different types of classes allow different students to use their abilities more effectively.

Learning about Job Opportunities

There are several sources that you can use to learn about job openings (see Figure 14.1 on page 378).

Advertisements. The most common way to learn about job openings is through advertisements placed by employers. Most newspapers and trade magazines have sections of their classified section devoted to advertising job opportunities. Often these sections are divided in subsections devoted to specific types of jobs—for example, Professional, Sales, Clerical. An increasingly popular source for advertising job openings is the Internet. Advertisements,

like people, come in many types and shapes. The advertisements not only announce the job opening and information about the position, they often also represent the image of the company, as you can see in Figure 14.1 (Rawlinson, 1988). One study found that ads displaying the company emblem and other illustrations attract the greatest number of applicants, while those ads that have specific information such as salary range and company telephone number attract the best qualified applicants (Kaplan, Aamodt, & Wilk, 1991).

These advertisements fall into three general categories, and Aamodt (1996) gives some pointers about how to respond to each type. Some ads ask applicants to *respond by calling.* In these cases the organization wants to quickly screen applicants or to hear the applicant's telephone voice. When answering these ads, (1) practice your first few sentences, and (2) be prepared for a short interview by having a copy of your résumé and a paper and pencil handy. Indicate that you are interested in learning more about the position and describe your past experience and knowledge of the company. Remember, you have only a short time to make a good impression. A second type of ad requests that people *apply in person.* In these cases, the organization wants to see the person and may require him or her to complete an application. In these cases, (1) be pleasant to the people you come in contact with, (2) be prepared for an on-the-spot interview, (3) dress as if you were going to an interview, and (4) take a résumé and paper and pen with you. Finally, other advertisements ask applicants to *send a résumé.* In these cases, send a cover letter with your résumé, indicating your interest and most relevant experience. In all cases, respond to many advertisements and act promptly. Employers often have a limited time in which to fill a position.

Situation-Wanted Advertisements. You don't have to wait for an employer to advertise for a position. Situation-wanted ads are those

Finding a Job That Fits

One of the authors worked for several years in the human resources department of a large company. One of his jobs was to help employees adjust to their jobs and to find new positions for employees who were unhappy or unproductive in their present position. He often discussed with employees how they decided to enter a particular profession. And he was struck by the number of people who failed to use available resources to help them make a decision. Sally was a typical case.

Sally had been a good but not exceptional student in high school. She held a number of part-time jobs, but no subject or job particularly interested her. When she graduated, college seemed to be the "most logical" option to her, and she chose to attend a university that many of her friends had chosen. In college her attention was focused on getting her degree and doing well enough to "keep my parents off my back." She tried a few majors and finally settled on journalism "because I was tired of changing and had to choose something to graduate."

As graduation time approached, she was a bit panicked about the process of a job. She talked with a number of her friends, and "we all decided that working in advertising would be fun." She interviewed with a number of firms and took a job that seemed interesting and was located in a "nice place." She quickly realized that she "hated" advertising, but she had little idea what she wanted to do

or what options were open to her. Needless to say, Sally was unhappy and unmotivated.

Fortunately, Sally's case had a happy ending. She talked with a job counselor (this author) and took a number of interest tests. These sources pointed her toward fashion design. But before rushing her decision, she read a number of books on fashion design, visited two design firms in the area, and talked with a number of people working in these firms. From these discussions she learned that the fashion world was highly competitive, but she identified a unique niche in the industry—designs for elderly people. She spent the next two years taking night and weekend classes at a local college in the areas of design and geriatric behavior. She enlisted the aid of two of her professors who had contacts in the industry to help her secure a job.

Sally found a job and over the years advanced in the company to the position of senior designer. This happy ending has an even happier sequel. Each year on his birthday, the author receives a card with a note of thanks for his help in guiding her *and* a new shirt "designed for the mature life!"

There are a wide variety of sources that we can use to help us make wise choices about our careers. Too often, however, we overlook these sources, instead making spur-of-the-moment decisions that may not be best for us.

---

where you indicate that you are available for a job, listing your qualifications and interests. Studies of situation-wanted ads found that nearly 70 percent of the applicants were contacted (sometimes by employment agencies) and 21.5 percent of the applicants received job offers (Williams & Garris, 1991; Willis, Miller, & Huff, 1991).

Campus Recruiters and Job Fairs. Most colleges have company recruiters visit campus, and many hold job fairs where several companies will have booths with recruiters who will discuss their company and job opportu-

nities. Large companies will sometimes hold their own job fairs when they have several positions available in different types of work areas. These methods allow the applicant to learn more about the company before making a formal application, and they allow the recruiter to develop an impression of the applicant. In some cases, recruiters may hire an applicant on the spot, so this contract should be treated as an interview.

Employment Agencies. Employment agencies serve as matchmakers for both employers and applicants. They generally have a file on

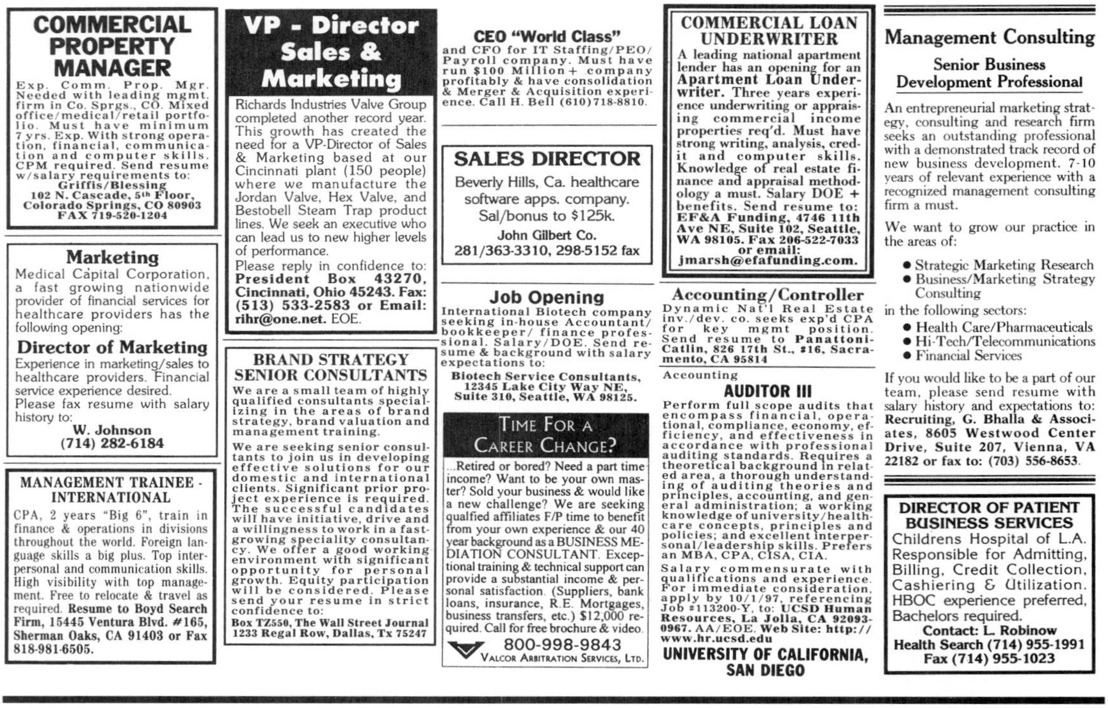

COMMERCIAL PROPERTY MANAGER

Exp. Comm. Prop. Mgr. Needed with leading mgmt. firm in Co. Sprgs., CO. Mixed office/medical/retail portfolio. Must have minimum 7 yrs. Exp. With strong operation, financial, communication and computer skills. CPM required. Send resume w/salary requirements to:
Griffis/Blessing
102 N. Cascade, 5th Floor,
Colorado Springs, CO 80903
FAX 719-520-1204

Marketing

Medical Capital Corporation, a fast growing nationwide provider of financial services for healthcare providers has the following opening:

Director of Marketing

Experience in marketing/sales to healthcare providers. Financial service experience desired.
Please fax resume with salary history to:
W. Johnson
(714) 282-6184

MANAGEMENT TRAINEE - INTERNATIONAL

CPA, 2 years "Big 6", train in finance & operations in divisions throughout the world. Foreign language skills a big plus. Top interpersonal and communication skills. High visibility with top management. Free to relocate & travel as required. **Resume to Boyd Search Firm, 15445 Ventura Blvd. #165, Sherman Oaks, CA 91403 or Fax 818-981-6505.**

VP - Director Sales & Marketing

Richards Industries Valve Group completed another record year. This growth has created the need for a VP-Director of Sales & Marketing based at our Cincinnati plant (150 people) where we manufacture the Jordan Valve, Hex Valve, and Bestobell Steam Trap product lines. We seek an executive who can lead us to new higher levels of performance.
Please reply in confidence to: **President Box 43270, Cincinnati, Ohio 45243. Fax: (513) 533-2583 or Email: rihr@one.net.** EOE.

BRAND STRATEGY SENIOR CONSULTANTS

We are a small team of highly qualified consultants specializing in the areas of brand strategy, brand valuation and management training.

We are seeking senior consultants to join us in developing effective solutions for our domestic and international clients. Significant prior project experience is required. The successful candidates will have initiative, drive and a willingness to work in a fast-growing speciality consultancy. We offer a good working environment with significant opportunity for personal growth. Equity participation will be considered. Please send your resume in strict confidence to:
Box TZ550, The Wall Street Journal
1233 Regal Row, Dallas, Tx 75247

CEO "World Class"

and CFO for IT Staffing/PEO/Payroll company. Must have run $100 Million+ company profitably & have consolidation & Merger & Acquisition experience. Call H. Bell (610)718-8810.

SALES DIRECTOR

Beverly Hills, Ca. healthcare software apps. company.
Sal/bonus to $125k.
John Gilbert Co.
281/363-3310, 298-5152 fax

Job Opening

International Biotech company seeking in-house Accountant/bookkeeper/finance professional. Salary/DOE. Send resume & background with salary expectations to:
Biotech Service Consultants,
12345 Lake City Way NE,
Suite 310, Seattle, WA 98125.

TIME FOR A CAREER CHANGE?

...Retired or bored? Need a part time income? Want to be your own master? Sold your business & would like a new challenge? We are seeking qualfied affiliates F/P time to benefit from your own experience & our 40 year background as a BUSINESS MEDIATION CONSULTANT. Exceptional training & technical support can provide a substantial income & personal satisfaction. (Suppliers, bank loans, insurance, R.E. Mortgages, business transfers, etc.) $12,000 required. Call for free brochure & video.
800-998-9843
VALCOR ARBITRATION SERVICES, LTD.

COMMERCIAL LOAN UNDERWRITER

A leading national apartment lender has an opening for an **Apartment Loan Underwriter.** Three years experience underwriting or appraising commercial income properties req'd. Must have strong writing, analysis, credit and computer skills. Knowledge of real estate finance and appraisal methodology a must. Salary DOE + benefits. Send resume to: **EF&A Funding, 4746 11th Ave NE, Suite 102, Seattle, WA 98105. Fax 206-522-7033 or email: jmarsh@efafunding.com.**

Accounting/Controller

Dynamic Nat'l Real Estate inv./dev. co. seeks exp'd CPA for key mgmt position. Send resume to **Panattoni-Catlin, 826 17th St., #16, Sacramento, CA 95814**

Accounting

AUDITOR III

Perform full scope audits that encompass financial, operational, compliance, economy, efficiency, and effectiveness in accordance with professional auditing standards. Requires a theoretical background in related area, a thorough understanding of auditing theories and principles, accounting, and general administration; a working knowledge of university/healthcare concepts, principles and policies; and excellent interpersonal/leadership skills. Prefers an MBA, CPA, CISA, CIA.

Salary commensurate with qualifications and experience. For immediate consideration, apply by 10/1/97, referencing Job #113200-Y, to: **UCSD Human Resources, La Jolla, CA 92093-0967.** AA/EOE. **Web Site: http://www.hr.ucsd.edu**

UNIVERSITY OF CALIFORNIA, SAN DIEGO

Management Consulting

Senior Business Development Professional

An entrepreneurial marketing strategy, consulting and research firm seeks an outstanding professional with a demonstrated track record of new business development. 7-10 years of relevant experience with a recognized management consulting firm a must.

We want to grow our practice in the areas of:

- Strategic Marketing Research
- Business/Marketing Strategy Consulting

in the following sectors:

- Health Care/Pharmaceuticals
- Hi-Tech/Telecommunications
- Financial Services

If you would like to be a part of our team, please send resume with salary history and expectations to: **Recruiting, G. Bhalla & Associates, 8605 Westwood Center Drive, Suite 207, Vienna, VA 22182 or fax to: (703) 556-8653.**

DIRECTOR OF PATIENT BUSINESS SERVICES

Childrens Hospital of L.A. Responsible for Admitting, Billing, Credit Collection, Cashiering & Utilization. HBOC experience preferred, Bachelors required.
Contact: L. Robinow
Health Search (714) 955-1991
Fax (714) 955-1023

FIGURE 14.1 Classified Advertisements for Job Openings

job openings and applicants looking for positions. Private agencies make their money by charging either the applicant or the employer an amount (usually 10–30 percent) of the applicant's first year salary when they are able to secure a position for the applicant. State and local public agencies do not directly charge the employer or applicant. These agencies often serve as screening agents, identifying potential "matches" by interviewing and testing applicants and providing this information to the employers.

Employee Referrals. One common way of learning about jobs is through friends and acquaintances who work for companies. In fact, one survey found that 40 percent of the companies with over 100 employees had formal referral programs (Stewart et al., 1990). In many cases employees are paid a bonus, sometimes as high as several thousand dollars, when they identify an applicant who is eventually hired.

Employees of a company may be a good source of information about the company and job conditions, although an employee who is working for a recruiting bonus may be tempted to give you only a glowing picture. Although the picture is far from clear, research suggests that applicants hired through formal channels often work out very well (Aamodt & Carr, 1988; Caldwell & Spivey, 1983).

Applying for the Job

James Herriot spent weeks planning how he would apply for veterinarian positions. With so many applicants for each position, he knew he had to make a good impression to even secure an interview. Herriot's situation is similar to that most of us face. In many cases employers make a decision whether to pursue an applicant based on his or her letter of application and résumé.

Cover Letters. Cover letters indicate your interest in a position, highlight your most relevant experience, and indicate the supporting materials you are enclosing with the letter. In general, these letters should be short and to the point, generally not longer than one page. Use of proper form and avoidance of slang is advised (Aamodt, 1996). Although you should show your interest in the position, avoid sounding desperate or discussing personal circumstances ("I'm recently divorced" or "My husband is unemployed and our car just died"). If possible, craft your letter to be specific to each company, showing some knowledge about the company or position.

Résumé. Résumés typically list your skills and your history. In addition to including information about how an employer can contact you (address, telephone number, fax number, e-mail address), résumés generally outline your educational background, your employment experience, your skills (computer literacy, language skills), and important accomplishments and awards. Résumés should be attractive and easy to read, and they should be free of factual or grammatical mistakes. Although résumés should contain unusual information that make you stand out from other applicants, you should avoid information that is not directly related to the position and may alienate some potential employers, such as your membership in the National Rifle Association or your political party affiliation (Bonner, 1993).

EMPLOYEE SELECTION

We cannot know exactly why Siegfried Farnon hired James Herriot. According to Herriot's account, his initial meeting with Farnon was little short of a comedy that included fall-

ing into the back seat of the old Hillman and getting kicked by Mr. Sharpe's cantankerous cow. It seems that Farnon was impressed with how Herriot handled these adverse and embarrassing situations. Farnon's decision was based on his intuition that James Herriot would make a good vet and fit into the practice. Like Siegfried Farnon, an employer has several issues to consider when hiring. The aim is to identify an employee who will perform well in the company environment and is likely to stay with the company. High turnover is both costly and disruptive. Industrial/organizational psychologists have developed the field of *employee selection* to study how employers make hiring decision and to discover ways to improve these decisions. Unlike Farnon's situation, employers, decisions are guided by tested procedures and legal issues, but even with these guides and aids, skill (and maybe a dash of intuition) must be applied in interpreting the information about an applicant. With this point in mind, let's examine some of the techniques employers use to determine who to hire. Later in the chapter we will examine some of the legal issues that guide hiring.

Tests. There is a wide variety of tests that employers may give their prospective employees. One is the *intelligence test.* There is often a general assumption that the more intelligent a worker is, the better he or she will perform. While we might be tempted to accept this position; it does not always prove to be true. Clearly, some jobs require workers with a high degree of intelligence, but it is also possible to hire employees who are too intelligent for a job. If this happens, the worker will become bored and dissatisfied with the job. Hence, again we can see the need to fit the person to the job. Overall, research has found a relatively small relationship between general intelligence and such measures of job performance as promotions and work-related accidents (Schmidt et al., 1984).

Recently, personality tests have been developed to measure honesty and integrity and identify job applicants who will not steal from their employer and engage in other dishonest behavior (Muchinsky, 1993). The problem with many personality tests is that they were developed to diagnosis clinical disorders; their relationship to work behavior is not clear. It is also important that employers know what types of personality are relevant to their work situation. For example, what type of personality will aid a person in the role of college professor?

Overall, there is a weak relationship between tests and performance (Van de Vijver & Harsreld, 1994). In other words, tests are of some help in identifying good prospective employees, but alone they do not provide a good foundation for making hiring decisions. The issue of testing also raises several legal and ethical questions. For example, how fair is the test? Does it discriminate against some groups on bases that may be unrelated to the job? An advertising company may give employees a test requiring them to carry a 150-pound weight for two miles. This test could eliminate many women from consideration. Several court decisions (e.g., *Griggs* v. *Duke Power Company*) have ruled that the companies must prove that a test is fair and job related before it can be used.

Other issues involve privacy and confidentiality (American Psychological Association, 1990). An invasion of privacy could result if the test reveals something about the applicant that he or she wishes to remain private. This is especially critical when the information has no direct relevance to performance of the specific job the employee is applying for. A third issue is confidentiality: Who should have access to the test results? The American Psychological Association (1985) has developed a code of ethics designed to guide the use of tests, and court decisions have also been used to help ensure that testing is fair and ethical.

Interviews. Siegfried Farnon used the **interview** to gain information about James Herriot. Interviews are the most popular method used by employers for selecting employees. Although interviews involve face-to-face interaction, they can take many forms; some follow a set list of questions, while others, like Siegfried Farnon's on-the-job initiation, are very informal, and the questions differ from one applicant to the next. Interviews are considered tests by the Equal Employment Opportunity Commission and are subject to the same legal rules as other tests.

Interviews have two purposes. One is to gather information about the applicant; the other is to evaluate the applicant based on the information. Siegfried Farnon learned a great deal about James Herriot in their initial meeting, and he evaluated the young man very favorably. The Herriot example shows us another function, often unintended, of interviews. Applicants may have the opportunity to learn more about the job and their prospective employer if they get a *realistic job preview* (RJP). The RJP allows employees to see both the positive and negative aspects of the job so that they do not take a position with unrealistic expectations. In some cases, the realistic view of the job reduces employee turnover (Vandenberg & Scarpello, 1990).

Although interviews are the most popular method of employee selection, they are not necessarily the best way to choose employees. There are several reasons for this. First, research has shown that many of the most common questions asked by interviewers have little to do with the specific job performance (Bolles, 1995). Interviewers commonly ask prospective employees questions such as "What do you see yourself doing five years from now" or "How would you describe yourself?" Answers to these questions may lead the interviewer to like (or dislike) the applicant, but they have nothing to do with predicting job performance. Second, there is a tendency for *contrast effects* to be found in interviewer ratings. In other words, you may be evaluated more positively if your interview follows a poor applicant, but if the prior applicant was wonderful, your ratings could be hurt. (Armed with this knowledge, you might be tempted to avoid scheduling your interview after the most brilliant person in your class!) Third, there is a tendency for both a *negative information bias* and a *primary effect* to influence interviewers' judgments (Rowe, 1989). That is, negative information obtained during the interview is weighed more heavily than positive information, and early information is most influential. These effects occur because we often form quick impressions of others (hence the primacy effect), and because when there are many applicants for few positions, interviewers may look for reasons to reject an applicant.

Finally, many factors unrelated to the specific information exchanged during the interview can affect interviewers' judgments. Research indicates that interviewers sometimes rate applicants more highly if they are physically attractive (Dipboye, Fromkin, & Wilbak, 1975), if they are similar (personality and/or attitude) to the interviewer (Foster, 1990), and if they are good *nonverbal* communicators (hold eye contact, have firm handshake, nod their head when listening). One study found that interviewers rated obese job applicants, especially women, lower than nonobese applicants (Pingitore et al., 1994). This effect was found even when the information supplied by the applicants was the same. And the effect was especially strong when the interviewer was satisfied with his or her own body shape.

Many steps have been shown to enhance the quality of decisions made by interviewers. One is training. For example, simply being cautioned about contrast effects reduced this bias by 20 percent in one study (Wexley et al., 1972). Structured, as opposed to unstructured, interviews resulted in better decisions because interviewers were forced to stick to job-related questions (Huffcut & Arthur, 1994).

Letters of Recommendation. Many jobs require applicants to have letters of evaluation sent by their professors or by people for whom they have worked. In theory, these letters are supposed to give information about the applicant's past performance, identifying his or her strengths and weaknesses. Although commonly used, letters of recommendation are poor predictors of job performance (Muchinsky, 1993). The reason is that the letters are almost always uniformly positive. We might expect this because the applicant generally chooses who writes the letter; few of us would ask someone to write a letter for us if we believed that person would write a negative letter. In addition, people are generally reluctant to write negative letters. This reluctance has increased dramatically in recent times with laws that allow applicants access to their job files. For a letter to be confidential, an applicant must sign a waiver that specifically gives up the right of access to these letters. These laws were designed to protect people from having their careers ruined by letters that were unfair and untruthful. Unfortunately, in protecting the rights of the applicants, the laws have reduced the value of the letters because evaluators are especially unwilling to say negative things if they feel the applicant might see their statements (Ceci & Peters, 1984). This overwhelming tendency toward positive statements has also increased the damage that can be caused by a negative statement in a letter of recommendation.

Assessment Centers. If you apply for a job and learn that the company would like you to attend an *assessment center,* don't panic. Assessment centers are structured so that a prospective employee performs several job-related tasks and is evaluated by a number of trained assessors. A typical assessment center involves four to six assessors examining

10 to 20 applicants over a three-to five-day period. At the end of the period, the assessors meet to compare judgments. Assessment centers have received relatively high marks for forecasting job performance (Klimoski & Strickland, 1987), but they are costly and not totally free of bias.

Biographical Information.   The psychologist Paul Muchinsky (1993) states that "If an Academy Award were given for the 'most consistently valid predictor,' biographical information would be the winner" (p. 120). Biographical information is the information that typically is obtained on application forms, asking applicants about their past experience and success. A good application form involves questions related to job-related background and avoids irrelevant questions such as "How many brothers and sisters do you have?" Biographical information is useful because it reviews past behavior, and there is strong support for the old adage that "the best predictor of future behavior is past behavior of a similar kind." The challenge in developing a valid application form is to determine which behaviors are most relevant to the job an applicant will be performing (Brown & Campion, 1994). A company may make poor decisions if it believes that willingness to work extra hours is critical to job performance, when in fact ability to interact with clients is the true factor that determines job performance. Therefore, a great deal of planning and research is required in developing and interpreting a useful application form.

ON THE JOB

James Herriot accepted Siegfried Farnon's offer as soon as it was given. He had known Siegfried for only a few hours and didn't know what Siegfried would expect of him. He had heard stories that many of his classmates cleaned house and washed automobiles for their employers. Many left their jobs after a few months. Herriot didn't know if he would be happy with his new job, and how worried he should be about satisfying Siegfried's expectations. The concerns and fears that Herriot experienced are felt by almost everyone who accepts a new job. The concerns generally center around how management treats employees and whether the individual will be satisfied with the job.

Job Training

Once Herriot accepted the position, a frightening thought gripped him: Now that I have the job, what do I do? Many of us will experience this same sinking feeling when we get our first job. After spending years in the classroom reading and listening to lectures, our main concern will be to get a good job. Once we land that plum, we suddenly realize that we've never held such a job before. Self-doubts will begin to invade our minds as we ask ourselves if we will be able to apply our years of learning. Our fears will increase as we look around and think that everyone else seems to know what they are doing.

In March 1996, the president of the IBM Corporation stated that he was becoming increasingly frustrated with the education process in the United States. He argued that he wanted colleges and universities to produce students with broad general skills, such as the ability to communicate and write effectively and to think about and evaluate issues. His company, he said, would train employees in specific job skills. It is becoming increasingly common for large companies to have their own job training programs. In developing these programs, companies undertake a careful analysis of themselves. This analysis includes an *organization analysis,* which involves identifying where training is needed and will be accepted within the company (Broadwell, 1993). The next step is to conduct a *task analysis,* which involves identifying specific jobs and determining the skills needed to perform those jobs. For example, a receptionist may need computer skills, interpersonal skills, and the ability to organize schedules. Finally, a *person analysis* is necessary to determine which employees need training and in what areas training is needed.

Once an organization decides where training is needed, there are a multitude of types of training that are available. The most common is *on-the-job training.* In this type of training, the employee begins working under the watchful eye of an instructor, often an established employee. The instructor will give advice and be available to answer questions as they arise. Siegfried used this method with James; he went on calls with James but only intervened when James needed help. Another method, often used in the trade professions (plumbing, carpentry, electrical trades) is *apprentice training.* This type of training involves the new employee being assigned for a long period of time to one skilled worker. The apprentice serves as a helper watching the skilled worker perform the job. The apprentice is slowly given more responsibility until, at the end of the apprenticeship, the worker is promoted. The apprenticeship is more like the teacher–student relationship than the on-the-job training method.

Other training methods involve *lectures* and *classes* that focus on the specific job and "how-to-do-it" methods. More recently, companies have employed *computer-assisted instruction* in which an employee is taught about the job and often tested by a computer terminal (Bass & Barrett, 1981). In this method, as the person sits at a keyboard, the computer flashes messages on a screen and the person responds by using the keyboard. Muchinsky (1987) describes one computer-assisted program that begins by flashing the message "Good Morning." If the person fails to push a key in a short time, the computer flashes, "What's the matter—kind of grumpy today?"

Recently, investigators have found that computer-assisted training, even when complex motor skills are involved, can be very effective when done in small groups (Shebilske et al., 1996). Remember that most employers do not expect new employees to know everything about the job. Learning and training continue on the job in a variety of ways.

How Well Are You Doing? Performance Appraisal

You have your job and your training. Now you're ready to begin working. The next issue you face is determining how well you are doing. *Performance appraisal* involves evaluating how well a person is performing on the job. This may seem to be simple exercise, but it is actually quite complex and involved. One concern of many employees is that they are often unsure what the employer expects from them. James Herriot raised this concern a number of times. For a time, he felt like he was only Siegfried's assistant, and he worried that he was not independent enough to please Siegfried. When he did do more on his own, he feared that Siegfried would be disappointed in him each time he was unable to cure an animal, even when it was clear that the animal was terminally ill. An important part of the employment setting is *goal setting.* Research has found that employees often perform better and feel more satisfied with their jobs when concrete and specific goals are high but reasonable (Kaufer et al., 1994). In other words, telling someone to "do your best" is not terribly comforting. In many cases, employers will work with employees to develop specific goals (i.e., produce a daily average of 700 widgets, be absent from work fewer than 12 days a year). The positive impact of goal setting is especially evident for tasks that are simple and repetitive. In addition to having a clear goal, it is also important that employees receive regular *feedback* on how well they are doing and how they are evaluated (Locke & Latham, 1990).

The typical performance appraisal involves a supervisor evaluating an employee. However, recently many organizations have realized that the supervisor may know only one part of an employee's activities. They have

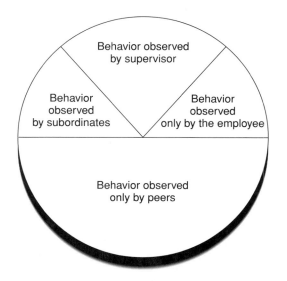

FIGURE 14.2   Who Observes Employee Performance?

Source: Reprinted from *Applied Industrial/Organizational Psychology* by Michael G. Aamodt. Copyright © 1996, 1991 by Brooks/Cole Publishing Company, Pacific Grove, CA 93950, a division of International Thomson Publishing Inc. By permission of the publisher.

adopted a *360-degree feedback* system that involves getting information from everyone, including the employee, about job performance (Hoffman, 1995). For example, as Figure 14.2 indicates, a waiter in a restaurant interacts with his supervisor, the cooks, other waiters, and patrons of the restaurant. A 360-degree feedback appraisal involves getting input from each of these people in addition to a self-rating from the waiter himself (Smither et al., 1995).

In addition to knowing who is making the appraisal, research has shown that it is important to know what is being evaluated. Some performance appraisal systems (such as those you might be asked to fill out in a restaurant, Figure 14.3) focus on *traits*. Unfortunately, the trait system is often too general to be very useful: How, for example, do you instruct an employee to be "more happy"? Other appraisal systems focus on specific *behaviors*. In this case our waiter might be rated on how often he smiles, how often he fills cus-

tomer's water glasses, or how accurate his billing is. Behavior feedback is more specific and more useful, and it can be used to help employees improve specific behaviors.

In a third type of performance appraisal, an employee is evaluated on the *results* of his or her work (Planchy & Planchy, 1993). Although this might seem like a relatively straightforward process, it can be complex. In the case of James Herriot, if Siegfried were to conduct a results-based appraisal, he would have to determine what results were important to him. Was he concerned with how many cases James took (quantity), how many animals James was able to cure (quality), how

---

McBurger Queen Restaurants

Dear Customer:

We value your business and strive to make each of your visits a dining pleasure. To help us reach our goal, we would appreciate your completing this card and placing it in our suggestion box on your way out.

1. Was your food cooked properly?   Y N
2. Was your server friendly?   Y N
3. Was your server efficient?   Y N
4. Do you plan to return?   Y N

5. Who was your server? _____

Comments:
_____
_____
_____
_____

FIGURE 14.3   Customer Evaluation Card

Source: Reprinted from *Applied Industrial/Organizational Psychology* by Michael G. Aamodt. Copyright © 1996, 1991 by Brooks/Cole Publishing Company, Pacific Grove, CA 93950, a division of International Thomson Publishing Inc. By permission of the publisher.

much time and medicine James used in his cases (cost effectiveness), how often James or others were injured while James was treating an animal (safety), or how often James was ill and unable to work (attendance)?

As you can see, performance appraisal can be a complex activity. A good performance appraisal can help motivate employees, serve as the basis for developing a fair reward system, and help identify training needs of the organization.

Job Satisfaction

Periodically, James Herriot would look out over the valleys and moors of the Yorkshire Dales thinking about his job. He truly loved the smell of the fresh mowed hay and the clean air; he loved working with the animals and the people in Yorkshire; he enjoyed being a part of Siegfried's practice and his family. James Herriot was very satisfied with his job.

Although we can define **job satisfaction** as a pleasurable emotional state that results from feeling that your job is fulfilling, there are some important points to remember. First, there are a number of "parts" to our jobs, some of which we may like and others of which we may dislike. For example, we may be delighted with the work, pay, and supervisor while disliking our coworkers and

the environment in which we work. Hence, most measures of job satisfaction ask questions about many components of the job (Scarpollo & Campbell, 1983). In assessing your own job, you should determine the facets that make you happy and those that you do not like. A second point that we will discuss more fully in this chapter is the way in which people make decisions about satisfaction. In some cases we determine our satisfaction by deciding whether the job meets our expectations and desires; in this case, we use an internal standard. In other cases, we may use an external or social standard to determine our satisfaction. Are we getting as much as other people who are in positions similar to ours? There are a number of theories about job satisfaction. Most argue that we will be satisfied with our jobs to the extent that they meet our needs. However, needs can vary widely, including existence needs (putting food on the table), social needs, and self-esteem and personal growth needs (feeling valued, developing new skills). Some of these needs may be met by the task itself (e.g., responsibility, challenge, interesting work), while others are job related but not directly involved with the task (e.g., pay, security, coworkers). No single theory has captured all the elements that determine our satisfaction.

REVIEW QUESTIONS

1. What is the most common source that people use to learn about job opportunities?

   a. school counselors
   b. friends
   c. employees of companies
   d. advertisements

2. T or F: Interviews are the most common method used by employers to select employees.

3. Information, often obtained on application forms, about a perspective employee's job-

   related background and experience is called _____.

4. T or F: It is important to have all necessary job skills and knowledge before entering most jobs.

5. _____ involves evaluation of how well a person is performing the job.

Rewards. What would make you happier with your job? If we were asked this question, most of us would quickly respond, "More money." But is money really a major factor that determines our satisfaction with our job? It clearly wasn't for James Herriot. He began making 4 pounds a week (less than $20 in those days), and though his earnings did increase, he could have made a great deal more by moving to a large-city practice.

Many of us might feel that we could be happy with any job if it paid enough. Research shows that although pay does influence how happy people are with their jobs, money is only a factor that determines job satisfaction (Weiner, 1980). But the issue of pay is a complex one. For example, in Western industrial cultures, pay is often based on individual performance; two individuals who have the same job and qualifications may receive different pay because one performs better than the other. However, in some collective cultures, such as Japan, pay is determined by the group or team to which one belongs (Matsumoto, 1996). In other cultures, such as China, people are often paid on the basis of the time they have worked for the company, policy that minimizes competition within the company or institution. In these cultures, individual workers would be very uncomfortable to be singled out for higher pay or recognition, feeling that this treatment would embarrass or hurt the feelings of other group members. Even in situations where rewards are based on individual performance, rewards can be of many types. For example, rewards may include money, time off, praise, work conditions (an office with a window), or getting your name on an Employee of the Month plaque.

Although many of us equate rewards with job satisfaction, investigators have raised a note of caution with this simple view (Deci, 1975). According to this position, there are two basic types of motivation that guide work behavior and influence job satisfaction. **Extrinsic motivation** comes from factors external to the individual. People can be motivated to work by extrinsic factors such as pay, threats, or pressure from coworkers. Thus our previous focus on "more money" was an extrinsic factor.

But **intrinsic motivation** is also an important factor in work behavior. There are two bases for intrinsic motivation. First, people have a need to see themselves as *controlling their own behavior*. That is, people want to see themselves as deciding when and how they will act. The second base for intrinsic motivation is that people want to see themselves as *being capable and competent*. Intrinsic rewards make workers feel in control and competent. Numerous studies have shown that intrinsic rewards—such as increased choice, opportunity to see the finished results of work, and opportunities to make input into the job process—increase satisfaction with the job (Staw, 1976; Deci, 1971). Therefore, when we speak of rewards we must refer to them in the broadest sense, which includes both extrinsic and intrinsic forms of satisfaction.

Another interesting issue concerns the relationship between extrinsic and intrinsic motivation. It seems that as extrinsic rewards increase, intrinsic motivation may decrease (Deci, 1975; Lepper, Greene, & Nisbett, 1973). Consider the situation where you jog because you enjoy running and the feeling you have after a good run (intrinsic rewards). Someone notices that you have the potential to be a world-class runner and offers you $1,000 to enter a marathon race. You do well, and the promoter now offers you $10,000 to run in another marathon. You will soon find yourself running for the money; extrinsic motivation now guides your behavior. At the same time your intrinsic motivation may well decrease; you will not enjoy running so much for the good feeling it gives you as for the external rewards it brings. Clearly, the danger here is that an activity you once enjoyed and controlled now controls you. You'll run as long as you receive money.

The task faced by management is to provide workers with enough extrinsic rewards to satisfy their needs and reward performance while also structuring the job so that there are sufficient intrinsic rewards.

Expectations. The night that James Herriot and Siegfried Farnon had their first discussion in the pub was an important one. James not only got his job offer that night; he also came away with a number of expectations about the veterinary practice. Siegfried was careful to tell James the problems he was having and how difficult it was to make a go of a new practice. But Siegfried couldn't hide his enthusiasm; he told James of his grand plans and the exciting possibilities that existed for the practice. Even though he knew the realities of the situation, James focused on the enthusiastic hopes. The only time James reports being dissatisfied with his job was during the first few weeks.

The expectations we have about people or events are often the internal standard by which we judge those people or events. The same process holds true when we judge how satisfied we are with our jobs. It's not an accident that the greatest period of dissatisfaction with a job occurs during the first year and that the young are most dissatisfied. It's at these times that people have the highest expectations about their jobs. Research has found that people get most of their information about their jobs from interviewers (Bray, Campbell, & Grant, 1974). Interviewers generally paint positive pictures of their organizations and the jobs they're offering. They also stress how selective their organization's hiring practices are. So the newly hired person believes that he or she is special and has chosen a super place to work. But new employees are generally not given a great deal of freedom, nor are they given the most exciting jobs. So what the employee finds often does not match his or her expectations. The result is a period of dissatisfaction during the early period on the job.

Older employees know the organization better and have more realistic expectations, so they are less often in the position of having their expectations disappointed. In other words, satisfaction is often determined by the fit between expectations about a job and what the worker finds the job to be.

Social Comparison. A friend of ours recently commented that she goes to her class reunions to determine how satisfied she is with her job and her life. As we discussed, she is using an external standard (other people) to judge her satisfaction. We discussed *social comparison theory* (Festinger, 1954; Goethals & Darley, 1977) in Chapter 3. According to this theory, when there is no measurable physical reality to go by we establish the value or correctness of an ability, characteristic, belief, or condition by comparing what we have to what others have. For example, you may receive an offer as a manager trainee for an annual salary of $35,000. Will you be satisfied with that salary? Chances are that you will be more satisfied with the $35,000 if you find that other trainees earn $32,000 than if you find they earn $40,000.

Social comparison plays an important role in determining job satisfaction. A person often compares his or her own salary, working conditions, office, and vacations with those of other *similar* workers. If your own conditions are better than those of other similar workers, you are likely to be happier than you would be if you find that your working conditions are worse than those of others. We can see this process at work in the Herriot example. Herriot reports that he was so happy with his new position in part *because* many of his classmates had no jobs or jobs that paid less and offered worse working conditions.

Equity. Another important question to ask in determining job satisfaction is whether or not we are getting from our job what we feel they are worth. **Equity theory** suggests that we determine our satisfaction with relationships or jobs by comparing the *inputs* we contribute with the *outcomes* we receive with the inputs and outcomes of others doing a similar job (Austin, 1986). We are most satisfied when the relationship between our inputs and outcomes is equal to that of others. If our ratio of inputs and outcomes is similar to the ratio of other workers, equity will result. Inputs can be in many forms, including hours worked, education, experience, and skills. Outcomes are also measured in many forms, such as pay, status, recognition, and office size/position.

The Importance of Job Satisfaction. We might ask: Why all this interest and concern with job satisfaction? Does it really matter if people are happy with their jobs? One place we might expect to see the effects of job satisfaction is in performance; there is a common saying that "the happy worker is a good worker." Though this relationship between happy worker and good work seems to make a lot of sense, there hasn't been much research to support it (Iaffaldano & Muchinsky, 1985). In fact, the reverse relationship is more often found: Good performance often leads to job satisfaction. There are two ways to explain this finding. First, good performance on the job generally results in higher rewards (salary, status), and these rewards increase the worker's satisfaction with his or her job (Porter & Lawler, 1968). Second, through good performance workers demonstrate their competence, and this feeling of competence enhances their view of their jobs.

Although we can't say that satisfaction necessarily leads to better performance, there are many other effects of satisfaction. First, people who are satisfied with their jobs are *less likely to be absent from work or seek other jobs* than are people who are dissatisfied with their jobs (Locke, 1976). This is a very important factor from management's viewpoint, since the training of new employees is very costly and time consuming. People who are happy with their jobs *tend to be healthier and live longer* than

dissatisfied workers (Palmore, 1969; Winter, 1987). This effect is easy to understand if we imagine the stress (see Chapter 5) placed on workers who must go every day to a job that they dislike. People's satisfaction with their jobs also influences their satisfaction with their lives in general. In a study conducted in Detroit automotive plants, investigators found a strong relationship between job satisfaction and a number of indices of *mental health,* including anxiety, tension, hostility, and personal morale (Kornhauser, 1965).

STRESS AND CRISES IN CAREERS

According to his books, James Herriot's transition into the working world was a smooth one. Although he had periodic doubts about his occupation, he enjoyed his work and, except for service in the Royal Air Force during World War II, spent over 40 years working at the veterinary practice in the Yorkshire Dales with Siegfried and Tristan. While most of us won't work in the same place for 40 years, we can anticipate a comfortable relationship with our careers and jobs. All of us will be subjected to stress in our jobs. In most cases this stress will not be great, but in other cases the stress will be the result of crises or significant changes in our careers. Career crises include career change, burnout, midlife crisis, and unemployment, and each career crisis involves considerable stress.

Stress in Working Conditions

Let us begin our discussion by focusing on the types of stress we are most likely to face in our working conditions. As you will recall, we discussed stress in detail in Chapter 5, and we will examine some of the environmental stressors in more detail in Chapter 15. Our interest here is some of the causes for stress in our working environment.

Throughout his books, James Herriot mentions the stress he experienced in his working conditions. One major source of

Studying Job Performance: The Hawthorne Effect

This laboratory is the one common to many investigators who study work and organizational issues: the workplace. And the study we focus on is one of the classic ones that illustrated some of the perils of conducting research in this and other settings. In the 1920s Elton Mayo and his colleagues at the Hawthorne Plant of the Western Electric company were interested in steps that could be taken to improve worker productivity. Women workers in the plant produced electrical switching devices. The researchers took one group of women and moved them to a separate room where they could be studied. They introduced a number of steps that they thought would improve productivity such as adding more rest periods and improving lighting. Each of these innovations did result in increased productivity. So far, so good.

The researchers were also interested in determining if deteriorating work conditions would hurt worker productivity. So they introduced steps to reduce the quality of the work setting. They reduced the number of work breaks and lowered the lighting in the room. Surprisingly, these "negative" interventions also led to increased productivity.

How can we explain these results? Comments from the women indicated that their behavior was influenced by the feeling that their company had taken special interest in them, and the realization that they were being observed (Roethlisberger & Dickson, 1939; see also Bramel & Friend, 1981 for other explanations). The study not only suggests that recognition can affect worker behavior, it also illustrates that people may behave differently when they know that their behavior is being observed. This latter finding, known as the *Hawthorne effect*, has led researchers in the laboratory and field to take steps to reduce this bias in their studies.

---

stress was the *cold;* Herriot cites being numb with cold while spending hours delivering a calf in a freezing barn. He recounts the time he caught pneumonia from standing in a frozen creek helping a farmer move a horse that had broken its leg. Most of us will not face such extreme cold in our work, but we may well have to work in cold or drafty offices. Even these levels of cold can distract our attention, cause numbness, and increase our reaction times (Ellis, 1982). *Heat,* on the other hand, can also decrease our performance by distracting us, causing us to feel irritable, and increasing our aggressiveness toward other employees (Anderson & Anderson, 1985). *Fatigue* and *boredom* are sources of stress often found in the workplace. Fatigue is more than simply being tired because we did not get a good night's sleep. Fatigue can result from being faced with too many demands from the job or it can result because the job is monotonous and boring. Fatigue causes our physiological system to "slow down," and it depresses our physical, mental, and emotional functioning. When we are fatigued, it is difficult to concentrate and we become careless. Other sources of stress in the workplace can include *crowding, isolation, noise, unpredictable* or *difficult work schedules,* or *ambiguous task demands.*

Stress not only reduces work performance, but it also increases the chance of *accidents.* The National Safety Council (DeReamer, 1980) has published some alarming figures that show why industry is so concerned with accidents: Loss of life from work accidents in the United States this century has far exceeded that from wars, floods, tornadoes, earthquakes, and other natural catastrophes *combined.* One American worker dies every 8 minutes from an industrial accident. And approximately 2 million people-years are lost annually because of work accidents.

Accidents result from two sources: unsafe conditions and unsafe acts. And work stress increases the chance of unsafe acts. In 1971, the Occupational and Safety Health Act (OSHA) was passed to step up work condition standards and protect workers. The law lists over 5,000 safety and health standards, some as specific as to dictate the height at which a fire extinguisher should be hung. Over 100,000 inspections are made each year by government inspectors acting under this law. Companies can be fined for violating the law. OSHA has made employers more aware of safety and health problems on the job, and it has motivated some important changes in the workplace to reduce stress and accidents. But we need only look at newspaper headlines to see that there is still much to be done in both these areas.

Career Change

As we discussed in Chapter 5, any change in our lives will be stressful. A change as dramatic as a career change will be very stressful even if it is a welcome change. Career changes don't only result in a change in the type of work we perform; they may also mean a change in our daily routine, our friends and acquaintances, and our financial condition. Despite the stress involved, however, career changes often have very positive results. People find new challenges and new opportunities to develop and display their skills. Adjustment to a new career can be a very positive experience.

If we look at the human development process, we might expect that a change in career should occur more often than it does. In most cases, people must choose an occupation during their early twenties. The needs and desires of a 20-year-old are very different from those of a person in his or her forties. Thus an interesting question to ask is why people don't change careers more often.

There are many answers to this question. One is that the decision to move from the known to the unknown is very difficult to make. Staying with a known job usually provides security, even if the job isn't satisfying.

A second answer concerns the commitment process that occurs in most jobs and companies (Salancik, 1977). According to *cognitive dissonance* theory, people strive to keep their actions and attitudes consistent (Festinger, 1957). People want to see themselves as acting consistently and rationally. For many people, the decision to change careers is to admit that they made an incorrect choice and worked hard to enter an unsatisfying career. This is a difficult confession for many people to make. In addition, by committing employees to their jobs through pay and retirement plans, employers often make it difficult for people to change jobs. Workers build up incentive pay and credit toward retirement that would be lost if they changed jobs. The result is that some workers are trapped in jobs by their desires to maintain consistency and by the reward structure of the workplace.

The number of people who make career changes is increasing, however. According to one study of college faculty members, there are a number of issues that drive career change (Simpson, 1990). One is the technological changes associated with the job. Many older professors were trained before the advent of computers and other advanced technology needed for teaching and research. In addition, there has been an explosion of information, requiring tremendous effort to "remain current" in their field. Many faculty are faced with making changes in the way they perform their jobs, and this transition point has led many to examine whether they are happy with their profession. A second important motivator for career change is personal interest. As we grow older and have a variety of experiences, our interests change. Indeed, James Herriot found that although he still enjoyed vet medicine, he also developed a desire to write. This change in interest led him to embark on a career that involved book writing and lecturing. Other career changes result from changing situations in the organization or institution. An employee may be faced with a new supervisor or chairperson whom he finds difficult or unpleasant. The company may go through *downsizing* or *reduction in force* (RIF) in which it eliminates positions or replaces workers with machines or computers. For example, automobile companies have installed robots in many plants that can assemble automobiles, reducing the number of employees needed in the plant.

Although career changes can be accompanied by a great deal of stress and bad feelings, Simpson (1990) found that most faculty members who experienced career changes reported being happy with their new positions. Their choice of a new career was based on the perceived advantages (money, freedom, challenge) of the new career and their estimation of their success in the career. Many companies have instituted training programs and counseling services to help employees train for new careers and help them choose satisfying careers.

Burnout

One of the most satisfying parts of many jobs is working with others. However, sometimes it can be very frustrating. We may find people unable to perform as we want them to, or people may not be appreciative of our help. James Herriot relates a number of cases where he labored all night to save a farmer's animal only to be told by the farmer that he didn't do his job well. These types of experiences may lead to a condition called **burnout.**

Burnout occurs when people lose sympathy for the people with whom or for whom they are working and become exhausted and cynical (Meier, 1983). The worker experiencing burnout feels fatigued, depressed, and irritable. He or she may experience a wide range of psychosomatic symptoms (see Chapter 4), such as headaches, ulcers, and nausea. Burnout is especially likely to occur in people in the helping professions—teachers, social workers, nurses, doctors, counselors, and psychologists. Managers in business are also prone to burnout. Often it's the conscientious and successful worker who experiences burnout.

Unemployment

The recession of the 1980s added the terms *unemployed* and *laid off* to our everyday vocabularies. Previously, only blue-collar workers were faced with the grim prospects of unemployment. Recently, though, we have seen white-collar workers such as managers, technicians, and professionals suddenly faced with the prospects of unemployment.

Loss of employment has many dramatic effects. The loss of income requires dramatic changes in lifestyle; for some people, it means the loss of homes and other valued possessions. Status and self-esteem are also negatively affected. The unemployed begin to have doubts about their abilities. They must not only ask why they were laid off, but also must face the unsettling prospect that they can't easily find other jobs. They may feel that their skills are unwanted. A third result of unemployment is a change in their daily pattern of living. A person no longer gets up in the morning with the prospect of spending 8 to 10 hours at his or her job. New ways of spending time must be found. This problem is often made worse when an unemployed person sees friends going to work. As a result of all these factors, unemployment increases the likelihood of alcoholism and mental and physical disorders (Plant, 1967). Suicide rates increase during periods of high unemployment. Symptoms of these problems are most likely to be observed soon after the person becomes unemployed and after a year of unemployment.

Recently, a number of new ways of combating the problems of unemployment have been attempted. Many employers have hired counselors to help their laid-off employees get new jobs. Government and industry have established retraining programs to help the unemployed train for new occupations where opportunities of employment are higher. Counseling is often offered to the unemployed and their families to help them cope with the stresses of being out of work. In some cases, employers have attempted to forewarn workers of the possibilities of layoff so they can be better prepared both emotionally and psychologically.

Improving Working Conditions

The fact that our modern world has added stress and complexity to our work situation has not gone unnoticed by employers. To help employees adjust to their rapidly changing jobs, enhance job satisfaction, and improve productivity, many companies have introduced a variety of innovations to the workplace. Some of these changes involve the job itself and can be viewed as having four basic dimensions: variety, autonomy, identity, and feedback (Hackman & Lawler, 1971). The original model of job design was to make the job as simple as possible, on the belief that this simplification would enable employees to learn the job and prevent errors. More recently, however, the trend has been toward *job enlargement* (increasing the number and variety of jobs workers perform) and *job enrichment* (increasing worker's control over planning and performance). To achieve these goals, companies have turned to employees to help plan and design their jobs (Muchinsky, 1993). Techniques such as Quality Circles and Total Quality Management (TQM) have been developed to expand employee input into company and job planning (Schmidt & Finnigan, 1993).

Other innovations focus the work schedule and setting. To help the job fit better into employees' needs, some companies have adopted *compressed work weeks* (working longer hours but for fewer days) or *flextime* schedules (having blocks of free time during the day). For example, a flextime schedule might involve working 7 a.m.–noon and 4 p.m.–7 p.m. This schedule would allow you to have lunch with your family and/or do your shopping and errands during the middle of the day. These hours would also enable you to avoid heavy rush-hour traffic. Another innovation is the introduction of *job sharing,* which involves two or more people sharing the same job. This option is especially attractive to couples who have young children or experience trouble finding two jobs in an area. For example, a university may have one opening for a professor to teach four courses. A couple who both have degrees in the area of need might share the position so that one person taught two courses in the morning and the other taught two courses in the afternoon. This schedule would give both people a position but would allow someone to be at home all day. Other attempts to accommodate employees with small children include developing *child-care* facilities on the job site so that parents can work and also ensure that their children are cared for.

Still another technique involves designing a job so an employee can *work at home.* Many jobs, such as sales positions, do not require the employee to be in an office, but do require that he or she be in contact with the office. Given the availability of telecommunications such as mobile telephones and e-mail, employees can be in constant contact with their home office. However, they can avoid wasting time in making unnecessary trips to the office. The company gains in this arrangement because it does not have to supply office space that is rarely used. In addition, the opportunity to use the work at home arrangement increases the number of employees that a company may hire. A recent article in the *Wall Street Journal* (April 11, 1996) discussed the increasingly common situation of couples in which one partner is ready for retirement and the other is younger and at the peak of his or her career. The opportunity to work at home allows the couple to move to an area where the retired partner can fulfill his or her needs and the working partner can contribute to the workforce in a suitable position. In fact, the authors are acquainted with a book editor who works out of his home office thousands of miles from his company, while his wife enjoys her retirement by painting wildlife.

It is becoming increasing clear that the future of job planning will not only involve advances and changes in technology but will also include designing jobs and situations to enhance employee–job fit.

WOMEN AT WORK

James Herriot began practicing veterinary medicine in 1937. At that time, very few women were veterinarians; in fact, only around 25 percent of American women held jobs outside the home. World War II created many dramatic changes in American society. Although the traditional view was that "a woman's place was in the home," the war forced many men to leave their jobs to join the armed forces. This created a severe labor shortage in the United States, and women entered the workforce in great numbers, taking on "traditional male" jobs. By 1945, women made up nearly 37 percent of the workforce. The trend of women working outside the home has increased since that time, fueled by the need of two wage earners in families, the increase in the number of single women with families, and the desire of women to take jobs that meet their interests and abilities. By 1988, 56 percent of women worked outside the home and estimates are that 90 percent of women will hold a job outside the home at some time in their lives (Matthews & Rodin, 1989).

The changing face of the workplace has created a number of conflicts. The traditional value of "the women's place in the home" has been challenged by the equally fundamental value that everyone should be free to choose their course of life and expect equal and fair treatment in doing this. A second conflict has been that women who work outside the home are also expected to fulfill the role of homemaker. This *role conflict* (see Chapter 13) has not only created considerable stress for women, but it often results in women adding outside employment to their full-time housework requirements.

In addition to these problems, many women have faced resistance when they enter the workforce, especially when they choose jobs that have been typically filled by men. In some cases, the resistance results because they are seen as competitors for jobs that should "rightfully go to men." In other cases, they have faced stereotypes that suggest that women are too weak, too emotional, or not committed enough to perform some jobs. These stereotypes are held despite the lack of evidence to support them (Muchinsky, 1993).

The resistance to women in the workforce has shown itself in many areas, most of which are illegal (see pp. 394–395) and counterproductive to work behavior. Women are generally paid less than men, even when they do comparable work and have similar qualifications. Women often face a *glass ceiling*, or failure to be promoted to high-level positions once they are hired by an organization. A third problem is *sexual harassment*, which is defined as "deliberate and unwanted sexual behavior that is unwelcome to its recipient, as well as sex-related behaviors that are hostile, offensive, or degrading (Fitzgerald, 1993, p. 1070)." Sexual harassment includes, but is not limited to, the threat of losing one's job to force sexual cooperation or using sexual behavior such as jokes or unwanted touching that make the workplace aversive. Sexual harassment not only reduces productivity, but it can also result in depression, headaches, and other stress-related symptoms (Hesson-McInnes & Fitzgerald, 1992).

As we will see, problems such as these and others involving other groups have moved concerns about work behavior out of the workplace and into the courts. The last forty years have witnessed a stream of laws and court decisions designed to protect workers and ensure fairness in work settings. The position of women in the workplace has improved, but inequities remain. Some advocates also have raised the concern that all the attention focused on outside employment has produced a tendency to overlook the important work of women within the home. This work makes both social and economic contributions and deserves recognition. The basic proposition of the doctrine of fairness is that all people should have opportunities to choose a career (including homemaking) that will be fulfilling to them, and they should receive fair compensation for their work.

DISCRIMINATION IN THE WORKPLACE

As we have seen, women must fight discrimination to enter many occupations and professions. In 1977, there were over 180 occupations in the United States in which fewer than 20 percent of the workers were women (Baker et al., 1980). Women's salaries for performing the same jobs as men averaged less than those earned by men. Similar cases, and even more extreme cases, of disproportionate representation are true for African Americans or members of other ethnic and racial minority groups. In many cases, these startling figures are the result of intentional efforts to keep minorities and women out of certain occupations. In other cases, this unequal distribution of jobs across subgroups is the result of unintentional causes such as word-of-mouth recruitment (McCormick & Ilgen, 1980). In all cases, the result in **job discrimination,** which limits people's job opportunities because of their race, sex, religion, color, or national origin. The people discriminated against aren't the only ones to suffer; society as a whole suffers. The result of job discrimination is that the best talent may not be employed in positions where it is most useful.

Dating back to the post–Civil War era, legislation has been passed that was aimed at combatting discrimination. However, the law that stands out as the boldest attempt to correct job discrimination is Title VII of the Civil Rights Act of 1964, amended by the Equal Employment Act of 1972. These laws described what was fair business practice and outlined appeal procedures that could be followed by

someone who felt that he or she was being unjustly treated. They also defined the *protected groups* and applied to all personnel functions including selection, training, promotion, retention, and evaluation. Title VII states:

It shall be an unlawful employment practice for an employer—

(1) to fail or refuse to hire or to discharge any individual or otherwise to discriminate against any individual with respect to his compensation, terms, conditions, or privileges of employment, because of such individual's race, color, religion, sex, or national origin; or

(2) to limit, segregate, or classify his employees or applicants for employment in any way which would deprive or tend to deprive any individual of employment opportunities or otherwise adversely affect his status as an employee because of such individuals race, color, religion, sex, or national origin.

Title VII also established the Equal Employment Opportunity Commission (EEOC) to enforce the law. The commission conducts investigations on its own initiative or when a complaint is brought to it by an individual or by a group. The enormous size of its job can be seen in the fact that the EEOC was processing almost 70,000 cases a year by the mid-1970s (Ash & Kroeker, 1975).

In 1967, the government passed an age discrimination act that extended to people age 40 and over the protection granted other groups in the original Civil Rights Act. There have been hundreds of cases testing the limits of the civil rights laws. In *Bakke* v. *University of California,* the court ruled that whites can be the victims of discrimination and that the medical school must accept Bakke because he was originally denied admission because of his race (white). The Americans with Disabilities Act (1990) extended protection to people with disabilities. The law makes it illegal to discriminate in hiring practices such as using tests that unfairly discriminate against protected groups. The law also aims at ensuring fair treatment on the job in such areas as compensation and promotion.

The Civil Rights Act and resulting court rulings have made a tremendous difference in opening employment opportunities to a large number of people who were previously the targets of discrimination. There is still, however, a great deal of debate and confusion about the grounds that employers can use in their selection and evaluation process.

While the Civil Rights Act is a law, *affirmative action* programs, which are also aimed at reducing discrimination, are voluntary agreements between employers and government agencies. Affirmative action recognizes that past inequities and discrimination can only be overcome by taking positive steps to recruit members of minority groups. These programs ask employers to set minority hiring goals and then vigorously recruit minority group members. Employers may visit college campuses that have a high percentage of minority or women students, and they often advertise in newspapers or magazines frequently read by the targeted group. Because affirmative action is not a law, companies who do not have such programs cannot be sued, but the government can pressure these companies by withholding contract or grants until affirmative action programs are developed.

In March 1996, the Fifth U.S. Circuit Court of Appeals ruled that a University of Texas affirmative action program discriminated against white applicants in an effort to boost minority enrollment in its law school. The ruling has broad implications for all affirmative action programs, raising legal and ethical issues about how a company or institution may design recruitment programs to attract members of one group without unfairly discriminating against members of other groups.

The Civil Rights Act and affirmative action programs have had a great influence in bringing equality into the workplace, but there is still a long way to go. Despite antidiscrimination efforts such as Title VII, the task of reducing discrimination and its effects remains of major importance today. Minorities and women are still underrepresented in many occupations and overrepresented in unemployment statistics. The task of reducing discrimination doesn't simply mean opening up job opportunities to minorities and women. It involves training minorities and women for the jobs. It involves changing the self-images of women and members of minority groups, who for years have been told that they don't have the ability, much less the opportunity, to perform certain jobs and who have been denied admission to the training programs that would give them the skills they need. Underscoring this last point are a number of studies that found women were less attracted to their jobs and to the companies when they felt they got their jobs because of their gender rather than because of their job-related qualifications (Chacko, 1982; Heilman & Herlihy, 1984).

RETIREMENT

As James Herriot approached the age where it was physically more difficult for him to perform the duties of his practice, he had to face the possibility of retirement. His response was to reduce his involvement in his vet practice and to engage in a new activity, writing. He loved to write and he loved the practice of veterinary medicine, so his choice of writing about his experiences as a vet was a natural and satisfying activity for him.

For many workers, the mere mention of the word **retirement** sends shivers up their spines. Many people don't look forward to retirement. For one thing, they view it as a period when they will have to give up something they enjoy and that gives them a sense of accomplishment and of contributing to society, their work. More likely, however, many of the negative feelings about retirement are the result of it being associated with old age and eventual death (Streib & Schneider, 1971). Despite these pessimistic views, however, research suggests that retirement is not experienced as negatively as people anticipate.

Streib and Schneider (1971) interviewed 4,000 people before and after they retired. Almost one-third found retirement more enjoyable than they had expected, and only 5 percent found it to be worse.

The key to successful retirement is substituting enjoyable activities for the time previously spent at work (Lowenthal, 1972). Interestingly, women often adjust better to retirement than men do because the role of homemaker is an acceptable activity for women to take on after they've quit their jobs. Men adjust better if they share in the housework, but unfortunately some men feel that housework is demeaning. Well-planned leisure activities such as travel or gardening also help make retirement enjoyable. A third popular substitution is another job more suited to the individual's physical and psychological needs. James Herriot followed this route when he chose to write. Research has found that 73 percent of people who consider work to be a major source of satisfaction in their lives find another job after retirement (Streib & Schneider, 1971).

One of the issues hotly debated today is whether or not retirement should be mandatory at a certain age. On one hand, it seems senseless to deny job opportunities to someone who is capable and willing to work. On the other hand, it has been argued that having a mandatory retirement age allow people to better plan for retirement (Botwinick, 1977). Issues such as this and others related to retirement are becoming of increasing importance in today's society. A process referred to as the "graying of society" is taking place: the proportion of older people in American society is rapidly increasing. In 1978, there were 24 million people aged 65 years and older; by the year 2000, there will be 32 million people in this category. One reason for this change is the declining birth rate in America. A second reason is that there have been major advances in health care; the health of today's 55-year-old compares favorably with that of people who were 40 or 45 in 1970 (Rosow & Zager, 1980). Therefore, we will see an increasingly large number of people entering retirement over the next decade. It is becoming more important for us to understand the stresses and the changes people undergo when they retire. Research is now being conducted on how to make the transition into retirement a happy and satisfying one.

REVIEW QUESTIONS

6. Pay, recognition, and high status are examples of _____ motivation.

7. According to equity theory, we compare our inputs and outputs with those of other people in our situation. Equity theory suggests that we will be _____ with our job if we are receiving considerable more rewards from our job than other employees, despite the fact that everyone's input is similar.

8. T or F: Research has shown that as extrinsic rewards increase, intrinsic motivation may decrease.

9. Many employers have taken steps to improve working conditions. Some of these efforts focus on redesigning jobs. _____ involves increasing workers' control over planning and performance.

10. T or F: Taking a job in the outside workforce frees most women from the demands of their traditional role as homemaker.

SUMMARY

1. People's jobs have a number of influences on their lives. The money they make determines their standard of living. The job also influences how they will spend much of their time, since most people work 8 hours a day. Jobs also influence where people live, who they associate with, the nature of their daily routine, and even the topics of their social conversations.

2. People are motivated to work for a number of reasons. In addition to working to survive, people hold jobs to establish their independence and personal identity, to enhance their self-esteem, and to strive toward self-actualization.

3. To make an informed decision about an occupation, a person can seek advice from counselors, take ability and interest tests, and engage in internships or summer work programs. Parents who provide a supportive and understanding environment can greatly help their children make informed choices about their careers. Some parents, however, hinder the decision-making process by trying to determine the occupations their children enter.

4. There are many sources from which to learn about job opportunities. Advertisements in newspapers or trade magazines are the most common source. Others include placing "situation wanted" ads so that prospective employers will call you, campus recruiters and job fairs, employment agencies, and employee referrals.

5. Employers use a number of techniques to select employees. Some employers use personality, intelligence, or ability tests. In using such tests, it is important that the information collected be relevant to the job and that the test not violate an applicant's right to privacy by examining nonjob related areas. Interviews are considered tests by the Equal Employment Opportunity Commission. Although interviews are the most common selection method,

they may not be the best technique because interviewer bias may influence the outcome. Biographical information that contains data about an applicant's job-related background and success is the most valid means of employee selection.

6. Much, if not most, learning about a job occurs on the job. Many large companies have formal job training programs. The most successful programs are developed after undertaking an organizational analysis, task analysis, and person analysis. Training programs may involve apprenticeships, lectures, and computer-assisted training.

7. Performance appraisal involves evaluating how well a person is performing a job. Although this appraisal is typically performed by a supervisor, other techniques include evaluations from everyone the employee has contact with on the job, including the employee himself or herself. Appraisals may focus on personality traits, behaviors or results of performance.

8. Job satisfaction is influenced by rewards (extrinsic and intrinsic), the fit between expectations and actual job conditions, the comparison between working conditions of people holding similar jobs, and perceptions of fairness (equity). Good performance often leads to increased satisfaction in one's job. People who are satisfied with their jobs are less likely to be absent from work or to look for other jobs. They are also more likely to be physiologically and psychologically healthy.

9. Some workers face important crises in their working lives. Career change because of job dissatisfaction is stressful for some people because it is often difficult to abandon one's desire for consistency and security. Burnout occurs when people lose sympathy for the people with whom or for whom they are working and become exhausted and cynical. Some people experience a difficult transition period between their late thirties and mid-forties where they feel that their lives haven't amounted to much and that the future holds no new challenges. People in any occupation may face unemployment include economic loss, loss of status and self-esteem, change in daily pattern of living, and increased likelihood of mental and physical illness.

10. In an effort to improve productivity and worker adjustment, many companies have undertaken steps to improve working conditions. Some of the steps include job enlargement (increasing the number and variety of jobs workers perform) and job enrichment (increasing worker's control over planning and performance). Other steps include making work schedules more flexible, allowing employees to work at home, and providing child-care facilities at the work site.

11. The trend for women to work outside the home has increased dramatically over the past fifty years. More than 56 percent of adult women in the United States now hold jobs outside the home. Women who hold these jobs often face special obstacles.

12. Job discrimination results when members of minority groups and women are underrepresented in a particular occupation due to prejudice against people on the basis of race, sex, religion, color, or national origin. Title VII of the Civil Rights Act of 1964 has been the most important law aimed at combating job discrimination.

13. Retirement is often viewed negatively because it is a sign of old age and involves giving up the work that people enjoy and that gives them fulfillment and status in our society. Successful retirement can be achieved by finding enjoyable substitutes for work, becoming involved in well-planned leisure activities, or engaging in new types of work suitable to a retired person's stage of life.

CRITICAL THINKING QUESTIONS

1. In many respects, choosing a college and choosing a major involves a process similar to that of choosing a job. Review how you made these decisions. As you look forward to choosing a job, what can you learn from your past choices (successes and mistakes) that can improve how you choose a job?

2. Apply the knowledge you have about how employers are attempting to improve the job situation to your own position as a student. How might you restructure your role as student to increase your satisfaction as a student and improve your performance (learning) as well as that of other students?

3. An interesting technique used in many conflict situations is role playing. The technique involves asking people to take the position of others in the conflict situation and to respond to the conflict from their position. In undertaking this exercise, people often see more clearly how and why others behave in the situation. Debbie Jones, a mother of two young children, is faced with adding a second income to help support her family. She has accepted a job as a supervisor of telephone repairs. Most of the people who work in this division are men who have never had a woman supervisor. If you are a male, take the role of Debbie. How do you feel as you enter the workplace? How do you act, and what issues are you most likely to be sensitive to? If you are female, take the role of one of the repairmen. Ask yourself the same questions as you confront Debbie. Now develop a plan that you think might reduce the conflicts and anxieties that could arise in the situation.

MATCHING EXERCISE_____

Match each term with its definition.

a. self-actualization
b. realistic job preview
c. assessment centers
d. performance appraisal

e. job satisfaction
f. extrinsic motivation
g. intrinsic motivation
h. burnout

i. job enrichment
j. job enlargement

1. Method of employee selection that involves having a prospective employee perform several job-related tasks and be evaluated by a number of trainers
2. A pleasurable emotional state that results from feeling that one's job is fulfilling
3. A state of developing one's potential and being able to use one's creative abilities
4. Motivation to perform a task that comes from factors external to the individual
5. An examination of a job that enables an employee to see both its positive and negative sides
6. Increasing the worker's control over planning and job performance
7. Evaluating how well a person is performing a job
8. Motivation to perform a job arising from degree of control one has over own behavior and feeling capable and competent
9. State that results when one loses sympathy for the people with whom or for whom one is working, accompanied by exhaustion
10. Increasing the number and variety of jobs that workers perform

Answers to Matching Exercise

a. 3   b. 5   c. 1   d. 7   e. 2   f. 4   g. 8   h. 9   i. 6   j. 10

ANSWERS TO REVIEW QUESTIONS_____

1. d
2. true
3. biographical information
4. false
5. Performance appraisal

6. extrinsic
7. dissatisfied
8. True
9. job enrichment
10. False

CHAPTER 15

LIVING WITH OUR ENVIRONMENT

Apache Ranchers

Herman Lehmann

On a warm day in May 1870, 11-year-old Herman Lehmann, his brother, and two sisters ran into the fields to scare the birds away from the new wheat. Herman's family had recently moved to a farm in Mason County, Texas, and they were hoping for a good harvest. The Lehmanns were fairly typical of the Germans who immigrated to Texas in the nineteenth century. They spoke only German and saw few other people because the farm was located several miles off the main road.

After the children had dispatched the birds, they began playing in the field. They were completely absorbed in their games when, all at once, they were surrounded by Native Americans with frightening painted faces. The children screamed and ran, but Herman never made it to the house. The chief of the Apache raiding party, Carnoviste, grabbed him and forced him to the ground. Herman was now a captive of the Apaches.

As the raiding party headed north, the country became increasingly barren. For four days of traveling day and night they found no food or water. On the fourth day, they came to a small creek and the whole party drank. On that day they also found a herd of antelope and shot several. The remainder of the trip went on in a similar fashion; they ate and drank only when the plains provided food and water.

Finally, they arrived at the Apache village, which was located near a large lake somewhere in New Mexico. The village contained nearly 2,500 people. Such a large concentration of people occurred only where water was abundant. In most cases the environment allowed only at few hundred people to camp together.

Herman became the property of Chief Carnoviste; he waited on the chief and cooked his food. In return, the chief taught the boy Apache ways. Herman learned to ride; to shoot a bow; to make poison arrows from a concoction of rattlesnake venom, skunk musk, and prickly weed; and to make shields from buffalo hide. Carnoviste taught him how to read the signs of his surroundings. He learned to forecast the weather by looking at spider webs. In dry weather the webs were thick, long, and high; before a rain the webs were low, short, and thick.

Herman also learned Apache manners. He wouldn't enter another Indian's camp area without being invited. He learned that even though there was only one "room" in a teepee, certain areas were used for specific purposes; there were private areas that a visitor didn't enter.

Despite the fact that the Apache village contained more people than Herman had ever seen in one place, he felt bitterly lonely. He reports never crying "while I was being tortured, nor when I ran the gauntlet, nor when I nearly drowned. In those times I gave a yell of defiance or a snarl of vengeance, but... in my loneliness and desolation, I wept" (Greene, 1972, p. 18).

In less than a year Herman Lehmann had completely adapted to his new social and physical environment. He became an Apache named Enda, member of a small band of Apaches that raided in Texas, New Mexico, Kansas, and Mexico. After a number of years, he became a subchief and led numerous raids on white settlers and soldiers.

The Apache raiders led a nomadic life, always traveling in search of water and food. During summers they followed the game into the Rocky Mountains. As winter began, they moved south. The size of the band was determined by the availability of food; when game was abundant, large concentrations of Apaches gathered together. As the years passed, the number of white settlers increased and game became increasingly scarce. Many of the Native American tribes were killed or herded onto reservations.

Five years after Herman's capture, Carnoviste was killed and Herman had to flee from the Apaches so as not to be killed and buried with his master. By this time, his last thought was to return to the whites; he hated them and had spent the last five years killing them. For six months after his flight from the Apaches, Herman wandered the plains living on whatever food his environment provided him. Soon he began to yearn for human companionship and started searching for another band he could join. He was able to locate a small Comanche hunting party. Although the Comanches regarded him with some suspicion in the beginning, they soon accepted him, and Herman assumed the Comanche name Montechena. The Comanches lived a life similar to that of the Apaches and traveled a similar territory.

The great white net, however, began to draw tighter, and Herman's group of Comanches was finally captured and sent to the Fort Sill reservation. Herman concealed himself among his Indian brothers so that the soldiers wouldn't see that he was a white captive and send him back to the white settlement. At Fort Sill, Herman was adopted and hidden by the great Comanche chief Quanah Parker.

Nevertheless, Herman was soon discovered by his captors. After some inquiry, the whites identified Herman and located his family. The Lehmanns had moved to Loyal Valley, Texas, but they had never given up hope of finding Herman alive.

There was a great deal of rejoicing when they learned that Herman had been found after almost nine years.

Herman returned to Loyal Valley to assume the way of white people. He was 20 years old and totally unprepared for what he found. The customs of the whites were strange to him. The whites owned land and grew their own food. Permanent settlements had sprung up where the whites lived with hardly any breathing room between them. White people lived in houses with many rooms rather than in one-room tepees. The "iron horse"— the steam locomotive—ran on steel tracks and connected the communities. The telegraph allowed people to communicate with each other even though they were many miles apart.

THE ENVIRONMENT AND HUMAN BEHAVIOR

The life of Herman the Apache was ruled by the environment. What and when Herman drank and ate were determined by the environment. Herman's food in the desert consisted of snakes, lizards, and small rodents. The grassy plains provided him with a diet of antelope, mustang, and buffalo. The environment determined where Herman made camp and how many others camped with him. The weather also determined Herman's home, as the Apaches often moved to mountainous areas during the spring and summer and to the flatlands as the cold winter blew into the mountains. For Native Americans the environment was master, and they acknowledged this in their ceremonies and religion.

The situation for Herman the white man was very different. At the end of the nineteenth century and into the twentieth century, white people thought they had nature under their control. Strong houses were built to withstand the weather and allow their inhabitants to live in one place regardless of the whims of the environment. Through agriculture and the domestication of animals, the settlers determined their diet rather than depending on the environment for their menu. If the land didn't readily supply water, a well could be dug to extract water from the reluctant earth. As more settlers moved onto the frontier, cities and towns were built and roads were carved through the wilderness. If a forest stood where the settlers wanted a town, the forest would be eliminated.

As technology improved and widened its sphere of influence, so did human mastery over the physical environment. Lakes and canals were constructed; irrigation allowed farming in many desert areas. Mountains were leveled or moved to make way for new towns. Bridges were built over rivers that once stymied travel and those rivers became the sewers and garbage dumps for the refuse of cities and industries. Much of this drastic change happened in the lifetime of Herman Lehmann.

Because of the control we have over our environment, most of us take it for granted and pay little attention to the effects it has on us. It often takes a disaster like a flood or a nuclear accident like the one in Chernobyl, Russia, in late 1985 to focus our attention on our physical environment. However, we will see in this chapter that our physical environment influences almost every aspect of our lives. Our environment affects our health, influences who we have as friends, serves as one of the major reasons we go to war, and determines the enjoyment we get out of daily activities such as viewing a movie or watching an athletic contest. Some of the features of our environment such as the amount of space we have or the way furniture in a room is arranged are very visible to us. Others, such as the amount of electricity in the air, are not visible. But even these environmental features can influence us. For example, research has shown that our social relations and performance on tasks can be influenced by the degree of electrical charges in the air around us (Baron, 1987a, 1987b). Given these effects of our environment, it is important for us to examine this topic to develop a better understanding of our adjustment to our social and physical world.

Perceiving Our Environment

When we discuss our environment, we might believe that we are discussing an entity that is seen by everyone in the same way and has the same effects on everyone. Indeed, this is not the case. Our responses to the environment are not determined solely by its physical characteristics, but by our perceptions of the environment.

For example, when you drive home from school this afternoon, you may get caught in a traffic jam that turns your normal 15-minute trip into a 20-minute trip. If you come from a small town, you perceive the traffic to be terrible and begin to think that this town is becoming very crowded. But if you're from a large city, your perceptions of this trip home will be very different. You will be amazed at how quickly the traffic is moving and begin to wonder where everyone has gone.

Our view of our present environment is affected both by our expectations and previous experiences as well as by the physical characteristics of the situation. In one demonstration of this effect, subjects first worked in either a highly crowded situation or a noncrowded environment (Webb & Worchel, 1993). They were then led to believe that their next environment would be crowded or not crowded. Finally, all subjects were placed in a very crowded work setting and asked to rate their environment. Although all subjects were rating the same environment, those who had been in a previous crowded situation rated the present environment as more crowded than subjects who came from a noncrowded situation.

A second important feature of perceiving our environment is that we are selective in our attention. Our environment contains more information than we could possibly comprehend at one time, so we narrow down our focus by paying attention only to certain aspects. If you look at the desert where Herman Lehmann lived as an Apache, you might focus on the lack of people, trees, and houses; to some eyes, it might have been a desolate, barren place. Herman, whose concern was survival, focused on the places that could provide protection and on parts of the desert that might be hiding game or water. A third person who was a naturalist would see the varied types of trees and plants that dotted the desert. The point is that although each of us may be faced with the same physical environment, we may well focus on different features of the world around us and interpret it differently.

Even more important is the fact that we respond to our perceptions and interpretations of the environment rather than its physical features. For example, a friend of ours recently told of taking his date to a highly recommended restaurant. The tables were small and very close together, and the only light in the place came from small candles at each table. Our friend felt crowded and feared

Adapting to Environmental Change

Several years ago one of the authors lived in a small rural county. The county was relatively poor and most people made their living by farming or commuting to jobs in neighboring counties. Then one of the farmers discovered a large deposit of rock on his farm. This rock could be used for building roads, and it had considerable value. He was approached by a company that proposed setting up a large quarry on his land to mine the rock. The quarry would bring new jobs to the community and bring significant tax revenue to the county. The quarry met federal government guidelines aimed at protecting the immediate environment.

At first everyone was excited by the prospects. The county planned to build a new school with the tax revenues and unemployment dropped as people were hired to work in the quarry. But after a few months, this joy was tempered by some sober realities. Although the quarry met legal requirements, its impact was still felt in many unanticipated ways.

The increased use of the county roads by the heavy trucks not only caused traffic problems but also created large potholes in several roads. Residents were forced to find other routes for their travel, which often meant longer trips to reach their destinations. Dust from the quarry blew onto neighboring land and crop output was reduced. The dust also got into people's homes, on their cars, and into their lungs. Health problems rose, and the only happy person was the fellow who owned the local car wash. His business tripled.

Several of the children began having problems in school. They complained that they could not study at home because of the noise from the quarry. A local chicken farmer found that his hens produced fewer eggs because they were upset by the trembling ground that resulted when the quarry blasted

to break up rock. Some residents complained about the eyesore that resulted from the giant hole in the ground. One stated that she never knew how important the view of rolling hills had been as she drove to and from her house until it was gone.

A town meeting was called to discuss these environmental problems. The residents realized the price they were paying for this change to their environment. At first, there were loud demands to close the quarry and "fill that damned hole." But as discussions progressed, a plan was developed. The quarry owners volunteered to plant a row of trees so the quarry would not be visible to passersby. The county imposed restrictions on the quarry so that blasting and rock crushing could only take place during the midday hours, when most people were away from home and the children were in school, outside hearing range of the quarry. The quarry operators were required to install large sprinklers to water the rock and reduce dust. Unfortunately, nothing could be done to help Mr. Davis's chickens, but even he adjusted. He converted much of his operation to turkeys, who seemed less affected by the periodic ground quakes.

Most important, the people in the county became more aware of the importance of their physical environment and how a change to the environment in one place could have a ripple effect into other locations and into the lives of people not directly involved in the change. The county developed a zoning plan to protect the environment and a review board to oversee future development plans. The quarry owners also learned of the wide impacts the quarry had on its neighbors. When they proposed another quarry in another county, their proposal included steps to reduce its impact.

---

eating food that he could not see. He was uncomfortable and wanted to leave as quickly as possible. His date found the setting romantic and intimate. She desired to prolong the meal as long as possible. Needless to say, the social encounter was not a happy event for

the couple. Both people faced the same environment, but they perceived it differently and their different reactions were based on their unique perceptions.

We should make one final point before going on. A frequently asked question is: "What is the best environment?" There is no simple answer. In fact, before even beginning to form an answer, we would have to raise other questions: "The 'best' environment for whom and for what activity?" In short, the best environment is the one with the best **person–environment fit** (Altman, Lawson, & Wohlwill, 1984). The environment cannot be considered without paying attention to who will be using it and the types of activities that will take place in it. A physical setting suitable for strangers waiting for an appointment with a physician would not be suitable for friends who wanted to have an intimate discussion. Thus, we cannot give a recipe for designing a room, home, or other setting to promote adjustment. Rather, we must work to develop settings that fit a purpose and the people who will use that setting. Later in this chapter we will see the disastrous results when the person–environment fit goal is not taken into account when considering our physical environment.

Isolation and Privacy

An interesting example of the importance of environmental perceptions and person–environment fit can be found when we consider isolation and privacy. Both of these conditions result from a lack of social interaction, yet one is experienced negatively and avoided, and the other is viewed positively.

When Herman was 16, his master Carnoviste was killed and Herman fled the Apaches. After many days of travel, he found a narrow canyon that offered shelter and plenty of food and water. All his physical needs were satisfied in this place, but soon he began to miss being with other people. Herman worked hard to overcome his feeling; he set about doing small jobs such as making arrows, and he even began to draw pictures in the sand. As his longing for other people grew, he found himself talking to his horse and to wolves that visited the canyon. Finally, he moved from his

canyon home in search of other people. Eventually he joined the Comanches.

Most of us never experience periods of social isolation. In fact, as a classroom demonstration, one of the authors asked students to spend three hours alone in a small room. The students could read and relax: their only requirement was that they not interact with anyone. This relatively short period of isolation was experienced by most students as uncomfortable and "weird." Time seemed to go by very slowly, and many students stated that they listened for noises that would indicate that other people were "out there." The experience increased students' awareness of how little time they spend alone.

There have been some studies on the effects of social isolation and we also have the reports of hermits, explorers, and prisoners in solitary confinement. These sources suggest a number of points about the effects of isolation. First, the effects of social isolation are most dramatic early in the isolation and begin to decline slowly as time passes. After long periods of isolation, the individual may enter a schizophrenic-like state of apathy where little matters. Second, socially isolated individuals often become preoccupied with thoughts of other people; they think, dream, and even hallucinate about other human beings. Third, isolated individuals who are able to occupy themselves with physical or mental activities suffer less than individuals who are unable to occupy themselves. Finally, one curious effect is that after lengthy periods of social isolation, people tend to experience discomfort when confronted with others. One study found that subjects kept greater distance between themselves and others and took longer to initiate conversations after isolation compared to conditions where they had not been isolated (Worchel, 1986a).

The studies on social isolation point out the significance of our environment for our adjustment. A varied environment that includes other people is important for our psychological well-being. Such variety is especially important for children since their psychological development is strongly affected by their social milieu. But variety and richness in our environment is important for adults as well.

Turning to the other side of the same coin, we find that there are times when isolation from others is both desired and beneficial. Simply "getting away" can give us the opportunity to reflect and relax. This "getting away" is often referred to as a search for privacy.

The difference between the positive situation of privacy and the negative situation of *social isolation* or loneliness involves the perception of choice. In fact, Ittelson and colleagues defined privacy as "an individual's freedom to choose what he will communicate about himself and to whom he will communicate it in a given circumstance" (1974). Thus, *privacy* involves the perception that social isolation is chosen rather than forced upon us. Some elderly people may choose to live in retirement homes because their physical and economic circumstances require it; they may experience their relative isolation as a worthwhile "retreat" from the cares of formerly busy lives. *Forced isolation,* on the other hand, is a condition in which we have no control over our environment or feelings. In these cases, isolation exists despite our desire for interpersonal interaction. People who are simply "dumped" in nursing homes may suffer greatly from the loss of their power of choice as well as from their undesired isolation.

While social isolation and the resulting loneliness can have a destructive effect on us, privacy has a very constructive effect. First, privacy allows us personal autonomy by providing us with the opportunity to control the environment. Second, it allows us to evaluate ourselves by providing the chance to withdraw from others. Third, it gives us a chance to release emotional tensions that are caused by everyday life. Most of us have had the desire to scream or cry to release our tensions. In most cases we are reluctant to do this in front of other people. In private, however, we feel freer to "let it all hang out." Finally, privacy allows us limited and protected communication by giving the choice of when and with whom we will share our thoughts.

The degree of privacy we seek (or have) is affected by many variables, including our age, sex, and culture. Children, for example, often have little privacy. Parents think nothing of walking into a child's room whenever they wish. However, as we get older, we expect to have more privacy; you would probably be very disturbed if your parents, siblings, or friends walked into your room without asking permission when you had closed your door. Indeed, many of us would be upset if our room was invaded even when we were not there. Culture, too, is important. Western cultures such as the United States and Germany afford people a great deal of privacy. Our homes are constructed with rooms having locking doors and soundproof walls, and there are clear rules that should be followed if people want to enter our space. On the other hand, Mediterranean cultures and Arabic cultures afford people considerably less physical privacy. Rooms often have no doors and it would be considered rude to close a door if one existed. In fact there is not even an Arabic word for privacy (McAndrew, 1993). However, even in these cultures there are norms about how one signals others to keep away, and certain areas of the house are considered private.

The important point is that social isolation can be experienced as either uncomfortable and negative (loneliness) or as positive and desired (privacy). We can construct our physical environment to help regulate the degree of social interaction we have. You may use such signs as an open door to signal that you desire social interaction. Adjusting to our world is aided by considering the amount of social interaction (or social isolation) we desire and the places where we desire that interaction.

PHYSICAL SPACE AND BEHAVIOR

As the preceding discussion suggests, the use of territory (our room, our furniture, our possessions) has a strong influence on our social interactions and adjustment to our environment. Therefore, an understanding of our territorial behavior is important for learning about the relationship between our environment and our behavior.

Territoriality

While Herman Lehmann was with the Apaches, he spent most of his time searching for game with small hunting parties of 10 to 15 people. They didn't choose their hunting grounds haphazardly. Their first consideration was to find areas where game would most likely be found. Their second consideration was whether other Apache groups had staked out the area. If there were signs that another band had already claimed an area, Herman's band would move on to hunt elsewhere.

When Herman returned to the whites, he found different customs of territorial behavior. The white settlers claimed personal ownership over land. Their claim gave them not only the right to farm, hunt, and live on a piece of land, but also the right to sell it or pass it on as a gift. At first, the settlers marked their territory by placing stakes or piles of rocks at the boundaries. As more settlers moved into the area, barbed wire fences and "NO TRESPASSING" signs marked a land owner's borders.

Almost every type of animal, two-legged or four-legged, exhibits territorial behavior. **Territoriality** involves claiming exclusive use of areas or objects. Such exclusiveness usually occurs within species, not between them: Only members of the same species are restricted from a claimed piece of territory. (Thus, a person who owns a piece of ground usually won't object if birds stake their own claims on property.) Once a territory is claimed, the "owner" will defend it even if he or she must resort to aggression.

While animals usually claim a single circumscribed area as their own, human territorial behavior is often more complex. For example, we may claim ownership over several nonadjacent pieces of property: home, office, beach home, mountain retreat. Humans often show territorial behavior over a wide range of objects as well: stereos, clothes, jewelry, furniture, tools, cars, boats, houses, land—even friends, lovers, and spouses are sometimes treated as "owned objects." It might be interesting for you to list the number of objects over which you display territorial behavior—things you would defend if someone tried to claim them. No doubt the list will be quite long.

Another aspect of human territorial behavior is the number of types of territories involved. Altman (1975) suggests that humans have three types of territories. **Primary territories** are exclusively owned and controlled by individuals and groups. These primary territories are central to the lives of those individuals. For example, your home would be your primary territory. Of all their territories, individuals are most attached to and protective of their primary territory.

Secondary territories include properties that are less central: The individual can't claim ownership over them. People become very emotionally attached to these territories, nevertheless, and attempt to control them. Your "regular" seat in a classroom may be your secondary territory; even though you don't own it, you feel entitled to occupy it and may become disturbed if someone else takes it. A similar case may be made for your seat at the dinner table; in many families, individuals have their "own" seats at the table.

The third type of territory is **public territory;** this includes property over which individuals do not feel ownership. They do, however, feel that they have control over the territory while they are occupying it. A spot

Reactions to Loss of Secondary Territory

One of the more predictable behaviors of college life is the tendency for students to "claim" certain seats in a classroom. On entering the classroom, they immediately head for their seat. This seat represents their secondary territory. Students don't feel that they own the seat, but they do feel that they should have that seat at a specific time period. To understand the extent of secondary territorial behavior, try the following exercise. Wait until midway through the semester, after students have laid claim to their place in the classroom. Get to class early and take a seat that is usually occupied by someone else. Watch that student's reaction when he or she enters the classroom. Chances are that the student will go toward his or her regular seat and react with some confusion when he or she finds it occupied by you. The student will likely search for another place that has not been occupied by anyone else during the semester (after giving you a dirty look and other signs that you have done something wrong). After class, ask the student how he/she felt on finding the space occupied.

The secondary territorial behavior serves the important function of helping establish order in the classroom. Students do not need to make a decision every day on where they will sit. Their seating helps establish predictable social interaction patterns. Students can anticipate who they will interact with during the class, and they may have entered into predictable patterns such as expecting to exchange books or notes with people who usually sit next to them. Your intrusion has altered all this and added uncertainty to their environment.

---

on the beach, for example, may be viewed as public territory. Individuals often claim a spot for themselves and feel that no one should intrude on it while they are occupying it. When they leave, however, the territory goes "up for grabs," and others may occupy it.

It is important to understand the various types of territories because people respond differently to invasions of each type. Uninvited trespassing on primary territories such as one's home or bedroom is likely to be met with stern rebukes and angry words. As the territory becomes less central, the responses to invasion will be less severe. Territorial behavior is so ingrained in us that we often don't recognize it directly. For example, you may have a feeling of growing irritation at a guest who, while visiting your room, sits down on your bed and begins to chat. This person may be friendly enough, but you still find yourself feeling increasingly tense and upset without understanding the basis for your reactions. It is very possible that these feelings are in response to the guest's invasion of your primary territory, your bed.

Functions of Territoriality. When the white settlers arrived in the Texas plains area, they were constantly baffled by the Native Americans. Despite their superior weapons and, in most cases, superior numbers, the settlers had a very difficult time beating them in combat or capturing them. The Native Americans used hit-and-run tactics, and they seemed to know which spots were advantageous for encounters and which were not. Herman Lehmann reports that he was amazed at how the Apaches could "disappear" into the environment, while the white settlers seemed to stand out against the land. One clear difference between the Apaches and the settlers was that the Apaches were fighting on their own territory; they had lived and hunted the plains for years and were very familiar with it. The settlers, on the other hand, were newcomers, and they were not as familiar with the land.

This example illustrates one function of territoriality: protection. Individuals are better able to protect themselves on their own territory than on foreign territory. A large part of this ability may be a function of familiarity. The Apaches knew every rock and crevice in their hunting area. Because of this, they knew not only when and where to fight and hide, but also the most likely places to find game and water. Observations of animal behavior show that in most cases animals fighting in their own territory defeat an intruder (Carpenter, 1958). Edney (1975) found that the residents in their own rooms generally took the leadership role, whereas the visitors reported feeling uncomfortable and were willing to take a more submissive role.

An indication of the protective function of territory is the fact that the elderly and victims of crime often retreat into their homes (territory) and may even refuse to venture into the outside world. They feel safe in their own territory. Taking this discussion a step further, we can better understand why crimes such as burglary and assault that occur in our homes are so devastating (Rosen, 1987). We not only suffer the immediate effects of the crime, but we must also come to grips with the realization that our territory, which we thought was safe, is not. If we cannot feel safe in our homes, where can we feel safe?

Another important aspect of territoriality is that it increases social order. Having a clear division of property reduces friction and misunderstanding between individuals; you know what is yours and have marked it, and your neighbor has done the same. Thus you are less likely to argue over who can plant a tree on a particular piece of property or who has control over an object such as a lawn mower or an automobile. In an interesting study, Rosenblatt and Budd (1977) found that married couples showed more territorial behavior than did unmarried couples who were living together. Presumably married couples knew they would be together for a long time and attempted to reduce the areas of possible conflict by arriving at a clear agreement about territories. For example, married couples were more likely than cohabiting couples to have a clear understanding about who slept on what side of the bed, who sat at a particular place at the dinner table, and to

whom a particular side of the closet belonged.

Having territory also helps us achieve privacy. We can escape from others when we have the exclusive control of an area. You can see this function when you think about how relaxed you felt when you finally were inside the safe confines of your home or room after a particularly hectic day.

Territoriality also helps control aggression. The poet Robert Frost wrote that "good fences make good neighbors." When individuals or groups have clear agreement about boundaries, they can avoid conflict by staying on their own side. Unfortunately, while territorial boundaries often control aggression, they can be the source of aggression when the parties disagree over where the boundaries should be drawn. Numerous wars have been started when countries disagreed about where boundaries should be drawn; in some cases the disagreement involved only a few miles of land.

Finally, territory helps us establish and advertise our identity. You can most easily understand this function by walking through a dormitory and looking at occupied rooms. Some rooms may be decorated with pictures of solitary outdoors activities such as hiking, boating, or skiing; other rooms may be decorated with posters of travel; still others have walls plastered with the portraits of rock stars. Each person is using the territory to show who he or she is. Similar signs of identity can be found in offices and on mailboxes. A person can also signal his or her identity by choosing to live in a rural setting or in a high-rise apartment. Thus, even before meeting a person, we can tell much about that person from his or her territory.

Some Practical Effects of Territorial Behavior. Some interesting studies have been made of the everyday effects of territorial behavior. One study found that a home was less likely to be burglarized if it displayed clear signs of being someone's territory (Brown,

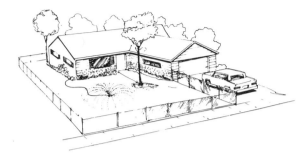

FIGURE 15.1   The Appearance of a Home Can Influence Its Chances of Being Burglarized (left, nonburglarized; right, burglarized).

1979). As Figure 15.1 shows, the home that had a fence marking its boundary and separating it from the street, clear indications of ownership (name plate and address signs), and indications of occupancy was less likely to be the target of a burglary than the home that didn't have these territorial markings. Territorial signals probably increase burglars' fears of being caught. Burglaries may also have been thwarted by people's natural reluctance to invade another's territory.

In another study Worchel and Lollis (1982) found that residents in both the United States and Greece were more likely to pick up litter that was in their primary territory than litter that was in public territory. This effect was found even when the litter in the public territory was unsightly and detracted from the beauty of the people's own territory. Worchel and Lollis suggested that an effective way to control litter would be to change people's perceptions and make them believe that they controlled public places. For example, people in a neighborhood could be given control over a local park and told that they were responsible for its maintenance.

REVIEW QUESTIONS

1. Understanding the relationship between the environment and behavior involves realizing that our behavior is influenced by our _____ of the environment as well as by its physical characteristics.

2. In order to define a "good" environment, we must consider the _____.

3. Social interactions can be characterized by our willingness to engage in them and the opportunities for interaction that are presented. Choosing not to engage in social interactions is called _____, while not being allowed the opportunity to interact is called _____.

4. _____ involves claiming exclusive use of areas or objects and defending that area or object from other members of the same species.

5. Territories can be defined by the degree to which individuals own and control them. _____ territories, such as homes, are exclusively owned and controlled by individuals.

6. Which of the following effects can be thought of as resulting from territoriality?

   a. protection
   b. privacy
   c. psychological advantage
   d. all the above

How Territorial Is Your Family?

One of the interesting features of environmental behavior is that it often goes unnoticed. We take much of this behavior for granted until someone violates our expectations or norms. This is especially true of territorial behavior. Francis McAndrew (1993) developed the following list of questions that will demonstrate how territorial your family is. As you answer these questions consider the rules and procedures your family has developed to protect each member's territory. It is also the case that the amount of territory one controls is associated with that person's power (Wartenberg, 1992). In your review of your family's territorial behavior, determine if the relationship between power and territory holds in your household.

1. Do the members of your family lock the bathroom door?
2. Do people sit in the same chairs at the table for every meal?
3. Do family members knock before entering each other's rooms?
4. Does your family close bedroom doors at night when they are sleeping?
5. Are there any special rooms at home (for example, a den, an office, workshop) that are used only by one individual?
6. Is there a chair that "belongs" to one individual in the living room or TV room?
7. Does anyone in your family have his or her own telephone or television?

Finally, every sports fan and gambler is familiar with the term "home court advantage." Numerous studies on a variety of sporting events have shown that the team playing on its home field is more likely to win. The home team players are more familiar and comfortable with the environment. They know how the ball will bounce, where the lighting is poor, and the effect of the wind on the ball. They also have the support of the crowd. There have been a number of cases where the visiting team has accused the home team of making the environment especially difficult such as keeping the visiting team's locker room cold or giving them hard benches to sit on. Gamblers give better odds to the home team. One situation in which the home court advantage does not occur is in critical or championship games (Baumiester, 1985). In these cases the visitor seems to have a slight edge. There are a number of reasons for this effect: One is that the pressure on the home team may be too great for them to perform well; they not only have the pressure of the championship game, but the crowd is watching every move they make. This pressure may cause them to choke and lose the contest.

Personal Space

Territoriality involves *fixed territory*, such as rooms and object. But we also show territorial behavior to the *mobile territory* that always surrounds us. Some years ago, Edward Hall (1959, 1966), an anthropologist, observed people from many different cultures interacting in numerous situations. He noticed patterns in the way people utilized space when interacting. Within each culture there seem to be unwritten customs regulating how close

TABLE 15.1 Keeping Your Distance: Hall's Spatial Zones for Different Types of Interpersonal Relationships

DISTANCE	APPROPRIATE RELATIONSHIPS AND ACTIVITIES
Intimate distance (0 to 1½ feet)	Intimate contacts (e.g., making love, comforting) and physical sports (e.g., wrestling)
Personal distance (1½ to 4 feet)	Contacts between close friends, as well as everyday interactions with acquaintances
Social distance (4 to 12 feet)	Impersonal and businesslike contacts
Public distance (more than 12 feet)	Formal contacts between an individual (e.g., actor, politician) and the public

Source: Based on Hall, 1963. (Reproduced by permission of American Anthropological Association, *American Anthropologist, 65,* 5:1003–1026, 1963.)

individuals approach each other. As we will see, the degree of distance varied from culture to culture and was influenced by the nature of the interaction. It seemed to Hall, however, that all individuals felt a certain sense of ownership of the space immediately surrounding them and that others avoided trespassing upon this space. Hall coined the term **personal space** to denote these "bubbles of space" that people keep around them when they are interacting.

Hall identified four sizes of interaction distance, or bubbles of space, each with a close and far phase. The size of one's personal space is determined by the type of interaction taking place. As can be seen in Table 15.1, the intimate distance (0 to 18 inches) is generally used by close friends for comforting, making love, and telling secrets. On the other hand, the public distance (12 feet and more) is used by people in very formal gatherings and is the distance accorded important public figures. It might be very instructive for you to make note of the distances at which you interact with various people. Usually we are not conscious of the different distances we keep, since our spacing occurs almost reflexively. But if you make a conscious effort to observe your own behavior and that of others, you should be able to observe the uniformity of spacing behavior in interactions.

Functions of Personal Space. One of the interesting aspects of much of our territorial behavior is that it has important survival and adjustment functions. For example, territoriality influences species survival by separating individuals and allowing them intimate knowledge of a defined area. It has been argued that personal spacing behavior also plays a role in survival. As you can see, the distance kept in most interactions involves a space that keeps another person "at arm's length" and allows for observation of their arms and legs. In an earlier time, when arms and legs were the main weapons available, this spacing served a protective function.

Another important function of personal space behavior is communication. Our spacing behavior is related to communication in two ways. First, we can communicate specific messages, such as attraction, through our use of space. It has been shown repeatedly that we stand closer to people we like than to those we dislike (Gifford and O'Conner, 1986). Thus we can "tell" others how much we like them and how comfortable we are with them by how close we place ourselves when interacting. You may observe how sensitive others are to the communication aspects of personal space. Simply place a greater than usual interaction distance between yourself and an intimate friend. Chances are that your friend will not directly ask why you are using this larger distance. But it is likely that this spacing will make your friend uncomfortable, and he or she may soon ask: "What's wrong? Are you angry?"

Space also has a more indirect effect on communication. In Chapter 9, we discussed the wide range of messages that can be communicated nonverbally through the use of eye contact, body posture, and hand movements. Spacing behavior determines which of these nonverbal channels can be used in communication. For example, if you are communicating with someone at the public distance (greater than 12 feet), you may hear his or her voice and see hand movements, but you will have difficulty determining if that person is making eye contact, leaning slightly forward or backward, frowning or smiling, seething or remaining calm. On the other hand, when you communicate at the intimate distance (0 to 18 inches), you should have no trouble picking up messages communicated through facial expression and eye contact, but you may be too close to notice arm and hand movements.

Another interesting way to look at the communication effects of interpersonal spacing is to examine the classroom. A number of studies have focused on how seating position affected students' participation in classroom discussions and their grades (Stires, 1980; Kinarty, 1975; Sommer, 1967). As Figure 15.2 shows, students seated in the front and middle rows of seats in classrooms are most likely to participate actively in class discussions. In these positions, students are most likely to be able to hold eye contact with the instructor and see his or her face clearly. (It has also been found that students who choose the middle seats in the classroom are most likely to get the best grades in class.) As you can guess,

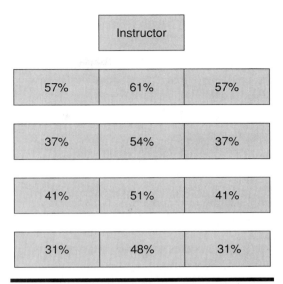

FIGURE 15.2 The Participators: Relation between Class Seating and Participation

Source: Sommer, R. Classroom ecology, *Journal of Applied Behavioral Science,* 1967, 3, 500. Copyright 1967 by NTL Institute Publications.

there are two ways to interpret these results. On one hand, good students may simply choose the middle rows of seats. On the other hand, it could be argued that students who are in the middle rows feel more a part of the class and receive more visual and verbal contact with the instructor than do students at the back of the class.

Factors Influencing Personal Space. We have already pointed out that the type of interaction and the type of relationship between people affect the size of personal space. A number of other factors influence the size of personal space. It is important to understand these factors since they will make you aware of why others may be using spacing that is not comfortable for you.

Ethnicity and culture have strong effects on the amount of personal space an individual will require to be comfortable. Numerous investigators have observed that Latin Americans, Arabs, Greeks, and the French have closer personal spaces than do Americans, Germans, the English, and the Swiss (e.g., Hall, 1966; Willis, 1966; Watson & Graves, 1966). To see the potential importance of this difference, consider the intriguing story about a Latin American and a North American who were conversing at a party. After exchanging a few pleasantries, the Latin American moved closer and closer to the North American. As the conversation progressed, the North American became uncomfortable with this distance and moved backward to restore a North American personal space limit. The Latin American countered these backward movements by continually moving closer to the North American. The result was the "Latin waltz": the Latin American moved closer each time the North American moved backward. During the course of the conversation, the two "waltzed" across the room, even though they were unaware of their behavior. This action was not the result of either party's being impolite or rude. Rather, the Latin American had a closer personal space norm than the North American, and each time the Latin American tried to establish comfortable spacing, the North American moved back in an effort to conform to a different personal space norm.

This story may be amusing, but Worchel, Cooper, and Goethals (1993) point out that cultural variations in personal space can have serious implications. In many cities, individuals from different cultures interact. Clearly, there are differences in language and customs that may make these interactions difficult. It is also possible that differences in personal space requirements add to the stress associated with these interactions. For example, an individual from a German background may find it very uncomfortable to interact with a Latin American because they have difficulty establishing satisfactory interpersonal spacing. The Latin American wants to interact at a close range, whereas the German desires a great deal of space. Friction is likely to develop between the two since each may view the other as rude. Actually both are attempting to establish spacing that is comfortable and acceptable to individuals from their different cultures. This type of conflict is more likely to be found in cities such as New York and San Francisco, which have a great deal of cultural heterogeneity, than it is in cities such as Berlin and Tokyo where there is more cultural homogeneity.

The sex of the individual affects not only the size of personal space but also the shape of it. Females have smaller personal space zones than males (Hayduk, 1983). The distance between people in male–female pairs tends to be smaller than the distance between same-sex pairs. There has been a great deal of speculation about the reasons for this space difference. Western cultures have strong taboos against homosexuality, especially male homosexuality. Young boys are taught very early that they should not caress each other. There is a great deal less touching between a father and a son than between a mother and a daughter. This early training may instill in young children the belief that males should not interact at close distances even though such close interaction is permissible between females or between members of the opposite sex.

Men's discomfort with physical closeness is also seen when we compare the spatial behavior of people who are attracted to each other. Females interact at closer distances with other females they like than with other females they dislike. But attraction doesn't influence the distance at which males interact with other males. Most men in our culture usually don't feel comfortable being physically close to other men, except in "permissible" situations such as football games. It is also interesting that in mixed-sex pairs, women are more likely than men to move closer to a person they like; men are less likely to "make the first move" by moving physically closer to women who attract them. Overall, women are

Careful Where You Sit!: Personal Space in Men and Women

A number of variables affect our spatial behavior. One of the more interesting differences in spatial behaviors involves the responses of men and women. As we discussed, personal space is viewed as the bubble of space around us, and violations of this bubble causes us distress. But is the bubble of personal space the same for men and women? In order to examine this question, Fisher and Byrne (1975) chose the library for their laboratory. They had experimental accomplices (male or female) wait by the library stacks until they spotted a student sitting alone at a table. The accomplice then approached the table and took a seat that was either (1) directly adjacent to the student, (2) one seat away, but on the same side of the table, or (3) directly across the table from the student. The accomplice pretended to study for five minutes and then left the library. Shortly afterwards, an experimenter approached the student and stated that he or she was studying students' feelings about the library. The student was asked to complete a questionnaire that asked how they felt about the library and about the other person who had been sitting at their table.

The results were quite interesting. Male students reported feeling most crowded when the "invader" had taken the seat across the table from them. They also liked the invader least when he or she took the seat across the table. On the other hand, females were most disturbed when the accomplice chose the seat adjacent to them. They felt most crowded and liked the "invader" the least under these conditions. Interestingly, these results were found whether or not the invader was male or female.

It is difficult to explain why males are most bothered by frontal invasions of their space, whereas females are most bothered by side violations. The investigators suggest that men may interpret the frontal invasion as being competitive, while females view the side invasions as a demand for unwanted affiliation. Regardless of the reason, the results have implications for social interactions and planning of furniture in rooms. For example, if the room is to be occupied by men, care should be exercised to arrange furniture to avoid frontal violations. If the room is to be occupied by women, the arrangement should protect against side violations.

---

more likely than men to respond to attraction by moving physically closer to the other person (Fisher et al., 1984).

Another interesting finding regarding sex differences in spatial behavior is that males seem most concerned with protecting their frontal space, while females are most sensitive about the space at their sides (see the accompaning Lessons from the Laboratory). For example, Byrne, Baskett, and Hodges (1971) found that given a choice, males prefer to position themselves across from friends, whereas females choose to position themselves next to friends.

The age of a person also influences personal space behavior. Children begin to develop consistent spatial behavior around the

age of 4 or 5, and the size of the child's personal space increases as he or she grows older. Adultlike spatial norms generally develop as the child reaches puberty. Although adults generally respect the spatial rights of other adults, they don't show the same respect for children's space. Surely you've witnessed a stranger walking over to a child and rubbing his hair or pinching her cheeks while saying "Aren't you cute!" Adults also don't seem to be bothered by invasions of their personal space by children under the age of 10 (Fry & Willis, 1971). But children over the age of 10 who invade an adult's personal space make the adult uncomfortable.

Many environmental factors also influence the space we place between ourselves and others. For example, we interact at closer distances in large compared to small rooms (White, 1975), in square compared to rectangular rooms (Worchel, 1986a), and outside compared to inside (Cochran et al., 1984). We use closer distances in rooms with high ceilings than in rooms with low ceilings (Savinar, 1975). And we allow others to come closer in settings likely to provoke anxiety (doctor's office, waiting room in dean's office) than in less anxiety-provoking settings (Long, 1984). The point should be clear: Many features of our physical environment affect the distance at which we carry out our social interactions.

This discussion should alert you to the fact that spatial behavior is often complex and influenced by many variables. We can't flatly state that a certain distance is proper in a certain type of relationship. The appropriate distance is influenced by factors such as the age, sex, and culture of the people involved in the interaction. Although we can't supply a table of proper distances, we can alert you to the fact that these variables influence spacing behavior.

Responses to Violations of Personal Space.

Since Herman Lehmann spent many of his formative years with the Indians, he was probably unfamiliar with the white norms of personal space. As a result, it is likely that he violated many of these customs when he returned to the white world. Such violations were probably met with a variety of responses.

One of the most common responses to violations of personal space is stress. People whose personal space is violated report feeling tense and anxious (Worchel & Teddlie, 1976). Physiological functions such as galvanic skin response, heartrate, and blood pressure also increase when personal space is violated.

People also attempt nonverbal compensations for these violations. Argyle and Dean (1965) had subjects converse with an experimental confederate at distances of 2, 6, and 10 feet and then observed subjects' responses behind a one-way mirror. They found that the closer the confederate stood, the less eye contact the subject kept. Other research has shown that people respond to spatial violations by leaning backward or turning their shoulder toward the violator. All these responses communicate discomfort to the violator and serve to reduce the intensity of interaction. If the violation continues, people take flight and completely avoid the other person.

People generally do not like the invaders of their personal space. In an interesting study showing this effect, Konecni (1975) had a confederate violate the personal space of a subject. Next, the confederate dropped some personal objects. If the confederate had violated the subjects' personal space, subjects were less likely to help pick up the dropped objects than they were if the confederate hadn't violated their personal space.

There are, however, exceptions to this effect. A violation of personal space can lead to increased attraction to the intruder if we see the intruder as making a friendly overture. Here again we see that people respond in line with their perceptions and interpretation of environmental events.

Density and Crowding

Herman Lehmann spent his early days on an isolated farm or roaming the plains with the Apaches and Comanches. Even after returning to the white world, he spent his remaining days in the sparsely populated area of Mason County, Texas. He never lived in a densely populated area or experienced prolonged feelings of crowding. This is not the case, however, for a large number of people throughout the world. With the coming of the industrial age, people began to flock to centralized areas to reap the fruits of the amazing new technological inventions and to partake of the readily available employment opportunities. At the same time, the world's population began to grow tremendously, and today this rate of growth is both staggering and frightening. Ehrlich (1968) points out that in 1650 the world's population was about 500 million. By the time of Herman's birth in the late 1850s, over 1 billion people inhabited the earth; it took 200 years for the world's population to double. When Herman died in 1932, there were 2 billion people in the world; the population had doubled in just 80 years. Ehrlich estimated that it now takes only 35 years for the world's population to double. If this estimate is correct, it means that the number of people living on earth will double twice during our lifetimes.

Given these figures and the fact that the size of the earth is constant, the amount of space available to the average person is shrinking and will continue to shrink. In recent years psychologists, biologists, and sociologists have begun to ask how this diminishing availability of space will affect human behavior and adjustment. Two major but related concepts have been developed to characterize and categorize the effects of limited space on behavior.

The first term is **density,** which is the amount of space available to a person. The density of a room can be found by dividing the number of square feet contained in the room by the number of people occupying the room. For example, if there are 50 students in your classroom of 500 square feet, the density is 10 square feet per person.

The second term is **crowding.** Crowding is not a physical measure. Rather, it describes the psychological state of a person. We feel crowded to a greater or lesser degree; we don't feel density. Crowding and density are often related, but this isn't always the case.

When we think of crowding on a world level, our concerns probably focus on shortages; too many people means too little food, energy, housing, and other resources that make our lives comfortable. These are important concerns, but psychologists have examined a somewhat different issue related to crowding: How does crowding influence our behavior? Some of the earliest research on this question looked at animals, not at people. One investigator observed a colony of rats that were confined to a pen for a long period of time. The animals had sufficient food, water, and nesting material, and they rapidly reproduced. But as the density in the pen increased, gross distortion in the rats' behavior occurred. Nest-building behavior was severely disrupted. The females failed to take proper care of their young, and many of the offspring died of neglect. Abnormal sexual behavior developed, as male rats would attempt copulation with immature rats or engage in homosexual behavior. Aggression increased until "it was impossible to enter the room without observing fresh blood spattered about the room from tail wounds" (Calhoun, 1962). Females had complications with pregnancies, and many developed cancer of the sex organs and mammary glands. The death rate among females was 3½ times greater than that for males.

Sociologists have examined statistics of human behavior in high-density urban areas. A number of these studies seem to indicate that as the density of an area increases, negative effects such as crime, infant mortality, disease, mental illness, and juvenile delinquency also increase (Schmitt, 1957, 1966). These data are certainly alarming.

Concern about such statistics has motivated a number of investigators to study the effects of density on human behavior. The results of these studies, however, cast some doubt on the premise that high density alone leads to adjustment problems. For example, Schmitt (1963) compared Hong Kong, with 2,000 people per acre the most densely populated city in the world, with New York City, which has a density of fewer than 450 people per acre. He found that the mortality rate in

New York City was twice as large as that in Hong Kong, hospitalization for mental illness was ten times greater in New York City than in Hong Kong, and the number of murder and manslaughter cases in New York City was six time greater than in Hong Kong. Even some of the early laboratory studies, in which groups of people were often packed into rooms so that their reactions and performance of tasks could be observed, suggested that high density didn't always cause people to feel uncomfortable or to perform poorly.

Conditions Affecting Crowding.   All of this presents quite a confusing picture; sometimes people (and animals) react very negatively to high density, and other times they don't. This situation has the makings of a good mystery story; the challenge is to discover the critical ingredients that make people feel crowded and uncomfortable. The answer cannot be the amount of space by itself.

To solve this mystery, consider the following common situations. In the first situation, you are going to the library to study for an important exam coming up the next morning. You arrive rather early, spread your materials out, and begin to thumb through some books. Soon others arrive and you find yourself sandwiched between two people; you are forced to place your belongings under your chair. Even though the library is not completely filled and the density is not particularly high, you may feel cramped and crowded and have trouble concentrating. Now place yourself at a football game. The stadium is filled and people are jammed around you; the density is many times greater than in the library. The game has started and the score is very close. On each critical play, the fans erupt with cheering; you even find yourself hugging the stranger sitting next to you. Do you feel as crowded in this situation as in the library? Probably not. You are likely to report feeling excited and exhilarated at the football game and unlikely to report feeling

terribly crowded. So high density doesn't always lead us to feel crowded. What, then, are the other differences in these two situations that could determine when people will feel crowded?

One difference is the focus of your attention. In the library you are focusing on the other people, while at the football game you are watching the action on the field. It has been found that we are more likely to feel crowded and uncomfortable when we are paying attention to other people being too close to us (Worchel & Brown, 1984).

A second difference revolves around the issue of control. At the library you expect to be able to control the space at your table. Control in this situation is important to accomplishing your task of studying. At the football game you don't expect to have control over more space than your own seat, and as long as you can see the game, control of space is not important.

High density leads us to feel crowded when we have no control over the environment or have less control than we want. To demonstrate this effect, Rodin et al. (1978) had four people wait until they spotted a single individual waiting for an elevator at the Yale University library. When the doors opened, the four confederates in the experiment and the unaware subject entered the elevator. In some cases, the four people positioned themselves so that the subject was standing next to the control panel and could control the elevator. In other cases, they stood so that the subject couldn't reach the controls. When the elevator stopped and the four confederates had departed, the experimenter asked the subject how crowded he or she had felt during the ride. Subjects who had no control (were not near the control panel) reported feeling more crowded and perceived the elevator as being smaller than subjects who had control over the movement of the elevator. Thus it seems that you are more likely to feel crowded in a situation that limits your control than in one in which you can still influence your environment.

A third difference involves desire for privacy. At the library you wanted privacy, but privacy isn't one of your goals when you go to a football game. As we can see, our need for privacy and solitude varies according to the situation. Crowding results when our desired level of privacy is greater than the level of privacy we have in a given situation (Altman, 1975).

As you will remember, we discussed earlier in the chapter how people's expectations and past experience affect feelings of crowding. Specifically, when we have just been in a crowded environment, we will experience a new environment as more crowded than if we have come from an uncrowded situation. Likewise, if we don't expect to be crowded, we will be especially uncomfortable in a high-density situation (Webb & Worchel, 1993).

Effects of Crowding.   Given that we know some of the conditions that cause us to feel crowded, we can now examine how crowding affects our behavior. The first point that comes to mind is that when we feel crowded we are also likely to feel uncomfortable. In fact, the most consistent finding in research is that conditions that lead to crowding also cause us to feel uncomfortable and anxious; people do not like feeling crowded. Interestingly, one study found that even the anticipation of feeling crowded elicits a negative mood (Baum & Greenberg, 1975).

Numerous studies have shown that we are likely to perform more poorly on tasks when we feel crowded. These studies examined tasks such as working puzzles, mazes, and anagrams and solving problems in human relations. Two results are especially striking. First, crowding has the most negative influence on complex tasks and relatively little influence on simpler tasks. This finding suggests clearly that if you are going to work on a complex problem, such as one that re-

quires reasoning or intense concentration, you should be careful to seek an environment in which you will not feel crowded. A second finding is that males are more affected by crowding than females (Stokols et al., 1973). The research indicates that whereas the performance and emotional state of males is negatively affected by crowding, these effects are not reliably found with females. The specific reason for this puzzling finding is not clear. Worchel (1978) has postulated that because females have smaller personal space requirements, they may not feel crowded in a density that causes males to experience crowding.

Another consistent finding is that crowding leads to a deterioration in interpersonal relationships, especially with males. People who are crowded don't like each other as much as do uncrowded people. One research project asked dormitory residents how much they liked their roommates (Baron et al., 1976). Half the subjects were living under crowded conditions (three students in a room built for two), while the other half were living two to a room and were less likely to experience crowding. The "triples" liked their roommates less than the students living in pairs. Other research found that aggression was greater from subjects who were crowded than from uncrowded subjects.

Space and Adjustments

Our discussion illustrates how widespread our spatial behavior is, but how can a better understanding of spatial behavior help our adjustment process? There are several important points to raise on this issue. First, because spatial behavior is so automatic, it is often overlooked. For example, you may find that you are uncomfortable with your roommate, but you can't put your finger on why. He or she is always friendly and willing to help you, but you feel uneasy. On closer examination, you might find that your roommate unwittingly violates your space. He or she might interact at a distance that makes you uncomfortable, he may violate your space by touching you when talking with you, or she may not respect your territory (such as leaving her books on "your side" of the room). Another example is that you might find yourself especially uncomfortable in a classroom. If you examine your experience, you might see that you have that class just after getting off a crowded bus. Your previous experience with crowding causes you to feel more crowded in the classroom.

Second, a knowledge of spatial behavior may make you more sensitive to why others respond to you as they do. You may better understand why your girlfriend finds you to be a cold person because you always keep large distances when interacting with her. You may better understand why your roommate gets so furious when she finds you studying at her desk. You can use your knowledge of spatial behavior to help make others feel more comfortable with you. Greater sensitivity to spa-

tial behavior may help you learn things about others that you overlooked before. For example, you might quickly scan your professor's office to determine what the decorations tell you about him or her. Does she have pictures of skiing on her wall or posters depicting fine art? This knowledge may help you "break the ice" when you begin your interaction or simply help you feel more comfortable with your professor. And if you travel to a foreign country, you may not jump so quickly to the conclusion that the people of that country are rude because they push you or stand too close.

Knowledge about spatial behavior, then, will help you better understand your behavior and that of others and help you avoid embarrassing situations or drawing unwarranted conclusions about the behavior of others or your own behavior. Overall, this knowledge will help you gain greater control and understanding of your actions and those of others.

REVIEW QUESTIONS

7. According to Hall, people will avoid trespassing upon the area immediately surrounding another person. This area is called _____.

8. Hall identified different interaction distances that are determined by the type of interaction occurring. Provide the term used by Hall to describe the distances under which the following interactions are likely to occur.

   a. telling secrets, making love, wrestling: _____ distance

   b. distance for formal interactions and for important public figures: _____ distance

9. Personal space requirements are not universal. Three factors related to the determination of interactional distances are _____, _____, and _____.

10. T or F: Women in general interact at closer distances than men.

OTHER ENVIRONMENTAL INFLUENCES

Noise

Herman Lehmann spent his life on the Texas plains. He rarely had to experience the high-density situations that many of us face on a

daily basis. Another feature of Herman's environment was quiet. The noises that Herman heard were, for the most part, those made by nature: the sound of animals, the whisper of the breezes, the crackle of fire, and the boom of thunder. The one exception to this was Herman's encounter with the iron horse." He reports that a raiding party of which he was a part came upon two ribbons of steel running across the plains. They puzzled over this discovery until they were startled by a loud noise. The noise pierced their ears and frightened them. Their fright increased when they looked up and saw "a huge one-eyed iron devil breathing fire and smoke" rushing down the tracks after them.

If Herman considered the noise of the oncoming train to be deafening and painful, we can only imagine his response to rush hour in the center of a large city! In recent years, we have become concerned with the noise pollution in our environment. Our technology has advanced to the point where we can make bigger and faster vehicles and larger machines to do our work, but an increase in noise has accompanied this achievement. In many of our factories, workers are able to perform their jobs only by wearing earplugs that dampen the noise. It is interesting and somewhat disturbing to note that almost all the noise we hear today is the by-product of humans and their machines; only a small part of the noise most of us hear is caused by the natural environment.

The sounds of our world are created by changes in air pressure. These changes in pressure affect a small membrane in our ears. The changes in the membrane caused by these pressures are transmitted to our brains through a series of three small bones, a hollow canal filled with fluid, and the auditory nerve. A sound becomes a **noise** when it is unwanted by the listener because it is unpleasant, bothersome and interferes with activities. Thus, while the latest rock song may seem like music to one person, it may be noise to another.

One of the most measurable effects of noise is hearing loss. In 1972 the U.S. Environmental Protection Agency (EPA) estimated that close to 3 million Americans suffered hearing loss caused by loud noises. The EPA conducted hearing tests for high-frequency sounds on a youthful population

and found that 3.8 percent of sixth graders, 10 percent of ninth and tenth graders, and a staggering 61 percent of college freshmen failed the test. It is possible that some of this hearing loss was caused by listening to loud rock music; individuals often expose themselves to music that reaches 110 to 120 decibels for hours on end, and research indicates that exposure to this loud noise for only 30 minutes a day may have serious consequences for hearing. In a shocking testimony to the effect of noise, one group of researchers (Rosen, Bergman, Plestor, El-Mofty, & Satti, 1962) found that 70-year-olds in quiet Sudanese villages have the hearing abilities of 20-year-olds in the United States. Other evidence shows that taking drugs such as antibiotics and even aspirin may result in increased effects of noise and cause greater hearing loss (Kaloff, 1982).

Another area of concern has been the effects of noise on people's performance of various tasks. A number of carefully controlled studies have been conducted to determine the influence of noise on task performance (Glass & Singer, 1972). The initial results were quite surprising; noise, even fairly loud noise, didn't significantly impair a subject's performance. People seemed to adapt very quickly to the noise and after a while even their psychological functioning was unaffected by it. You may be familiar with this adaptation response (often called *habituation*) if you live close to a busy street or a railroad track. At first you are very bothered by the noise and may have some trouble functioning. But after some time you adapt and become almost unaware of it. You don't "hear" it again until a friend visits and questions how you can "stand all this noise."

However, the story does not end here. More careful study found that people's work was hurt by noise that was unpredictable and uncontrollable. Anyone who has tried to read while workers are using a jackhammer can understand this effect! Your reading will be suddenly interrupted by the machine-gun sound of the hammer. When the sound stops, you go back to reading, only to be jolted again by the noise. You can't predict when the noise will return, and soon you find yourself listening for the next burst rather than concentrating on your reading. Another interesting fact is that we are also affected by the aftereffects of noise. After being bombarded by unpredictable and uncontrollable noise, we find it difficult to work even in a quiet environment; Finally, not all noise affects us the same way. Background noise that involves conversation seems to be the most disruptive; in this case we are not only distracted, but we focus our attention on trying to determine what is being said (Topf, 1985) .

Not all people are affected by noise to the same degree. Some people are more easily distracted than others. Most disturbing is the fact that children fall into the "easily distractible" category, and research has found dramatic effects of noise on children. One demonstration of the insidious effects of noise is seen in a study that examined the reading ability of children living in a large high-rise apartment complex situation over a highway in New York City (Cohen, Glass, & Singer, 1973). The children on the lower floors were exposed to more noise than were children on the upper floors. The researcher found that the children living on the lower floors had more hearing problems and poorer reading ability than did the children living on the upper floors. Another set of studies found that children whose school was in the noisy flight path of the Los Angeles airport performed more poorly and had higher blood pressure than children in quiet schools (Cohen et al., 1982). This effect was especially strong for students who had been in the school for less than two years. And a large study of German children found that those children living close to a noisy airport had higher physiological stress levels (heart rate) and performed more poorly on reading and memory tasks than did children in quieter

neighborhoods. The children in the high noise areas were less likely to persist on tasks when they were frustrated.

Noise also influences how we interact with other people. Consider the last time you were at a party where loud music was playing and many people were talking. How did you interact with other people? The noise probably affected your conversations, for one thing, because it's difficult to hear when loud music is playing. We practically have to yell to be heard, so we avoid talking about important or intimate subjects, and our conversations tend to be short. Also, because the noise is irritating, we may take out our discomfort on other people. It has been shown that noise leads people to be more aggressive (Geen & O'Neal, 1969). Along these same lines, we are less likely to offer help to others in a noisy environment. In one study an accomplice dropped an armload of books in front of an unsuspecting person (Matthews & Cannon, 1975). In half the cases a loud lawnmower was running, and in the other half it was not. People were much more likely to help in the quiet environment than in the noisy one.

So the loud noises we've created in our environment can have profound effects on us. Remember these effects when you have the opportunity to choose where you will live or work. Certainly we can't eliminate noise-producing phenomena, but we can use our knowledge of the effects of noise to guide the design and placement of our highways, airports, factories, and machines.

Weather

Herman Lehmann's Apache and Comanche bands ranged the plains and deserts of Texas, New Mexico, and Mexico, where it's not uncommon for daytime temperatures to remain well above 90 degrees for weeks on end. The Apaches and Comanches were considered to be the bravest warriors. They were among the last tribes to be conquered by the whites. Nu-

TABLE 15.2   Effect of Relative Humidity on Experienced Temperature

RELATIVE HUMIDITY (%)	THERMOMETER READING (°F)					
	41°	*50°*	*59°*	*68°*	*77°*	*86°*
	Effective Temperature					
0	41	50	59	68	77	86
20	41	50	60	70	81	91
40	40	51	61	72	83	96
60	40	51	62	73	86	102
80	39	52	63	75	90	111
100	39	52	64	79	96	120

merous factors certainly contribute to the aggressiveness of a people, and there is some evidence that temperature may be one of them.

Heat has been the one most widely studied weather variable related to human behavior. When most of us think of heat, we focus only on temperature; we can imagine the sweltering temperatures that Herman endured in the desert. But the temperature isn't the only factor that influences how we feel. As can be seen from Table 15.2, relative humidity—the percentage of moisture in the air—also affects how hot we feel. The desert where Herman roamed had low humidity, so while the above 90 degree temperatures were hot, they weren't as uncomfortable as they would have been in areas that have high humidity. Wind, on the other hand, tends to reduce the discomfort of heat.

Heat is a weather variable worthy of study because the environments in which many of us live are becoming hotter. Cities are generally 10 to 20 degrees (F) hotter than rural areas because of a high concentration of automobiles, asphalt, buildings, and air conditioning units. One investigator (Hurt, 1975) concluded that air conditioners in downtown Houston, Texas, put out enough waste heat (heat blown out of buildings) in 8 hours to boil ten pots of water the size of the Astrodome!

Much of the concern with heat has focused on its effect on aggression. The U.S. Riot Commission (1968) reported that most riots occur during the summer months; in fact, the commission found that in the riot-plagued year of 1967 all but one riot started when daytime temperatures were over 80 degrees F. We can explain the relationship between heat and aggression by viewing heat as a frustration. Hot temperatures cause people to feel uncomfortable and irritable, and they react to little frustrations by striking out at people and things around them. Additional research shows that, up to a point, aggression increases as temperature increases (Harries & Stadler, 1988; Anderson & Anderson, 1985). There is some disagreement about the point at which it becomes so hot that aggression decreases. We can imagine, however, that at very hot temperatures people don't want to interact with each other; their attention in these very hot environments turns to keeping cool.

As a final note on the relationship between heat and aggression, examine the results presented in Figure 15.3. An analysis of over 800 baseball games indicates that pitchers pitch more aggressively and hit more batters as the temperature rises (Reifman, Larrick, & Fein, 1991). So the next time you take a stroll through your neighborhood or step up to the plate to bat, you might want to cast an eye on the thermometer to determine your chance of performing these activities safely!

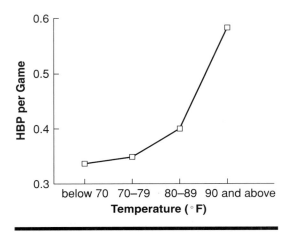

FIGURE 15.3 Mean Number of Players Hit by a Pitch (HBPs) in Games Played below 70° F (*n* = 176), between 70° F and 79° F (*n* = 315), between 80° F and 89° F (*n* = 224), and at 90° F and above (*n* = 111).
Source: R. Sommer (1967).

In addition to influencing our chances of being a target of aggression, high levels of heat also affect our performance on tasks. Some evidence indicates that our ability to perform mental tasks is reduced if we spend over two hours in temperatures over 90°F, and our ability to do moderate physical work is reduced if we spend over an hour in those same temperatures (Fisher, Bell, & Baum, 1984). On the other hand, performance of many tasks is also negatively affected in temperatures below 55°F. Interestingly, people seem to be able to adapt to extreme temperatures over time so that the effects are reduced. Thus, if you had lived in a warm southern climate for a long period of time and were suddenly transported to Greenland, you would have greater difficulty performing tasks in that very cold climate than would someone who had been living in Greenland since birth.

Weather is an important factor in surveys, which appear in popular magazines, that rate the quality of life in various cities in the United States. These surveys argue that weather affects our activities and social inter-

actions. For example, people often remain inside their homes or offices during periods of rain, while they will spend more time outside during warm sunny periods. In fact, some people suffer from a disorder known as **seasonal affective disorder** (**SAD**), a form of depression associated with low levels of light. This disorder is common in the fall and winter when there are fewer hours of daylight. People suffering SAD tend to become socially withdrawn, sleep a lot, have low energy levels, and gain weight during low-light periods (Wehr et al., 1989). SAD can be effectively treated by placing people in bright lights for several hours a day during the winter and fall (Heerwagen, 1990).

THE CONSTRUCTED ENVIRONMENT

During his life as a Native American, Herman Lehmann spent most of his days and nights in the open. When he traveled with the Apaches and Comanches, he slept under the stars. His home while in the villages usually consisted of a one-room teepee or hogan. The Apaches and Comanches didn't build permanent buildings, and the temporary structures they did build were made from materials available in the immediate environment. They weren't encumbered by bulky furniture; they ate, sat, and slept on the ground.

This experience is quite different from our own environment, with its wide variety of houses and towering buildings. Within these structures are rooms of almost every size, shape, and color, and the variety of furniture design and arrangement seems limitless. Just as other aspects of the environment influence our behavior, so too does the design of our buildings and rooms. In fact, it seems as if almost every detail of the constructed environment can guide our actions and interactions.

Environmental psychology has played one of its most important roles in helping us design our constructed environments to reduce stress and promote health and adjust-

Weather and Your Behavior

There is considerable evidence that human behavior is influenced by such weather-related variables as temperature, light, and even seasons. Some of us are more affected by weather than are others. To determine the extent that you are affected by weather, try the following exercise. Choose one or two days each week during the semester and chart the weather on those days. List the temperature range for the day, the number of hours of daylight, and other conditions (such as storm, rain, sunny, cloudy, snow, etc.). Also describe your behavior during each of the designated days. Indicate how you generally felt, how you spent your time (number of hours studying, in social activities, etc.), the number of hours you slept, and any indicators of your performance (grades on tests taken on the designated day, number of times others indicated you showed insight or made good points during a discussion, etc.). Then relate your behavior and feelings to the weather conditions.

Did you sleep more during low light days than long light days? Was your performance better during moderate days than on cold or very hot days? Did you feel depressed when there was little sunlight during the day? This exercise will give you some insight into how you are affected by the weather, and it may help you plan your activities to take advantage of your findings.

ment (Stokols, 1995). One of the clearest examples of this influence occurred in St. Louis in the late 1950s. In 1954, 43 eleven-story high-rise apartment buildings were erected on a 57-acre tract as a governmentally assisted public housing project. The buildings of the Pruitt-Igoe project were beautiful, and they received awards for their architectural design. Each apartment had the most modern facilities, and the nearly 12,000 residents were assured adequate space. All signs suggested that the project should be a huge success and could revolutionize the building of housing projects (see Figure 15.4). But the high hopes for the Pruitt-Igoe project were shattered before long. In a few years, the complex resembled a battlefield; windows in many of the apartments were broken or boarded; the elevators became piled with human waste; gang warfare broke out, and residents were afraid to leave their apartments after dark; rape and robbery were common. An exodus from the complex began, and officials couldn't find people willing to move into the apartments.

By 1970, only 16 of the 43 buildings were occupied, and in April 1972 city officials ordered demolition of the entire project.

How could this monument once praised as the greatest advancement in subsidized housing end in such utter failure? The general answer is that even though the project looked beautiful and was well designed from an architectural standpoint, it didn't fit the needs of the people who lived there. Residents complained that the long hallways in the building didn't foster interaction between neighbors, and consequently they often felt lonely. Parents pointed out that living in high-rise buildings made it impossible to supervise their children in the playgrounds. Imagine a parent trying to watch out of a window on the eleventh floor as his or her child plays below. Newman (1972) also argued that there was too much **indefensible territory** in the project. Indefensible space includes areas that can't easily be marked or observed; consequently people fear entering them. Residents of the Pruitt-Igoe project were afraid to enter the

FIGURE 15.4 The Pruitt-Igoe complex was hailed as an architectural wonder and a great advance in low-income housing when it was built.

However, a few years after it was built, Pruitt-Igoe resembled a battlefield. It did not fit the needs of the people who lived there, and it was eventually demolished.

elevators because they often couldn't see who was in them, and once the doors closed they were at the mercy of other passengers. The Pruitt-Igoe story shows that we must design our environment to meet the needs of the people who will inhabit them.

On a smaller scale, research has shown that physical aspects of a single room can affect our emotions and behaviors. Desor (1972) found that subjects perceived a rectangular room to be more spacious than a square room, although the actual number of square feet in the two rooms was the same. A number of in-

vestigators compared "open offices," where workers are separated only by low partitions, to the small, closed office design, where each worker has his or her own office. The results of this research suggested that whereas workers in the open offices interacted with more people, workers in the smaller offices formed closer friendships with a small number of people. Workers in the open offices felt less crowded and perceived the area to be more spacious than did workers in the small offices (Wells, 1972; Sommer, 1974). But the open-office workers felt they had less privacy and

TABLE 15.3 Relation among Moods and Colors

Blue	secure, comfortable, tender, soothing, calm, serene
Red	exciting, protective, defending, defiant
Orange	distressed, upset
Black	despondent, powerful
Purple	dignified
Yellow	cheerful

Source: Wexner (1954).

noisier conditions than workers in the smaller, closed offices. Even the color of a room may affect our behavior because people associate various moods with various colors, as Table 15.3 demonstrates. In one study, people became more physiologically aroused (higher galvanic skin response) when watching red slides than when watching green slides (Wildon, 1966).

Moving closer to home, we can point out that the type of dormitory in which students live affects their behavior in a number of ways. Generally, students live in one of two types of dormitories. In the corridor dormitory bedrooms are arranged along a hallway (see Figure 15.5). Residents share a bathroom and a common lounge. A second type, the suite dormitory, is arranged more like a typical apartment, with three or four bedrooms arranged around a lounge or living area and students in the suite sharing bathroom (see Figure 15.5). Although the amount of space students have is the same in both types of dormitories, the effects on the residents are very different. Suite residents both feel and exercise more control over their environment than do corridor residents (Baum & Valins, 1977). They can decide who can enter their lounge and bedrooms better than corridor residents can. Students in the corridor dorms feel more crowded than suite residents do, have more

unwanted social encounters, and feel less control over their living situations. Their response is to withdraw into their rooms and not try to improve common areas such as bathrooms and lounges.

In the past, too many mistakes have been made by designing buildings and rooms to look pleasing to the eye with little attention given to making the design fit people's needs and behavior. The necessity of fitting design to behavior should be kept in mind when you choose a home or an apartment. A wise choice will facilitate your adjustment to your new environment and should make your life more enjoyable and carefree. A poor choice will add complication and annoyance.

The Arrangement of Furniture

It may be difficult, if not impossible, for many of us to change the size, shape, or color of the room in which we live. However, in most cases, we can influence the arrangement of furniture which can have a noticeable effect on behavior.

Sommer and Ross (1958) describe how the supervisors in a geriatric ward of a Canadian hospital carpeted and painted the dayroom and installed new furniture in an effort to facilitate greater interaction among the patients. These efforts were unsuccessful, however, as the patients sat in the dayroom "like strangers in a train station waiting for a train that never came" (Sommer & Ross, 1958). The new furniture had been lined up in rows so that the patients could only sit side by side or back to back. Sommer and Ross felt that the arrangement of furniture inhibited interaction, and they placed groups of chairs in a circular fashion around tables instead. After a few weeks, interaction among patients had doubled, and use of the dayroom had greatly increased.

Furniture can be arranged so that interaction is either fostered or inhibited. Chairs that are placed close together in a circular or other

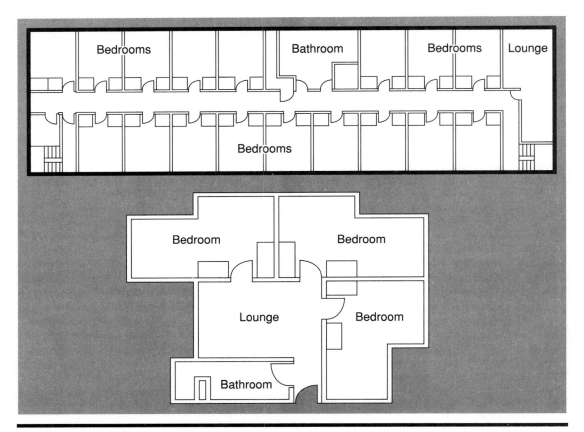

FIGURE 15.5 Floor Plan of a Corridor-Style Dormitory (top) and a Suite-Style Dormitory (bottom)
Source: Adapted from Baum, A. & Vallns, S. (1977). *Architecture and social behavior: Psychological studies in social density.* Hillsdale, N.J.: Erlbaum.

"facing" manner to invite social interaction. People are much less likely to interact when they occupy chairs that are spread out or placed side by side. You can see the effect of this arrangement by watching strangers in a waiting room or airport lounge. The side-by-side arrangement eliminates most eye contact, and people spend much of their time reading or staring straight ahead. Just as the design of a room or building should fit the needs of the inhabitants, so too should the arrangement of furniture. If the room is one in which social interaction is likely to take place or is desired, the furniture should be placed so

that individuals can conduct conversations and hold eye contact. On the other hand, if the desire is to reduce social interactions (such as in a library), chairs should be arranged in a side-by-side or back-to-back fashion.

The Urban Environment

A discussion of the relationship between environment and human behavior wouldn't be complete without an examination of the most visible human contribution to the environment: the city. Herman Lehmann probably never saw a city. While living with the Apaches and Comanches, he rarely saw concentrations of more than a thousand people. When these groups gathered, they rarely left permanent effects on the earth's surface. Even after returning to the whites, Herman avoided large crowds. Thus he never experienced the phenomenon of life in a large city.

Many discussions of urban life often deteriorate into an argument about whether it is "good" or "bad." This type of argument is futile; urban centers have both positive and negative influences on human behavior. Instead of arguing the merits of the city, we need to understand its effects on human behavior and how these effects are perpetuated.

One word that can be used to describe the urban environment is *diversity*. Large cities host almost every type of architecture, person, entertainment, work vehicle, neon sign, and noise known to humans. This variety offers nearly unlimited opportunities for cultural stimulation, learning, shopping and eating. The immense size of cities gives the individual a degree of anonymity, and in this lies freedom. An unwritten code in many cities is "I won't bother you if you don't bother me." Thus an individual can practice his or her trade, openly express his or her opinion, and wear whatever he or she chooses, so long as the practice doesn't directly interfere with others. A visit to a large city will quickly show that this freedom is extensively exercised by city dwellers!

Although this freedom has many positive effects, unfortunate consequences result when the freedom changes into disregard and lack of concern for others. In most cities, some people are forced to live in woefully inadequate conditions. Harris and Lindsay (1972) reported that 24 percent of urban welfare families in the United States had no running water, and 22.4 percent had no private use of a bathroom with a shower. Incidence of disease such as tuberculosis, heart disease, and syphilis is higher in inner-city areas than in suburbs.

Visitors to large cities are often prone to describe city dwellers as cold and unfriendly. Many of us have read newspaper accounts of someone who was in need of help but whose cries were ignored by passing city dwellers. Can we blame the urban environment for these behaviors? Stanley Milgram (1970) suggests that, yes, the urban environment may indeed be responsible for these responses. He points out that the city is a complex environment; the urbanite is confronted with a huge array of sounds, people, and sights. According to Milgram, humans can cope with only a limited amount of stimulation. When the stimulation becomes too great, the individual must protect himself or herself by filtering some of it out. This filtering often involves not paying attention to many of the people or activities in the environment.

Another way to deal with this great variety is to place objects into categories and respond to the category rather than to the individual objects. For example, instead of dealing with each individual you meet, you may place them into two categories: friends and strangers. You then respond to friends in one way and to strangers in another way. Each time you meet a person, you need only determine whether he or she is a friend or stranger. Once you make this decision, your behavior is predetermined; you ignore strangers and greet friends warmly. This categorization may explain why people in cities are less likely to help others and are perceived as being "cold." Once a person is placed in the "stranger" category, he or she is ignored, and the request for help goes unnoticed. This seems a crass way to behave, but we must remember that a city dweller encounters as many as 220,000 people each day. He or she would never make it from the subway to the office if each person were greeted and a decision about each person's needs and health were made in each encounter!

Adjustment to the complex city environment can also be aided by developing very ritualized and organized patterns of behavior. As a city dweller, you might rise every morning at the same time, eat the same food for breakfast, catch the same subway or bus to work, eat lunch at the same time and place, and so on. Once your routine is established, you do not need to spend time making decisions. The problem with this approach is that anything that forces a change in your routine becomes very frustrating and confusing. For instance, a blackout or strike creates havoc; decisions that are rarely made must be dealt with and the whole life pattern must be reorganized.

At the risk of sounding too anti-city, we must mention some additional problems posed by city life. First, cities are noisier than rural areas. An EPA study showed that even the quietest times in an inner-city apartment are noisier than the noisiest times in small towns. The large concentration of motor vehicles, machines, and people add to the pollution of cities. One investigator has reported that just living in New York city is equivalent to smoking 38 cigarettes a day (Rotton, 1978). And cities tend to be more stressful than other environments. Stress results because movement is often impaired by traffic and other people, there is a great deal of contact with strangers, it is often difficult to find your way around, and the environment is often unpredictable and uncontrollable.

MAKING OUR WAY THROUGH OUR ENVIRONMENT: COGNITIVE MAPS

Our environment is a complex maze of buildings, roads, and natural and built structures. There are literally thousands of bits of information in our surroundings. Think about your own neighborhood. There are some obvious points that stand out. These might include houses, roads, stores, hills, rivers, and maybe even a rusting junk car on the corner. Now take a look at your environment. You

will likely find many additional fixed objects such as trees, fences, sidewalks, traffic lights, and signs. In addition, many "mobile" objects are in place now that may be gone tomorrow. These include parked cars and trucks, kids playing in the yard, the pit bulldog in front of the red house, and the pile of sand and lumber on the sidewalk. If you expand your vision beyond your neighborhood, the amount of information multiplies many times. Each of us is faced with the task of organizing this information so we can describe our environment and navigate through it. How we do this is an interesting area of study.

Investigators have found that each of us has a mental image of our environment, a **cognitive map** (Matlin, 1989). This map is an image of the salient features of our environment. This image is organized along certain principles. First, our map is more detailed in areas that are familiar to us. For example, you may be able to draw a very detailed picture of your neighborhood, including every house, tree, and fence on your block. However, your map of an area that you visit infrequently will be less detailed. It might have just a few major buildings and roads.

Second, as Figure 15.6 playfully suggests, we exaggerate the size of familiar locations. We see our own neighborhood or city (or state, or nation) as being larger than it is in comparison with unfamiliar areas. Third, certain features help organize our maps (Lynch, 1960). We use **paths** (roads, rail lines), **edges** (rivers, shorelines, large fences), **districts** (Chinatown, university district) , **nodes** (major intersections) , and **landmarks** (tall buildings, mountains).

These maps are important in many respects. First, we use them to find our way through our environment. Because you have a relatively clear cognitive map of your city, you can find most places even without a detailed road map. In fact, you may have no idea of the names of many of the streets you use, but you

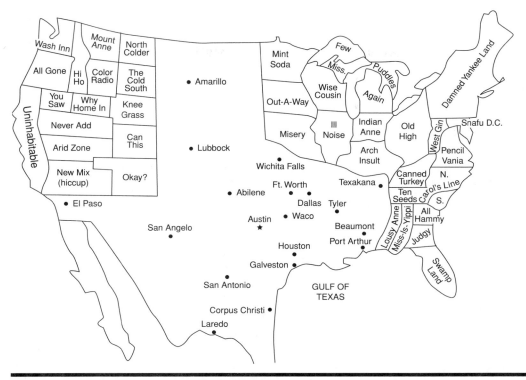

FIGURE 15.6 A Texan's View of the United States
On our cognitive maps we tend to exaggerate the size of areas that are highly familiar to us.

know that to get to the grocery store you turn right at the corner with the Burger King and then make a left at the corner with the large billboard. Second, these maps give us a sense of security and control in our environment. We know where we are and feel we can make our way to our destination (McAndrew, 1993).

The importance of cognitive maps holds an important lesson for people planning an environment. It is much easier to develop a good cognitive map of cities (or neighborhoods) that have clear markers such as major paths, edges, and landmarks than areas that do not have these markers. For example, cities that have clearly visible landmarks such as the Empire State Building in New York City help people orient themselves, just as do ma-

jor loops such as those found in Houston. Likewise, a square grid of streets is easier to visualize than is a layout that includes streets that meander in twists and turns. A recognized downtown area or a distinct shopping mall serves as a reference point better than randomly placed strip shopping areas.

Community and city planners are taking heed of these lessons from environmental psychology (Stokols, 1995). Layouts of areas are being designed with central reference points and landmarks, clearly girded streets, and identifiable boundaries. Landscaping is designed to be both pleasing to the eye and pleasing to the mind. The aim of these efforts is to design areas to make people feel secure and help them navigate through their territory.

GUARDIANS OF THE ENVIRONMENT: BEING A GOOD PARTNER

Up to this point, we have focused on how our environment influences our behavior. We must also realize that we are entrusted with protecting our environment. You need only take a look at your community to see how good (or poor) a job we have done with this responsibility. In many respects we have been poor partners. We have polluted our rivers and air. We have removed much of the natural beauty of our surroundings by destroying forests, leveling natural hills, and filling in drainage areas. This behavior is in stark contrast to that of the Apache Indians of Herman's day. A young chief of the Cayuses commented in 1855, "The Great Spirit, in placing men on earth, desired them to take good care of the ground, to do each other no harm."

As we have rushed to add humanmade structures to our environment, we are cautioned by research that shows that humans find beauty in nature. We find forest and natural water areas as attractive. There is also evidence that being in wilderness areas or even viewing pictures of wilderness reduces our stress levels and lowers heart rate and blood pressure.

There are several areas where our behavior can help our environment. One such area is litter. One ton of solid waste is generated each year for every man, woman, and child in the United States. Litter is not only unsightly, it can also destroy creeks and ponds, kill wildlife, and invite rodents and other unwanted pests. Most of us think very little about throwing a candy wrapper out of the car window, believing that just this little bit of litter cannot hurt. This thinking is exactly that found in Hardin's Tragedy of the Commons, described in Chapter 13. This kind of problem, as we also saw in Chapter 13, is known as a **social dilemma**. The social dilemma pits individual benefits against group benefits.

Individuals are motivated by both greed (wanted to get as much as possible) and fear (that others will violate the rules and get more). In the case of litter, you might be motivated by the desire to keep your automobile clean and the fear that even if you don't litter, others will litter. Why should you be the only chump who follows the path designed to benefit others, when they do not follow this path?

Approaches to reducing littering behavior have followed many courses. Often people are threatened with stiff fines for littering. In addition, education programs teach people not to litter and the consequences of littering. Still other approaches involve giving people clear instructions about not littering and making waste baskets available. Finally, other attempts include making people feel that the territory on which they might dispose of litter is their own: "These are YOUR roads. Keep them clean." (Worchel & Lollis, 1982). Similar approaches have been used to stop pollution, whether it be pollution by factories or individual automobiles.

Another issue related to being a good partner with the environment is the use of natural resources. Most of us think nothing about jumping into our automobile to go down the block for a few groceries. Once at the grocery store, we happily package our groceries in plastic or paper sacks which we throw in the trash once arriving home. Our evening at home involves cooking dinner while the television blares unwatched in the adjoining room. We drink a couple of soft drinks and throw away the aluminum containers. Then we go to bed without a single pang of guilt at having unnecessarily wasted natural resources.

The last three decades have seen an increasing concern with protecting our environment through conservation. Conservation involves avoiding the needless use of natural resources, especially energy, and recycling items that can be reused. One of the barriers to conservation often is that we simply don't know how our behavior affects the environment or how effective our efforts to conserve actually are. In other words, we get little or no immediate feedback on the effects of our behavior. Most of us have no idea how much we might save by taking shorter showers or washing our clothes in cold rather than hot water. We might be able to figure this out by comparing our monthly electric bills, but this results in a long delay between the behavior and the feedback. Some investigators have found that placing electric meters near appliances helps people conserve energy (Darley, 1978). In this way people can see immediately how much electricity they are using and how much they are saving.

A second barrier to conservation is often habit. We have simply learned to be comfortable with one pattern of behavior. For example, Europeans often stare in disbelief at the size of American cars. Although we may not need an automobile of this size or power, Americans have grown comfortable with this large size. Conservation, in this case, involves changing habits. Unfortunately, we don't readily change our energy-consuming habits; it often takes a crisis (like the oil embargo in the 1970s) or some other forceful factor (rapidly increasing cost) to bring about change.

In addition to using less, reusing objects is a critical component of conservation efforts. Recycling paper or metals like aluminum re-

duces the amount of energy used (it takes less energy to make paper from recycled paper than from wood), reduces pollution, creates less solid waste and water pollution, and helps preserve our natural environment. Despite these advantages, Americans are not doing a good job in their recycling efforts. Although some European countries recycle over 50 percent of their wastepaper, the United States recycles only 29 percent of its wastepaper. And if we were to place the aluminum cans discarded in the United States end to end, the line would circle the earth 164 times (Miller, 1990). Many of the programs designed to promote recycling rely on rewards. One study found that students were more likely to recycle if they were given lottery tickets (with a high potential payoff) than if they were offered small cash rewards. Some states have passed "container laws" that require cash deposits on every aluminum can or bottle sold in the state. In these states, nearly 90 percent of the cans and bottles are recycled as long as the refund is at least 5 cents a container (McAndrew, 1993).

Although we have only scratched the surface in this discussion, each of us can play an important role in protecting our environment. Much of the destruction of our environment is caused by humans. Because our environment affects the quality of our life and health, we must guard it against destruction.

REVIEW QUESTIONS

11. T or F: Crowding and density are simply two terms for the same condition.

12. The most bothersome noises are _____ and _____.

13. _____ are the mental images that people form of their environments that help them find their way through unfamiliar settings.

14. T or F: Giving people immediate feedback about the impact of their behavior on the environment can increase efforts of conservation.

SUMMARY

1. Adjustment involves not only dealing with our social situation; we must also adjust to our physical environment. Our reaction to our environment is affected by our perceptions of it, not just its absolute physical characteristics. In order to determine the "best" environment, we must strive for the best person–environment fit.

2. Feeling isolated from others and having to interact with others more than we want can be uncomfortable. Privacy involves the individual's freedom to choose what, when and to whom he will communicate. Our physical environment often affects the degree of privacy we can obtain, and we can construct our environment to help us obtain our desired level of privacy.

3. Territoriality involves claiming exclusive use of areas or objects. Investigators observe that humans have three types of territory that vary according to the degree of control and sense of ownership: primary, secondary, and public. Territorial behavior has a number of functions in our adjustment. It affords us protections, it enhances social order and predictability, it helps us achieve a desired level of privacy, it controls aggression, and controlling territory helps us establish and advertise our identity.

4. Personal space is a factor of the "mobile" territory that always surrounds us. We strive to protect this space, although its size is affected by many factors including the type of interaction we are having, our age, our sex, and our culture. Violations of our personal space cause us to feel aroused and uncomfortable, and we will respond by trying to regain proper spacing.

5. Density is a physical measure of the amount of space available to a person in a particular environment. Crowding, on the other hand, is a psychological state that is based on people's feelings about their spatial condition. Crowding results when we lose control over opportunities to regulate our spacing, when our actual privacy is less than our desired privacy, and when our present amount of space is less than our expectations and previous amount of space.

6. Noise is sound that is unpleasant and bothersome. Noise that is unpredictable and uncontrollable is most likely to interfere with task performance. There is also evidence that noise has aftereffects; our performance in a quiet area will be worse if we were previously in a noisy environment.

7. Research on weather has largely concentrated on temperature. There are indications that high temperature (between 90–100°F) may increase aggression, and extreme temperatures (both hot and cold) can inhibit task performance. Other research has shown that weather variables such as number of cloudy days can affect our moods.

8. The design of our homes, dormitories, or apartments affects our behavior and our social interactions. For example, open offices encourage more social interaction, but they can reduce individual privacy. In large complex cities, people often attempt to reduce the complexity by categorizing others into groups rather than viewing them as individuals, reducing the amount of social interaction, and ignoring many aspects of their environment.

9. In order to navigate through our environment, we form cognitive maps. These maps emphasize unique characteristics of the environment such as rivers, tall buildings, and major roads. Environments with clear markers help us adjust to the setting and reduce the chances that we will feel disoriented when not in familiar surroundings.

10. We are the guardians of our environment, and therefore it is important that we protect our environment. Such behaviors as avoiding litter, developing careful plans for develop-

ment, controlling pollution, and conserving resources are important to the future of our environment. However, these behaviors present us with social dilemmas because they require placing group needs over individual needs.

CRITICAL THINKING QUESTIONS

1. An important goal of architects and city planners is not only to develop structures and neighborhoods that are pleasing to the eye, but ones that help people adjust and feel comfortable. Unfortunately, these designers are often unaware of or ignore research in such areas as human territorial behavior and cognitive mapping. Taking this research into account, consider the role of a city planner or architect. How would you design a home, a dormitory, and a neighborhood to promote the residents' adjustment? Be specific in your suggestions.

2. Because the impact of the environment on our behavior is often overlooked, most of us pay little attention to it. Think for a moment about some of the less evident characteristics of your environment, such as the weather and the type of land features (mountains, desert, rivers, lakes). How would your daily life change if you lived in a location that had very different weather and land characteristics?

3. The quality of our lives is closely associated by the quality of our physical environment. Yet many people are unwilling to take steps to protect their environment. How would you develop a program that would encourage people to take better care of their environment?

MATCHING EXERCISE

Match each term with its defintion.

a. person–environment fit
b. privacy
c. territoriality
d. primary territory

e. personal space
f. density
g. crowding
h. noise

i. seasonal affective disorder
j. indefensible space
k. cognitive map

1. amount of space available to an individual in a particular setting
2. claiming exclusive use of areas or objects
3. space surrounding individuals that they believe they should control
4. psychological feeling that results when amount of space an individual has is less than the amount of space desired
5. form of depression associated with low light
6. areas that cannot be easily marked or observed
7. mental image of the environment
8. sound that is experienced as unpleasant and bothersome and interferes with activities
9. matching the environment to the person who will use it and the activities involved
10. areas that are exclusively owned and controlled by individuals or groups
11. ability to regulate interactions, controlling what will be communicated and to whom

Answers to Matching Exercise

a. 9   b. 11   c. 2   d. 10   e. 3   f. 1   g. 4   h. 8   i. 5   j. 6   k. 7

ANSWERS TO REVIEW QUESTIONS

1. perceptions
2. person–environment fit
3. privacy, isolation
4. territoriality
5. primary
6. d
7. personal space
8. **a.** intimate
   b. public

9. culture, age, sex
10. true
11. false
12. uncontrollable, unpredictable
13. cognitive map
14. true

Ability test a test designed to examine an individual's reasoning, memory, mechanical, math, or psychomotor skills

Acceptance the final stage in the dying process, in which people feel at peace and able to accept the fact that they are dying

Actor–observer bias the tendency for people to attribute their own behavior to external, situational factors and other people's behavior to internal, personal characteristics

Actual self one's self image, based on how one sees oneself

Adjustment a complex personal process that involves learning about oneself, setting goals, and coping with social and situation demands

Affect feeling or emotion

Affiliation being close or interacting with other people

Agoraphobia an anxiety disorder characterized by fear and avoidance of open, crowded, or other public spaces

AIDS Acquired Immune Deficiency Syndrome, resulting from a virus that attacks the body's immune system and makes the individual very susceptible to a wide variety of diseases

Alcoholics Anonymous a self-help program for alcoholics with many groups across the country; follows the "12-step" program

Alzheimer's disease a disease associated with aging, which involves the progressive deterioration of the brain

Amnesia complete or partial loss of memory

Amphetamines psychoactive stimulant drugs, such as Benzedrine, Methedrine, and Dexedrine, and a newer street form, methamphetemine hydrochloride ("crystal meth")

Anal stage Freud's second stage of development, discussed by Erikson, beginning around the age of 18 months with toilet training

Anger and resentment the second stage in the dying process, in which people feel unfairly stricken and say, "Why me?"

Anorexia nervosa an eating disorder in which the person, usually a woman, loses a great deal of weight, has an exaggerated fear of gaining weight, distortions about her body size or shape, and amenorrhea

Anxiety generalized feelings of fear and apprehension

Anxiety disorders psychological disorders including anxiety states, phobias, and obsessive-compulsive disorders; characterized by intense fear the individual cannot manage

Anxiety state a psychological disorder characterized by constant feelings of extreme anxiety and worry interspersed with short periods of intense panic

Assertiveness training a behavior modification technique in which a person is trained to act appropriately assertive in interpersonal situations

Asthma a psychological disorder in which breathing becomes difficult

Attachment the need to be with another person and to be approved of by that person

Attribution the process of labeling physiological arousal as a particular emotional state

Autogenic training reducing muscle tension by focusing on one's own suggestions that one's muscles and limbs are getting warm and heavy and that one's breathing is becoming regular

Autonomic nervous system (ANS) the body system comprised of the brain and neurons that connect the brain to the body; includes two divisions: sympathetic nervous system and parasympathetic nervous system

Barbiturates psychoactive drugs that depress the central nervous system and cause addiction; not commonly used in clinical practice as they have been replaced by newer antianxiety medications

Bargaining the third stage in the dying process, in which people strive to stay alive to reach a particular event

Beavers Systems Model a model that describes a continuum of family functioning, from optimal through severely dysfunctional

Behavior therapy a form of therapy based on the principles of reinforcement, which focuses on changing behavior rather than analyzing feelings

Behaviorists psychologists who believe that behavior is determined by rewards and punishments in the external environment

Being motive the motivation to grow and develop

Bipolar disorder also known as "manic-depression," an affective disorder characterized by cycling mood states

Birth control any method used to prevent the conception of children

Body language nonverbal communication of emotions by posture, positioning, and facial expressions

Borderline personality disorder a personality disorder characterized by intense emotions and extreme behaviors, with an inner sense of emptiness

Bulimia an eating disorder characterized by very heavy binges of eating followed by purging through self-induced vomiting or laxatives, and a perceived lack of control over eating

Burnout the state that results when a person loses sympathy for others with whom he or she works and becomes exhausted and fatigued

Career the progress or general course of work activity through a person's life or through some phase of it

Caring the feeling that another person's satisfactions and well-being are as important as one's own

Catatonic schizophrenia a type of schizophrenia marked by disturbances in motor behavior

Catharsis the process whereby an act of aggression reduces the desire for further aggression

Circumcision an operation, often performed shortly after birth, that removes the foreskin from the penis

Classical conditioning a form of conditioning in which a formerly neutral stimulus is paired with a stimulus that elicits a response, so that the neutral stimulus acquires the capacity to elicit the response

Client centered therapy Carl Rogers' nondirective approach to psychotherapy, which emphasized unconditional positive regard, empathy, and congruence in the therapy relationship

Cocaine a psychoactive stimulant drug that produces intense euphoria, heightened sensations, and a number of negative effects upon overdose or withdrawal

Coercive power the capacity to deliver threats and punishments to force compliance from another individual

Cognitive conservatism the ego's tendency to maintain its beliefs and to perceive the beliefs it currently holds as the ones that it has held for a long time

Cognitive dissonance theory (1) a relationship among cognitions such that one cognition follows from the opposite of another; or (2) a feeling of discomfort resulting from inconsistent thoughts

Cognitive maps mental images of a city or other area

Cognitive therapy a type of psychotherapy that focuses on analyzing and changing faulty thinking patterns

Collective culture culture that emphasizes interdependence and the paramount importance of one's group

Commitment in Thibaut and Kelley's theory of the stages of relationships, the stage in which people decide to be special or exclusive partners in a relationship

Companionate love love based on intimacy and commitment, but lacking passion

Comparison level the standard by which the outcome level of interactions in a relationship is evaluated based on all the outcomes a person knows about through his or her own or another's experiences

Comparison level for alternatives the lowest level of outcomes a person will accept in a relationship; the level of outcomes in the next available relationship

Complementarity having opposite but congruent needs

Compulsion a recurring, ritualistic behavior pattern experienced as irresistible

Conditions of worth in Carl Rogers' theory of personality, the standards that a child must live up to in order to get approval from parents and to feel worthy

Conflict theory the theory that prior to a decision the choices spread in value so that a person can make a decision between them

Conformity a change in behavior or belief toward a group as a result of real or imagined group pressure

Congruence in psychotherapy, the matching of a therapist's inner feelings with what he or she expresses overtly

Conscience   in Freudian theory, that part of the superego containing prohibitions and restrictions

Consummate love   love based on intimacy, commitment, and passion

Contraception   methods of birth control used to prevent conception

Conventional level of morality   morality based on conformity to rules and values learned from authority

Coping mechanism   conscious and deliberate efforts to manage stressful situations

Correspondence bias   the tendency to disregard situational or external factors that are plausible causes of a person's behavior

Corridor dormitory   a dormitory in which bedrooms are arranged along a long hallway

Crowding   a psychological state of stress that results when people are too close

Culture-bound disorders   mental disorders found in some cultures or societies but not in others

Culture   a set of attitudes, values, and beliefs shared by people and communicated from one generation to the next; often centers on ways of adapting to the environment

Cultural orientation   at mid-life, an interest in spiritual and cultural matters as opposed to the gratification of instincts and gaining more experience

Cyclothymia   fluctuating and troublesome mood states that are not as extreme as those in bipolar disorder

Deficiency motive   a motive instigated by some psychological deficit experienced as an inner drive to obtain what is missing

Deindividuation   a condition whereby the individual becomes "submerged into the group" and feels relatively anonymous

Delirium tremens   physical sensations that accompany withdrawal from alcohol, including profuse sweating, nausea, disorganized thinking, and sometimes hallucinations

Delusion   a false belief held by a person without any objective evidence

Denial   an ego-defense mechanism in which an individual refuses to acknowledge an external source of threat

Density   a physical measure of the space available to an individual in a certain area

Depressive disorders   disorders characterized by low mood, lack of energy, loss of interest in normal activities, and sleep disturbances

Discrimination   negative, often aggressive behavior, aimed at a target of prejudice

Diffuse anxiety   the experience of dread without being able to identify the reason for the feeling

Disorganized schizophrenia   a type of schizophrenia marked by regressive, fragmented thinking and behavior

Disparagement   a mode of enhancing one's self-esteem by degrading and criticizing others

Displaced aggression   an angered individual's attack on a target that was not responsible for the frustration

Displacement   an ego-defense mechanism in which anger felt toward a powerful person is expressed in the form of aggression against a person who cannot retaliate

Dissociative disorders   psychological disorders in which there is loss of memory and recognition of one's past behavior and experience, or splitting of awareness

Dissonance theory   the theory that people are made uncomfortable by inconsistent cognitions and have a drive to reduce the discomfort by changing a cognition

Door-in-the-face effect   a persuasion technique in which a target is more likely to comply with a request after refusing to comply with an excessively large request

Double-bind   a situation characterized by paradoxical communication, dependence on the communicator, and inability to metacommunicate

Dream   in Levinson's theory, the goal toward which one sets one's life in early adulthood

Dream analysis   a psychoanalytic technique for uncovering and working with unconscious wishes, fears, and conflicts

DSM-IV   Diagnostic and Statistical Manual, 4th edition; the classification system for mental disorders currently used in the United States

Dysthymia   a mild form of depression

Ego   the structure of the psyche that notices, perceives, remembers, and helps the individual cope with reality

Ego-ideal   in Freudian theory, that part of the superego containing aspirations and values

Ego-identity   a positive sense of self and of the role one can play in society

Electroconvulsive therapy   a treatment for depression in which electric current is passed through the head, inducing a seizure of electrical activity in the brain

Emotion a complex state of feeling involving conscious experience, internal and overt physical responses, and motivation to action

Emotion-focused coping an approach to dealing with stress that involves not becoming preoccupied with the stress and not allowing one's emotions to be dominated by stress-arousing situations

Empathic understanding in psychotherapy, the therapist's capacity to view the world from the client's point of view and to understand his or her feelings

Encounter group therapeutic groups emphasizing personal growth through authentic communication and through the expression of personal feelings about oneself and others

Endocrine system the body system that includes glands that secrete hormones directly into the bloodstream

Equity a state that results when one person's ratio of inputs and outcomes is the same as that of another person

Equity theory a theory that suggests that individuals compare the relationship between their inputs and outcomes with those of other parties to determine the fairness (and satisfaction) of a relationship

Erectile dysfunction often called impotence, a dysfunction involving a male's failure to have or maintain an erection long enough to have sexual intercourse

Erotica sexually arousing material that rarely involves violence and is not degrading to women, men, or children

Evolutionary psychology a set of ideas relating human behavior to natural selection and evolutionary adaptation

Experimental therapy a type of psychotherapy, such as client-centered therapy and process-experiential therapy, that focuses on emotional experiencing

Expert power the power an individual derives by being seen as possessing special insight or knowledge about a particular area

Extinction the process by which a conditioned response gradually disappears when the unconditioned stimulus or reinforcer is removed

Extrinsic motivation the desire to perform work based on external factors such as pay or threats

Family life cycle the stages of growth and change through which a family progresses

Family therapy therapy involving a couple, a parent and child, or a whole family, in which the established interactional system is analyzed

Feedback in encounter groups, other people's reactions, expressed in terms of their own feelings, to one's behavior or statements

Fetal alcohol syndrome a birth defect involving learning, behavioral, and other physiologically-based symptoms due to prenatal exposure to alcohol; *fetal alcohol effect* is a milder condition also related to prenatal exposure to alcohol

Flooding a behavior therapy technique in which a person is put into a feared situation in order to extinguish the fear response

Foot-in-the-door effect a persuasion technique in which a target is more likely to comply with a large request after agreeing to a small request

Free association a psychoanalytic technique in which the patient verbalizes whatever thoughts or feelings come in mind, without censoring them

Gender identity the inner feeling of being male or female

Gender role the habits, traits, and behaviors that are stereotypically identified as "masculine" or "feminine"

Gender schemas cognitive structures about gender that organize our thinking and perceptions

General adaptation syndrome (GAS) in Selye's theory, the body's reaction to threat, consisting of (1) an alarm stage marked by a mobilization of the body's resources, (2) a resistance stage marked by the organism's attempts to protect itself, and (3) an exhaustion stage in which the organism can no longer resist the threat

Generalized anxiety disorder an anxiety disorder characterized by chronic and diffuse anxiety, worry, and physiological arousal

Generalization a process by which a person comes to fear other stimuli that are associated with an original fearful event

Generativity a concern for establishing and guiding the next generation

Genital herpes a sexually transmitted disease caused by a virus that during its active phase results in small blisters on the genitals

Gestalt therapy a form of humanistic group or individual psychotherapy emphasizing personal integration and taking responsibility for one's own life

Goal an object or condition that a person desires to obtain

Gonorrhea a sexually transmitted disease caused by a bacterium, which results in pain during urination and a discharge of pus or blood

Group polarization a process whereby group discussion causes an individual to make a more extreme decision than he or she would make alone

Groupthink a group situation that results in groups making poor decisions; conditions such as a strong central leader, high group cohesiveness, and a sense of invulnerability make groupthink more likely

Guidance counselor a person trained to help students choose occupations to fit their interests and abilities

Hallucination a perception or mental image occurring without any external stimulus to cause it

Hardy personality a behavioral approach that views stress as a challenge rather than a threat, and consequently reduces the likelihood of coronary heart disease

Health psychology a branch of psychology that relates behavior to physical health

Heroin a psychoactive opiate drug that produces a range of effects including pain relief, calming or narcotic effects, physiological and psychological addiction, and severe withdrawal symptoms

Heterosexuality sexual relations between two people of the opposite sex

Hierarchy a ranked list of anxiety-provoking situations ranging from terrifying to minimally threatening

Homophobia negative attitudes toward homosexual individuals and behavior

Homosexuality sexual relations between two people of the same sex

Humanists psychologists who believe that humans are basically good and, left on their own, will strive to be positive forces within society

Hypnosis an induced psychological state of deep relaxation and suggestibility

Hypochondriasis constant worrying about physical symptoms; caused by anxiety

Hysteria a disorder marked by physical symptoms, such as paralysis, mutism, or tics, that have no organic or physical basis

Id the structure of the psyche that instinctively and unconsciously seeks pleasure and satisfaction of bodily needs

Ideal self the picture of the self that one would like to be

Idealized performance acting as if one supports and conforms to ideal standards of good conduct more than one actually does

Identification (1) a process by which a person adopts a pattern of behavior in an attempt to be like someone he or she admires; (2) an ego-defense mechanism in which anxiety is reduced by identifying with a high status individual or institution

Identity confusion lack of a clear sense of self and of what one is capable of accomplishing in society

Immune system a physiological system that destroys disease-causing organisms

Implosion a behavior therapy technique in which the client is asked to imagine as vividly as possible the most frightening situation possible; gradually, the anxiety response to the situation extinguishes

Individualistic culture a culture that emphasizes the importance of personal independence and personal responsibility

Intervention a strategy used by alcohol counselors, family, and friends to help an alcoholic person break through denial and begin treatment

Incubation a period of time in which a phobic reaction intensifies as a person avoids the original stimulus

Indefensible space an area that cannot be easily marked, observed, or controlled

Interview the most popular method used by employers to select employees; involves face-to-face interaction; may be formal, centering on a set of predetermined questions, or informal, with questions differing from one applicant to another

Induced abortion termination of pregnancy by removing the immature fetus from the uterus

Informational influence the power of the group to influence a member's behavior through the member's desire to obtain information about the "correct" way to believe or behave

Informational power   power derived by the possession of a specific piece of information

Ingratiation   attempts by an individual to enhance his or her image in the eyes of another by expressing attitudes that he or she thinks the other person wants to hear

Instinct   an innate program that determines an organism's behavior in a given situation

Institutionalization   in Thibaut and Kelley's theory of the stages of relationships, the stage in which there is some formalization of commitment

Intellectualization   an ego-defense mechanism in which the individual reacts to a stressful situation in a detached and analytical manner

Interest test   a test designed to compare an individual's interests with those of successful people in a wide variety of occupations

Interpersonal distance   the distance people keep between themselves and others when interacting

Intimacy   a close emotional relationship characterized by deep caring for another person

Intrinsic motivation   the desire to perform based on internal factors, such as the wish to control one's own behavior and to demonstrate competence

Job discrimination   limiting people's job opportunities because of their race, sex, religion, color, or national origin

Job satisfaction   a pleasurable emotional state that results from feeling that one's job is fulfilling

Kinesiology   the study of communication through body movements

Latency period   according to Freud and Erikson, a long stage during middle and late childhood in which children attempt to develop intellectual, athletic, artistic, and social skills

Leader   an individual who influences the activities of a group

Learned helplessness   a condition that exists when an individual feels that behavior has no impact on environment; results in giving up and becoming very passive in the face of stress

Legitimate power   power an individual derives from occupying a particular role or position

Locus of control   Rotter's notion of a generalized expectation that outcomes in life are either within one's control (internal locus of control) or controlled by outside forces, such as luck or powerful others (external locus of control)

Logotherapy   Frankl's therapy, which emphasized helping clients find meaning in their lives

Loneliness   a state of mental stress and anxiety that results when people either erect mental barriers to wall themselves off from others or are afraid to break down existing barriers

Love   (1) mature love: a positive emotion about another person involving caring, attachment, and the desire for intimacy; (2) romantic love: a strong, often fleeting positive feeling about another person that has a physiological arousal component

Mania   an extreme mood of elation, well-being, and euphoria

Marijuana   a psychoactive drug that produces a mild high, euphoria, and changes in memory, concentration, and coordination

Mask   the attempt by an individual to hide one emotion by displaying another

Masturbation   self-manipulation of one's genitals to orgasm

Menopause   the time in a woman's life when menstruation ceases and she is no longer capable of reproduction

Metacommunication   a communication about another communication

Micromomentary expressions   barely visible facial expressions that show emotions one is attempting to control during interaction with another

Model   in social learning theory, a person who performs or models a behavior that can be observed and learned by another person

Moral realism   in Piaget's theory of moral development, the strict and literal application of rules with no thought of intentions and possible mitigating circumstances

Moral relativism   in Piaget's theory of moral development, the considering of intentions in evaluating the morality of behavior

Mutism   an inability to speak; associated with hysteria

Neurasthenia   chronic tiredness, exhaustion, or fatigue

Neutralize   to attempt to conceal an emotion from another

Noise   sound that is unwanted by the listener because it is unpleasant, bothersome, and interferes with activities

Nonspecific urethritis   an inflammation of the male urethra similar to gonorrhea but that cannot be treated with penicillin

Nonverbal communication sending messages through body language without talking

Normative influence the power of the group to influence a member's behavior through the member's fear that he or she will be rejected for failing to follow the group's direction

Norms general rules that apply to everyone in a group and specify what must be done and when it must be done

Obedience conforming to direct orders from a high-status individual

Observational learning learning that takes place when a person observes a model performing a behavior

Obsession a recurring thought or image experienced as uncontrollable intrusions into consciousness

Obsessive-compulsive disorder a mental disorder characterized by intrusive thoughts and repetitive urges to perform some corrective behavior

Obsessive-compulsive personality disorder a personality disorder characterized by emotional coldness, rigidity, and perfectionism

Occupation the specific form our choice of work takes

Operant a behavior that has been acquired on the basis of reinforcement

Operant conditioning the process of learning in which a response or change in behavior is strengthened with a reinforcer

Oral stage Freud's first stage of development, discussed by Erikson, spanning approximately the first year of life, in which the child primarily needs nourishment and physical comfort

Orgasm an intense physical and emotional experience often occurring at the climax of a sex act, such as intercourse or masturbation

Orgasmic dysfunction a female's inability to experience an orgasm, even when there is normal sex interest and drive

Ostracism in Sullivan's theory, the rejection of an individual by a group that finds him or her different and undesirable

Outcome level the average level of outcomes that is experienced in a relationship

Overcompensation effect a tendency to overcorrect for an initial incorrect impression and to overemphasize the most recent information

Paradoxical communication a message that contradicts itself

Paralanguage aspects of speaking, such as pace of speech and tone of voice, which qualify the meaning of what is stated

Paranoid schizophrenia a type of schizophrenia marked by delusions of grandeur and/or persecution

Personal space the space individuals keep when interacting with others; there is often a feeling of ownership of the space directly around an individual, and uninvited intrusions are met with retreat or hostility

Person–environment fit a view that the "best" environment is the one that matches the environment to the needs of the person who will use it

Personification in Sullivan's theory, young children's vague images about themselves that contain both "good me" and "bad me" elements

Person perception the process of forming impressions of other people

Phallic stage Freud's third stage of development, discussed by Erikson, spanning ages 3 to 4, when the child is interested in his or her sexual organs and develops strong attachments to the parent of the opposite sex

Phobia an intense fear of a particular behavior, object, or place that poses no immediate threat to the individual

Polygraph a machine, often called a lie detector, that records changes in heart rate, blood pressure, and galvanic skin responses

Pornography sexually arousing art, literature, or films

Postconventional level of morality morality based on consensus within society or self-chosen ethical principles

Post-traumatic stress disorder a mental disorder characterized by a variety of physical and psychological anxiety symptoms, which arise in response to a major trauma

Power-expressive rapes rapes in which men attempt to assert and show power and dominance over women

Power-reassurance rapes rapes in which men who feel insecure about their power and worth attempt to make themselves feel better by overcoming uncertainty about their power

Preadolescence   in Sullivan's theory of development, the years just before adolescence, starting at about age 9, when children first establish intimate relationships with same-sex peers

Preconventional level of morality   morality based on obedience, punishment, and reward

Prejudice   an unjustified negative attitude toward a person based solely on the individual's membership in a group

Premature ejaculation   a male's inability to delay ejaculation long enough to penetrate and satisfy his partner at least 50 percent of the time

Premenstrual syndrome (PMS)   a condition involving irritability, depression, fatigue, water retention, and other symptoms that affect a minority of women in the days preceding menstruation

Primacy effect   an impression of another that is most heavily influenced by the earliest information received about the person

Primary process   in Freudian theory, the imagining of objects or behaviors that will gratify the id

Primary territory   areas or objects that are exclusively owned or controlled by individuals and are of central importance in their lives

Privacy   the ability to regulate social interactions, controlling what will be communicated, and to whom

Private acceptance   changing both attitudes and behavior to be more congruent with group norms

Process-experimental therapy   a type of psychotherapy that focuses on understanding and processing affective experiences

Problem-focused coping   an approach to dealing with stress that involves correctly indentifying the causes of stress and taking steps to reduce them

Projection   an ego-defense mechanism in which an individual's unacceptable thoughts or impulses are attributed to others

Proxemics   studies concerned with how people position themselves in social interaction

Proximity   one person's geographical closeness to another person; an important factor in influencing interpersonal attraction

Psychodynamic psychotherapy   a type of psychotherapy that addresses inner psychological dynamics and conflicts

Psychoeducational group therapy   a form of group therapy in which clients and their families are given and provide for each other support and education about mental illness

Psychophysiological disorder   a disorder in which the individual shows physical symptoms that have psychological causes

Psychosis   a more severe form of psychological disorder, marked by severe disturbances in thought and loss of the ability to function in society

Psychotherapy   a treatment for psychological disorders that focuses on the behavior, cognitions, and/or emotions of the client

Psychotropic medication   prescription drugs that affect mental processes and provide relief from the symptoms of some psychological disorders

Public compliance   conformity in which an individual changes only overt behavior to follow the group

Public territory   an area that individuals control only while occupying it

Radical behaviorism   B. F. Skinner's philosophy that psychologists should only discuss behavior and not thoughts and feelings because behavior is all that they can observe

Rational-emotive therapy   Albert Ellis' approach to psychotherapy, which focuses on the process of learning that our belief that we have to live up to other people's expectations of us is debilitating and irrational

Rationalization   an ego-defense mechanism by which people convince themselves and others that their behavior was performed for socially desirable reasons

Reactance theory   a psychologically motivational state that results when a person feels his or her freedom has been threatened or eliminated

Reaction formation   an ego-defense mechanism in which anxiety is reduced by repressing one set of feelings and over-emphasizing an opposite set of feelings

Reappraisal   a strategy of coping that involves changing the way one thinks about a stressful situation; often involves attempting to see positive as well as negative aspects of the situation

Recategorization   the process of changing one's mental picture of the social world that involves redrawing group or category boundaries

Recency effect   the heavy influence of the most recent information about another person in the creation of one's impression of that person

Recovery   the final stage in the grieving process in which one begins to put suffering behind and tries to continue an active life

Referent power   the power an individual derives from being admired and liked

Reflected appraisal   the process through which we imagine how other people evaluate us and form our self-concept in response to their appraisals

Regression   an ego-defense mechanism in which an individual reacts to a stressful situation by reverting to childish or juvenile behavior

Reinforcer   a desired stimulus that strengthens a behavior; a reward

Relative humidity   the percent of moisture in the air

Relaxation   a response marked by tensionless muscles and breathing, which is used in systematic desensitization; relaxation is incompatible with feeling anxiety

Repression   an ego-defense mechanism in which unwanted thoughts or impulses are driven from one's consciousness

Residual schizophrenia   a type of schizophrenia marked by extreme withdrawal, apathy, and odd beliefs or behaviors, but not necessarily outright psychotic episodes

Resistance   in Freudian psychoanalysis, the patient's avoidance of thinking about or discussing anxiety-provoking thoughts or feelings

Retarded ejaculation   a male's inability to ejaculate during intercourse

Reward power   the capacity to give positive reinforcements to achieve compliance from another person

Role conflict   the internal conflict that results when the behavioral expectations of an individual's role in one group contradict the behavioral expectations of another group to which the individual belongs

Roles   a set of norms that define how an individual in a particular position should act

Sampling   in Thibaut and Kelley's theory of the stages of relationships, the process of looking over the possibilities and then deciding on a person with whom to attempt to form a relationship

Sandwich generation   family members who are caring for both children and elderly parents at the same time

Scapegoat   a person or group that people blame for their troubles and toward whom they displace aggression

Schema   an organization of knowledge, such as a belief, derived from past experience, which we use to interpret new experience or information

Schizoid personality disorder   a personality disorder characterized by pervasive detachment from others and restricted emotions

Schizophrenia   a psychosis marked by disintegration of normal thought processes

Seasonal Affective Disorder (SAD)   depressive symptoms brought on by biological responses to seasonal changes, particularly the decrease in the hours of daylight during winter

Secondary territory   areas or objects to which individuals are emotionally attached, which they feel they control exclusively; they do not, however, own these territories or objects

Self-actualization   striving to reach personal potential and using abilities in a creative way

Self-appraisal   examining one's self to identify positive and negative points, hopes and aspirations, goals, and social and physical environments in which one exists

Self-concept   one's perceptions of one's abilities, goals, and aspirations and one's overall feeling of worth

Self-disclosure   revealing to others private information about one's beliefs, attitudes, feelings, and life history

Self-efficacy   the belief that one can handle stress and is in control of one's environment

Self-esteem   the degree to which one likes and respects oneself

Self-fulfilling prophecy   a prophecy or prediction that may not be inevitable but that leads to certain behaviors that make it come true

Self-in-relation theory   a recent theory that the psychological development of females occurs in relation to other people, resulting in a more interconnected adult personality

Self-schema   a belief about the kind of person one is

Self-identify   the image one has of oneself; generally includes personal identity (traits and characteristics) and social identity (derived from groups to which one belongs)

Self-serving bias   the tendency to perceive or interpret events to enhance one's self-esteem

Sense of autonomy   a sense of control over one's body and a feeling that one is free to act independently

Sense of basic mistrust   in Erikson's theory, the child's feeling that the world cannot be counted on and that he or she is inadequate to meet its demands

Sense of basic trust   a basic feeling of trust in oneself and the environment and the feeling of adequacy in meeting external demands

Sense of guilt   in Erikson's theory, the child's sense that his or her wishes, desires, and actions are inappropriate and immoral

Sense of industry   the child's sense of control, power, and competence in achieving desired goals

Sense of inferiority   in Erikson's theory, the child's feeling that he or she has little worth and is inferior to others

Sense of initiative   the child's sense of having some control over objects and other people, along with the ability to act creatively

Sense of integrity   a sense of peace with oneself and others and the acceptance of responsibility for one's life

Sense of isolation   in Erikson's theory, a feeling of distance from others and an alienated and cynical attitude toward humanity

Sense of shame and doubt   in Erikson's theory, a child's feeling that he or she may not have the capacity to control bodily functions and act autonomously

Sexual dysfunction   sexual problems that are frequent or long-lasting

Sexual fantasy   a thought or daydream that is sexually stimulating

Sexual orientation   the preference for same (homosexual), opposite (heterosexual), or both (bisexual) sex partners

Sexually transmitted diseases   physical diseases transmitted through sexual contact

Shock   the stage in the grieving process in which a person tries to deal with the surprise and finality of another person's death

Similarity-attraction   a theory that people are attractive to others who have attitudes, appearance, background, or desires in common

Simple phobia   singular fears, such as fear of heights, closed spaces, snakes, etc.

Simulate   to attempt to display emotions that seem appropriate to the situation but that are not genuinely felt

Social comparison   the process of evaluating ourselves by comparing ourselves to others

Social comparison theory   a theory that argues that individuals engage in comparing themselves with others (usually similar others) to develop their self-image; social comparison is most likely to occur in situations involving social reality

Social dilemma   the conflict that results when an individual must choose between alternatives that benefit the self and those that benefit the group

Social exchange theory   a theory that views social relationships in economic terms, such as inputs, costs, and outcomes

Social influence   the exercise of power or the use of reinforcers by a person or group to influence the behavior of others

Social interaction   relating to or interacting with other people

Social isolation   a condition in which other people are not present in the environment

Social learning theory   a theory of personality and behavior that emphasizes observational learning during social interaction

Social phobia   strong fears of public situations in which one might be embarrassed

Social power   the capacity to influence others and resist influence from others

Social reality   a situation in which there is no predetermined (physical) measure of quality, requiring that one use the behavior of others to determine truth or quality

Social support   support offered by other people that helps deal with stress; can involve information, resources, or emotional support

Sound   changes in air pressure that affect the membrane in the ear and are perceived by the person

Stereotype   a representation of a group or category that involves simplified generalizations

Sterilization   a method of birth control that makes the individual incapable of reproduction

Stress   a condition that results when one perceives that one's well-being or integrity is threatened, and that one must devote all one's resources to coping with that threat

Sublimation an ego-defense mechanism in which sexual and aggressive urges are channeled into socially acceptable behavior

Suffering the stage in the grieving process following shock in which the greatest suffering and loneliness are experienced

Suite dormitory a dormitory arranged like an apartment in which a small number of bedrooms are placed around a common living area

Superego the structure of the psyche that contains the parents' morals, ideals, and values

Syphilis a sexually transmitted disease caused by a spiral-shaped bacterium, which causes chancres on external or internal sex organs

Systemic desensitization a behavior therapy technique in which the client is taught to relax, is presented with a hierarchy of anxiety-arousing situations, and learns to relax even when contemplating the most threatening situation

Systemic stress stress whose effects can be seen throughout the body in the form of damaged organs

Territoriality behavior involving claim to exclusive use of areas or objects

Testes the main male internal sex organs, which produce androgens and sperm

Testosterone a male hormone that has a range of effects in the body and brain

Theory a systematic statement that explains why events occur

Theory X a traditional theory of management that holds that workers are lazy and dishonest and must be watched carefully

Theory Y a theory of management that states that workers want to contribute and achieve and that the role of management is to create a positive work environment

Theory Z a management theory espoused by Japanese companies that views workers as being adopted into a family rather than simply hired to do a specific job

Tics spasmodic jerking or involuntary twitches associated with hysteria

Tolerance a term applied when a person must take more and more of a drug to achieve the desired effect

Token economy a form of behavior therapy in which desired behavior is rewarded with tokens that can be used to purchase reinforcers

Transference in psychoanalytic therapy, the process by which the patient projects onto the therapist his or her attitudes toward significant others and acts toward the therapist as he or she may have acted toward those others

Transsexual a person who has the inner experience of being of a different sex (male or female) than his or her biological sex

Type A behavior responses to stress that include becoming hostile, competitive, and time-driven; a link has been established between this type of behavior and coronary heart disease

Unconditional positive regard in psychotherapy, complete acceptance of the client by the therapist along with the therapist's warm caring for the client as a human being, with no conditions attached

Undifferentiated schizophrenia a type of schizophrenia marked by thought disorder but not paranoia, catatonia, or other symptoms

Vaginismus a dysfunction resulting when the muscles surrounding the vagina involuntarily constrict to inhibit penetration by the penis during intercourse

Voice stress analyzer a machine that records tremors in speech that reflect stress and tension

Withdrawal physical symptoms, such as sweating, shaking, and nausea, that accompany the cessation of an addictive drug; specific withdrawal symptoms vary by drug

Work some disciplined activity that gives one a feeling of personal accomplishment and that makes a contribution to society

Working alliance the sense of collaboration between the therapist and client, involving agreement on the tasks and techniques of therapy as well as emotional bonds and trust

Aamodt, M. G. (1996). *Applied industrial/organizational psychology* (2nd ed.). Pacific Grove, CA: Brooks/Cole.

Aamodt, M. & Carr, K. (1988). Relationship between recruitment source and employee behavior. *Proceedings of the 12th Annual Meeting of International Personnel Management Assoc.*, 143–146.

Abramson, L., Seligman, M. E. P., and Teasdale, J. (1978). Learned helplessness in humans: Critique and reformulation. *Journal of Abnormal Psychology, 87*, 32–48.

Adorno, T., Fenkel-Brunswick, E., Levinson, D., & Sanford, R. ((1950). *The authoritarian personality.* New York: Harper Row.

Ahlburg, D., & DeVita, C. (1992). New realities of the American family. *Population Bulletin, 47.* Washington, DC: Population Reference Bureau.

Akersrtedt, T. (1991). Sleepiness at work: Effects of irregular sleep hours. In T. Monk (Ed.), *Sleep, sleepiness, and performance.* New York: Wiley.

Alexander, F., & French, T. (1946). *Psychoanalytic psychotherapy.* NY: Ronald Press.

Alicke, M., Smith, R., & Klotz, M. (1986). Judgements of physical attractiveness: The role of faces and bodies. *Personality and Social Psychology Bulletin, 12*, 381–389.

Altman, I. (1975). *The environment and social psychology.* Monterey, CA: Brooks/Cole.

Altman, I., & Haythorn, W. W. (1965). Interpersonal exchange in isolation. *Sociometry, 28*, 411–426.

Altman, I., Lawson, M., & Wohlwill, R. (1984). *Elderly people and the environment.* New York: Plenum Press.

American Psychiatric Association (1994). *Diagnostic and statistical manual of mental disorders* (4th ed.). Washington, DC: Author.

American Psychological Association (1990). Ethical principles of psychologists. *American Psychologist, 45*, 390–395.

Anderson, C., & Anderson, D. (1985). Ambient temperature and violent crime: Tests of linear and curvilinear hypotheses. *Journal of Personality and Social Psychology, 46*, 91–97.

Anderson, C. M., Griffin, S., Rossi, A., Pagonis, I. Holder, D. P., & Treiber, R. (1986). A comprehensive study of the impact of education vs. process groups for families of patients with affective disorders. *Family Process, 25*, 185–206.

Anderson, C. M., Reiss, D. J., & Hogarty, G. E. (1986). *Schizophrenia and the family: A practitioner's guide to psychoeducation and management.* New York: Guilford.

Andreasen, N., Flaum, M., Swayze, V. W., Tyrell, G., & Arndt, S. (1990). Positive and negative symptoms in schizophrenia: A critical reappraisal. *Archives of General Psychiatry, 47*, 615–621.

Andreasen, N., Swayze, V. W., Flaum, M., Yates, W. R., Arndt, S., & McChesney, C. (1990). Ventricular enlargement in schizophrenia evaluated with computed tomographic scanning: Effects of gender, age, and stage of illness. *Archives of General Psychiatry, 47*, 1008–1015.

Argyle, M. (1991). *Cooperation: The basis for sociability.* London: Routledge.

Argyle, M. (1992). *The social psychology of everyday life.* London: Routledge.

Argyle, M., & Dean, J. (1965). Eye-contact, distance, and affiliation. *Sociometry, 18*, 289–304.

Aries, D. (1976). Interaction patterns and themes of male, female, and mixed groups. *Small Group Behavior, 7*, 7–18.

Aries, E. (1987). Sex and gender. In P. Shaver & C. Hendrick (Eds.), *Gender and communication* (pp. 149–176). Newbury Park, CA: Sage.

Aries, E. (1996). *Men and women in interaction.* NY: Oxford University Press.

Arnold, G. (1994, June). Into the black. *Spin, 10*, 34–37, 40.

Aronson, E. (1992). The return of the repressed: Dissonance theory. *Psychological Inquiry.* Santa Cruz, CA.

Aronson, E., & Bridgeman, L. (1979). Jigsaw groups and the desegregated classroom: In pursuit of common goals. *Personality and Social Psychology Bulletin, 5*, 438–446.

Aronson, E., & Linder, D. E. (1965). Gain and loss of esteem as determinants of interpersonal attractiveness. *Journal of Experimental Social Psychology, 1,* 156–171.

Aronson, E., Wilson, T. D., & Akert, R. M. (1997). *Social Psychology* (2nd ed.). Reading, MA: Longman.

Asch, S. (1956). Studies of independence and conformity: I. A minority of one against a unanimous majority. *Psychological Monographs: General and Applied, 40,* 1–70.

Ash, P., & Kroeker, L. (1975). Personnel selections, classification, and placements. *Annual Review of Psychology, 26,* 481–508.

Athanasiou, R., Shaver, P., & Tavris, C. (1970, July). *Psychology Today,* pp. 39–52.

Attridge, M., Berscheid, E., & Simpson, J. A. (1995). Predicting relationship stability from both partners versus one. *Journal of Personality and Social Psychology, 69,* 254–268.

Austin, W. (1986). Justice in intergroup conflict. In S. Worchel & W. Austin (Eds.). *Psychology of intergroup relations.* Chicago: Nelson Hall.

Backman, K. W. (1981). Attraction in interpersonal relationships. In M. Rosenberg & R. Turner (Eds.), *Social psychology: Sociological perspectives.* New York: Basic Books.

Bailey, J. M., & Martin, N. G. (1995, September). *A twin registry study of sexual orientation.* Paper presented at the annual meeting of the International Academy of Sex Research, Provincetown, MA.

Bailey, J. M., & Pillard, R. C. (1991). A genetic study of male sexual orientation. *Archives of Genetic Psychiatry, 48,* 1089–1096.

Baker, M. et al (1980). *An interdisciplinary approach to women's studies.* Monterey, CA: Brooks/Cole.

Bandura, A. (1965). Behavior modification through modeling procedures. In L. Krasner & L. P. Ullman (Eds.), *Research in behavior modification.* New York: Holt, Rinehart and Winston.

Bandura, A. (1982). Self-efficacy mechanism in human agency. *American Psychologist, 37,* 122–147.

Bandura, A. (1983). Self-efficacy determinants of anticipated fears and calamities. *Journal of Personality and Social Psychology, 45,* 464–469.

Bandura, A. (1986). *Social foundations of thought and action: A cognitive theory.* Englewood Cliffs, NJ: Prentice Hall.

Bandura, A., Ross, D., & Ross, S. (1961). Transmission of aggression through imitation of aggressive models. *Journal of Abnormal and Social Psychology, 63,* 575–582.

Bandura, A., Ross, D., & Ross, S. A. (1963). Imitation of fil-mediated aggressive models. *Journal of Abnormal and Social Psychology, 66,* 3–11.

Bardwick, C. (1971). *The psychology of women: A study of bio-cultural conflicts.* New York: Harper & Row.

Baring-Gould, W. S. (1967). *The annotated Sherlock Holmes.* New York: Clarkson N. Potter, Inc.

Baron, R. (1987a). Effects of negative ions on cognitive performance. *Journal of Applied Psychology, 72,* 131–137.

Baron, R. (1987b). Effects of negative ions on interpersonal attraction: Evidence for intensification. *Journal of Personality and Social Psychology, 52,* 547–553.

Baron, R. A., & Byrne, D. (1981). *Social psychology: Understanding human interaction* (3rd ed.). Boston: Allyn and Bacon.

Baron, R. S., Cutrona, C. E., Hicklin, D., Russell, D., & Lubaroff, D. (1990). Social support and immune function among spouses of cancer patients. *Journal of Personality and Social Psychology, 59,* 344–352.

Baron, R., Mandel, D., Adams, C. & Griffin, L. (1976). Effects on social density in university residential environments. *Journal of Personality and Social Psychology, 3,* 434–446.

Barrett, N. (1979). Women in the job market: Occupations, earnings, and career opportunities. In R. Smith (ed.). *The subtle revolution: Women at work.* Washington, D.C.: The Urban Institute.

Basow, S. A., & Kobrynowicz, D. (1993). What is she eating? The effects of meal size on impressions of a female eater. *Sex Roles, 28,* 335–344.

Bass, B., & Barrett, G. (1981). *People, work, and organizations* (2nd ed.). Monterey, CA: Brooks/Cole.

Baum, A., & Greenberg, C. (1975). Waiting for a crowd: The behavioral and perceptual effects of anticipatory crowing. *Journal of Personality and Social Psychology, 32,* 667–671.

Baum, A., & Valins, S. (1977). *Architecture and social behavior: Psychological studies in social density.* Hillsdale, NJ: Erlbaum.

Baumeister, R. (1985, April.) The championship choke. *Psychology Today,* 48–52.

Baumeister, R. F., & Hutton, D. G. (1987). Self-presentation theory: Self-construction and audience pleasing. In B. Mullen & G. R. Goethals (Eds.), *Theories of group behavior.* New York: Springer-Verlag.

Baumeister, R. F., & Leary, M. R. (1995). The need to belong: Desire for interpersonal attachments as a fundamental human motivation. *Psychological Bulletin, 117,* 497–529.

Baxter, L. A. (1988). A dialectical perspective on communication strategies in relationship development. In S. Duck (Ed.) *Handbook of personal relationships.* New York: Wiley.

Beall, A. E., & Sternberg, R. J. (Eds.). (1993). *The psychology of gender.* NY: Guilford Press.

Beavers, W. R. (1982). Healthy, midrange, and severely dysfunctional families. In F. Walsh (Ed.), *Normal family processes* (pp. 45–66). New York: Guilford.

Beavers, W. R., & Hampson, R. B. (1990). *Successful families.* New York: Norton.

Beck, A. T. (1967). *Depression: Clinical, experimental and theoretical aspects.* New York: Harper & Row.

Beck, A. T. (1976). *Cognitive therapies and the emotional disorders.* New York: International Universities Press.

Beck, A. T. (1978). *Depression inventory.* Philadelphia, PA: Center for Cognitive Therapy.

Beck, A. T. (1991). Cognitive therapy: A 30-year retrospective. *American Psychologist, 46,* 368–375.

Beck, A. T., Rush, A. J., Shaw, B. F., & Emery, G. (1979). *Cognitive therapy of depression.* New York: Guilford.

Becker, J. B., & Breedlove, S. M. (1992). Introduction to behavioral endocrinology. In J. B. Becker, S. M. Breedlove, & D. Crews, D. (Eds.), *Behavioral endocrinology* (pp. 3–38). Cambridge, MA: MIT Press.

Belenky, J., Clinchy, B., Goldberger, N., & Tarule, J. (1986). *Women's ways of knowing.* New York: Basic Books.

Bell, A. P., & Weinberg, M. S. (1978). *Homosexualities: A study of diversity among men and women.* New York: Simon & Schuster.

Belsky, J., Perry-Jenkins, M. & Crouter, A. (1985). The work-family interface and marital change across the transition to parenthood. *Journal of Family Issues, 6,* 205–220.

Bem, D. J. (1972). Self-perception theory. In L. Berkowitz (Ed.), *Advances in experimental social psychology. Vol. 6.* New York: Academic Press.

Bem, D. J. (1996). Exotic becomes erotic: A developmental theory of sexual orientation. *Psychological Review, 103,* 320–335.

Bem, S. L. (1981). *Bem Sex Role Inventory professional manual.* Palo Alto: Consulting Psychologists Press.

Bem, S. L. (1985). Androgyny and gender role schema: A conceptual and empirical integration. In T. B. Sanderegger (Ed.), *Nebraska symposium on motivation: Psychology of gender* (pp. 179–226). Lincoln, NE: University of Nebraska Press.

Ben-Ari, R., & Amir, Y. (1988). Intergroup contact, cultural information, and change in ethnic attitudes. In W. Striebe et al (Eds.), *The social psychology of intergroup conflict.* Berlin: Springer-Verlag.

Benbow, C. P. (1988). Sex differences in mathematical reasoning ability in intellectually talented preadolescents: Their nature, effects, and possible causes. *Behavioral and Brain Sciences, 11,* 169–232.

Bennett, L. (1968). *What manner of man: A biography of Martin Luther King, Jr.* Chicago: Johnson.

Benoit, J. (1987). *Running tide.* New York: Knopf.

Berg, J. H., Stephan, W. G., & Dodson, M. (1981). Attributional modesty in women. *Psychology of Women Quarterly, 5,* 711–727.

Berscheid, E. (1985). Interpersonal attraction. In G. Lindsay & E. Aronson (Eds.), *Handbook of social psychology* (2nd ed.). *Vol. 2.* (pp. 413–484). New York: Random House.

Berscheid, E., Dion, K., Walster, E., & Walster, G. W. (1971). Physical attractiveness and dating choice: A test of the matching hypothesis. *Journal of Experimental Social Psychology, 7,* 173–189.

Berscheid, E., & Walster, E. (1974). A little bit about love. In T. H. Huston (Ed.), *Foundations of interpersonal attraction.* New York: Academic Press.

Berscheid, E. & Walster, E. (1978). *Interpersonal attraction.* Reading, Mass.: Addison-Wesley.

Berscheid, E., Dion, K., Walster, E., & Walster, G. W. (1971). Physical attractiveness and dating choice: A test of the matching hypothesis. *Journal of Experimental Social Psychology, 7,* 173–189.

Bettelheim, B. (1958). Individual and mass behavior in extreme situations. In E. E. Maccoby, T. M. Newcomb & E. L. Hartley (Eds.), *Readings in social psychology.* New York: Holt, Rinehart and Winston.

Blanchard, E. and associates (1990). A controlled evaluation of thermal biofeedback and thermal biofeedback combined with cognitive therapy in the treatment of vascular headache. *Journal of Consulting and Clinical Psychology, 58,* 216–224. ABC News, June 17, 1995.

Block, J. (1976). Issues, problems, and pitfalls in assessing sex differences: A critical review of *The psychology of sex differences. Merrill-Palmer Quarterly, 22,* 383–388.

Bluen, S., Barling, J., & Burns, J. (1990). Predicting goals, performance, job satisfaction, and digression by using achievement strivings and impatience–irritability dimensions of Type A behavior. *Journal of Applied Psychology, 75,* 212–216.

Blysma, W. H., & Major, B. (1994). Social comparisons and contentment. *Psychology of Women Quarterly, 18,* 241–249.

Bochner, S. (1994). Cross-cultural differences in the self concept: A test of Hofstede's individualism/collectivism distinction. *Journal of Cross Cultural Psychology, 25,* 273–283.

Bolles, R. (1995). *What color is your parachute?* Berkeley, CA: Ten Speed Press.

Bond, M. (1996). Surveying the foundations: Approaches to measuring group, organizational, and national variation. Paper presented at Conference on Work Motivation, Kubbutz Ein-Gedi, Israel.

Bonner, J. (1993). Measurement of resume content preference. Unpublished M.A. thesis, Radford University, Radford, VA.

Boston Women's Health Book Collective. (1979). *Our bodies, ourselves.* New York: Simon & Schuster.

Botwinick, J. (1977). Intellectual abilities. In E. Birren & K. Shaie (Eds.), *Handbook of the psychology of aging.* New York: Van Nostrand.

Bouchard, T. and others (1990). Sources of human psychological differences: A Minnesota study of twins reared apart. *Science, 250,* 1055–1059.

Bouchard, T. J., Jr., Lykken, D. T., McGue, M., Segal, N. L., & Tellegan, A. (1990). Sources of human psychological differences: The Minnesota study of twins reared apart. *Science, 250,* 223–228.

Bouchard, T. & McGue, M. (1990). Genetic and environmental influences on adult personality: An analysis of adopted twins reared apart. *Journal of Personality, 58,* 263–295.

Bowlby, J. (1969). *Attachment and loss. Vol. 1.* New York: Basic Books.

Bradbury, T. N. & Fincham, F. D. (1990). Attributions in marriage: Review and critique. *Psychological Bulletin, 107,* 3–33.

Bradt, J. (1989). Becoming parents: families with young children. In B. Carter & M. McGoldrick (Eds.), *The changing family life cycle.* (pp. 237–254). New York: Gardner.

Bramel, D., & Friend, R. (1981). Hawthorne, the myth of the docile worker, and class bias in psychology. *American Psychologist, 36,* 867–87.

Braver, S., Wolchik, S., Sandler, I., Sheets, V., Fogas, B., & Bay, C. (1993). A longitudinal study of noncustodial parents: Parents without children. *Journal of Family Psychology, 7,* 9–23.

Bray, J. H., & Hetherington, E. M. (1993). Families in transition: Introduction and overview. *Journal of Family Psychology, 7,* 3–8.

Bray, D., Campbell, R., & Grant, D. (1974). *Formative years in business: A long-term AT&T study of management lives.* New York: Wiley Interscience.

Brehm, J., & Brehm, S. (1981). *Psychological reactance: A theory of freedom and control.* New York: Academic Press.

Brehm, S. S. (1992). *Intimate relationships.* New York: McGraw-Hill.

Brehm, S. S., & Kassin, S. M. (1996). *Social psychology* (3rd ed.). Boston: Houghton Mifflin Company.

Brewer, M. (1991). The social self: On being the same and different at the same time. *Personality and Social Psychology Bulletin, 17,* 475–482.

Brewer, M., & Kramer, R. (1985). The psychology of intergroup attitudes and behavior. *Annual Review of Psychology.* New York: Annual Review Incorporated.

Brewer, M. & Miller N. (1988). Contact and cooperation. When do they work? In P. Katz & D. Taylor (Eds.). *Towards the elimination of racism: Profiles in controversy.* New York: Plenum.

Brislin, R. (1993). *Understanding culture's influence on behavior.* Fort Worth: Harcourt Brace Jovanovich.

Broadwell, M. (1993). Seven steps to building better training. *Training, 30,* 75–81.

Brody, G. H., Stoneman, Z., & Flor, D. (1996). Parental religiosity, family process, and youth competence in rural, two-parent African-American families. *Developmental Psychology, 32,* 696–706.

Brown, B. (1979). Territoriality and residential burglary. Paper presented at the American Psychological Association meeting, New York.

Brown, B., & Campion, M. (1994). Biodata phemenology: Recruiter's perceptions and use of biographical information in resume screening. *Journal of Applied Psychology, 79,* 897–908.

Brown, B., & Lohr, A. J. (1987). Peer-group affiliation and adolescent self-esteem: An integration of ego-identity and symbolic-interaction themes. *Journal of Personality and Social Psychology, 52,* 47–55.

Brown, G. W., & Harris. T. (1978). *Social origins of depression.* London: Tavistock.

Brown, R. (1988). *Group process: Dynamics within and between groups.* Oxford, England: Basil Blackwell.

Brubaker, T. (1990). Families in later life: A burgeoning research area. *Journal of Marriage and Family, 52,* 959–982.

Bryant, J. (1985). Testimony on the effects of pornography: Research findings. Paper presented at the U.S. Justice Department Hearings, Houston.

Buehlman, K. T., Gottman, J. M., & Katz, L. F. (1992). How a couple views their past predicts their future: Predicting divorce from an oral history interview. *Journal of Family Psychology, 5*(3 & 4), 295–318.

Buffone, G. W. (1984). Running and depression. In M. Sachs & G. Buffone (Eds.), *Running as therapy: An integrated approach.* Lincoln, NE: University of Nebraska Press.

Buhler, C. (1972). The course of life as a psychological problem. In W. R. Looft (Ed.), *Developmental psychology: A book of readings.* New York: Holt, Rinehart and Winston.

Bullock, W. A., & Gilliland, K. (1993). Eysenck's arousal theory of introversion-extraversion: A converging measures investigation. *Journal of Personality and Social Psychology, 64,* 113–123.

Bumpass, L., & Sweet, J. A. (1989). Children's experience in single-parent families: Implications of cohabitation and marital transitions. *Family Planning Perspectives, 6,* 256–260.

Burnett, S. A. (1986). Sex-related differences in spatial ability: Are they trivial? *American Psychologist, 41,* 1012–1014.

Buss, A. H. (1980). *Self-consciousness and social anxiety.* San Francisco, CA: W. H. Freeman.

Buss, D. M. (1988). The evolution of human intrasexual competition: Tactics of mate attraction. *Journal of Personality and Social Psychology, 54,* 616–628.

Buss, D. M. (1988). The evolutionary biology of love. In R. J. Sternberg & M. L. Barnes (Eds.), *The psychology of love.* (pp. 100–118). New Haven, CT: Yale University Press.

Buss, D. M. (1989). Sex differences in mate preference: Evolutionary hypothesis tested in 37 cultures. *Brain and Behavioral Sciences, 12,* 1–49.

Buss, D. M. (1994). *The evolution of desire.* New York: Basic Books.

Buunk, B., Doosje, B., Jans, L., & Hopstaken, L. (1993). Perceived reciprocity, social support, and stress at work: The role of exchange and communal orientation. *Journal of Personality and Social Psychology, 65,* 801–811.

Byrne, D. (1982). Sex without contraception. In D. Byrne & W. A. Fisher (Eds.), *Adolescents, sex and contraception.* Hillsdale, NJ: Lawrence Erlbaum.

Byrne, D., Baskett, C., & Hodges, L. (1971). Behavioral indicators of interpersonal attraction. *Journal of Abnormal and Social Psychology, 61,* 137–149.

Byrne, D., Clore, G., & Smeaton, G. (1986). The attraction hypothesis: Do similar attitudes affect anything? *Journal of Personality and Social Psychology, 51,* 1167–1170.

Caldwell, D., & Spivey, W. (1983). The relationship between recruiting source and employee success: An analysis by race. *Personnel Psychology, 36,* 67–72.

Calhoun, J. F. (1962). Population and social density. *Scientific American, 206,* 139–148.

Carksadon, M., & Roth, T. (1991). Sleep restriction. In T. Monk (Ed.), *Sleep, sleepiness, and performance.* New York: Wiley.

Carli, L. L. (1989). Gender differences in interaction style and influence. *Journal of Personality and Social Psychology, 56,* 565–576.

Carpenter, C. R. (1958). Territorality: A review of concepts and problems. In A. Roe & G. Simpson (Eds.), *Behavior and evolution.* New Haven, CT: Yale University Press.

Carter, B. & McGoldrick, M. (Eds.) (1989). *The changing family life cycle.* New York: Gardner Press.

Carver, C. et al. (1993). How coping mediates the effects of optimism on distress: A study of women in the early stage of breast cancer. *Journal of Personality and Social Psychology, 65,* 375–390.

Caspi, A. Bolger, N. & Eckenrode, J. (1987). Linking person and context in the daily stress process. *Journal of Personality and Social Psychology, 52,* 184–195.

Cate, R. M., & Lloyd, S. A. (1988). Courtship. In S. Duck (Ed.), *Handbook of personal relationships.* (pp. 409–427). New York: Wiley.

Cattell, R. B. (1950). *Personality: A systematic, theoretical, and factual study.* New York: McGraw-Hill.

Cattell, R. B. (1966). *The scientific analysis of personality.* Chicago: Aldine.

Cattell, R. B. (1972). The 16 PF and basic personality structure: A reply to Eysenck. *Journal of Behavioral Science, 1,* 169–187.

Cattell, R. B. (1973). *Personality and mood by questionnaire.* San Francisco, CA: Jossey-Bass.

Ceci, S. & Peters, D. (1984). Letters of reference: A naturalistic study of the effects of confidentiality. *American Psychologist, 39,* 29–31.

Chacko, T. I. (1982). Women and equal employment opportunity: Some unintended effects. *Journal of Applied Psychology, 67,* 119–123.

Chaiken, A. L., & Derlega, V. J. (1976). Self-disclosure. In J. W. Thibaut, J. T. Spence, & R. C. Carson (Eds.), *Contemporary topics in social psychology.* Morristown, NJ: General Learning Press.

Cherlin, A. J. (1981). *Marriage, divorce, and remarriage.* Cambridge: Harvard University Press.

Clark, M. S., & Mills, J. (1979). Interpersonal attraction in exchange and communal relationships. *Journal of Personality and Social Psychology, 37,* 12–24.

Clarke, A. (1952). An examination of the operation of residual propinquity as a factor of mate selection. *American Sociological Review, 27,* 17–22.

Clay, R. A. (1995). Working mothers: Happy or haggard? *APA Monitor, 26,* 1.

Clements, M. (1996, May). Strange bedfellows. *Harper's Bazaar,* pp. 138–145.

Cochran, C., Hale, W. & Hissam, C. (1984). Personal space requirements in indoor versus outdoor locations. *Journal of Psychology, 117,* 121–123.

Cohen, L. (1987, November). Diet and cancer. *Scientific American,* 128–137.

Cohen, S., Glass, D. & Singer, J. (1973), Apartment noise, auditory discrimination, and reading ability in children. *Journal of Experimental Social Psychology, 9,* 407–422.

Cohen, S., Krantz, D., Evans, G. & Stokols, D. (1982). Community noise, behavior, and health: The Los Angeles Noise Project. In A. Baum & J. Singer (Eds.), *Advances in environmental psychology* (Vol. 4). Hillsdale, NJ: Erlbaum.

Cohen, S., Tyrrell, D., & Smith, A. (1993). Negative life events, perceived stress, negative affect, and susceptibility to the common cold. *Journal of Personality and Social Psychology, 64,* 131–140.

Collet, L. (1990). After the anger: what then? *Family Therapy Networker, 14,* 22–31.

Collins, R., & Coltrane, S. (1995). *Sociology of marriage and the family.* Chicago: Nelson Hall.

Coltrane, S. (1989). Household labor and the routine production of gender. *Social Problems, 36,* 473–490.

Coltrane, S. (1990). Birth timing and the division of labor in dual-earner families. *Journal of Family Issues, 11,* 157–181.

Comer, R. J. (1992). *Abnormal psychology.* New York: W. H. Freeman.

Consumer Reports. (1995, November). Mental health: Does therapy help? 734–739.

Cooley, C. H. (1922). *Human nature and the social order.* New York: Scribner.

Cox, A. J. (1986). "Aunt Grace can't have babies." *Journal of Religion and Health, 25,* 73–85.

Coyne, J. C., Kahn, J., & Gotlib, I. H. (1987). Depression. In T. Jacobs (Ed.), *Family interaction and psychopathology* (pp. 509–534). New York: Plenum.

Cozby, P. C. (1972). Self-disclosure, reciprocity, and liking. *Sociometry, 35,* 151–160.

Cozby, P. C. (1973). Self-disclosure: A literature review. *Psychological Bulletin, 79,* 73–91.

Cozzi, C. (1986). The shelter. *Family Therapy Networker, 10,* 30–35.

Cramer, P. (1990). *The development of defense mechanisms: Theory, research, and assessment.* New York: Springer-Verlag.

Cramer, P. (1996). *Storytelling, narrative, and the thematic apperception test.* New York: Guilford Press.

Crandall, C. S. (1988). Social contagion of binge eating. *Journal of Personality and Social Psychology, 55,* 588–598.

Crawford, M., & English, L. (1984). Generic vs. specific inclusion of women in language: Effects on recall. *Journal of Psycholinguistic Research, 13,* 373–381.

Crawford, M. (1989). Feminist epistemologies and women's ways of knowing. In M. Crawford & M. Gentry (Eds.), *Gender and thought* (pp. 128–145). New York: Springer-Verlag.

Crawford, M. (1995). *Talking difference.* London: Sage.

Crits-Cristoph, P., & Barber, J. P. (1991). *Handbook of shortterm dynamic psychotherapies.* New York: Basic.

Crosby, F. J., Pufall, A., Snyder, P. C., O'Connell, M., & Whalen, P. (1989). The denial of personal disadvantage among you, me, and the other ostriches. In M. Crawford & M. Gentry (Eds.). *Gender and thought* (pp. 79–99). New York: Springer-Verlag.

Cutrona, C. (1990). Stress and social support—in search of optimal matching. *Journal of Social and Clinical Psychology, 9,* 3–14.

Dahl, A. S., Cowgill, K. M., & Asmundsson, R. (1987). Life in remarriage families. *Social Work, 32,* 40–44.

Daley, P. (1975) *The fantasy game: How male and female sexual fantasies affect our lives.* New York: Stein and Day.

Daly, M., & Wilson, M. (1988). *Sex, evolution, and behavior.* (2nd ed.). Belmont, CA: Wadsworth.

Darley, J. (1978). Energy conservation techniques as innovations and their diffusion. *Energy and Building, 1,* 339–343.

Darley, S. A., & Cooper, J. (1972). Cognitive consequences of forced noncompliance. *Journal of Personality and Social Psychology, 24,* 321–326.

Darling, C. A., Davidson, J. K. & Passarello, L. C. (1992). The mystique of first intercourse among college youth: The role of partners, contraceptive practices, and psychological reactions. *Journal of Youth and Adolescence, 21,* 97–117.

Daubman, K. A., Heatherington, L., & Ahn, A. (1992). Gender and the self-presentation of academic achievement. *Sex Roles, 27,* 187–204.

Davison, G. C., & Neale, J. M. (1994). *Abnormal psychology* (6th ed.). New York: Wiley.

DeAngelis, T. (1996). Fathers strongly influenced by culture. *APA Monitor, 26,* 1, 39.

Deane, E. (Executive Producer). (1992). *The Kennedys.* [Film]. (Available from Corporation for Public Broadcasting, 1320 Braddock Place, Alexandria, VA.)

Deaux, K. (1979). Self-evaluations of male and female managers. *Sex Roles, 5,* 571–581.

Deci, E. L. (1971). Effects of externally mediated rewards on intrinsic motivation. *Journal of Personality and Social Psychology, 18,* 105–115.

Deci, E. L. (1975). *Intrinsic motivation.* New York: Plenum.

Demare, D., Lips, H. M., & Briere, J. (1993). Sexually violent pornography, anti-women attitudes, and sexual aggression: A structural equation model. *Journal of Research in Personality, 27,* 285–300.

DeReamer, R. (1980). *Modern safety and health technology.* New York: Wiley.

Derlega, V. J., & Berg, J. H. (1987). *Self-disclosure: Theory, research, and therapy.* New York: Plenum Press.

Derogatis, L. (1988). The unique impact of breast cancer and gynecologic cancers on body image and sexual identity in women. In J. Vaeth (Ed.), *Body image, self-esteem, and sexuality in cancer patients.* Basel: Krager.

Desor, J. A. (1972). Toward a psychological theory of crowding. *Journal of Personality and Social Psychology, 21,* 79–83.

DiAngelis, T. (1996). Exercise gives a lift to psychotherapy. *American Psychological Association Monitor, 27,* 24–25.

Diener, E., Diener, M., & Diener, C. (1995). Factors predicting the subjective well-being of nations. *Journal of Personality and Social Psychology, 69,* 851–864.

Dies, R. R. (1995). Group psychotherapies. In A. Gurman & S. Messer (Eds.). *Essential psychotherapies.* (pp. 488–522). New York: Guilford.

Diggs, P. July 12, 1994. Personal communication.

Dindia, K., & Allen, M. (1992). Sex differences in self-disclosure: A meta-analysis. *Psychological Bulletin, 112,* 106–124.

Dion, K. L., & Dion, K. K. (1988). Romantic love: Individual and cultural perspectives. In R. J. Sternberg & M. L. Barnes (Eds.), *The psychology of love.* New Haven, CT: Yale University Press.

Dipboye, R., Arvey, R., & Terpstra, D. (1977). Sex and physical attractiveness of raters and applicants as determinants of resume evaluations. *Journal of Applied Psychology, 62,* 288–294.

Dipboye, R., Fromkin, H., & Wilbak, K. (1975). Relative importance of applicant sex, attractiveness, and scholastic standing in evaluation of applicant resumes. *Journal of Applied Psychology, 60,* 30–43.

Donat, P. L., & D'Emilio, J. (1992). A feminist redefinition of rape and sexual assault: Historical foundations and change. *Journal of Social Issues, 48,* 9–22.

Donne, J. (1624). *Devotions upon emergent occasions.*

Donnerstein, E., & Berkowitz, L. (1981). Victim reactions in aggressive erotic films as a factor in violence against women. *Journal of Personality and Social Psychology, 41,* 710–724.

Donnerstein, E., Linz, D., & Penrond, S. (1987). *The question of pornography: Research findings and policy implications.* New York: Free Press.

Dornbusch, S., Carlsmith, J. M., Bushwall, S., Ritter, P., Liederman, H., Hastorf, A., & Gross, R. (1985). Single parents, extended households, and the control of adolescents. *Child Development, 56,* 326–341.

Dorris, M. (1989). *The broken cord.* New York: Harper & Row.

Dovidio, J., & Gaertner, S. L. (Eds.). *Prejudice, discrimination and racism.* New York: Academic Press.

Doyle, A. C. (1930). *The Complete Sherlock Holmes.* Garden City, NY: Doubleday.

Doyle, J. A. (1995). *The male experience.* Dubuque, IA: Wm. C. Brown.

Doyle, J. A., & Paludi, M. A. (1995). *Sex and gender.* Madison, WI: Brown and Benchmark.

Dryden, W. (1992). *Integrative and eclectic therapy.* Buckingham, PA: Open Press.

Durand, V. M., & Barlow, D. H. (1997). *Abnormal psychology.* Pacific Grove, CA: Brooks/Cole.

Durkheim, E. (1951). *Suicide: A study in sociology,* trans. J. Spaulding & G. Simpson. New York: Free Press.

Dutton, D., & Aron, A. (1974). Some evidence for heightened sexual attraction under conditions of high anxiety. *Journal of Personality and Social Psychology, 30,* 510–517.

Dutton, D. G. (1992). Theoretical and empirical perspectives on the etiology and prevention of wife assault. In R. V. Peters, R. J. McMahan, & V. L. Quinsey (Eds.), *Aggression and violence throughout the life span* (pp. 191–221). Newbury Park, CA: Sage.

Duvall, E. M. (1977). *Marriage and family development* (5th ed.). Philadelphia: Lippincott.

Eagly, A. H. (1987). *Sex differences in social behavior: A social role interpretation.* Hillsdale, NJ: Erlbaum.

Eagly, A. H. & Wood, W. (1985). Gender and influenciability: Stereotype versus behavior. In V. O'Leary, R. Unger & B. Wallston (Eds.), *Women, gender, and social psychology,* Hillsdale, NJ: Erlbaum.

Eagly, A. H., Ashmore, R. D., Makhijani, M. G., & Longo, L. C. (1991). What is beautiful is good, but...: A meta-analytic review of research on the physical attractiveness stereotype. *Psychology Bulletin, 110,* 107–128.

Eccles, J. (1989). Bringing young women to math and science. In M. Crawford & M. Gentry (Eds.), *Gender and thought* (pp. 36–58). New York: Springer-Verlag.

Edney, J. J. (1975). Territoriality and control: A field experiment. *Journal of Personality and Social Psychology, 31,* 1108–1115.

Edwards, R. (1995, September). Psychologists foster the new definition of family. *APA Monitor, 26,* 38.

Ehrlich, P. (1968). *The population boom.* New York: Ballantine.

Eisenberg, L. (1995). Is the family obsolete? *The Key Reporter, 60,* 1–5.

El-Sheikh, H., & Klaczynski, P. (1993). Cultural variability in stress and control: An investigation of Egyptian middle-class, countryside, and inner-city girls. *Journal of Cross Cultural Psychology, 24,* 81–98.

Ellis, A. (1962). *Reason and emotion in psychotherapy.* New York: Lyle Stuart.

Ellis, A. (1979). The basic clinical theory of rational-emotive therapy. In A. Ellis & R. Grieger (Eds.). *Comprehensive handbook of RET.* New York: Springer.

Ellis, H. D. (1982). The effect of cold on the performance of serial choice reaction time and various discrete tasks. *Human Factors, 24,* 584–598.

Erikson, E. H. (1963) *Childhood & Society.* New York: Norton.

Erikson, E. H. (1968). *Identity: Youth and crisis.* New York: Norton.

Evans, D. A., et al. (1989). Prevalence of Alzheimer's disease in a community population of older persons: Higher than previously reported. *Journal of the American Medical Association, 262,* 2551–2556.

Exercise gives a lift to psychotherapy. (1996, July). *APA Monitor, 27,* 24.

Eysenck, H. J. (1952). The effects of psychotherapy: An evaluation. *Journal of Consulting and Clinical Psychology, 16,* 319–324.

Eysenck, H. J. (1953). *The structure of human personality.* New York: Wiley.

Eysenck, H. J. (1967). *The biological basis of personality.* Springfield, IL: Thomas.

Eysenck, H. J. (1982). *A model for intelligence.* Berlin: Springer-Verlag.

FDA approves Paxil for treating additional disorders. (1996, July). *APA Monitor, 27,* 4.

Fagot, B. I. (1978). The influence of sex of child on parental reactions to toddler children. *Child Development, 49,* 459–465.

Fagot, B. I. (1984a). The consequences of problem behavior in toddler children. *Journal of Abnormal Child Psychology, 12,* 385–396.

Fagot, B. I. (1984b). Teacher and peer reactions to boys' and girls' play styles. *Sex Roles, 11,* 691–702.

Fairburn, C. J., Jones, R., Peveler, R. C., Hope, R. A., & O'Connor, T. (1993). Predictors of 12-month outcome in bulimia nervosa and the influence of attitudes to shape and weight. *Journal of Consulting and Clinical Psychology, 61,* 676–698.

Faller, K. C. (1989). Why sexual abuse: An exploration of the intergenerational hypothesis. *Child Abuse and Neglect, 13,* 543–548.

Fast, I. (1993). Aspects of early gender development: A psychodynamic perspective. In A. E. Beall & R. J. Sternberg (Eds.), *The psychology of gender* (pp. 173–193). New York: Guilford.

Feist, J., & Brannon, L. (1988). *Health psychology.* Belmont, CA: Wadsworth.

Festinger, L. (1954). A theory of social comparison process. *Human Relations, 7,* 117–140.

Festinger, L. (1957). *A theory of cognitive dissonance.* Evanston, IL: Row Paterson.

Festinger, L., Schachter, S., & Back, K. (1950). *Social pressures in informal groups: A study of a housing community.* Stanford, CA: Stanford University Press.

Fiedler, F. E. (1978). Recent developments in research on the contingency model. In L. Berkowitz (Ed.), *Group process.* New York: Academic Press.

Fisher, J., Bell, P., & Baum, A. (1984). *Environmental psychology.* New York: Holt, Rinehart and Winston.

Fisher, J., & Byrne, D. (1975). Too close for comfort: Sex differences in responses to invasions of personal space. *Journal of Personality and Social Psychology, 32,* 15–21.

Fisher, J., & Fisher, W. (1992). Changing AIDS risk behavior. *Psychological Bulletin, 111,* 455–474.

Fishman, C. (1988). *Treating troubled adolescents.* New York: Basic.

Fiske, S. T., & Taylor, S. E. (1991). *Social cognition.* New York: McGraw-Hill.

Fitzgerald, L. (1993). Sexual harrassment: Violence against women in the workplace. *American Psychologist, 48,* 1070–1076.

Ford, C., & Beach, F. A. (1951). *Patterns of sexual behavior.* New York: Paul Hoeber.

Forsyth, D. (1990). *An introduction to group dynamics* (2nd ed.). Pacific Grove, CA: Brooks/Cole.

Foster, M. (1990). A closer look at the relationship between interviewer–interviewee similarity and ratings in a selection interview. *Applied H. R. M. Research, 1,* 23–26.

Frank, J. D. (1961). *Persuasion and healing.* Baltimore, MD: Johns Hopkins Press.

Freeman, A., Pretzer, J., Fleming, B., & Simon, K. M. (1990). *Clinical applications of cognitive therapy.* New York: Plenum.

French, H. W. Psychiatry's terra incognita: healing in Africa. *New York Times,* December 1, 1995, Section A, Page 4.

French, J., & Raven, B. (1959). The bases of social power. In D. Cartwright (Ed.), *Studies in social power.* Ann Arbor, MI: University of Michigan Press.

Freud, A. (1946). *The ego and the mechanisms of defense.* New York: International Universities Press. [First German Edition, 1936.]

Freud, S. (1940). *An outline of psychoanalysis.* In Vol. 23 of the *Standard edition.* London: Hogarth.

Frey, K. S., & Ruble, D. N. (1987). What children say about classroom performance: Sex and grade differences in perceived competence. *Child Development, 58,* 1066–1078.

Fried, S. (1993). *Thing of beauty: The tragedy of superstar Gia.* New York: Simon & Schuster.

Friedman, M., & Rosenman, R. (1974). *Type A behavior and your heart.* New York: Knopf.

Frieze, I. H. (1983). Investigating the causes and consequences of marital rape. *Signs, 8,* 532–553.

Fromm, E. (1956). *The art of loving.* New York: Harper & Row.

Fry, A., & Willis, F. (1971). Invasion of personal space as a function of age of the invader. *Psychological Record, 21,* 383–389.

Fulmer, R. M. (1977). *Practical human relations.* Homewood, IL: Irwin.

Fulmer, R. M. (1988). Lower-income and professional families: A comparison of structure and life cycle processes. In B. Carter & M. McGoldrick (Eds.), *The changing family life cycle* (pp. 545–578). New York: Gardner.

Funder, D. C. (1995). On the accuracy of personality judgement: A realistic approach. *Psychological Review, 102,* 652–670.

Gaertner, S., Mann, J., Dovidio, J., Murell, A., & Pomare, M. (1990). How does cooperation reduce intergroup bias? *Journal of Personality and Social Psychology, 59,* 692–704.

Gaines, D. (1994, June 2). Suicidal tendencies: Kurt did not die for you. *Rolling Stone, 59–61.*

Garcia-Coll, C. (1990). Developmental outcome of minority infants: A process-oriented look at our beginnings. *Child Development, 61,* 270–289.

Garn, S. M. (1975). Bone loss and aging. In R. Goldman & M. Rockstein (Eds.), *The physiology and pathology of human aging.* New York: Academic Press.

Garner, D. M., Garfinkel, P. E., Schwartz, D., & Thompson, M. (1980). Cultural expectation of thinness in women. *Psychological Reports, 47,* 483–491.

Gatchel, R. & Baum, A. (1983). *Introduction to health psychology.* Reading, MA: Addison-Wesley.

Gatz, M., & Hurwicz, M. L. (1990). Are old people more depressed? Cross-sectional data on Center for Epidemiological Studies depression scale factors. *Psychology and Aging, 5,* 284–290.

Geen, R., & O'Neal, E. (1969). Activation of cue-elicited aggression by general arousal. *Journal of Personality and Social Psychology, 11,* 289–292.

Gelles, R. J., & Cornell, C. P. (1985). *Intimate violence in families.* Beverly Hills, CA: Sage.

Gergen, K. J. (1971). *The concept of self.* New York: Holt, Rinehart and Winston.

Gerrard, M. (1982). Sex, sex guilt, and contraceptive use. *Journal of Personality and Social Psychology, 42,* 153–158.

Giambra, L. M., & Martin, C. E. (1977). Sexual daydreams and quantitative aspects of sexual activity: Some relations for males across adulthood. *Archives of Sexual Behavior, 6,* 497–505.

Gifford, R., & O'Conner, B. (1986). Nonverbal intimacy: Clarifying the role of seating distance and orientation. *Journal of Nonverbal Behavior, 10,* 207–214.

Gilbert, D. T., Giesler, R. B., & Morris, K. A. (1995). When comparisons arise. *Journal of Personality and Social Psychology, 69,* 227–236.

Gilligan, C. (1982). *In a different voice.* Cambridge, MA: Harvard University Press.

Gilligan, C. (1977). *In a different voice: Psychological theory and women's development.* Cambridge, MA: Harvard University Press.

Gilmore, M. (1994). *Shot in the heart.* New York: Doubleday.

Gilmore, M. (1994, June 2). The road from nowhere: Walking the streets of Aberdeen. *Rolling Stone,* 44–46.

Ginsberg, E. (1966). *The development of human resources.* New York: McGraw Hill.

Glass, D., & Singer, J. (172). *Urban stress: Experiments on noise and social stressors.* New York: Academic Press.

Glenn, N. (1975). Psychological well-being in the postparental stage: Some evidence from national surveys. *Journal of Marriage and the Family, 37,* 105–110.

Glick, P. C. (1984). Marriage, divorce, and living arrangements: Prospective changes. *Journal of Family Issues, 46,* 563–576.

Goethals, G. R., & Darley, J. M. (1977). Social comparison theory: An attributional approach. In J. M. Suls & R. L. Miller (Eds.), *Social comparison process: Theoretical and empirical perspectives.* Washington, DC: Hemisphere/Halsted.

Goethals, G. R., Messick, D. M., & Allison, S. T. (1991). The uniqueness bias: Studies of constructive social comparison. In J. Suls & T. A. Wills (Eds.), *Social comparison: Contemporary theory and research.* Hillsdale, NJ: Erlbaum.

Goffman, E. (1955). On face-work: An analysis of ritual elements in social interaction. *Psychiatry, 18,* 213–231.

Goffman, E. (1959) *The presentation of self in everyday life.* Garden City, NY: Anchor Books.

Goffman, E. (1967). *Interaction ritual: Essays on face-to-face behavior.* Garden City, NY: Doubleday.

Gold, J. (1994, June). Into the black. *Spin, 10,* 38–40.

Golde, P., & Kogan, N. (1959). A sentence completion procedure for assessing attitudes toward old people. *Journal of Gerontology, 14,* 355–363.

Goldstein, M. J., & Miklowitz, D. J. (1995). The effectiveness of psychoeducational family therapy in the treatment of schizophrenic disorders. *Journal of Marital and Family Therapy, 21,* 361–376.

Goodwin, F. K., & Jamison, K. R. (1990). *Manic–depressive illness.* New York: Oxford University Press.

Gottesman, I. (1991). *Schizophrenia genesis.* New York: Freeman.

Gould, M., Wunch-Hitzig, R., & Dohrenwend, D. (1981). Estimating the prevalence of childhood psychopathology. *Journal of the American Academy of Child Psychiatry, 20,* 462–476.

Gray, J. (1994). *Men are from Mars, women are from Venus.* Hampton: Chivers North America.

Greenberg, L. S., & Safran, J. D. (1987). *Emotion in psychotherapy.* New York: Guilford.

Greene, A. (1972). *The last captive.* Austin: Encino Press.

Greeno, C. G. (1989). Gender differences in children's proximity to adults. Unpublished doctoral dissertation. Stanford University, Stanford, CA.

Greenwald, A. G. (1980). The totalitarian ego: Fabrication and revision of personal history. *American Psychology, 35,* 603–613.

Griffitt, W. & Gray, P. (1969). "Object" evaluation and conditioned affect. *Journal of Experimental Research in Personality, 4,* 1–8.

Groth, A. N., & Birnbaum, H. J. (1979). *Men who rape: The psychology of the offender.* New York: Plenum.

Groth, A. N., Burgess, A. W., & Halmstrom, L. L. (1977). Rape: Power, anger, and sexuality. *American Journal of Psychiatry, 134,* 1239–1243.

Gruber, V., & Wildman, B. (1987). The impact of dysmenorrhea on daily activity. *Behavior Research and Therapy, 25,* 123–128.

Guccione, B. (1994, June). Top spin. *Spin, 10,* 16.

Gump, B. B., & Kulik, J. A. (1995). The effect of a model's HIV status on self-perceptions: A self-protective similarity bias. *Personality and Social Psychology Bulletin, 21,* 827–833.

Hall, E. T. (1959). *The silent language.* New York: Fawcett.

Hall, E. T. (1966). *The hidden dimension.* New York: Doubleday.

Hall, J. A., & Braunwald, K. G. (1981). Gender cues in conversation. *Journal of Personality and Social Psychology, 40,* 99–110.

Hamilton, N. (1992). *JFK.* New York: Random House.

Hammerschlag, C. (1988). *Dancing healers.* New York: Harper and Row.

Hardin, G. (1968). The tragedy of the commons. *Science, 162,* 1243–1248.

Hare-Mustin, R., & Maracek, J. (1988). The meaning of difference: gender theory, post-modernism, and psychology. *American Psychologist, 43,* 455–464.

Hare-Mustin, R., & Maracek, J. (Eds.). (1990). *Making a difference: psychology and the construction of gender.* New Haven, CT: Yale University Press.

Harkins, E. (1978). Effects of the empty nest transition: A self-report of psychological well-being. *Journal of Marriage and the Family, 40,* 549–556.

Harlow, H. (1971). *Learning to love.* New York: Albion.

Harnish, R. J., Abbey, A., & DeBono, K. G. (1990). Toward an understanding of "the sex game": The effects of gender and self-monitoring on perceptions of sexuality and likability in initial interaction. *Journal of Applied Social Psychology, 20,* 1333–1344.

Harragan, B. L. (1987). *Games mother never taught you: Corporate gamesmanship for women.* New York: Warner.

Harries, K., & Stadler, S. (1988). Heat and violence: New findings from Dallas field data. *Environment and Behavior, 18,* 346–368.

Harris, R., & Lindsay, D. (1972). *The state of cities.* New York: Praeger.

Hastorf, A., & Cantril, H. (1954). They saw a game: A case study. *Journal of Abnormal and Social Psychology, 49,* 129–134.

Hatfield, E. (1988). Passionate and companionate love. In R. J. Sternberg & M. L. Barnes (Eds.), *The psychology of love.* New Haven, CT: Yale University Press.

Hatfield, E., & Sprecher, S. (1986). *Mirror, mirror ... The importance of looks in everyday life.* Albany, New York: State University of New York Press.

Hatfield, E., Sprecher, S., & Traupmann, J. (1978). Men's and women's reactions to sexually explicit films: A serendipitous finding. *Archives of Sexual Behavior, 7,* 583–592.

Hatfield, E., Utne, M. K., & Traupmann, J. (1979). Equity theory and intimate relationships. In R. L. Burgess & T. L. Huston (Eds.), *Social exchange in developing relationships.* New York: Academic Press.

Hayduk, L. (1983). Personal space: Where do we now stand? *Psychological Bulletin, 94,* 293–335.

Heatherington, L., Daubman, K. A., Bates, C., Ahn, A., Brown, H., & Preston, C. (1993). Two investigations of "female modesty" in achievement situations. *Sex Roles, 29,* 739–753.

Heatherton, T., & Weinberger, J. (1994). *Can personality change?* Washington, DC: American Psychological Association.

Heerwagen, J. H. (1990). Affective functioning, "light hunger," and room brightness preferences. *Environment & Behavior, 22* (5), 608–635.

Heider, F. (1944). Social perception and phenomenal causality. *Psychological Review, 51,* 358–374.

Heilman, M., & Herlihy, J. (1984). Affirmative reaction, negative reaction? Some modifying considerations. *Organizational Behavior and Human Performance, 33,* 204–213.

Helmreich, R., Spence, J., & Pred, R. (1988). Making it without losing it: Type A, achievement motivation, and scientific attainment revisited. *Personality and Social Psychology Bulletin, 14,* 495–504.

Hendricks, J., & Hendricks, C. D. (1975). *Aging in mass society.* Cambridge, MA: Winthrop.

Henley, N. M. (1989). Molehill or mountain? What we know and don't know about sex bias in language. In M. Crawford & M. Gentry (Eds.), *Gender and thought* (pp. 59–78). New York: Springer-Verlag.

Henley, N. M. (1977). *Body politics.* Englewood Cliffs, NJ: Prentice-Hall.

Henley, N. M., Gruber, B., & Lerner, L. (1988). Effects of masculine generic usage on attitudes and self-esteem. Unpublished manuscript.

Hepworth, J. T., & West, S. G. (1988). Lynchings and the economy: A time-series reanalysis of Hovland and Sears (1940). *Journal of Personality and Social Psychology, 55,* 239–247.

Herriot, J. (1972). *All creatures great and small.* New York: Bantam Books.

Hersher, L. (Ed.), (1970). *Four psychotherapies.* New York: Appleton-Century-Crofts.

Hessen-McInnes, H., & Fitzgerald, L. (1992). Modeling sexual harrassment: A preliminary analysis. Paper presented at APA/NIOSH Conference on Stress in the 90's. Washington, DC.

Heston, L. L., & White, J. A. (1991). *The vanishing mind: A practical guide to Alzheimer's disease and other dementias.* New York: W. H. Freeman.

Hetherington, E. M. (1972). Effects of father absence of personality development in adolescent daughters. *Developmental Psychology, 7,* 313–326.

Hetherington, E. M. (1993). Virginia longitudinal study of divorce and remarriage. *Journal of Family Psychology, 7,* 39–56.

Higgins, T. (1990). Personality, social psychology, and person-situation relations: Standards and knowledge activation as common language. In L. Pervin (Ed.), *Handbook of personality: Theory and research.* New York: Guilford.

Hill, C. T., & Stull, D. E. (1987). Gender and self-disclosure: Strategies for exploring the issues. In V. J. Derlega & J. H. Berg (Eds.), *Self-disclosure: Theory, research, and therapy.* New York: Plenum.

Hinkle, S., & Scholpler, J. (1986). Bias in the evaluation of in-group and out-group performance. In S. Worchel, & W. Austin (Eds.), *Psychology of intergroup relations.* Chicago: Nelson Hall.

Hite, S. (1976). *The Hite report: A nationwide study of female sexuality.* New York: Macmillan.

Hobart, C. W. (1958, May). The incidence of romanticism during courtship. *Social Forces, 36,* 363–367.

Hochschild, A. (1989). *The second shift.* New York: Viking.

Hoffman, R. (1995). Ten reasons you should use 360-degree feedback. *HR Magazine, 40,* 82–85.

Hofling, C., Brotzman, K., Dalrymple, S., Graves, N., & Pierce, C. (1966). An experimental study of nurse-physician relationships. *Journal of Nervous and Mental Disease, 143,* 171–180.

Hofstede, G. (1980). *Culture's consequences: International differences in work-related values.* Beverly Hills, CA: Sage.

Hofstede, G. (1986). Cultural differences in teaching and learning. *International Journal of Intercultural Relations, 10,* 301–320.

Hofstede, G. (1991). *Culture and organizations: Software of the mind.* London: McGraw Hill.

Hollander, E. P. (1985). Leadership and power. In G. Lindzey and E. Aronson (Eds.), *Handbook of social psychology* (3rd ed.). New York: Random House.

Holmes, T., & Masuda, M. (1974). Life change and illness susceptibility. In B. Dohrenwend & B. Dohrenwend (Eds.), *Stressful life events: Their nature and effects.* New York: Wiley.

Holmes, T., & Rahe, R. (1967). The social readjustment rating scale. *Journal of Psychosomatic Research, 11,* 213–218.

Horvath, A. O., & Greenberg, L. S. (1994). *The working alliance.* New York: Wiley.

Horvath, A. O. (1995). The therapeutic relationship: From transference to alliance. *In Session: Psychotherapy in Practice, 1,* 7–17.

Howard, J. W., & Dawes, R. M. (1976). Linear prediction of marital happiness. *Personality and Social Psychology Bulletin, 2,* 478–480.

Huffcutt, A., & Arthur, W. (1994). Hunter and Hunter (1984) revised: Interview validity for entry-level jobs. *Journal of Applied Psychology, 79*, 184–190.

Hunt, M. (1974). *Sexual behavior in the 1970s.* Chicago: Playboy Press.

Hurt, H. (1975). The hottest place in the whole U.S.A. *Texas Monthly, 3*, 50ff.

Hyde, C. (1986). Ethics, religion, and sexuality. In Hyde, J. S. *Understanding human sexuality.* New York: McGraw-Hill.

Hyde, J. (1981). How large are cognitive differences? *American Psychologist, 36*, 892–901.

Hyde, J., Fennema, E., & Lamon, S. J. (1990). Gender differences in mathematics performance: A meta-analysis. *Psychological Bulletin, 107*, 139–155.

Hyde, J., & Linn, M. (1988). Gender differences in verbal ability: A meta-analysis. *Psychological Bulletin, 104*, 53–69.

Iaffaldano, M., & Muschensky, P. (1985). Job satisfaction and job performance: A meta-analysis. *Psychological Bulletin, 97*, 251–273.

Inaba, D. S., & Cohen, W. E. (1990). *Uppers, downers, and all arounders.* San Francisco: CNS Productions.

Insko, C. & associates (1980). Social evolution and the emergence of leadership. *Journal of Personality and Social Psychology, 39*, 431–439.

Ittleson, W., Proshansky, H. Rivlin, L., & Winkel, G. (1974). *An introduction to environmental psychology.* New York: Holt, Rinehart and Winston.

James, W. (1908). *The principles of psychology.* New York: Holt.

Jamison, K. (1993). *Touched with fire: Manic–depressive illness and the artistic temperament.* New York: Free Press.

Jamison, K. (1995). *An unquiet mind.* New York: Knopf.

Janis, I. (1972). *Victims of groupthink: A psychological study of policy decisions and fiascos.* Boston: Houghton Mifflin.

Janis, I. (1982). *Groupthink* (2nd ed.). Boston: Houghton Mifflin.

Jecker, J., & Landy, D. (1969). Liking a person as a function of doing him a favor. *Human Relations, 22*, 371–378.

Johnson, B. D. (1991, May 13). Madonna: The world's hottest star speaks her mind. *Maclean's, 104*, 44–49.

Johnston, L., Bachman, J., & O'Malley, P. (1992). Student drug use, attitudes, and beliefs: National trends 1975–1992. Rockville, MD: National Institute on Drug Abuse.

Jones, E. E. (1990). *Interpersonal perception.* New York: Freeman.

Jones, A. & Crandall, R. (1986). Validation of a short index of self-actualization. *Personality and Social Psychology Bulletin, 12*, 63–73.

Jones, E. E. (1964). *Ingratiation.* New York: Appleton-Century-Crofts.

Jones, E. E., & Nisbett, R. E. (1971). *The actor and the observer: Divergent perceptions of the causes of behavior.* Morristown, NJ: General Learning Press.

Jones, E. E., Rock, L., Shaver, K. G., Goethals, G. R., & Ward, L. M. (1968). Pattern performance and ability attribution: An unexpected primacy effect. *Journal of Personality and Social Psychology, 10*, 317–341.

Jordan, J., Kaplan, A., Miller, J. B., Stiver, I., & Surrey, J. (1991). *Women's growth in connection.* New York: Guilford.

Jourard, S. M. (1971). *Self-disclosure: An experimental analysis of the transparent self.* New York: Wiley.

Jourard, S. M., & Freidman, R. (1970). Experimenter-subject distance and self-disclosure. *Journal of Personality and Social Psychology, 25*, 278–282.

Jung, C. G. (1971). Psychological types. In H. Read, M. Fordham, & G. Adler (Eds.), *Collected works. Vol. 6.* Princeton, NJ: Princeton University Press. (Originally published 1921.)

Jung, C. G. (1960). The structure and dynamics of the psyche. In *The Collected Works* (Vol. 8). New York: Pantheon.

Jussim, L., Eccles, J., & Madon, S. (1996). Social perception, social stereotypes, and teacher expectations: Accuracy and the quest for the powerful self-fulfilling prophecy. In M. P. Zanna (Ed.), *Advances in Experimental Social Psychology, Vol. 28* (pp. 281–388). Boston: Academic Press.

Kalish, R. A. (1982). *Late adulthood: Perspectives on human development.* Monterey, CA: Brooks/Cole.

Kanfer, R., Ackerman, P., Murtha, T., Dugdale, B., & Nelson, L. (1994). Goal setting, conditions of practice, and task performance: A resource allocation perspective. *Journal of Applied Psychology, 79*, 826–835.

Kaniasty, K., & Norris, E. (1993). A test of a social support deterioration model in the context of a natural disaster. *Journal of Personality and Social Psychology, 64,* 395–408.

Kaplan, A., Aamodt, M., & Wilk, D. (1991). The relationship between advertising variables and applicant responses to newspapers advertisements. *Journal of Business and Psychology, 5,* 383–395.

Karasawa, K. (1995). An attributional analysis of reactions to negative emotions. *Personality and Social Psychology Bulletin, 21,* 456–467.

Karney, B. J., Bradbury, T. N., Fincham, F. D., & Sullivan, K. T. (1994). The role of negative affectivity in the association between attributions and marital satisfaction. *Journal of Personality and Social Psychology, 66,* 413–424.

Kaslow, N. J. & Celano, M. P. (1995). The family therapies. In A. S. Gurman & S. B. Messer (Eds.), *Essential psychotherapies* (pp. 343–402). New York: Guilford.

Kassin, S. (1995). *Psychology.* Boston: Houghton Mifflin Company.

Kaufman, J., & Zigler, E. (1987). Do abused children become abusive parents? *American Journal of Orthopsychiatry, 57,* 186–191.

Kelley, H. H. (1950). The warm-cold variable in first impressions of persons. *Journal of Personality, 18,* 431–439.

Kelley, H. H., & Thibaut, J. W. (1978). *Interpersonal relations: A theory of interdependence.* New York: Wiley Interscience.

Kelman, H. C., & Hamilton, V. L. (1989). *Crime of obedience.* New Haven, CT: Yale University Press.

Kenrick, D. T. (1994). Evolutionary social psychology: From sexual selection to social cognition. *Advances in Experimental Social Psychology, 26,* 75–121.

Kenrick, D. T., Sadalla, E. K., Groth, G., & Trost, M. R. (1990) Evolution, traits, and the stages of human courtship. *Journal of Personality, 58,* 97–116.

Kenrick, D. T., & Trost, M. R. (1993). The evolutionary perspective. In A. E. Beall and R. J. Sternberg (Eds.), *The psychology of gender.* New York: Guilford.

Kernis, M., & Wheeler, L. (1981). Beautiful friends and ugly strangers: Radiation and contrast effects in perception of same-sex pairs. *Personality and Social Psychology Bulletin, 7,* 617–620.

Kessler, I. I. (1979). On the etiology and prevention of cervical cancer. A status report. *Obstetrics and Gynecological Survey, 34,* 790–794.

Kinarty, E. L. (1975). The effect of seating position on performance and personality in a college classroom. Unfinished doctoral dissertation.

Kinder, D. R., & Sears, D. O. (1981). Prejudice and politics: Symbolic racism versus racial threats to a good life. *Journal of Personality and Social Psychology, 40,* 414–431.

Kinsey, A. C., Pomeroy, W. B., & Martin, C. E. (1948). *Sexual behavior in the human male.* Philadelphia: W. B. Saunders.

Kinsey, A. C., Pomeroy, W. B., Martin, C. E., & Gebhard, P. H. (1953). *Sexual behavior in the human female.* Philadelphia: W. B. Saunders.

Kipnis, D. (1992). Does behavior traditionally change practitioners' behaviors as well as the behaviors of people they are trying to help? In S. Worchel, W. Wood & J. Simpson (Eds.), *Group process and productivity.* Newbury Park, CA: Sage.

Klimoski, R., & Strickland, W. (1987). Assessment centers—validity or merely prescient? *Personnel Psychology, 30,* 191–202.

Kobasa, S., Hilker, R., & Maddi, S. (1979). Who stays healthy under stress? *Journal of Occupational Medicine, 21,* 595–598.

Kohlberg, L. (1981). *Essays on moral development: Vol. 1. The philosophy of moral development.* New York: Harper & Row.

Kohlberg, L. (1984). *Essays on moral development: Vol. 2. The psychology of moral development.* New York: Harper & Row.

Konecni, V. (1975). The mediation of aggressive behavior: Arousal level versus anger and cognitive labeling. *Journal of Personality and Social Psychology, 32,* 706–712.

Kornhauser, A. (1965). *Mental health of the industrial worker.* New York: Wiley.

Koss, M. Dinero, T. E., Seibel, C., & Cox, S. (1988). Stranger and acquaintance rape: Are there differences in the victim's experience? *Psychology of Women Quarterly, 12,* 1–23.

Koss-Chioino, J. D., & Canive, Jose J. M. (1995). Cultural issues in relational diagnosis: Hispanics in the United States. In F. Kaslow (Ed.), *Handbook of relational diagnosis and dysfunctional family patterns* (pp. 137–151). New York: Guilford.

Kramer, P. (1993). *Listening to Prozac—A psychiatrist explores mood-altering drugs and the meaning of the self.* New York: Viking.

Krestan, J., & Bepko, C. (1980). The problem of fusion in the lesbian relationship. *Family Process, 19,* 277–290.

Kroeber, T. C. (1963). The coping functions of the ego mechanisms In R. W. White (Ed.), *The study of lives.* New York: Atherton Press.

Lakoff, R. (1975). *Language and women's place.* New York: Harper & Row.

Lamb, M. (1986). *The father's role: Applied perspectives.* New York: Wiley.

Landy, D., & Aronson, E. (1969). The influence of the character of the criminal and his victim on the decisions of simulated jurors. *Journal of Experimental Social Psychology, 5,* 141–152.

Landy, D., & Sigall, H. (1974). Beauty is talent: Task evaluation as a function of the performer's physical attractiveness. *Journal of Personality and Social Psychology, 30,* 299–304.

Langer, E. J. (1989). *Mindfulness.* Reading, MA: Addison-Wesley.

Langer, E., & Rodin, J. (1976). The effects of choice and enhanced personal responsibility for the aged: A field experiment in an institutional setting. *Journal of Personality and Social Psychology, 34,* 191–198.

Langer, E., Janis, I., & Wolfer, J. (1976). Reduction of psychological stress in surgical patients. *Journal of Experimental Social Psychology, 11,* 155–165.

Larazus, R. (1981, July). Little hassles can be hazardous to health. *Psychology Today,* 58–62.

Lash, J. P. (1971). *Eleanor and Franklin: The story of their relationship, based on Eleanor Roosevelt's private papers.* New York: Norton.

Lauer, J. C., & Lauer, R. H. (1985, June). Marriages made to last. *Psychology Today,* pp. 22–26.

Lazarus, R. (1993). From psychological stress to the emotions: A history of changing moods. *Annual Review of Psychology, 44,* 1–21.

Lazarus, R., & Delongis, A. (1983). Psychological stress and coping in aging. *American Psychology, 38,* 245–254.

Lazarus, R., & Folkman, S. (1987). Coping and adaptation. In W. Gentry (Ed.), *The Handbook of Behavioral Medicine.* New York: Guilford.

Leary, M. R. (1995). *Self-presentation: Impression management and interpersonal behavior.* Dubuque, IA: Brown & Benchmark.

Lecuyer, R. (1976). Man's accommodation to space. *Travail Humain, 39,* 195–206.

Leeper, M., Green, D., & Nisbett, R. (1973). Undermining children's intrinsic interest with extrinsic rewards: A test of the "overjustification" hypothesis. *Journal of Personality and Social Psychology, 28,* 129–137.

Leff, J. P. (1976). Schizophrenia and sensitivity to the family environment. *Schizophrenia Bulletin, 2,* 566–74.

Leff, J. P., & Vaughn, C. E. (1985). *Expressed emotion in families: Its significance for mental illness.* New York: Guilford.

Leigh, B., & Stall, R. (1993). Substance abuse and risky sexual behavior for exposure to HIV virus: Issues, methodology, and prevention. *American Psychologist, 48,* 1035–1045.

Leisor, B. M. (1979). *Liberty, justice, and morals: Contemporary value conflicts* (2nd ed.). New York: Macmillan.

Leland, J. (August 26, 1996). The fear of heroin is shooting up. *Newsweek,* pp. 55–56.

Lenney, E. (1977). Women's self-confidence in achievement settings. *Psychological Bulletin, 84,* 1–13.

Leo, J. (1987, January 12). Exploring the traits of twins. *Time,* p. 63.

Lerner, M. J. (1970). The desire for justice and reactions to victims. In J. Macauley & L. Berkowitz (Eds.), *Altruism and helping behavior.* New York: Academic Press.

LeVay, S. (1993). *The sexual brain.* Cambridge, MA: MIT Press.

LeVay, S. & Hamer, D. H. (1994). Evidence for a biological influence in male homosexuality. *Scientific American, 270* (5), 44–49.

Levin, R. J., & Levin, A. (1975, September). Sexual pleasure: The surprising preferences of 100,000 women. *Redbook,* pp. 51–58.

Levine, P. (1996). Eating disorders and their impact on family systems. In F. W. Kaslow (Ed.), *Handbook of relational diagnosis and dysfunctional family patterns* (pp. 463–476). New York: Wiley.

Levinger, F. (1983). Development and change. In H. Kelley et al., *Close relationships.* San Francisco: Freeman, 1983.

Levinson, D. J. (1978). *The seasons of a man's life.* New York: Knopf.

Levinson, D. J. (1985). The life cycle. In H. I. Kaplan & B. J. Sadock (Eds.), *Comprehensive text-*

book of psychiatry/IV. Baltimore, MD: Williams & Wilkins.

Levinson, D. J. (1986). A conception of adult development. *American Psychologist, 41,* 3–13.

Levitt, E. E., & Klassen, A. D., Jr. (1973). *Public attitudes toward sexual behaviors: The latest investigation of the institute for sex research.* Bloomington: Indiana University Press.

Lewinsohn, P. M. (1975). Engagement in pleasant activities and depression level. *Journal of Abnormal Psychology, 84,* 718–721.

Lieberman-Cline, N. (1992). *Lady magic.* Champaign, IL: Sagamore.

Linehan, M. M., & Kehrer, C. A. (1993). Borderline personality disorder. In D. H. Barlow (Ed.), *Clinical handbook of psychological disorders: A step-by-step treatment manual.* (2nd ed.). New York: Guilford.

Linville, P. W. (1982). The complexity-extremity effect and age-based stereotyping. *Journal of Personality and Social Psychology, 42,* 193–211.

Lips, H. (1988). *Sex and gender.* Mountain View, CA: Mayfield.

Lipsey, M., & Wilson, D. (1993). The efficacy of psychological, educational, and behavioral treatment: Confirmation from meta-analysis. *American Psychologist, 48,* 1181–1209.

Locke, E. A. (1976). The nature and causes of job satisfaction. In M. Dunnette (Ed.), *Handbook of industrial and organizational psychology.* Chicago: Rand McNally.

Locke, E. A., & Latham, G. (1990). *A theory of goal setting and task performance.* Englewood Cliffs, NJ: Prentice Hall.

Loftus, E. F. (1979). The malleability of human memory. *American Scientist, 67,* 313–320.

Loftus, E. F., & Klinger, M. R. (1992). Is the unconscious smart or dumb? *American Psychologist, 47,* 761–765.

Long, G. (1984). Psychological tension and closeness to others: Stress and interpersonal distance preferences. *Journal of Psychology, 117,* 143–146.

Lott, A. J., & Lott, B. E. (1974). The role of reward in the formation of positive interpersonal attitudes. In T. Huston (Ed.), *Foundations of interpersonal attraction.* New York: Academic Press.

Lowenthal, M. F. (1972). Some potentialities to a life cycle approach to the study of retirement. In F. Carp (Ed.), *Retirement.* New York: Behavior Publications.

Luft, J. (1969). *Of human interaction.* Palo Alto, CA: National Press Books.

Lynch, K. (1960). *The image of the city.* Cambridge, MA: MIT Press.

Lynn, M., & Oldenquist, A. (1986). Egoistic and nonegoistic motives in social dilemmas. *American Psychologist, 41,* 529–534.

Lytton, H., & Romney, D. (1991). Parent's differential socialization of boys and girls: A meta-analysis. *Psychological Bulletin, 109,* 267–296.

MacLeish, A. (1965). *The Eleanor Roosevelt story.* Boston: Houghton-Mifflin.

Madden, M. E. (1987). Perceived control and power in marriage: A study of marital decision making and performance. *Personality and Social Psychology Bulletin, 13,* 73–82.

Maccoby, E. E. (1990). Gender and relationships: A developmental account. *American Psychologist, 45,* 513–520.

Maccoby, E. E., Buchanan, C. M., Mnookin, R. H. & Dornbusch, S. M. (1993). Postdivorce roles of mothers and fathers in the lives of their children. *Journal of Family Psychology, 7,* 24–38.

Maccoby, E. E., & Jacklin, C. N. (1974). *The psychology of sex differences.* Stanford, CA: Stanford University Press.

Maddux, J. E., & Rogers, R. W. (1983). Protection motivation and self-efficacy: A revised theory of fear appeals and attitude change. *Journal of Experimental Social Psychology, 19,* 469–479.

Madigan, S. (1994). Body politics. *Family Therapy Networker, 18,* 27.

Madey, S. DePalma, M., Bahrt, A. & Beirne, J. (1993). The effects of perceived patient responsibility on characterlogical, behavioral, and quality-of-care assessments. *Basic and Applied Social Psychology, 14,* 193–214.

Madonna (1992). *Sex.* New York: Warner Books.

Mahler, M. (1979). *The selected papers of Margaret Mahler* (Vols. 1, 2, 3). New York: Jason Aronson.

Maier, R. A. (1984). *Human sexuality in perspective.* Chicago: Nelson-Hall.

Major, B., Cozzarelli, C., Sciacchitaro, A., Cooper, M., Testa, M., & Mueller, P. (1990). Perceived social supports, self-efficacy, and adjustment to abortion. *Journal of Personality and Social Psychology, 59,* 452–463.

Major, B., McFarlane, D., & Gagnon, D. (1984). Overworked and underpaid. *Journal of Personality and Social Psychology, 47,* 1399–1412.

Major, B., & Testa, M. (1989). Social comparison processes and judgments of entitlement and satisfaction. *Journal of Experimental Social Psychology, 25*, 101–120.

Malamuth, N. (1984). Violence against women: Cultural and individual cases. In N. Malamuth & E. Donnerstein (Eds.), *Pornography and sexual aggression.* New York: Academic Press.

Malinowski, B. (1941) Man's culture and man's behaviour. *Sigma Xi Quarterly, 29*, Nos. 3, 4.

Marcia, J. E. (1966). Development and validation of ego identity status. *Journal of Personality and Social Psychology, 3*, 551–558.

Marcia, J. E. (1980). Identity in adolescence. In J. Adelson (Ed.), *Handbook of adolescent psychology.* New York: Wiley.

Marks, G., Miller, N., & Maruyama, G. (1981). Effect of targets' physical attractiveness on assumptions of similarity. *Journal of Personality and Social Psychology, 41*(1), 198–206.

Mas, C. H., Alexander, J. F., & Turner, C. W. (1991). Dispositional attributions and defensive behavior in high- and low-conflict delinquent families. *Journal of Family Psychology, 5*, 176–191.

Maslow, A. H. (1954). *Motivation and personality.* New York: Harper & Row.

Maslow, A. H. (1970). *Motivation and personality* (2nd ed.). New York: Harper & Row.

Masters, W. H., & Johnson, V. E. (1966). *Human sexual response.* Boston: Little, Brown.

Masters, W. H., & Johnson, V. E. (1970). *Human sexual inadequacy.* Boston: Little, Brown.

Mathews, K. & Cannon, L. (1975). Environmental noise level as a determinant of helping behavior. *Journal of Personality and Social Psychology, 32*, 571–577.

Mathias, B. (1986). Lifting the shade on family violence. *Family Therapy Networker, 10*, 20–29.

Matsomoto, D. (1996). *Culture and psychology.* Pacific Grove, CA: Brooks/Cole.

Matsumoto, D., & Fletcher, D. (1994). Cultural influences on disease. Unpublished paper, San Francisco State University. [Cited in Matsumoto, 1996.]

Matthews, K., & Rodin, J. (1989). Women's changing work role: Impact on health, family, and public policy. *American Psychologist, 44*, 1389–1393.

McAdams, D. P. (1990). *The person: An introduction to personality psychology.* New York: Harcourt Brace Jovanovich.

McBroom, W. H. (1981). Parental relationships, socioeconomic status, and sex role expectations. *Sex Roles, 7*, 1027–1033.

McCaul, K., Sandgern, A., & O'Neill, L. & Hinz, V. (1993). The value of the theory of planned behavior, perceived control, and self-efficacy expectations for predicting health-protective behaviors. *Basic and Applied Social Psychology, 14*, 221–252.

McCollough, P., & Rutenberg, S. (1989). Launching children and moving on. In B. Carter & M. McGoldrick (Eds.), *The changing family life cycle* (pp. 285–310). New York: Gardner Press.

McConahay, J. B. (1986). Modern racism, ambivalence and the Modern Racism Scale. In J. F. Dovidio & S. L. Gaertner (eds.). *Prejudice, discrimination, and racism: Theory and research* (pp. 91–125). Orlando, FL: Academic Press.

McCormick, E., & Ilgen, D. (1980). *Industrial psychology,* 7th ed. Englewood Cliffs, NJ: Prentice-Hall.

McCrae, R. R., & Costa, P. T., Jr. (1987). Validation of the five-factor model of personality across instruments and observers. *Journal of Personality and Social Psychology, 52*, 81–90.

McCrae, R. R., & Costa, P. T., Jr. (1991). Adding *liebe und arbeit:* the full five-factor model and well-being. *Personality and Social Psychology Bulletin, 17*, 227–232.

McCrae, R. R., Zonderman, A. B., Costa, P. T., Jr., Bond, M. H., & Paunonen, S. V. (1996). Evaluating replicability of factors in the revised NEO personality inventory: Confirmatory factor analysis versus procustes rotation. *Journal of Personality and Social Psychology, 70*, 552–556.

McGhee, W., & Thayer, P. (1961). *Training in business and industry.* New York: Wiley.

McGill, D., & Pearce, J. K. (1982). British families. In M. McGoldrick, J. G. Pearce, & J. Giordano (Eds.), *Ethnicity and family therapy.* (pp. 457–482). New York: Guilford.

McGoldrick, M. (1989). The joining of families through marriage: The new couple. In B. Carter & M. McGoldrick (Eds.), *The changing family life cycle* (pp. 209–234). New York: Gardner Press.

McGoldrick, M., & Carter, B. (1989). Forming a remarried family. In B. Carter & M. McGoldrick (Eds.), *The changing family life cycle* (pp. 399–429). New York: Gardner Press.

McGrath, J. E. (1988). *The social psychology of time.* Newbury Park, CA: Sage.

McKim, W. A. (1991). *Drugs and behavior* (2nd ed.). Englewood Cliffs, NJ: Prentice-Hall.

McMullen, S., & Rosen, R. C. (1979). Self-administered masturbation training in the treatment of primary orgasmic dysfunction. *Journal of Consulting and Clinical Psychology, 47,* 912–918.

McNulty, S. E., & Swann, W. B., Jr. (1994). Identity negotiation in roommate relationships: The self as architect and consequence of social reality. *Journal of Personality and Social Psychology, 67,* 1012–1023.

McWhirter, D. P., & Mattison, A. (1984). *The male couple: How relationships develop.* Englewood Cliffs, NJ: Prentice-Hall.

Mead, G. H. (1934). *Mind, self, and society.* Chicago: University of Chicago Press.

Mead, M. (1935). *Sex and temperament in three primitive societies.* New York: Morrow.

Meier, S. T. (1983). Toward a theory of burnout. *Human Relations, 36,* 899–910.

Mendolia, M., & Kleck, R. (1993). Effect of talking about a stressful event on arousal: Does what we talk about make a difference? *Journal of Personality and Social Psychology, 64,* 283–292.

Merton, R. K. (1957). *Social theory and social structure.* New York: Free Press.

Meyer, S. L., Murphy, C. M., Cascardi, M., & Birns, B. (1991). Gender and relationships: Beyond the peer group. *American Psychologist, 46,* 537.

Milgram, S. (1963). Behavioral study of obedience. *Journal of Abnormal and Social Psychology, 67,* 376–386.

Milgram, S. (1965). Some conditions of obedience and disobedience to authority. *Human Relations, 18,* 57–76.

Milgram, S. (1970). The experience of living in cities. *Science, 167,* 1461–1468.

Miller, L. C. (1990). Intimacy and liking: Mutual influence and the role of unique relationships. *Journal of Personality and Social Psychology, 59,* 50–60.

Miller, J. B. (1976). *Toward a new psychology of women.* Boston: Beacon.

Minuchin, S. (1974). *Families and family therapy.* Cambridge, MA: Harvard University Press.

Minuchin, S. & Fishman, H. C. (1981). *Family therapy techniques.* Cambridge, MA: Harvard University Press.

Minuchin, S., Rosman, B. L., & Baker, L. (1978). *Psychosomatic families.* Cambridge, MA: Harvard University Press.

Mirowsky, J., & Ross, C. E. (1987). Support and control in Mexican and Anglo cultures. In M. Gaviria & J. D. Arana (Eds.), *Health and behavior: Research agenda for Hispanics* (pp. 85–92). Chicago: University of Illinois Publications Services.

Mischel, W. (1973). Toward a cognitive social reconceptualization of personality. *Psychological Review, 80,* 252–283.

Mischel, W. (1990). Personality dispositions revisited and revised: A view after three decades. In L. A. Pervin (Ed.), *Handbook of personality: Theory and research* (pp. 111–134). New York: Guilford Press.

Mitchell, J. E., Matsukami, D., Eckert, E. D., & Pyle, R. L. (1985). Characteristics of 275 patients with bulimia. *American Journal of Psychiatry, 142,* 482–488.

Moitoza, E. (1982). Portugese families. In M. McGoldrick, J. G. Pearce, & J. Giordano (Eds.), *Ethnicity and family therapy* (pp. 412–437) New York: Guilford.

Monaghan, E. P., & Glickman, S. E. (1992). Hormones and aggressive behavior. In J. B. Becker, S. M. Breedlove, & D. Crews. (Eds.). *Behavioral endocrinology* (pp. 261–286). Cambridge, MA: MIT Press.

Money, J. & Tucker, P. (1975). *Sexual signatures.* Boston: Little, Brown.

Money, J. (1987). Propaedeutics of diecious G-I/R: Theoretical foundations for understanding dimorphic gender-identity/role. In J. Reinisch, L. A. Rosenblum, & S. A. Sanders (Eds.). *Masculinity/femininity: Basic perspectives* (pp. 13–28). New York: Oxford University Press.

Montville, L. (1995, December 4). Love story. *Sports Illustrated,* pp. 34–41.

Moreland, R., & Levine, J. (1989). Newcomers and Oldtimers in Small Groups. In P. Paulus (Eds.), *Psychology of group influence.* (2nd ed.). Hillsdale, NJ: Erlbaum.

Moreland, R., & Zajonc, R. (1982). Exposure effects in person perception: Familiarity, similarity, and attraction. *Journal of Experimental Social Psychology, 43,* 395–415.

Mori, D., Pliner, P., & Chaiken, S. (1987). "Eating lightly" and the self-presentation of femininity. *Journal of Personality and Social Psychology, 53,* 693–702.

Morris, M. W. & Peng, K. (1994). Culture and cause: American and Chinese attributions for social and physical events. *Journal of Personality and Social Psychology, 67,* 949–971.

Morse, S. J., & Gergen, K. J. (1970). Social comparison, self-consistency and the concept of self. *Journal of Personality and Social Psychology, 16,* 148–156.

Moscovici, S. (1994). Three concepts: Minority, conflict, and behavioral style. In S. Moscovici, A. Mucchi-Fiani, & A. Maass (Eds.), *Minority influence.* Chicago: Nelson Hall.

Moscovici, S., & Mugny, G. (1983). Minority influence. In P. Paulus (Eds.), *Basic group process.* New York: Springer-Verlag.

Mowrer, O. H. (1971) Freudianism, behavior therapy, and self-disclosure. In E. Southwell & M. Merbaum (Eds.), *Personality: Readings in theory and research* (2nd ed.). Monterey, CA: Brooks/Cole.

Muchinsky, P. (1993). *Psychology applied to work.* Pacific Grove, CA: Brooks/Cole.

Mullen, B., Rozell, D., & Johnson, C. (1996). The phenomonology of being in a group: Complexity approaches to operationalizing cognitive representation. In J. Nye & A. Brower (Eds.), *What's social about social cognition?* Thousand Oaks, CA: Sage.

Mundy, C. (1994, June 2). The lost boy. *Rolling Stone,* 51–53.

Murphy-Berman, V., & Berman, J. (1993). Effects of responsibility for illness and social acceptability on reaction to people with AIDS: A cross-cultural comparison. *Basic and Applied Social Psychology, 14,* 215–230.

Murstein, B. I. (1986). *Paths to marriage.* Beverly Hills, CA: Sage.

Napolitan, D. A., & Goethals, G. R. (1979). The attribution of friendliness. *Journal of Experimental Social Psychology, 15,* 105–113.

National Institute on Alcohol Abuse and Alcoholism. (1989). Alcohol and trauma. *Alcohol Alert,* No. 3. Rockville, MD: Author.

National Institute on Alcohol Abuse and Alcoholism. (1990, January). *Alcohol and the female reproductive system.* Rockville, MD: Author.

National Institute on Alcohol Abuse and Alcoholism. (1992). Genetics of alcoholism. *Alcohol Alert,* No. 18. Rockville, MD: Author.

National Institute on Drug Abuse. (1991). *Third triennial report to Congress on drug abuse and drug abuse research.* Rockville, MD: Author.

Nemeth, C. (1989). The stimulating properties of dissent: The case of recall. Paper presented at the third workshop on Minority Influences, Pengia, Italy.

Nemeth, C. J. (1992). Minority dissent as a stimulant to group performance. In S. Worchel, W. Wood, & J. Simpson (Eds.), *Group process and productivity.* Newbury Park, CA: Sage.

Nemeth, C. J. (1994). The value of minority dissent. In S. Moscovici, A. Mucchi-Faina & A. Maass (Eds.), *Minority influence.* Chicago: Nelson Hall.

Nevin, R. W. (1970). *Pregnancy and emotional state.* Edgartown, MA: School Street.

Newcomb, T. M. (1961). *The acquaintance process.* New York: Holt, Rinehart and Winston.

Newhill, C. (1990). The role of culture in the development of paranoid symptomology. *American Journal of Orthopsychiatry, 60,* 345–356.

Newman, O. (1972). *Defensible space.* New York: Macmillan.

Nisbett, R. E., Caputo, C., Legant, P., & Marecek, J. (1973). Behavior as seen by the actor and as seen by the observer. *Journal of Personality and Social Psychology, 27,* 154–164.

Nishimoto, R. (1988). The cross-cultural analysis of psychiatric symptom expression using Langer's twenty-two item index. *Journal of Sociological and Social Welfare, 15,* 45–62.

Nolen-Hoeksema, S. (1991). Responses to depression and their effects on the duration of depressive episodes. *Journal of Abnormal Psychology, 100,* 569–582.

Nolen-Hoeksema, S., & Morrow, J. (1991). A prospective study of depression and distress following a natural disaster: The Loma Prieta earthquake. *Journal of Personality and Social Psychology, 61,* 115–121.

Norman, W. T. (1963). Toward an adequate taxonomy of personality attributes: Replicated factor structure in peer nomination personality ratings. *Journal of Abnormal and Social Psychology, 66,* 574–583.

Normoyle, J., & Lavrokes, P. (1984). Fear of crime in elderly women: Perceptions of control, predictability, and territory. *Personality and Social Psychology Bulletin, 11,* 191–202.

Norton, A. J., & Moorman, J. E. (1987). Current trends in marriage and divorce among American women. *Journal of Marriage and Family, 49,* 3–14.

Oates, S. B. (1982). *Let the trumpet sound: The life of Martin Luther King, Jr.* New York: Harper & Row.

Oliven, J. F. (1974). *Clinical sexuality.* Philadelphia: J. B. Lippincott.

Orbach, S. (1986). *Fat is a feminist issue.* New York: Berkley Publishing Corporation.

Osborne, R. (1996). *Self: An eclectic approach.* Boston: Allyn and Bacon.

Owen, P. (1984). Prostoglandin synthetase inhibitors in the treatment of primary dysmenorrhea: Outcome trials reviewed. *American Journal of Obstetrics and Gynecology, 148,* 96–103.

Palmore, E. (1969, Winter). Predicting longevity: A follow-up controlling for age. *The Gerontologist,* 247–250.

Papastamos, S., & Mugny, G. (1989). Synchronic consistency and psychologization in minority influence. Paper presented at the third workshop on Minority Influences, Pengia, Italy.

Paunonen, S. V., Jackson, D. N., Trzebinski, J., & Forsterling, F. (1992). Personality structure across cultures: A multi-method evaluation. *Journal of Personality and Social Psychology, 62,* 447–456.

Peck, J. S., & Manocherian, J. R. (1989). Divorce in the changing family life cycle. In B. Carter & M. McGoldrick (Eds.), *The changing family life cycle* (pp. 335–369). New York: Gardner Press.

Pegalis, L. J., Shaffer, D. R., Bazzini, D. G., & Greenier, K. (1994). On the ability to elicit self-disclosure: Are there gender-based and contextual limitations on the opener effect? *Personality and Social Psychology Bulletin, 20,* 412–420.

Pendlebury, W. W., & Solomon, P. R. (1996). Alzheimer's disease. *Clinical Symposia, 48,* (3), 1–32.

Pennebaker, J. W., Colder, M., & Sharp, L. K. (1990). Accelerating the coping process. *Journal of Personality and Social Psychology, 58,* 528–537.

Peplau, L. A., Rubin, Z., & Hill, C. T. (1977). Sexual intimacy in dating relationships. *Journal of Social Issues, 33*(2), 86–109.

Perls, F. S. (1969). *Gestalt therapy verbatim.* Moab, UT: Real People Press.

Pervin, L. (1968). Performance and satisfaction as a function of person–environment fit. *Psychological Bulletin, 69,* 56–68.

Pettigrew, T. F. (1959). Regional differences in anti-Negro prejudice. *Journal Abnormal and Social Psychology, 59,* 28–36.

Piaget, J. (1965). *The moral judgment of the child.* New York: Free Press. [Original American edition, 1932.]

Pingitore, R., Dugoni, D., Tindale, R., & Spring, B. (1994). Bias against overweight job applicants in a simulated employment interview. *Journal of Applied Psychology, 79,* 909–917.

Pinsof, W. M. & Wynne, L. C. (1995) The efficacy of marital and family therapy: an empirical overview, conclusions, and recommendations. *Journal of Marital and Family Therapy, 21,* 583–613.

Pinsof, W. B. & Catherall, D. R. (1986). The integrative psychotherapy alliance: Family, couple, and individual therapy scales. *Journal of Marital and Family Therapy, 12,* 137–151.

Pirke, K. M. (1995). Physiology of bulimia nervosa. In K. D. Brownell & C. D. Fairburn (Eds.), *Eating disorders and obesity* (pp. 261–265). New York: Guilford.

Planchy, R., & Planchy, S. (1993). Focus on results, not behavior. *Personnel Psychology, 72,* 28–30.

Plant, T. (1967). *Alcohol problems: A report to the nation by the cooperative commission on the study of alcoholism.* New York: Oxford University Press.

Plomin, R. (1989). Environment and genes: Determinants of behavior. *American Psychologist, 44,* 105–111.

Pollok, E. (April 11, 1996). Ambition imbalance: She wants to work, he wants to golf. *Wall Street Journal,* p. 1.

Porter, L., & Lawler, E. (1968). *Management attitudes and performance.* Homewood, IL: Dorsey.

Powlishta, K. K. (1987, April). The social context of cross-sex interactions. Paper presented at biennial meeting of the Society for Research in Child Development, Baltimore, MD.

Prentice-Dunn, S., & Rogers, R. (1989). Deindividuation and the self-regulation of behavior. In P. Paulus (Eds.), *Psychology of group influence.* (2nd ed.). Hillsdale, NJ: Erlbaum.

Preto, N. G. (1989). Transformation of the family system in adolescence. In B. Carter & M. McGoldrick (Eds.), *The changing family life cycle* (pp. 255–283). New York: Gardner Press.

Quattrone, G. A., & Jones, E. E. (1980). The perception of variability with in-groups and outgroups: Implications for the law of small numbers. *Journal of Personality and Social Psychology, 38,* 141–152.

Radford, M., Mann, L., Ohta, Y., & Nakane, Y. (1993). Differences between Australian and Japanese students in decisional self-esteem, decisional stress, and coping styles. *Journal of Cross-cultural Psychology, 24,* 284–297.

Rawlinson, H. (1988). What do classified ads say about you? *Recruitment Today, 1,* 47–52.

Reed, D., & Weinberg, M. S. (1984). Premarital coitus: Developing and established sexual scripts. *Social Psychology Quarterly, 47,* 129–138.

Regier, D. A., Narrow, W. E., Roe, D. S., Mandersc-heid, R. W., Locke, B. Z., & Goodwin, F. K. (1993). The defacto US Mental and Addictive Disorders Service System: Epidemiological Catchment Area prospective 1-year prevalence rates of disorders in services. *Archives of General Psychiatry, 50,* 85–94.

Reifman, A., Larrick, R., & Fein, S. (1991). Temper and temperature on the diamond: The heat-aggression relationship in major league baseball. *Personality and Social Psychology Bulletin, 17* (5), 580–585.

Reiss, D. (1981). *The family's construction of reality.* Cambridge, MA: Harvard University Press.

Rescorla, R. A. (1987). A Pavlovian analysis of goal-directed behavior. *American Psychologist, 42,* 119–129.

Risman, B. (1989). Can men "mother?" Life as a single father. In B. J. Risman and P. Schwartz (Eds.), *Gender in intimate relationships* (pp. 155–164). Belmont, CA: Wadsworth.

Roberts, P., & Newton, P. M. (1987). Levinsonian studies of women's adult development. *Psychology and Aging, 2* (2), 154–163.

Robin, A. L., Koepke, T., & Moye, A. (1990). Multidimensional assessment of parent-adolescent relations. *Psychological Assessment: A Journal of Consulting and Clinical Psychology, 2,* 451–459.

Robinson, F. P. (1970). *Effective study.* New York: Harper & Row.

Robinson, J. P., Shaver, P. R., & Wrightsman, L. S. (1991). *Measures of personality and social psychological attitudes.* San Diego, CA: Academic Press.

Robinson, J. L., Kagan, J., Reznick, J. S., & Corley, R. (1992). The heritability of inhibited and uninhibited behavior: A twin study. *Developmental Psychology, 28,* 1030–1037.

Rockers, models, and the new allure of heroin. (August 26, 1996). *Newsweek* (pp. 50–54)

Rodin, J., Solomon, S. & Metcalf, J. (1978). Role of control in mediating the perceptions of density. *Journal of Personality and Social Psychology, 36,* 988–999.

Roethlisberger, F., & Dickson, W. (1939). *Management and the worker.* Cambridge: Harvard University Press.

Rogers, C. R. (1951). *Client-centered therapy: Its current practice, implications, and theory.* Boston: Houghton Mifflin.

Rogers, C. R. (1959). A theory of therapy, personality and interpersonal relationship, as developed in the client-centered framework. In S. Koch (Ed.), *Psychology: A study of science.* New York: McGraw-Hill.

Rogers, C. R. & Sanford, R. C. (1989). Client-centered psychotherapy. In H. I. Kaplan and B. J. Sadock (Eds.), *Comprehensive textbook of psychiatry* (Vol. 1, 5th ed.), Baltimore, MD: Williams and Wilkins.

Rook, K. S. (1987a). Reciprocity of social exchange and social satisfaction among older women. *Journal of Personality and Social Psychology, 52,* 145–154.

Rook, K. S. (1987b). Social support versus companionship: Effects of life stress, loneliness, and evaluations by others. *Journal of Personality and Social Psychology, 52,* 1132–1147.

Rosen, G. M. (1987). Self-help treatment books and the commercialization of psychotherapy. *American Psychologist, 42,* 46–51.

Rosen, S., Bergman, M., Plestor, D., El-Mofy, A., & Satti, M., (1962). Prebycusis study of a relatively noise-free population in the Sudan. *Annals of Otology, Rhinology, and Layrangology, 71,* 727–743.

Rosenbaum, M. F. (1986). The repulsion hypothesis: On the nondevelopment of relationship. *Journal of Personality and Social Psychology, 51,* 1156–1166.

Rosenblatt, P. C. & Budd, L. G. (1975). Territoriality and privacy in married and unmarried cohabiting couples. *Journal of Social Psychology, 97*(1), 67–76.

Rosenblatt, P. C. & Budd, L. G. (1977). Territoriality and privacy in married and unmarried couples. *Journal of Social Psychology, 44,* 112–118.

Rosenthal, N. E., & Blehar, M. C. (Eds.) (1989). *Seasonal affective disorders and phototherapy.* New York: Guilford.

Rosenthal, R., & Jacobson, L. (1968). *Pygmalion in the classroom: Teacher expectation and pupils' intellectual development.* New York: Holt, Rinehart and Winston.

Rosenthal, R. (1973). The Pygmalion effect lives. *Psychology Today, 7,* 56–63.

Ross, C. E., & Mirowsky, J. (1987). *Children, child care, and parents' psychological well-being.* Paper presented at the annual meeting of the American Sociological Association, New York.

Rotter, J. B. (1966). Generalized expectancies for internal vs. external control of reinforcement. *Psychological Monographs, 80* (Whole No. 609).

Rotter, J. B., Chance, J. E., & Phares, E. J. (1972). *Applications of a social learning theory of personality.* New York: Holt, Rinehart, and Winston.

Rotton, J. (1978). Air pollution is no choke. Unpublished manuscript, University of Dayton.

Rowe, P. (1989). Unfavorable information and interview decision. In R. Elder & G. Ferris (Eds.), *The employment interview.* Newbury Park, CA: Sage.

Rubin, L. B. (1979). *Women of a certain age.* New York: Harper Colophon.

Rubin, Z. (1970). Measurement of romantic love. *Journal of Personality and Social Psychology, 16,* 265–273.

Rubin, Z. (1973). *Liking and loving: An invitation to social psychology.* New York: Holt, Rinehart and Winston.

Russell, D. (1984). *Sexual exploitation: Rape, child sexual abuse, and workplace harassment.* Beverly Hills, CA: Sage.

Safran, J. D., & Greenberg, L. S. (1991). *Emotion, psychotherapy and change.* New York: Guilford.

Salancik, G. R. (1977). Commitment is too easy! *Organizational Dynamics, 6,* 62–80.

Samuelson, C., & Messick, D. (1988). Inequities in access to and use of shared resources in social dilemmas. *Journal of Personality and Social Psychology, 51,* 962–967.

Sanchez-Ku, M., Wahlquist, S., & Worchel, S. (1996). *Working in multinational work teams.* Paper presented at International Work Teams Conference, Dallas, TX.

Sargent, J., Liebman, R., & Silver, M. (1985). Family therapy for anorexia nervosa. In D. M. Garner & P. E. Garfinkel (Eds.), *Anorexia nervosa and bulimia* (pp. 257–279). New York: Guilford.

Sato, K. (1987). Distribution of the cost of maintaining common resources. *Journal of Personality and Social Psychology, 23,* 19–31.

Savinar, J. (1975). The effect of ceiling height on personal space. *Man–Environment Systems, 5,* 321–324.

Scarpello, V., & Campbell, J. (1983). Job satisfaction: Are the parts there? *Personnel Psychology, 36,* 577–600.

Scarr, S., Phillips, K., & McCartney, K. (1989). Working mothers and their families. *American Psychologist, 44,* 1402–1409.

Schaubroeck, J., & Williams, S. (1993). Type A behavior pattern and escalating commitment. *Journal of Applied Psychology, 78,* 862–867.

Schlenker, B. R., Dlugolecki, D. W., & Doherty, K. (1994). The impact of self-preservations on self-appraisals and behavior: The power of public commitment. *Personality and Social Psychology Bulletin, 20,* 20–33.

Schmidt, W., & Finnigan, J. (1993). *TQManager: A practical guide for managing a total quality organization.* San Francisco: Jossey Bass.

Schmitt, N., Gooding, R., Noe, R., & Kirsch, M. (1984). Meta-analysis of validity studies published between 1964 and 1982 and the investigation of the study of characteristics. *Personnel Psychology, 37,* 402–422.

Schmitt, R. C. (1957). Density, deliquency, and crime in Honolulu. *Sociology and Social Research, 41,* 274–276.

Schmitt, R. C. (1963). Implications of density in Hong Kong. *Journal of the American Institute of Planners, 29,* 210–217.

Schmitt, R. C. (1966). Density, health, and social disorganization. *Journal of the American Institute of Planners, 32,* 38–40.

Schneider, D. J. (1973) Implicit personality theory: A review. *Psychological Bulletin, 79,* 294–309.

Schreiber, F. R. (1973). *Sybil.* New York: Warner.

Schriesheim, C., Tepper, B., & Tetrault, L. (1994). Least preferred co-worker score, situational control, and leadership effectiveness: A meta-analysis of contingency model performance predictions. *Journal of Applied Psychology, 79,* 561–573.

Schultz, D. A. (1984). *Human sexuality* (2nd ed.). Englewood Cliffs, NJ: Prentice-Hall.

Schwartz, F. N. (1989). *Breaking with tradition: Women and work: The new facts of life.* New York: Warner.

Seccombe, K. (1991). Assessing the costs and benefits of children: Gender comparisons among childfree husbands and wives. *Journal of Marriage and Family, 53*, 191–202.

Segal, M. W. (1974). Depression and learned helplessness. In R. J. Friedman and M. M. Katx (Eds.), *The psychology of depression: Contemporary theory and research.* New York: Halsted.

Selby, H. A. (1975). Semantics and causality in the study of deviance. In M. Sanches & B. Blount (Eds.), *Sociocultural dimensions of language use* (pp. 11–24). New York: Academic Press.

Seligman, J. (1989, Winter/Spring Special Edition). Variations on a theme. *Newsweek, 114*, 38–46.

Seligman, M. E. P. (1975). *Helplessness: On depression development and death.* San Francisco: Freeman.

Seligman, M. E. P. (1991). *Learned optimism.* New York: Knopf.

Seligman, M. E. P. (1995). The effectiveness of psychotherapy: The Consumer Reports study. *American Psychologist, 50*, 965–974.

Seligman, M. E. P., Abramson, L., Semmel, A., & Von Baeyar, C. (1979). Depressive attributional style. *Journal of Abnormal Psychology, 88*, 242–47.

Selye, H. (1974). *Stress without distress.* Philadelphia: Lippincott.

Selye, H. (1976). *The stress of life.* New York: McGraw-Hill.

Selzer, M. L. (1971). The Michigan Alcoholism Screening Test: The quest for a new diagnostic instrument. *American Journal of Psychiatry, 127*, 1653–1658.

Seuss, Dr. [Theodore Geisel] (1984). *The butter battle book.* New York: Random House.

Shaffer, D. R., Pegalis, L. J., & Bazzini, D. G. (1996). When boy meets girl (revisited): Gender, gender-role orientation, and prospect of future interaction as determinants of self-disclosure among same- and opposite-sex acquaintances. *Personality and Social Psychology Bulletin, 22*, 495–506.

Shaver, P. R., Hazan, C., & Bradshaw, D. (1988). Love as attachment: The integration of three behavioral systems. In R. J. Sternberg & M. L. Barnes (Eds.), *The psychology of love* (pp. 68–99). New Haven, CT: Yale University Press.

Sheehan, S. (1982). *Is there no place on earth for me?* New York: Houghton Mifflin.

Sheehan, S. (1995, February 20, 27). The last days of Sylvia Frumkin. *New Yorker*, 200–211.

Sherif, M., Harvey, O., White, B., Hood, W., & Sherif, C. (1961). *Intergroup conflict and cooperation: The Robber's Cave experiment.* Norman, OK: University of Oklahoma Press.

Sherwood, A., Light, K., & Blumenthal, J. (1989). Effects of aerobic exercise training on hemodynamic responses during psychosocial stress in nonmotensive and borderline Type A men: A preliminary report. *Psychosomatic Medicine, 51*, 123–136.

Shotland, L. R. (1992). A theory of the causes of courtship rape: II. *Journal of Social Issues, 48*, 127–143.

Siegel, S. J., & Alloy, L. B. (1990). Interpersonal perceptions and consequences of depressive–significant other relationships: A naturalistic study of college roomates. *Journal of Abnormal Psychology, 79*, 361–373.

Sifneos, P. E. (1987). *Short-term dynamic psychotherapy.* New York: Plenum.

Simmel, G. (1950). The stranger. In K. H. Wolff (Ed.), *The sociology of Georg Simmel.* Glencoe, IL: Free Press.

Simmel, G. (1955). *Conflict.* New York: Free Press.

Simon, H. B. (1991). Exercise and human immune function. In R. Ader, D. E. Felton, & N. Cohen (Eds.), *Psychoneuroimmunology* (2nd ed.), pp. 869–895. New York: Academic Press.

Simpson, E. (1990). *Faculty renewal in higher education.* Malabar, FL: R. E. Krieger.

Skinner, B. F. (1938). *The behavior of organisms.* New York: Appleton-Century-Crofts.

Skinner, B. F. (1958). *Science and human behavior.* New York: Macmillan.

Skinner, B. F. (1971). *Beyond freedom and dignity.* New York: Knopf.

Smith, B. M. (1991). *Values, self, and society.* New Brunswick, NJ: Transaction Press.

Smith, E. J. (1982). The black female adolescent: A review of the educational, career, and psychological literature. *Psychology of Women Quarterly, 6*, 261–288.

Smith, M. L., Glass, G. V., & Miller, T. I. (1980). *The benefits of psychotherapy.* Baltimore, MD: Johns Hopkins Press.

Smither, J. et al. (1995). An examination of upward feedback program over time. *Personnel Psychology, 48*, 1–34.

Snow, M. (1992). *Take time to play checkers: And other wise words from kids.* New York: Penguin.

Snyder, M. (1987). *Public appearances/private realities: The psychology of self-monitoring.* New York: W. H. Freeman.

Snyder, M., Tanke, E. D., & Berscheid, E. (1977). Social perception and interpersonal behavior: On the selffulfilling nature of social stereotypes. *Journal of Personality and Social Psychology, 31,* 64–67.

Solomon, P. R., Knapp, M. J., Gracon, S. I., Groccia, M., & Pendlebury, W. W. (1996). Long-term tacrine treatment in patients with Alzheimer's disease. *The Lancet, 348,* 275–276.

Solomon, T., Mikulinger, M., & Hobfoll, S. (1988). Effects of social support and battle intensity on loneliness and breakdown during combat. *Journal of Personality and Social Psychology, 23,* 19–31.

Sommer, B. (1983). How does menstruation affect cognitive competence and psychophysiological response? *Women and Health, 8,* 53–90.

Sommer, L., & Ross, H. (1958). Social interaction on a geriatric ward. *International Journal of Social Psychiatry, 4,* 128–133.

Sommer, R. (1967). Small group ecology. *Psychological Bulletin, 67,* 145–152.

Sommer, R. (1974). *Tight spaces: Hard architecture and how to humanize it.* Englewood Cliffs, NJ: Prentice-Hall.

Sorenson, R. (1973). *Adolescent sexuality in contemporary America.* New York: World.

Spark, R. F., White, R. A., & Connolly, P. B. (1980, October 3). Impotence is not always psychogenic. *Journal of the American Medical Association, 243*(8), 1558.

Spence, J. T. (1984). Masculinity, femininity, and gender-related traits: A conceptual analysis and critique of current research. In B. A. Maher & W. B. Maher (Eds.), *Progress in experimental personality research* (pp. 1–97). Orlando, FL: Academic Press.

Spitzer, R. (1989). *DSM III–R casebook.* Washington, DC: American Psychiatric Press.

Spritzer, R. L., Gibbon, M., Skodol, A. E., Williams, J. B. W., First, M. B. (Eds.). (1994). *DSM-IV casebook.* Washington, DC: American Psychiatric Press.

Stampfl, T. G. (1967). Implosive therapy. In S. G. Armitage (Ed.), *Behavior modification techniques in the treatment of emotional disorders.* Battle Creek, MI: V. A. Publication.

Stanley, J. P. (1977). Paradigmatic woman: The prostitute. In D. L. Shores & C. P. Hines (Eds.), *Papers in linguistic variation* (pp. 301–321). Tuscaloosa, AL: University of Alabama Press.

Starr, M. (1995, December 4). Brave heart, broken heart. *Newsweek,* pp. 70–71.

Stasser, G. (1992). *Pooling of unshared information during group discussion,* In S. Worchel, W. Wood, & J. A. Simpson (Eds.), *Group processes and productivity* (pp. 48–67). Newbury Park, CA: Sage.

Statistical Abstracts of the United States. (1992). Washington, DC: U.S. Government Printing Office.

Staw, B. B. (1976). *Intrinsic and extrinsic motivation.* Morristown, NJ: General Learning Press.

Steiner, I. D. (1972). *Group process and productivity.* New York: Academic Press.

Stephens, R. S., Roffman, R. A., & Simpson, E. E. (1994). Treating adult marijuana dependence: A test of the relapse prevention model. *Journal of Consulting and Clinical Psychology, 62,* 92–99.

Sternberg, R. J. (1986). *Intelligence applied: Understanding and increasing your intellectual skills.* San Diego, CA: Harcourt Brace Jovanovich.

Stewart, R., et al. (1990). Employee's references as a recruitment source. *Applied H. R. M. Research, 1,* 1–3.

Stires, L. (1980). Classroom seating location, student grades, and attitudes: Environment or selection? *Environment and Behavior, 12,* 87–110.

Stock, W. E., & Greer, J. H. (1982). A study of fantasy-based sexual arousal in women. *Archives of Sexual Behavior, 11,* 33–47.

Stokols, D. (1995). The paradox of environmental psychology. *American Psychologist, 50*(10), 821–837.

Stokols, D., Rall, M., Pinner, B., & Schopler, J. (1973). Physical, social, and personal determinants of the perception of crowding. *Environment and Behavior, 5,* 87–110.

Storms, M. D. (1981). A theory of erotic orientation development. *Psychological Review, 88,* 340–353.

Straus, M. A., & Gelles, R. J. (1986). Societal change and change in family violence from 1975 to 1985 as revealed by two national samples. *Journal of Marriage and the Family, 48,* 465–479.

Strauss, J., & Ryan, R. (1987). Autonomy disturbances in subtypes of anorexia nervosa. *Journal of Abnormal Psychology, 96,* 254–258.

Strauss, N. (1994) The downward spiral: The last days of Nirvana's leader. *Rolling Stone,* June 2, 1994, #683, 35–43.

Streib, G., & Beck, R. (1981). Older families: A decade review. *Journal of Marriage and the Family,* 42, 937–956.

Streib, G., & Schneider, G. (1971). *Retirement in American society: Impact and process.* Ithaca, NY: Cornell University Press.

Strong, S. R., & Claiborn, C. D. (1982). *Change through interaction.* New York: Wiley.

Styron, W. (1990). *Darkness visible.* New York: Random House.

Sugarman, D. B., & Hotaling, G. T. (1989). Violent men in intimate relationships: An analysis of risk markers. *Journal of Applied Social Psychology,* 19, 1034–1048.

Suls, J., & Wills, T. A. (1990). *Social comparison: Contemporary theory and research.* Hillsdale, NJ: Erlbaum.

Szapocznik, J., Kurtines, W. M., & Fernandez, T. (1980). Bicultural involvement and adjustment in Hispanic American youth. *International Journal of Intercultural Relations,* 4, 353–366.

Tajfel, H. (1970). Experiments in intergroup discrimination. *Scientific American,* 223, 96–102.

Tajfel, H. (1982). *Social identity and intergroup relations.* Cambridge, England: Cambridge University Press.

Tajfel, H. & Turner, J. (1986). The social identity theory of intergroup behavior. In S. Worchel & W. Austin (Eds). *The psychology of intergroup relations.* Chicago: Nelson Hall.

Tannen, D. (1990). *You just don't understand.* New York: Ballantine.

Tavris, C., & Sadd, S. (1977). *The Redbook report on female sexuality.* New York: Delacorte.

Taylor, S. E. (1989). *Positive illusions: Creative self-deception and the healthy mind.* New York: Basic Books.

Taylor, S. (1986). *Health psychology.* New York: Random House.

Terborg, J. (1977). Validation and extension of an individual differences model of work performance. *Organizational Behavior and Human Performance,* 18, 188–216.

Terzian, J., & Cramer, K. (1970). *Mighty hard road: The story of Cesar Chavez.* New York: Doubleday.

Tesser, A. (1993). The importance of heritability in psychological research: A case of attitudes. *Psychological Review,* 100, 129–142.

Thibaut, J. W. & Kelley, H. H. (1959). *The social psychology of groups.* New York: Wiley.

Thompson, A. P. (1983). Extramarital sex: A review of the research and literature. *Journal of Sex Research,* 19, 1–22.

Thorndike, E. L. (1898). *Animal intelligence: An experimental study of the associative process in animals.* Psychological Review Monograph Supplement, 2(4, Whole No. 8).

Thornton, B. (1977). Toward a linear prediction model of marital happiness. *Personality and Social Psychology Bulletin,* 3, 674–676.

Thornton, A. (1989). Changing attitudes toward family issues in the United States. *Journal of Marriage and Family,* 51, 873–893.

Tieger, T. (1980). On the biological basis of sex differences in aggression. *Child Development,* 51, 943–963.

Toffler, A. (1970). *Future shock.* New York: Random House.

Tolstoy, L. (1918). *Anna Karenina.* Cambridge: Oxford University Press.

Toman, W. (1988). *Family therapy and sibling position.* Northvale, NJ: Aronson.

Topf, M. (1985). Personal and environmental predictors of patient disturbance due to hospital noise. *Journal of Applied Psychology,* 70, 22–28.

Torrey, E. F. (1983). *Surviving schizophrenia: A family manual.* New York: Harper and Row.

Touhey, J. C. (1972) Comparison of two dimensions of attitude similarity on heterosexual attraction. *Journal of Personality and Social Psychology,* 23, 8–10.

Trepper, T. S., & Niedner, D. M. (1995). Intrafamily child sexual abuse. In F. Kaslow (Ed.), *Handbook of relational diagnosis and dysfunctional family patterns* (pp. 394–406). New York: Guilford.

Triandis, H. C. (1993). The contingency model in cross-cultural perspective. In M. M. Chemers & R. Ayman (Eds.), *Leadership theory and research: Perspectives and directions* (pp. 167–188). Boston: Academic Press.

Triandis, H. C. (1994). *Culture and social behavior.* New York: McGraw-Hill.

Triandis, H. C., Bontempo, R., Villareal, M., Asai, M., & Lucci, N. (1988). Individualism and collectivism: Cross-cultural perspectives on self-ingroup relationships. *Journal of Personality and Social Psychology,* 54, 323–338.

Troll, L. E. (1971). The family of later life: A decade review. *Journal of Marriage and the Family,* 33, 263–290.

Troll, L. E. (1975). *Early and middle adulthood.* Monterey, CA: Brooks/Cole.

Tuckman, B. W. (1965). Developmental sequences in small groups. *Psychological Bulletin, 63,* 384–399.

Turner, J., Oakes, P., Haslam, S., & McGarty, C. (1994). Self and collective: Cognition and social context. *Personality and Social Psychology Bulletin, 20,* 454–463.

Uleman, J. S., Newman, L. S., & Moskowitz, G. B. (1996). People as flexible interpreters: Evidence and issues from spontaneous trait inference. In M. P. Zanna (Ed.), *Advances in Experimental Social Psychology, Vol. 28* (pp. 211–279). Boston: Academic Press.

Ullman, S. E., & Knight, R. A. (1993). The efficacy of female resistance to strategies in rape situations. *Psychology of Women Quarterly, 17,* 23–28.

Unger, R. K. (1979). *Female and male.* New York: Harper & Row.

U.S. Center for Disease Control and Prevention. Atlanta, Ga. Unpublished data.

U.S. Riot Commission, (1968). *Report of the National Advisory Commission on Civil Disorders.* New York: Bantam.

Van de Vijer, F., & Harsveld, M. (1994). The incomplete equivalence of paper-and-pencil and computerized versions of general aptitude tests. *Journal of Applied Psychology, 79,* 852–859.

Vance, E. B., & Wagner, N. N. (1976). Written descriptions of orgasm: A study of sex differences. *Archives of Sexual Behavior, 5,* 87–98.

Vandenberg, R., & Scarpello, V. (1990). The matching model: An examination of the process underlying realistic job preview. *Journal of Applied Psychology, 75,* 60–67.

Vaughn, E. (1993). Individual and cultural differences in adaptation to environmental risks. *American Psychologist, 48,* 673–680.

Vetter, B., & Babco, E. (Eds.) (February 1986). *Professional women and minorities.* Washington, DC: Commission on Professionals in Science and Technology.

Videbeck, R. (1960). Self-conception and the reactions of others. *Sociometry, 23,* 351–362.

Video Turns Big Profit for Porn Products. (1982, March 10). *Variety, 306,* 35.

Vincent-Roehling, P., & Robin, A. L. (1986). Development and validation of the family beliefs inventory: A measure of unrealistic beliefs among parents and adolescents. *Journal of Consulting and Clinical Psychology, 54,* 693–697.

Volk, S., Schulz, H., & Yassouridis, A. (1990). The influence of two behavioral regimins on the distribution of sleep and wakefulness in narcoleptic patients. *Sleep, 13,* 136–142.

Vonnegut, M. (1975). *The eden express.* New York: Praeger.

Walsh, A. (1990, April) *FARE: Fraternity acquaintance rape education.* Paper presented at Southeastern Psychological Association Convention, Atlanta.

Walsh, F. (1989). The family in later life. In B. Carter & M. McGoldrick (Eds.), *The changing family life cycle* (pp. 312–334). New York: Gardner Press.

Walster, E. (1965). The effect of self-esteem on romantic liking. *Journal of Experimental Social Psychology, 1,* 184–197.

Walster, E., Walster, B., Abraham, D., & Brown, A. (1966). The effect on liking of underrating or overrating another. *Journal of Experimental Social Psychology, 2,* 70–84.

Walster, E., Berscheid, E., & Walster, G. W. (1973). New directions in equity research. *Journal of Personality and Social Psychology, 25,* 151–176.

Walster, E., & Prestholdt, P. (1966). The effect of misjudging another: Over-compensation or dissonance reduction? *Journal of Experimental Social Psychology, 2,* 85–97.

Walster, E., Walster, G. W., & Traupmann, J. (1978). Equity and premarital sex. *Journal of Personality, 36,* 82–92.

Walster, E., & Walster, G. W. (1978). *A new look at love.* Reading, MA: Addison-Wesley.

Walster, E., Walster, G. W., & Berscheid, E. (1978). *Equity: Theory and research.* Boston: Allyn and Bacon.

Walster, E., Walster, G. W., Piliavin, J., & Schmitt, L. (1973). Playing hard to get: Understanding an elusive phenomenon. *Journal of Personality and Social Psychology, 26,* 113–121.

Washington Post (1996, March 13). In insecure times, Americans waiting longer to tie the knot.

Watson, J. B. (1925). *Behaviorism.* New York: Norton.

Watson. O., & Graves, T. (1966). Quantative research in proxemic behavior. *American Anthropologist, 68,* 971–985.

Webb, W., & Worchel, S. (1993). Prior experience and expectation in the context of crowding. *Journal of Personality and Social Psychology, 65,* 512–521.

Wehr, T. A. & Rosenthal, N. E. (1989). Seasonality and affective illness. *American Journal of Psychiatry, 146* (7), 829–839.

Weinberger, D., Scarr, S., & Waldman, I. (1992).The Minnesota transracial study: A follow-up of IQ test performance at adolescense. *Intelligence, 16,* 117–135.

Weiner, R. D. (1979). The psychiatric use of electrically induced seizures. *American Journal of Psychiatry, 136* (12), 1507–1517.

Weiner, N. (1980). Determinants and behavioral consequences of pay satisfaction. A comparison of two models. *Personnel Psychology, 33,* 741–757.

Weiner, M. J., & Wright, F. E. (1973). Effects of undergoing arbitrary discrimination upon subsequent attitudes toward a minority group. *Journal of Applied Social Psychology, 3,* 94–102.

Weisbard, E. (1994). Revolutionary debris. *Spin, 10,* 40.

Weisburd, D. E. (1990). Planning a community-based mental health system. *American Psychologist, 45,* 1245–1248.

Weiss, D. L. (1983). Affective reactions of women to their initial experience of coitus. *Journal of Sex Research, 19,* 209–237.

Welch, J. Notes on The Messiah. Columbia Masterworks M2S607. Library of Congress R59–1290.

Wells, B. (1972). The psycho-social influence of building environment: Sociometric findings in large and small office spaces. In R. Gutman (Ed.), *People and buildings.* New York: Basic Books.

West, C., & Zimmerman, D. H. (1985). Gender, language, and discourse. In T. A. vanDijk (Ed.), *Handbook of discourse analysis: Vol. 4. Discourse analysis in society.* (pp. 103–124). London: Academic Press.

Wexley, K., Yukl, G., Kovacs, S., & Sanders, R. (1972). Importance of contrast effects in employment interviews. *Journal of Applied Psychology, 57,* 233–236.

Wheeler, L., Reis, H. T., & Bond, M. H. (1989). Collectivism–individualism in everyday social life: The middle kingdom and the melting pot. *Journal of Personality and Social Psychology, 57,* 79–86.

White, L., & Edwards, J. N. (1990). Emptying the nest and parental well-being: An analysis of national panel data. *American Sociological Review, 55,* 235–242.

White, M. (1975). Interpersonal distance as affected by room size, status, and sex. *Journal of Social Psychology, 95,* 241–245.

White, R. W. (1964). *The abnormal personality.* New York: Ronald Press.

Williams, J. D., & Jacoby, A. P. (1989). The effects of premarital heterosexual and homosexual experience on dating and marriage desirability. *Journal of Marriage and Family, 51,* 489–497.

Williams, R., & Garris, T. (1991). A second look at situation wanted advertisements. *Applied H. R. M. Research, 2,* 33–37.

Willis, F. (1966). Initial speaking distance as a function of the speakers' relationship. *Psychonomic Science, 5,* 221–222.

Willis, S., Miller, T., & Huff, G. (1991). Situation-wanted advertisements: A means for obtaining job information and inquiries. *Applied H. R. M. Research, 2,* 27–32.

Wills, T. A. (1981). Downward social comparison principles in social psychology. *Psychological Bulletin, 90,* 245–271.

Wilson, B. A. (1987). *Rehabilitation of memory.* New York: Guilford Press.

Wilson, G. T., & Lawson, D. M. (1978). Expectancies, alcohol and sexual arousal in women. *Journal of Abnormal Psychology, 87,* 358–367.

Winch, R. F. (1958). *Mate selection: A study of complementary needs.* New York: Harper & Row.

Winter, D. G. (1987). Leader appeal, leader performance, and the motive profile of leaders and followers: A study of American presidents and elections. *Journal of Personality and Social Psychology, 52,* 196–202.

Wiseman, C. V., Gray, J. J., Mosimann, J. E., & Ahrens, A. H. (1992). Cultural expectations of thinness in women: An update. *International Journal of Eating Disorders, 11,* 85–89.

Wolpe, J. (1958). *Psychotherapy by reciprocal inhibition.* Stanford, CA: Stanford University Press.

Wood, J. V. (1996). What is social comparison and how should we study it? *Personality and Social Psychology Bulletin, 22,* 520–537.

Worchel, S. (1978). The experience of crowding: An attributional analysis. In A. Baum & Y. Epstein (Eds.), *Human response to crowding.* Hillsdale, NJ: Lawrence Erlbaum.

Worchel, S. (1979). Cooperation and the reduction of intergroup conflict: Some determining factors. In W. Austin & S. Worchel (Eds.), *The social psychology of intergroup relations.* Monterey, CA; Brooks/Cole.

Worchel, S. (1986a). The influence of contextual variables on interpersonal spacing. *Journal of Nonverbal Behavior, 10,* 230–254.

Worchel, S. (1986b). The role of cooperation in reducing intergroup conflict. In S. Worchel & W. G. Austin (Eds.), *The psychology of intergroup relations.* Chicago: Nelson Hall.

Worchel, S., & Arnold, S. (1973. The effects of censorship and attractiveness of the censor on attitude change. *Journal of Experimental Social Psychology, 9,* 365–377.

Worchel, S., & Brown, E. (1984). The role of plausability in influencing environmental attributions. *Journal of Experimental Social Psychology, 20,* 86–96.

Worchel, S., & Lollis, M. (1982). Reactions to territorial contamination as a function of culture. *Personality and Social Psychology Bulletin, 8,* 365–370.

Worchel, S., & Rothgerber, H. (1997). Changing the stereotype of stereotypes. In R. Spears, P. Oakes, N. Ellemers & S. Haslam (Eds.), *The social psychology of stereotyping and group life.* London: Blackwell.

Worchel, S., & Shebilske, W. (1996). *Psychology: Principles and applications,* (5th ed.). New York: Prentice-Hall.

Worchel, S., & Teddlie, C. (1976). The experience of crowding: A two-factor theory. *Journal of Personality and Social Psychology, 34,* 30–40.

Worchel, S., Andreoli, V. A., & Folger, R. (1977). Intergroup cooperation and intergroup attraction: The effect of previous interaction and outcome of combined effect. *Journal of Experimental and Social Psychology, 13,* 131–140.

Worchel, S., Cooper, J., & Goethals, G. R. (1991). *Understanding social psychology.* (5th ed.). Monterey, CA: Brooks/Cole.

Worchel, S., Coutant-Sassic, D., & Grossman, M. (1992). A Developmental Approach to Group Dynamics: A model and illustrative research. In S. Worchel, W. Wood, & J. Simpson (Eds.), *Group process and productivity.* Newbury Park, CA: Sage.

Worchel, S., Coutant-Sassic, D., & Wong, F. (1993). Toward a more balanced view of conflict: There is a positive side. In S. Worchel & J. Simpson (Eds.), *Conflict between people and groups.* Chicago: Nelson Hall.

Worchel, S., Grossman, M., & Coutant-Sassic, D. (1994). Minority influence in the group context: How group factors affect when the minority will be influential. In S. Moscoria, A. Mucci-Faina, & A. Maass (Eds.), *Minority influence:* Chicago: Nelson Hall.

Wulf, S. (1995, December 4). Short but sweet program. *Time.*

Yalom, I. (1985). *The theory and practice of group psychotherapy* (3rd ed.). New York: Basic Books.

Yukl, G. (1982). Innovations in research on leader behavior. Paper presented at Eastern Academy of Management, Baltimore, MD.

Zajonc, R. (1968). Attitudinal effects of mere exposure. *Journal of Personality and Social Psychology, 9,* 1–27.

Zastrow, C. (1992). *Social problems: Issues and solutions* (3rd ed.). Chicago: Nelson Hall.

Zillman, D. (1984). *Connections between sex and aggression.* Hillsdale, NJ: Erlbaum.

Zillman, D. (1996). Sequential dependencies in emotional experience and behavior. In R. D. Kavanaugh, B. Zimmerberg, & S. Fein (Eds.), *Emotion: Interdisciplinary perspectives* (pp. 243–272). Mahwah, NJ: Lawrence Erlbaum Associates.

Zimbardo, P. (1970). The human choice: Individuation, reason, and order versus deindividuation, impulse, and chaos. In W. Arnold & D. Levine (Eds.), *Nebraska symposium on motivation.* Lincoln, NE: University of Nebraska Press.

Zimbardo, P. G. (1971). The psychological power and pathology of imprisonment. Statement prepared for the U.S. House of Representatives Judiciary Committee. Unpublished manuscript, Stanford University.

Zimbardo, P. G. (1990). *Shyness.* Reading, MA: Addison-Wesley.

Zimbardo, P. & Leippe, M. (1991). *The psychology of attitude change and social influence.* New York: McGraw Hill.

Zullow, H., & Seligman, M. E. P. (1985). Pessimistic ruminations predict decrease in depressive symptoms: A process model and longitudinal study. Unpublished manuscript.

Index

Photo Credits

Page 1, Courtesy of Centron Films, Lawrence, Kansas
Page 22, Library of Congress
Page 48, Archive Photos
Page 78, Courtesy of Old Dominion University
Page 107, Reprinted with permission from *Thing of Beauty* by Stephen Fried
Page 143, AP Photos/Robert Sorbo/Wide World Photos
Page 169, Courtesy of Gould Farm
Page 197, Archive Photos
Page 227, AP Photos/PBS/Wide World Photos
Page 253, Pascal Roundeau/Allsport
Page 281, Topham/The Image Works
Page 310, Corbis-Bettmann
Page 338, Rod Lamkey, Jr./Liaison International
Page 370, AP/Wide World Photos
Page 400, Corbis-Bettmann
Page 426, Corbis-Bettmann

Text Credits

Page 82—Items from the Bem Sex Role Inventory (BSRI) reproduced by permission of the Distributor, Mind Garden, Inc., P.O. Box 60669, Palo Alto, CA 94306 from the **Bem Sex Role Inventory** by Sandra Lipsitz Bem. Copyright 1978 by Consulting Psychologists Press. All rights reserved. Further reproduction is prohibited without the Distributor's written consent.

Page 122, Table 5.2—Crown copyright is reproduced with the permission of the Controller of Her Majesty's Stationery Office.

Page 129, Figure 5.6—Copyright © 1993 by the American Psychological Association. Reprinted with permission.

Page 136, Figure 5.8—R. Paffenbarger, A. Wing, & R. Hyde, Physical activity as an index of heart attack in college alumni. *American Journal of Epidemiology, 108,* 161–175, 1987.

Page 152—Michigan Alcoholism Screening Test, Copyright 1971 the American Psychiatric Association. Reprinted by permission.

Page 180—From the *Beck Depression Inventory.* Copyright © 1978 by Aaron T. Beck. Reproduced by permission of Publisher, The Psychological Corporation, San Antonio, Texas. All rights reserved. "Beck Depression Inventory" and "BDI" are registered trademarks of The Psychological Corporation.

Page 263—From *Self-Consciousness and Social Anxiety* by Arnold Buss © 1980 by W. H. Freeman and Company. Used with permission.

Page 350, Figure 13.2—From Berkowitz, *Advances in Experimental Social Psychology*, Vol. 15, New York: Academic Press, 1982, p. 153.

Page 412, Table 15.1—Reproduced by permission of the American Anthropological Association from *American Anthropologist 65:5,* October 1963. Not for further reproduction.

Page 413, Figure 15.2—R. Sommer. Classroom Ecology, *Journal of Applied Behavioral Science*, 1967, 3, p. 500. Copyright 1967 by NTL Institute Publications. Reprinted by permission of Sage Publications, Inc.